Praise for

AS THOUSANDS CHEER

■ □ ■

"Bergreen, with thoroughness and fairness, tells the whole story. . . . A painstaking, professional, and ultimately satisfying biography"

—*The Los Angeles Times Book Review*

"Revealing . . . Stirring . . . Bergreen vividly depicts Berlin's life in its various stages—as a Tin Pan Alley tunesmith, a World War I recruit, a Broadway showman, and a Hollywood composer."

—*Parade*

"What a life, and what a book."

—*The Daily Mail*

"A compelling biography . . . *As Thousands Cheer* presents a vivid portrait of the man and his era."

—*The Cleveland Plain Dealer*

"The next Berlin biographer will face daunting competition. . . . Bergreen has got down what seems to be the whole story, and he tells it fairly and compassionately."

—*The Washington Post Book World*

"Laurence Bergreen's book contains some fascinating minor curiosities and it digs deeper into explaining Berlin the man."

—*The Spectator*

"A remarkable feat . . . An intriguing look at a troubled, misunderstood, intense talent . . . Very informative"

—Larry King, *USA Today*

PENGUIN BOOKS

AS THOUSANDS CHEER

Laurence Bergreen was born in New York City and educated at Harvard University. His first book, *Look Now, Pay Later: The Rise of Network Broadcasting* (1980), was followed in 1984 by his critically acclaimed *James Agee: A Life* (Penguin). He has written for numerous publications, including *Esquire*, *Newsweek*, *The New York Times*, and *American Film* magazine, and lives in New York City with his wife and children.

AS THOUSANDS CHEER

The Life of IRVING BERLIN

by

LAURENCE BERGREEN

PENGUIN BOOKS

PENGUIN BOOKS
Published by the Penguin Group
Viking Penguin, a division of Penguin Books USA Inc.,
375 Hudson Street, New York, New York 10014, U.S.A.
Penguin Books Ltd, 27 Wrights Lane, London W8 5TZ, England
Penguin Books Australia Ltd, Ringwood, Victoria, Australia
Penguin Books Canada Ltd, 2801 John Street,
Markham, Ontario, Canada L3R 1B4
Penguin Books (N.Z.) Ltd, 182–190 Wairau Road,
Auckland 10, New Zealand

Penguin Books Ltd, Registered Offices:
Harmondsworth, Middlesex, England

First published in the United States of America by
Viking Penguin, a division of Penguin Books USA Inc., 1990
Published in Penguin Books 1991

1 3 5 7 9 10 8 6 4 2

A portion of this book first appeared in *Esquire*.

Photograph on frontispiece: Irving Berlin as he appeared on the cover of *Time* in May 1934. Courtesy of Museum of Modern Art/Film Stills Archive.

Grateful acknowledgment is made for permission to reprint the following works:

Letters from the Shubert Archive.

Excerpt from "Beauty Parade" by permission of *Mad* magazine. © 1961 by E. C. Publications, Inc.

THE LIBRARY OF CONGRESS HAS CATALOGUED THE HARDCOVER AS FOLLOWS:
Bergreen, Laurence.
As thousands cheer : the life of Irving Berlin/by Laurence Bergreen.
p. cm.
Includes bibliographical references.
ISBN 0–670–81874–7 (hc.)
ISBN 0 14 01.0398 8 (pbk.)
1. Berlin, Irving, 1888–1989. 2. Composers—United States—Biography. I. Title.
ML410.B499B5 1990
782.1'4'092—dc20 89-40677

Printed in the United States of America

To Betsy, Nick, and Sara

Acknowledgments

During the final decades of his life, Irving Berlin was preoccupied with preserving his privacy. His obsession meant he would not authorize his biography, nor would he cooperate with anyone writing an article about him—let alone a book. He often said that he wanted no account of his life to appear until after he died. True to form, he declined to speak directly with me, despite numerous requests that I made over a period of several years.

Now, after his death on September 22, 1989, at the age of 101, the time has come to tell the story of the greatest songwriter in our nation's history—Irving Berlin.

In the course of my research for this biography, I was fortunate to encounter a number of people who are knowledgeable on the subject of popular music in general and Irving Berlin in particular. I wish to single out for special mention Miles Kreuger, the president of the Institute of the American Musical in Los Angeles, and James T. Maher, a historian and editor of *American Popular Song*. Their assistance has been crucial to this book.

My literary agent, Wendy Weil, has been remarkably sensitive and supportive ever since the beginning of this project. I am grateful for her expertise in negotiating all aspects of publishing this work and for her friendship and understanding.

At Viking Penguin, I had the good fortune to work with Amanda Vaill. The manuscript has benefited from her scrupulous editorial attention, and I have delighted in her wit, her professionalism, and her unquenchable enthusiasm.

I conducted approximately two hundred interviews for this book, the vast majority of them held face-to-face. I would like to thank the following individuals for generously sharing their reminiscences: George Abbott, Eddie Albert, Alan Anderson, Ernest Anderson, Edward A. Berlin, Jay Blackton, Joan Bennett, Pandro S. Berman, Al Brackman, Oscar Brand, Carol Bruce, Irving Caesar, Sammy Cahn, Saul Chaplin, Don Chandler, Goldie Clough, Mynna Granat Dreyer, Jack Elliott, Nanette Fabray, Leonard Feist, the late John Green, Stanley Green, Evelyn Haynes, Mary Healey, Jack Hirshberg, William C. K. Irwin, Ed Jablonski, E. J. Kahn, Helmy Kresa, Miles Kreuger, Maurice Kusell, Burton Lane, the late T. Newman Lawler, Harold Leventhal, Dorothy Lindsay, Robert Lissauer, Kathleen Lombard, William Mackay, James T. Maher, Alan Manson, Gerald Marks, Allyn Ann McLerie, Ward Morehouse, Russell Nype, Hermes Pan, Ezio Peterson, Thomas Pryor, Milton Rosenstock, Nick Savano, Sidney Sheldon, Arthur Shimkin, Al Simon, Gary Stevens, Ezra Stone, JoAnn Young, Magda Volges, Walter Wager, John Wallowitch, Ian Whitcomb, Gil Wiest, and David L. Wolper.

I interviewed a number of other individuals who talked about Irving Berlin on an anonymous basis, and they, too, have my thanks.

Librarians and archivists around the country helped me to locate documents that shed light on Berlin, his collaborators, and his times. Ned Comstock of the Archives of Performing Arts at the University of Southern California gave me access to the Warner Brothers and Arthur Freed Collections. Thanks also to Sam Gill of the Margaret Herrick Library of the Academy of Motion Picture Arts and Sciences in Beverly Hills and to Leith Adams of USC.

In New York City, the Performing Arts Research Center of the New York Public Library proved to be an essential resource. At the Shubert Archive, Maryann Chach guided me toward valuable documents. Faith Coleman aided my research at the Museum of the City of New York. At the Library of the Association of the Bar of the City of New York, curator Anthony P. Grech expedited my work. At ASCAP, Mike Kerker proved helpful. Stephen Siegel of the 92nd Street Y, Zachary Baker of the YIVO Institute for Jewish Research, and Michelle

Anish of the Blaustein Library of the American Jewish Committee all assisted my research into Berlin's Russian origins. At the New York Society Library, I was able to locate a number of long-forgotten theater memoirs. The resources of the New-York Historical Society and the New York Sheet Music Society also proved useful.

At the Museum of Modern Art, I screened a number of films with scores by Berlin. The museum's Film Stills Archive, under the direction of Mary Corliss, supplied photographs. My thanks to James Snyder, friend of many years, for expediting my research at MOMA.

Much of my inquiry into the history of the Mackay family was conducted at the Bryant Library in Roslyn, Long Island, where archivist Anthony Cucchiara brought the Clarence H. Mackay papers to my attention, as well as numerous photographs of the family.

Acknowledgment as well goes to Jennie Rathbun and Rodney Dennis of the Houghton Library of Harvard University, for granting me access to the papers of Alexander Woollcott; Dr. John Gable, executive director of the Theodore Roosevelt Association; the Motion Picture Division of the Library of Congress; Emmett D. Chisum of the University of Wyoming at Laramie; the Smithsonian Institution for supplying a photograph of Berlin's transposing piano; the Manuscript Division of the Library of Congress; the State Historical Society of Wisconsin in Madison; and the Peabody Museum of Salem, Massachusetts, for providing a photograph of the ship that brought a young immigrant named Israel Baline to the New World. I also wish to acknowledge my debt to Gerald Bordman's masterful chronicle of the Broadway stage, *American Musical Theatre*.

Several research assistants contributed to the scope of this book: Bryan Hammond in London; Devorah Cutler in Los Angeles; and Julia McDonald, Kelly Reynolds, and Susan Goldsmith in New York.

Susan Shapiro painstakingly transcribed the recordings of many of the interviews I conducted, and later she became a valued researcher and sounding board. Her efforts deserve a special salute.

A number of other people lent their support to this project in various ways. My sister-in-law, Joan Freeman, and her husband, Rob Alden, allowed me extended use of their home during my frequent visits to Los Angeles for research. As if that were not enough, they looked after me when I was laid low by pneumonia during one of these trips. Genealogist Marsha Dennis located government records pertaining to Berlin and his family history. David Fox of the *Los Angeles Times* supplied contacts and advice. Jack Hirshberg kindly permitted me to draw on the transcript of a lengthy interview he conducted with Berlin in 1954. Composer Max Lifchitz, a former holder of the Irving Berlin Fellowship at the Juilliard School of Music, was particularly helpful in analyzing various songs by Berlin; I have had frequent recourse to Max's insights. I have relied on Daniel Dolgin, Darrell Fennell, and James Rowe for legal advice; my thanks to them all.

Edmund Morris, the authorized biographer of Ronald Reagan, graciously interviewed the former president on my behalf for this book. I wish to extend thanks to both Edmund and his wife, Sylvia Morris, biographer of Clare Booth Luce, for bringing correspondence between Berlin and Luce to my attention.

Thanks are also due to Scott Anderson, Julian Bach, Irwin Bazelon, Stephen Chodorov, Joyce Johnson, Joseph Kanon, Eric Levin, Noirin Lucas, Larry Maslon, Marion Meade, Patricia Millman, Jennifer Smith, Steve Tager, Chuck Verrill, Richard Newberger, Louis Sheaffer, Joseph Thanhauser, and Ellen Wallenstein.

Most of all, I am grateful to my wife, Betsy, whose unfailing support and clarity of vision have helped me throughout the preparation of this book, and to our children, Nick and Sara, whose innocent questions caused me to think about my subject in new ways.

Contents

■

PART THREE:
Acclaim
(1924–1945)

PART FOUR:
Retreat
(1946–1989)

PART ONE

DISCOVERY

1888–1914

■ □ ■ □ ■ □ ■

CHAPTER 1

Lost Souls

On the morning of September 13, 1893, the SS *Rhynland*, a four-masted transatlantic passenger ship, arrived at the port of New York, where it was greeted by clear skies and cool weather. Owned by the Belgian Red Star Line, the fifteen-year-old vessel had departed Antwerp eleven days before with a full complement of passengers. Most were planning to take what the American customs authorities euphemistically called a "protracted sojourn" in the United States; in other words, they were immigrants.

A mixture of nationalities jostled for space aboard the *Rhynland*; Germany, France, and Belgium were all well represented, but the vast majority of the passengers were Russian Jews, who comprised the poorest, dirtiest, and most desperate group. They traveled not singly, as did the other nationalities, but in large family groups of six, eight, or more. Since they were so numerous and so poor, they had bought the cheapest passage available: steerage, at thirty-five dollars a head.

To accommodate the growing number of immigrants coming to the New World, the *Rhynland* made the New York–Antwerp run on a regular basis. This particular voyage had been routine. There had been several deaths en route among older passengers, who were less able to withstand the emotional and physical rigors of the voyage. More importantly, however, there had been no outbreak of the most feared disease of the era, cholera. In recent days, other ships had not been so lucky; the infected vessels had reached New York only to be sent away.

At the time of the *Rhynland*'s arrival, immigrants were pouring into New York at the rate of thousands a day, and the immigrant authorities were struggling to process them all. Until the end of 1891, less than two years before, newcomers had disembarked on an island near the Battery, at the southern tip of Manhattan, where they were received in a huge structure called Castle Garden—a former concert hall, where Jenny Lind had once entertained. However, overcrowding and a corruption scandal among New York City officials had recently prompted the Federal government to take over the immigration process and to open a larger facility on Ellis Island. The *Rhynland*'s passengers followed the new routine, disembarking at a pier and riding with their baggage on a barge to Ellis Island, to await examination for evidence of disease.

Ellis Island could handle as many as five thousand immigrants a day, though often three times that number arrived. For overburdened health officials and immigrants alike, the place was purgatory, and the new arrivals could only guess whether heaven or hell awaited them. Despite the torrent of arrivals and the Babel of tongues, which vastly complicated paperwork, passage through Ellis Island could be remarkably swift. Healthy immigrants usually made it through in a day, and few were forced to spend even one night there.

Among the *Rhynland*'s complement of Russian-Jewish passengers arriving at Ellis Island that day was the family of Moses Beilin, as a clerk casually spelled their surname. (The proper spelling was "Baline.") Since the family spoke only Yiddish, communication with the local authorities was often inexact. Traveling with the forty-six-year-old Moses, according to the ship's manifest, were his wife, Lena (carelessly transcribed as "Leo"), their six children, and eight pieces of luggage: the sum of the possessions they brought to America. Moses belonged to a venerable profession; he was a cantor—a man of God and a musician—but to appear more desirable and employable in the eyes of the immigration authorities, he gave his occupation as that of "kosher butcher."

According to the one surviving photograph of Moses, he was a short man with large, burning dark eyes and the full facial hair of an

Orthodox Jew. His nose was straight and strong, seeming to add authority to his small physique, and he wore a skullcap. His wife, Lena, two years younger, was larger, and in her photograph she looks dour and careworn, her expression as uncompromising as her husband's was open and searching. She listed no occupation for herself, but their two eldest children, fifteen-year-old Sarah and fourteen-year-old Sifre, improvised the calling of "servant" for themselves. Then came the older of the two boys, eleven-year-old Benjamin, followed by "Baroke" (probably a corruption of Becky or Rebecca), who was ten; another girl, Chasse, who was eight; and finally, the baby of the family, five-year-old Israel. At the time, his forehead bore the scar left by a pen knife that had fallen on him during the voyage.

In years to come, two of these immigrant children would change their names. Chasse would call herself Augusta, or Gussie. And Israel would change his name to Irving—Irving Berlin.

No matter what he called himself, though, he would always be a creature of crowds and the emotions they generated. This immigration was the first of many mass movements in which he would participate throughout his life. He would always live among crowds, take most of his ideas from them, and win fame and money by setting what the crowds believed to music. But for now, as an immigrant youth, he was going along with the crowd unconsciously, following the dictates of his family, who were in turn obeying the imperatives of history.

Young Israel, the rest of the family, and their eight pieces of luggage passed inspection on September 14, the day after they arrived. Once they were released by the Immigration Bureau, they took a short ferry ride to another crowded island, Manhattan, where they were immediately confronted with the complexities of surviving in New York. Among Israel's earliest memories was a predictable sense of awkwardness and insecurity. "We spoke only Yiddish and were conspicuous for our 'jew clothes,' " he later recalled with characteristic directness. Implicit in his observation was the belief that if his family members were to survive, they would have to adopt American ways, and not just in matters of dress and language; to cling to the old would consign them to eternal exile.

Israel, or Izzy, as he was soon called, found the transition easier to make than did his parents. As immigrants, they were truly strangers in a strange land; three-quarters of the city's population consisted of immigrants and their children. Germans and Irish predominated, while the Balines, as Eastern European Jews, belonged to the fastest-growing immigrant group. As a group they faced immense difficulties in trying to get established; nearly a third of them gave up the struggle to survive in America and returned to the lands they had fled, bringing back with them tales of disillusionment and heartbreak. Many who did stay became known as *farloyrene menshen*, "lost souls," who spent the balance of their days in a trance of alienation and drudgery. Such would be the lot of Moses and Lena Baline.

Like many other greenhorns, the Balines relied on a relative to serve as their guide to New York until they could fend for themselves. The eight Balines were taken by theirs straight to a waiting basement apartment on Monroe Street, in the heart of the Lower East Side. Izzy's new neighborhood was the most crowded in the city: nearly seven hundred inhabitants per acre. And it was among the ugliest—"a gray stone world of tall tenements, where even on the loveliest spring day there was not a blade of grass," according to one Yiddish writer, who continued: "The air itself seems to have absorbed the unique Jewish sorrow and pain, an emanation of thousands of years of exile." This sorrow was anything but stagnant; it was perpetually disturbed by crowds, filth, and an assortment of mutually unintelligible languages—Polish, Italian, and various dialects of Yiddish.

In that less charitable era, outsiders called the Lower East Side "Jewtown," and the Balines were typical inhabitants. They possessed no lucrative trades, were poor to the point of desperation, and were closely knit. The harsh environment had a way of bringing Jewish families together rather than fragmenting them; as the process of assimilation took hold, their closeness became their principal means of coping with the New World. And there was another, subtler effect; it made for a closeness and sense of intimacy that would stay with Berlin and countless other Lower East Side Jews like him throughout their lives. When extreme hardship forced him to leave his family, he stayed within walking distance, and even when he could afford to marry and start his own family, he remained as close to them as he had been to his parents and older siblings. This sense of intimacy would infuse many of his most successful love songs, stressing such absolutes as eternity, perfection, and completeness.

Like nearly all other immigrant Jews, the Balines were tenement dwellers, at a time when the crowded buildings were becoming a national scandal. One magazine of the day termed them "great prisonlike structures of brick . . . with narrow doors and windows, cramped passages and steep rickety stairs." Smells in tenements were often overwhelming. In winter, fumes from coal stoves, gas from lamps, and vapors from boilers plagued residents; and in the summer, the smell of decomposing garbage and human and animal waste was inescapable. The combination of overcrowding and inadequate sanitation promoted a variety of diseases, especially diphtheria, croup, measles, and tuberculosis. Among the first to call attention to these conditions was the crusading journalist Jacob Riis, a Danish-born immigrant who had grown up on the Lower East Side. At the time the Balines were struggling for a foothold, he wrote his ground-breaking exposé, *How the Other Half Lives*, describing in grisly detail the problems immigrants faced on the Lower East Side. He came away angry and despairing at the conditions he found: "The story of inhuman packing of human swarms, of bitter poverty, of landlord greed, of sweater [sweatshop] slavery, of darkness and squalor and misery, which these tenements have to tell, is equalled, I suppose, nowhere else in the civilized world." For the Balines, the Melting Pot quickly turned into an Inferno.

Burdened by the large number of mouths to feed, the family's place in this wretched environment remained marginal. After spending a few weeks in the basement on Monroe Street, they moved to permanent quarters in a Civil War-vintage brownstone at 330 Cherry Street. The Balines' building had been designed as a single dwelling, and it was subsequently divided into apartments. The eight members of the family, plus a lodger they took in to earn extra money, shoehorned themselves into three rooms on the third floor. The only relief from their packed quarters was the fire escape, the roof, or the street.

Because of this overflow of humanity, the ghetto streets, where Izzy would romp, and later try to earn a few coins, and eventually begin his musical career, played a crucial role in his life; he received more of an education there than he did anywhere else. Even by Lower East Side standards, Cherry Street was so disreputable and dangerous that many took care to avoid it. In this neighborhood, the closer to the East River a street lay, the more desirable it was considered; Cherry

Street, several blocks from the river, was hemmed in on all sides. Even Izzy's patch of sky was darkened by the looming presence of the Brooklyn Bridge.

Yet Cherry Street had a colorful history. Before it became a haven for immigrants like the Balines, it had been one of the most prestigious addresses in the city. In the early eighteenth century, actual cherry trees had stood on the site, which was then known as Cherry Garden. At the time, it lay at the northern limit of settled Manhattan; beyond it stretched farms belonging to the Roosevelt family. No. 1 Cherry, at the corner of Franklin Street, served as George Washington's first place of residence after he became president in 1789. (The mansion was torn down in 1856.) And by the Civil War, Cherry Street had metamorphosed into a fashionable shopping district boasting a Brooks Brothers and a Lord & Taylor. Twenty years later the street's character changed drastically with construction of the tenements and the Italian, Irish, and Jewish immigrants they attracted. One Cherry Street immigrant described his tenement as a "pigsty reaching up to the sky." The fragrance of cherry blossoms had yielded permanently to the stench of poverty and overcrowding.

Despite the filth, young Izzy was content with his environment. "Everyone should have a Lower East Side in their lives," he was fond of saying in years to come, when success had dulled the sharper edges of his memories of the neighborhood. Still, he was sincere. Primitive his surroundings certainly were, but his family protected him against them. As its youngest member, he had the luxury of living out at least a brief childhood before throwing himself into the struggle to survive. He was more at home in New York than any of the other Balines; he was young enough to adapt, to survive, perhaps even to thrive. "You never miss luxury until you've had it," he said. "I never felt poverty because I'd never known anything else. I was a boy with poor parents, but let's be realistic about it: I didn't starve; I wasn't cold or hungry. There was always bread and butter and hot tea."

This remarkably sunny perception of his boyhood came in part from the protected status he enjoyed, and in part from his own disposition; from his earliest youth until well into middle age, he would demonstrate a remarkable flexibility and resilience. Far better than the older members of his family, he learned the uses of adversity.

▪ ▪ ▪

Izzy's acceptance of the harsh living conditions in the New World was echoed by many of his neighbors, for as bad as things were on Cherry Street, the situation had been far more desperate in Russia, especially for Jews. On March 1, 1881, seven years before Izzy was born, revolutionary terrorists assassinated Czar Alexander II. Under his reign Jews had managed to eke out a precarious existence in Russia, but restrictions crippled their lives. They confined Jews to a Pale of Settlement reaching from the Black Sea to the Baltic Sea. They barred Jews from owning large amounts of land, holding important government posts, and entering many influential professions. As a result, most Jews led an uneasy existence on the margins of Russian society, where anti-Semitism was the norm.

After the assassination the new czar, Alexander III, abolished even the limited freedoms granted to Jews. His aggressive brand of anti-Semitism gave rise to a wave of pogroms throughout the Pale. Inflamed by fantastic tales of evil Jewish rites, government agents destroyed and burned Jewish settlements, eventually driving much of their population beyond the borders of Russia.

Moses and Lena Baline brought their large family into the world during these unsettled times. Moses had been born in January 1846, his wife in August 1849. After they wed, they had their children in swift succession—six in ten years. Sarah, their first, was born in May 1878; Sifre the following year; Benjamin in September 1881; Rebecca in March 1883; Chasse in April 1885; and finally Israel, on May 11, 1888. By that time, Moses was forty-two and his wife thirty-nine.

At the time of Israel's birth, the family lived in the town of Mohilev, about one hundred and twenty-five miles east of Minsk, the capital of White Russia. The exact birthplace of Irving Berlin has long been the subject of confusion. It is usually given as "Temum" or "Temun," often described as a town in Siberia: an error that Berlin let stand for decades. In fact, there is no such town in Siberia, and it was highly unlikely that Jews would have found themselves in Siberia in the first place, since it was outside the Pale.

However, Berlin's immigration and naturalization papers told a substantially different story. He filled these out in the United States under oath when he applied for permanent U.S. citizenship, and on them he listed his actual birthplace: Mohilev. The registration for his second marriage—another document where no myth making was allowed—confirmed this town as his birthplace. His willingness to let the error stand was but one instance of the many myths—some inspired by minor vanities, others invested with greater significance—that he would create throughout his life as he struggled to invent and revise his identity.

As a *chazzan*, or cantor, in Mohilev, Moses Baline sang during religious services. His was a highly visible and significant function, for in Orthodox synagogues, then as now, musical instruments were banned and choirs hidden; as a result, the cantor served as the primary source of musical stimulation. The melodies and prayers Moses chanted were largely traditional. Some cantors, blessed with big voices, took liberties with their interpretations, and in this way became celebrities commanding high salaries. Nothing suggests Moses ever attained such status; nevertheless, a cantor was an honorable calling, and cantors' sons traditionally aspired to the same profession. Moses' grandfather and father had both been cantors, and it seemed likely that his son Israel would eventually become one, as well. Then the fabric of Jewish life in Russia began to come apart.

The Balines might have been able to withstand the reduction of the Jews' civil freedoms and remain in Russia, but the pogroms threatened their lives. One night, their wooden home was destroyed, along with other Jewish dwellings. As an adult, Berlin admitted to no memories of his first five years in Russia except for one: he was lying on a blanket by the side of a road, watching his house burn to the ground. By daylight the house was in ashes, and Moses Baline had no choice but to join the exodus of Jews from Russia. It is doubtful he expected to find greater success or wealth in America than he had known in Mohilev; he was simply trying to preserve his life and his family.

For Moses more than any of the other members of the Baline family, moving to America actually entailed a reduction in status. Never again would he find steady work—as a cantor or anything else. Not in New York, where many immigrant Jews hastened to cast off traditional forms of worship along with their long coats and skullcaps. And never again would Moses be able to support his family. Instead, he became a part-time *shomer*, a kosher poultry inspector; the trade was fast becoming a sinecure for "lost souls" like Moses. The job could have been worse; he could have wound up plucking chickens. Or it could have been better, and he might have aspired to become a *shochet*, or slaughterer. Instead, he inspected the carcasses of animals to make certain they had been killed in the ritually correct manner. Eventually, the assimilation of Jews lessened the demand for this occupation, as well, and Moses resorted to a manual trade he was ill-equipped to undertake: house painting. It was punishing work for a man to take up in middle age.

To augment the family's income, Lena became a midwife, assisting with home births in their Lower East Side neighborhood. Three of the daughters—Rebecca, Sarah, and Augusta (formerly Chasse)—found occasional employment wrapping cigars, another common trade for immigrant women. (The fourth Baline daughter, Sifre, died young.) The oldest of the boys, Benjamin, toiled in a sweatshop, piecing together shirts.

Izzy worked as well, hawking the rowdy *Evening Journal* on the street. This newspaper was a typical Hearst publication of the 1890s, thriving on screaming headlines and jingoism. Once, when he was reading an extra copy on a pier that jutted into the East River, a crane unloading coal from a barge accidentally knocked him into the river. He might have drowned if an alarmed bystander, an Irishman, hadn't jumped into the water to pull him to shore. Izzy was rushed by ambulance to a hospital, where he recovered from inhaling the river water. Throughout the ordeal he'd held on to the five pennies he'd earned during the day by selling newspapers.

Izzy supplemented his slender earnings by doing business with a nearby junk shop, selling off a precious family heirloom in order to bring a little money into the household. "I used to go there selling bits and pieces of an old brass samovar that my mother had brought from Russia and kept under the bed," he later remembered of the junk shop. "I'd get five and ten cents for the pieces and kept selling them until the entire samovar had disappeared." Every evening, when he and the rest of the Baline children came home from work, they would deposit the coins they had earned that day into Lena's outspread apron.

Eventually Izzy conquered the East River, filthy as it was. Like other neighborhood children, he would take off his clothes and hide them under a pier, moving quickly to avoid the police, who would look askance at a naked boy. He would dive into the river and swim to Brooklyn, fighting treacherous currents all the way. Throughout his life, he would excel at swimming; even in his late fifties, when he was touring the world in a wartime revue, he would startle his companions by diving off the deck of a troop ship straight into the Pacific Ocean.

When Izzy was not peddling newspapers or junk, he attended public school, beginning at age seven. He brought little enthusiasm to the experience, and he met with little success in the classroom. Said one teacher of Izzy Baline's demeanor: "He just dreams and sings to himself." He also attended *cheder*, or religious school, to prepare for his *bar mitzvah*, again with a notable lack of enthusiasm. Whatever else he might be, he was not much of a student, though he did enjoy singing in a synagogue with his father on the High Holy Days. "I suppose it was singing in *shul* that gave me my musical background," he recalled. "It was in my blood."

Though Moses could no longer find work as a cantor, he still sang when he could, and he taught his youngest child the rudiments of the profession. Throughout his life, Berlin composed a number of songs testifying to the joy of music, a joy he conceived singing with his father. "Let Me Sing and I'm Happy" was how he put his feelings in one title. Whether writing about a ragtime band, a simple melody, or the latest dance craze, he constantly extolled the life-affirming qualities of music and song.

The liturgical songs he heard his father sing were often designed to celebrate holidays, and public celebrations—not only Jewish but gentile—became another source of fascination, especially Christmas. "I did not have a Christmas," he later wrote. "I bounded across the street to my friendly neighbors, the O'Haras, and shared their goodies. Not only that, this was my first sight of a Christmas tree. The O'Haras were very poor and later, as I grew used to their annual tree, I realized they had to buy one with broken branches and small height, but to me that first tree seemed to tower to Heaven." The tree seemed to remind the boy of himself, who was also small, but who, in his mind's eye, was infinitely larger, at least at Christmas time.

Holidays provided a respite from the steadily increasing problems of the Baline household. Money was always in short supply, and now illness threatened to wipe out what little they had. In September 1900, Moses came down with chronic bronchitis, possibly aggravated by acrid fumes he had inhaled while painting. Too sick to be cared for by his family, he moved into a "rest home," where he died at nine-forty A.M. on July 19, 1901, "of chronic bronchitis terminating in exhaustion & arterio sclerosis."

Two days later, Moses Baline, age fifty-three, was buried in Washington Cemetery, not far from New York City, leaving behind his wife and five children.

■ □ ■ □ ■ □ ■

CHAPTER 2

Prince and Pauper

Less than two months before his father's death, Israel turned thirteen, and a photograph of him taken at the time, probably to commemorate his *bar mitzvah*, shows the effect of this difficult period. For the first and only time in his life, his face is puffy and flabby looking; his features recede into folds of flesh. His expression is evasive, and his eyes are ringed with dark circles. It is an uncharacteristic pose for this normally feisty and resilient youth.

His family shared his misery. After eight years in New York, they were in even worse condition than at the time of their arrival. In search of freedom they had gone halfway around the world and lost a daughter and father in the process. They were still living at 330 Cherry Street, near the bottom of the social ladder, and they had no reason to believe their lot would ever improve.

With Izzy approaching the age of fourteen, when he could legally leave school, he, along with many other ghetto children desperate to earn money, turned his back on both formal education and his family. The Balines could no longer afford the luxury of keeping him in school. As his friend and confidant, theater critic Alexander Woollcott, later wrote, Izzy realized that "he contributed less than the least of his sisters and that skeptical eyes were being turned on him as his legs lengthened and his earning powers remained the same. He was sick with a sense of his own worthlessness." It was at this point that he left home, or, as he put it, "went on the bum." Through this painful and dangerous rite of passage, he would gradually discover his sense of self and worth in a difficult and demanding world.

He was now a foot soldier in the city's ragged army of immigrants. Along the Bowery and nearby side streets an entire subindustry of lodging houses had sprung up to shelter the thousands of homeless boys choking the Lower East Side streets. They were not settlement houses or charitable institutions; rather, they were Dickensian in their meanness, filth, and insensitivity to ordinary human needs. They were, in effect, warehouses for unwanted human beings. (Jacob Riis was especially outraged by the avaricious lodging houses catering to youths like Izzy Baline and did much to publicize their inadequate conditions.) Fifteen cents bought Izzy a night's stay; a set of filthy yellow sheets cost twenty-five cents extra. The bed on which he slept often crawled with lice. Primitive bathing facilities were located in the basement boiler room, where he could also wash his clothes and dry them on the furnace. For his money Izzy usually got a locker in which he could store his belongings, but often as not they would be stolen as he slept or in his absence—not that he owned much of value. He wore used clothes that he had purchased for a few pennies in neighborhood bargain basements.

Izzy endured these living conditions for two years, moving from one lodging house to another, always on the Lower East Side, within blocks of his family's Cherry Street apartment. He spent a full year residing at one calling itself The Mascot, located near the corner of Bayard Street and the Bowery. There, he recalled, "You got a cubby-hole to sleep in, one open at the top, and you were always scared that somebody would reach over and steal your pants." Izzy had little interest in expressing indignation or instigating a social crusade; he gave no thought to the damage these living conditions could inflict on him or anyone else. Nor did he betray even the slightest self-pity at the loss of his entire adolescence. He remained an Everyman, thinking no further than his next meal, his next bed.

As a survival technique, this habit of denial buttressed him in the daily struggle for survival, though it couldn't protect him from a pervasive sense of shame over his living conditions. When he signed the lodging houses' register books he used the name "Cooney" rather than his own.

He kept up tenuous relations with his family, though not so close as his geographical proximity to Cherry Street would suggest. His mother missed her youngest child terribly, and days would pass without her hearing from him. Occasionally a neighbor dropped by to inform her that he had caught a glimpse of Izzy and supply her with the location, yet by the time she got there, he had always moved on, and she saw nothing but a vista of anonymous passersby jostling for space on the sidewalk.

Izzy's resolve to tough it out in the lodging houses constituted an immense leap, as critical in its way as his father's decision to leave Russia had been. For better or worse he was free of his family's constraints and the world they had imported from Russia, free not only of their demands, but also their language and religious rituals. Furthermore, the decision to leave home was the first real step Izzy took on his own. It was a daring move, for he possessed few survival skills; his slender education and immaturity meant that formal employment was out of the question. His only proven ability was the one he had acquired thanks to his late father's vocation: singing.

He possessed a raspy tenor voice that he managed to instill with nervous energy, and with it he planned to earn enough money to pay for his lodging-house accommodations. Along with other youngsters in similar straits, youngsters who wanted to use their voices rather than their backs to earn a few pennies, he went to the saloons on the Bowery to sing to the customers. These itinerant musicians were known as buskers, and they were a constant feature of the Lower East Side. Izzy's audience was a different breed from the kind of people he had previously known: mainly sailors, prostitutes who catered to them, and a scattering of Irish and German laborers. Before this indifferent crowd he would sing a few of the popular ballads he had picked up on the street and committed to memory, songs such as the popular tearjerker "Mansion of Aching Hearts." As he sang he hoped the customers would pitch a few pennies in his direction.

Moving from one Bowery saloon to the next, Izzy encountered sordid aspects of the city from which his family had previously shielded him. During the course of the next two years, he became familiar with the range of saloons crowding the Bowery, from McKeons at No. 20 to the aptly named Morgue (No. 25) and "Biggie" Donovan's Saranac, where beer cost five cents a glass and hard liquor ten. There customers called for a stack of reds (whiskey) or whites (gin) when they were not being disturbed by frequent brawls or young buskers like Izzy Baline. He especially disliked a nameless saloon at No. 9 Bowery. "A terrible joint," he remembered, "inhabited by the drunkenest sailors and the oldest hags [prostitutes]. But I went there and passed the hat." He preferred to hang out at Brodie's (No. 112), where the owner, a former boxer, had made himself into a local hero by jumping off the Brooklyn Bridge and living to tell about it.

Many of these Bowery saloons had semiprivate back rooms devoted to prostitution, gambling, and opium smoking, and Izzy gained an arm's length familiarity with these activities. No. 57 Bowery, for instance, housed one of the neighborhood's better-known brothels, Diamond Lottie's, whose proprietress Izzy fondly remembered for the diamond set in her front tooth. He ventured out of the neighborhood on Saturday nights to sing at MacAlear's waterfront saloon, where he received his biggest nightly take: fifty cents.

It was in these seamy surroundings that the runaway boy received his real and lasting education, not in *cheder* nor a public school classroom. For the first time in his life, he was among a largely non-Jewish population. Culturally, he was beginning to emerge from the ghetto, learning the language of the street rather than the synagogue or a Russian village. Music was his sole source of income and independence, and he learned to gauge the kind of songs that would appeal to his disparate and indifferent audiences, for his survival depended on their approval. Well-known tunes expressing simple sentiments were the most reliable.

From the time Izzy went on the bum, he planned to move up and move out of the Bowery. All around him he saw the human wreckage of those who had not found an avenue of escape. "The bums and riffraff stayed and died off. Others like myself were only waiting to get the hell out of here," he noted.

After a strenuous year of busking on the Bowery, Izzy received what seemed to be his chance to escape when he landed a role in the chorus of a musical called *The Show Girl*. It was the first time he had found employment in the theater; he had made the transition from cantor's son to chorus boy, a rapid if uncertain advance. At the time, the height of the 1902 season, the American musical was enjoying a brief flowering. On Broadway, the Irish entertainers Victor Herbert and George M. Cohan—now merely names to Izzy, later his friends and mentors—held sway with their lavish and often foolish productions noted for their large casts—often as many as a hundred—and sparse scenery.

As a member of the chorus, Izzy left the Lower East Side for the first time, to participate in the show's out-of-town tryouts, but when the production reached Binghamton, New York, he was let go. He returned ignominiously to New York ahead of the show itself, which opened in May and soon closed.

His experience with the production, though curtailed, led to his next job. In addition to his duties as a member of the chorus, Izzy had also occasionally served as a "boomer," or song plugger: a hired hand who sat in the audience, disguised as a paying customer, and who applauded furiously when the cast sang the choruses of songs. A dedicated boomer even tried to encourage the audience to stop the action onstage by repeating the choruses or singing along with the none-too-surprised actors.

On the strength of this experience, Izzy gathered the resolve to approach Harry Von Tilzer, one of the best-known and most prolific songwriters of the day, for employment as a boomer. Von Tilzer, in fact, had written the weepy "Mansion of Aching Hearts" Izzy had been singing in Bowery saloons. Successful and famous by the time he reached thirty, Von Tilzer was, like so much else in the infant popular music field, something of an illusion. There was nothing German about him, any more than there would be about Irving Berlin. He had grown up in Indianapolis as Harry Gumm. (Later, his niece Frances would change her name to Judy Garland.) Although he could neither read nor write music, he claimed to have composed eight thousand songs; in any event, two thousand of them were published, at least a dozen of which sold more than a million copies of sheet music during the course of his career. One of his most recent hits was the 1900 smash, "A Bird in a Gilded Cage," for which he had written the music, though he is best remembered today for "I Want a Girl Just Like the Girl Who Married Dear Old Dad."

Less well known today are Von Tilzer's "coon" songs, the then universally accepted name for black or "race" music. As Izzy discovered, whites wrote much "black" music; songs such as Gumm's "Rufus Rastus Johnson Brown" were reliable sellers. Von Tilzer named another one of his "coon" songs "Alexander (Don't You Love Your Baby No More?)." A common "coon" appellation was Alexander, supposedly a comically grand name for a black man to possess. Von Tilzer's multiple masquerade—an American posing as German, a white man composing black music—reflected the overwhelming influence of ethnicity on popular music.

Publishing "coon" songs was one instance of Von Tilzer's commercial cunning; another was his decision to start his own publishing company to ensure that he collected all the royalties that were coming to him. The offices were located at 42 West 28th Street, just south of Herald Square. This was an innovative choice of location, and within a decade other music publishing companies would honeycomb the district; for now many were scattered around town or in other major cities, especially Chicago. With its elements of youthful success, ignorance of formal musical technique, and mastery of the music publishing business, all carried out under an assumed name, the Von Tilzer story served as a model for the career that Izzy Baline would soon begin to make for himself.

He began by offering his lung power to Von Tilzer, who immediately put him to work as a boomer in Tony Pastor's famous music hall, where Izzy gained his first exposure to vaudeville. Pastor was the first impresario to promote vaudeville to a wide audience, insisting that the various comedy, music, acrobatic, and animal acts he presented maintain a wholesome tone—a formula that attracted huge crowds to his 14th Street theater. It was here that Harrigan and Hart, Lillian Russell, and Delehanty and Hingler (the most popular dance team of the day) performed on their way to national eminence.

Izzy's job, for which he earned five dollars a week, consisted of plugging a song in Pastor's newest act, The Three Keatons. Ma played the saxophone, Pa told jokes, and their child, Buster (later the silent-screen star), was, in the words of one critic, "tossed around by his parents and even bounced against the scenery in a most entertaining manner."

Once again, the job proved to be short-lived. Izzy's term of employment ended with the conclusion of the Keatons' run at Tony Pastor's, and he returned to the anonymous ranks of the Bowery buskers. Everything was as it had been before his brief fairy tale job as a boomer, except that he was now better known, at least to his gypsy colleagues. His particular friend of the moment was the self-proclaimed "Mayor of Chinatown," Chuck Connors. In reality Connors lived with his sister in a shabby house on Doyers Street in Chinatown. Dressed in his habitual brown derby and green jacket, he eked out a living conducting tours of the neighborhood for curiosity seekers from uptown.

Under Connor's influence, Izzy drifted into more exotic territory than he had previously known; Chinatown enjoyed a national reputation as a haven for prostitution, especially in the form of the dreaded "white slave trade"; and opium dens. Helped by its association with the Chinese and vice, opium earned a reputation as the most glamorous and notorious drug of the era. Expressing a widely shared revulsion, Jacob Riis noted, "There are houses, dozens of them, on Mott and Pell Streets, that are literally jammed, from the 'joint' in the cellar to the attic, with these hapless victims of a passion which, once acquired, demands the sacrifice of every instinct of decency to its insatiate desire."

However, there was a decided ambivalence about the public's reaction to opium and the China subculture where it prospered. Riis's uplifting horror was matched by an equally widespread frisson of titillation as Chuck Connors and promoters like him cultivated Chinatown's lurid reputation to attract the tourist trade. Since opium was as legal as chop suey at the time, its use was widespread and often innocuous. Olliffe's Drugstore at No. 6 Bowery served as the center of legitimate distribution in the area; believed to be the oldest pharmacy in the United States (established in 1805), it was more of a local landmark than a scandal.

Through Connors, Izzy came to the attention of one of the best-known buskers in Chinatown, an older man who went by the name of Blind Sol. Because of his handicap, he needed guidance in making the rounds of the saloons and cafés where he sang. Occasionally a prostitute took pity on Blind Sol and escorted him; at other times, a helpful young busker. Eventually Izzy had his chance to feel the weight of Blind Sol's hand on his shoulder as they pushed through the doors of a saloon and tried to get the attention—and the loose change—of the besotted patrons.

Working with Blind Sol turned out to be a mixed blessing. The old man commanded a large audience, but he usually had to divide his earnings with the piano player in each establishment they visited. A good night's work netted Izzy no more than fifty cents. The only advantage of this arrangement was that Izzy became acquainted with the pianists, whom he coaxed to show him a musical trick or two.

▪ ▪ ▪

By now Izzy was approaching sixteen, and he had been drifting through a twilight of saloons and lodging houses for over three years, with little to show for his efforts. In early 1904 Chuck Connors again came to his aid by recommending the young man for a full-time job in a new café that had just been started by another Chinatown luminary, Mike Salter.

Located at 12 Pell Street, in the heart of Chinatown, the establishment was officially known as The Pelham Café, though everyone called it by the proprietor's nickname, "Nigger Mike's." (Like "coon," the epithet "nigger" was widely used and not considered shockingly offensive, but make no mistake, it still carried a racist sting.) Nigger Mike was no blacker than Izzy Baline; he was a Russian Jew with an olive complexion. Best known as a ward heeler and political fixer, he also dealt in alibis. His preferred method of exculpating cronies was to persuade a prostitute who was not otherwise engaged to dress in conservative clothing and pose as the suspect's mother. The ruse generally worked, except when Salter enlisted an obviously Irish "mother" to plead for the release of her obviously Jewish or Italian "son." Mike was stocky and rough spoken and bragged of having killed ten men, but he was genial enough, except when he drank—as Izzy would eventually discover.

Like much else that Izzy encountered, The Pelham Café was a misnomer; the place was actually a dance hall and bar designed to cater to the tourist trade slumming through Chinatown in search of opium dens and notorious criminals. The café happened to be located in territory fought over by two rival gangs, an Irish-Italian pack known as the Five Pointers and a Jewish gang called the Eastmans, after their leader, "Monk" Eastman. Gang members occasionally dropped in at the café, and respectable ladies and gentlemen came from uptown, often under the guidance of Chuck Connors, in the hope of rubbing elbows with them. However, it was disappointingly obvious that the café's clientele consisted primarily of tourists and locals rather than lords of vice. Not that the establishment was entirely innocent; the upstairs housed a brothel run by an "opium fiend" who went by the name of Chinatown Gertie. Her domain consisted of a small, dark room, her opium pipe, and her kimono, and she allowed tourists to gawk at her, though they had to pay fifty cents for the privilege. Gertie then split the proceeds with Connors and other guides.

Izzy discovered that Nigger Mike's was but one of many "resorts"—as such establishments were called—in the neighborhood. Nearby, on Doyers Street, stood Mike Callahan's renowned Dance Hall and Sailor's Drinking Place, its door guarded by "Big Jerry," a reputed gunslinger. There were several opium dens within walking distance. At Jimmy Pong's, upward of fifty Chinese huddled in bunks, smoking opium and attracting tourists.

An energetic rivalry sprang up among the resorts, which vied for patrons on the strength of the atmosphere they provided. Next to the proprietor, the Pelham's best-known fixture was known simply as Sulky, a dour barkeeper who regularly gave loans to the café's patrons and kept his accounts in an accurate, though wet ledger stored beneath the bar. After Sulky, in terms of reputation, came the house pianist, Mike Nicholson, who usually went by the name of Nick. Occasionally other pianists substituted, including Lukie Johnson. This black musician brought a new sound into the café, a syncopated style of music called ragtime.

At the bottom of the hierarchy came the singing waiters; it was an unassuming job, but Izzy was glad to have it. There is no evidence to suggest that it required a great deal of musical ability; an ingratiating manner and a good pair of lungs were the important elements. Once again he sang a mixture of sentimental Irish ballads borrowed from Broadway shows (and often written by George M. Cohan), and he displayed a new talent that quickly attracted attention: an ability to devise blue parodies of these songs. This rude but effective brand of showmanship endeared him to the café's patrons, which in turn endeared him to Nigger Mike, for a time.

Occasionally Izzy ran errands for his boss, often to Olliffe's drugstore, to obtain a purgative compounded of calomel and jalap. Mike would give the mixture to an unruly patron, if necessary. At the drugstore, Izzy befriended a clerk, another immigrant Jewish youth, whose name was Joseph Schenck. At the time, Schenck was studying for his pharmacist's degree with the help of a Russian-English dictionary. Later, he would abandon the field for the movie industry, where he would exert a crucial influence over Izzy's career. But for now, he was, like Izzy, in search of an avenue of escape from the rigors of the ghetto.

Izzy worked punishing hours at the café, from eight in the evening until six the following morning. Despite the ungodly hours, Izzy was delighted with the job because the pay was good—seven dollars a week plus tips—and the atmosphere lively. The patrons pitched coins; drank Salter's cheap whiskey; sang along with Izzy and two other waiters, Bullhead Lawrence and Kutch Kutchinsky; and danced to the tunes "Professor" Nick Nicholson banged out on the piano. The music was in constant ferment; the fox trot is generally believed to have been created on the floor of Nigger Mike's by Chuck Connors; while the ungainly "mayor" would have had a difficult time developing a dance step, he popularized it as part of his duties.

Life as a singing waiter could be strenuous. Another employee by the name of Jubal Sweet recalled the sight of seventeen-year-old Izzy Baline trying to sing and collect tips at the same time: "Now a singing waiter couldn't be stooping over every time a coin hit the floor. Spoil his song, like—see? No, he'd keep moving around easy, singing all the time, every time a nickel would drop he'd put his toe on it and kick it or nurse it to a certain spot. When he was done he had all the jack in a pile, see?" Maneuvering for money, Izzy acted "nervous like," according to Sweet, "and he had a neat flip of the ankle. Like you'd brush a speck offa the table with your fingers."

Izzy succeeded in this demanding job on the strength of his likability. He repeatedly displayed a knack for recruiting a protective figure who would make it his business to look out for the lonely youth. First there had been Chuck Connors, then Mike Salter, and now one of the other waiters, Kutch Kutchinsky, "sort of took to the kid and seen to it that nobody stuck nothing [to him]," as Sweet put it. Despite his acceptance, Izzy was never one of the boys. He neither drank nor caroused, and while he was sociable enough, there was a certain reticence about him. Nor did he confide in anyone; he accepted help, but he kept his own counsel.

■ ■ ■

By the following year, 1905, Nigger Mike had made a success of his resort, and Izzy had become a fixture along with Chinatown Gertie. Throughout, Chuck Connors kept the establishment on his itinerary, and it attracted an ever-widening circle of tourists. Just how wide its fame had spread became evident in November, when Connors conducted a tour of Chinatown for a large and prestigious group headed by Prince Louis of Battenberg. A rear admiral in the British Navy, the prince, who was related by marriage to King Edward VII, had recently sailed into the Port of New York aboard his flagship, the HMS *Drake*, and had since, according to the *New York World*, "captured New York and its society."

On Saturday evening, November 18, 1905, the prince dined with August Belmont, the financier; saw a hit play, Clyde Fitch's *Her Great Match*, at the Criterion Theatre; and just before midnight assembled a group to tour Chinatown under Connor's guidance. Owing to the reputed danger of Chinatown, the royal party included two detectives, and owing to the prince's fame, eighteen reporters. Exchanging his formal attire for a "rough tweed suit, a travelling cap, and stout tan shoes" and a golf cap, the prince rode downtown in a carriage. He alighted in Chinatown, where he tasted chop suey, visited a mission on Doyers Street, and at around one o'clock in the morning entered The Pelham Café, followed by his entourage.

Instantly, the grinning Professor Nicholson played "Strike Up the Band, Here Comes a Sailor." The prince expressed his pleasure, and the Professor responded with a tune that sounded something like "God Save the King." Mike Salter then sauntered forward and offered free drinks to his royal guest and the rest of the party, but the wealthy Belmont, who had built a subway system, insisted on picking up the tab. Emboldened, Nigger Mike requested a favor: "Prince, you can do the folks of Chinatown a favor. Just whisper to your friend, Mr. Belmont, that a subway would be a good thing for the district." As the conversation threatened to become awkward, two other members of the royal party, Lady Susan Townley and Mrs. John R. Drexel, asked Nigger Mike to bring on his popular singing waiters.

As the crowd of reporters watched, "two waiters, called Izzy and Bullhead, were introduced as 'the best singers in Chinatown,' " reported the *World*, "and they sang a song, the chorus of which runs:

> Gee, but this is a lonesome town.
> Nothing to do but hang around
> Everything looks dreary
> Everyone looks weary:
> No one here with a friendly clutch.
> No one to stand for a hurry touch.
> The best you get is a frozen frown—
> Gee, but this is lonesome town."

Prince Louis praised the waiters' effort, and, as he jostled with the reporters, noted that it did not apply to him. "I have had a delightful time, not dreariness, not weariness, and not one bit lonesome."

In their capacity as waiters, Izzy and Bullhead proceeded to serve beer to the visitors; this time Prince Louis paid. He then gave Izzy a ten-cent tip, and the young waiter announced he would frame the coin and hang it on the wall at The Pelham Café. By now it was time for the prince to leave as "banjos, cornets, wheezy piano and a hundred hoarse voices were making fearful and wonderful discord for 'God Save the King.' "

The royal progress made front-page news in the New York dailies for the next two days, in the process dragging a self-possessed young singing waiter known to the public only as "Izzy" into the limelight, along with his employer and several proprietors of opium dens the prince had visited. Izzy's first brush with publicity offered a compelling instance of the power of the press to create an image or reinforce a legend. As his ambition began to awaken, it was a lesson he would remember.

Among the reporters who covered the royal visit was twenty-three-year-old Herbert Bayard Swope of the *New York Herald.* In later years, when Swope became one of the most prominent newspapermen of his generation, he would often be credited as the first journalist to introduce the phenomenon known as Izzy Baline to the public, but in fact the singing waiter never appeared in Swope's account, though he did in others'. Nevertheless, the two became acquainted, forming the first of several literary friendships that would play a crucial role in furthering Izzy's career and creating an image acceptable to the public. (Years later the singing waiter and Prince Louis's son were to meet again, as well, under vastly different circumstances.)

The next flurry of excitement at Nigger Mike's revolved around the murder of a regular patron called Hobnailed Casey, who was known for conspicuously cleaning his nails at his table with a large and dangerous-looking knife. One evening Casey picked a fight with piano-playing Professor Nicholson, and so enraged Mike's assistant, one Frisco Joe, that Joe suddenly retrieved a gun from the icebox where it was stored and shot Casey to death on the street. Izzy was at the scene, and he relayed the tragic occurrence to Sulky, the bartender, who, Izzy noticed, had already crossed off Casey's fifty-dollar debt.

"Did you do that when you heard the shot?" Izzy asked.

"I did it when I saw Joe take the gat out of the ice box," Sulky replied.

Despite such distractions, Izzy continued to sing at Nigger Mike's and, for the first time, to entertain an ambition beyond that of earning enough money to last him the week. "Once you start singing, you start thinking of writing songs—it's as simple as that," he claimed. More precisely, Mike Salter did the thinking for him and suggested that Izzy and the Professor come up with an original song as a means of attracting still more publicity for The Pelham Café.

There was nothing original about the idea; over at a rival resort, Callahan's, on Doyers Street, the resident pianist, Al Piantadosi, had recently made a name for himself (and his place of employment) by writing the music for an Italian dialect song, "My Mariucci Take a Steamboat," with lyrics by the bar's bouncer, Big Jerry. That Big Jerry could write passable lyrics came as a surprise to all who knew him, and even more remarkably, a reputable publishing firm, Ted Brown, printed the song. And more startling still: the song became popular, enjoying a brief vogue in New York.

Rising to the challenge to devise a song that would do the same for Nigger Mike's, Izzy tried his hand at lyrics, sticking to the Italian dialect genre that had proved so successful for Al and Big Jerry. Izzy had a reputation for being fast and clever with words, but the words for this, his first song, came slowly and with great effort, when they came at all. Titled "Marie from Sunny Italy," the song was riddled with howlers and awkward rhymes.

For all his singing experience, Izzy was unable to read or write music; the task of composing the melody fell to the pianist, Professor Nicholson, who had also assisted the lyricist with the rhymes. Although Nicholson quickly pieced together a tune, he was embarrassed to explain that he felt less secure writing it, even though he was perfectly capable of reading whatever sheet music was placed in front of him. So the task of transcription fell to a third person, an anonymous violinist.

The gang at Nigger Mike's expected that "Marie from Sunny Italy" would achieve the same success as the song that had inspired it, and their hopes soared when Joseph W. Stern, the well-known music publishers, bought it, though the firm paid only seventy-five cents for the right. Izzy's share came to thirty-seven cents, a relatively insignificant amount compared to his earnings as a singing waiter. The sheet music appeared in May, about the time Izzy turned nineteen, adorned with a handsome illustration of an Italian youth serenading his loved one aboard a gondola. Of greater importance than anything else about this otherwise routine song was the name of the lyricist as it appeared on the title page: not Izzy or Israel Baline, but "I. Berlin."

Izzy had chosen his professional name with considerable care. It was sufficiently similar to his real name to be unmistakably his, but at the same time it had a formal, Teutonic ring. A nineteen-year-old singing waiter who adopted this name plainly had aspirations that extended well beyond Chinatown. Nor was it necessarily an entertainer's name; there was nothing breezy or familiar about it. With such a name, Izzy was not so much trying to conceal his identity as enlarge on it. His choice of a new name marked the beginning of his effort to create a persona for public consumption, and during the next five decades, he would continue to redefine and reinvent himself, using materials that came readily to hand. Yet those who knew him well enough or went back with him to his Lower East Side days would continue to call him Izzy Baline, and he would, on occasion, refer to himself by that name in their presence, or sign his letters "Izzy." The custom indicated his need for a few people before whom he would not be obliged to enact the demanding role of Irving Berlin, but simply revert to his canny, coarse, nervous, and pragmatic self.

When "Marie from Sunny Italy" was published, his good friend Joe Schenck bought the first copy, though not many more were sold. The song quickly disappeared, and Izzy returned to temporary obscurity at Nigger Mike's. Much later, he declared that his effort deserved its fate: "It went the way of all imitation." He went on to observe, "It was an important song, though, because it did get me out of Chinatown." His imprecise recollection to the contrary, this one song didn't achieve that elusive goal. He would have to write more and better songs before he left, songs that would outdo even Al Piantadosi's biggest hit, "I Didn't Raise My Boy to Be a Soldier."

At this embryonic stage in his songwriting career, Izzy found more success with his spontaneous, risqué parodies than with more formal attempts. One of his crowd pleasers was a takeoff of a well-known song by a young composer named Max Winslow: "Are Ye Comin' Out Tonight, Mary Ann?" Winslow worked as a "professional manager" for Harry Von Tilzer, Berlin's one-time employer; in his job, Winslow functioned as a talent scout and liaison to the music business. It was in his professional capacity that he journeyed down from West 28th Street to Pell Street and Nigger Mike's, where he heard Izzy's salacious version of "Are Ye Comin' Out Tonight, Mary Ann?" Winslow was impressed by the singing waiter's facility with words and his rousing style of performance—which had the customers beating the table tops in time with the tune. Winslow went back to Von Tilzer and tried to persuade the publisher to hire the singing waiter as a fifteen-dollar-a-week staff lyricist, but Von Tilzer refused.

However, Izzy and Winslow became fast friends. Together they rented a small, sparsely furnished room on East 18th Street, just off Union Square, and at last Izzy's years in Lower East Side lodging houses were permanently behind him. Though they had moved only blocks from Chinatown, culturally they lived in another, far more respectable world. For the first time in his life he had, at least when Winslow was not around, a room of his own.

Izzy's manner of dress changed as radically as his living conditions and became as formal and reserved as his adopted name. He cast off the starched white apron of the singing waiter and dressed in the most fashionable and expensive suits he could afford, suits with tight trousers and fancy lapels. A tie and celluloid collar were the rule; Izzy would never be one to loll about in casual clothes. He preferred to groom himself for eventual success, proudly displaying a diamond pinky ring he had purchased cheaply from a traveling salesman at Nigger Mike's. He made regular visits to barbershops frequented by entertainers, where, in addition to his usual haircut and shave, he saw to it that his thick hair, usually an unruly black mass, was pomaded to a respectable gloss. Though he wanted above all else to be an entertainer, he had no interest in living or looking like a Bohemian.

His new attitude showed up in his work, where it stirred envy among the other waiters: first a new name, then the fancy clothes. Izzy had suddenly gone uptown, and they disliked the way he reminded them of their inferior social status. In time, they gained revenge on him with a cruel prank.

Among the more insidious professional hazards of life as a singing waiter was the temptation to sleep on the job; and Izzy had occasionally succumbed. Several times before, patrons had taken advantage of him by removing his diamond ring, promising to return it to him on the condition that he bring them a bottle of champagne, *gratis*. Now, in the atmosphere of envy surrounding him, the joke soured. The next time Izzy leaned his head on the bar and fell asleep, Bullhead Lawrence removed the waiter's prized diamond ring as an accomplice quietly took twenty-five dollars from the cash register. The two of them then shook Izzy awake, pointed to the register, and accused him of permitting a robbery to occur. Bullhead later said, "He ran to the till and saw that it was empty, and his ring was gone."

When Mike learned of the theft, he had, unfortunately, been drinking, and in that quarrelsome mood he summarily fired the upstart singing waiter. Izzy never complained about the unfair treatment; in a sense, Mike had done him a favor, and it was time to move on.

CHAPTER 3

Tin Pan Alley

The reputation of I. Berlin, singing waiter and occasional lyricist, proved sufficient to win its owner a new position early in 1908, but at better wages and in a classier establishment. The proprietor was Jimmy Kelly, a former boxer and bouncer at Nigger Mike's, and his restaurant was located "uptown," that is to say at 14th Street and Union Square, close to the burgeoning music publishing industry. Berlin now found himself working in a neighborhood far better than what he had known, yet it, too, possessed notorious enclaves. "The headquarters of the Hip Song Tong [gang] used to be across the way," he remembered, "and one of their buildings was occupied by Chinese and their white women."

Despite the vice flourishing around him, he remained a detached bystander and an innocent. When he sought relaxation, he went not to a brothel or a bar, but to a barbershop. Still, his speech was as profane as that of his counterparts and as redolent of Lower East Side slang. He spoke freely of wops, sheenies, micks, niggers, and chinks, though there was nothing remarkable about such terms before the First World War. And his accent remained pure Cherry Street, insistent and harsh. He flattened his *a*'s and turned his final *r*'s to mush. He spoke rapidly, if occasionally indistinctly, and radiated nervous energy; he was as high strung as a whippet, teeming with plans, schemes, hunches, and notions—all related to the music business. And he was eager to ingratiate himself with whomever he thought might help him achieve his goals. He was willing to talk with anyone, consider any idea, but he made up his mind in a flash, and once he did, could rarely be dissuaded.

His sociability was largely confined to his business dealings. Approaching his twentieth birthday, he was as much a loner as ever; he had one close friend in Max Winslow, but he lacked a steady girlfriend or other significant relationship. He viewed his clamorous surroundings with the same amused tolerance he had displayed on the Lower East Side, but his genuinely naïve outlook, despite its inherent limitations, would prove an asset in the songwriting trade, where cheerfulness and sentimentality were at a premium. Berlin feared no evil because he saw no evil.

At Jimmy Kelly's he concentrated less on performing and more on mastering the rudiments of the craft of songwriting, but he was severely handicapped by his lack of musical training. Gradually, though, he devised various strategies to make up for this limitation. At first, he worked out a simple *modus operandi* with the restaurant's pianist: Berlin would hum a melody, and the pianist would transcribe it. But literal transcriptions of his melodies lacked the polish and flair that more successful songwriters imparted to their creations. Berlin decided to look beyond a literal-minded transcriber for actual collaborators—anyone from whom he might be able to learn a few tricks of the trade: rhyme schemes, for one thing, and harmony, not to mention tips as to what the publishers were buying. (Love songs were the one absolute staple, but it would be several years until Berlin made his first memorable contribution to this genre.) Among his earliest collaborators was Maurice Abrahams, another aspiring young songwriter. Together they composed "Queenie, My Own," a love song that quickly found a buyer (motion picture executive Carl Laemmle) but no audience. Berlin tried again with other collaborators, to little avail.

He had to wait until the last week of 1908 to receive some real encouragement. Finally Marie Cahill, a star known for her feisty stage portrayals, bought a song for which he had contributed the lyrics, "She Was a Dear Little Girl," and added the number to her hit show *The Boys and Betty*, which told of a woman who flees her husband for the temptations of Paris. Berlin's song did not belong in the show's original score, which had been composed by Silvio Hein; it was an "interpolation": a number added after the opening. It was then common practice for stars to interpolate songs during a show's run to fatten their roles or enliven dull spots in the evening. As a result, many musical shows changed substantially after opening night, and often their biggest hits came from the ranks of interpolations rather than the original score. Berlin would often employ this practice to advance his reputation as a songwriter.

As Irving Berlin the neophyte songwriter struggled, his roommate, Max Winslow, growing restless under the constraints of the Von Tilzer office, developed a sideline as a coach for female vocalists. He rapidly distinguished himself in this field by encouraging his pupils to adopt a unique and marketable style of singing. In time, his students became known throughout the business as "Winslow's Singles." He also applied his keen judgment to Berlin, recognizing that what his friend's raw talent required was a touch of class. To this end, Winslow introduced him to a new collaborator, who proved to be far more sophisticated than any of Berlin's Chinatown cronies.

Edgar Leslie had come to New York from Stamford, Connecticut. Unlike the majority of younger tunesmiths, he was educated (at the prominent Cooper Union) and a white Protestant. He wore his ethnic and cultural distinctions like a suit of armor and usually couched his observations in crisp, sardonic terms, earning the nickname "Sourpuss." However, he possessed a kind, generous-looking face that became animated when he discussed his two great musical loves, English music hall songs and operettas by Gilbert and Sullivan. The lyrics for which he is best remembered were generally upbeat, as exemplified by his song, "For Me And My Gal." In contrast to this literate, cultivated, and socially secure young man, Berlin was severely provincial; a new suit of clothes did little to conceal his many rough edges and nothing to hide his mounting ambition.

Together they wrote a song entitled "Wait, Wait, Wait," which they took to Winslow, who in turn recommended it to his boss, Von Tilzer, who liked the song enough to publish it. Thanks to the tutelage he received from Leslie, this song met with a modest commercial success, and its coauthors earned two hundred dollars in royalties—a trifling sum compared to the thousands of dollars a hit could reap, but the amount was sufficient to persuade Berlin he had a future as a songwriter for the great Von Tilzer. Just then, however, Winslow decided to leave Von Tilzer for a new firm calling itself the Seminary Music Company. At his suggestion the firm's misleading title was changed to reflect the names of its two founders, Waterson and Snyder.

Henry Waterson and Ted Snyder made for an ill-matched pair, and at first glance they appeared unlikely to succeed in the highly competitive popular music racket. The middle-aged Waterson—who spelled his last name "Watterson" when it suited his mood—financed the operation. He knew far more about diamonds, in which he dealt, and horses, on which he regularly placed substantial bets, than he did about music. He was almost entirely deaf and could scarcely appreciate his much younger partner's musical facility. For Waterson, musical ignorance posed no obstacle; if Von Tilzer could become rich and famous as a music publisher without reading a note of music, why couldn't Henry Waterson accomplish the same goal without being able to hear one?

The younger man, Snyder, was, at the moment, a red-hot property, thanks to the recent success of his instrumental, the "Wild Cherries Rag." Only twenty-five, Snyder had composed a string of hits even before "Wild Cherries," and he was eager to find other songwriters to publish. Suddenly, both Winslow and a popular performer named Amy Butler started telling him about a singing waiter going by the name of Irving Berlin and his risqué parodies. Butler was so enthusiastic she persuaded Snyder to cross Union Square and hear the foul-mouthed waiter for himself. Snyder listened and stroked his chin; he was not overwhelmed. He knew that a popular songwriter lived or died by his ability to *give the public what it wanted*, to set a prevailing public sentiment to music. But the singing waiter's act, funny and energetic as it was, posed a serious problem: the lyrics were too suggestive to print, and that liability alone meant that no publisher would touch him. Berlin wasn't trying to *give the public what it wanted*, and until he did, Snyder was at a loss to make use of him.

Meeting with these mixed reactions, Irving stayed on at Jimmy Kelly's, where by now he was less of a waiter and more of a resident entertainer. There he was approached by a now-forgotten song-and-dance man who needed an Italian comic dialect number for his act at Tony Pastor's. Berlin agreed to write the lyrics—clean lyrics—for ten dollars, and for the first time he sought inspiration not in other songs but in a topical event: the 1908 Olympic Games in London. The talk of the games was an Italian marathon runner named Dorando Pietri, who would have won his race had the crowd not surged forward and pushed him toward the finish line. This infraction disqualified Pietri, and victory went instead to a New Yorker, J. J. Hayes. The Olympics inspired several other topical songs that year, but Berlin's was the only one to ignore the feats of the athletes in favor of a fictional situation he devised in which a hapless Italian-American barber bets his entire shop on Dorando, only to see him lose. This stroke of invention marked the first time Berlin displayed any originality in his songwriting and demonstrated his knack for casting an overwhelming public event in simple terms with strong emotional appeal.

By the time Berlin finished his elaborate set of lyrics, however, the nameless song-and-dance man had changed his mind. On the advice of Amy Butler, the composer hastened with his material to the offices of Waterson & Snyder, where his name was known, if not yet highly regarded. Waterson, though unable to hear, could at least read; he approved the lyric and agreed to pay its author twenty-five dollars, tune included. Thinking he could later devise one with the aid of the pianist at Jimmy Kelly's, Berlin claimed he had already worked out the melody. "Just you trot into the next room to the arranger and he'll take down your tune for you," Waterson offered. With his twenty-five dollars and a link to the new firm at stake, Berlin forced himself to improvise a tune on the spot; fortunately, it was adequate for a song in which the lyrics were preeminent.

Waterson's staff transcriber took down a rough approximation of Berlin's tune, matched it with the lyrics, and when the result was published, it proved to be a bona fide hit in New York, if not the rest of the country. Despite its success, Berlin waited two years before he attempted to write music again; until then, he preferred the safer arena of lyrics.

Collaborating again with Edgar Leslie, Berlin sought to capitalize on "Dorando" 's success with another comic dialect song. This time Leslie proposed the subject matter. Thanks to his familiarity with opera, he had learned of a scandal created by a recent production of Richard Strauss's *Salome*; it seemed that the "Dance of the Seven

Veils" had more in common with burlesque than with the Bible. Exploiting this ripe topic, Leslie and Berlin made the song as risqué as they dared. ("We did it to see whether we could get away with it," Berlin commented.) As with "Dorando," they recast the material in strictly local, ethnic terms. A certain Sadie Cohen, who happens to be a striptease artist, scores a hit with her "Dance of the Seven Veils," to which her boyfriend, the prudish Moses, takes exception.

Today this song seems to be nothing more than a quaint piece of ethnic stereotyping, but at the time, its facile rhymes raised a genuine issue confronting immigrant Jews: the threat of seduction away from the old paths into the godless and immoral behavior of American urban life. It was an issue Berlin faced every day as he moved ever deeper into a show business demimonde populated with jugglers, comics, song-and-dance men, and chorus girls. So far, the fastidious young man had managed to hold out against their lure.

"Sadie Salome, Go Home," as the song was called, ran up a tidy sale for Waterson & Snyder: three thousand copies, enough to inspire the company to offer Berlin a contract as a staff lyricist. Finally, here was his chance to make a break with the singing waiter trade. The document, however, spelled out their business relationship in considerable and, for the uneducated Berlin, often incomprehensible detail. Displaying a characteristic sense of caution and patience that would mark many of his future business dealings, he decided to show the contract to a lawyer friend who frequented Jimmy Kelly's; the lawyer urged him not to sign. Instead, Berlin proposed a simpler and more reliable agreement to write lyrics for Waterson & Snyder at a salary of twenty-five dollars a week, plus royalties. The firm accepted, and he became, at last, a journeyman wordsmith.

▪ ▪ ▪

It was Berlin's good fortune to enter the popular music field as it was embarking on a period of enormous prosperity. During previous decades, the music industry had been diffuse, provincial. Publishers were scattered across the country. Boston was home to the firm of Oliver Ditson, with its encyclopedic song catalogue; Root and Cady was headquartered in Chicago; Baltimore had its publishers, as did Philadelphia, where Lee & Walker flourished. Beginning in 1881, however, the music publishers began to converge on New York; that year two brothers founded the influential firm of T. B. Harms, and others quickly followed their lead. Many publishers flourished because they generally bought songs outright and paid composers little or no royalties. Copyright laws that could have protected starving composers were either not enforced or had yet to be written.

This climate of exploitation led to a number of tragic endings for some of the best-known American songwriters of the era. The most accomplished and admired of them all, Stephen Foster, died in 1864, an impoverished alcoholic, leaving behind a string of timeless classics such as "Oh, Susanna," "Jeannie With the Light Brown Hair," and "The Old Folks At Home." And Foster had been the first American songwriter to receive even meager royalties. Many other lesser figures also died broke; Hart Danks, composer of "Silver Threads Among the Gold," ended his days in a shabby apartment in New York, where he wrote his farewell message: "It's hard to die alone." Another songwriter, Richard Gerard, wound up working in the New York post office to earn his keep and to the end of his life carried cards identifying himself as the coauthor of the "world famous 'Sweet Adeline.' " Meanwhile, their publishers flourished.

The hits on which publishers thrived were usually sentimental ballads extolling motherhood, home, and faithful sweethearts; an occasional cad met with his comeuppance in these songs, or a woman sank into a sinful way of life, but generally the songs meant to reassure. They stood in sharp contrast to the harshness of urban life; offering escape to a simpler time and place, they were inevitably nostalgic. The exception to the prevailing philosophy of songwriting was the occasional song inspired by real events, everything from the Olympics, as Berlin demonstrated, to fire fighters and, in 1842, the first water pumped into New York. Temperance, the Abolitionist movement, and women's suffrage all inspired an outpouring of musical expression.

The public bought these offerings as much for the brightly colored illustrations adorning the sheet music covers as for the music and lyrics within. Alert to the promotional value of cover art, music publishers commissioned and purchased all rights to the illustrations and reproduced them by means of an innovative technology known as lithography. No less an artist than Winslow Homer turned out sheet music covers in his younger days.

Gradually the major publishers began to relinquish their near-monopoly on profits. The turning point occurred in 1892, when the New York firm of M. Witmark & Sons sent songwriter Charles K. Harris a royalty check for eighty-five cents. Outraged by the paltry sum, he immediately established his own publishing company, for which he wrote "After the Ball." The song quickly became the biggest hit of its time, earning Harris as much as $25,000 a week, and eventually selling five million copies.

Other songwriters hastened to emulate Harris's stunning example. Songwriters such as Edward Marks, Paul Dresser (brother of novelist Theodore Dreiser), Joseph Stern, Harry Von Tilzer, and Charles B. Ward all became publishers, joining the ranks of other, more traditional firms such as Shapiro, Bernstein & Company and the Leo Feist Music Publishing Company. Many, such as Waterson & Snyder, congregated around Union Square. As a group, they made more money than the previous generation of tunesmiths would have thought possible. In his first year of operation, for instance, Von Tilzer's firm sold over five million copies of sheet music.

Songwriters not fortunate enough to become their own publishers still eked out a precarious living. Under the provisions of the 1909 Copyright Act, they sold their songs as work for hire; the publisher wound up owning the copyright. Often a copyright of negligible value at the time of a song's first publication soared in value months or even years later, especially when the movies began asserting their insatiable appetite for music and their formidable ability to popularize previously obscure songs.

Part of the credit for the boom in sheet music belonged not to the publishers or songwriters but to the retail outlets where the music was sold; they, too, became an important part of the business, and of the retailers, none was more important than the F. W. Woolworth chain. Frank Woolworth himself loved music and played several instruments (poorly). In the early 1890s he prevailed on reluctant local store managers to start selling sheet music; by the First World War, the chain sold 200 million copies of sheet music annually.

To maintain this level of sales, publishers cultivated star performers who could popularize the songs. Most singers received their copies for free, and they often received coauthorship credit simply for agreeing to promote a song written entirely by others. Such promotion expenses, often running to tens of thousands of dollars per song, were required to attract a performer of the stature of Eddie Cantor or Al Jolson, who could give it the boost needed to sell millions of copies.

But publishers did more than pin their hopes on the whims of performers. They employed scores of song pluggers to demonstrate tunes in Woolworth's and on the premises of the publisher itself. Previously, such pluggers—including Berlin, during his stint at Tony Pastor's—had worked in vaudeville theaters, coaxing an audience to sing along with a show; now they played and sang in department stores, calling attention to the latest sheet music. Pluggers were known for their piercing voices and stamina. They migrated from store to store throughout the day, hoping to entice customers into buying the publishers' latest offering. Their musical demonstrations were not confined to stores alone; enterprising pluggers sang on the streets as their busker forbears had. Still others held forth from elevated train platforms, saloons, theater balconies, pool halls—almost anywhere a crowd gathered.

As a songwriter Berlin developed a more skeptical view of the value of plugging:

> I have heard it asserted that a song isn't written—that it is plugged—but that isn't true by any degree of reasoning [he wrote]. Plugging gives a quick verdict on a song and advertises it; but no matter what you do, you can't make a success out of a bad song. By consistent plugging you can get a certain revenue out of a fair song—but that's all. In the end it doesn't pay. Plugging has its big value in making a success out of a good song.

To serious students of music, the trifles from which publishers reaped such rich rewards were hardly songs at all; they were the bastard offspring of cynicism and greed, and they contained all the poetry of an assembly line. For the word- and tunesmiths, that was just the point: the stuff was simple enough to churn out by the yard, and anyone could grasp it. Though the results tended toward sameness and blandness, publishers made no apology for adhering to childishly simple formulas. The prevailing philosophy was best expressed by Charles K.

Harris, who listed six conditions for a successful song. "When writing popular songs," he advised, "always bear in mind that it is to the masses, the untrained musical public, that you must largely look for support and popularity. Therefore, do not offer them anything which in subject matter or melody does not appeal to their ears. To do so is just so much time thrown away." He also cautioned: "Watch your competitors," and "Take note of public demand." Furthermore: "Avoid slang and vulgarisms; they never succeed." (Berlin's "Dorando" proved Harris wrong on that point, at least.) He offered hints about craft: "Many-syllabled words and those containing hard consonants, wherever possible, must be avoided." One recommendation Berlin did take to heart: "In writing lyrics be concise; get to your point quickly, and then make the point as strong as possible." Numerous Berlin hits would illustrate the wisdom of this last directive, if not the others.

As a student of songwriting, Berlin soon learned more specific formulas than those expressed by Harris, formulas detailing the actual musical construction of a popular song; and these were as rigid, as subtle, as intricate, and as widely observed as the rules governing the construction of a sonnet.

Songs generally began with a verse or recitative to assist the singer in making a transition from speaking to singing. The verse established the song's premise and gave the performer a chance to slip into character for the more lyrical and emotional chorus, which formed the heart of the song. This was the truly memorable section, the part the audience would whistle after the curtain came down or hum without thinking the next morning. It was also the most complex. The chorus, or refrain, varied in length. In the nineteenth century, it was usually eight or sixteen bars long, while verses ran as long as sixty-four bars. Then Stephen Foster popularized the convention of marrying eight-bar verses to an eight-bar chorus in songs such as "Go Down, Moses" and "Camptown Races"; these were early "coon" songs, or songs based on black models. For his English-influenced compositions, such as "Beautiful Dreamer," Foster adopted a more sophisticated sixteen-bar chorus, which he constructed in four sections of four bars each. It was this latter form—simple, symmetrical, and inevitable—that served as the model for popular songs at the time Berlin entered the field. And it remained the standard until Berlin smashed the mold with his ground-breaking hit, "Alexander's Ragtime Band," with its chorus of thirty-two effervescent bars.

Eventually, the thirty-two-bar chorus gained widespread acceptance, and it was on such choruses that Berlin lavished most of his wit, imagination, and skill as a composer. Like its sixteen-bar predecessor, it was built of four sections of equal length; the first eight bars stated the song's principal melody, and the second eight usually repeated it, note for note, even though the words often changed. The repetition proved useful for driving the song deep into the listener's memory. Then, just when the chorus threatened to become monotonous, the third section, often called the release, or bridge, offered a variation or a refreshing mirror image of the principal melody. Finally, the end of this brief escape inevitably led to a reiteration of the melody that had already been heard twice.

This rigid formula often proved to be a creative straitjacket. With a limited selection of acceptable themes (motherhood, courtship, and rural nostalgia) and only eight notes in the scale, songs often sounded alike. At the same time, the copyright laws, stringently enforced by litigious publishers jealously guarding their catalogue, insisted that songs had to be different from one another.

Yet many songs did borrow freely from others. One trick of the songwriters' trade was to quote snatches of several public domain songs in the course of a tune. A prominent instance of this technique occurred in the 1923 hit, "Yes, We Have No Bananas," which was a pastiche of at least five other songs. And Berlin himself quoted Stephen Foster to splendid effect in "Alexander's Ragtime Band." Despite the occasional daring flourish, Berlin adhered to conventional songwriting practices as strictly as the next composer, right through his 1,500 published songs, yet he would prove himself a master at devising subtle harmonies and variations on accepted models: musical fingerprints that imparted freshness and originality to his songs.

None of this musical craftsmanship came quickly or easily to him. At the time he went to work for Waterson & Snyder, he restricted his efforts to lyrics alone and left the music to those better qualified to compose it. He studied the efforts of other composers, especially those of Stephen Foster, who quickly became Berlin's idol as a songwriter, if not a businessman. Berlin later paid Foster the singular compliment of hanging his portrait on the wall of his office. Songs on the order of Foster's classics, Berlin recognized, were deceptively simple; they were easy enough to play and sing (that was the idea), but devilishly hard to write.

Compounding the problem of writing a good song was the problem of selling it to a publisher, which usually meant the composer had to endure a gauntlet of rejection. One veteran song plugger described what it took to survive: "You've got to have all the gall, you've got to have a hide like an alligator, you've got to have unlimited self-confidence, you've got to believe that because you wrote it, it's the best." Customers were too crude, the pace too frantic, the competition too intense for a thin-skinned, sensitive songwriter to survive.

In search of zealots able to survive constant rejection, publishers did more than rely on their staff composers and lyricists; they roamed the streets of Union Square, Chinatown, and the Bowery—Berlin's three haunts—in search of new tunes and new musical trends. Since many were former songwriters themselves, they knew the value of being in touch with the street, both to find and sell their wares. "The best songs came from the gutter," Edward B. Marks, the publisher, insisted. "There was no surer way of starting a song off to popularity than to get it sung as loudly as possible in the city's lowest dives. If a publisher knew his business, he always launched a sales campaign by impressing his song on the happily befogged consciousness of the gang in the saloons and beer halls." Berlin knew the streets, if little else; the years he had spent barging into Bowery saloons and entertaining the customers at Nigger Mike's served as an ideal apprenticeship for a career as a popular songwriter.

By now he had graduated from the street to the marketplace. Waterson & Snyder, like most other publishers, functioned as a wholesaler and retailer, talent scout, and factory dedicated to the mass production of music. Easy access was the rule. Virtually anyone claiming to be a songwriter could enter a publisher's office, give his music to a waiting plugger, and obtain a brief audition. Once in a great while he might even sell his song, generally for ten or fifteen dollars. Or he might join forces with one of the many singers loitering in publishers' offices, waiting for songs that they could work into their acts. In less than a decade, the rapidly increasing number of publishers and the size of their operations necessitated moving to larger quarters, and virtually the entire industry migrated uptown, along with the city's theater district. By 1910 many established publishers had abandoned Union Square for a short stretch of West 28th Street between Fifth Avenue and Broadway. (Waterson & Snyder were one of the few who remained downtown.) The district quickly became the focus of this fast-growing, but still remarkably compact industry. Visiting his brother Paul Dresser in the neighborhood one day, Theodore Dreiser noted the profusion of activity accompanying the creation of popular songs:

> Three or four pianos give to each chamber a parlor-like appearance. The walls are hung with the photos of celebrities, neatly framed. In the private music rooms, rocking chairs. A boy or two waits to bring *professional copies* at a word. A salaried pianist or two wait to run over pieces which the singer may desire to hear. . . . And then those "peerless singers of popular ballads," as their programs announce them, men and women whose pictures you will see upon every song-sheet, their physiognomy underscored with their own "Yours Sincerely" in their own handwriting. Every day they are here, arriving and departing, carrying the latest songs to all parts of the land.

Immigrant desperation to survive fueled much of the young industry's success. By the time publishers took over West 28th Street, the Irish, who had arrived in New York a generation or two earlier, were now yielding control of the entertainment industry to the Jews, who infused the business with their own brand of vigor.

Among those tracking the rise of immigrant Jews in the field of popular music was a journalist and songwriter named Monroe Rosenfeld. In 1909, desperate for money, he wrote a series of articles about the flourishing new breed of music publishers, their pluggers, transcribers, and staff lyricists. Walking through the district, he listened to the cacophony created by pianists banging away beside open windows, vocalists belting out hits-in-the-making, and composers endlessly repeating a melody or phrase. To Rosenfeld's ears, the noise sounded like the clatter of pots and pans in a busy kitchen, and he proceeded to give his articles and the street the name by which it has since been known: Tin Pan Alley.

▪ ▪ ▪

Berlin made himself an Alley fixture with remarkable alacrity. In his first year as a professional lyricist, he set a pattern of extraordinary productivity that he would maintain for half a century. In 1909, he wrote the words for over two dozen published songs, as well as countless others that never reached the public. He set himself a goal of writing as many as four or five songs during his nightlong work sessions, and he constantly assessed and judged his handiwork, often harshly.

Of the songs that he did publish, fully half were set to music composed by his employer, Ted Snyder. They were mostly forgettable efforts, even by Alley standards, but two of them developed into bona fide hits that made Irving Berlin a name to be reckoned with, at least during the season in which they were published.

The first of these hits had its genesis in an ordinary incident that occurred late one spring: "One night, in a barber shop, . . . I ran into George Whiting, a vaudeville actor, and asked him if he could go to a show with me. 'Sure,' he said; and he added with a laugh, 'My wife's gone to the country.' " For Berlin, this offhand remark proved to be a moment of inspiration, as he later recalled for a theatrical magazine.

> Bing! *There* I had a common place familiar title line. It was singable, capable of humorous upbuilding, simple, and one that did not seriously offend against the "sexless" rule; for wives and their offspring of both sexes, as well as their husbands, would be amused by singing it or hearing it sung.
>
> I persuaded Whiting to forget the theatre and to devote the night to developing the line with me into a song.

Berlin went on to divulge something of his thought processes while giving birth to a Tin Pan Alley product, at the same time dropping clues about his ferocious appetite for work:

> Now, the usual and unsuccessful way of handling a line like that is to dash off a jumble of verses about the henpecked

husband, all leading up to a chorus running, we'll say, something like this:

My wife's gone to the country,
She went away last night.
Oh, I'm so glad! I'm so glad!
I'm crazy with delight!

Just wordy, obvious elaboration. No *punch*! All night I sweated to find what I knew was there, and finally I speared the lone word, just a single word, that *made* the song—and a fortune. Listen:

My wife's gone to the country!
Hooray!

Hooray! ["Hurrah!" in the actual song] That lone word gave the whole idea of the song in one quick wallop. It gave the singer a chance to hoot with sheer joy. It *invited* the roomful to join in the hilarious shout. It everlastingly put the catch line over. And I wasn't content until I had used my good thing to the limit. "She took the children with her—Hooray! *Hooray!*"—and so on.

Ted Snyder supplied a serviceable melody for Berlin's lyrics, and the firm rushed out the song in time for the seasonal boost it required. Their faith in the song lead them to place a half-page advertisement in a recently established trade journal calling itself *Variety*.

WEATHER NOTES—Look Out for a Cyclone!
"MY WIFE'S GONE TO THE COUNTRY"
("HURRAH—HURRAH")
Discovered by the "It" Song Explorers,
IRVING BERLIN, GEO. WHITING AND TED SNYDER.

And that faith quickly turned out to be justified; the song sold 300,000 copies, and its vogue proved strong enough for the *New York Evening Journal* to commission still more verses to run in its pages. In an impressive display of verbal dexterity and endurance, the twenty-one-year-old lyricist obliged not with the six verses required but with one hundred, all of them elaborating the theme of a husband rejoicing in his temporary liberation from domestic tyranny.

Despite his relative inexperience, Berlin realized how ephemeral his newfound reputation might be. "Song writing all depends on the public," he explained to a reporter who had come to interview the newest name in Tin Pan Alley. "The thing it likes one minute it tires of the next. . . . You must be able to switch your lyre to something else. If not, a new writer will take your place and your star, which rose so suddenly, will set as rapidly as it came up." Few others would find so little to enjoy in sudden success.

Although the song helped established Berlin as a songwriter, it had a less benign effect on his collaborator, George Whiting. After the song became a hit, his wife took its implications rather more literally than he had intended and sued him for divorce. Years later, he wrote "My Blue Heaven" in an effort to atone and win her back.

From Berlin's point of view, the hit song's chief shortcoming was the number of collaborators with whom he had to share royalties. For his subsequent hit, he devised a way around this problem—and his nagging lack of musical ability—by writing words for a melody in the public domain, Mendelssohn's "Spring Song," which was enjoying a new life as a popular strain. Berlin cannily seized on the tune, simplified it according to a Tin Pan Alley formula, and wrote conventional courting lyrics to accompany it.

Berlin claimed sole authorship for this stunt, and it proved to be a crowd pleaser, making the rounds of New York City "lobster palaces," lavish restaurants where patrons devoured lobster and champagne and entertainers sang the latest hits. "Night after night one can hear the 'lobsterites' applauding some hoarse-voiced girl singing this arrant nonsense in the cafes," lamented one disgruntled music critic of Berlin's latest effort. "But when some exquisite selection from 'Aida' or 'Madame Butterfly' is stingily given there is a contrasting lack of enthusiasm."

"That Mesmerizing Mendelssohn Tune" did not depend on critics for its popularity. It sold even more copies than "My Wife's Gone to the Country"—over half a million—and a year after publication it continued to sell thousands of copies each month. Berlin, who recognized how shallow an achievement it was, could only shake his head in wonder as he suddenly started earning more money than he could spend. Rather than boast of his cleverness on this occasion, he took his song, and the Alley mentality that had fostered it, to task.

"Of course sentimental ballads are still good. They always will be. But we are not producing any living songs," he complained to a journalist who had intended only to lionize young Irving, not witness this exercise in self-chastisement. The songwriter went on to caution, "These things I am writing are only for the brief career of the vaudeville stage. They will be a hit for a week or two. Then they will be forgotten and new ones will take their place. But I cannot think of a song in years that has come to stay." He reminded the reporter that "folks are still singing 'Swanee River' and 'My Old Kentucky Home.' It's something to be known like Stephen C. Foster." At the cost of dismissing his current work, Berlin declared ambitions that went beyond the narrow commercial boundaries of Tin Pan Alley.

Even his failures were noteworthy because they presaged some of his later successes. One song concerned Christmas. It was a Tin Pan Alley truism that holidays offered ideal occasions for songs, and Berlin followed this conventional wisdom when he tried his hand at "Christmas Time Seems Years and Years Away." On this occasion, his effort was a flop, though he would, of course, turn his attention to Christmas again, to greater effect. But his willingness to write such a song now, in 1909, demonstrated how far the process of assimilation had already gone. Not that he had any intention of converting; under his assumed name, he simply relished the opportunity to write songs on any theme he wished, in any dialect he preferred. Unlike Izzy Baline, who was irrevocably rooted in the Lower East Side, Irving Berlin had no particular identity; he could portray, in turn, an Italian, Irishman, German, Jew, Black—whatever suited his whim and whatever he decided the market demanded.

Black music, especially, captivated his imagination, and he began to explore the music he had heard Lukie Johnson playing down at Nigger Mike's: ragtime. Berlin had remained friends with the talented black pianist, and attempted to penetrate the mystique surrounding the unique and compelling sound of the music he played. As a student of Stephen Foster, who had repeatedly adapted the black music and black subjects of his day, Berlin sensed ragtime was worth taking seriously and adapting to Tin Pan Alley formulas. However, he lacked sufficient training to grasp the intricacies of "ragged time," or syncopation, which formed the basis of this style of music. Furthermore, ragtime had been in retreat ever since its heyday ten years earlier, when it had come up from the South, spread through the cities of the Midwest, and then burst on the scene in New York. The best-known ragtime composer, Scott Joplin, of Sedalia, Missouri, had attracted widespread attention with his gentle and reflective rags, but in the last two years the black composer had been in retreat in New York City, where he was attempting to write an entire opera in ragtime. Meanwhile, Joplin's wife supported him by running a boardinghouse, and his health failed as syphilis attacked his brain. While Joplin toiled in obscurity, any number of black ragtime pianists, including Berlin's friend Lukie Johnson, continued to play it, even though ragtime was considered passé.

Circulating primarily among whites rather than Blacks, Berlin sensed that the word *ragtime*, if not the actual music as Scott Joplin would have defined it, was making a comeback. On white tongues, it suggested far more than just syncopation—rather, a new, free-swinging, and irreverent attitude toward life. Enlisting Ted Snyder to provide the required syncopated melodies, Berlin ingeniously tried to revitalize ragtime by adapting it to different ethnic modes—white ("That Opera Rag"), Italian ("Sweet Marie, Make a Rag-a-Time-Dance with Me"), and even Jewish ("Yiddle on Your Fiddle Play Some Ragtime"). The variety was enough to make a ragtime purist gag.

Even Berlin's frequent misfires possessed some residual value. In Tin Pan Alley parlance, they were trunk songs: songs to be saved for the future. And even if they were not resurrected, they could still yield useful bits and pieces for new songs. In the early stages of his career, Berlin was sufficiently organized to maintain an active backlog of trunk songs, to which he turned when he required inspiration and which he freely cannibalized. Some of these early songs contained musical phrases or dramatic ideas that he first isolated, then expanded into a full-fledged "new" hit. The more Berlin wrote, the more his songs were informed by the discarded ghosts of his earlier tunes.

Yet the craft of popular songwriting, for all the tangible benefits it had begun to bestow, still failed to satisfy Irving. His years as a busker and singing waiter had conditioned him to believe that great songs were made by performers and audiences, not by composers toiling in solitude. He was too active, too high-strung, to spend the rest of his career behind a desk or seated before a piano in a practice room at Waterson & Snyder; he needed a stage to feel fully himself. "When you're a singer—when I say singer, that doesn't necessarily mean a good singer," Berlin explained, "you get to know the feel of a song, and that helps you, if you have a talent for songwriting."

When he contemplated singing now, however, his thoughts turned not to the sawdust-strewn floor of a Lower East Side saloon but to the Broadway stage.

■ □ ■ □ ■ □ ■

CHAPTER 4

Reinventing Ragtime

Broadway producers are generally more respected than loved, and among producers, many are more feared than respected. The most powerful producers during Irving Berlin's career, the Shubert brothers, belonged to a category by themselves: they were loathed by the many performers, managers, and theatrical professionals who dealt with them. In fact, the two brothers loathed each other with as much spiteful glee as they loathed the rest of the world; when they were done humiliating their business partners, they would turn on one another. This ruthless duo, just coming into their ascendancy at the time Berlin sought their assistance, was to rule Broadway throughout the songwriter's career, producing over two hundred shows and influencing countless others; no other theatrical organization could match the Shuberts' clout. To many, the name Shubert was synonymous with Broadway.

The children of immigrants, they shared with the songwriter a deprived and precarious background. Originally, there had been three Shubert brothers, born in Lithuania of an alcoholic peddler. Driven from their home by pogroms, the family settled in Syracuse, New York, where Sam, the oldest of the siblings, gained a toehold in the theater by selling programs. In time, he progressed to manager and theater owner, while his two younger brothers, Levi (who became Lee) and Jacob (later J. J.), followed him into the business. Together, they learned to contend with the reigning theater dynasty of their youth, the despised Klaw and Erlanger syndicate. When the syndicate welshed on a deal, the Shuberts challenged and eventually supplanted it by adopting many of its bullying tactics. As the Shubert dynasty expanded, the brothers leased, managed, and built theaters throughout New York City, and their activities propelled the theater district uptown from Union Square to Herald Square, and finally to the Broadway–Times Square area.

Nothing, not even Sam's death in a train accident in 1905, stopped the Shubert juggernaut. Lee, the older of the two surviving brothers, concentrated on buying and maintaining theaters, while J. J. fancied himself a flawless talent spotter. They cared little that others disliked them; in fact, they went out of their way to antagonize or belittle Broadway figures who were better known than they. A classic Shubert confrontation occurred in 1915, when Berlin's friend Alexander Woollcott, then a drama critic for *The New York Times*, had the temerity to term a Shubert comedy "quite tedious." This mild rebuke prompted the brothers to demand that the *Times* send another critic to the next Shubert offering. Rising to the challenge, Woollcott paid for his own ticket, but at the door, he found his path blocked both by a doorman and J. J. himself.

If the young team of Irving Berlin and Ted Snyder was going to launch a stage career, the two men would have to contend with the Shuberts. Seeking a spot in the lineup of a Shubert-backed show, they were fortunate to obtain an audition with the intransigent J. J. Not yet thirty, the impresario held court in an ostentatious office. When Berlin and Snyder appeared before him, he scarcely took notice of them, preferring to remain behind his massive, intimidating desk and dictate letters to a stenographer.

J. J.'s reception unnerved Berlin, even though he was accustomed to singing in hostile surroundings. But now he was particularly eager to please, and he could barely concentrate enough to remember his own lyrics. The audition proceeded uncertainly until he reached what should have been his drawing card, the lusty "Hurrah"s punctuating the chorus of "My Wife's Gone to the Country." Surely J. J. would remember that hit fondly. When Berlin opened his mouth to sing, his mind went blank, his throat seized up, and the audition came to a humiliating conclusion. As far as the talent-spotting Shubert was concerned, Irving Berlin was nothing more than a singing waiter with a fancy stage name and some fast-fading novelty tunes to his credit; the Shuberts preferred big acts. So ended the first encounter of their long and acrimonious relationship.

On the heels of the rejection, Irving decided that if he could not persuade a producer to put him onstage, he could at least bring his songs to the notice of established performers. He haunted the vaudeville and burlesque theaters in search of singers he thought could benefit from his material, and he would approach them backstage after their acts to discuss business or, if necessary, buy them a drink. On one of these outings, he spotted a talented young comedienne named Fanny Brice, who, like so many young performers, came from the Lower East Side. Unlike Berlin, Brice had been born there and had taken the trouble to learn the Yiddish accent she employed onstage to get laughs. Berlin went to his trunk and retrieved "Sadie Salome, Please Go Home," a number whose dialect inflections perfectly suited her talents. With this song in her repertoire, she attracted the attention of a rising young impresario, Florenz Ziegfeld, Jr., who rushed to enlist her services in one of the earliest editions of his annual *Follies*, where she scored a success with another of Berlin's ethnic specialty songs, "Good-bye, Becky Cohen." In the end, such songs gave Brice's career more of a boost than they did Berlin's.

Still unwilling to relinquish his dream of establishing himself as a performer, Berlin made a second attempt, this time meeting with unexpected luck. On September 27, 1909, a musical hodgepodge entitled *The Girl and the Wizard* opened. Casually relating the story of a German gem dealer who meddles in his nephew's love life, it featured a strident and risqué song called "Oh, How That German Could Love," by Berlin and Snyder.

Berlin got his chance to perform this predictable exercise not before a Broadway audience but before a microphone. The young Columbia Graphophone Company, headquartered in Bridgeport, Connecticut, signed him to a singing contract. Adopting a stage German accent, he flailed away at the tune, trying to wring all the innuendo he could from it. The recording, considered Berlin's first, was not a success, and his studio career came to a quick end.

Meanwhile, his songs continued to turn up on Broadway, generally in shows *not* produced by the Shuberts. On January 6, 1910, a modest hit called *The Jolly Bachelors* opened at the Broadway Theater, with a score including three Berlin-Snyder tunes, including yet another attempt to conjure the magic of ragtime, "Stop That Rag (Keep on Playing, Honey)," a romantic, or "spooning" song.

Despite this accomplishment, Berlin still failed to appear onstage himself. Part of the blame belonged to the Shubert brothers, but part could be laid to Berlin's limitations as a performer. As Irving Berlin, songwriter, he could be all things to all people, supplying whatever type of song the occasion demanded, whether it was Christmas or ragtime or "coon." As a performer, he was irrevocably Izzy Baline, whose slight physique and high voice made little impression. In a confined, controlled situation, he was able to convince by sheer force of will, but in the open spaces of a theater, he was simply lost.

Fortunately, his reputation as a songwriter continued to grow, even as he vainly pursued a stage career, and his fortune began to mount in Tin Pan Alley fashion: a penny at a time. For each copy of sheet music sold, he earned a royalty of one cent for his work as a lyricist, while his collaborator, generally Ted Snyder at this time, earned another cent. The rest of the wholesale price of the sheet music, another three to five cents, went directly to the publisher. Thus the 600,000 copies that his hit tune "My Wife's Gone to the Country" eventually sold brought Berlin personally $6,000 in royalties, while his publisher kept another $30,000.

Berlin's growing financial success soon attracted press attention. On July 10, the raffish and popular *New York World* introduced the neophyte songwriter to its readership in a lengthy feature headlined:

> THE MAN WHO IS "MAKING THE COUNTRY HUM"
> HE WROTE "MY WIFE'S GONE TO THE COUNTRY"
> AND OTHER MODERN CLASSICS AND IS GETTING RICH

The star treatment he received was highly unusual, as it was usually reserved for performers; songwriters, in general, did not enjoy the same visibility. But Berlin suddenly and unwillingly became the exception to this rule. The paper hailed him as "the most successful songwriter of the year" and breathlessly disclosed that he had "cleaned up $15,000 in the past year." Not only that, but "the wealth was still rolling in on him." The *World* went on to remind the public that only "eighteen months ago he was a waiter in 'Nigger Mike's' Pelham Café, in Pell Street, New York."

Berlin's success was expressed entirely in terms of his songs' overwhelming popularity and the money he earned from them. Nothing was said, now or for years to come, about the songs themselves. Though he aspired to emulate Stephen Foster's example, Berlin's songs were seen not as handcrafted, unique creations, but as manufactured products. When Berlin became impatient with this method of accounting, he seemed ungrateful. Wasn't it enough to be so popular? Who could ask for anything more?

The accompanying photograph in the *World* showed the twenty-two-year-old composer looking businesslike in a dark suit and celluloid collar, but hardly more than fourteen. His slight build, combined with his innocent, open expression, conveyed an impression of extreme youth. Now fully grown, he stood just five feet six inches, and he weighed less than one hundred and twenty-five pounds.

Taking advantage of the celebrity conferred by this article, Berlin and Snyder finally persuaded a producer to present them on Broadway, but the engagement turned out to be more of a learning experience than a stage triumph. The two did not get their own show; nor did they receive star billing. Instead, they appeared as one of many acts in a revue entitled *Up and Down Broadway*, with a score written principally by another composer, Jean Schwartz.

The revue was a characteristically casual affair, with a loosely knit story concerning Greek gods who descend on the New York theater scene. In the midst of this amiable shambles, Berlin and Snyder sang two of their collaborations, "That Beautiful Rag" and "Sweet Italian Love." This frantic activity occupied their evenings throughout the summer and part of the fall, as well, and the experience proved sufficient to satisfy Berlin's thirst for performing, at least for a while. He preferred to concentrate his energies and talents on mastering the business and craft of songwriting, leaving the performing of his works to others who were better able to put them across to an audience.

Shortly after the curtain rang down for the last time on *Up and Down Broadway*, Berlin exchanged grease paint for an eyeshade, accepting an opportunity to extend his knowledge of the music business. In October 1910 he accompanied his boss, Henry Waterson, to London to visit their firm's British representative, Bert Feldman. They departed New York aboard the *Lusitania*; five years later a German submarine would sink the ocean liner and bring the United States close to entering a world war, but this crossing was as uneventful as Berlin's first transatlantic voyage aboard the *Rhynland* eighteen years before. He was returning to Europe, if not in triumph, at least as a respectable businessman.

In London Feldman provided Berlin with an insider's view of the British music publishing business. The composer found an industry as old-fashioned as Tin Pan Alley was modern. American-style promotion—newspaper advertisements, interviews with important industry figures, and song pluggers—did not exist. Music publishers could be downright secretive about their activities. In this publicity vacuum, music hall stars reserved for themselves the glory and the responsibility of making or breaking songs. It was an antiquated system, but it had the virtue, Berlin discovered, of being far less expensive than maintaining an army of pluggers.

Berlin also had an opportunity to study British music hall songs firsthand, rather than learn about them from Edgar Leslie. In Bloomsbury he met with a popular songwriting team, D. Eardly-Wilmot and Hermann Lohr, whose "Little Grey Home in the West" was a hit with English audiences. Under the influence of this ballad in particular and English songwriting in general, Berlin learned to write a new style of song. His ample repertoire of Jewish, "coon," Italian, German, and pseudo-ragtime songs was soon increased by rather loftier "English" ballads such as "Dreams, Just Dreams." Within months of his return from England, these separate categories would begin to cross-pollinate, with exciting musical results, as Berlin learned to combine several styles in the span of a single song.

The voyage to England endowed Berlin with another, less tangible benefit; he temporarily escaped his reputation as a former singing waiter. In England no one knew or cared much about his origins, and no one dared call him "Izzy." He was Mr. Berlin, and the formality suited him. Furthermore, the English accepted him as a popular *American* composer, whereas in New York he was constantly reminded that he was really Izzy Baline, a Russian immigrant, whose "Americanness" was manufactured. Although in fact he had yet to file his naturalization papers to make his American citizenship official, his identification with his adoptive homeland was by now complete, as the reception he received in England demonstrated.

▪ ▪ ▪

As 1910 drew to a close, Berlin could look back on his fast-growing catalogue of songs with satisfaction. All told, he had published over thirty titles that year, twenty of them in collaboration with the indefatigable Snyder. Even at this breakneck pace, during which he managed to bring a new song before the public every other week, he still found the time to advance his performing career. Yet the profusion of titles, many of uneven quality, marked him as a highly talented novice with pronounced hack tendencies. Though he yearned to write songs on a par with the best of Stephen Foster's efforts, he realized that Tin Pan Alley practices discouraged that sort of high-flown, noncommercial aspiration. At the same time, he was getting the knack of various commercial genres. Rail though he might against the ephemeral nature of his songs, he was willing and able to deliver whatever would sell: spooning songs ("Kiss Me, My Honey, Kiss Me," "When I Hear You Play That Piano, Bill"), "coon" songs ("Colored Romeo"), and dialect songs. None of these efforts contained the slightest indications of Berlin's inner convictions, moods, or point of view; they were tailored to fit the demands of the marketplace. Similarly, his ethnic songs did not result from his need to vent personal prejudice. Instead, they represented the norm in vaudeville entertainment and in society at large, where assimilation was barely an aspiration for most immigrants, and ethnicity, like poverty, was a fact of life.

Where Berlin's Jewish dialect songs often depicted their subjects as money grubbing, his "coon" songs emphasized the sexual prowess of blacks, along with their instinctive musical ability; again, this was not a personal statement by Berlin but a reflection of the prevailing vaudeville and minstrel show conventions. Unlike ragtime or jazz, the "coon" song was not a black invention; it was the product of the bigoted white imagination. When Berlin and Snyder sat down to write a raunchy "coon" number entitled "Alexander and His Clarinet," they were describing, with the help of numerous *double entendres*, yet another highly sexed "coon." The idea behind the song derived from a long line of "Alexander" songs instigated by Harry Von Tilzer in 1902, and he, in turn, had borrowed the Alexander character from a popular turn-of-the-century minstrel act, Montgomery and Stone. The two white entertainers, who performed in blackface, were sure to get a laugh whenever they started calling each other "Alexander," a name their audiences considered too grand for a black man.

For all its tongue-in-cheek salaciousness, this song failed to catch on. However, another risqué tune published the same year, "Call Me Up Some Rainy Afternoon," developed into a minor hit and contained the seeds of more mature songwriting than Berlin had previously exhibited. Rather than purveying yet another tiresome ethnic stereotype, it functioned as a parody of the conventional spooning song, telling of a young coquette who teases her suitor. When the suitor responds to her offer, he finds, to his chagrin, that she is singing the same sweet song to another man. This touch—surprising, comic, and plausible—marks the first time the listener can sense that Berlin is speaking from his own feelings and experience rather than parroting yet another stereotype for public consumption. An anomaly for now, the poignant lyrics foretold the subtle love songs Berlin would write a dozen years later.

"Call Me Up Some Rainy Afternoon" exhibited still another distinctive feature: Berlin had written both the lyrics *and* the music. Ever since he had begun to publish songs, Irving had been vexed by the problem of how to earn royalties as both a composer and a lyricist. His answer was not to acquire the rudiments of music theory but to extend his playing ability—not that he was much of a performer. He banged on the keyboard in the energetic, thumping style of a vaudeville pianist accompanying a sweaty chorus line. Like many self-taught musicians, he hit only the black keys, which were easier for his untrained hands to control. He called them "nigger keys," and the pianos he used, "nigger pianos." Both terms were standard Tin Pan Alley jargon. His use of these expressions, repugnant though they were, suggested his unconscious identification with untrained and intuitive black musicians. From Nigger Mike's to nigger keys, Berlin cast his lot with black music.

Playing on the black keys alone restricted him to the key of F-sharp major, but Berlin refused to change his habits. "The black keys are right there under your fingers," he explained in his defense, adding with a faint sneer reserved for the educated few, "The key of C is for people who study music." His protest to the contrary, playing only the black keys deprived him of the ability to explore a wide range of musical subtleties. Nor could he embellish his tunes with harmonies. Without some way of manipulating his melodies, he would never be able to call himself a songwriter, and he would never be able to match the standard set by Stephen Foster.

Fortunately, he stumbled across a mechanical invention that vastly extended his ability to express himself musically. It was a common enough device in 1910. For over a hundred years, the English concern of Norris and Hyde had been selling a piano that could change keys when the performer moved a lever concealed beneath the keyboard. Later, the Calvin Weser Company of New York introduced the device to the United States, calling it a transposing piano. It was not a particularly expensive contraption; Weser sold its upright grand version for only one hundred dollars. George M. Cohan owned three, and every publishing house on Tin Pan Alley had them.

Inevitably, Berlin tried composing on a transposing piano. He could still play "nigger piano," he discovered, but by flipping the lever, he could sample any key he wished. The device freed him to develop the harmonies, nuances, rhythms, and fill notes he needed to embellish his tunes. At the touch of a lever, he could test a chord or a phrase in a different key; he could experiment with interactions between words and melodies without having to seek out a collaborator whose patience and endurance was as great as his. Much to Berlin's satisfaction, when he had finished, he did not have to trouble himself with the task of writing down the result; he simply played the finished product for a transcriber, whose contribution was now drastically reduced.

Even with this wonderful gadget at his disposal, he still began the process of composing in the most basic way: with his voice. "I get an idea," he explained, "either a title or a phrase or a melody, and hum it out to something definite. When I have completed a song and memorized it, I dictate it to an arranger." There was one other musical element that often eluded the niceties of notation, and Berlin felt he possessed it as a birthright. "I know rhythm," he insisted. "There is one of the great qualities, for rhythm is a big part of any . . . song. It's the swing."

Working at his transposing piano, Berlin found the songs now came easily; he composed not merely one a day, as other prolific composers boasted they did, but as many as *five*. He maintained the unorthodox hours to which he had become accustomed during his years as a singing waiter. "I am working on songs all of the time, at home and outside and in the office," he said. "I gather ideas, and then I usually work them out between eight o'clock at night and five in the morning." If he was moved to write during the day (afternoons, inevitably, for Berlin slept the mornings away), he explained, "I pull down the window-shades and work by artificial light, strumming away by ear in the key of F Sharp, or using a transposing keyboard."

Though he composed every note, Berlin was still unable to write down the songs he played and memorized, but he made certain that no one mistook his transcribers for collaborators. "There is the fellow who creates the song," he maintained, "and there is a fellow who is a technical man, just the same as someone who's skilled at typing your letter. Now you may not be able to type your own letter, but somebody else can do it for you. But they can't make it up for you."

Once he became comfortable with what he called his "trick piano," Berlin went beyond simply defending his role as "the fellow who creates the song" to boasting that his lack of musical education constituted an asset. "In my ignorance of the laws of music," he wrote in *The Green Book Magazine*, "I have often broken all laws, and the result was an original twist. In popular songs, a comparative ignorance of music is an advantage also, in that, my vocabulary being somewhat limited through lack of education, it follows that my lyrics are simple."

His penchant for parading his ignorance before the public made him seem, paradoxically, all the more appealing and comprehensible to ordinary Americans, who often regarded music as remote, effete, and European. Music suggested waltzes, a pince-nez, and a bearded professor speaking a foreign language. Berlin, in contrast, was vigorous and down-to-earth. He claimed he knew no more about music than anyone—and less than many. He was no haughty eccentric artist threatening the established order. He belonged to what he always called "the mob"; he was the man who called the tune to which ordinary folks danced, and as long as they paid him he was content. As he repeatedly stated, he was in the music business to make money, and that, too, was a sentiment Americans could readily understand and endorse. All in all, he made an ideal candidate for musical man of the people.

▪ ▪ ▪

With his increased control over songwriting, thanks in large part to the trick piano, Berlin returned immediately to the intriguing genre of ragtime—the devil's music, music to be played in a brothel or a saloon, and all the more thrilling for that. He proposed to do more than copy Joplin's stately, introspective rags. "Classic" ragtime, the sensation of 1899, no longer sounded exciting to his ears. From his vantage point in 1910, it sounded like parlor music, containing more echoes of hymns than whorehouses. Berlin wanted his version of ragtime to reflect the stress, confusion, and excitement of urban existence; it would be meant more for dancing than listening.

The common element in the two versions was ragged time, or syncopation. It was a music of contrasts: the irregular accents of the melody went against the regular accents of the beat, like a hiccup. Originally an African rhythm, it underwent gradual refinements in the South even before Joplin adapted it into sonata form. Ragtime gained further popularity when the pianist and singer Ben Harney introduced it to New York City in February 1896, and it quickly became a vaudeville staple, fanning out across the nation along with the growing vaudeville circuits. By the time Berlin heard ragtime, it sounded conventional, though not soothing. To ears conditioned by European waltzes, its inherent contrasts made it sound nervous and steam powered. Syncopation introduced tension into the music, a sense of activity and conflict that sounded entirely modern. It was jagged and pulsing music, echoing the rhythms of manufacturing and the assembly line. For traditionalists, it symbolized whatever was new about the twentieth century and whatever was wrong with it. Yet it could also enliven a tired tune and, Berlin discovered, it functioned smoothly with the accents of ordinary American speech, whose inflections and contractions often echoed syncopated rhythms. Though a hybrid, ragtime came to be regarded as indigenous American music, and to Berlin, *the* American form of music. "Syncopation is the soul of every American," he proclaimed, "and ragtime is a necessary element of American life. Pure unadulterated ragtime is the best heart-raiser and worry banisher that I know—and I've seen from experience that it's better than mediums as a cure."

Despite the exuberance of this statement, Berlin found ragtime difficult to reintroduce to the public, especially compared with the instant success of his early hits. Now, for the first time, he was attempting to create a musical fashion rather than follow one, and he discovered that innovation required greater patience than imitation did—though it could reap greater rewards.

The "ragtime" melody Berlin devised on the trick piano was actually a march: a safe choice, for a march suggested ragtime without incurring the liability of being ragtime. His melody employed only a brief jumpy phrase of actual syncopation. A bugle call enlivened it, as did a phrase borrowed from "Swanee River," by Berlin's favorite composer, Stephen Foster. There were unorthodox features, as well. The chorus lasted twice the usual length, a full thirty-two bars. Its length reflected Berlin's belief that the chorus was by far the most memorable part of a song; therefore, the longer the chorus, the more indelible the impression left by the song. "Short choruses, I argue, are over too quickly; they don't carry enough sustained interest," he stated. Even more daring, the song suddenly changed key in midcourse, but this violation of formula songwriting imparted a pleasing variety to the melody and offered a distraction from its relentless march tempo.

So intent was Berlin on showing off his newfound expertise as a composer that he chose the risky course of offering the song as an instrumental, though he did endow it with an evocative title, "Alexander's Ragtime Band." The "Alexander" marked it as another "coon" song, but Berlin relied on the word *ragtime* to sell the tune. He knew, of course, that it contained almost no syncopation, but he nonetheless wished to associate himself with this daring buzzword. Stranger still, when the sheet music was later published, with a pink-and-green illustration of a bandstand, the members of the band looked white, and Alexander himself had been reborn as their white bandleader.

With its mixed ancestry, the instrumental failed to find an appreciative audience. Berlin initially offered it to a short-lived cabaret calling itself the *Folies Bergère*, for which he was already writing music. These *Folies* belonged to producer Jesse Lasky. Lasky's sister would later marry Samuel Goldwyn, the movie producer, and Lasky would become an influential name in Hollywood, but for now, his hopes were bound up in this knockoff of the French original.

Berlin had previously supplied the show with three lackluster songs, "I Beg Your Pardon, Dear Old Broadway," "Spanish Love," and "Down to the Folies Bergère." He then auditioned his new instrumental, "Alexander's Ragtime Band," for Lasky on a conventional piano, his heart pounding as his fingers hammered the keys. Since Lasky was slow to make up his mind, Berlin had to play the song three times.

Finally, he ventured to ask the impresario, "You think it's good?"

"I wouldn't go so far as to say that," Lasky replied. "But I might be able to use it."

On the opening night of the *Folies*, the orchestra flailed away at Berlin's instrumental, but the song made little impression. Later in the show, a performer whistled it—again, to no avail. Lasky dropped it from the score, and Berlin came to regard it as a "dead failure."

Defeated, Berlin shelved the troublesome instrumental and went on to try his hand at composing a string of novelty songs capitalizing on various dance crazes that were sweeping the city. The failure of one problem song did nothing to slow his frantic pace of composition. His 1911 songs, over forty titles in all, consisted of the familiar mixture of dialect, novelty, and pseudo-ragtime numbers. He occasionally collaborated, but for the most part the songs were entirely his, and all the more assured for that.

And he continued to write for Broadway shows, becoming associated with the reckless and driven producer, Florenz Ziegfeld, Jr., who was destined to wield immense influence over Berlin's career in particular and the Broadway stage in general. Though the name Florenz Ziegfeld evokes a distinctly European sensibility, Flo actually hailed from Chicago, where his strict father ran the respected Chicago Musical College. But Flo was a rebel and a prankster. He despised classical music and all its stifling trappings; he detested the air of pompous virtuousness with which classical musicians (especially his own father) cloaked themselves. Flo much preferred raw spectacle. He first acquired his taste for show business when Buffalo Bill and Annie Oakley visited Chicago in 1883, and he played hookey from school to watch them again and again. Here were performers the audience did not require a college degree to understand. Their appeal was universal, and they were wholly American.

Though his lowbrow tastes were formed, Flo was still too young to be free of his father's influence. As treasurer of the Chicago College of Music, Flo acquired a reputation for financial irresponsibility, harbinger of a lifelong habit. His father had no choice but to fire him, and when Flo was later given the task of signing acts for the 1893 Columbian Exposition in Chicago, of which his father happened to be music director, the twenty-six-year-old junior Ziegfeld made his true tastes known by enlisting an army of vaudeville-style acrobats and, most difficult of all for the Ziegfeld senior to bear, *circus* bands.

Flo wasn't content simply to embrace popular culture; he also flouted the conventional midwestern morality of his youth. Eventually, he found a companion in his revels, Anna Held, whose background was as exotic as he would have liked his own to have been. A former chorus girl, she claimed to have been born in Paris, though it is more likely that she was born in Warsaw, the daughter of a Jewish glove manufacturer. Her varied career took her through the Yiddish theater and later the music halls of Paris, and she had endured a brief, unhappy marriage. Ziegfeld spotted her during a talent-scouting trip to London, and they soon began a love affair. They planned to marry, but Held's Catholic husband refused to grant her a divorce; instead, Ziegfeld and Held lived together for years in a common law union.

Despite Ziegfeld's disdain for high culture, there was enough of the professor in him still to drive him to select the best talents available, and on the strength of this ability, he was now establishing himself as the most celebrated of a new breed of flesh peddler: *impresario* was the term he preferred. The idea for the *Follies* actually belonged to Anna Held rather than Ziegfeld. She thought a Parisian-style revue, patterned after those in which she had once performed, would be just the thing to attract American audiences. But as his longtime scenarist Harry Smith recalled, "Mr. Ziegfeld was not especially enthusiastic about the idea and he apparently considered the French *revues* rather stupid affairs, which they often are." Ziegfeld knew what he liked: animal acts, acrobats, and an occasional Strong Man—*stunts*. And a revue was, in comparison, too European, too sophisticated.

However, in 1907, the waning Klaw and Erlanger syndicate decided to devote one of their theaters, the New York, to a vaudeville show followed by an hour-long revue on the roof garden. The so-called "Jardin de Paris," where the revue was to take place, consisted of nothing more than a few rows of folding chairs stretching beneath a tin roof. It was here, amid these dreary surroundings, that Ziegfeld staged his first revue, working on a shoestring budget of $13,000. He was so indebted to Anna Held's advice that he called his first chorines not Ziegfeld Girls but Anna Held Girls. By opening night the vaudeville acts had disappeared from the bill, and Ziegfeld's revue later became successful enough to move to its own theater.

Despite this professional success, Ziegfeld and Held's tempestuous union deteriorated, and the two would part for good in 1913, when Held would resume her stage career with the assistance of Ziegfeld's rivals, the Shubert brothers.

Now, in 1911, Ziegfeld was a forty-four-year-old presence on Broadway with the best of his career still before him. He was short, with a long nose, sad eyes, and a thick mane of hair swept back; he dressed himself to sleek perfection in suits and spats and brought the same polish to the acts he presented. His *Follies* had become an institution, and though their quality fluctuated from year to year and they spawned numerous imitations (such as Jesse Lasky's short-lived venture), Ziegfeld's version remained preeminent, thanks to his relentless insistence on presenting the best acts and the most beautiful flesh he could find. Actually, he was canny enough to take the old burlesque performers, with their sweaty bosoms, thick legs, sour breath, and general air of seediness, and wrap them in yards of gossamer. A master of packaging, he maintained that his soft-core presentations were dedicated to "glorifying the American girl," not exploiting her. The hypocrisy worked, and the gimmick made his spectacular revues palatable to audiences, who gladly fell in step with his charade. To be sure, he had a better eye than the old-fashioned managers he supplanted; he filled a stage with as many as fifty seductive chorines, and he displayed them amid settings that suggested a luxurious brothel. At the urging of Anna Held, he discovered that Americans would excuse the *Follies'* naughtiness if the show were presented with a Continental flourish.

He was also superstitious, especially about the number thirteen, which he considered a lucky talisman. He named his early revue *Follies of 1907* to fulfill his requirement for a title with exactly thirteen characters. Holding to this formula, he omitted his name until June 1911, when he felt ready to tempt the fates by lengthening the title to include himself; and from then on, he presented the *Ziegfeld Follies*. He failed to exercise similar care about paying his performers. He was habitually in debt to some of the biggest names in show business, but he was able to persuade stars to work for him because he obviously appreciated their talents—in contrast to other impresarios, such as the Shuberts.

Frenzy marked Ziegfeld productions. He often threw his *Follies* into rehearsal with only Act One written, figuring that the librettist could write the remainder of the material as the show took shape. He threw in and tossed out songs with the same lack of caution; often the tunes that managed to remain in the show were those that had been written backstage, at the last minute, with the performers waiting for their lyrics and the musicians for their lead sheets. He treated his stars in the same cavalier fashion; they entered and exited the cast at a furious rate, both before and after opening night.

His preferred method of communication was the telegram, for which he became renowned. After giving instructions over the phone or in person, he inevitably repeated the instructions verbatim in a wire, and he expected instant compliance. Ziegfeld's telegrams were as long as letters, usually five hundred words or more, and he sent them to everyone who worked for him—to Eddie Cantor, W. C. Fields, and Fanny Brice—but *not* to Irving Berlin. The impresario quickly discovered that the songwriter would do precisely what he had been told to do, in the shortest possible time, without being reminded. "He treated Berlin with the utmost respect," noted Ziegfeld's longtime secretary Goldie Clough, who sent the legendary telegrams for her boss.

Despite his financial duplicity, Ziegfeld's drive for perfection helped him acquire an air of respectability, as if the chorus girls he displayed were vestal virgins he was guarding for their own protection.

In private, though, he was a relentless womanizer; his office was often the scene of his seductions. To ensure privacy, he developed a system for locking his door. He could open it from within, but only Goldie, his secretary, could open it from the outside. Once, when she forgot to lock the door, a telegram messenger boy walked into Ziegfeld's office and ran out, crying, "He's laying a girl on the desk!"

Berlin refused to partake of Ziegfeld's feast. He was glad to contribute songs to the *Follies*, but he displayed little appetite for chorus girls. He was simply too shy. Though he overcame this sensitivity when he performed, he seemed to evaporate when he was offstage. "A skinny little guy, very quiet," remembered Goldie of the composer. "Rarely spoke, and when he did, his voice was very quiet. He sort of blended into the scenery; you hardly ever knew he was there." His shyness also shielded him against demanding personalities like Ziegfeld, who, like everyone else, respected the diminutive songwriter's reserve, especially when he repeatedly redeemed himself through his music. Ziegfeld also rewarded Berlin's punctual creativity by paying the songwriter with unusual promptness.

Berlin contributed four songs to the 1911 edition of the *Ziegfeld Follies*, and they enlivened an otherwise lackluster score. His standout number, "Woodman, Spare That Tree," served as a mock lamentation for the esteemed black comedian Bert Williams, and to Berlin's credit, it was more of a comic than a "coon" song. It was also one of Berlin's last collaborative efforts. Lyricist Vincent Bryan took his inspiration from the famous poem by George Pope Morris. "It was built around someone who had this slippery elm," Berlin later recalled, "and his wife couldn't climb up there to catch him. It was very funny in those days, and it still is a funny song."

Invigorated by his success with the *Ziegfeld Follies*, Berlin returned to his problem song, "Alexander's Ragtime Band," deciding he might have better luck with it if he included words that could help sell the idea of ragtime to audiences. He quickly jotted down the kind of old-fashioned "coon" lyrics that came easily to him now that he was functioning as his own composer.

> Writing both words and music [Berlin explained two years later] I can compose them together and make them fit. I sacrifice one

for the other. If I have a melody I want to use, I plug away at the lyrics until I make them fit the best parts of my music and vice versa.

Nearly all other writers work in teams, one writing the music and the other the words. They either are forced to fit some one's words to their music or some one's music to their words. Latitude—which begets novelty—is denied them, and in consequence both lyrics and melody suffer.

Three-fourths of that quality which brings success to popular songs is the phrasing. I make a study of it—ease, naturalness, every-day-ness—and it is my first consideration when I start on lyrics. "Easy to sing, easy to say, easy to remember and applicable to everyday events" is a good rule for a phrase.

Although "Alexander's Ragtime Band" mixed black, white, ragtime, and even military musical flourishes, Berlin's lyrics smoothly integrated these disparate elements. Nevertheless, Berlin, Snyder, and Waterson all lacked faith in the song; only Max Winslow sensed its potential. He persuaded Snyder to accompany him on a visit to a Broadway producer, Aaron Hoffman, who was assembling a revue called *The Merry Whirl*, but when they reached his office at the Columbia Theatre, the errand boy misunderstood their names, and Hoffman inadvertently dismissed the two callers before they were able to pitch Berlin's song.

On the subway the following morning, Winslow bumped into Hoffman and asked why Hoffman had sent the two men away. Apologizing for the confusion, Hoffman persuaded Winslow to return that afternoon. Winslow's persistence paid off; Hoffman liked "Alexander's Ragtime Band" enough to put it in the revue, which opened in May of 1911. "The verdict of the first night crowd at the Columbia was that 'Alexander' made *Merry Whirl* that season," wrote *Variety*. But the rest of the show was so lame that it soon closed, threatening to drag Berlin's song with it into obscurity.

Then, in defiance of the usual sales pattern for a hit, the song began to catch on outside New York. The development caught Berlin off guard. He was experienced enough to realize how hits were made: they began in New York, in the cafés or in a Broadway revue, and they trickled down to the bars and finally the streets—only then did they spread out of town, often with a touring company of a hit show. Yet "Alexander's Ragtime Band" swam upstream, reversing the usual pattern. It quickly caught on with performers around the country. In Chicago especially it became identified with the "coon shouter" (or singer) Emma Carus, famed for her "female baritone." It soon worked its way back to New York and Lew Dockstader's minstrel show, where Al Jolson (another former singing waiter who achieved fame) belted it out with his characteristic intensity.

The ubiquitousness of "Alexander's Ragtime Band" was due in large part to the efforts of Max Winslow, who ensured that Waterson & Snyder got professional copies in the hands of performers and that the firm's staff of seventy-five pluggers kept the song tinkling in the ears of music buyers in stores. The tune's success helped advance Winslow's career, as well. He quickly became known as "the man who discovered Irving Berlin," a title Berlin himself allowed to stand, for when even the songwriter himself had given up on "Alexander's Ragtime Band," Winslow had taken over and coaxed it to fame.

These repeated exposures eventually had a cumulative impact on the sheet music sales. The song sold, Berlin wrote, "in only a mild, pale-pink way for the first three months. Then, suddenly, it took heart and went like hot-cakes." By midsummer it sold a respectable 500,000 copies, and by year's end, a full million. The next year, it would sell another million copies, and not just in the United States. English audiences, especially, took to it with the same enthusiasm American audiences had. To Europe Berlin and his rags belonged not only to Tin Pan Alley and the music hall but to a larger pattern: the emergence of native American music during the years immediately preceding the First World War. The best-known member of the new movement was Antonín Dvořák, whose Symphony in E Minor (*From the New World*) drew on American spirituals and folk songs. In Connecticut the unknown Charles Ives struggled to incorporate the sounds of American bands and marches into his orchestral fantasies. And Scott Joplin, now composing an entire opera in ragtime, *Treemonisha*, lent further strength to the movement. With the exception of Ives, these composers were all outsiders. A Black, a Jew, a Czech: all of them had had sufficient exposure to European culture to want to challenge it.

Together these efforts inspired a widely held sense that American music should and could throw off German and Viennese influence to embrace jazz, blues, ragtime, and even the minstrel show—just as

Berlin was doing in the Tin Pan Alley vernacular. Initially, he had no sense of belonging to a larger pattern, least of all one encompassing classical music; yet without intending to, he became a prominent exponent of the nativist movement in American music. Four years later, when he finally awakened to his role, he began to champion American music with as much enthusiasm as he had promoted his rags. "The reason our American composers have done nothing highly significant is because they won't write American music," he told critic Julian Johnson in 1915. "They're as ashamed of it as if it were a country relative. So they write imitation European music which doesn't mean anything. Ignorant as I am, from their standpoints, I'm doing something they all refuse to do: I'm writing American music!"

It was not a role Berlin had sought, that of a revolutionary American artist; he'd merely wanted a hit song. But once cast in the role of a modern American composer, he discovered astonishing fringe benefits. The English, for instance, considered Berlin not merely the popularizer of the word *ragtime*, but the inventor of that type of music and the composer of all other rags. It was an impression Berlin did nothing to discourage, not with the royalties accruing at a faster rate than he had ever experienced. "Alexander's Ragtime Band" would eventually outsell every other song of its day, earning its twenty-three-year-old composer an imposing $30,000 in royalties. Beyond that, its success established him in the public mind as the quintessential Tin Pan Alley composer. In September *Variety* proclaimed the song "the musical sensation of the decade."

Though he professed to be "flabbergasted" by the international popularity the song achieved, Berlin was capable of stepping back and coolly analyzing the reasons for the song's success. The popularity was thrilling, but it was also a useful case study. "I humbly began to study my own song, asking myself, 'Why? Why?' " he noted in 1915,

> And I got an answer. The melody . . . started the heels and shoulders of all America and a good section of Europe to rocking. The lyric, silly though it was, was fundamentally right. Its opening words, emphasized by immediate repetition—"Come on and hear! Come on and hear!"—were an *invitation* to "come," to join in, and "hear" the singer and his song. And

> that idea of *inviting* every receptive auditor within shouting distance became a part of the happy ruction—an idea pounded in again and again throughout the song in various ways—was the secret of the song's tremendous success.

Not everyone agreed with Berlin's reasoning. An insidious rumor, at first whispered, later spoken aloud, began to circulate: Irving Berlin did not write all his songs by himself. The rumor insisted that he employed a ghostwriter, variously called a "little colored boy," or a "little nigger boy," who actually wrote the melodies for him. "Alexander's Ragtime Band," particularly, came under suspicion. The rumor had its own logic; it explained his affinity for "coon" songs, the ferocious output, and the irony of a musical illiterate composing numerous hit songs. Since he could not write musical notation, he possessed no manuscripts that could demonstrate his authorship. Furthermore, ghostwriting was a common Tin Pan Alley practice. Everybody did it; why not Berlin?

"Songwriters don't steal, at least those of reputation don't," he retorted. "Why should they? But the public, by some freak of mind, would rather believe that the fellow who is getting the credit isn't the one who is doing the work." He proceeded to address the specific charge against him. "Some one started the report that I had paid a negro ten dollars for it and then published it under my own name," Berlin wrote.

His furious response contained a challenge of his own:

> I asked them to tell me from whom I had bought my . . . successes—twenty-five or thirty of them. And I wanted to know, if a negro could write "Alexander," why couldn't I? Then I told them if they could produce the negro and he had another hit like "Alexander" in his system, I would choke it out of him and give him twenty thousand dollars in the bargain.
>
> If the other fellow deserves the credit, why doesn't he go get it?

Since no one was willing to be choked, the rumor faded, at least from Berlin's ears.

Those who knew the conscientious composer realized the rumor was nonsense. His desire for control over his songwriting was so great that he was emotionally incapable of entrusting the work to others. When the rumor pointed to Lukie Johnson, the black pianist at Nigger Mike's, as one of Berlin's ghostwriters, Johnson denied involvement. Still, the rumor refused to die. Even Berlin's boss, Henry Waterson, believed it—not that Waterson cared. Business was business, and no matter how he did it, Berlin brought money into the firm.

Despite the controversy, Berlin quickly and inevitably became known as "The Ragtime King," although the actual nature of ragtime music continued to elude this untrained musician. "You know," he eventually confessed, "I never did find out what ragtime was."

By which he meant that the dictionary definition:

> **rag·time** (rag′tim′), *n. Music.* **1.** rhythm in which the accompaniment is strict two-four time and the melody, with improvised embellishments, is in steady syncopation.

said it all, while completely missing the point. He had the satisfaction of knowing that in the public mind, ragtime had undergone another metamorphosis. No longer the preserve of Scott Joplin or Ben Harney and their followers, it was now identified with the excitement generated by the music of Irving Berlin.

■ □ ■ □ ■ □ ■

CHAPTER 5

Love and Death

In the spring of 1911, when Berlin's reputation as The Ragtime King began to soar, he received a signal honor: an invitation to join the elite show business fraternity known as the Friars' Club. The event marked his formal acceptance by the show business establishment, but it caused considerable anxiety, as well, for the shy songwriter.

The Friars was a highly public organization whose members were dedicated to the art of self-promotion. Though a fixture of the city's show business subculture, the club had been in existence for just seven years. It was the creation of New York press agents who sought to deter imposters from using phony critics' credentials to gain entrance to opening nights. The press agents began to meet regularly, and they eventually invited theater owners and star performers such as George M. Cohan to join their number.

As the club expanded, it inaugurated a popular annual dinner to introduce new members to the public and their show business colleagues. Newcomers such as Berlin were required to give an afterdinner speech. The prospect of addressing some of the better-known faces on the New York entertainment scene made Berlin's small frame quiver with anxiety. For once his listeners would consist not of the uncritical, often inebriated audiences to which he was accustomed, but of other theater professionals.

The banquet took place at the opulent Hotel Astor on lower Fifth

Avenue. George M. Cohan, still a great force on Broadway, led the festivities. Just ten years older than Berlin, Cohan always insisted his birthday was July 4, 1878, as a way of proclaiming that patriotism was his birthright, though the actual date was July 3. A mere fact could not be allowed to stand in the way of a larger truth. Cohan prided himself on doing it all: he wrote the books, music, and lyrics for his shows, as well as starring in them, and he prided himself on his resourcefulness. When asked if he could write a show without a flag in it, Cohan retorted that he could write without anything except a pencil.

With the possible exception of Harry Von Tilzer, Cohan exerted the greatest influence over the arc of Berlin's career. The key to Cohan's larger-than-life reputation lay with his loudly proclaimed patriotism. Many of his best-known shows and songs illustrated patriotic themes and reveled in heartfelt—if shameless—flag waving. He brought similar enthusiasm to bear in promoting the other institution in which he believed, show business, which he celebrated in his razzle-dazzle song, "Give My Regards to Broadway."

To Berlin and the rest of the Friars assembled at the Astor, Cohan incarnated American show business: hard sell and soft shoe, emotional, frenetic, and relentlessly cocky. His marriage, too, symbolized the predominant ethnic influences on show business, since the Irish entertainer was married to a Jewish star, Ethel Levey. This reciprocity between the Irish and the Jews made an impression on Izzy, who would later emulate it in his own marriage.

Broadway chronicler Rennold Wolf began the evening's festivities by "roasting" the renowned Cohan with a few well-chosen barbs designed to puncture the great man's self-esteem. Then it was Cohan's turn to rise and present the newest member of the Friars to the audience. Every bit as tough and street smart as the songwriter, Cohan spoke bluntly to the assembled actors, singers, vaudevillians, and comedians; Irving Berlin, he said, was a "Jew boy that had named himself after an English actor [Henry Irving—or so Cohan supposed] and a German city."

After this awkward start, Cohan conceded that "Irvy writes a great song," though professional rivalry made the sentiment difficult to express. "He writes a song with a good lyric that rhymes, good music,

music you don't have to dress up to listen to, but it is good music. He is a wonderful little fellow, wonderful in lots of ways. He has become famous and wealthy without wearing a lot of jewelry and falling for funny clothes. . . . He is uptown," Cohan continued, "but he is there with the old downtown hardshell. And with all his success, you will find his watch and his handkerchief in his pockets where they belong."

Then it was Berlin's turn to offer justification for the accolades he had just received. He positioned himself before a curtain that concealed a piano and a musician who played a syncopated melody Berlin had dashed off the previous night. The song's self-deprecatory message earned the goodwill of the self-centered entertainers. "Mr. Berlin's 'Friar-speech' was a marvel of ingenuity," noted *Variety*'s correspondent, "and the melody contained more 'tricks' of composition (according to Irving's own admission) than any ten numbers he had ever written." Despite the song's favorable reception, Berlin remained "wobbly on his feet up to the moment he finished it." Whatever agony the performance cost Berlin, he demonstrated an unerring sense of occasion. He had managed to compose a song that simultaneously expressed his feelings and the overall mood of an event.

After the ordeal of Berlin's acceptance "speech" had ended, the band came to life, playing the most recent hits published by Berlin's firm; later in the evening, the musicians began to play tunes of other publishers, over Max Winslow's strenuous objections. Berlin was too dazzled to mind, too engrossed by the contortions of the dancers as they attempted the latest dance steps. A new craze was in the making, and Berlin would soon play as central a role in it as he had in ragtime.

A relatively private triumph, the Friars' banquet quickly led to a more public type of exposure, as Berlin participated in the Friars' *Fourth Annual Frolic*, an all-star revue that opened in New York and went on a brief tour of the Midwest. In its short life, the *Frolic* had quickly acquired a reputation for extreme length, unpredictability, and disorganization. Seats for the fundraising event cost more than double the going Broadway rate, an astonishing five dollars. Berlin's appearance in the show, singing his new "coon" song, "Ephraham Played Upon the Piano," made such an impression that audiences demanded several encores.

All this, and the Friars were still not done with Berlin. The final annual rite consisted of a parade up Broadway. Berlin donned a top hat for the occasion, and a photograph taken of him marching along the street shows him in rare form, grinning from ear to ear. "This is the life," the excited young man wrote on the photograph. In this time of success chasing success, it seemed as if his luck would never fail, nor his sure touch as a composer falter, nor his public acclaim ever fade. And his luck did hold, at least for a while.

The year of marvels rolled on. When the *Frolic* returned to New York after its midwestern tour, Berlin became an attraction in his own right. In September, as the worst of the summer heat relented, he appeared for one week in Hammerstein's Victoria Theatre. This was a Times Square variety house, owned by Willie Hammerstein, whose son, Oscar II, would one day write lyrics to rival Berlin's. In 1911 the Victoria often presented various celebrities to the public whether they could perform or not; they made it to the Victoria on the strength of their fame.

Berlin received the full star treatment. Outside the theater, his name was in lights; within, a life-sized photograph of the man billed as "The Composer of a Hundred Hits" occupied the lobby. This description was more of a prediction than an accurate evaluation of Berlin's accomplishments at the time, but it demonstrated how completely Berlin the phenomenon, the man-who-cannot-write-music-only-hits, overshadowed the intense, workaholic composer who continued to spend his nights composing, his mornings sleeping, and his afternoons selling. Berlin's act, the second-to-last of the evening, filled sixteen minutes, during which he displayed the range of his dialect songs and a new ragtime number, "That Mysterious Rag." In contrast to the informality of the songs, he wore tails, and he left the chore of piano playing to his new musical secretary, Cliff Hess.

Despite the haste with which Berlin had assembled his act, he succeeded in winning over Victoria's impatient audiences. *Variety*'s young editor, Sime Silverman, came away with this impression: "To see this slim little kid on stage," he wrote, "going through a list that sounded like all the hits in the world, is something to think about. Mr. Berlin looks so nice on the platform all the girls fall for him immediately. He did make some hit." So much so that the audience applauded right through the following act, in the hope that he would return for an encore. Berlin declined every time. His popularity was gratifying, but his being exhibited as a freak was not precisely to his taste.

News of Izzy Baline's uptown triumph reached his former place of employment, Nigger Mike's, where Chuck Connors, still conducting guided tours of colorful houses of vice, assembled a party of two hundred rowdy Chinatown fans. They ventured uptown to attend a matinée at the Victoria Theatre, caught Berlin's act, then loitered on the sidewalk until the start of the evening performance, hoping to catch a glimpse of their Izzy, hoping that Izzy still remembered them. Finally he appeared—briefly—and satisfied them that success had not changed him. "Gee, Izzy," complained one, "we've been hanging around this bum joint three hours trying to get a chance to pinch that swell picture of you in the lobby."

Whether jest or threat, the remark reminded Berlin of the social and economic gulf he had crossed since Mike Salter had fired him. Nor was Berlin, at this early stage in his career, eager to look over his shoulder. He had methodically severed all links to Cherry Street and the world of the Lower East Side. His older siblings had married and were pursuing conventional careers as merchants, tradesmen, or homemakers. The once overcrowded Cherry Street apartment where he had spent his boyhood was now occupied only by his mother, and as soon as he could afford to, he moved her out, as well. In 1913, flush with royalties from his hit songs, he purchased a home for her at 834 Beck Street in the Bronx, in an area considered to be "the country," at least by Lower East Side standards. Izzy's ability to buy his mother a house was, within the family, far more tangible proof of his success than any sheet music with his American name on it or newspaper clipping.

Berlin took particular pride in this accomplishment, which came as a surprise to his mother. When the house was ready for occupancy, he took a taxi down to Cherry Street, where he told his mother, in Yiddish, "I want you to come for a ride."

"I can't," she said. "I have to get supper."

Her son insisted, and they entered the cab. They headed north, out of the city, until they finally pulled up in front of a "country" house. His mother was so disoriented she had to ask where they were. "The Bronx," Berlin said as he escorted her into the house. But Lena continued to protest that she had to get home to make supper until Berlin explained to her that she *was* home, and a maid would be available to cook her supper. Lena Berlin would live in the house until her death in 1922.

Berlin, too, had moved. No longer needing to share modest quarters with Max Winslow, he left Union Square for a handsome bachelor suite at 216 West 112th Street, in the midst of a growing middle-class Jewish neighborhood, two blocks north of Central Park. In his selection of a new home, Berlin indicated his desire for quiet and respectable bourgeois surroundings; he was far from the distractions and temptations of Broadway or Union Square. His choice of neighborhood also suggested his desire to insulate himself from the swelling Berlin image. He was fully cognizant of the value of publicity to his career; without constant attention he could scarcely continue to flourish as a composer. He tirelessly recounted the tales of his Lower East Side youth for reporters; he knew which stories would get him valuable inches of newspaper columns as surely as he knew which keys to strike on his trick piano. But the public posturing, while exhilarating, required effort. The real Berlin—Izzy Baline—remained aloof, shy, and insecure about his place in the musical landscape. His fame paradoxically caused him to remain alone and a loner.

To consolidate his sense of belonging, he petitioned the New York State Supreme Court, through his lawyer, Max Josephson, to change his name officially. In the application, dated November 16, 1911, he gave his original name as "Irving Baline" rather than Israel. On the first day of the New Year, his name became the same in the eyes of the law as it was on Tin Pan Alley: Irving Berlin. The change amounted to copyrighting a property of great worth. As Berlin's petition explained, "The musical compositions . . . have been uniformly successful and have earned vast sums of money both for your petitioner as the composer and the Ted Snyder company." As a result, "the name has become exceedingly valuable, and the name Irving Berlin on a musical composition tends to increase the sale thereof." To clinch his argument, he stretched the truth by claiming he had been going under his "exceedingly valuable" name for thirteen years, when in fact it had been fewer than four.

Berlin ended 1911, his year of marvels, with one last achievement. In December he finally acquired a title commensurate with his professional status. Henry Waterson made him a partner in the company whose success had been largely due to Berlin's efforts. In recognition of this fact, Waterson placed the composer's name ahead of Snyder's; henceforth, the company would be known as Waterson, Berlin & Snyder. The corporation was officially formed on December 13, with its business address as 112 West 38th Street. Of five shares in the company, three belonged to Waterson, while Berlin and Snyder each held one.

To commemorate the occasion and, incidentally, to cajole extra publicity for the firm, Waterson threw a champagne party and invited the press to attend. However, what should have been another triumph soon turned into a highly public embarrassment for the thin-skinned composer when Waterson, his tongue loosened by alcohol, decided to make a speech that included a joke at Berlin's expense. "You know, Irvy," he said before the reporters, "there's a story circulating on Broadway—that the reason you can turn out so much golden ragtime is because you got your own colored pickaninny tucked away in a closet." Mention of this stubborn rumor in front of the press, even in jest, shocked Berlin into silence and cast a pall over the proceedings. He never forgave Waterson the insult, and he began planning for the time when he would be able to leave the firm and start his own publishing company.

Meanwhile, he took consolation in the financial rewards of the partnership. In addition to his royalties as a composer and lyricist, he earned a share of the firm's profits. His increased earning ability only encouraged him to drive himself harder than before. Vacations or other distractions were anathema. He worked in the office, at home, on the subway, or as he walked along the street. "If I loaf a week or two, it takes me two weeks to get into the swing of work again," he told a journalist. "This is a business, and I'm in it to make money."

The money was, in its way, as intoxicating as music. By his own calculations he had earned $100,000 from his hit songs in only three years, and it seemed to him that he was now writing songs that might last longer than a season or two before they faded into obscurity. His ragtime hits, he estimated, might even last—that is, continue to sell—for a full ten years, "long enough for me." When the mood was upon him, he prided himself on his contempt for the finer things, as if they posed an obstacle to his success. "I don't write church lyrics on the side," he told a journalist, "have no passion for flowers, and never read Shakespeare in the original Greek."

Talking tough was standard Tin Pan Alley practice, but when repeated in the newspapers, it cast doubt on his integrity and motives and inspired critics to find reasons to disparage his music. The *New York Herald* charged that The Ragtime King had " 'ragged' more money from the public's unsentimental pockets than possibly all the writers of real poetry since the days of Thomas Chatterton," and went on to lament: "Decrepit pianos will jingle from the banks of Saskatchewan to the shores of the Yukon; from the shacks at Panama to the remoter homes of Brooklyn and New Jersey."

Neither the charge of commercialism nor the rumors of a black ghostwriter deflected Berlin from his singleminded devotion to the musical marketplace; he listened only to the sales figures of his songs, and since they instructed him to churn out more rags, he hastened to obey, long after their freshness faded. "That Dying Rag," "Whistling Rag," "The Ragtime Mocking Bird," and even "Alexander's Bag-Pipe Band" were designed to exploit ragtime's popularity, and when the flow ceased, another composer wrote a tune entitled "Izzy, Get Busy, Write Another Ragtime Song."

Rather than maintain an inevitably short-lived status as The Ragtime King, Berlin entertained grander schemes for syncopation. And, in a break with his usual penchant for working in privacy, he lobbied in the press on behalf of his new project. "If I live long enough," he told the New York *Dramatic Mirror*, "I shall write an opera completely in ragtime. I have not yet fully developed my story but it will of course be laid in the South." As late as 1915, Berlin was still talking of his plans for an operatic triumph, offering a few more tantalizing details. "I'm going to prove you can syncope for people's hearts as well as their toes," he insisted. "I shall write my own lyrics, as I always do. And I don't want the critics to find my grammar crooked. . . . When I begin to write seriously, I want no silly lyrics." The following year, 1916, he was still promising: "A grand opera in syncopation may sound like a joke now—but someday it's going to be a fact—even if I have to write one."

And then—nothing.

Even as he promoted his ragtime opera, he searched for the next musical trend that he could exploit. He attempted to infiltrate Broadway, but his timing was poor. Theaters had been wallowing in a slump since the previous year; only Ziegfeld had managed to thrive in the face of the cycle of shorter runs and higher costs that was driving other producers out of business. Berlin experienced the problem firsthand when he contributed seven songs written with collaborators to *The Sun Dodgers*, yet another musical about high society; the show lasted only twenty-nine performances and none of Berlin's songs gained wide circulation.

Berlin had better luck when he turned his attention to the new dance crazes flourishing in the cafés and music halls—not the decorous waltzes favored by orchestras sawing away in hotel ballrooms—but a new breed of vigorous, highly sexual, and (once again) black-inspired dances whose names alone had shock value: the rag, rock, turkey trot, monkey, maxixe, half-in-half, lame duck, gotham gobble, humpback rag, bunny hug, ostrich, and come-to-me-tommy. To see them was even more shocking than pronouncing their names, for the dancers actually pressed their loins together on the dance floor, in full view of the public. In the press and from pulpits, self-appointed guardians of public morality decried this dancing bestiary. A 1910 issue of *Harper's Weekly* pricked readers' concern with the question, "Where Is Your Daughter This Afternoon?" (She might be dancing the turkey trot—and that could lead anywhere.) Matters became so serious that a New York grand jury investigated, and after due deliberation arrived at a "presentment condemning the turkey trot and kindred dances and laying particular stress upon the fact that the hotels and cafés allow such dances."

Meanwhile, Waterson, Berlin & Snyder scented inspiration for a profitable new line of songs.

Berlin attempted to exploit the craze by writing a generic dance tune with a deceptively casual title: "Everybody's Doin' It Now." With this song, he managed to avoid identification with a particular step, which might die out at any time, and instead comment on the entire phenomenon. The lyrics shamelessly repeated a word that had taken on horridly suggestive connotations: *it*. To assert that everybody was doing *it* was tantamount to claiming that everybody was copulating, but Berlin was willing to run the risk of opprobrium for the sake of a making *it* the basis of a hit. The song also furnished an accurate depiction of the dance style of the moment: shimmying shoulders, snapping fingers, and the joyful growl, "It's a bear."

For once, the songwriter relished his creation and boasted of its wonders.

> "Everybody's Doin' It" is an example of phrasing at its best, with the added glory of being a marvelous title. It had the advantage of being a catch-phrase, one that would apply to almost anything, that the public and the newspapers would pick up and use. That one point had "made" more than one song.
>
> It was an idea out of the air. I wanted a dance song; everybody was doing it. I just sat down and wrote the thing as it was. It was the dance craze put to music and words.

Emboldened by success, Berlin grew impatient for the song to move. "Nearly all of my best-sellers began to grow beards before the public noticed them," he lamented. Although "Alexander's Ragtime Band" had taken the better part of the previous year to find an audience, he noted in wonder that "Everybody's Doin' It Now" took as long as several weeks to catch on. The composer need not have worried, for once the song did catch on, it became a fixture not only in dance halls, but also in parlors, where it was considered the standard tune of the dance craze.

Popularity concealed peril. Waterson, Berlin & Snyder became enmeshed in legal controversy created by their assertion that "Everybody's Doin' It Now." A New York Commission on Amusements and Vacation Resources for Working Girls was formed to investigate the situation, and it found, in good Puritan fashion, evidence of "reckless and uncontrolled dances" that could create "an opportunity for license and debauch." The commission's talk was buttressed by legal action. In New Jersey a woman was sent to jail for doing the turkey trot in the afternoon; fifteen other hapless women were fired when their boss spied them dancing on their lunch hour. When the commission searched for culprits responsible for encouraging this moral turpitude,

Waterson, Berlin & Snyder soon came to their attention, and the firm was placed at the head of a watch list. Furthermore, several of the firm's pluggers had been excluded from various music stores; the charge: taking excessive liberties with women. Henry Waterson responded to these problems by attempting to take retaliatory legal action, and Berlin reacted by composing harmless novelty tunes such as "Jake! Jake! The Yiddisher Ball Player."

▪ ▪ ▪

The continuing success of "Everybody's Doin' It Now" lured troops of aspiring singers to the 38th Street offices of Waterson, Berlin & Snyder, where they came in search of free "professional copies" of the firm's music and searched for the next hit to bring before the public. Among these hopefuls was a twenty-year-old unknown named Dorothy Goetz. (Her older brother, Ray, had collaborated on several tunes with Berlin, notably the unsuccessful *Sun Dodgers* suite, though he had better luck with other partners.) When she finally got her chance to meet with Mr. Berlin himself, she began to plead for a song, any song, from the great composer. Said Berlin of the encounter, "She had hardly begun to speak when another Broadway adorable swept into the room. As soon as she heard what she [Dorothy] was asking, she rushed across to the desk, [and] pulled her away, shouting: 'No. No. I want it.' "

Now that she was so close to her idol, Dorothy was not about to relent. "Dorothy was a woman of spirit," Berlin recalled. "She swung around a haymaking left and slapped the newcomer across the face." A full-fledged melee ensued as the two women began pulling one another's hair. Berlin, who hated histrionics, tried to stop the fight, but he found that in the face of their fury, he was "powerless to separate them." At the same time, he thought the quarrel funny: "They were scratching, tearing hair and shouting in lovely voices that they wanted to sing my song. Well, I had dreamed of people fighting for the right to sing my stuff—but this was the first time I saw that dream come true."

When the singers were separated, Berlin gave the song to the intruder. Before Dorothy had a chance to complain further, he invited her on a date; within several weeks they were deeply in love. It was the twenty-three-year-old Berlin's first experience with romance, and he pursued Dorothy in headlong fashion throughout the early months of 1912. She was short, with soft brown curls, dark eyes, and a large, inviting mouth. Berlin learned that Dorothy's father, Edward, lived in Buffalo, New York, and her mother, Mary, had been born in Canada and later emigrated to the United States. Dorothy had lived most of her life in Buffalo and had only recently come to New York to advance her singing career.

For the fastidious Berlin, love inevitably meant marriage. The only potential obstacle he faced concerned religion; Dorothy was not Jewish, but the difference scarcely registered with Berlin, especially now that he was in love. For Dorothy, Irving Berlin was as good a catch as she was likely to make. Among the most eligible bachelors on Tin Pan Alley, he also possessed the virtue of steadfastness. He was not given to late-night parties, casual liaisons, or other unsettling forms of behavior—except for his by now ingrained habit of working through the night. Berlin's success, especially his $100,000 annual income, created the only hint of discord in their relationship. Rumors inevitably spread that Dorothy was marrying the songwriter for his money. There was no indication that Berlin's money mattered to Dorothy—though his reputation certainly did—but to her parents at home in Buffalo, their prospective son-in-law's wealth *did* matter, as would eventually become embarrassingly apparent.

Within several weeks of their meeting, Berlin proposed, and the two traveled to Dorothy's home in Buffalo, where they were married in a simple ceremony in February. To escape the cold weather, the couple took their honeymoon in Cuba, then a popular and fashionable resort. While they were there, an epidemic of typhoid fever broke out: a serious matter in an era before antibiotics. Shortly after their return to New York City, Dorothy fell ill.

In preparation for married life, Berlin had moved again, leaving 112th Street for new and luxurious quarters in the Chatsworth, a well-known apartment building at 72nd Street and Riverside Drive. It was a status address, and here the young couple expected to live in a manner befitting Berlin's reputation. Instead, Dorothy languished in the new apartment with a worsening cold and a persistent fever. Throughout the spring Berlin attempted to work, but he would rush home to find his new wife's condition slowly worsening. According to his confidant Woollcott, "The doctors and the decorators were jostling each other in the hallway of this shiny new home, while the anxious bridegroom was locked up in the front room trying ludicrously to fulfill his contracts for jaunty songs long overdue."

In contrast to his pathetic domestic situation, Berlin's most recent songs continued to gain momentum. He acknowledged the popularity of "Everybody's Doin' It" by tearing himself away from Dorothy to take a brief star turn at the Victoria Theatre during the last week in April. "Everybody is doing it or doing something when this popular song writer sings this ragtime classic," exclaimed the *New York Telegraph*'s critic, who tried to review the show but found himself instead carried away by the music, along with everyone else in the theater: "The musicians in the orchestra begin swaying while playing their instruments, the curtain is raised and behind the scenes stage hands are discovered 'doing it' with chairs, brooms or whatever they may be handling when the strains of this contagious tune strikes them."

No amount of turkey trotting could dispel the specter of illness. Dorothy's health continued to fail, and by the beginning of June, she developed pneumonia and came under the constant supervision of a Park Avenue physician, Dr. L. Korff. There was nothing that he or anyone else could do on her behalf, and she died on the morning of July 17, scarcely five months after she had wed Berlin. Her age was just twenty years and four months. The cause of death was variously given as pneumonia and typhoid fever. The marriage, so unexpected and impetuous, was over almost before it had begun. Berlin had known love, briefly, though he had never gotten his chance to enjoy a normal married life, or the children that would have followed.

At five o'clock the following afternoon, a Thursday, brief services for Dorothy were held at the Berlin apartment; the following day, the body was sent to Buffalo for internment. The funeral took place at Forest Lawn on Friday, under gray skies, with the surviving members of Dorothy's family in attendance.

The tragically brief marriage yielded a pitiful coda. Among the few bits of tangible evidence of the marriage was a pawn ticket for jewelry that Berlin had given to Dorothy's sister Ethel. The ticket made the rounds of the Goetz family; Mary took it from Ethel, and then when

Mary was divorced, her husband, Edward, took it from her. The entire matter wound up in court, where the Goetz family, now in disarray, continued to squabble, as if recovering the jewelry could bring Dorothy back to life. Dorothy was gone, and with her the Goetz family's hopes of having an illustrious (and prosperous) songwriter in the family. Berlin remained friendly with Ray, who helped the young widower through the early stages of mourning, but the rest of the family had to contend with an unredeemed pawn ticket and the unfulfilled expectations it symbolized.

▪ ▪ ▪

In all externals, the loss appeared to have little effect on his career, and he immediately tried to return to his life as it had been before he met Dorothy. However, he needed only to return home to the apartment where she had spent the last months of her life to be reminded of her. Occasionally he turned his attention to songwriting—it had gotten him through tough times in the past—but initially, composing failed to relieve his sorrow. He turned out several joyless and mechanical numbers for the dance craze, and they inevitably fizzled. He was rarely seen during August, spending much of his time in seclusion at home. Meanwhile, Ray Goetz, who had briefly been his brother-in-law and remained his friend, decided to take Berlin abroad as a step toward recuperation. Berlin agreed, on the condition that he combine business with pleasure.

Strengthened by the knowledge that his life had some direction, he returned to his trick piano for solace, and this time attempted to write about his wife's death rather than avoid it. The result, a ballad called "When I Lost You," was unlike any song Berlin had previously written. It was an exceedingly simple and stately waltz employing a bittersweet harmony underneath the melody; diminished seventh chords added further melancholy. It was the only song Berlin ever admitted had a basis in the events of his life.

The composer was too much a creature of Tin Pan Alley not to see the song's obvious commercial merit, and it was duly published by his company. Berlin was in no condition to plug a song of this nature, but since his wife's death was widely known, many song buyers knew the story behind the song. It began to sell, and by the following year, it became his first hit ballad as the public snapped up a million copies of his grief.

Though begun amid solemn circumstances, the song quickly became more grist for the Tin Pan Alley mill. The back page of Waterson, Berlin & Snyder's sheet music often contained an advertisement for other songs published by the firm. "When I Lost You" succumbed to the same crass promotional treatment. A headline stated:

> IRVING BERLIN THE SONG GENIUS OF THE WORLD
> SAYS THIS IS THE BEST SONG
> I EVER WROTE

Beneath the headline was a photograph of the bereaved "song genius" himself, dressed in white tie and tails, pointing at an excerpt from the hit ballad. At the bottom of the page came the phrase, "For Sale by All Dealers." Dorothy's death, or to be more specific, Berlin's feeling about her death, was now one more item for sale on Woolworth's shelves.

It would be a mistake to conclude that the ordeal of his wife's death left Berlin untouched, or that he quickly rebounded and picked up his life just where he had left off before he had met her. It would be twelve years until he contemplated matrimony again, and he would then be a changed man, capable—on the evidence of songs he would write at the time—of serious and deeply meditated love. But the brashness that had characterized his whirlwind courtship with Dorothy would be a thing of the past. During the twelve years his widowhood would last, he became more inward, not in the sense of becoming introspective, a mental habit he despised, but less trusting of the world around him: his friends, his business partners, even himself. Her death also reinforced his dedication to the craft of songwriting, for it seemed the only reliable thing left to him. So much else had failed him—his homeland, his family, his singing career, his early marriage—there was little beside songwriting on which he could rely with absolute assurance.

For this reason, when he regained his confidence as a songwriter with "When I Lost You," he returned to composing with a vengeance, starting with a tune that quickly established itself as a surefire vaudeville hit, "When That Midnight Choo Choo Leaves for Alabam'." It was syncopated, it was upbeat, and it demonstrated that Berlin had recovered his knack for writing a crowd pleaser, even if it was not the ragtime opera he had been promising his public.

The public expected hits from Berlin, not an opera. In England, especially, his popularity was reaching its crest. Columnist Rennold Wolf noted that " 'Alexander's Ragtime Band' is even now second in popularity in London only to 'God Save the King,' and his 'Everybody's Doin' It' has displaced all of the native music hall songs in general favor." As a nod in the direction of Berlin's popularity, an entire London revue called itself "Everybody's Doin' It."

Wolf's claim that Berlin was even more popular in England than in the United States was exaggerated, but only slightly, and the adulation abroad gave further impetus to Goetz's plan to spirit away the composer. However, Berlin was still in no condition to travel or to meet his English admirers, even though the occasion promised to be pleasant. The trip was postponed until the following summer.

Remaining in New York, he dedicated himself to his publishing business and avoided further vaudeville engagements. One of the few events he allowed himself to be lured from his home to attend was a "beefsteak dinner" at Keen's Chop House, on West 44th Street. It was held by an ad hoc organization calling itself the United Songwriters of America. The occasion was meant to be festive, but Berlin, for once daring to fly in the face of popular sentiment, contributed a bittersweet ode overflowing with melancholy and with scorn for the entire business of songwriting. The ode concluded:

> Popular song, you will never be missed
>   Once your composer has ceased to exist,
> While Chopin, Verdi, Beethoven and Liszt
>   Live on with each generation.
> Still, though you die after having your sway,
>   To be forgotten the very next day,
> A rose lives and dies, in the very same way—
>   Let that be your consolation.

In its decorous way, this was an extraordinary outburst, unlike anything Berlin had ever written, or would write. In it he articulated misgivings that he generally held in check. It was verbose, it was cynical, it employed negative words Berlin avoided such as "hate" and "worthless," and its ideas were far more complex than Berlin, with his urge to crystalize a widely held point of view, was usually given to express. Its emphasis on the fragility and mortality of a song strongly suggests that Berlin's melancholy state of mind was as much the result of Dorothy's death as his disillusionment with Tin Pan Alley. This was not the Berlin who callously boasted that he was in the business for the money; his ode indicated a sensitivity and seriousness of purpose to which he rarely admitted.

Shortly after the ode, Berlin, revealing a new, more dedicated side of himself, explained that he composed "under a nervous strain, and more often than otherwise I feel as if my life depends on my accomplishing a song." But he kept his sense of desperation out of his music, which, with its emphasis on domestic comedy, became almost perversely escapist. When Waterson, Berlin & Snyder opened an office in Chicago, the composer-businessman went to visit and found the branch "in desperate need of some new numbers." He quailed before the prospect. He had only recently turned out three hits in rapid succession: "When I Lost You," "When the Midnight Choo Choo Leaves for Alabam'," and "At the Devil's Ball," but, he realized, "that fact didn't alter cases: the branch needed at least two new songs; it was up to me to write them."

Adopting a *modus operandi* to which he would have frequent recourse in the future, he holed himself up in his suite at the Hotel Sherman and, barely taking the time to eat or sleep, composed two songs concerning the domestic pleasure he himself sorely lacked. The first began, like so many of his songs, with a current phrase that had caught his fancy: "Snooky-Ookums."

> I liked its freakishness and the characteristic humor it suggested. I had thought what a laugh would be sent up by a song wherein a half-sized man gurgled baby-talk to a whale of a woman. There I had my idea and my title, and I went to work on them. Without the melody, the lyrics sound like a summer-resort on a moonlight night. But both are in the character, and together they emphasize the idea for all it's worth.
>
> Listen:

All the day he calls her
"Snooky-ookums! Snooky-ookums!"
All the day they talk like babies.
She's his jelly-elly roll;
He's her sugey-ugar bowl . . .
All night long the neighbors shout:
"Cut it out! Cut it out!"
They cry, "For goodness' sake, don't keep us awake
With your snooky-ooky baby-talk."

> Terrible, eh? Sounds funny, doesn't it? Put it with the melody, though, and you'll find it matches up better. . . . Lyrics look scraggly in cold print, for that's not what they were written for.

Berlin was correct on both counts. But he still needed another song to help launch the Chicago office. This time inspiration came from a completely unexpected direction. The Greco-Turkish War was then much in the news, and it prompted the songwriter to start daydreaming about Turkish harems. He tried various melodies to underscore the point, but "it was like stretching steel." He began humming. Nothing. Eventually he went to his trick piano, and soon, he recalled, "I got something that sounded like 'Dum te-de dum.' And I had it: In my harem." On this slender foundation, he built the rest of the song, though even he found it difficult to sing such fluff with a straight face. To increase the song's comic potential, he concocted Yiddish and Irish dialect verses. The result, he knew, was ridiculous, "but ridiculously funny" nonetheless.

To test the songs' effectiveness, he performed them both before a lively crowd at the College Inn. The audience's shouts of approval confirmed what he had suspected: the Chicago office of Waterson, Berlin & Snyder had two new hit songs to attract business.

■ ■ ■

Berlin returned to New York to find the British again claiming his attention. In February 1913 the novelist Arnold Bennett published a lengthy article in the London *Times* criticizing American popular music:

> There is no doubt that there is at present one class of creative and executive artists whom the public in the United States is disposed to idolize and enrich—namely, the composers and singer of "rag-time." . . . It is the music of the hustler, of the feverishly active speculator; of the "sky-scraper" and the "grain-elevator." Nor can there be any doubt about its vigor—vigor which is, perhaps, empty sometimes and meaningless, but, in the hands of competent interpreters, brimming over with life.

Bennett's cultural chauvinism led him to doubt ragtime's black pedigree. He suggested that the African music from which "ragtime" was derived was actually an adaptation of "British folk-songs introduced to the Negro by his English masters," and, as a result, it "represents not the lazy, sensuous, pleasure-loving 'nigger' element but the modern American at his most characteristic, full of energy." To Berlin such complex critical cavils as Bennett's counted for nothing. In the final analysis only the sales figures of his songs mattered, and at the time "Alexander's Ragtime Band" had sold over 500,000 copies in England alone, and Berlin's other ragtime and Dixie songs were selling with as much "purposeless energy."

Come June, Berlin extricated himself from the snares of the music publishing business. He sailed for England and his postponed engagement at the Hippodrome, accompanied by his musical secretary, Cliff Hess. On arriving in London, he installed himself at the Savoy Hotel, a full-blown celebrity on this, his second, trip to England, and to demonstrate the point he held an American-style press conference on June 19. For an English composer, this sort of self-promotion was simply not done; but Berlin was more than a mere composer, he was a phenomenon, and he had designs on achieving for himself the solo performing career he had never quite managed to bring off back home. His timing could not have been better; ragtime was at its peak in London, and Berlin had the delightful sensation of finding his reputation here precisely where it had been in New York two years earlier, when "Alexander's Ragtime Band" first burst on the scene, and before Dorothy had died. No Arnold Bennett rushed forward to attempt to discredit him now as he described his compositional techniques.

"I hum the songs, that's all," he said as the English reporters jotted down his every syllable. "Hum them while I am shaving, or in my bath, or out walking. I hum them and fix my own words to them, until they're fixed clearly in my mind; and when I have got the rhythm I want I call in an 'arranger' [Cliff Hess]. I don't know anything about harmony; but I can make tunes."

For the habitually insecure Berlin, no amount of praise could compensate for his conviction that he was being tested by the British and would be found wanting. It was a bold performance, far more brash than the one he would later give at the Hippodrome, and, to Berlin, even more important. In his run at the Hippodrome, he could reach only a few thousand people, at most; through the newspapers he could reach the entire country.

At first the strategy worked as well as he could have hoped. In terms that Berlin himself could scarcely have improved upon, the *Daily Express* introduced this prodigy to the English public in bold headlines:

**£20,000 A YEAR
FROM
RAGTIME**

GENIUS WHO DICTATES
SYNCOPATED
MELODIES

FIVE TUNES A DAY.

"Go where you will," the *Express* correspondent exhorted, "you cannot escape from the mazes of music he has spun. In every London restaurant, park and theatre you hear his strains; Paris dances to it; Berlin sips golden beer to his melodies; Vienna has forsaken the Waltz, Madrid flung away her castanets, and Venice has forgotten her barcarolles. Ragtime has swept like a whirlwind over the earth and set civilization humming. Mr. Berlin started it."

Now it was London's turn to be astonished by the Berlin legend: the impoverished boyhood, the apprenticeship as a singing waiter, and the peculiar fact that ragtime's best-known exponent could neither read nor write music. His youth caught the English by surprise; Mr. Berlin, they had assumed, would naturally be a mature individual. "It is almost impossible to believe that this boy—he looks nineteen—lathering his face to an unconscious tune one morning, four years ago, hit on the jerky, spasmodic bars of 'Alexander's Ragtime Band.' "

After the initial wave of acclaim, a backlash gradually set in, as the English press caught its collective breath and submitted Berlin's more extravagant claims to scrutiny. His breezy explanation of his compositional techniques (or lack of same) created a considerable amount of incredulity and envy. The *Times* warned: "to announce that he is here in London is to give a hint to many that here is their wished-for chance of having Mr Berlin's blood."

Much to the glee of the bloodthirsty, Berlin made one mistake during his press conference; it seemed insignificant at the time, but now it returned to haunt him. To prove himself in front of the reporters, he recalled, "I was foolish enough to tell them I would write both the words and music of a song for which they were to suggest a title." One of the journalists proposed "The Humming Rag." Berlin disappeared into his suite and devised a tune to go with this all-purpose title within an hour.

There followed a misunderstanding that would have been comic if it had not further inflamed his anxieties. He summoned the reporters to his suite, where he played the tune with a single finger on his piano, while Hess took it down. Irving thought he was showing off; making music to order was standard operating procedure on Tin Pan Alley, and the young pro was proud of his ability to crank out so many bars of music in a fixed span of time, as if he were a machine. But the English journalists were less impressed by Berlin's speed than they were by the solitary finger with which he played. From then on, a new rumor took flight: Irving Berlin could play the piano with only *one* finger. This rumor, groundless though it was, became so persistent that years later, when Chico Marx heard that Berlin had cut his finger, the comedian snapped, "Well, that won't hurt *his* piano playing."

Not until 1950, when Berlin played his piano in public in connection with a plagiarism suit, was the rumor fully dispelled. In London it supplied his detractors with just the evidence they needed to demonstrate that he was nothing but a hustling, hard-sell sham. Critics dubbed him "The Swanky Yankee," but English theater-goers cared little about the number of fingers Berlin employed to play the piano; they responded to his ragtime rhythms.

Faced with the possibility of losing favor, Berlin resolved to make a gesture of good will toward his English audience. On the eve of his debut at the Hippodrome,

> I discovered that all of my songs were known in England and that I needed a new one for an opening number. I wanted something that would give London a local flavor, yet would carry out the syncopated idea. I had used the word 'raggedy' in another song, not a success. I just liked it. I felt free to use it again, and with it and the London-interest suggestion, I went to work and stayed up most of the night composing "The International Rag."

By four in the morning, when the London streets were deserted and attendants at the Savoy Hotel were nodding off at their posts, he hit his stride. He now had the new rag roughed out and began dictating to the ever-reliable, ever-present Hess. Then other guests at the hotel began to awaken and complain about the strange "raggedy" sounds emanating from the songwriter's suite. The composer, knowing that still more work lay ahead, lurched toward the bathroom, grabbed a handful of towels, and threw them "into the piano to deaden its resonance." As daylight stole across the city, Berlin completed the chorus and began work on another verse. The song was finished just in time for the first performance, that afternoon, and by then he was exhausted from the ordeal. "I sweat blood," he said of this method of composing. "Absolutely. I sweat blood between 3 and 6 many mornings, and when the drops that fall off my forehead hit the paper they're notes."

Berlin's performance at the Hippodrome later that day caught both British audiences and critics by surprise. They had expected heavy, bombastic fare in their own music hall tradition; such was the treatment Berlin's own hits were accorded by English performers. Yet the songwriter's performance was by comparison muted and modest; it did not call to mind skyscrapers, grain elevators, and quick-buck artists. With the imperturbable Cliff Hess accompanying him, Berlin sang "The International Rag" and all the other hits for which he was known abroad: "Alexander's Ragtime Band," "Everybody's Doin' It," and "When I Lost You." If his voice was weak, his timing and diction were, as always, impeccable; his sense of conviction unassailable.

Even the critic for the *Times*, which had earlier torn ragtime to pieces in the most civilized manner, now conceded Berlin's legitimate musical ability. Addressing his detractors, the newspaper insisted that "once they have seen and heard him on the stage, only the most truculent could wish to have Mr Irving Berlin's blood. . . . In his mouth they [the songs] become something very different from the blatant bellowings we are used to." Yet the *Times* could not resist finally putting Berlin in his place. "All their quaintness, their softness, their queer patheticalness come out," it said of his rags. "They sound, indeed, quite new, and innocently, almost childishly pleasing, like a negro's smile."

The Ragtime King's understated performance had confounded his idolaters and detractors alike. His penchant for surprise added to the fascination he engendered. On arriving in England, he had been boastful when modesty would have better suited the occasion; in performance the "queer patheticalness" of his songs won over the audience. There were further paradoxes: the recently widowed composer churning out a parody love song such as "Snooky-Ookums," for instance, or the Tin Pan Alley hustler contemplating his ethereal ragtime opera. These apparent non sequiturs were symptoms of his breathtakingly rapid evolution. Even as he played the role of The Ragtime King in London, his mind raced ahead to an ambitious new project in New York.

PART TWO

RECOGNITION

1914–1924

■ □ ■ □ ■ □ ■

CHAPTER 6

Broadway Bound

When Berlin returned to New York in July 1913, he had the satisfaction of knowing that with the exception of the annoying "one finger" misunderstanding, his English engagement had been an outstanding success. At the same time it marked his farewell to his prosperous reign as The Ragtime King, not because he was deposed, but because he chose to abdicate the role. Dance, he knew, was the coming thing—not the wild animal dances with their funny names and suggestive steps, but an elegant new type of ballroom dancing.

An agile young couple, Vernon and Irene Castle, was transforming dance the way Berlin had once transformed ragtime: repackaging it in a form acceptable to mainstream white audiences. They demonstrated to Americans that it was possible to be graceful and romantic without being European; they had discovered a straightforward American way to express affection without looking silly and self-conscious. The Castles set a standard of elegance and affability. And they made dance respectable. Their career was brief, but exceedingly bright, and the American public would not see their like again until Fred Astaire began dancing to songs composed by Irving Berlin. The American dances spawned in the craze of 1912–1914 had been too sensual, too African to gain universal acceptance; they were as divisive as the suffragette movement, with which they were often linked. In both cases women threw off restraints to proclaim an independence that the *ancien régime* found grotesque, threatening.

Then the Castles, Berlin's counterpart in dance, appeared on the scene and tamed the outrageous dances and their precarious dives, pelvic thrusts, and violent rhythms. The Castles slowed the tempos, simplified the rhythms, restrained the gestures, and made the movements seem altogether healthy. Soon "experts" were claiming that dancing, far from destroying morality, aided weight loss. Berlin was not above briefly trying to capitalize on this craze-within-a-craze. "Dance and Grow Thin" was surely as trivial a song as he ever wrote, yet even this effort was catchy, well-done, and redeemed by a faint suggestion of mockery concerning the craze it sought to exploit. But the Castles' appeal didn't pretend to be utilitarian; it was purely emotional. Americans wanted to be swanky, and the Castles proved it was possible.

Like Berlin, they learned their craft from black models, who diligently schooled them. The Castles' fourteen-piece band, going under the diplomatic name of The Syncopated Society Orchestra, consisted primarily of blacks. Their highly capable director, James Reese Europe, an Alabama-born Black, was a star in his own right. Big Jim Europe had come to fame championing the cause of a distinctly American black music; his ability and credibility were sufficient to earn him a date in Carnegie Hall in 1912, conducting an all-black orchestra of one hundred twenty-five musicians, including seven pianists and a chorus of one hundred fifty.

Europe conducted the Syncopated Society Orchestra whenever the Castles danced, he wrote most of the music to which they danced, and he even showed the Castles *how* to dance, convincing the athletic Vernon to move more slowly, more gracefully. He worked with the Castles on refining the fox trot, and the result became the nation's standard version. Even as he toned down the Castles' dance steps, Europe's music remained true to its black origins by emphasizing the back beat. Like other black musicians, he was uncomfortable with the term *ragtime*. "There never was any such music as ragtime," he insisted. It was "merely a nickname or a fun-name given to Negro rhythm by our Caucasian brother musicians." He much preferred the term *syncopation* to describe his music.

On the strength of their popularity, the Castles built an empire of dance halls. They also performed, commanding the highest salaries of their day. And they taught—the Vernon Castle School of dancing opened its doors at 26 East 46th Street. Their book, *Modern Dancing*, quickly became a fixture in homes across the country. They made dance instruction films, and they contributed an outpouring of articles to the popular press, spreading the gospel of dance. Americans everywhere—not just in New York—pored over photographs showing the slinky couple going through the fox trot step by step and tried to make sense of diagrams depicting dancing footprints linked by a string of dots and dashes.

Irene, especially, became a public icon, setting fashions in matters only distantly related to dance. She had a shrewd sense of how to manipulate symbols, and she knew how to make naughty into nice. With her thin, supple physique, she shattered the popular preference for plump, heavy-limbed female entertainers; the flappers who would appear on the scene in a few years owed their emphasis on a slender silhouette to her. She bobbed her red hair and created an instant yet tenacious style throughout the country. She smoked cigarettes and legitimized that practice for women. She wore men's riding pants and popularized that fad, as well. When she was seen carrying a lapdog, lapdogs suddenly became a necessity for the fashionable woman.

Promoting themselves as the ultimate romantic American couple, the Castles were not quite what they seemed. It was true that Irene Foote hailed from New Rochelle, but her husband Vernon was English, and his real name was Blyth, not Castle. He was a confirmed Francophile and fond of daredevil stunts. All physical activity came to him with the greatest of ease, whether it was polo, tennis, or dancing. He was every bit as slender as Irene, with deep-set eyes and thick blond hair.

Shortly after they wed, the couple fled to Paris, where, after a period of starvation, they became an attraction at the Café de Paris, where they performed the outrageous turkey trot and grizzly bear. When they returned to the United States in 1912, the Castles, as the couple had rechristened themselves, were able to command ten times their former salary. Vernon spent many profitable evenings starring in *The Lady of the Slipper* on Broadway, then dancing the rest of the night away with his wife Irene at Louis Martin's café.

Making dance respectable (at last) was the key to the Castle's success. "Refinement is the key note of their method," noted their publicity. They tamed the turkey trot into the fox trot and avoided dips that would reveal Irene's legs or thrust their pelvic regions together. At the same time they brought a distinctly modern humor and intimacy to their dancing; it was romantic rather than throbbingly and threateningly sexual, and most reassuringly of all to American audiences, they did not take themselves seriously. "If Vernon ever looked into my eyes with smoldering passion during the tango, we should have both burst out laughing," Irene said. Everyone breathed a sigh of relief along with the Castles.

Their American charm and sense of humor appealed mightily to audiences, who were, at long last, beginning to tire of European operettas and to seek homegrown fare. Ever since the Hungarian composer Franz Lehár's musical confection *The Merry Widow* had become the sensation of the 1907 season on Broadway, two years after its debut in Vienna, American musicals had struggled for audience acceptance. Even George M. Cohan, a leading figure on Broadway, felt pushed aside by the European invader and its imitations. But a combination of isolationist sentiment and intellectual ferment combined to reeducate public taste. Though Berlin had set his sights on a ragtime opera, many thought the time for a syncopated musical had come; it would be American, it would be ragtime, and it would be popular. The only question was: who would produce such a spectacle?

The honor fell to the most dignified impresario of the era, Charles Dillingham. His father was an Episcopal clergyman, and the young Dillingham had paid his dues as a drama critic for the *New York Evening Sun* before making the leap to play writing and finally producing. Now, when he decided to pair Irving Berlin with the Castles, he was taking what seemed an inevitable step.

In the post-*Merry Widow* era it would not do to mount another revue with vaudeville-style acts thrown together as dramatic non sequiturs; Dillingham required at least a semblance of a story to give the show an up-to-date feeling, and for that he turned to the premier librettist of the American musical stage, Harry Smith. Smith belonged to the breed of scenarist who would sit backstage, typewriter propped on his wobbly knees, tapping out a new second act for a show on a moment's notice. In his lengthy career, he wrote the librettos for over three hundred shows this way, casually including whatever material the stars or producer requested. Given these conditions, no one expected him to be a fount of literature, but he was fast, and in this unselfconscious era, speed and adaptability outweighed consistency.

Smith was no primitive. By the time Dillingham asked him to work on a show for the Castles, the scenarist had thirty years' experience, and when he wasn't busy concocting his whirlwind plots, he doted on his first love, fine books; in fact, he named his autobiography *First Nights and First Editions*. With his encyclopedic knowledge of ancient plays, many of which could be recycled for current consumption, he brought a scholarly approach to the often nonsensical business of writing scenarios. Indeed, much of his work consisted of loosely adapting long-forgotten scripts by others.

On this occasion Dillingham gave him an antique French play, *Round the Clock*, with instructions to convert it into a "new musical entertainment." Smith made short work of the script; it was but one of four he wrote in the span of a single month, and its plot was so slender that the program credit for it read, "Book (if any) by Harry B. Smith." Since the resulting scenario was designed to exploit the talents of the Castles, Smith gave it a catch-all title, *Watch Your Step*.

Finally, Dillingham announced his choice of composer: Irving Berlin. The challenge was considerable, for there were to be no interpolations in this unified score. Dillingham's offer opened up much broader horizons than Berlin, as an untrained musician, had dared contemplate. In accepting it, the composer was making the most audacious gamble of his career. Until now he had written his songs one at a time, and the success or failure of a single song had little lasting impact on his reputation. There would always be a chance to redeem himself with the next song. But now, with a complete score to compose, his entire reputation was on the line. He had only one chance to impress the audience, and as Berlin knew from his experience trying to make a hit of "Alexander's Ragtime Band," even a good song can require many performances in different circumstances before it finally catches on.

More than Berlin's personal reputation was at stake. "It was the first time Tin Pan Alley got into the legitimate theater," he noted. If he proved he could write a hit score, Tin Pan Alley would gain a valuable new foothold on Broadway; if he failed, or even if he did not succeed instantly, on opening night Tin Pan Alley would lose its most prestigious showcase. There was good reason to believe Berlin was overreaching. Of course he had demonstrated his gift for writing hits, but as an untrained musician, he lacked the skills to assemble a complete score. It was one thing to concoct a song with a catchy thirty-two-bar chorus; it was another to sustain an entire evening's entertainment.

The task of composing the score occupied Berlin throughout the heat of the summer of 1914. He worked relentlessly, usually at night, always at home, and always with Cliff Hess faithfully transcribing his melodies. The completed score contained eighteen songs, half his output for the entire year.

The opening night was set for December, and by that time events over which Berlin had absolutely no control began to work in his favor. On June 28, 1914 the Austrian Archduke Francis Ferdinand was assassinated in Sarajevo, Yugoslavia. With the specter of war looming in Europe, President Woodrow Wilson steered the nation on a course of isolationism; the last thing Americans wanted was to become involved in a foreign war. Berlin, along with the rest of Tin Pan Alley, sensed a growing public antipathy toward all things German, including German (or Viennese) operettas such as *The Merry Widow*. Suddenly the name Berlin had chosen for himself seven years earlier began to sound unpleasantly Teutonic, but it was too late to change his name again; it had become too valuable a property. However, isolationism worked in his favor; for the first time in the young century there existed an agreeable climate for major and self-consciously American art forms, and in his role as the composer and lyricist for *Watch Your Step*, Berlin was there to take advantage of it—if he could.

When the show went into rehearsal, Harry B. Smith was immediately taken by the young songwriter. Smith had himself written lyrics for six thousand songs, but even he was impressed by Berlin's facility:

> He is a genius in inventing unexpected rhymes. Most bards would think it hopeless to attempt to find a rhyme for "Wednesday"; but Mr. Berlin found one. In one of the songs in this piece, a matinée idol describes his persecution by women and

alludes to the elderly worshippers who attend the afternoon performances:

"There's a matinée on Wednesday,
I call it my old hens' day."

At a Hippodrome dress rehearsal, the composer, Raymond Hubbell, defied Berlin to find a rhyme for "orange." A few minutes later the song writer came down the aisle, stopped the orchestra rehearsal, which Hubbell was directing, and said, "I've got it."

"Brother Bill and I once stole a cellar door;
And Bill was eating an orange
He stole the hind hinge
And I stole the fore hinge."

Despite Berlin's rapid pace of work, *Watch Your Step*, at least in rehearsals, seemed destined to be a flop. The production was bedeviled not only by its own ambitiousness, but also by the inevitable cast changes, which continually threw it into disarray. Among the original members of the company was W. C. Fields, then nearing his comic peak. He was so good, in fact, that he upstaged the Castles during a tryout at the Empire Theater in Syracuse, New York. Observing his show thrown out of balance, Dillingham fired Fields on the spot; the producer was paying the Castles more than he was paying Fields, and it was they whom audiences would come to see, not Fields. In the end Dillingham wanted to protect his investment. Such changes took their toll. Harry Smith recalled one of the actresses in the cast, despairing over the hash that *Watch Your Step* threatened to become, intone at a dress rehearsal, "I went to church this morning and burned candles for the success of this piece; but, personally, I think it will be a [blank-blank] failure."

Even the songs lacked pizzazz, for all Berlin's skill at rhyming. He faced greater problems than he ever had. It was one thing to interpolate songs in a show, another to have the entire weight of the show resting on his score. It was not enough for the songs to shine in their own right, to stop the show and inspire the audience to demand encores; they had to fit into the action and, even more difficult, they had to be consistent with the characters who sang them. In addition to the problems of integrating his score, Berlin was grappling with the large orchestra. Composing through the night on his trick piano, he gave scant thought to instrumentation. He had no idea how to write for a clarinet as opposed to a violin, or how to handle percussion, but in performance, instrumentation became crucial, and not even Cliff Hess could help here, for his expertise began and ended with the piano. Fortunately, Dillingham had enlisted the services of Frank Sadler, a well-known orchestrator, who gave the grateful young composer a short course in writing for Broadway shows. "My songs were all ragtime," he said. "They were written for a piano and ten, as we used to call a vaudeville orchestra. Frank Sadler arranged them for a twenty-piece band and did it with real taste. I learned a lot from him."

The issue of which instruments belonged in a dance orchestra was fast becoming as controversial as the dance craze itself. Until *Watch Your Step*, the predictable "piano and ten" included a first violin, bass, first and second cornet, trombone, drums, viola, second violin, clarinet, and flute; they were all rooted in the nineteenth century. After *Watch Your Step*, the dance band underwent a rapid transition to the twentieth century. The saxophone made an appearance, then the banjo, and a piano accordion; the violins were banished to the concert hall. With his playing restricted to the piano, Berlin was grateful to turn over the chore of instrumentation to an expert, preferring to concentrate on melodies and lyrics. He was completely comfortable working with both a transcriber and an arranger, though he insisted their help did not in any way detract from the sole credit he demanded and received for the music. As a Tin Pan Alley product, he was accustomed to performers adapting his music. "In this way American music is completely different than European music," he offered in his defense. "There they start from the ground up and the composer knows all phases—writing, arranging and orchestration. Here someone creates it and someone else dresses it up."

With the Castles, Berlin, and Dillingham involved, and its ambition to overtake the European operetta widely known, expectations for *Watch Your Step* ran higher than for any other musical in the 1914 season. When the show finally opened on December 8 at the New Amsterdam Theater, the audience was prepared to react strongly. As the curtain rose on Act One, they were confronted with a "law office de danse," where stenographers typed in syncopated time. To the strains of Berlin's "Minstrel Parade," a group of distinctly countrified folk appeared, awaiting the reading of a will of one of their relatives. The will bequeathed $2 million to any relative who managed to avoid falling in love. One relative, Ernesta Hardacre (Sallie Fisher), insisted on her innocence by explaining that her mother "gave me two white rabbits, and then some unknown person sent me six more little ones." Then a rival claimant appeared, Joseph Lilyburn, played by the great Vernon Castle himself, "the human jack-knife," as a critic described him. Singing "I'm a Dancing Teacher Now," Castle sent up the entire dance craze he had fostered.

As a plot, it wasn't much, but then Harry B. Smith was merely supplying a frame for the Castles' dancing and Berlin's music. With a lack of logic so characteristic of Smith's scenarios, the action suddenly shifted to a stage door, a change of scene that served as an excuse for the entire production to turn into a backstage musical. Finally, Irene Castle appeared, not even attempting to fit into a role, but simply as herself. It came as a shock to the audience when she began to sing "Show Us How to Do the Fox Trot," for her voice lacked the polish of her dancing, but once she began to move, she put to rest all doubts about her ability to hold the stage.

Act Two opened with a song that was so simple and direct in its appeal that many considered it the finest in the score—though it was far from that. In "Let's Settle Down in a One-Horse Town," Berlin had contributed yet another variation on that Tin Pan Alley staple: rural nostalgia. Like patriotism, yearning for the simpler life was a reliable sentiment, especially on Broadway.

On the slenderest of pretexts, the scene shifted to the Metropolitan Opera, where a mock production was in progress. In the boxes of the famed Diamond Horseshoe, women filed their nails and men watched the stock market ticker or read a newspaper. In the midst of this jaded, indifferent audience, the ghost of Verdi appeared, and he was angry, for he had discovered the chorus of the opera singing his classics in syncopation. He urged them not to "hurdy-gurdy Mr. Verdi," but his protest fell on deaf ears. A stand-in Caruso also appeared, matching his voice against the caterwauling syncopated chorus. Finally, Verdi voiced his protest to some of the better-known melodies from his operas, especially *Rigoletto*, but the stubborn company replied with a ragtime obbligato.

This exceptionally clever parody demonstrated Berlin's savvy, if not his compositional skill. Ever since writing "Sadie Salome, Go Home," he had displayed a gift for parodying the pretensions of opera, but never before had he launched such a broad-based musical assault. Nor was his "Ragtime Opera Medley" another thirty-two-bar formula exercise. It went on and on, a prodigious display of musical wit and inventiveness. The sheet music for this number alone ran to seventeen pages; nothing quite like it had ever been seen or heard before, and its high spirits satisfied both opera lovers and haters alike. Yet it was not the ragtime opera he had been promising his public; if anything, it was a persuasive demonstration of the folly of such a grandiose project. The gigantic parody amounted to a dialogue Berlin had been carrying on with "serious" or "classical" music since he had begun composing, and it explained, for anyone who cared to interpret, why Berlin could never write such an opera himself.

In the next scene, Algy Cuffs (Charles King), one of the claimants to the will, encounters his friend Kilgobbin. "Hello, old man!" he calls. "Been to the theatre tonight?" And Kilgobbin replies: "Yes, we went to the opening of 'The Onion Girl.' " Then Kilgobbin gives his cue. "That one song was a crackerjack," he says. "How does it go?"

Algy's girlfriend proceeds to sing a tantalizing bit of the song, a sprightly, syncopated tune about a "musical demon." Then the entire company *whistles* the song—whistling being yet another short-lived craze Berlin was determined to exploit.

Kilgobbin, curmudgeon that he is, complains: "Oh, this new music gives me a pain. Why don't they spring some of the old stuff of the Harrigan and Hart days. That was music!"

The audience, of course, instantly recognized the names of Harrigan and Hart, the premier Irish comic duo of Berlin's youth, and the sentimental ballads with which they were associated.

"I know the kind you mean," Stella says, and she proceeds to sing what seems, at first, to be an entirely separate tune. And then, a minor but charming musical miracle took place, as the two songs, so incompatible at first hearing, were sung in unison, with the jittery ragtime tune weaving in and out of the flowing melody. This trick was designed to show off Berlin's musical dexterity, and it proved that beyond dispute. Even better, the song called "Play a Simply Melody," suggested that the traditional English ballad, reminiscent of Stephen Foster and, by extension, America's rural past, could coexist harmoniously with ragtime's jagged rhythms. This was an unusual proposition, especially at a time when it was widely assumed that the two forms of music and the disparate ways of life they represented—one raffish, the other genteel—were mutually exclusive.

Since the two parts of this complex song fit together as neatly as a Chinese puzzle, it was remarkable that Berlin, who had no knowledge of harmony, managed to bring it off. The feat required an extremely acute musical ear, an ability that Berlin had acquired with years of practical experience. In fact, the words proved more difficult for Berlin to match than did the melodies. "The musical part didn't give me any trouble," he said. "The difficulty was getting two lyrics so that they didn't bump into each other."

As soon as the curtain rang down and the furious applause commenced, Berlin and everyone else associated with *Watch Your Step* realized that the show, for all the trouble it had caused during rehearsal, was a bona fide hit. By the time the reviews came out in the morning, it was apparent that it was *the* success of the 1914–1915 season.

Throughout the performance, Berlin, good Jewish boy that he was, sat in the audience with his mother, Lena, who had come down from her home in the Bronx for the occasion, and several of his sisters. The impression Izzy's show made on his mother can only be imagined. She still spoke no English and had only the faintest notion of the kind of work her son actually did, but if he could accomplish all this without being able to read a note of music, then it was true that all things were possible in America.

For Berlin, it had been anguish to sit out the show, hearing his music performed by the flashy twenty-piece orchestra and trying to gauge its effect on the first-night audience. At least that particular Gehenna had ended, though he would soon have to endure the reviews. In the midst of the tumult, he heard a cry: "Composer! Composer!"

The audience wanted him; he was as much a star as the Castles or George M. Cohan. He walked up the aisle, mounted the stage, and acknowledged the applause. When the composer appeared before them, the audience drew its collective breath. He looked tiny, and although he was now a twenty-six-year-old widower, he scarcely seemed out of his teens. He made a brief speech of thanks, but his words were drowned out by the roar of approval. The occasion was more than a ritual acknowledgment of his accomplishments; it was a coronation by acclamation, confirming the fact that Berlin had made the leap from Tin Pan Alley to the legitimate theater. *Variety*'s man marveled. The audience, he wrote, "would probably not have believed it had they been told that this youth, who composed the music of 'Watch Your Step' and was then thanking the throng in a '$2 Broadway house,' had less than seven years before, unknown and unheard of, sung songs in a 'dump' on Chatham Square."

After the applause it was expected of Berlin that he would celebrate. "Seldom has a successful first night occurred in New York when the one most responsible for it could not be found after the performance at the most famous Broadway restaurant, the center of a large and admiring crowd," *Variety* advised. He was young, single, and extremely successful; here was his chance to dandle a chorus girl on each knee. Instead, he escorted his mother and sisters from the theater, put them in the car he had hired for the occasion, and took each of them to her home. And when he was alone, he went straight to his apartment where Cliff Hess joined him. The two of them remained there in suspended animation until three o'clock in the morning, when two acquaintances, both journalists, came to pay their respects. Still Berlin refused to exult. At his friends' urging, he played through several of the songs in the show; it was a quiet performance, his way of retrieving the score from the huge cast and orchestra and demonstrating that it was, after all, *his* score they'd sung. His friends gloated over Berlin's career prospects now that he had composed a Broadway hit, but Berlin, who knew how quickly defeat could follow success and who had been conditioned to take nothing for granted, refrained from making predictions. He would say only that he "hoped the show would get over for Mr. Dillingham's sake." Berlin then reached the anticlimactic finish of this celebration by turning to his new collection of "exquisite chinaware" and displaying it to his small circle of friends.

Berlin's utter lack of demonstrativeness, his aw-shucks attitude, came naturally to him; he discovered a knack for playing the role of composer as popular hero to the hilt, and he was learning how to turn his innate sense of reserve to his advantage. He was fully aware of the impression he gave by sitting with his mother and sisters on opening night, then dropping them off, one by one, and going home alone afterward. It was exactly the impression he had wanted to give: the hardworking, industrious immigrant minding his own business and taking nothing for granted. And then, after dazzling all Broadway with his modesty, he could return to his lair and count his royalties. Despite signs to the contrary, therefore, he recognized the significance of this, his first Broadway success. Thirty years later, when *Life* magazine asked him to list the highlights of his career, he placed the opening night of *Watch Your Step* first.

Then came the reviews. At the time, reviewers, who were often anonymous, tended to view productions with a great deal more charity than do reviewers today. Even allowing for this climate of critical indulgence, *Watch Your Step* and especially Berlin's score fared well in the press, where it proved to be a bigger attraction than the Castles, as *The New York Times'* headline indicated the morning after the opening:

'WATCH YOUR STEP'
IS HILARIOUS FUN

Irving Berlin's Revue at the
New Amsterdam Is Fes-
Tivity Syncopated.

The word that jumped out at the company was *revue;* they had hoped to present a "syncopated musical show," as the program described it. And now they had been demoted to the status of revue, or even worse, "vaudeville done handsomely," according to *The New York Times*, which paid strict attention to the matter of genre.

Yet Berlin's music, no matter in what form it was presented, clearly carried the evening, according to the *Times*. "More than anyone else," its anonymous reviewer concluded, " 'Watch Your Step' belongs to Irving Berlin. He is the young master of syncopation, the gifted and industrious writer of words and music for songs that have made him rich and envied . . ." *Variety* concurred that Berlin had definitely arrived on New York's theatrical scene, insisting that the composer "stands out like the Times building does in the Square. That youthful marvel of syncopated melody is proving things in 'Watch Your Step,' firstly that he is not alone a rag composer, and that he is one of the greatest lyric writers America has ever produced."

The only trick Berlin hadn't managed to pull off was the one expected of him: to write an *integrated* musical comedy, an American riposte to *The Merry Widow.* After all was said and done and danced and sung, *Watch Your Step* remained a revue. Part of the responsibility surely belonged to Smith's scattershot libretto and Dillingham's emphasis on presenting a gargantuan spectacle. But part belonged to Berlin, as well, and his willingness to obey an irresistible urge to display his musical wit, even when it meant burying the one indisputably distinguished song in his score, "Play A Simple Melody."

Although *Watch Your Step* ran for 175 performances and then embarked on a profitable national tour, it was not quite the milestone in musical comedy that it might have been. Berlin's score failed to yield the one universally recognized hit for which Tin Pan Alley had hoped, and it fell short of greatness. But critics and audience alike agreed that the show was great *fun.*

Nonetheless, Berlin had brought syncopation to Broadway, and that was reason enough for the first-nighters to acclaim him. Indeed, Berlin's ovation all but buried the reception accorded the Castles, whose dancing had been the show's *raison d'être;* one notice devoted only a few brief words to the couple, near the end: "There is dancing by Mr. and Mrs. Castle." The Castles had simply proved to be themselves; Berlin had stretched himself and given birth to a new persona.

Berlin was more than a successful songwriter, and *Watch Your Step* amounted to more than an outsized hit. For once the measure of Berlin's achievement could not be taken in terms of the numbers that meant everything on Tin Pan Alley: so many copies of sheet music sold, so many dollars earned in royalties. Berlin moved well beyond those indices, not that they didn't still apply to him; on Tin Pan Alley they would *always* apply, and he would always take them seriously, but he belonged to another category—a legend-in-the-making. This exceedingly private man, who had retreated to his apartment to display his collection of chinaware to a few friends on the night of his Broadway success, was poised to become public property, a figure in the public domain. It would be several years until Berlin would lift his head from the narrow columns recording sales of his sheet music and gaze on the forbidding dimensions of this role.

For now the press pointed the way, and when he hesitated, well-meaning celebrities, attracted by his sudden fame, tried to nudge him in the right direction. Suddenly everyone wanted a piece of him. Giacomo Puccini wished to collaborate on an opera, according to an Italian newspaper. From England George Bernard Shaw announced that he had written lyrics for Mr. Berlin to set to music. It was impressive yet intimidating, the way these luminaries threw themselves at him, actually treating him as an equal. But the former singing waiter harbored serious doubts that he belonged in their select number. What could he offer Puccini—a selection of comic Italian dialect songs such as "Dorando"? Or perhaps Berlin could play a little "nigger piano" to divert the composer of *La Bohème*. Not knowing precisely how to proceed, he asked Ray Goetz to speak with the composer; the two briefly met, and the matter went no further. And as for Shaw, he was merely a name to Berlin, who automatically assumed that he did not belong on that man of letters' exalted plane. Irving was condemned to be popular.

In New York a publication called *Music and Theatre Gossip* seriously proposed adapting Berlin's life story to a silent film. The publication had the title picked out—*Rag-ing It to Glory*—and Berlin's twenty-six years were neatly compartmentalized, reel by reel. This was the year of D. W. Griffith's *Birth of a Nation*, and although the would-be screenwriter entertained similarly epic aspirations for Berlin's life, he found it a stretch to portray the details of the songwriter's brief life on the same cinematic scale.

> "Reel" 1: Young Irving is seen at play with his Lower East Side companions. Although the son of a rabbi, he is raised sort of *ad lib* like so many other East Side boys. He gravitates

to a cheap Chinatown "joint." Taken by his rather pleasing voice the habitués throw him money. In time he is given a permanent job as waiter and entertainer.

"Reel" 2: Always "on the job," young Berlin calls on Max Winslow, professional manager of a music publishing house. Mr. Winslow gives him a new song to put on that evening and promises to visit the "joint" with a bunch of the boys, who will throw him some coin if he "does it good!" Winslow finds Irving parodying the words of the original song when he reaches the café that evening and is further attracted to the bright young fellow. He decides to take him "under his wing."

"Reel" 3: Irving is now living with Mr. Winslow in his East Eighteenth Street apartments—and has secured a better engagement at Kelly's on Fourteenth Street. He persists that he can write his own songs and Winslow tries in vain to get him a permanent job with his (Winslow's) own employers. In the meanwhile, Irving gets one or two songs published which net him a little money.

"Reel" 4: Winslow switches to another music publishing house, and places a number of Irving's songs. They catch on. Hit follows hit. Two million copies of "Alexander's Ragtime Band" are sold in this country alone. Irving is taken into the concern, the present name of which is Waterson, Berlin & Snyder Co. Charles Dillingham invites him to write the lyrics for a new musical comedy.

"Reel" 5: . . . Irving Berlin, the songwriting kid, responding modestly to the calls of a large first-night audience for "composer." "Watch Your Step" an assured success. Irving scores seven big song hits in one night.

"Reel" 6: At the conclusion of "Watch Your Step," Irving bundles his mother and sister into a taxicab, takes them all home, then repairs to his own apartment on West Seventy-first street with no other companion than Mr. Cliff Hess, his private secretary. Later that night a few of his more intimate friends seek him out in his beautiful apartments to congratulate him on his latest success.

It never occurred to the author of this scenario that it might prove difficult to reenact a songwriter's life in a *silent* movie. The journalist also appeared to be ignorant of Berlin's tragically brief marriage to Dorothy Goetz; nevertheless, he was among the first to be carried away by the legend fast forming around the young composer.

No silent movie about Berlin's young life was ever released; the songwriter cringed at the prospect. Throughout his career emissaries from Hollywood would pester him with the idea. At first it was presented to him as an honor, later as an obligation, but either way Irving, with his mania for control, would never turn over his own life to others. His loathing of the prospect ran deep, a primitive fear that the result would wrest his identity from his control. As long as he collected royalties, he was content to let his music loose in the world, but Irving himself required cushioning against the impact of his celebrity. Later he would restrict even the performances of his songs, as if he were determined to expunge all evidence of his memory from the public record.

■ □ ■ □ ■ □ ■

CHAPTER 7

The Great American Composer?

The artistic temperament is a disease that affects amateurs.
G. K. CHESTERTON

On parochial Tin Pan Alley, Berlin's Broadway success engendered rancor and envy, even at his own firm of Waterson, Berlin & Snyder. Ted Snyder, his former songwriting partner, resented the way his former protégé now overshadowed him; he hoped Berlin would take him along, offer him connections, throw him a bone, but Irving, he discovered, was interested only in Irving. Berlin accorded the same treatment to his other songwriting partner, Edgar Leslie, who resented it with equal fervor.

Henry Waterson's conduct posed even more serious problems. Berlin had always been annoyed by the way the firm's senior member had joked with reporters about the embarrassing rumors of a "colored boy" who composed Berlin's songs. Now Berlin discovered that Waterson was skimming profits to pay gambling debts incurred at the racetrack. It seemed likely that if Waterson persisted in his addiction to gambling, the business would go bankrupt. The meticulous Berlin would never tolerate such unprofessional conduct in a business partner. Several weeks before the opening of *Watch Your Step*, therefore, he found time to withdraw quietly from the firm where he had made his mark as a songwriter; publicity generated by the Broadway show obscured a move that would otherwise have been the talk of the Alley.

On November 17, 1914, the songwriter formed his own firm, Irving Berlin, Inc., with offices at 1571 Broadway. The location, far from the West 28th Street music publishers but in the heart of the theater district, revealed where his interests now lay. The old firm, Waterson, Berlin & Snyder, continued to exist for several more years, and with its extensive plugging staff it remained the logical choice for promoting his individual vaudeville songs. The new company handled his more sophisticated material, especially scores for revues and musicals.

Berlin could now afford to bankroll his own business; he owned three shares of the concern, with two partners, including his lawyer, Max Josephson, owning one share apiece. Through the vehicles of his two companies, he straddled Tin Pan Alley and Broadway, and while he was a product of the former, he aspired to become an even bigger presence in the latter. If ultimately overambitious, his plan was sound, even necessary, for Waterson, Berlin & Snyder eventually did go bankrupt, and for just the reason he'd feared: Waterson's gambling.

He spent little time at either office. He was no longer interested in hearing the cacophonous parade of singers, pluggers, and lyricists who trudged through a music publisher's office; he sequestered himself at home, where he became absorbed in self-improvement. A Broadway composer, a man to whom Puccini and Shaw wrote to offer their services, ought to be educated, he told himself, and not in music alone. Like a businessman or statesman preparing to play a significant role in the world's affairs, Berlin set about building his vocabulary. "I never had a chance for much schooling," he now explained with endearing candor, "so I couldn't read the good books I wished to because I had to look up too many of the big words. I'm taking time now to look those words up. I'm trying to get at least a bowing acquaintance with the world's best literature, and some knowledge of history, and all of the famous dead people." *All of the famous dead people:* the phrase revealed an impenetrable core of intellectual naïveté. His course of self-improvement had a practical side, as well: "I'm a little bit commercial in so doing. . . . I want to enlarge my vocabulary, with a definite purpose of bigger, better writing."

To this end he painstakingly began to gather tokens of the finer things of which he had been deprived during his youth, items that he chose carefully and selected with a shrewd collector's eye. He fancied books especially. He purchased a complete set of the works of Shakespeare, which he was sure to display to any critic who came to interview him. Later, when a collector offered him "many thousands of dollars" for the set, Berlin refused to sell. He also acquired a life of Abraham Lincoln containing letters by Lincoln himself and autographed editions of any famous literary work he could find. He invested in art: paintings by George Inness, an American artist then in vogue, and carved ivory from the Orient and France. Despite Berlin's passion for collecting, visitors to his apartment found it notable not for its plenty, but for its restraint. It was subdued to the point of austerity, displaying the simplicity and sense of control that Berlin brought to bear on his songs.

And when he left his home in search of relaxation, he avoided the cafés and theaters where he would be recognized, where people could approach him with good wishes that concealed offers, proposed business dealings, and dubious investment opportunities; instead, he socialized in private with other theater and vaudeville performers. One whom he permitted to befriend him was Elsie Janis, a former vaudeville child star. Her mother had been a friend of Mrs. McKinley, the president's widow, and the family had even visited the White House, but the dark-haired, vivacious Elsie much preferred the company of actors to that of politicians.

A protégée of "Charley" Dillingham, as she called him, she lived with her mother in an imposing mansion in Tarrytown, New York, not far from the Hudson River. Irving occasionally visited the eighteenth-century manor house, strolled across its eleven acres, played tennis on its court, and swam in its pond. In the great library, before a large fireplace, on a vast polar bear skin, he sprawled contentedly, living in a dream of luxury.

Elsie's manor house became his second home, and he wiled away the evenings there—not with Elsie, but at a piano, working. "Many nights," she recalled, "we would go to sleep to the tune of a new Berlin hit which Irving, in the drawing room below, would thump at until dawn!" She was plainly stuck on him, and as he composed in the room downstairs from her, she fancied that she was the one inspiring his songs—though there is no evidence to suggest that she did. Still, she wrote: "There was one song that I absolutely claim as mine. It was called 'Don't Wait Too Long.' Never a sensational hit, but after all there are so few people to whom it might apply."

Poor driven Irving—unable to relax, to let go of his music even for one night and permit himself to reciprocate Elsie's affection. As much as she pined for Irving, though, Elsie was not the marrying kind, not since her parents had gotten divorced and her brother had shot himself during an ocean voyage. She advised Irving and her other friends that if they insisted on getting married, they should enjoy two happy years together, have a baby, and call it quits. Berlin, of course, had other ideas.

On the evenings that he was marooned in town, Irving frequented concert halls, where he submitted himself to the spell cast by the current Russian composers, with whom he felt a spiritual affinity: Rimsky-Korsakov, Borodin, and Moussorgsky. Inspired by their worthy examples, he continued to promise himself and his public a *magnum opus* in the form of a ragtime opera, though by now his declarations had the impure air of a hoax about them. Still, the opera existed in his imagination, if not on paper, as distant music. It was a form of muse, a master song to which he turned for inspiration when the time came to write his actual tunes. It was a complex and lengthy agglomeration of melodies, parodies, and vernacular expression. At times this master song could sound like a symphony; at other times like a piano and ten.

The closest he ever got to transcribing this constantly evolving master song was the seventeen-page operatic parody in *Watch Your Step*, but he kept borrowing excerpts from the master song for his conventional tunes, editing the excerpts to fit into conventional Tin Pan Alley formats. It was an essential part of his melodic genius that he had access to his master song, and that he could imagine it with such force he could actually hear it and take from it and use it to give his compositions so much life and originality. At the same time, it was frustrating never to be able to deliver the whole thing to the public, but he lacked the technical skill to assemble it, and so he resigned himself to selecting tantalizing excerpts. They sounded complete enough by themselves, but to Berlin, they were only part of a much larger musical creation that he alone could hear and whose breadth he alone could appreciate.

Years later, Berlin alluded to the essential unity of all his songs when he remarked that he may have published over one thousand songs (and written several times more), but they were all variations on a few themes. In the last analysis, he insisted, he had only five or six different "key" songs that he kept dressing up in different guises throughout his career. "The five most important songs I ever wrote, structurally," he said in 1947, near the end of his active songwriting career, "were 'Alexander's Ragtime Band,' 'Everybody Step,' 'What'll I Do?,' 'A Pretty Girl Is Like a Melody,' and 'Cheek to Cheek.' Those were the key songs of forty years of song writing, and I'll tell you why." This was Irving trying to intellectualize and not doing a convincing job of it. He was never quite sure what these terms meant, exactly; for him a song was a *sound*, a *feeling*, not an intellectual exercise. But he did have specific ideas about the sounds:

> From the harmonic or rhythmic form of 'Alexander's Ragtime Band,' I got 'Ragtime Violin,' 'Everybody's Doin' It' and 'Syncopated Walk.' From the rhythmic form of 'Everybody Step,' I got 'Pack Up Your Sins,' 'Puttin' on the Ritz,' and . . . 'Top Hat, White Tie and Tails.' Using the same rhythmic pattern as 'A Pretty Girl Is Like a Melody,' I wrote 'Say It with Music,' 'Lady of the Evening,' 'Crinoline Days,' and 'Soft Lights and Sweet Music.' The basic song always suggested four or five others, each a bit different but basically the same.

Perhaps he feared that if he harnessed his muse and wrote his ragtime opera, he would use up his master song and use up himself in the process. And so he exercised common sense and restricted himself to songs, a genre he knew he could sell, at the cost of his grander, operatic vision. Because the standards he set for himself were so high, he remained perpetually dissatisfied. A conscientious craftsman, he realized how far short of the ideal his handiwork fell. A pretty girl once accosted him at a party, exclaiming, "Oh, Mr. Berlin, I guess there's no one who has written as many hits as you have."

And the songwriter replied, "I know there's no one who has written so many failures."

This penchant for self-criticism hindered his creative output. In

1915 his output of songs declined for the first time, and the new songs marked a retreat from the flights of imaginative fantasy that had been the hallmark of his score for *Watch Your Step.* Despite the waning of the ragtime craze, he returned to the genre, writing songs for established performers who labored to keep its spirit alive. Among the best known was Belle Baker. A Russian Jew like Berlin, her real name was Bella Becker. As a former player in Jacob Adler's esteemed New York Yiddish Theatre, she had managed to overcome her physical limitations—a short and stocky physique—to establish herself as a vaudeville star. She knew how to put a song across, laughing and crying almost simultaneously and compelling an audience to listen.

Berlin was so fond of her singing that he occasionally visited the Palace Theatre, where she topped the bill, and when she sang one of his songs, she'd point to the audience, the spotlight following her finger until it alighted on the diminutive figure of Berlin himself, who would stand, receive the enraptured audience's tribute, and sing an extra verse or two, much to their delight. This was the kind of raw music Berlin understood, not so rarefied as musical comedy or opera. He was completely in his element at the Palace, with its rowdy atmosphere, so unlike the decorum of a Dillingham show. Here he knew whether or not the demonstrative audience liked his song *as it was sung;* he didn't have to wait until end of the show to hear the reaction. His impatient temperament thrived on that kind of instant feedback.

The search for a new type of song to please this unpretentious crowd led him back to his old specialty, the ethnic song, to which he now brought a new sophistication. For Belle Baker he concocted "Cohen Owes Me Ninety-Seven Dollars," the story of an elderly Jew who lies near death and offers his last words of wisdom to his son. The maudlin opening verse leads the audience to expect that the old man will deliver the fruits of a lifetime, but instead, all the old man really can think of is his business.

As if to atone for the coarse fun of an ethnic song, Berlin's next song, a ballad, was as florid and high-toned as any he wrote; yet for all the differences, it, too, dwelled on the last wishes of an elderly man, and it, too, was designed for the vaudeville circuit to help fill the gap left by ragtime. It was also something of a con job, though Berlin turned out to be as much a victim as his audience.

The song first occurred to Irving when an acquaintance, the playwright Wilson Mizner, mentioned the bittersweet tale of a Chicago lawyer, Charles Lounsbery, who had recently died destitute in a home for the mentally ill, and had left behind an unusual will. "I leave to children exclusively," read the will, "the dandelions of the field and the daisies thereof, with the right to play among them freely, according to the custom of children." Subsequent clauses elaborated on this inspirational theme: children were also bequeathed "the long, long days to be merry in, in a thousand ways, and the Night and the Moon," and so on.

"There's a great idea for a song in that, and I would give a lot for the rights to it," Berlin said to Mizner.

He ceased worrying about rights when the story came to his attention a second time, in a magazine article. If he didn't get his version out soon, Berlin decided, someone else would. His lyrics—"Respectfully dedicated to the memory of Charles Lounsbery, whose legacy suggested this song"—dwelled on trees, flowers, mem'ries, and babies. Such cloyingly benevolent sentiments made "When I Leave the World Behind" a guaranteed "sob song," in Tin Pan Alley parlance.

Berlin gave the song to Fritzi Scheff, a well-known Viennese prima donna who had become a vaudeville star. When she introduced it at the Palace, the composer was there in the audience, and when she finished, he rose and sang it several more times. After this tryout he brought the song to the attention of a singer known for outsized dramatic statements: Al Jolson. Like Berlin, the Lithuanian-born singer was the son of a cantor—Asa Yoelson was his real name—and on the strength of his passion and earsplitting delivery, he stood at the pinnacle of the tumultuous vaudeville hierarchy. Every songwriter of repute wanted Jolson; the man could guarantee hits like no one else, as Jolson knew. The problem was that Jolson, along with other vaudeville stars, could command an extra fee—usually *sub rosa*—of over a hundred dollars a week simply to include one song in his act. Berlin bitterly resented performers who took advantage of this mercenary climate, but if he wanted a hit, he had no other choice than to go along with the current practice.

As expected, Jolson milked tears from the audiences with his rendition of "When I Leave the World Behind." Later, Belle Baker and other vaudeville stars replicated his success. Meanwhile, Berlin waited silently and somewhat uncomfortably for the other shoe to drop: for Lounsbery or his estate to demand a share of the royalties. But no such avariciousness disturbed this orgy of altruism, and Irving eventually discovered why: there had never been a Charles Lounsbery, nor any will. The document had been concocted by a certain Willston Fish as a lark, and Berlin and his audiences had all been happily duped.

The back-to-back successes of "Cohen Owes Me Ninety-Seven Dollars" and "When I Leave the World Behind" helped Berlin regain his bearings. He ceased tormenting himself with unattainable visions of a ragtime opera and concentrated on consolidating his position as a composer of hits, just hits, and as such he saw himself as part of a generation of immigrants, along with Jolson and Baker, who were giving the nation its indigenous music. Though critics were inclined to recognize the contributions of black musicians, Berlin was quite certain that his group deserved to be center stage, not Blacks.

"Our popular song writers and composers are not negroes," he declared several years later. "Many of them are of Russian birth or ancestry. All of them are of pure white blood. As in the case of everything else American, their universally popular music is the product of a sort of musical melting pot." This was an important point to Berlin and many other successful immigrants; they hastened to proclaim their identity as Americans rather than Jews, Russians, or Lithuanians. Their music had nothing to do with reinforcing their cultural distinctiveness; on the contrary, it was a route to the American mainstream. "Their distinctive school," Berlin said of the Russian Jews who had come to dominate popular music, "is a combination of the influences of Southern plantation songs, of European music from almost countless countries and of the syncopation that is found in the music of innumerable nationalities—found even in the music of the old master composers."

He insisted that songwriting was a business like any other. "It's not a matter of inspiration with me at all," he said. "Generally I decide in a very prosaic way that I'm going to write something, and then I sit down and do it." There was no mystery; it was all a matter of hard work. "Of course," he admitted on second thought, "very often ideas occur to me when I'm not hunting for them—but then I shouldn't say that, for I'm always hunting for them. I'm something like the writer who said to me the other day that he had to sleep in the daytime, because he laid awake and thought up songs all night!" So there was a "musical demon" at work in Berlin after all, gnawing at him, keeping him awake night after night. He had said as much in "Play a Simple Melody," but he permitted himself to uncork the genie only when he composed; at other times he camouflaged it behind his pragmatic veneer: "Usually, writing songs is a matter of having to pay bills and sitting down to make the money to pay them with."

Irving's attempt to de-romanticize songwriting masked his profound anxieties over the state of the popular music business. In a few short years, Tin Pan Alley had become the victim of its own success; the industry was suffering from the spiraling costs of production and promotion. Even his own Waterson, Berlin & Snyder was teetering on the verge of bankruptcy, and he attempted to explain how this could have happened.

> The publisher sells his songs to the jobber or "the trade" for six and a half cents a copy. He pays a cent a copy royalty to the men who have written the song. This leaves him a gross of five and a half cents a copy on the song. Out of this he must care for a tremendous overhead expense; the printing costs him a cent a copy; he has advertising he must keep up; he has branches and branches-staffs in a half-dozen cities; he maintains a staff of eight or nine piano-players in his home office, and staffs of two or three in his branch offices; he keeps a force of "pluggers" or "song boosters"—who go over the cities singing his songs in motion-picture theaters and cafés—at work; he employs a force of "outside men" whose duty it is to get his songs sung by the stage; and then, on top of it all, he . . . has recommenced paying performers to sing his songs. . . . I know one publisher who has paid out more than fifty thousand dollars a year to vaudeville singers to have them put on his songs. . . .

Much as Berlin deplored the practice, he subscribed to it himself. But the recent increase in the amount of money required to launch a song alarmed him; the situation was so bad, he felt, that there was room for only a handful of hits, to which a publisher was forced to devote all his resources.

> This cutthroat competition, which has resulted recently in the failure of a number of publishing firms, operates in spite of the fact that it has become more and more difficult to make money out of the song-publishing business. Under present conditions a publisher loses money on a song unless he sells more than three hundred thousand copies. (I mean, by this, a song he has advertised and "plugged"—one he is betting on as a success.) He must sell between five hundred thousand and six hundred thousand to make a fair profit.

And the likelihood of a publisher's consistently reaching that level of sales, Berlin implied, was remote indeed.

The cranky veteran songwriter, who had published his first song all of seven years before, went on to insist that beginners need not apply; the business was already overcrowded. Trying to write songs outside the Alley was futile, for "the amateur has no knowledge of the workings of the trickiest game in the game world." Amateurs were advised to stay away. Berlin claimed, "Our publishing house has never received, from an amateur, a usable idea, either in lyrics or melody; and we have examined thousands of manuscripts."

His boasting to the contrary, Berlin's musical judgment often proved erratic. To his peril, he ignored the "amateurs" he professed to disdain, partly out of his inherent shyness. One day in 1915, he found himself confronted with a young brother and sister dance team, Fred and Adele Austerlitz, who had come from Omaha and were still in their teens. They had recently changed their professional name to Astaire and had begun to work their way up the vaudeville ladder, opening for shows on the Orpheum and Keith circuits; and they had gained acclaim when they played the Palace in Chicago. They owed much of their early success to the Castles, who had whetted the public's appetite for dance, but Fred, especially, preferred the knockabout exuberance of vaudeville to the Castles' restrained ballroom dancing. The pair had devised an act called "Fred and Adele Astaire in New

Songs and Smart Dances," toured the country with it, and were commanding a salary of $350 a week.

Whenever they passed through New York, Fred visited the publishers on Tin Pan Alley, looking for songs, as did so many other performers. An admirer of Berlin's, he naturally visited Waterson, Berlin & Snyder, but he found it difficult to get in to see the renowned songwriter, who gave preferential treatment to the big names like Jolson and Baker. Unable to meet Berlin and to inspire him to write a song just for his act, young Fred settled for a "stock" item: "I Love to Quarrel with You." It would be another fifteen years until Astaire was at last able to capture Berlin's attention.

Another talented teenager whom Berlin turned away called himself George Gershvin, and like Berlin, he was a Russian Jew who'd grown up on the Lower East Side. Though he was only ten years younger than Berlin, George belonged to a different generation. He had been born on this side of the Atlantic, for one thing, and he was assimilating into the American mainstream at an even faster rate than Irving. The teenager's father, Morris, had changed the family's name from Gershovitz, and George, who was now eighteen, would soon modify it again, to Gershwin. Though his upbringing was humble, he hadn't been scarred by life the way Berlin had. Music was a natural expression of George's enthusiasm and talents, whereas for Berlin it had been a tool for survival. As a result, George maintained a more flexible attitude toward his art; he was equally fascinated and equally adept at both popular and classical forms; he could talk about "Alexander's Ragtime Band" and Chopin in the same breath; for him the world of opera and concert halls, though still remote, was an attainable goal. The musical boundaries that existed for a man of Berlin's background and musical experience did not hold true for young George. But at that time, the young man who would become George Gershwin wanted nothing so much as to get a job at Waterson, Berlin & Snyder as a plugger or, if he were truly fortunate, as Berlin's transcriber.

More persistent than most aspirants, he actually got to audition several of his songs before the master himself. It was an interesting encounter. Unlike Berlin, Gershwin possessed a ferocious musical technique and had studied with a reputable teacher, Charles Hambitzer, who had pronounced him a genius. He had already acquired a distinctive, hammering style of playing, the legacy of an earlier job: cutting piano rolls for the Standard Music Company in New Jersey. The player piano was a new technology that helped to spread music; for the first time people who had no ability or inclination to play could hear music performed on an instrument they owned. Gershwin himself had cut rolls for a number of prominent composers of the era, including Louis A. Hirsch, Jerome Kern, and of course, Irving Berlin. When he played for Berlin, then, a considerable amount of talent and experience went on display.

Still, the master's response was tepid. "Not bad. I'd say you have some talent," Berlin said. Subjecting the young man to another test, he hummed a song. The young Gershwin played a note-perfect rendition on the piano. "You can have a job as an arranger and musical secretary," Berlin offered. "What's your name?"

After Gershwin introduced himself, Berlin caught him up short. "Don't take it. You've got more talent than an arranger needs."

Berlin might have been polite, or he might have been right, but in either event, Gershwin did not get the job; instead, he became a plugger at a new Tin Pan Alley establishment, Remick's. He, too, would have further dealings with Berlin.

The songwriter's shortsightedness extended to business matters as well as his appraisal of talent. In lamenting the increasing difficulty of earning a profit in Tin Pan Alley, he expressed views shared by many other publishers and composers. Although publishers earned substantial royalties from sheet music and later piano rolls, much of their output was performed in public without so much as a penny being paid to them. Restaurants, hotels, and ballrooms routinely played their songs and made money from patrons who'd come to hear the music, dance to it, or eat to it. The establishments insisted they were merely plugging the songs and giving their publishers free publicity, but composers, especially, did not see matters the same way. They heard their music being performed, and they knew they were not being paid.

Among the most concerned was Victor Herbert, the boisterous Irish-American composer of hit songs and operettas. From the start of his career, he had paid careful attention to his contracts and skillfully advanced himself from cellist to conductor and finally composer. On the night of April 1, 1915, he and several of his collaborators happened to attend a cabaret show at a popular New York establishment, Shanley's Broadway Restaurant, where they listened to a performance of "Sweethearts," a song they knew well because they'd written it. And they hadn't authorized Shanley's to perform it.

Herbert and his publisher, G. Schirmer, commenced a suit against Shanley's for copyright infringement, but there seemed to be little prospect of a successful outcome. In the past few years a number of similar lawsuits had failed to bring comfort to composers and publishers. They had argued that such infringement amounted to public performance for profit, and they had gone down to defeat on that basis. This time, a brilliant lawyer, Nathan Burkan, represented the composers and publishers, and he employed a different strategy. He contended that the Shanley's performance violated the dramatic licensing protection afforded by copyright law. When they lost again, Burkan took the case all the way to the United States Supreme Court, where Justice Oliver Wendell Holmes delivered the majority opinion. "If the rights under the copyright law are infringed only by a performance where money is taken at the door, they are very improperly infringed," he wrote about restaurants such as Shanley's that were obviously using music to lure patrons. "If music did not pay, it would be given up. If it pays, it pays out of the public's pocket. Whether it pays or not, the purpose of employing it is for profit, and that is enough." The decision, so sweeping and unexpected, became something of a magna carta for Tin Pan Alley. Composers would no longer have to submit to the tyranny of performers who claimed they were only publicizing the music.

The surprising legal victory for publishers and composers breathed new life into a foundering organization devoted to protecting such rights: the American Society of Composers, Authors, and Publishers (ASCAP). Given Berlin's preoccupation with the difficulty of making an honest dollar on Tin Pan Alley, ASCAP's mission seemed likely to win his support. However, during its crucial formative period, he refused to endorse the organization, as did many other prominent songwriters. The year before, when ASCAP had held an organizational dinner at Luchow's Restaurant, thirty-five songwriters were expected to attend the event, but just nine actually appeared. Victor Herbert was among the few who did, while Berlin, Jerome Kern, and others stayed away. They perceived ASCAP as a union, and they resisted the influence a union might exert over their businesses or even their songwriting.

To a composer, the most intimidating aspect of ASCAP was its plan to collect royalties on behalf of its members and then distribute them several times a year. Berlin was accustomed to collecting his own royalties rather than relying on the good intentions of an external organization, and he had difficulty understanding what tangible benefits ASCAP could offer him. Such was the problem with ASCAP: it was so comprehensive and sophisticated that Tin Pan Alley publishers failed to grasp how it could benefit them. Locked into their primitive, every-man-for-himself mentality, music publishers instinctively resisted the idea of cooperating with one another.

Though an attentive and shrewd businessman, Berlin was not a sophisticated one, and he resisted innovation. By now his understanding of how the music business functioned had been formed; the mold was set at an early age, and throughout his career he was reluctant to change—more than reluctant. Berlin publicly denounced any new ideas, no matter how inevitable they were, radio being the best example. As a result, his publishing company would become more of an anachronism with each passing decade. To Irving, it would always be the summer of 1911 on Tin Pan Alley, and "Alexander's Ragtime Band" was just beginning to take the country by storm.

▪ ▪ ▪

Berlin's remedy for bad business conditions remained, as always, a hit song, and he doggedly pursued this goal throughout the year. Both ragtime and the dance crazes had lost momentum, and he turned his attention to reflecting the national mood in song. The leading public issue of the moment was of course the war in Europe. Berlin's instincts were combative, and the prevailing sentiment, pacifism, did not come naturally. Still, he had to give the public what it wanted.

In 1914 he had embarrassed himself with a clumsy antiwar fantasy entitled "Stay Down Here Where You Belong," in which the devil counsels his son to remain in hell rather than risk going to war with mankind. Berlin later recognized how seriously he had erred with this song. Decades later, Groucho Marx, the comedian, took a liking to the tune and occasionally sang it in public—to Berlin's chagrin. "Every time I see him," the songwriter said, "I stick my hand in my pocket and ask him, 'How much if you don't sing it?' "

Although Berlin's execution was faulty in this case, pacifist sentiments could be commercial, given the right treatment. The following year, his former rival from his days at Nigger Mike's, Al Piantadosi, wrote the melody for a million-copy hit that expressed the same idea in language to which people could relate: "I Didn't Raise My Boy to Be a Soldier." Encouraged by its success, Irving tried again with another fantasy, "While the Band Played an American Rag," and again failed to strike the right note.

The fault could not be laid to Berlin's politics, if he had any at the time; while the war raged in Europe, America remained an isolationist bastion. In their frequent moments of self-congratulation, Tin Pan Alley professionals often cited the maxim by the Scottish politician Andrew Fletcher of Saltoun concerning songwriting—"I care not who makes a country's laws, so long as I can make its songs"—as justification for their efforts, but as the cannier among them, such as publisher Edward Marks, realized, "Popular songs reflect events and moods; they never compel them."

It would seem that Berlin's patriotism was merely a commercial ploy to sell songs, but, in fact, it was only now that he began to see himself as more of an American than an immigrant. His patriotism was a genuine belief, one of the few he ever held outside the values of Tin Pan Alley. His first marriage had failed him, his homeland had destroyed his family, his parents had provided little comfort; in his exceedingly uncertain world, the United States offered a sanctuary and had made him rich. In comparison with foreign governments, it was incredibly benign, especially in its attitude toward Jews and other immigrants. These values made a genuine impression on him, and he took them as seriously as he did the copyright laws that permitted him to grow rich.

Nor was Berlin alone in his beliefs. Many other Jews, especially the commercially successful ones of his generation, hastened to identify themselves with what they perceived as "American" values. Being Jewish had only served to ensnare them in centuries-old persecution; what could they possibly gain by reasserting their faith now? As Berlin realized, being American and successful were practically synonymous.

Furthermore, the outbreak of war in Europe, a war that could spread to the United States, encouraged the songwriter to assert his hard-won Americanness. He commenced a lengthy three-step process to become a naturalized citizen, beginning with his filing a Declaration of Intention on September 23, 1915, in the process formally renouncing his "allegiance to Nicholas II, Emperor of all the Russias." This document alone did not make Berlin, the man who came to incarnate popular American music, an American; it merely started the clock on a two-year-long process that would culminate with his taking the oath of allegiance.

At the time Irving filed his declaration, Charles Dillingham, the producer of *Watch Your Step*, came forward with an invitation to compose the score for a new Broadway show, tentatively titled *Blow Your Horn.* From the start the production was intended as a sequel to Berlin's first Broadway success the year before. Harry Smith would again write the libretto, but this time the Castles would have no role in the production. Vernon, always the romantic, had left show business to prepare himself for war. The beginning of 1916 found him studying aviation in Newport News, Virginia. When he received his pilot's license, he planned to sail for England, where he expected to see action. Meanwhile, Irene remained at their home in Manhasset, Long Island, fretting over his characteristically impulsive decision to abandon show business for the false glory of war.

The star of the new show was a French actress, Gaby Deslys, who had recently made a name for herself in the United States in appearances with Al Jolson. Few claimed to perceive much talent in Gaby, but she did wear the most elaborate, outsized hats ever seen onstage, and her lavish life-style stirred malicious gossip wherever she went. Though not much of a singer herself, she would be buttressed by two entertainers familiar to New York theatergoers, Harry Fox and Blossom Seeley.

Billboard disclosed plans for the show on September 2. Berlin was instantly faced with the problem of writing the score on an extremely tight schedule, even for him, with an opening night scheduled in December, little more than a year after *Watch Your Step.* Once again the demands of a musical comedy ran counter to his interests and abilities as a composer of hit songs; the irregular nature of the score suggests that he hastily wove together old and new material.

Smith, on the other hand, took this assignment to heart, and his libretto, for once unified, told of a chorus girl (played by Marion Sunshine) who aspires to replace a leading lady who has recently married and retired from the stage. Coached by a helpful assistant (Harry Fox), who was, perhaps, patterned after Max Winslow, she undergoes various vicissitudes and finally accomplishes her goal. For all its frivolity, this was a standard plot for the era. The travails of chorus girls were a staple subject matter in the early days of musical comedy, and of course the virtuous little creatures always triumphed in the end. This turn of events was not especially farfetched. One of the actual chorus girls, for instance, a nineteen-year-old friend of Gaby's named Marion Davies, would soon become famous as William Randolph Hearst's mistress as a result of her appearance in this production.

The show's out-of-town tryouts began in Philadelphia on December 1, and it immediately met with an enthusiastic reception; Dillingham and Berlin seemed poised to duplicate the success of *Watch Your Step* when it opened at the Globe Theatre on Christmas Day. By this time, the show had undergone significant changes. The title had been changed to *Stop! Look! Listen!*, and the seductive Gaby Deslys's role had been drastically reduced to a single turn, in which she offered yet another variation on ragtime, commenting on it from the French perspective in "Everything in America Is Ragtime." The score's emphasis on ragtime indicated how much it owed to *Watch Your Step*. And another song, "When I Get Back to the USA," was actually patterned after the earlier show's "Play a Simple Melody." The newer song, attempting to exploit the nation's isolationist spirit, told of a homesick American abroad who yearns to return home. His lament rebounds off a pulse-quickening rendition of "My Country, 'Tis of Thee." Again, Berlin had set his mind to the creation of an authentic American song—as opposed to an American style of music—and again he'd missed the mark; but he was getting closer all the time.

Two of the songs Harry Fox introduced became staples in the Berlin catalogue: "The Girl on the Magazine Cover" and "I Love a Piano." The first was a glamorous, all-purpose production number that could take its place in nearly any revue of the day; its sole purpose was to extol feminine beauty, and this it did with grace and a sense of occasion. As Joseph Santley sang before a giant reproduction of *Vogue* magazine, four showgirls—Justine Johnstone, Pickles St. Clair, Eileen Percy, and Marion Davies—sprang to life and walked off the page.

One member of the audience was transfixed by this particular scene. He sat in the second row of the orchestra night after night, devouring the sight of Justine Johnstone and Marion Davies parading across the stage. Finally, he screwed up his nerve and sent a note backstage to Johnstone, an invitation to dinner with William Randolph Hearst, who was, as any showgirl would know, the huge, brash, wealthy, and immensely influential newspaper publisher; at fifty-two, he was the *id* of American journalism.

"I can't go out with Hearst," said Johnstone to Davies. "Why don't you go?"

Davies substituted, and the meeting marked the beginning of her celebrated affair with Hearst. Berlin's "The Girl on the Magazine Cover" made a great impression on Davies, as well. Later, when she was living with Hearst at San Simeon, she held a sumptuous party and for the evening's climax restaged this number.

For sheer staging virtuosity, "I Love a Piano" outdid all the other songs in the score. The set for this number consisted of an immense keyboard running from one end of the stage to the other. Before it, six pianists pounded away on six pianos, playing the melody to this song about the love of music. Berlin had captured another piece of his master song in "I Love a Piano," and he was quite taken with the tune; for the next forty-five years he would insist it was his best effort. Certainly it ranked with his best. Like "Alexander's Ragtime Band" and "Play a Simple Melody" before it, this was a song about the possibilities of music; the earlier songs had highlighted its effect on listeners, while "I Love a Piano" told the story from the performer's point of view.

Although *Stop! Look! Listen!* did not cause quite the sensation that *Watch Your Step* had, it met with a generally favorable reception. "Contains a wealth of cleverly written songs, a remarkable cast of vaudeville headliners, wondrous costumes, a couple of carloads of impressionistic scenery, and entertainment enough to 'make' three shows of its type," said *The New York Clipper*. And Berlin's "Everything in America Is Ragtime" came in for special commendation as a "fine example of good lyric construction and more than equals the best that Gilbert and Sullivan or Geo. M. Cohan ever wrote in the way of operatic ensembles." But for the critic of *The New York Dramatic Mirror*, the appeal of Berlin's ragtime was already wearing thin. "There is no glowing, sensuous, extravagant appeal," he complained. "It is wholly ragtime, noisy, overdone ragtime from the opening chorus to the final number."

Initially, the show was a commercial success, grossing $20,000 a week, with not a single empty seat in the house, but it soon turned into a demonstration of how an unhappy cast can sabotage a successful production. Among the members of the company was Gaby's sometime lover and would-be manager, Harry Pilcer, who resented the leading lady's reduced role in the production. At the same time, he wanted a piece of her salary. The two began fighting during every performance. As a result of this tension, Gaby's performances, never stellar to begin with, quickly deteriorated, and she was soon staggering through her role, muffing her lines, and throwing the entire production out of balance. As word of her lapses spread, the size of the audience quickly decreased until by February, only weeks after the opening, Dillingham was losing money. Since he could not salvage the show, he exercised his producer's prerogative and closed it at the beginning of March, with Gaby still having four weeks remaining in her contract.

Though Berlin could do nothing to prevent this debacle, his reputation emerged unscathed. His hit songs, especially "I Love a Piano," flourished even as the show deteriorated. He had demonstrated that his success of the previous years was no fluke; he consolidated his reputation as a Broadway composer. Two months later, when his former mentor, George M. Cohan, opened *The Cohan Revue of 1916*, the show creaked in comparison with the gleaming, up-to-date *Stop! Look! Listen!*, though it, too, featured a syncopated score.

While Berlin's show was smarter than Cohan's, it lacked the polish and unity of another musical that had opened just two days before it, *Very Good Eddie*, with a book by an English journalist named Guy Bolton and a score principally by another rising young popular American composer, Jerome Kern. Kern's songs weren't particularly showy—though at least one, "If I Find the Girl," was a true showstopper—but unlike Berlin's they grew out of dramatic events and enlarged upon them. As an American musical comedy, one of the first of a recognizable genre to which there would soon be an outpouring of contributions, *Very Good Eddie* represented the state of the art.

The famous theater housing *Very Good Eddie* enhanced the show's appeal. The Princess, on West 39th Street, was a tiny place, with only 299 seats; those fortunate enough to obtain a ticket reaped special rewards, even though they had to forsake elaborate sets and a line of fifty chorus girls shimmying in front of the footlights.

Critics tried to group them together: Kern and Berlin, the next generation of Broadway composers. But Berlin resisted the notion of seeing his name bracketed with anyone else's; he wrote his own music and lyrics, published his own songs, and on occasion, performed them himself. He displayed scant interest in developing the collaborative skills required by a musical. Kern, for his part, admired Berlin greatly and was glad to ride his coattails, if only he could grasp them. Irving, though, felt no community of purpose with Kern or any other composer on the scene. The idea of devoting an entire evening to telling one story simply didn't register with him; that was the task of opera, not show business. The two men traveled divergent paths, Kern refining the art of the musical, Berlin tirelessly perfecting the technique of the hit song.

▪ ▪ ▪

In the summer of 1914, President Wilson had officially proclaimed the United States a neutral power, even though Great Britain was at war with Germany. The nation's isolationist mood had a lasting impact on popular entertainment, creating a political vacuum in which revues and musical comedies concocted by Berlin and the rest of the theater community flourished. At the same time, their avoidance of political and social realities condemned such productions to oblivion. Even the sinking of the *Lusitania* by a German submarine in May 1915, a hugely provocative event, failed to disturb the national torpor. A mood of uneasy escapism persisted on Broadway throughout 1916, prompting producers to rely on froth and more froth to lure patrons.

Reflecting this trend, Berlin's output for 1916—over two dozen titles—failed to include one song of enduring merit, though his momentum was such that no one seemed to notice the sudden drop in the quality of his latest offerings. He established a rhythm of moving from one Broadway score to the next, his reputation and income secure. The two events—Berlin's successful career and the tragic potential of war engulfing the nation—still seemed entirely unconnected. Reflecting the temper of Broadway, he embarked on one of the more frivolous episodes of his career by returning to Ziegfeld's orbit.

Profiting handsomely from the public's apparently insatiable thirst for escapism, Florenz Ziegfeld had recently expanded his empire to include the Century Theatre at Broadway and 62nd Street. It was old, it was cavernous, and it was reputed to be unable to return a profit to its owner. Along Broadway it was known as "the house of misfortune," for many a show had faltered on its boards, and many a producer had gone broke trying to fill it. "Folks shook their heads. They said the Century was too big and too far from the beaten track," noted Alexander Woollcott. "They began to speak of it spookily, as though the Century were haunted by the ghosts of disappointed adventurers under its roof. Yet there has remained with all concerned a deep conviction that if some thoroughly attractive entertainment were to be housed there, the huge and costly theatre would draw people from the ends of the earth."

Buoyed by the success of his *Follies*, Ziegfeld wanted to stage a *Follies*-type revue in the Century, but on a more spectacular scale than anything he had previously mounted. He re-christened his American girl "The Century Girl" and began assembling a giant revue in her honor; true to Ziegfeld's paradoxical nature, it was both inane and awe-inspiring, childish and hugely complex. To assist him in this venture, Ziegfeld enlisted the support of Charles Dillingham, a move that endowed the project with instant credibility, now that two of Broadway's biggest impresarios were pooling their resources.

Continuing to think in terms of twos, the superstitious Ziegfeld then decided to employ a pair of composers to write the score for *The Century Girl*: Victor Herbert and Irving Berlin. It was miraculous that the two men got along as well as they did, for the Dublin-born Herbert, then fifty-eight, was in every way Berlin's opposite. He possessed an extravagant temperament, drank hugely, had a florid complexion and large girth to show for it, and enjoyed a reputation as a brash womanizer who considered any woman he met his for the taking. On being introduced to Goldie Clough, Ziegfeld's twenty-one-year-old secretary, he grabbed her breasts and exclaimed in his Irish accent, "Oh, nice fresh meat!" An older secretary, accustomed to his rudeness, chased him away. Such coarse behavior was beyond Berlin, even though there were girls everywhere—chorus girls, secretaries, and pliant young hopefuls of every description. They talked with flat midwestern accents that hinted at the small towns they'd recently escaped, smoked cigarettes, bobbed their hair like Irene Castle, would dance any animal dance, and knew what was expected of a girl who wanted to get ahead in show business and become the next Hazel Dawn. Jolson, Ziegfeld, and Herbert all took advantage, but not Berlin; he could not be tempted.

Herbert's relationship with Ziegfeld was a tormented one, so much so that when Herbert died eight years later, it was said that Ziegfeld was responsible, that he hadn't paid the royalties he owed the composer, and thus had driven him to an early grave. "Victor was constantly trying to see Mr. Ziegfeld," Clough recalls, "And Mr. Ziegfeld wouldn't see him. One day he came into my office, which was right outside of Mr. Ziegfeld's office. 'I must see Flo,' he said in his accent. 'It's very important.' And I said: 'But he's not in, Mr. Herbert.' And he said, 'I don't care. I will wait.' And just then the door to Mr. Ziegfeld's office opens and out comes a beautiful girl. You could see Mr. Ziegfeld sitting at his desk, and Victor turns purple with rage. He didn't even go into Mr. Ziegfeld's office. He ran out of the building. And the next day we heard he was dead. Somebody in his family said, 'Goldie upset Victor so much by lying to him and saying that Mr. Ziegfeld wasn't there.' "

Still, those were the orders Ziegfeld had given her, and she had followed them. But remaining in his good graces did little to assuage her misery and sense of guilt; she cried for days afterward.

Though Ziegfeld spared the young composer such brutal treatment, Irving nonetheless felt deeply insecure around Herbert, who possessed a formidable command of musical technique. He could play various instruments, he could read a score, and he could conduct the orchestra during rehearsals of *The Century Girl*—none of which Irving could do. When the two of them met for lunch at the Lambs' Club, a theatrical fraternity similar to the Friars, but more subdued, Berlin delicately broached the topic. "Victor, I'm a bit worried," he said. "People say that if I studied music, it would overwhelm me."

"Irving, you have nothing to worry about. You have a natural talent for putting music and words together—mind you, a little science wouldn't hurt."

That gentle suggestion prompted Berlin to begin a course of formal musical training; at last he would acquire the technical expertise necessary to composing Broadway scores—and, incidentally, lay to rest the ubiquitous rumors of black ghostwriters composing songs for him.

But when Berlin began to study music, he immediately ran into problems. "I tried to learn how to read and write music," he recalled much later, "but I found I was not a student. Besides, in the time I spent taking lessons I could have written a few songs. Writing music is something that must come naturally; of course you can do it well or badly. Song writing is technical and simple, at the same time." Determined, Berlin tried to master music in the traditional manner: "I studied and practiced for two days and then gave it up."

Instead of studying he purchased a grand piano; it occupied pride of place in his apartment, but he rarely played it and never composed on it, for the instrument lacked the ability to change keys at the touch of a lever. It was to his reliable trick piano that he turned when the urge to compose came over him, but he kept this device out of sight for the time being, as if it were a secret vice. When he posed for a formal portrait, attired in spats and a three-piece suit, looking the part of the boy-wonder-composer-tycoon, he sat before a concert grand, the artist at his canvas, as if that were where he worked his musical magic, but the instrument was merely a prop. Irving Berlin did indeed love a piano, as he said in the song, but not this sleek beauty. He loved a battered upright with a funny lever tucked beneath the keyboard, to which he remained furtively devoted.

The curtain rang up on Ziegfeld's gamble to resurrect the Century at precisely 8:25 P.M. on Monday night, November 6. Since it was election eve, and a war loomed, the play was filled with political references. Both the incumbent, Woodrow Wilson, and his Republican challenger, Charles Evans Hughes, campaigned on platforms promising to keep the country out of the war, and the revue contained bizarre echoes of the popular preference for peace coupled with a militant form of patriotism.

As the theater darkened, Victor Herbert himself stepped into the orchestra pit and began to conduct the score he had written with Berlin.

Yet it was apparent as soon as the curtains parted that the show would succeed on the strength of its costumes and sets rather than its score, for this was the revue that introduced in its first scene the theatrical image for which Ziegfeld is best remembered: a "celestial staircase" devised to display the girls vertically as well as horizontally. Conceived by the Viennese designer Joseph Urban, the staircase extended from a trapdoor on the stage floor, through which emerged representations of women of all ages, who then began to ascend past pink and purple clouds, as Herbert's music wafted from the orchestra pit. Audiences beheld stars such as May Leslie, who portrayed the warrior queen Boadicea, Marjorie Cassidy (Helen of Troy), Semone D'Herlys (Cleopatra), Hazel Dawn (Joan of Arc), Margaret Morris (Catherine of Russia), Flo Hart (Marie Antoinette), Lillian Tashman (Empress Josephine), and finally, the star of stars, Hazel Dawn as the Century girl herself, who appeared to an inevitable standing ovation.

The next scene, scored by Berlin, proved to be as peculiar as the first, for it portrayed both of the show's composers on stage. John Slavin took the part of Berlin, and Arthur Cunningham that of Victor Herbert. Together they conducted a music lesson in the "garden of a modern girls' school." Once again Berlin devised a counterpoint song, a contrivance that had quickly become one of his trademarks. As Herbert, Cunningham sang a traditional love song entitled "Kiss Me Again," while Slavin, as Berlin, overtook him with ragtime. As a theatrical device, the gimmick still worked, but it was losing freshness with each repetition.

Even the intermission proved to be spectacular, more of a diversion than a respite from the show. A marimba band played while patrons danced. Ziegfeld also broke with established practice by permitting the men (and only the men) in the audience to smoke, "even down in the first row of the orchestra," commented the *Times* with some wonder. It was apparent to everyone that Ziegfeld's charm had worked once again. "The curse is off the Century," Woollcott decided; still, he had his doubts: "How long any management not royally endowed and not altogether mad can afford to give such prodigal entertainment on so staggering a scale is not for us to ask." There was scarcely time for the bedazzled opening-night crowd to realize there was no book—what little dialogue they'd heard amid the theater's poor acoustics was credited to "Everyman." Ziegfeld's technique was simply to overwhelm his audience with one elaborate setting after the other.

The centerpiece of the second act belonged to Irving Berlin, who contributed one of his most lavish and forgettable songs, a duet called "Alice in Wonderland." Hazel Dawn and Irving Fisher sang to each other as a chorus representing the characters in the story filled the stage. Once again the setting was the true star, with Urban offering an uncanny imitation of the original Tenniel illustrations. It was in such production numbers that Berlin's lack of musical training was most apparent, for orchestration carried the music in a scene like "Alice in Wonderland," and Berlin's strengths lay in melody and rhythm. He was, for once, out of his depth. The second act also included a Ziegfeld-style acknowledgment of the war in Europe, and it was cast in his distinctive style of fatuous allegory. Herbert's "When Uncle Sam Rules the Waves" began with a backdrop of endless blue. Eventually more staircases appeared, and the same set of actresses ascended them, this time dressed to represent various American territorial interests such as Hawaii and Puerto Rico.

There ensued another intermission and more dancing to the marimba band Ziegfeld had thoughtfully provided.

The audience was growing surfeited and weary by the time the third act began, and even the unashamedly partisan Woollcott was thinking that whole parts of the revue "must be lopped off before it can settle down for the season." Most of the act belonged to Herbert, but at least Berlin was allowed to have the last say in the grand "matrimonial finale," a wedding set in a crystal palace. While the orchestra played Berlin's "On the Train of a Wedding Gown," lights played over the scene, which refracted the beams into dazzling, multicolored rays, and a "procession of the laces of the world" (English, French, and, inevitably, American) filled the Century's outsized stage.

When the curtain rang down on this scene, it was 12:45 in the morning, and the revue had run over four hours. But the audience was delighted; New York had never seen anything quite like it (and *see* was the operative word, for the show's effect was primarily visual, secondarily musical, and hardly verbal at all). Other producers and theaters noted for their chorus lines had aspired to this sort of grandiose spectacle, but only Ziegfeld had the resources and zeal to bring it off convincingly. *The Century Girl* marked the culmination of a tradition rather than a continuation; it was an event: the ultimate girlie show, a spectacle of gigantic but meaningless proportions.

The next morning, Election Day, 1916, brought word to the street that *The Century Girl* had justified Ziegfeld's faith and the expense involved. " 'THE CENTURY GIRL' A HUGE SUCCESS" proclaimed the *Times*' headline. "Handsome Entertainment, Like a Much-Magnified 'Follies,' Opens the Greatest of Music Halls." This was precisely the kind of notice that all concerned with the show had hoped for, and Woollcott was glad to oblige, describing the evening as "glorified beyond anything we had in the music hall world and multiplied by ten" and declaring that the Century Theatre "is *the* place to go." (In contrast, the paper accorded a decidedly mixed reception to George Bernard Shaw's latest play, *Getting Married*, which opened the same night at the Booth Theatre.)

Such was the power of Ziegfeld to make a reputation that Berlin was more frequently mentioned as being represented on stage in a skit than as one of the show's two composers. Berlin's by now passé reputation as The Ragtime King had been revived all for the greater glory of Ziegfeld. Unlike *Watch Your Step* of two seasons before, this triumph belonged to Ziegfeld, and Berlin was but one more star paying him tribute. The producer had come a long way from his first *Follies* on a windswept rooftop beneath a tin shed, but his young composer, in contrast, was going nowhere. After imitating *Watch Your Step* in two shows in a row, he found himself in grave danger of becoming yesterday's sensation: Irving Berlin, the onetime King of Ragtime.

Although his songs had fared badly, Berlin was a man on whom nothing was lost—an ability to absorb all that engaged his interest was part of his genius—and at the moment he was learning a variety of extramusical lessons. He would soon take the Ziegfeld approach and transform it, inject it with a healthy, bracing shot of masculinity, and turn it into political theater. Within two years Berlin would return to the giant Century with his own production, employing what he had learned during this stint—with one important exception: his large cast would contain not a single woman, beautiful or otherwise. By then history would have caught up with him and transformed him into something more than a popular entertainer.

▪ ▪ ▪

As Berlin struggled to rediscover himself musically, he led a life that was prosperous and well-organized, if a bit empty. He had his spacious apartment on West 72nd Street, his two offices—one on Broadway, the other on Tin Pan Alley—and a car he used occasionally to drive to Atlantic City, New Jersey, on brief respites from work. A domestic creature, he was not given to travel for its own sake; his most stimulating excursions were journeys around his own room, his musical reveries. He held fast to his methodical bachelor existence, with a cook and a valet to attend to his needs. They left the premises at midnight, and he stayed up until three or four in the morning, composing. He avoided parties and the temptations offered by ever-present chorus girls, preferring to comport himself with the dignity and reserve of a sober businessman rather than a Tin Pan Alley tunesmith.

Irving Caesar, an exuberant young songwriter from the Lower East Side, considered Berlin's reserve "part of his genius," for he was able to "husband his resources." The shamelessly extroverted Caesar envied Berlin's "instinct for self-preservation." Caesar believed that in a field noted for careers cut short by alcohol, neglect, and personal excess, Berlin's ability to stay above the fray counted as much as his talent and determination. A dedicated student of the mob, he never considered himself one of its members.

Although he cushioned himself against the world, and his work habits further isolated him, he at least permitted himself the luxury of friendship, if not love, with Constance Talmadge, a silent-movie actress and sometime fortune hunter. They'd met through Irving's pal from the Lower East Side, Joseph Schenck.

Joe had risen considerably from his status as an errand boy at Olliffe's Drugstore. After taking over the Palisades Amusement Park in New Jersey with his brother Nicholas, he entered the movie business, first as an exhibitor in partnership with Marcus Loew (one of the founders of the Metro-Goldwyn-Mayer studio), and later as a powerful independent producer. His first real success came about when he persuaded the notorious and beautiful Evelyn Nesbit—former wife of Harry Thaw, the man who shot the celebrated architect Stanford White—to star in a motion picture. At the time Nesbit was afraid that Thaw, who had escaped from prison, would kill her next. For Schenck, the scandal meant great publicity, and for Nesbit the offer to star in a movie meant protection from her insanely jealous former husband. The resulting movie, *Redemption*, was shot in two weeks, brought Schenck a $200,000 profit, and launched him as a major producer.

Schenck disliked California, to which most of the film industry was migrating, and remained in New York, where he became acquainted with three sisters, Norma, Natalie, and Constance (or "Dutch," as everyone called her) Talmadge. Of the sisters, Schenck fancied Norma, and he thought the tall, willowy Dutch, with her mop of red curls and irrepressible smile, would appeal to Irving. All three girls had grown up in Brooklyn, and their father, a circus roustabout, deserted the family when they were still children. Their mother, Margaret (known to all as Peg), became a classic stage parent, determined to push her three daughters into show business. In Norma's case, she had succeeded splendidly. Smitten with her, Schenck was devoting all his time and energy to producing a movie in which she starred, *Panthea*.

Despite the attention he bestowed her, Schenck could not bring himself to propose to Norma; he was terrified of being rejected. He tried to recruit Irving to act as a scout. "Come around to the studio tomorrow and meet this Norma Talmadge," he said. "Try and find out if I have a chance, will you?"

The next morning, Irving did as asked. Between takes of the movie, he chatted with Norma, and over lunch he gave his impressions to Schenck: "Joe, that girl is crazy about you. The sooner you propose, the better." Schenck proposed that afternoon, and Norma accepted.

The sole remaining obstacle to matrimony was Norma's mother, Peg, who did not consider Schenck good marriage material; charming he might have been, but it was obvious he was a gambler and a wastrel. To remove her from the scene, Irving arranged to accompany Peg to the theater one night; meanwhile, Schenck drove Norma to Stamford, Connecticut, where they were married by a justice of the peace. For the next two months, they continued to live apart for fear of arousing Peg's wrath; when Schenck finally did break the news to her, she had no choice but to accept the inevitable.

Natalie, who was the least successful in show business, eventually married Buster Keaton, then entering his prime as a vaudeville star.

It appeared that two of the Talmadge girls had achieved their dream, but Norma discovered that her husband Joe could be as brutal as he was charming. He once beat her so badly during a transatlantic crossing that she never left her cabin during the voyage. And Natalie endured her share of marital woes with Keaton.

And then there was Dutch. At the time Schenck introduced her to Berlin, Irving was young, but Dutch was younger, only sixteen years old. Still, she was—briefly—the best known of the three Talmadge sisters, thanks to her appearance as a "mountain girl" in the Babylon sequence of D. W. Griffith's eccentric epic, *Intolerance* (1916). Dutch dallied with Irving as she did with a number of other suitors. Her adolescent flirtatiousness alternately charmed and exasperated him; to express his ambivalent feelings about her, he dubbed her "The Virtuous Vamp." The epithet, acute as were so many of Berlin's seemingly off-the-cuff remarks, stuck fast. Dutch's friend, the dark, diminutive Anita Loos, later wrote a scenario for Dutch entitled *The Virtuous Vamp*, which became a successful movie and defined her screen persona.

Loos, who could be serious on occasion, was struck by Berlin's quietly fanatical devotion to songwriting, even in the midst of socializing. "I sometimes used to sit beside Irving at his tiny piano and listen while he composed," she recalled. "He would go over and over a lyric until it seemed perfect to my ears. Then he'd scrap the whole thing and begin over again. When I asked Irving what was wrong, he invariably said, 'It isn't *simple* enough.' "

His search for musical simplicity was driven by the sublimation of his erotic impulses. While his friends frolicked in bed, Irving remained at his piano. Denied personal fulfillment by the death of his first wife, he took refuge in music; his songs, paradoxically, brought him closer to other people, especially women, while holding them at a distance. He'd established a pattern of attraction to impulsive, narcissistic women, such as Elsie Janis and now Dutch, whose warmth and gregariousness made them seem so appealing, but these emotionally immature women could never fulfill his need for total commitment.

Despite the interest Berlin displayed in Dutch—and Loos believed he was in love with her—the Talmadge girl stubbornly refused to commit herself to him. To Irving, who could be as Victorian as the century in which he had been born, fidelity mattered greatly in any serious relationship, but the Virtuous Vamp had the looks and inviting manner that enabled her to play one suitor off another. Of course she was still young, practically a child, despite her apparent maturity; she could hardly be expected to choose wisely. Joe Schenck, Dutch's mother Peg, and Anita Loos all joined forces to pressure the girl to return Berlin's affections. That way all three daughters would be married to men who were rich and successful, and their mother would at last have found her revenge for the indignity her ne'er-do-well husband had inflicted on the family years before.

Yet Dutch hesitated, and to her friends' alarm, she initiated another romance, this time with a Greek tobacco importer named John Pialogiou. He was prosperous, but still, he was no Irving Berlin. Said the woman who badly wished to be Irving's mother-in-law, "I just can't understand Dutch. It isn't a question of choosing between little Irving and some gorgeous Greek god. But why pick a guy who looks like a Greek waiter?"

▪ ▪ ▪

While Berlin remained caught in a romantic quandary, and his career lost momentum, world events began to move at a frantic pace. The day after *The Century Girl* opened to acclaim, the presidential election, held November 7, gave an exceedingly narrow margin of victory to Woodrow Wilson, who still vowed to keep the United States out of the war in Europe. He promised "peace without victory," even as tales of unimaginable carnage on the battlefield drifted back to the United States, instilling a nationwide *frisson* of horror and revulsion against the war, coupled with a growing fatalism that the United States was by now doomed to be dragged into the conflict sooner or later. In February 1917, Germany resumed unrestricted submarine warfare and permitted the United States to send just one ship to England a week. Under such provocation, patriotism soared, and the war to be avoided at all cost now became an inevitability. On April 2 Wilson denounced submarine combat as "warfare against mankind," and four days later the United States formally declared war against Germany. At the time there were only 200,000 men in uniform, but the number soon began to rise dramatically, eventually involving nearly five million Americans directly—their wives and families, often severely affected as well, amounted to several times that number.

Responding with Pavlovian urgency to this mass movement, Tin

Pan Alley began to crank out a new type of war song, accepting the inevitability of conflict and offering wishes for a favorable outcome. "Just a Baby's Prayer at Twilight" and "Hello, Central, Give Me No Man's Land" brought a tear to the eye, while "K-K-Katy" attempted a droll depiction of a newly drafted soldier's attempt to bid a stuttering farewell to his sweetheart. Berlin naturally began to devise songs about soldiers and for soldiers, even though he was not a soldier himself. Like wartime propaganda, they all relied on simplicity and repetition.

His first effort, "For Your Country and My Country," was, appropriately, aimed at recruiting soldiers. In later years he was given to explaining that "somebody in Washington" asked for a tune that would inspire soldiers to enlist, though there is no evidence that any government official directly contacted Berlin with such a request. Even if a trifle embroidered, the explanation suggests Berlin's desire to be aligned with the war effort in an official capacity. More than anything else, he relished the legitimacy that such a call, whether real or imagined, conferred on his efforts, and his sudden decision to write such songs marked still another milestone in his march toward assimilation. Under the czar's regime (now about to be toppled), conscription had long been an inflammatory issue for the Jews, who often resisted the call to serve by fleeing Russia. Yet here was Berlin advocating recruitment in his adopted country. The logical culmination of Berlin's Americanization would be for him to enlist in the Army, but he hesitated before making so drastic a step. After all, he figured he could be more effective in promoting the war effort in his role as an entertainer than as a soldier.

The song he fashioned for the occasion was appropriately martial and pulse quickening, but more than that it was aggressively masculine, in contrast to the ethereal fluff he'd been turning out to suit Ziegfeld's obsessive need to glorify (and ravish) the American girl. The bracing absence of sentimentality set Berlin's war songs apart from the ballads favored by other Tin Pan Alley patriots. He saw comedy where others merely wrung their hands. "They Were All Out of Step But Jim," the amusing observation of a proud mother watching her son march, managed to describe mobilization from the point of view of a soldier's family, a strategy endowing the song with fresh appeal.

For all his efforts to establish a new musical identity, Irving Berlin was still, in the public mind, best known as a ragtime phenomenon, not only in the United States but across much of Europe as well. From wartime France, Vernon Castle wrote to his wife of the nostalgia for prewar times that Berlin's music evoked. "There is a gramophone here playing all of the 'Watch Your Step' music and it makes me so homesick." Meanwhile, there was a "continual thunder of guns going outside." Castle tried to restrain himself as he listened to his officers attempt to sing "Play a Simple Melody," but he finally lost patience. "They didn't know how the rag part went until I showed them and now I realize I've made one of the biggest mistakes of the war! Every night they take sides and sing on one side 'Play a Simple Melody,' etc., and on the other 'Oh, You Musical Demon,' with the pianist playing an entirely different tune. It would all make an Indian uprising sound like real music." Meanwhile, the guns continued to roar and would soon threaten to drown out Berlin's music—to Vernon Castle and other homesick soldiers, the music of life itself.

In April the critic and novelist Carl Van Vechten, writing in *Vanity Fair*, damned the composer with faint praise in an article titled, "THE GREAT AMERICAN COMPOSER, His Grandfathers Are the Present Writers of Our Popular Ragtime Songs." To Van Vechten, Berlin was one of three noteworthy white ragtime artists—the other two being Edward B. Claypoole, now forgotten but known at the time for his "Ragging the Scale," and once again, Louis A. Hirsch, who was making a career by following in Berlin's footsteps all the way to Ziegfeld's *Follies*. Van Vechten was quite sure that Berlin, for all his money and acclaim, was merely a footnote to musical history, a common melodist whose music would win lasting fame only if a *real* composer such as Igor Stravinsky incorporated his songs and presented them to the public, "finally wrapped in the profundities of a fugue." Thanks to the judgments of critics such as Van Vechten, Berlin seemed to be trapped in the dying art of ragtime like a fly caught in amber.

He bid farewell to any lingering aspirations he might have had about becoming a "serious" musician; he knew his level by now, and he instinctively sought it. He signed on again with Ziegfeld for the 1916 edition of the *Follies*, not that he was happy with the result. He contributed but a single number to the show, "In Florida Among the Palms," a predictable exercise designed to exploit a craze for tropical settings. Worse, he had to share the limelight with his rivals Louis Hirsch and Jerome Kern, both of whom rose to the occasion and outdid Berlin with their efforts—Kern especially, with his "Have a Heart" and "When the Lights Are Low."

Kern, in fact, was soon to be everywhere. He was assembling no fewer than *three* new Broadway scores, *Have A Heart, Love o'Mike*, and, most memorably, *Oh, Boy!* (with its voluptuous "Till the Clouds Roll By"), all of which would open between January and February the following year. It seemed highly unlikely that Berlin or any other Broadway tunesmith would be able to catch up with this prolific composer, who was barely over thirty years of age and who, unlike so many other popular American composers, had enjoyed a comfortable New York childhood. To audiences seeking diversion at the theater from the press of war news, it appeared that the torch had irretrievably passed from Berlin to Kern.

Unwilling or unable to learn from that humbling experience, Berlin tried again the following year, contributing a number of songs to the *Cohan Revue of 1918* (which actually had its debut on New Year's Eve, 1917). Cohan's star was in decline, and once again, Berlin had little to show for another Broadway effort, though it was not for lack of trying. He sorely wanted to please his old mentor, the man to whom he owed much of his Broadway career. But Cohan's slapdash, what've-you-got-for-me-next attitude only served to increase Berlin's creative agony. "Cohan," wrote the critic Gilbert Seldes, "would knock out a song overnight, create the number for it the next morning, write a sketch between lunch and dinner, in between intervals of rehearsing, and was directing the entire production besides." The predictably slapdash production consisted largely of parodies of other hit shows, and Berlin, in a gesture of futility, resorted to devising ragtime songs; by now little else was expected of him.

Indeed, some of the best-known names associated with Berlin's heyday as a ragtime composer were dying off. On his return from France, Vernon Castle became a flying instructor in Texas, a seemingly safe posting. But as he was about to make a routine landing, he swerved to avoid another plane and plunged into a fatal crash. With this accident, the Castles' remarkable career ended as swiftly and improbably as it had begun. Irene Castle continued to dance, but her moment of glory had passed.

The deaths of two distinguished black musicians brought the final quietus to ragtime. Living in obscurity in Harlem, battling syphilis, Scott Joplin had labored for ten years on his ragtime opera, *Treemonisha.* Even as his reputation faded, his ambition soared. Joplin never lived to see more than a run-through of his opera, which had to wait until 1975 for a full-scale mounting. After completing it, he turned his attention to a musical comedy titled *If* (presumed to be lost) and then began his first symphony, on which he was working at the time of his death, April 1, 1917. Two years later, James Reese Europe, the Castles' collaborator and perhaps the most sophisticated of all black ragtime musicians, died following a stab wound in the neck, the tragic result of a scuffle with his drummer. He was only thirty-eight. On May 13, 1919, he received the first public funeral to be held in honor of a black man by New York City. By that time the term *ragtime* was all but dead, as well; a new musical buzzword had replaced it, one far more slippery than "ragtime" had ever been: *jazz.*

As early as January 1917, a Columbus Circle lobster palace by the name of Reisenweber's began to advertise a new type of entertainment, a "jasz band" [sic]. Within weeks Jimmy Durante, later known as a comedian but then working as a musician in Harlem, took his cue from the sign and assembled a "New Orleans Jazz Band" in *his* nightclub, using musicians imported from the South. Soon the New Orleans musicians began calling themselves the "Assassinators of Syncopation."

The jazz craze spread every bit as quickly as ragtime had. Irving, knowing that his livelihood as a composer depended on his ability to keep abreast of trends, watched closely. He made a fling at incorporating the term *jazz* in a song, much the way he had conjured syncopation in "Alexander's Ragtime Band," but "Mr. Jazz Himself," as Berlin named his song, met with nowhere near the same response; the former Ragtime King was not about to become Mr. Jazz. This was one type of popular music he would not be able to appropriate and exploit. Jazz would never be associated with Irving Berlin, not the way ragtime or any number of lesser musical fads had been. The new breed of jazz musician stood in approximately the same relationship to Irving Berlin as he did to European composers. As an established Tin Pan Alley composer, he belonged to the old guard, while they represented the next musical generation. The rise of jazz, in fact, offered still another indication that his moment in the public eye might well be ending.

Jazz, as Berlin discovered, was too free form to lend itself conveniently to Tin Pan Alley packaging in a couple of verses and a thirty-two-bar chorus. Much of the spirit of jazz derived from the way musicians improvised, and beyond that, the funny little virtuoso games they played with each other. They developed signature refrains, or "riffs": idiosyncratic assemblages of notes that gave new life to an old melody. The games jazz musicians played went way beyond the narrow Tin Pan Alley mindset: one jazz musician would imitate another's riffs and rhythms, even his body language, while still another would parody the imitation, and so on into the night.

As jazz developed, it seemed as if the musicians spoke a secret musical language to which only other jazz musicians and the initiated were truly privy. The "rules" of jazz changed constantly, and from state to state, city to city. Different types of jazz proliferated throughout the country: Chicago, New Orleans, New York, Kansas City—to name but a few of the major regional outposts. This chaotic state of affairs made for a musical Babel. The sophistication and complexity of jazz styles endeared it to intellectuals; it was later to be said, with only slight exaggeration, that for every (black) jazz musician, there were two (white) critics to explain what he was doing. All this virtuosity for virtuosity's sake bred a sanctimoniousness among jazz enthusiasts that clung to the music like a bad habit.

The situation stood in contrast to the monolith of Tin Pan Alley, concentrated as it was along a few blocks of West 28th Street. There was no such thing as a "regional" Tin Pan Alley song. Tin Pan Alley publishers, including Berlin, adapted all musical styles into their common musical language. Thus, Tin Pan Alley products were marketable in a way jazz would never be, because listeners, performers, composers, publishers, and distributors across the nation knew just what to expect.

Mr. Berlin, for instance, did not look kindly on performers who took excessive liberties with his compositions and tried to upstage the melodies. He painstakingly tailored his tunes to suit performers and revues, and he expected note-perfect renditions rather than show-offy little games or some hot saxophonist weaving a medley of songs by other composers into a Berlin tune with such skill that the audience forgot all about the song and hailed the musician. That was not what Irving had in mind when he spent his nights making his songs as simple as he possibly could.

Berlin's rigid approach to composition implied that he was no longer on the cutting edge of popular music, but by now he had forsaken innovation as a worthy goal. His drive to join the mainstream extended to all areas of his life, especially the unresolved question of his citizenship, as he resumed his legal quest to become a naturalized citizen, with the assistance of his lawyer, Max Josephson. On October 11, 1917, Berlin fulfilled the second of the three steps required by filing his Petition for Naturalization. And on February 6, 1918, he completed the process by taking the oath of allegiance: "I hereby declare, on oath, that I absolutely and entirely renounce and abjure all allegiance and fidelity to any foreign prince . . . and particularly to The Present Government of Russia, of whom I have heretofore been a subject." He further promised, "I will support and defend the Constitution and laws of the United States of America against all enemies, foreign and domestic; and that I will bear true faith and allegiance to the same." No mere formality, these were words to which he ascribed the utmost seriousness. America's most famous popular composer had finally become, shortly before his thirtieth birthday, an American citizen.

At his age he seemed an unlikely draft prospect. Surely the Army would bypass him on account of his celebrity alone. Yet he still wanted to lend his talents to the war effort, by writing songs, entertaining, whatever was required of him. Elsie Janis, following her appearance in *The Century Girl*, was reveling in the job of entertaining American troops in France; she implored him to join her in this capacity, a role pleasant enough to contemplate, the two of them singing and cavorting before homesick doughboys, then dashing off to restaurants and parties. Before he could make arrangements, he experienced what his friend Alexander Woollcott termed a "painful shock": he found himself drafted into the Army.

■ □ ■ □ ■ □ ■

CHAPTER 8

Sergeant Berlin

"I found out quickly I wasn't much of a soldier. There were a lot of things about army life I didn't like, and the thing I didn't like most of all was reveille," Berlin said of his first taste of the military. "I hated it. I hated it so much that I used to lie awake nights thinking about how much I hated it."

He had been assigned to Camp Upton, located in Yaphank, Long Island, where he became a member of the Twentieth Infantry, 152nd Depot Brigade. To an urban dweller like Berlin, Yaphank, a hundred miles from New York, seemed a hopelessly remote and desolate place. Dusty roads meandered aimlessly through flat, featureless potato fields, and the local inhabitants, mostly farmers and their families, wanted nothing to do with the tumult of New York City. The only excitement Berlin found was at Camp Upton itself, which functioned primarily as a staging area for soldiers bound for France. Most of the inductees came from New York, and like Berlin, they were often immigrants, generally draftees, with little desire to return to Europe and challenge the Hun; they were young men with lives to lead, careers to establish. To them the war came as more of an enforced vacation than a glorious cause.

Once drafted, the recruits found it incredibly inconvenient to be thrown together in barracks, forced to get up at dawn, and spend the day on KP duty or marching across a parade ground in close order drill. The desperate war overseas, if it entered the men's minds at all, seemed a remote and abstract conflict, at best. They went along because President Wilson told them to; they were hardworking, able-bodied, and cooperative (to a degree), but this was a war they could all live without. Nor did their soldier's pay—only thirty dollars per month—take the sting out of the indignity of Army life.

By the time Berlin entered the service in the spring of 1918, the prospects for victory were steadily improving. In July, the Battle of the Marne had finally brought the relentless German offensive to a standstill, and from this time on, American doughboys pouring into France helped drive the war to a swift conclusion. On November 11, the Germans signed an armistice agreement, bringing an end to hostilities but commencing a new and protracted phase of peace negotiations. With the war on the verge of concluding as Berlin donned his khaki uniform for the first time, there was little chance that he would ever be sent to Europe. However, even his experience of a noncombatant's rigidly structured and mindless life made a profound impression on him.

He considered himself a misfit from the start of his Army experience; everything about Army life went against his instincts. Patriotic or not, Berlin was indignant. Here they'd gone and taken him, a law-abiding citizen who earned his keep and then some and employed others who depended on him for their livelihood, taken him out of his thriving music publishing business and plunked him down in the middle of square miles of nothing and assigned him to peel potatoes, wash dishes, and generally carry out demeaning tasks he would have been embarrassed to ask his cook to perform at home.

Like everyone else at Camp Upton, he'd been beguiled by Cohan's "Over There." He'd expected to be one of the Yanks who were coming, who would play the hero and bring the war to a swift conclusion. But what did his dreary routine have to do with fighting a war? This utterly private man was now forced to share crowded sleeping quarters with dozens of other men, a situation he hadn't encountered since his days in Lower East Side flophouses. Neither did the strenuous physical drills suit his taste, nor his status as a humble private. He occasionally received weekend leave, when he was able to return to his apartment in New York, which now seemed more luxurious than ever to him, and to eat food prepared by his own cook exclusively for him, but the brief return to civilian life only made life at Camp Upton more difficult to bear.

He occasionally tried to cut corners and, in the process, assert his status. In one instance, he arranged for his valet to make his bunk and polish his Army issue items; all the while Berlin was on the field, enduring drill. "I really wasn't fitted to be a soldier," he soon concluded. "I was a songwriter," he told himself. "I knew entertainment."

Harry Ruby (originally Rubinstein), then a pianist working at Waterson, Berlin & Snyder, but soon to join Berlin, vividly remembered the worst problem his celebrated boss experienced: "Berlin gets into the Army at Upton, and now he's getting up with all the other soldiers, five A.M.! Irving had never gone to bed before two or three in the morning. He would work until two, three, and then sleep, and get up around ten. All of a sudden, he's getting up with the birds at five, and he's going out of his mind! This is not for him, believe me."

As much as Berlin detested barracks life, the experience proved to be a beneficial shock, for it gave him an entirely new range of experiences on which to draw for his songwriting; leaving the comforts of home turned out to be one of the best things that could have happened to him. Berlin sincerely "wanted to be a good soldier," as he recalled. "Every morning when the bugle blew I'd jump right out of bed, just as if I liked getting up early. The other soldiers thought I was a little too eager about it, and they hated me. That's why I finally wrote a song about it."

The immediate impetus for the song derived from a colonel at the camp, who, when he discovered a group of buglers practicing, asked them to play George M. Cohan's "Over There." The buglers found they were unable to play Cohan's song, for their instruments lacked sufficient notes. "Well," said the officer, completely unperturbed, "keep on trying."

Berlin decided to incorporate his hatred of the military mentality, of bugles, and, most of all, of getting up at the crack of dawn, in a song, and this time he struck a nerve. He discovered that soldiers everywhere, including the one who slept in the bed next to his, Private Howard Friend, felt precisely as he did about reveille. In contrast to the run-of-the-mill popular song extolling the grandeur of war, Berlin's plaintive "Oh! How I Hate to Get Up in the Morning," with its threat to "murder the bugler," bordered on the mutinous.

The song made the rounds at Camp Upton, where it gave expression to every soldier's self-deprecatory, antiheroic sentiments and quickly caught on. The soldier-songwriter's song of the Great War contained no reference to combat, President Wilson, freedom, peace, or even patriotism; instead, it focused exclusively on homely details such as hatred of the bugler; it was folksy without being a folk song, and its tone of comic grousing appealed not only to the soldiers of Camp Upton, who lived it, but also to the country at large. As a result, Berlin finally had his first hit war song. For once the timing of his message was right. The song's mutinous message wouldn't have been well received in the grim, early days of the war; it took the prospect of peace to permit the laughter the song required for its effect. The melody of a confident but nonbelligerent victor, it eventually sold a million and a half copies.

In addition, it was undeniably autobiographical, deriving directly from his observations and street-smart humor. "There is a song called 'The Star-Spangled Banner,' which is a pretty big song hit, too," Berlin later remarked, "but my answer to the question in the opening line of the national anthem is a loud 'No!' I can't 'see' anything 'by the dawn's early light.' My song about hating to 'get up in the mo-o-o-rning' was a protest written from the heart out, absolutely without the slightest thought that it would ever earn a cent."

Here, at last, was a hit that no one dared to attribute to a black musician in Harlem. Even though it set no musical fashion, it did accomplish the task of returning Berlin himself to favor. This was the song in which he finally cast off for good the fetters of ragtime that had bound him to so many ephemeral revues. "Oh! How I Hate to Get Up in the Morning" wasn't reminiscent of black music, or Jewish, or Italian, as so many of Irving's earlier songs had been; it was written in an "American" vernacular: simple, straightforward, masculine. Though he would continue to employ devices he'd learned from ethnic songs, such as syncopation, he would write no more of them. As a soldier-songwriter, he now belonged to a category by himself.

As "Oh! How I Hate to Get Up in the Morning" was catching on, most of the soldiers who had come to Camp Upton with Berlin departed for France, as expected, but Private Berlin stayed behind, earning promotion to the rank of sergeant; it seemed a special destiny lay in store for him. Major General J. Franklin Bell, the camp's commanding officer, ordered Berlin to his office and explained: "We want a new community house—a place where friends and relatives of you men can be made a little more comfortable when they come to visit. It could cost a lot of money—perhaps $35,000—and we thought perhaps you could put on a little show to make money." To comply, Berlin prevailed on his vaudeville friends to assuage their guilty consciences and make morale-boosting visits to Camp Upton, but he began to feel "this was running a little thin." Around the same time, he remembered, "the Navy did a show called *Boom Boom.* I read about it in *Variety*, and I thought: Hmm, this is my chance. So I went to a Colonel Martin, I think it was, who was on the staff of the commanding officer, . . . and asked him, 'Why can't we do a show here at Camp Upton?' "

So ran the official version. The *un*official version, according to Harry Ruby, Sergeant Berlin's colleague at Camp Upton, was that Berlin continually pestered the commanding officer for an opportunity to stage a vaudeville show to occupy the other show business draftees in the camp. And that request, according to Ruby, was motivated by Berlin's desire to find a way to avoid getting up at reveille. After Major General Bell agreed to Berlin's proposal, the songwriter went on to say, "Here's the thing, General. I write at night. Sometimes I work all night when I get an idea. And I couldn't do that if I had to get up in the morning at five, you understand."

"Why, you don't have to get up at five," replied the General. "You just forget about all that. *You write this show.*" And that was precisely the response he had hoped to hear. If the cost of sleeping late was writing a show *gratis*, he was prepared to proceed. Both the Army and Berlin got a fair amount from the deal; the Army would pay for all expenses incurred by the show, but in return, Berlin donated his services.

Realizing that whatever personnel he required would come free, Berlin contemplated a lavish Ziegfeld-style revue, conceived on a scale that the impresario would have approved. Furthermore, he wanted to stage it not on the base, as just another talent show, but on Broadway, as a full-blown theatrical event. In May the Navy had taken over the huge Century Theatre for sixteen performances of a show noted mainly for its all-too-believable female impersonators. Berlin naturally wanted the Century for his own revue, in which he planned to teach the Navy a trick or two about entertaining civilians. The only modest aspect of the production was to be the length of its run: eight performances only. To fill a theater of the Century's outsized proportions, Sergeant Berlin requested a crew of three hundred men for his show, the number evenly divided between performers and stage hands. Once the extent of Berlin's demand became known, Major General Bell quickly established a supervisory board consisting of three officers—Major J. John Brandreth, Captain James G. Benkard, and Lieutenant Basil Broadhurst—to oversee the ambitious project.

After holding auditions, Berlin started rehearsals for *Yip! Yip! Yaphank*, as he called his show, in June. Newspapers in New York carried advertisements for seats at prices ranging from fifty cents to two dollars.

As he began his nocturnal labors on the score, Berlin sent for Harry Ruby, who became the songwriter's musical secretary. Ruby moved out to Camp Upton and lived in the same barracks as Berlin. Now it was Ruby's turn to marvel at Berlin's ferocious work habits.

"He'd come up to me in the morning while I was out there at Yaphank with him," said Ruby, "and he'd say, 'Harry, got a pencil and some music paper?' and I'd say sure, and he'd say, 'Take this down,' and sing me a melody. . . . I'd ask him, 'When the hell did you write *that?*' and he'd say, 'Oh, I was up all night. Do you like it?' And I'd say it was great, and I'd play it back for him to hear what he'd dictated—and he'd listen, and he'd say, 'You got one chord wrong in there.' And he'd be right—he couldn't *play* the chord, but he could *hear* it all right!"

Berlin dictated a rich assortment of melodies that cast military experiences in human, even homely terms: "I Can Always Find a Little Sunshine in the Y.M.C.A.," "Kitchen Police," and "Dream On, Little Soldier Boy." In keeping with the show's vaudeville format, he even devised, amid these unlikely circumstances, a romantic show stopper, "Mandy," that would serve as the centerpiece of a minstrel section. After taking down the melodies and devising appropriate harmonies, Ruby turned over the songs to an arranger, who further elaborated them into orchestral parts. In all respects, Berlin's *modus operandi* was the same as it was for a conventional Broadway revue.

Finally, Berlin composed one unashamedly patriotic anthem,

which spoke of prairies and mountains and oceans white with foam. He called it "God Bless America," but even as he dictated it to Ruby, Berlin became insecure about its originality. "There were so many patriotic songs coming out everywhere at the time," Ruby recalled. "Every songwriter was pouring them out." As he wrote down the melody, Ruby said to Berlin, "Geez, *another* one?" Deciding that Ruby was right, that the song was too solemn to ring true for the acerbic doughboys, Berlin cut it from the score and placed it in his trunk. "Just a little sticky" was the way he described the song. "I couldn't visualize soldiers marching to it. So I laid it aside and tried other things."

As the score began to take shape, Berlin decided to try it out on his civilian friends, especially Dutch Talmadge, who continued to beguile him. Dutch responded to the invitation by assembling a party, including her sisters and Anita Loos. Together they traveled out to Yaphank and listened to Irving, seated at a piano, warble a lyric complaining, It was apparent that he was continuing to mine the same humorous vein he had discovered in "Oh! How I Hate to Get Up in the Morning."

Despite the winning songs, the visit did nothing to further Irving's suit with Dutch, who resumed making films for Joe Schenck and playing the coquette for her suitors. She surprised everyone by spurning Berlin and all the handsome young actors with whom she had been seen for the Greek tobacco importer.

In July *Yip! Yip! Yaphank* opened at Camp Upton's little Liberty Theatre, and Berlin endowed the occasion with all the publicity he could muster. He discovered that with the might of the United States Armed Forces behind him, he was able to command respect (and attendance) for his work as never before. A private train hired for the day transported seventy celebrities from New York to see the show, including vaudeville stars Al Jolson, Fanny Brice, and Will Rogers, and the female chorus of a Broadway revue entitled *Midnight Frolics*. The run-through, a scaled-down version of the revue, served its purpose, which was to win the approval of its military backers, especially Major General Bell, and the *Yip! Yip! Yaphank* company proceeded to take over the cavernous spaces of the Century Theatre.

It was now August, and the city sweltered in relentless heat and humidity, but the three hundred soldiers from Camp Upton yielded nothing to the weather. They bivouacked at the 71st Regiment Armory, at Park Avenue and 34th Street, and each day they marched uptown to the Century in military formation, rehearsed under the direction of Sergeant Berlin, and then marched back downtown to the Armory, where they remained under military discipline. Meanwhile, playbills appeared all over town, proclaiming, "UNCLE SAM PRESENTS *Yip Yip Yaphank*—a military mess cooked up by the boys at Camp Upton."

Opening night, August 19, found every seat in the huge old theater occupied. Outside, on Central Park West, soldiers equipped with rifles were stationed every few paces, while others guarded the entrances. This show of force might have seemed threatening had not each sentry been under orders to smile at the crowds. With an end to the war in sight, the members of the audience were inspired more by the desire to express their gratitude than by bellicose instincts. Once again vaudeville stars turned out in force; in addition to the familiar faces of Fanny Brice and Al Jolson, celebrity watchers noted the presence of George M. Cohan and the widowed Irene Castle. Ignored by the crowd, but of far greater importance to Sergeant Berlin, was the bulky, stooped figure of one other theatergoer, his mother, Lena Baline, who was also in attendance.

Within, a call of "Atten-shun!" brought the excited murmurs of the audience to a sudden halt, and every head, including those of the girls selling programs, snapped forward; the crowd rose in unison, stood more or less at attention, and waited as Major General Bell passed among them on the way to his box. And the show began.

Berlin had framed his revue with minstrel acts, but in his version, the traditional minstrel line wore khaki, and only the men on either end were in blackface. Acting as an interlocutor, a Captain McAllister informed the soldiers that they now faced a seasoned enemy, perched just over the footlights, an enemy they must bomb with jokes and vanquish with songs. The first tune struck an attitude of studied, comic irreverence that would be maintained throughout the evening: "You Can't Stay Up All Night On Bevo." "Bevo" was nonalcoholic wartime beer, and Anheuser-Busch, the brewers, actually paid Sergeant Berlin $10,000 to deride the stuff; Berlin promptly donated the "contribution" to the Army.

Since the revue intended to depict life at Camp Upton and to showcase the talents of some of its inhabitants, there ensued a procession of acrobats, jugglers, and dancers. There was even a boxing demonstration featuring Benny Leonard, the lightweight champion of the world. Recognizing how much theater was inherent in army life, Berlin cannily included a series of military drills. Set to his syncopated music, the drills became transformed into choreography as the soldiers marched in ever more complex formations.

In addition to these displays of talent, the revue included much silliness, as the soldiers, after demonstrating their finesse in intricate drills, became hairy-chested chorus girls parodying the lavish spectacles Ziegfeld had staged in the same theater. Individual soldiers tried to imitate leading ladies of the moment, such as Ann Pennington and Marilyn Miller. In response to this organized lunacy, the audience, according to one observer, "became a carefree mob that whistled, shouted and cheered every number, and joined in the choruses after the first encore. The enthusiasm and vigor of the boys on the stage and the stimulus of the songs swept everyone irresistably into the spirit of the evening. It was more like the last inning of a world-series ball game than anything else."

Although he had orchestrated all these onstage activities from behind the scenes, Berlin refrained from appearing onstage until the latter part of the revue. He gauged well the effect of a delayed entry, for by the time he *did* appear onstage, it was nearly eleven P.M., and the anticipation of the audience, which had been waiting several hours for a chance to see him, reached its highest pitch. His solo act, a reflection of his own self-contained, even isolated personality, made for a dramatic contrast to the foregoing excitement. The lights dimmed, and a Camp Upton-style tent appeared onstage. There were calls for "Sergeant Berlin," but he failed to materialize. Eventually two other soldiers dragged him out of the tent, asleep on his feet. "Of course there was a welcome that rocked the theater," wrote *Theatre Magazine*'s critic, "but to his credit as a good actor, there he stood, while his friends waited for a nod of recognition, staring dreamily ahead, and buttoning up his coat. Then he introduced, in his peculiar, plaintive little voice, the chorus that began: "Oh! how I hate to get up in the morning."

This mournful underplaying enthralled the audience. In the process he finally established a stage persona for himself, that of the feisty little common man buffeted by events over which he has no control but managing, through a sense of humor and innate toughness, to survive in an often insane world. Irving's slight build made the persona credible, and so did his Lower East Side accent. There was nothing slick about his thin, high voice; he could easily have been just another soldier, except that his timing was flawless, and his lament hilarious. "Some day I'm going to murder the bugler," he sang. "Some day they're going to find him dead." Except that in his mouth, the words came out sounding more like he'd "moidah dah buglah"—it was pure Cherry Street tough talk.

Berlin furthered his comical exploration of the soldier's unhappy lot in his last scene, where he sang of how he was making the world safe for democracy with a mop and a pail. Said one observer: "Every soldier in the audience who was doing his bit by peeling potatoes or picking weeds from the parade ground howled joyfully in response." Not everyone laughed, however. When two soldiers began to bully Berlin as part of the skit, his mother, from her vantage point in the audience, became concerned; to her the sight was alarmingly real, not comic. Why were these men pushing her Izzy around this way? And why was the audience laughing? And most of all, what were they saying? English remained a foreign tongue to her.

Throughout the entire evening, only one song fell flat, and it was, as Berlin had feared, the sentimental number "I Can Always Find a Little Sunshine in the Y.M.C.A." Invoking motherhood and the dubious pleasure of writing home, the ballad elicited boos and catcalls. But the second minstrel number, a "Darktown Wedding," quickly restored the audience to good humor. Intended as a grotesque, comic parody of a typical Ziegfeld "tribute" to the American girl, the scene contained one number that later became a Berlin standard: "Mandy."

The expression of a young suitor who wanted a minister handy so he could marry his Mandy, the song swooned with honorable romantic sentiment. And what did the impish Berlin do with this tender song and all these hairy-chested soldiers? He staged "Mandy" as a drag number with a blackface male chorus wearing ribbons and curls. And when the men began to sing of their yearning to marry, the spectacle was tasteless, it was racist, but it was also funny. Then, in the midst of the revelry, Mandy herself appeared onstage, and she was played by an actual woman, not a drag queen. Not only that, but the actress really *was* Black. Her unexpected appearance, according to observers, "fairly stopped the proceedings with a pair of eyes that would be worth a million dollars in the movies if they were topped with Pickford curls instead of Topsy pigtails."

After exploring the limits of theatrical absurdity, the company shed their blackface and costumes and rallied for the finale. Two hundred and seventy-seven soldiers—the entire Camp Upton company fortified with police reservists—crowded onstage wearing full battle gear. A song Berlin had hurriedly written to replace the "sticky" "God Bless America"—"We're On Our Way to France"—began. The soldiers suddenly streamed from the stage down ramps and through the aisles of the Century, rifles perched on the shoulders, and continued out the doors, as if they actually were on their way to France and perhaps to their deaths.

After this stunning conclusion, Major General Bell rose to address the audience. He thanked them all for their generosity, explained that the proceeds would be used to build a community house at Camp Upton, and then added: "I have heard that Berlin is among the foremost songwriters of the world," he said, "and now I believe it."

He then gestured to Sergeant Berlin, indicating that he should speak. Applause for Berlin began; they all loved that little man. It had taken upward of three hundred soldiers to pull this revue off, but Berlin had shaped the entire production, written the lyrics, composed the music, and staged the scenes, all the while tweaking Ziegfeld's bulbous nose and having a good time in the process. Though he had been onstage only a matter of minutes all evening, everyone knew he was the evening's mastermind. Berlin's reticence only inspired the audience to cheer more lustily for him; on and on the roar of approval continued, for a full ten minutes, while the songwriter groped for words. Spontaneity did not come easily to a man as disciplined as he, but he had to overcome his inhibitions and respond; his commanding officer's wishes had the force of an order. The cast came to his rescue by hoisting him onto their shoulders and parading their little hero around the stage.

The occasion proved to be more than another showbiz triumph, though. Without quite intending to, he had outstripped the conventional measurements of Broadway success and become a symbol to the audience and to the soldiers, an emblem of camaraderie, fun, and catchy tunes. Moreover, the night had promoted this tiny man to the status of an archetypal figure, the minstrel of Camp Upton, of the Great War, and by extension, of the country. For he, better than any other show business figure, had managed to capture the war in song—not the hideous blunders, needless deaths, and general horror of the war, which would become widely acknowledged once it had ended—but the gap-toothed, good-natured, aw-shucks spirit of a nation awakening from the long and perilous slumber of isolationism to its eminence as a world power. Wrote one entranced reporter of the event: "It may well be that no mortal theatre was ever so beautiful as the Century that hot night on August of 1918, and it is even more likely that no mortal show could ever have been quite so transcendentally wonderful, so altogether out of this world."

After the show, Berlin celebrated the occasion as only Berlin would: he slipped away from the crowd and took his mother to her home in the Bronx. During the ride, she finally confessed—in Yiddish—her astonishment that he had been released. Her son pressed her for an explanation. Released? "Yes," she answered, "by all the gangsters who got hold of you and carried you on their shoulders. How ever did you escape?"

▪ ▪ ▪

Though designed as a limited-run benefit talent show, *Yip! Yip! Yaphank* received the press coverage and publicity due a Broadway hit. In the morning New York was peppered with newspaper headlines proclaiming the show's success.

> 'YIP! YIP! YAPHANK' MAKES ROUSING HIT—All of the Numbers Are Patriotic and Its Chorus "Maidens" Are One Long Laugh. (*New York Times*)

> YIP YIP YAPHANK WINS!—Camp Upton Boys Make Big Advance on Manhattan Front. (*Brooklyn Eagle*)

The *Eagle* reserved special praise for the show's score: "To hear Irving Berlin sing, 'How I Hate to Get Up in the Morning' [sic] alone is worth a trip to Manhattan. There is more truth than poetry in the song and it came home strong to the boys under 45 in the audience last night, many of whom may be 'cussing' the bugler themselves, inside of a few short months."

Contributions poured in. Even E. F. Albee, the powerful vaudeville manager who rarely went to the theater himself, took sixteen friends and enjoyed himself so much that he donated one thousand dollars. Buying a seat for *Yip! Yip! Yaphank* at the highest possible price quickly became a patriotic duty. Before the acclaim died away, the revue's run was extended for another week and then for a full month, well into September. Since another show had already been booked into the Century, *Yip! Yip! Yaphank* moved to the Lexington Avenue Opera House, where the ovations continued, and the donations piled up. Expected to earn $35,000, the show eventually collected $83,000.

Camp Upton contingent's Cinderella existence on Broadway came to a startling conclusion. On closing night, the thirty-second performance, they received special orders. When the soldiers marched down the aisles singing "We're On Our Way to France" at the end of the performance, they continued marching to the street. At first the audience assumed this was all part of the show, but then the production's large crew began to follow the actors down the aisles, led by Sergeant Berlin. Gradually the crowd realized the soldiers actually were going to war, and there was considerable crying and fainting and cheering—a jumble of emotions coalescing into cheers that rang in the ears of the departing soldiers as they proceeded in formation to a troop carrier. They boarded without delay and departed for France.

This theatrical *coup* demonstrated Berlin's mastery of theatrical symbolism, a talent that grew out of his prowess as a songwriter but now went well beyond it. He displayed an intuitive grasp of how to manipulate potent political symbols and how to choose words to seize men's minds. When he was at the top of his form, writing from the heart rather than to a Tin Pan Alley formula, he had the gift of making his audience realize what was on their minds even before they'd acknowledged it to themselves. Songs such as "Oh! How I Hate to Get

Up in the Morning" or the mothballed "God Bless America" were poised on the cusp of consciousness; they crystalized and catalyzed public opinion. Berlin was as awed as anyone else by his power to command the public's attention, and he was exceedingly cautious, even timid, about using this power. He recognized that his reputation would never last if he attempted to extend popular opinion in an unfamiliar direction; to lend his prestige to an unpopular cause would be to risk losing it. His mission was to express latent thoughts and feelings, not to invent them.

■ ■ ■

When the war ended in November, the need for Camp Upton's community house—the original reason *Yip! Yip! Yaphank* had come into existence—suddenly evaporated. The structure was never built, and Berlin never did find out what became of the $83,000 he'd raised for Uncle Sam.

All things considered, though, Irving Berlin had had himself a very nice war. He had reaped vast good will and priceless personal publicity from *Yip! Yip! Yaphank*—the kind that could not be bought on Tin Pan Alley at any price. When he returned to civilian life at the beginning of 1919, he was recognized wherever he went, though this situation often led to keen embarrassment for him. When he attended a performance at the Broadhurst Theatre one evening, the man sitting next to him pointed him out to the rest of the audience, which burst into applause. And then his neighbor announced, "I'll give five hundred dollars to the Salvation Army if Mr. Berlin will sing to us." More cheers. Reluctantly, he took the stage and warbled "Oh! How I Hate to Get Up in the Morning," thinking he'd discharged his obligation—except that the man spoke once more: "I'll give another five hundred dollars if Mr. Berlin gives us another chorus." More applause, and Berlin had no choice but to comply yet again.

He soon discovered that his notoriety carried more serious hazards. He received a death threat and a kidnapping threat; anarchists were much in the news, and Berlin feared them, as well. At that same time, he tried to make light of the danger in a song, "Look Out for That Bolsheviki Man." Yet he did fear for his safety enough to equip himself with a bullet-proof Packard limousine, driven by a burley chauffeur-bodyguard. Occasionally they wandered as far as Atlantic City, where the songwriter sequestered himself in an oceanside hotel and churned out songs to keep his new company in business. More frequently, the Packard roamed the city after dark, skirting bums, anarchists, and fans alike.

Berlin was guarding himself against the sort of person he might have become. Which was the real Berlin? From now on, he would insist it was the one he invented—the ubiquitous, all-American, self-effacing celebrity. His songs became less daring, though no less successful. His first postwar hits traded on the success of his military numbers. "I've Got My Captain Working for Me Now," a fantasy of revenge enjoyed by numerous soldiers returning to civilian life, was popularized by Al Jolson into a fair-sized hit. In fact, the number of songs Berlin published shot up to his former pace of approximately two a month. On November 11 the Globe Theatre saw the premiere of *The Canary*, another Charles Dillingham–Harry B. Smith collaboration, complete with five new songs by Irving Berlin.

With his career revitalized by the success of *Yip! Yip! Yaphank*, he acted swiftly to consolidate his business interests. Using the trade publications as if they were his personal publicity organ, he announced that he would consider any firm that would pay him a salary of $75,000 plus a generous bonus. For a time it seemed he would sign on with the respectable firm of T. B. Harms, but Harms appeared to be in no hurry to commit itself. Berlin was a star, but everyone on Tin Pan Alley had seen stars come and go.

During the waiting period, Irving happened to play a new song he'd written about the Russian revolution, "That Revolutionary Rag," for a Harms executive. Harms expressed interest in the tune, and Berlin requested a transcriber to set down the music. In response, Harms quickly produced one of its best staff pianists, George Gershwin, to attend to the chore.

Since his last meeting with Berlin four years earlier, Gershwin had made only slight progress in the music field. He had published several songs, but he still earned his keep as an exceedingly talented house pianist. Gershwin not only took down Berlin's tune, but also devised an arrangement, and when he performed the version enhanced with the Gershwin touch, Berlin was astounded. "It was so good, I hardly recognized it!" he exclaimed. A compliment, on the surface, but actually, for the strict Berlin, the kiss of death.

The young pianist then reminded Berlin of their previous meeting, and once again he declared his desire to become Berlin's regular musical secretary. Gershwin still worshipped him, still considered him the quintessential Tin Pan Alley composer. What better place to complete his songwriting apprenticeship?

Again Berlin considered. This Gershwin, he knew, was simply too much of an original, too fast and too show-offy, to function as a musical secretary, a job that Berlin considered nothing more than clerical drudgery. The last thing he needed was a genius of an amanuensis who'd always remind him of his inferiority in matters of musical technique and "improve" the songs on which he'd labored through the nights. "Stick to your songs, kid," he advised.

This time around, Berlin's judgment was vindicated; Gershwin finally got his break later that year when several of his songs became hits, while "That Revolutionary Rag," which he'd improved beyond recognition, flopped. The song's failure also ended the possibility of a Berlin-Harms union.

Still, the encounter with Gershwin was sufficient to send Berlin on yet another futile search for the musical training he'd always lacked. This time he turned to a prominent teacher named Herman Wasserman, whom he had met at Camp Upton. The two men were about the same age, and they got along well enough during lessons, but the result was always the same; Berlin simply could not absorb Wasserman's pianism. They would try again, ten years later, with exactly the same results. Berlin was Berlin, and there was nothing to be done.

In May Berlin finally stopped tormenting himself with pointless musical lessons and fruitless negotiations with other publishing companies and decided to go into business with Max Winslow, who'd been patiently waiting for months. As a first step, Berlin dissolved the company he'd formed in 1914 to handle his Broadway scores, and on June 18 he incorporated the new Irving Berlin, Inc., with offices at 1607 Broadway.

The firm included a third partner, Saul Bornstein, an unlovely bully of a man who took charge of business activities, while Winslow stuck with his specialty as "professional manager" and Berlin composed songs as fast as he was able. Each of the men drew a salary of five hundred dollars a week, and Berlin earned considerable royalties on top of that sum, fully three times as much as he'd ever earned at his old firm: six cents on songs, eight on production numbers.

Nobody on Tin Pan Alley commanded a higher rate, but since Berlin was his own publisher, the arrangement was something of a shell game: the more he made as a songwriter, the less he made as a partner in the music business. Either way, though, he would not lose. Since the firm's catalogue included most of the songs he had composed since he'd formally entered the business ten years earlier, it was blessed with a fair chance of success from its first day in business.

The seat of Berlin's power seemed to be just another anonymous-looking office suite overlooking the cluttered, gray stretches of Broadway, but within, it had a peculiar life of its own. One visitor compared it to the "upstairs lobby of the leading hotel of a town of seven thousand": pale blue walls, a chandelier that was always lit, carved pillars. In the center stood a leather circular seat ringed with bright brass cuspidors, a few chairs, an oak table, and an opening in one wall through which a male receptionist was visible. And always, the muffled thumping of pianos and a crowd." Said another visitor: "You no sooner step out of that elevator web as it reaches the Berlin floor than you are immediately trampled underfoot by something that suggests a crowd in front of a baseball score-board, a mob scene, perhaps, in a William A. Brady melodrama, or a busy day at the gates of Ellis Island."

The hallway leading off the waiting room overflowed with theater people: "Slim-waisted, pasty-faced lads with incredibly nimble feet," noted Alexander Woollcott, "who stand askew and litter the floor with the nervous butts of their half-consumed cigarettes; small, squeaky actresses of ten or twelve towed by their belligerent mothers"—everyone *except* Mr. Berlin himself, who rarely mingled with the throng, even in these controlled circumstances. In the morning he was surely at home, sleeping; and he often worked at home in the afternoons, as well. In fact, the only time he could tolerate setting foot in his own office was at night, after everyone but his transcriber—in this period, a young man named Arthur Johnston—had gone home.

Berlin's transcriber occupied a dismal room appropriate to the low status Berlin accorded his role. Transcribers were, as Woollcott remarked, "Men who, when Berlin was born, knew more about music than he will ever know. . . . You can imagine their sentiments." And then, beyond the transcribers' den, lay the office of the professional manager; it was here that Winslow reigned behind a mahogany desk. He could, it was said, be mistaken for a bank president, "if it did not seem uncharacteristic of a bank president, in the midst of a conference, to throw back his head and clinch an argument by bursting into song with what is left of a once famous whiskey tenor."

Impressive as Winslow's office was, it paled in comparison to Berlin's lair, "a region of opalescent lamps, thick, yielding rugs and submerging divans." Here was the one real touch of luxury in the entire establishment, but it turned out to be more of an icon than an actuality, for Berlin was rarely, if ever, there. Its suggestion of the word *tycoon* made him feel ill at ease. Concluded Woollcott after beholding this display of pointless grandeur: "Life has prepared a throne for Irving Berlin but he is too vagrant, too self-critical and too humorous a person ever to be caught in the act of sitting in it."

To remind the public of his formidable position in the world of songwriting, Berlin offered, in the course of an interview with *The American Magazine*, "nine rules for writing popular songs." Charles K. Harris, in his heyday, had proclaimed there were six, but Berlin was determined to outdo him, as he was any other songwriter on the horizon.

Summarized, the rules ran as follows:

1. The melody should be within the range of most singers.
2. The title should be attention-getting and, in addition, repeated within the body of the song.
3. The song should be "sexless": able to be sung by men and women.
4. The song requires "heart interest."
5. And at the same time, it should be "original in idea, words, and music."
6. "Stick to nature," advised Berlin in his pragmatic way. "Not nature in a visionary, abstract way, but nature as demonstrated in homely, concrete, everyday manifestations."
7. Sprinkle the lyrics with "open vowels" so that it will be euphonious.
8. Make the song as simple as possible.
9. "The song writer must look upon his work as a business,

that is, to make a success of it, he must work and *work*, and then WORK."

The first eight rules could have come from the lips of any journeyman Alley tunesmith; it was the last rule that set Berlin apart. In the end, everything else flowed from the willingness to work, and as he himself realized, his ferocious devotion to work set him apart from many in the same field.

Not since "Alexander's Ragtime Band" had made him a nationally known figure had Berlin given himself over to boasting. Throughout 1919 and the following years, his confidence ran as high as it ever did—and so did his credibility. Whether in songwriting or in the music publishing business, Berlin did what he said he would do, and even after he finished his own compositions, he had plenty of energy and ideas left over to apply to others'. Indeed, he made what others would have considered an entire career out of doctoring the efforts by lesser figures.

Irving Berlin, Inc. published numerous songs by other composers; Berlin's output alone did not justify keeping such a large staff on his payroll, but no song received the Berlin imprimatur without first receiving the Berlin examination. If he found a song wanting, he tinkered with the lyric or fussed with the melody. He still had vast blind spots when it came to technical matters such as harmony, but he could inject syncopation into a tired rhythm or devise novel rhymes. He would even, in a flash of inspiration, dash off entirely new lyrics for a song composed by a lesser-known figure, but when the result was published, it would not credit Berlin; all credit still went to the original composer—whether he wanted it or not. Officially, Berlin did not collaborate; but as a publisher, he tinkered frequently with others' work.

There was considerable irony in this situation, for jealous tongues on the Alley still spread the rumor that Berlin, untutored and undeservedly lucky hack that he was, kept a black boy on his payroll, writing hit songs. In fact, the opposite was true: Berlin, the consummate Alley professional, functioned as a ghostwriter on many of the songs his company published—precisely how many will never be known, for he was not given to documenting such activity.

· · ·

By the time Berlin launched his company, records had become a major force in home entertainment. A popular record could sell as well as sheet music and of course returned royalties to the composers and performers. To the old guard on Tin Pan Alley, these black shellacked discs boded ill. Every record sold meant less sheet music bought—so ran the conventional wisdom. The fear was that a technological revolution would throw sheet music publishers out of business and render a generation of pluggers obsolete.

In Berlin's case, however, records provided a handsome new source of income and publicity for his next score. Cushioning himself against the risk of opening his own office, he returned to Ziegfeld's fold; composing for the venerable *Follies* was as sure a thing as a songwriter could hope for. Normally Ziegfeld divided his score among several composers, who all vied to outdo one another, but in this instance the impresario departed from his custom and assigned Berlin most—though not quite all—of the score. In doing so, Ziegfeld hoped to import much of the excitement Berlin's soldier show had generated ten months earlier. He even recycled some of the songs Berlin had written while at Camp Upton, and which had appeared in *Yip! Yip! Yaphank*, incidentally giving the songwriter another opportunity to earn royalties.

The Ziegfeld Follies of 1919, containing seven Berlin numbers, opened at the New Amsterdam Theatre on June 16. Since Ziegfeld was still superstitious, especially about the number 13, which he believed to be especially lucky for him, he held back Berlin's first song until the thirteenth "episode" in the show; it was a minstrel number sung by Eddie Cantor and the renowned black comedian Bert Williams. And the first act concluded with an opulent restaging of Berlin's paean to marriage, "Mandy," sung by the entire company, including a corps identified in the program as "The Follies Pickaninnies." This time around, the song, given an elegant performance by Marilyn Miller, achieved the popularity it had failed to find when sung by the soldiers in *Yip! Yip! Yaphank*.

The second and concluding act of the *Follies* belonged almost entirely to Berlin, and it began with a now-forgotten evocation of "Harem Life," in which "favorite wives" paraded before the audience, which was almost too preoccupied with Joseph Urban's exotic set to notice them. Later in the act, the songwriter returned to form when the tenor John Steele sang the consummate Ziegfeld song: "A Pretty Girl Is Like a Melody." The song became one of Berlin's great favorites; years later, he would write the editors of *Life* magazine, which was preparing an article about him, and declare it to be "the best individual song written for a musical"—not *my* best song, but *the* best. The song marked a distinct departure from his earlier melodies; it was neither a street-smart comedy number nor a traditional ballad, and it was slow and elegant, yet colloquial. He would return repeatedly to this type of song—flowing and serene—throughout the 1920s until it became his dominant mode (and, by extension, the dominant mode of popular music) during the decade.

Another song Berlin wrote for the evening, "You'd Be Surprised," spoke of a man much like Berlin—a man unassuming, perhaps a bit disappointing to behold, and yet when he was alone with a woman, he became surprisingly ardent. The songwriter was extremely fond of this creation. "Nothing could be more commonplace or bromidic than the line, 'You'd be surprised,' " he boasted.

> Every man, woman, and child in the English-speaking world has said it and heard it countless times.
>
> I know from the bales of unsuccessful songs I am constantly coming across exactly how the mentally lazy or the uninitiated would go about the work of building that line into a song. They would write a lyric concerning one or several of the innumerable surprising things of life. They would possibly—no, *probably!*—jumble up their song with *all* the surprising things they could think of, thereby losing simplicity. And the chorus would be just a noisy blah:
>
> You'd be surprised! You'd be surprised!
> I realized you'd be surprised!
> I must say that I recognized
> Surprised you'd be—you'd be surprised!

Berlin savagely dissected this clumsy parody of his chorus. "No punch again," he complained. "Just repetition, not *effective*, accentuating repetition. Words, noisy words."

In contrast, Berlin's version achieved its comic effects through juxtapositions between the unassuming suitor and his pleasantly outsized passion. This little dynamo of a song also had important consequences for Irving's fledgling music business. At the year's end, Eddie Cantor, who had sung it in the *Follies*, recorded it for the Emerson label. The result was Irving Berlin's first hit record, selling over 800,000 copies, equal to the number of sheet music copies sold.

Other songs by Berlin—"Prohibition," "You Cannot Make Your Shimmy Shake on Tea," "A Syncopated Cocktail"—dwelt on a topical theme: the newly passed Volstead Act, which led to a flourishing subculture of speakeasies and an equally flourishing new genre of Tin Pan Alley songs lamenting the advent of Prohibition.

By general consent, *The Ziegfeld Follies of 1919* was the suavest and most accomplished of all the revues the impresario ever mounted. "This edition of the 'Follies,' " commented *The New York Clipper*, "is the best ever."

Much of the reason for the *Follies'* continued eminence stemmed from Ziegfeld's daredevil approach to financing his productions. His conception of economics was every bit as fanciful as his presentation of chorus girls. In 1917, when a full-scale musical cost approximately $25,000 to mount on Broadway, Ziegfeld spent nearly $90,000 on his annual revue, and the following year, he spent $120,000. And now, in 1919, he overspent to the point of $170,000. To help defray his costs, he steadily increased ticket prices; for nearly half a century, two dollars had been widely observed as the top price for a New York show; Ziegfeld lifted it to $3.50.

After 1919 Irving devoted little energy to subsequent editions of the *Follies*. The songwriter's disaffection stemmed in part from Ziegfeld's seamy personal life, which had a way of visiting tragedy on those around him. The impresario had, over the years, conducted numerous affairs with young girls in his chorus lines; the relationships generally descended from lavish presents to temper tantrums within a few months. One of the girls who became ensnared in his web was named Olive Thomas. In 1915 the two had spent a few happy weeks on his yacht, drifting across Long Island Sound and drinking champagne. Meanwhile, Ziegfeld's second wife, Billie Burke (*another* gorgeous Ziegfeld Girl herself), vented her frustration in crying jags.

Flo's affair with the seventeen-year-old Olive Thomas ran into trouble when he began a simultaneous liaison with her closest friend, Anna Daly. In frustration Olive found herself a new lover, Jack Pickford. Brother of silent-screen star Mary Pickford, he was a wild young man with a fondness for liquor and fast cars; he promised to get Olive into pictures, and in 1917 they married. Just before they sailed for France in 1920 to make a movie, Olive, probably at Jack's urging, made out a life insurance policy naming him as the beneficiary. There was one other grim note attendant on their sailing: Olive was probably not aware that her husband was suffering from syphilis.

Soon after they arrived in Paris, where they stayed, inevitably, at the Ritz, Olive and Jack began arguing. Early one morning, Olive Thomas, age twenty-two, was found dead. Jack claimed that she'd accidentally poisoned herself with his syphilis medication, mistaking it for sleeping pills, but no evidence of the substance was found in her body. The finger of suspicion pointed at her husband, but he escaped being charged.

In mid-September Olive's remains were returned to the United States aboard the *Mauretania*. On this nightmarish voyage, Jack Pickford tried to jump overboard but was dragged to safety by another passenger. At about the same time, in New York, Olive's close friend (and Ziegfeld's former lover) Anna Daly took an overdose of Veronal. She later died at Bellevue Hospital, leaving behind a terse note about Ziegfeld. It read: "He doesn't love me anymore and I can't stand it and Olive is dead."

On September 29 Ziegfeld arranged a suitably theatrical funeral for Olive Thomas at St. Thomas Church in Manhattan. He prevailed on Berlin to attend and, more than that, to serve as an usher. Irving went along out of a mixture of loyalty and expediency, but the sordidness of Ziegfeld's inner circle—culminating in the pointless deaths of two young actresses—repelled him. At times Ziegfeld behaved liked Broadway's greatest producer; at other times like Broadway's greatest pimp. Here was another instance of the great divide separating the young songwriter from the Broadway establishment as personified by Ziegfeld. The impresario staged his salacious fantasies and permitted audiences the privilege of vicarious participation. Irving, in contrast, remained tenaciously private. He perceived show business as a way of growing rich rather than working off his libido. His morality was a function of his fierce desire for autonomy.

After the funeral he kept his distance from Ziegfeld, as one would from a fascinating but repugnant satyr. The occasional Berlin song would appear in subsequent editions of the *Follies*, as they dwindled in scale and importance, but he increasingly turned his energies to the idea that he might be able to out-Ziegfeld Ziegfeld—not by staging revues that were even more lavish and egomaniacal than the impresario's, but by bringing a more subtle type of musical spectacle to Broadway. Berlin had nothing against harmless harem fantasies, which were reliably commercial, but both he and the country had grown up and wised up since Ziegfeld had begun his *Follies*, and Berlin sensed that audiences were ready to respond to more sophisticated explorations of romance. To carry out his plan, he needed a new kind of partner, a producer who knew Broadway as well as Irving knew Tin Pan Alley. And he soon found him, thanks once again to his former mentor, George M. Cohan. Berlin had received a lot of help from the great man over the years: Cohan had put the young songwriter up for membership in the Friars, inspired him with patriotic themes, hired him to write the occasional song, and in general demonstrated how a Broadway star conducted himself. Now Cohan bestowed one last, precious gift, a daring and canny producer named Sam Harris, who would shape Berlin's career in the theater as Max Winslow had shaped it on Tin Pan Alley.

CHAPTER 9

From the Music Box to the Round Table

Sam H. Harris was a good sixteen years older than Berlin, though the canny producer was never one to get overly fussy about numbers. He knew a balance sheet could get in the way of a hell of a good time—or a hell of a good show. If you didn't have the money, ran Harris's credo, borrow it. And if borrowing didn't work, gambling might; Sam liked to play the horses even more than he liked the theater.

He was a short man; in his youth, he had parted his dark hair in the center and worn a mustache of nearly handlebar proportions. When he got older, and his hairline receded, his droopy, bulbous nose, which seemed nearly to touch his upper lip, dominated his features.

He was as much a product of the Lower East Side streets as Berlin was—maybe more so. He spent his childhood in an apartment at Mulberry and Bayard streets, and he'd been on his own since the age of eleven; early in life he developed a fondness for plunging into entrepreneurial schemes of daunting complexity, and he knew how to come out the other end with everyone he worked with liking him and admiring his pluck. He'd progressed from laboring in his father's tailor shop to managing a towel supply concern, but he served his real apprenticeship at the racetrack and in the vaudeville theaters. At Christmas time he assembled unemployed actors for a limited-run show, and everyone involved appreciated his knack for making something out of next to nothing.

His gambling instincts led him away from the stage to the boxing ring, where he briefly prospered as a fight promoter best known for his handling of "Terrible" Terry McGovern, featherweight champion of the world in 1900. Harris's other interests later asserted themselves, and he persuaded his fighter first to go on the stage, and then to put up the money for a racehorse. Soon Harris was busy assembling a stable of racehorses and watching his bank account dwindle. The fact was that Harris was a hell of a lot better promoter than a handicapper. He once entered four horses in a seven-horse race, only to see them finish in the fourth, fifth, sixth, and seventh places.

In the fall of 1904, Harris attended an outing on Staten Island of a theatrical organization known as the Words and Music Club. There a friend introduced him to the fabled George M. Cohan. The two became friends while playing baseball with apples plucked from a nearby tree, and several weeks later Cohan explained he was preparing a new show entitled *Little Johnny Jones*. Would Harris care to come in as a partner? Harris was flush at the moment: fourteen horses in his stable and a hundred thousand dollars in the bank. He was delighted to make this new association. But several months later, when the show was ready to go into production, Harris was broke, and so was Cohan. In desperation they went to see a friend of Harris's in Philadelphia and prevailed on him to lend the two $25,000; Harris's friend gave them the money in cash, and the partners lugged a suitcase filled with bills back to New York.

Little Johnny Jones was a success, but more than that bound the two men. Cohan was married at the time to the actress Ethel Levey, but after they divorced in 1907, he married a former chorus girl named Agnes Nolan; that same year Harris married Agnes's sister Alice. Now related by marriage, the team of Cohan and Harris produced an outpouring of plays until a bitter actors' strike in 1919 sundered the partnership. Since Berlin had gradually inherited Cohan's mantle on Broadway, the songwriter naturally inherited Cohan's flamboyant producer, as well.

During a brief period when he was on his own, Harris had come into possession of a theater, which he named after himself—the Sam H. Harris Theater—and he persuaded Irving that owning a theater was the way to go. Harris now wanted to *build* one and (Irving was sure to love this part) call it the Irving Berlin Theater. Harris emphasized the benefits of owning a theater: they could hire whom they pleased and they could be sure the management wouldn't cheat. Even better, they wouldn't have to deal with the demands of the obstinate Shubert brothers.

Berlin hesitated. The prospect of having his own theater appealed to his urge to control all facets of his career, but it was a daunting prospect. He knew precious little about theater management, and he had his hands full running his music publishing company. Still, the big names on Broadway were identified with specific theaters: Kern and the Princess, Dillingham and the Globe, and Ziegfeld and the New Amsterdam. In comparison Berlin had been a nomad, and he persuaded himself that Harris was right; on Broadway having a theater of one's own was the ultimate status symbol.

The theater's name required thought, however. Irving was reluctant to put his own name on it; he wanted his songs to be his monument, not a chunk of real estate, no matter how glamorous. Eventually he devised a title, and when he happened on Harris at the Friars' Club, he eagerly said, "If you ever want to build a theater just for musical comedy, why not call it the Music Box?" It was a name in Berlin's image, suggesting intricate, intimate, carefully crafted songs. Harris assumed the theater would be called "Irving Berlin's Music Box": still catchy enough. But the songwriter demurred. "That would be too much Berlin."

Harris characteristically took that simple conversation as the seal of a business relationship and went looking for a site on which to build the Music Box. Berlin, busy with his publishing business, knew nothing of Harris's initiative. In the raw, early spring of 1920, the composer took a brief working vacation in Palm Beach, Florida. The day after he returned to New York, Harris called him at home. Although it was noon, Berlin was fast asleep, following his usual custom.

"Irving, you remember that Music Box idea of yours?" asked Harris.

"Will I ever forget it?" replied the groggy songwriter. Nearly a year had passed since they'd begun talking about the theater, but it had never seemed quite real, not until this phone conversation.

"Well, I have just bought a piece of land on Forty-fifth Street across the way from the Astor, and I called you up to tell that you can have your Music Box whenever you want it."

Berlin moved quickly to take advantage of the offer; at the time Harris spoke, the site, for which Harris had paid $330,000, was occupied by a row of brownstone boarding houses. These were soon razed. As plans for the theater began to materialize, the Broadway theater community sensed that something unusual was taking shape in its midst. Designed by C. Howard Crane, a prominent architect based in Detroit, Michigan, the Music Box featured a dignified façade combining aspects of both French Provincial and Italian Renaissance architecture. A loggia and four imposing columns soon loomed above 45th Street, flanked on either side by pavilions. The gray Indiana limestone used for the exterior gave the structure a welcome sense of gravity that effectively offset its whimsical, if symmetrical design.

But it was the interior that caused most of the talk, for it was as lavish as any on Broadway, yet restrained, as far from burlesque, vaudeville, and Tin Pan Alley as a legitimate theater could get without becoming a concert hall. Berlin's painstaking insistence on understated luxury was evident throughout. Containing seating for 1,010, the auditorium was neither as intimate as the Princess nor as cavernous as a Ziegfeld showcase. The auditorium's color scheme represented the essence of tastefulness, circa 1920: antique ivory alternating with soft green throughout. Berlin and Harris took some liberties with the conventional auditorium design of the era by eliminating the first-floor boxes (along with the potential revenue they represented) and enhancing the appeal of the second-floor boxes, which were accented by ornamental iron rails finished in a grayish silver hue. The boxes flowed smoothly into the proscenium, giving the entire auditorium a decidedly sleek finish, as well as superior sight lines. The unusual chandeliers especially attracted notice; they were made of Dutch brass and amber crystals.

This splendid setting was not achieved without some sacrifice backstage, where a shallow work space threatened to cramp scenery and actors alike. However, a new counterweight system for moving scenery and lights alleviated the problem to an extent. Berlin's perfectionism extended even to the most neglected part of most theaters, the dressing rooms. Usually tiny, dark, and draughty cells or improvisations of leftover backstage space, they were an indignity actors had long had to bear, but the Music Box dressing rooms broke with this ignominious tradition; they were as lavish and carefully lit as the rest of the theater.

All this luxury and tastefulness and worship of the canons of good taste added greatly to the theater's expense. Harris had exhausted his reservoir of funds, and therefore Berlin would have to find a way to pay for a theater that the entertainment world was quick to condemn as folly. At the Friars' Club, actors reveled in gossip about the costly extravagance involved in the building of the Music Box. Said a comedian named Sam Bernard, "It stinks from class," while another observer pointed out: "The boys think they're building a monument, but they're building a tombstone." Berlin himself, with his customary simplicity, admitted he was in a "tough spot."

It seemed that Berlin, who had always done everything as cheaply as he could, had finally lost control of his finances. Mistakes on the part of the architect added to the theater's expense. Its handsome lobby, for instance, lacked a crucial feature: a box office. Once Berlin and Harris discovered this oversight, they ordered the contractors to cut into the freshly applied plaster and make room for a discreet window.

In need of a quick infusion of cash, the songwriter turned to an old and influential friend, Joseph Schenck, now prospering as a film producer.

"Joe, I'm in trouble," Irving began.

Schenck knew where the songwriter was leading, or so he thought. "O.K. Who is she?" he asked.

"It's not a girl. A theater."

The two men quickly cut a deal; Schenck gave Berlin the money required to finish the Music Box, and in return the producer became a partner in its managing triumvirate. Berlin added a condition of his own to the arrangement; he would buy out Schenck as soon as possible. No one, not even Schenck, gave Berlin much of a chance to make good on that promise. It was now being said that even if the Music Box was sold out during the first five years of its existence, it would still lose money. And the demise of the Music Box could well bring the rest of Berlin's music business crashing down on top of it. On Broadway and in the Alley, theaters and publishers went bankrupt all

The S S *Rhynland*: the ship that brought the young Irving Berlin, then known as Israel Baline, and the rest of his family to the New World in September 1893. (Peabody Museum of Salem, Massachusetts)

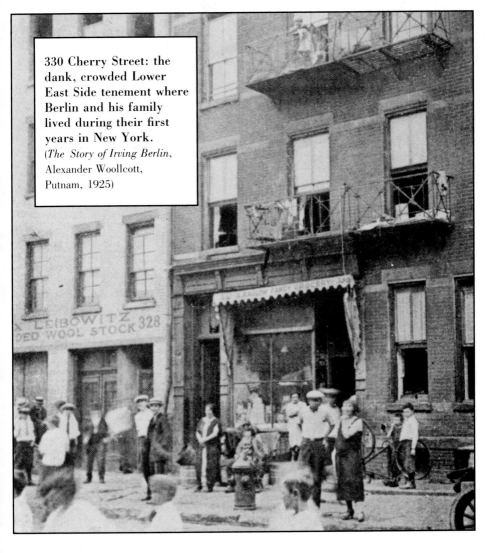

330 Cherry Street: the dank, crowded Lower East Side tenement where Berlin and his family lived during their first years in New York. (*The Story of Irving Berlin*, Alexander Woollcott, Putnam, 1925)

Lena Baline, the songwriter's mother. An outsider in America until the end of her days, she was baffled by her son's fame. (*The Story of Irving Berlin*, Alexander Woollcott, Putnam, 1925)

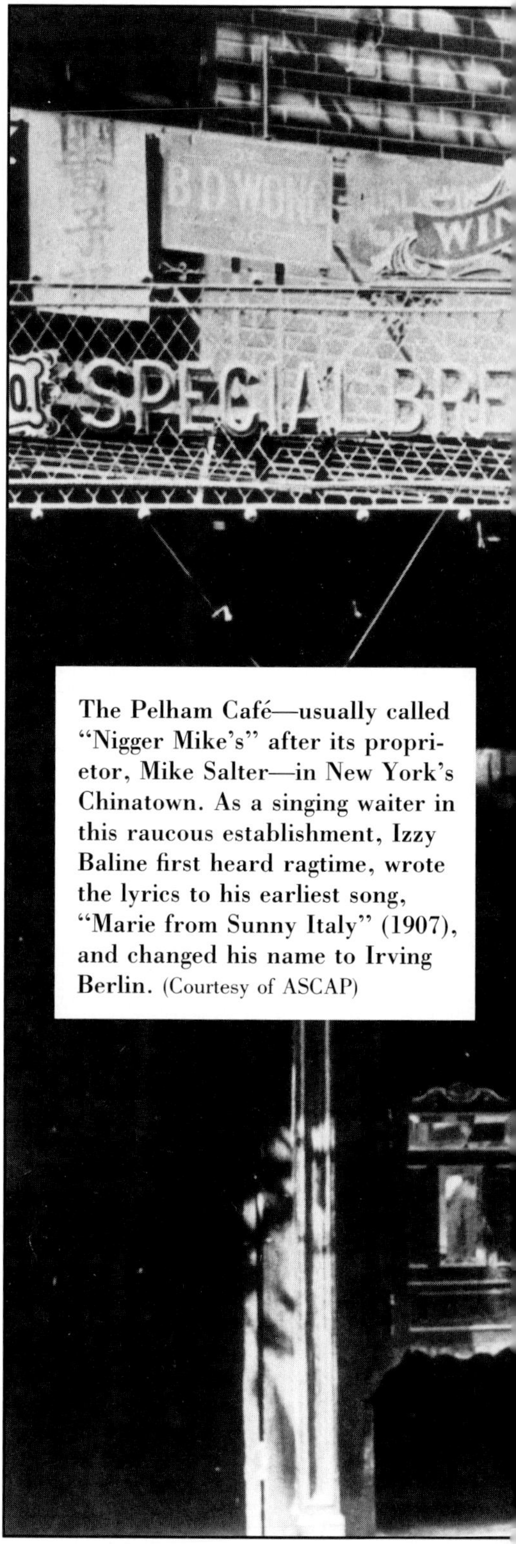

The Pelham Café—usually called "Nigger Mike's" after its proprietor, Mike Salter—in New York's Chinatown. As a singing waiter in this raucous establishment, Izzy Baline first heard ragtime, wrote the lyrics to his earliest song, "Marie from Sunny Italy" (1907), and changed his name to Irving Berlin. (Courtesy of ASCAP)

Israel Baline at age thirteen, near the time of his father's death. Soon after, he left home for good. (Courtesy of ASCAP)

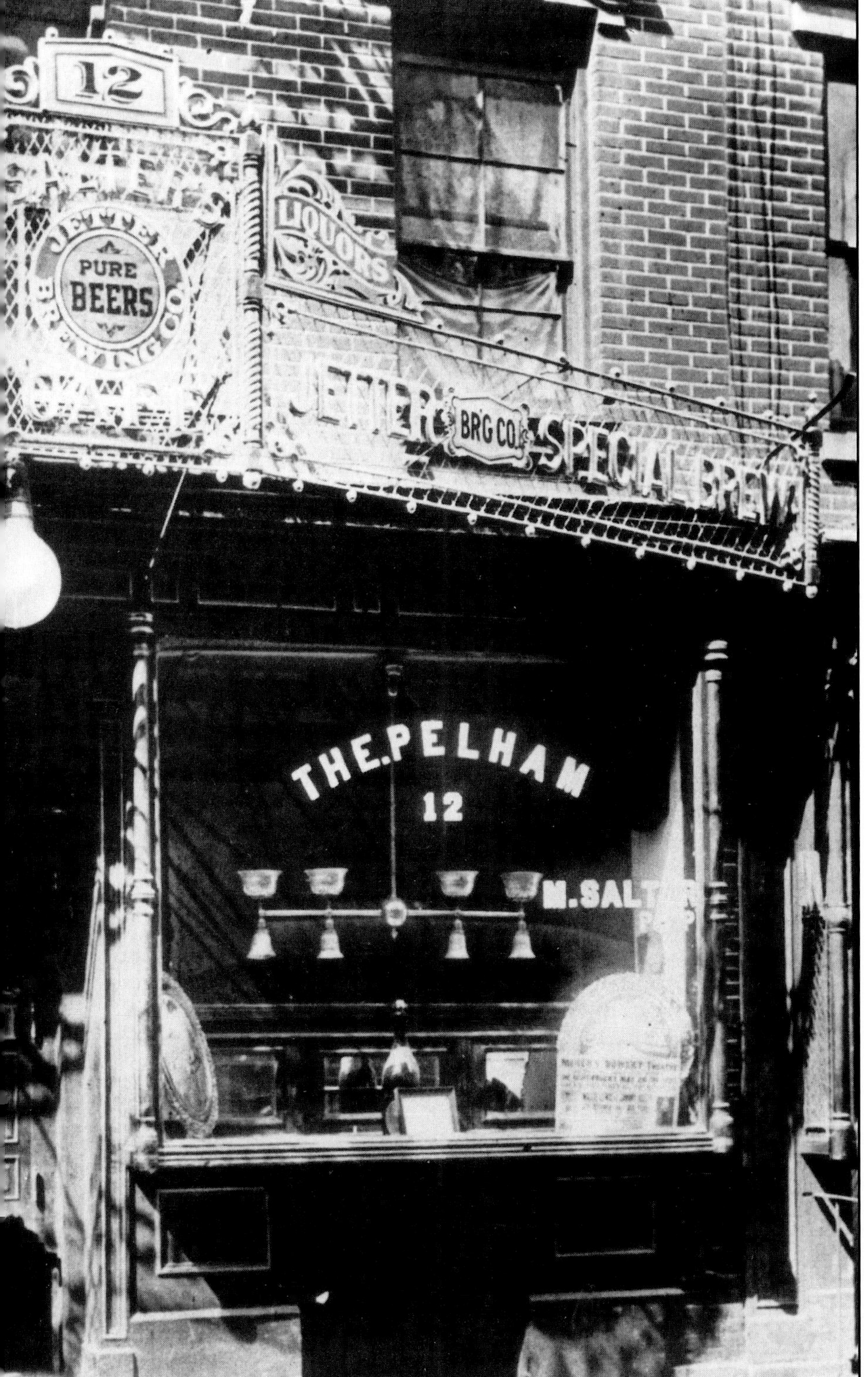
12
PURE BEERS
LIQUORS
BR'G CO.
SPECIAL BREW
THE.PELHAM
12

Berlin posing at a grand piano, on which he played only the black keys, at the time "Alexander's Ragtime Band" became a hit and established his reputation as a popular songwriter. (USC Library, Special Collections, Hearst Newspaper Collection)

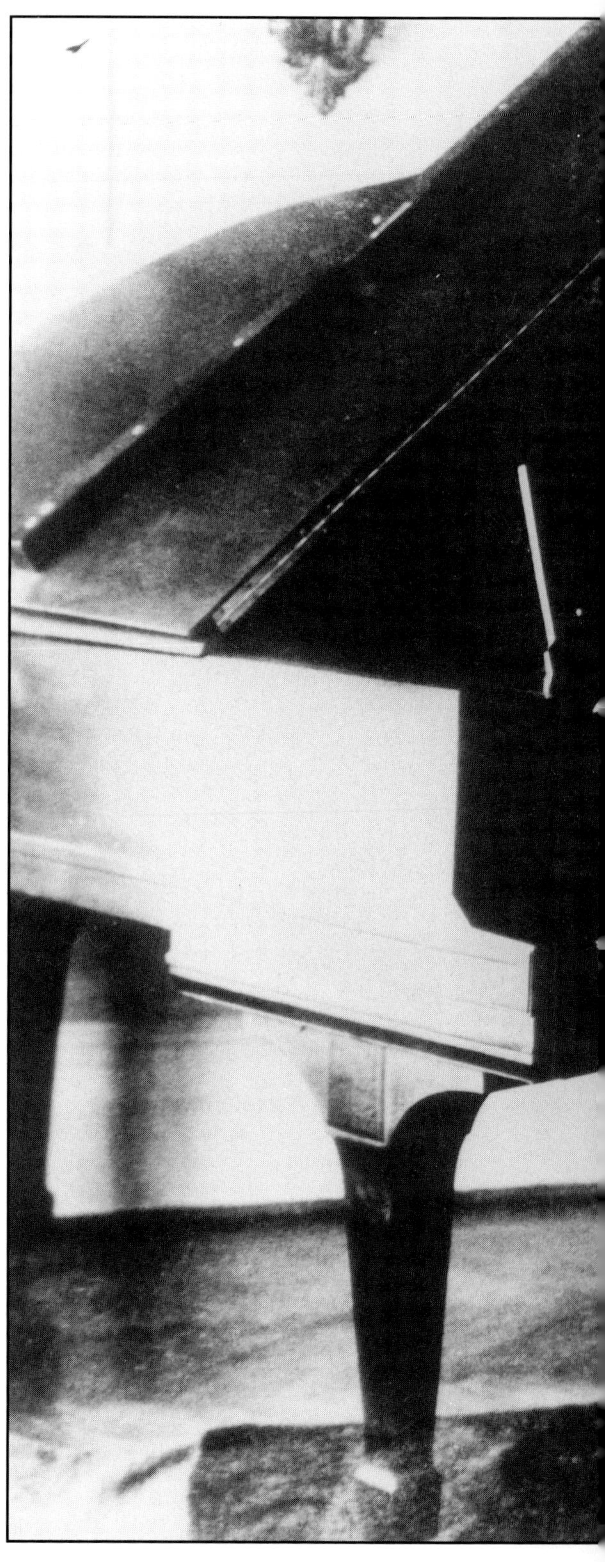

Berlin and Dorothy Goetz, his twenty-year-old first wife, on their honeymoon in Cuba, where she contracted a fatal case of typhoid fever. (Theatre Arts Collections. Harry Ransom Humanities Research Center. The University of Texas at Austin.)

ABOVE: **A 1916 actors' benefit drew leading members of the popular music establishment of the day, including Jerome Kern (far left), Oscar Hammerstein I (seated), John Philip Sousa (sixth from right), and Irving Berlin (far right).** (Courtesy of ASCAP)

FACING PAGE: **"This is the life." Berlin marches along Broadway in the annual Friars Parade, 1912.** (*The Story of Irving Berlin*, Alexander Woollcott, Putnam, 1925)

Icons of the age: Irene and Vernon Castle, the stars of Berlin's first Broadway show, *Watch Your Step*, in 1913, at the height of their fame and influence. (Billy Rose Theatre Collection, The New York Public Library at Lincoln Center. Astor, Lenox, and Tilden Foundations)

(Smithsonian Institution Photo No. 72–11195)

MADE EXPRESSLY FOR
IRVING BERLIN

One of the transposing pianos on which Berlin composed his hit songs and the label put on it by the manufacturer. The instrument now belongs to the Smithsonian Institution. Note lever beneath keyboard, used to shift keys. (Smithsonian Institution Photo No. 72–11193)

This is the life
Photo by

FACING PAGE: **Berlin as a soldier in the Great War—1918. A lifelong insomniac, his loathing of reveille at Camp Upton, Long Island, where he was stationed, inspired the perennial "Oh! How I Hate to Get Up in the Morning."** (Courtesy of ASCAP)

Berlin at the door of his theater, the Music Box, in 1925, flanked by two friends—the producer Sam Harris (left) and Jimmy Walker (right), the former Tin Pan Alley songwriter who was soon to be elected mayor of New York. (Courtesy of ASCAP)

The Music Box—built by Berlin, site of his famed Music Box Revues in the 1920s, and still in use today. Co-owner Sam Harris wanted the songwriter to name the opulent theater after himself, but Berlin refused. (*The Story of Irving Berlin*, Alexander Woollcott, Putnam, 1925)

Among the highlights of the first *Music Box Revue* (1921) were "The Eight Notes," chorus girls who became the notes of the scale and hovered about Berlin during his sole appearance onstage. (Courtesy of ASCAP)

Berlin's hit satirical revue, *As Thousands Cheer* (1933), rescued the songwriter's ailing reputation. Appearing in a sketch lampooning radio broadcasts of the Metropolitan Opera are (left to right) Leslie Adams, Helen Broderick, Clifton Webb, Marilyn Miller, and Jerome Cowan. (Billy Rose Theatre Collection, New York Public Library at Lincoln Center. Astor, Lenox, and Tilden Foundations)

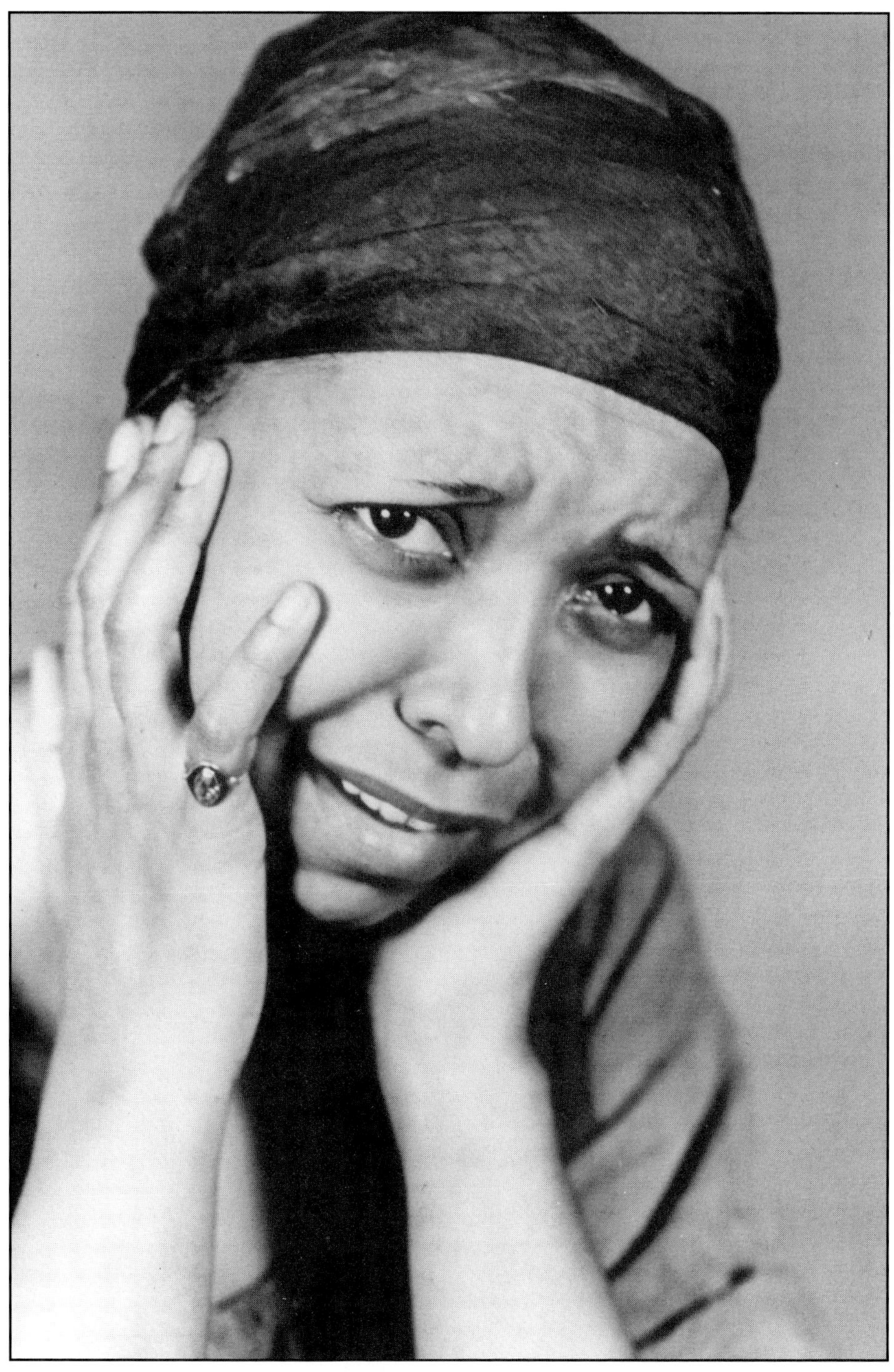

Ethel Waters singing "Supper Time," the lament of a wife and mother whose husband has been lynched, and the most daring song in Berlin's score for *As Thousands Cheer*. (Theatre Collection, Museum of the City of New York)

Interior of Harbor Hill, with Clarence Mackay's collection of armor on display; the armor now belongs to the Metropolitan Museum of Art. (Bryant Library Local History Collection, Roslyn, New York)

Harbor Hill, the Long Island estate where Ellin Mackay, Berlin's second wife, spent her youth. Designed by Stanford White at the turn of the century, the house cost $6 million dollars to construct, contained fifty rooms, and required a staff of 134 servants to maintain. (Bryant Library Local History Collection, Roslyn, New York)

Clarence Mackay surrounded by his three children: (left to right) Ellin, John, and Katherine. (Bryant Library Local History Collection, Roslyn, New York)

Newlyweds Irving Berlin and Ellin Mackay flee reporters, January 1926. (Bryant Library Local History Collection, Roslyn, New York)

Irving and Ellin sunbathing in Madeira during their honeymoon. . . . And with the eldest of their three daughters, Mary Ellin, in 1930. (The Illustrated London News Picture Library)

the time; it was an unpleasant but inevitable part of the business. In short, Berlin was taking the greatest risk of his career.

Adding to the pressure he felt was the oppressive knowledge that once the theater was finished, if it ever was, he would have to fill it with a revue. That had been the original point of the project, which tended to get overlooked by nearly everyone involved with it, except Berlin, on whose shoulders sole responsibility for the score and lyrics rested. Berlin being Berlin, no interpolations would be allowed. And once he completed the score for the *Music Box Revue of 1921*, he would immediately have to turn his attention to the score for the 1922 edition, and then 1923, and so on without respite. This was a tough spot, indeed, and with no prospect of his ever getting out of it. The Music Box would be the first and only Broadway theater ever built to accommodate the songs and scores of a single composer.

While Berlin fretted, the cost of building the Music Box mounted, eventually reaching $947,000, an astonishing sum for a theater of its modest size. And that was just for the building; the first edition of the revue would add another $188,000 to the cost: a similarly outlandish sum in a season when a fair-sized budget for a musical ran to around $50,000. A breakdown of the revue's budget reveals thousands of dollars spent on frivolous items such as rented jewelry and unspecified "missions abroad," in addition to more basic items:

Costumes	$66,783.09
Salaries & labor	29,020.54
Properties	22,614.71
Electrical supplies	10,701.85
Rental of pearls	10,115.00
Furniture	1,320.21
Orchestrations	2,269.63
Fares for missions abroad	2,170.00
Forfeited royalties	3,600.00
Office expenses	1,525.38
Miscellaneous	9,278.52
Scenery	28,214.09

In contrast to the anxious Berlin, the extroverted Harris had a better sense of how to handle the controversy surrounding the financial situation of the Music Box. Harris suspected that the widely publicized expense of putting up a million-dollar theater could only help generate interest. To attract still more attention, he prevailed on the songwriter himself to appear in the show; his brief appearance in *Yip! Yip! Yaphank* had been a highlight of that revue, and it made sense for Irving to try the same trick again. Berlin was not at all comfortable with the idea, clashing as it did with his notion of the omnipotent but invisible impresario who controlled every aspect of a production from a remote office, but he allowed himself to be persuaded.

Harris proceeded to issue a press release in which he pretended to chide Berlin:

> The young man who has puckered the lips of a nation into a whistling position, stimulated the hurdy-gurdy industry and increased the dividends of the graphophone and pianola companies is going to the stage. This does not mean that Mr. Berlin has written his last song. It simply means that he will have to get up a little earlier every day despite his predilection to slumber. Sam H. Harris announces that he [Berlin] will be a member of the company opening in The Music Box Revue. Mr. Berlin's present working day averages about twelve hours. And I felt that time was hanging heavily on his hands. Accordingly I offered him a job. I believe that everyone should work. Besides, he is a fine young fellow and I want to see him get ahead. When I expressed my feelings, he took the job.

Adding to the pressures on Berlin was a new concern: the proliferation of Broadway revues. Every other theater, it seemed, offered its brand of "follies" or "jollies" or what have you. The 1920 season alone saw the appearance of the *Broadway Brevities*, the *Greenwich Village Follies*, George White's *Scandals*, the *Frivolities*, the *Gaieties*—yearly editions all—along with coyly titled one-time-only revues such as *Tick-Tack-Toe* and *Hitchy-Koo*. And of course, the granddaddy of them all, Ziegfeld's *Follies*, returned to Broadway in June 1920, with a staggering eleven-dollar ticket price.

Even while his Music Box Theatre was rushed to completion, Berlin found the time to contribute several songs to the latest *Follies*, though he was far from dominating the evening as he had the year before. Despite the success of individual elements in this edition of the revue, a sense of obsolescence hung heavily over the spectacle. Ziegfeld's protégés (including Berlin) were gradually overtaking him, making for a cluttered field of song, spectacle, and chorus girls in various enticing states of undress. From Berlin's point of view the most alarming aspect of the situation was that many of these revues lost money during their New York runs. It was not until they went on tour, often with multiple companies filling theaters across the nation, that their producers managed to recoup their costs. The real demand for their frothy wares existed not on Broadway but out on the road, in Boston, Philadelphia, Chicago, Cleveland, and St. Louis—places that were starved for the latest import from New York. The Music Box revues would eventually tour also, but not so widely as their competition, for Berlin and Harris did not command the resources to manage multiple road companies. And the tours were not lucrative enough to make up for any shortfall in the New York run. But their revues did make obligatory stops in Chicago and even London, where Berlin's name, with or without ragtime, was a perennial draw.

By mid-September, the theater was finished, the box office installed, and the revue entered the final, frantic rehearsals under the direction of Hassard Short. The most elaborate scenic effect was a variation of Ziegfeld's celestial staircase: an elevator bearing sixteen chorus girls from a well hidden beneath the stage to the top of the proscenium. This elevator had become the talk of Broadway, for it was hideously expensive and notoriously fickle. But Short had made it an integral part of the revue's staging, and in time it was known as "Hassard Short's elevator." One afternoon, when Joe Schenck happened to enter the auditorium to observe a rehearsal, the device, fully loaded with its intended cargo, was stuck halfway between the stage and the ceiling, trapping the girls in midair.

"What's that?" Schenck asked Berlin, who cringed at the unexpected sight of his benefactor.

"Oh, that's just one of our little effects."

Schenck burst into laughter and slapped Irving on the back. "Never mind," he said. "It's no more than you or I would lose in a good stud game and never think of it again."

Such technical problems forced Berlin to delay the opening of the Music Box, originally scheduled for Monday, September 19, to Thursday, September 22. The pundits who had expected him to fail now felt even more sure of their predictions. The beleaguered cast took to calling the revue *The Harris and Berlin Worries of 1921*—a jest that eventually found its way into the script. And those were worrisome days for Irving. He was sleeping even less than usual. The weeks of draining his resources gave him a chronic case of indigestion, a symptom he took to calling his "songwriter's stomach." He grew rapier thin; the skin of his once boyishly puffy cheeks became taut, lines began to form around his eyes, his chin now jutted sharply, and he no longer looked younger than his thirty-two years. Always cautious, he made the rounds of doctors, searching for a physical cause for his inability to sleep and his loss of weight, but none was found.

On September 22, several hours before the curtain was due to rise, Berlin, outwardly contained but inwardly frantic, met Harris in a private suite in the Hotel Astor, near the Music Box. They were, as Berlin later recalled, two "very frightened men." They ate a light meal, speaking little. Occasionally they would rise from the table and walk to a window overlooking West 45th Street, look down, and study the exterior of the theater they had just finished building. As the sunlight faded and shadows began to engulf the Music Box, its amber sign flashed on, a beacon to the opening night crowd that would soon assemble and sit in judgment.

It was a warm, summerlike evening. It was now about eight P.M., the time specified on the tickets for the audience to begin taking their seats. Standing by the window, Harris and Berlin observed limousines pull up to the theater to discharge their wealthy, prominent, and carefully groomed passengers. Celebrities such as Douglas Fairbanks attracted a crowd of passersby, people who had no interest in the first *Music Box Revue* but who simply came to gawk at the scene. They overflowed the sidewalk and filled the street, blocking traffic until police arrived and pushed them aside; then they flowed into the doorways, and still more people leaned from windows to take in the sight of the crowd gathering in front of the new theater.

Finally Berlin and Harris realized they could delay no longer.

"Go to it, Irving," said Harris as they shook hands.

"Go to it, Sam."

Irving then dashed to the theater's dressing room to prepare himself for his onstage appearance. He wouldn't be singing tonight, but he had his lines to worry about. It was nearly half past eight, the theater was filled, and the show was about to start.

The first night of the *Music Box Revue of 1921* became one of the legendary Broadway openings of the decade. With its energy, irreverence, frivolity, and sensuality, the event incarnated the spirit of the Jazz Age, though jazz itself was one of the few trends Berlin hadn't incorporated into the revue. Next to it, Ziegfeld's *Follies* seemed sedate, even dated. "How could it miss?" wrote one critic about Berlin's great gamble. "One of the most beautiful theatres in the World; several well known authors [Frances Nordstrom, William Collier, Thomas J. Gray, and others] wrote the book; Irving Berlin contributed the score and lyrics; the cast reads like an Equity benefit performance. . . . How could it possibly miss?" As the comment suggests, the Music Box Theatre itself stole the show; the privileged members of the audience were so delighted to be there, basking in the glare of publicity, stupefied by the sense of occasion, that they proved to be a docile gathering.

Their attitude was typical of the times; throughout most of the 1920s, with rare and isolated exceptions, audiences and theatrical professionals alike anticipated nothing more of an evening in the theater than a rousing good time. People did not expect attending a performance to be strenuous, to change their lives, reflect social issues, or to satirize with too sharp an edge. The *Music Box Revue of 1921*, all fizz and froth, exemplified this code of behavior; it was the dramatic equivalent of a Prohibition-style nonalcoholic cocktail. It was, above all, exceedingly ingratiating. After having gambled all his financial resources on the theater, the last thing Berlin wanted to do was risk offending his patrons. No court jester quailing before an omnipotent, if complacent, monarch could have been more eager to please, more fearful of offending.

After the overture had quieted the audience, the first sketch, a send-up of bedroom farce, set the evening's jolly, knowing, and faintly ribald tone. The lights came up on an oversized bed in a lavish boudoir; here a pretty young woman (Florence Moore) was making bootleg cocktails for four male guests who were soon to arrive. After various phone calls announcing complications, the men are successively called upon to pose as her husband, and she eventually winds up hiding under the bed with her gentlemen guests. It will give an idea of the thinness of the show's material that this scene would later be considered the comic high point of the evening.

The next scene, featuring a popular singer named Wilda Bennett, proved to be equally reassuring, for it was a Ziegfeld-style tour de force of staging and cheesecake set against a giant black iridescent fan that filled the stage. "The climax to this episode," an enthralled reviewer wrote, "came when Miss Bennett and the girls who had marched down from the sticks of the fan were individually lifted into the air until each could pose as part of the color scheme of decoration."

This scene and three others consumed the lion's share of the show's outsized budget; each relied on Hassard Short's talent for filling a stage from one end of the proscenium to the other. The "Dining Out" sketch, for instance, featured chorus girls costumed as giant portions of food and even place settings.

Later, Berlin himself appeared onstage, his unruly black hair slicked to a fare-thee-well, surrounded by demure chorus girls called the "Eight Notes." They asked him the question that was on everyone's mind: how does Irving Berlin write a song? But this was no forum for a serious reply. Irving simply made light of his ability. He did not, as the audience might have expected, introduce a hit song himself, as he had in past revues. He was but one more splendid stage effect on display, along with the elevators and the costumes and chorus girls' legs.

The most striking of all the tableaux was titled "The Legend of the Pearls." (It was for this scene that Berlin and Harris had expended over $10,000 to obtain the necessary jewelry.) As Wilda Bennett sang, chorus girls dressed as giant pearls paraded across the stage before the astonished and gratified audience. Though it made little sense, the spectacle gradually overwhelmed and numbed the senses. This worship of luxury was precisely what the audience had wished to see.

Betwixt and between the comedy skits and the showstopping, I-can't-believe-what-I'm-seeing pageants, Berlin managed to work in two songs that would become enduring hits. "Everybody Step" was a cheerful, syncopated tune made to order for the high-pitched, girlish warbling of the three young Brox Sisters. Far more problematic was "Say It With Music," which Berlin hoped would emerge as the theme song of the entire revue. This particular song marked at least the third time he had cloned his then favorite tune, "A Pretty Girl Is Like a Melody"—the second instance being the previous year's "The Girls of My Dreams." Fortunately, Irving could copy from himself with impunity. This song, perhaps the most celebrated of all Berlin's *Music Box Revue* efforts, did not go over well in its initial exposure. "We had a terrible time trying to get applause," Berlin remembered. "I used to stand in the back of the house with Hassard Short and say, 'How can you like this?' And it was sung by Joe Santley, a great performer, and Wilda Bennett, a wonderful star and singer." Part of the reason for the song's poor reception can be laid to the relatively simple staging it received. Berlin had wanted the song to receive the attention he believed it deserved, but the audience, apparently, was more interested in spectacle.

Padded with comedy sketches, the show ran for three-and-a-half hours, and by the time the flushed and tired audience began to applaud the labors of Harris, Berlin, and company, it was midnight. For Berlin, however, the real test of the revue was just beginning; the enthusiasm of the first-night crowd was heartening, but reviews and subsequent ticket sales would tell the fate of both the revue and the theater housing it.

Audience demand for seats would have to be strong, for the show was as expensive to maintain as it had been to mount. The cost of keeping it on the boards came to over $19,000 each week. Berlin and Harris believed they would be able to support the cost because the notices were uniformly encouraging. " 'MUSIC BOX REVUE'—NEW BERLIN SHOW IS STAGE REVELATION" announced the influential *New York Clipper*. Other papers reinforced this message: "MUSIC BOX GETS UNDER WAY TO A FLYING START—IRVING BERLIN'S REVUE HAS DASH AND SPARKLE."

And with somewhat less accuracy, though with equal enthusiasm:

DAINTY PLAYHOUSETTE HAS
UPROARIOUS SHOW.

With Irving Berlin's Melodies,
Willie Collier's and Sam Bernard's Comedy
and Sam Harris' Direction
There's Nothing More To Be Desired.

The most significant review—in terms of its effect on both the show's fortunes and Berlin's life over the next several years—came from the typewriter of the *Times* drama critic, Alexander Woollcott, who was by now a Broadway celebrity in his own right. Within hours of the curtain's ringing down on the revue, his acclaim was on newsstands and doorsteps throughout the city. "The Music Box was opened last evening before a palpitant audience and proved to be a treasure chest out of which the conjurers pulled all manner of gay tunes and brilliant trappings and funny clowns and nimble dancers," he wrote in characteristically overheated prose. "Its bewildering contents confirmed the dark suspicion that Sam H. Harris and Irving Berlin have gone quite mad," by which Woollcott, in his persona as a jovial bully, meant that "they have builded them a playhouse in West Forty-fifth Street that is a thing of beauty in itself, and then crowded its stage with such a sumptuous and bespangled revue as cannot possibly earn them anything more substantial than the heart-warming satisfaction of having produced it all."

Despite these effusions, Woollcott entertained grave doubts about the production itself. He savaged the comic routines and had relatively little to say on the all-important subject of Berlin's songs, which, after all, were the crucial element in the revue. Still, there was a certain tune that had managed to overcome his resistance. "[Berlin] has written only one real song," Woollcott maintained—and how that barb, hidden though it was in a bower of praise, must have stung the composer. "It is called 'Say It With Music,' and by February you will have heard it so often that you will gladly shoot at sunrise any one who so much as hums it in your hearing."

The revue ran for forty-one weeks, during which time it reaped an average weekly gross revenue of $27,788, making for a profit of nearly $9,000, and a total for the entire run of almost $370,000. Berlin made additional money from the publishing arm of his business, which issued sheet music of the songs from the score of this and subsequent Music Box revues in a standard format.

Berlin now ran a vertically integrated machine for dispensing songs, managing every aspect from composition to theatrical presentation. Irving himself was given to saying that his best music had been composed during the era of the Music Box revues, but then he was always most enthusiastic about whatever occupied his time and energy at the moment. In fact, he was stretching himself dangerously thin; he had much in common with the circus performer who starts an ever-growing number of plates spinning on narrow poles and is then forced to divide his attention until the neglected plates come crashing down around his ears. The mania for control and the easy money to which Harris had access put Berlin in an inherently unstable position, for he had to devise an entirely new revue for his Music Box *every year.* The weeks were short, summer was a lost season on Broadway, and once a revue opened in the fall, it was time for him to start thinking and composing and hiring for next year's production.

Nor did mounting the productions grow easier with time. Each year the newest edition of the *Music Box Revue* teetered on the brink of chaos. Whenever the opening was postponed by even a day, the production's cost increased by $8,000. Two weeks' delay, and the prospect of that year's revue earning a profit would vanish.

Yet to Sam Harris—and especially to Berlin, now coming into his maturity at a time when the nation was embarked on an apparently endless binge of frivolity (reflected and encouraged by Broadway)—anything seemed possible. For a man who'd risen from immigrant to singing waiter to impresario, limits did not apply—at least not for now. The plates would spin and spin—a dazzling sight to behold.

▪ ▪ ▪

To signify his new, enhanced status, Berlin finally moved out of the Riverside Drive apartment where Dorothy had died in 1912 after only five months of marriage. He moved downtown, closer to the action, to a building at 29 West 46th Street. He did not simply rent an apartment, he bought the entire building, including the grocery store occupying the ground floor. The songwriter now had several tenants to worry about: the family running the store as well as five single dwellers. Despite the complication, the move made sense, for his new home was but a few minutes' walk from his precious Music Box.

He lavished attention on the decor of his duplex penthouse, which turned out to be even more striking than his previous apartment. One astonished party of visitors, the writing team of Guy Bolton and P. G. Wodehouse, described it in terms of a magical kingdom:

> There was a broad corridor that descended in a series of steps, each step an eight foot square platform, to the big living room that faced the street. Molded glass panels by Lalique lighted this handsome passage. These were fringed with big potted plants, and standing in front of two of them were tall wooden stands on which stood a pair of brilliant-hued toucans. They added the final touch of magnificence. . . .

Wodehouse and Bolton were not casual visitors. At this time, the spring of 1922, they were eager to harness the talents and reputation of this kingdom's renowned inhabitant, whom they found every bit as exotic and unexpected as his surroundings. They were plotting to transfer their skills from the tiny Princess, where they had collaborated with Jerome Kern, to the larger (and suddenly more prestigious) Music Box Theatre. So important was the issue to "Plum," as everyone called Pelham Wodehouse, that he was willing to lay aside his newly successful series of droll stories about an English butler named Jeeves to pursue the project.

Berlin's producer, Sam Harris, was amenable to the idea. Bolton and Plum were to write the book and Berlin the score for a new musical called *Sitting Pretty*. It promised to be a typical Wodehouse-Bolton knockabout affair, centering on the mixed up marriages of two sisters in an orphan asylum.

As the book began to take shape, Wodehouse and Bolton went to meet Berlin in the composer's new penthouse. Although they did not suspect it, the composer, whom they idolized, was more in awe of them than they were of him. These writers gave off a flinty aura of country club sophistication as if born to it, while Berlin was still in the process of laboriously acquiring his. He could be cordial with the likes of a Pelham Grenville Wodehouse, but never at ease; for that he needed a Sam Harris, a Max Winslow, someone who knew what it had been like down on the Lower East Side and Cherry Street, and who realized why Berlin had worked as hard as he had to get out of the old neighborhood.

After dinner Irving decided to show off his toucans to his guests; he extended his hand toward one, "which immediately proceeded to strike like an offended rattlesnake," according to the writers, "its terrifying bill missing the hand by the fraction of an inch."

"I'd be a bit more distant with those fowls if I were you. They're liable to take your finger off," Wodehouse recalled himself saying.

Berlin laughed and attempted to make a joke at his own expense. "And it might be the one I play the piano with." He figured that Wodehouse, like most of the English, assumed that he, Berlin, could play the piano with just one finger—the bitter legacy of a misunderstanding spread by the English press nearly a decade before. To demonstrate that he did know his way around a keyboard, Berlin turned to his trick piano and performed several songs intended for the score of *Sitting Pretty*. Here was Berlin the showman at work, the relentless, irresistible plugger of his own tunes. But when the show ended, he became Berlin, the wily businessman.

"This *Sitting Pretty* book," he said. "I've read it, and I think it's darned good. But . . ."

"But?" asked the writers.

Irving was concerned about the casting of the show. He had been hoping that a sensationally popular vaudeville team, the Duncan sisters, would star. In fact, he was hard pressed to imagine anyone else in the leading roles.

"Well, as I figure it out, it's no use without the Duncans," he explained. "The high spots come when the sisters, the rich one and the poor one, meet and do numbers together. With the Duncans these'll be smashes. We know what those babies can do with a number when they work it together. But without the Duncans . . ."

The discussion turned to the possibility of staging the show with other sister teams, but none appealed to Berlin. By the end of the evening, Wodehouse and Bolton realized that Berlin's insecurities about casting had gotten the better of him.

"Irving doesn't mean to write that score till he's sure we've got the Duncans," said Bolton to a dispirited Plum as they rode the building's tiny elevator to the street. "One show more or less means nothing to that bird. He can always make another million or so whenever he feels like it. Lucky devil!"

A million or so? It was true that he earned around $160,000 a year from his songwriting in the early 1920s, but most of his money was tied up in his music publishing business and the Music Box Theatre. The expense of maintaining those enterprises was great, and they could go under at any point. It happened on Broadway so frequently that bankruptcy sometimes seemed to be the logical outcome of success. He was not, at bottom, a gambler like Sam Harris. Concluding that *Sitting Pretty* without the Duncan sisters was simply too much of a gamble, he pulled out.

After Berlin had wriggled free of their grasp, Wodehouse and Bolton returned to their original partner, Jerry Kern, who agreed to compose the score for *Sitting Pretty*. The show eventually opened in the spring of 1924, *sans* Duncan Sisters. As Berlin had feared, it died a lingering death.

Having freed himself from the snares of this show, Berlin returned to his private musical obsession, opera. This time the impulse came from the reigning queen of the opera scene in Chicago, Mary Garden. Her emissary, Muriel Draper, asked herself, "Why we shouldn't have an American opera dealing with skyscrapers and bad whisky," and decided she would commission Irving Berlin to distill one.

Although he yearned to prove himself as a serious composer of opera, he approached the project with the flair of a Broadway impresario, giving an exclusive interview to the New York *Sun*. "JAZZ GRAND OPERA PROMISED BY BERLIN" ran the headline, which continued, "Plans Tentative, but Composer Is Determined." To the few who recalled Berlin's strident assertions ten years before that he was going to compose a great *ragtime* opera, this grandiose announcement had an uncomfortably familiar ring. "I am determined to do this as a serious composition," he announced, "and as soon as my more commercial undertakings are completed I mean to get at it, for it will take a lot of undivided time."

He proceeded to describe some of the elements of what the *Sun*'s correspondent termed the composer's "magnum opus," and to Miss Draper's dismay, it had little to do with "skyscrapers and bad whisky": "It is possible the scenes may be laid down South during the Civil

War, where sentiment in America seems naturally to turn. Whenever we write a song about the South, there is something romantic about it, even if the subject is in reality a mud hole." By giving his opera an historical setting, Irving figured, jazz would acquire respectability. "Whenever people hear of jazz they think of shaking shoulders," he complained. "I am convinced that eventually the great American opera will be written in that form. . . . I intend to do such a work, even if [I] have to produce it myself at the Music Box."

In the end, Berlin and his backers failed to agree on the contents of the opera, and the magnum opus never came to fruition. About one matter, however, he proved prophetic: what many consider to be the great American folk opera would employ a good deal of jazz and Black-influenced music. The work, still thirteen years in the future, would not be staged at the Music Box, nor would it be composed by Berlin. That particular laurel, of course, would go to Irving's energetic young admirer, George Gershwin, whose score for *Porgy and Bess* was performed before an audience for the first time on the evening of October 10, 1935, at the Alvin Theatre. By then Berlin would have forgotten his scheme concerning an opera of any kind—ceased to talk about it with enthusiastic journalists and ceased to imagine himself as anything other than what he was, the quintessential popular American songwriter.

▪ ▪ ▪

When he was not at the Music Box on West 45th Street or at home on West 46th Street, Berlin spent considerable time nearby, at the Algonquin Hotel, located on West 44th Street. Here he became a member of the celebrated (and self-celebrating) Round Table: a loose agglomeration of about fifty theater people, journalists, and artists who met regularly for lunch in the hotel's comfortable dining room, exchanged gossip, and coined and endlessly repeated witticisms. Most of them were young and vulnerable, veterans of the Great War who were struggling to gain a foothold in a chaotic world; their response was to form their own society, with its own standards. By the time Irving joined the group, in 1922, it had already been in existence for three years, under the informal guidance of Alexander Woollcott, whose personality it reflected. It was convivial, disorganized, bitchy, and even to many of its members, a tiresome but addictive institution. Indeed, some of the men, especially Woollcott, found their weekends without Round Table companionship so tedious that they started an offshoot, the Thanatopsis Literary and Inside Straight Club, which convened on Saturday afternoon to play cards and often did not break up until Monday morning.

Berlin was too self-contained and shy to become part of the Round Table's inner circle. In addition to Woollcott, who jealously guarded the primacy of his position, the insiders included Robert Sherwood, Marc Connelly, George S. Kaufman, and Heywood Broun—all playwrights; Dorothy Parker, Franklin P. Adams (better known as F.P.A.), Robert Benchley, Ring Lardner, Herbert Bayard Swope, and Donald Ogden Stewart—among the journalists and critics in attendance; as well as participants who were one of kind: Tallulah Bankhead; Harpo Marx; Jascha Heifetz; the actress Ruth Gordon; the exceedingly popular novelist Edna Ferber; Alice Duer Miller, a society figure as well as a novelist; the artist Neysa McMein; and an editor named Harold Ross, whose plan to start a magazine called *The New Yorker* struck Woollcott as highly implausible.

Despite Irving's position on the periphery, this society came to exert a profound influence over him. By 1925 both his career and his social life centered around its members. The Round Table's vivacious, ambitious regulars were more than a group of colleagues for Irving, they were a surrogate family—and a noisy, rambunctious family at that, complete with rivalries and gossip and secret alliances and betrayals. "Their standards were high," Ferber wrote of the Round Table's members, "their vocabulary fluent, fresh, astringent, and very, very, tough. . . . Casual, incisive, they had a terrible integrity about their work and a boundless ambition."

The first real signs of the Round Table's hold on Irving appeared in the spring of 1922. Shortly after joining the association, he participated in a peculiar Round Table theatrical production inspired by an internationally famous revue entitled *Chauve Souris*. On a Sunday night, when the revue's own 49th Street Theater was dark, the Round Tablers rented it and presented their version, a travesty called *No Sirree*. The public was invited, and *The New York Times* rose to the bait and reviewed the affair, though with a distinct lack of enthusiasm.

No Sirree consisted of one curiosity after another: Robert Sherwood singing Dorothy Parker's "Everlastin' Ingenue Blues," a chorus line populated by Tallulah Bankhead and Helen Hayes, and a rambling comic monologue by Robert Benchley called "The Treasurer's Report." The music accompanying these bizarre sights had been composed by the critic and composer Deems Taylor and featured offstage fiddling by Jascha Heifetz.

Berlin had the honor of conducting the orchestra, but he was too much of a theater professional not to indulge in a bit of talent scouting on the side. One of the few successful elements of the show happened to be Benchley's sly impersonation of a bumbling assistant treasurer who, having been called upon to give a report, suddenly finds himself enraptured by the sound of his own words. Bentley's stage persona, that of a gentle, befuddled middle-aged businessman, endowed the routine with wit and credibility.

Immediately after the show, Berlin and Sam Harris approached Benchley with an offer that the journalist claimed changed the course of his life. The partners found Benchley's monologue so amusing that they wanted to feature it in the next edition of the *Music Box Revue*. Benchley was astonished and unprepared, for his monologue had been entirely improvised. Furthermore, as a drama critic, he harbored doubts about the propriety of performing on Broadway. As a polite way of refusing Harris's and Berlin's request, Benchley named a ridiculously high fee for his services: five hundred dollars a week.

After briefly mulling over the terms, Harris replied, "Well, for five hundred dollars a week you'd better be awfully good." Thus Benchley, in spite of himself, became a member of the *Music Box Revue*'s elite company.

Having survived the rite of passage represented by *No Siree*, Irving found himself taken up by an extended Round Table set. The Round Table, did not, he discovered, exist solely at the Algonquin Hotel. Many members regularly convened at the lavish estate of Herbert Bayard Swope, with whom Irving renewed his friendship.

When they had first met, in 1905, Irving was still Izzy Baline, a singing waiter at Nigger Mike's, and Swope a young reporter covering the visit of Prince Louis Battenburg. Since then, Swope, adept at courting and manipulating the wealthy and powerful, had risen through the ranks of journalism, winning a Pulitzer Prize for war coverage in 1917, to become the executive editor of Ralph Pulitzer's *World.* He was more than influential, he was famous; his picture had been on the cover of *Time.* His bluff, gregarious manner invariably commanded respect. In 1928 he would retire from the *World*, cash in his stake in the newspaper for $6 million, and devote himself to financial and social pursuits.

The best-known chronicler of Long Island society, F. Scott Fitzgerald, is thought to have used Swope's estate on Great Neck, Long Island, as a prototype for the home of the enigmatic Jay Gatsby, the protagonist of his most accomplished novel, and there was more than a little of Gatsby in Swope. Both the real individual and the fictional character, while sociable enough, had an aura of mystery; both tended to conceal their origins. Though most people, including his children, were not aware of it, Swope was Jewish. And both Gatsby and Swope had a love of the endless, free-form party that seemed to spring up out of nowhere, like a summer storm: the emblem of the Jazz Age. The extravagant Swope would serve tea at six, dinner at midnight, supper at three o'clock in the morning, and champagne nearly all the time. With two shifts of servants attending to his guests 'round the clock, parties lasted for days on end.

Many of Swope's illustrious guests were devoted to croquet, which they played on their host's vast lawn. Their version of the game employed unusually heavy balls and steel-bound mallets supplied by the sporting goods concern of Abercrombie & Fitch. They played for hours, and when nightfall came, they illuminated the field with the headlights of their cars.

Irving, along with other Round Table members, frequently attended Swope's summer revels. The fascination, for many of the show business and literary people like Berlin, was mixing with Long Island society. Swope's hospitality afforded them entrée to exclusive parties, estates, golf courses—even private airfields. Berlin was one of the few Round Table members who was actually as wealthy as the socialites, but his profession and Cherry Street accent marked him as one of the entertainers rather than the entertained.

Though out of his element in the green expanses of Great Neck, he was at home at the other outpost of the Round Table: the West

57th Street studio of Neysa McMein. She was attractive enough to have caught the eye of Charlie Chaplin, who had been her lover. She befriended Irving, and while the two were close, their relationship proved to be yet another instance of the unconsummated liaisons he was given to forming. She was the same physical type to which he had been attracted on occasion in the past: tall and athletic looking, with striking red hair. "Beautiful, grave, and slightly soiled," was Woollcott's description of her.

Where Swope catered to the society aspirations of the Round Table, Neysa appealed to its Bohemian side. As Marjorie Moran McMein back in her hometown of Quincy, Illinois, she had changed her name to Neysa on the advice of a numerologist and proceeded to make her way to New York as a commercial artist. Eventually she became a sought-after illustrator for fashionable magazines such as *McCall's*, *Collier's* and the *Saturday Evening Post*, commanding as much as $2,500 for her covers.

Her studio became a salon where anyone from Berlin to Dorothy Parker and H. G. Wells could be found, usually drinking champagne while Neysa toiled at her easel. "A bleak, high-ceilinged room, furnished by the process of haphazard accumulation," said Woollcott of the place. "The population is as wildly variegated. Over at the piano Jascha Heifetz and Arthur Samuels may be trying to find what four hands can do in the syncopation of a composition never thus desecrated before. Irving Berlin is encouraging them. Squatted uncomfortably around an ottoman, Franklin P. Adams, Marc Connelly, and Dorothy Parker will be playing cold hands to see who will buy dinner that evening. . . . Chaplin or Chaliapin, Alice Duer Miller or Wild Bill Donovan, Father Duffy or Mary Pickford—any or all of them may be there."

Woollcott's description was an accurate one. Irving did often hover over Neysa's piano writing songs. One evening in November 1923, Parker and McMein gave a birthday party for another Round Table member, Donald Ogden Stewart. Irving came, hiding two clinking bottles of champagne under his coat. "While we all sat around, celebrating and drinking the champange," Stewart recalled, "Irving went to the piano and kept on playing the first part of a song he had written. It was called, 'What'll I Do?' But he hadn't been able to finish it. He played the part he had over and over, and we all liked it—but the best part of the evening was that after Irving had had enough of his champagne, he was finally able to finish the song that night." The song, telling of a bittersweet loneliness that no amount of partying and champagne could alleviate, subsequently became an important hit.

Berlin's penchant for composing when surrounded by friends had unforeseen but entirely fortunate consequences for him. After the opening of the *Music Box Revue*'s second edition, he was sued for plagiarizing "Pack Up Your Sins and Go to the Devil," the spirited song that concluded the show. Of all the tunes in the show, it was perhaps the least likely to have been plagiarized, for it was one of Berlin's distinctive two-part melodies (though this time it pitted rhythm against rhythm). The Round Table rallied to his side. When the matter came to trial, Jascha Heifetz, Neysa McMein, and the actress Lenore Ulric testified they had witnessed their friend laboring on this song nine months before the show opened, thus ruling out the possibility that he had plagiarized a melody composed at a later date. Backed by this impressive testimony, the songwriter was naturally acquitted.

Though membership in the Round Table bestowed many benefits on Irving, it consisted of more than an endless diet of witticisms, champagne, and croquet. A complex pathology afflicted its members. Many had drinking problems of varying degrees of seriousness; still others were beset by compulsive gambling. Hypochondriacal ailments also tormented Round Table members, including Irving, and they shared a physician who built a prosperous trade on treating them. Most insidious of all was the Round Table's tendency to hold its members in a perpetual adolescence, in which family obligations or significant relationships outside its charmed circle fell victim to loyalty to the Round Table's other members.

No one exemplified the Round Table's dark side—the relentless self-promotion, gambling, and hypochondria—better than its guiding spirit, Alexander Woollcott. Though only in his midthirties, he was already a pompous character of the first order. Best remembered for his vivid performance as Sheridan Whiteside in *The Man Who Came to Dinner* (written by that other Round Table member, George S. Kaufman, in collaboration with Moss Hart), Woollcott simply played himself onstage. Yet Woollcott's reputation as a blowhard and bully was deceptive. He was the grandson of the leader of a well-known but impecunious "cooperative society," or intellectual commune, known as the Phalanx, where he spent his earliest years. Later, at Hamilton College, he quickly distinguished himself, earning a Phi Beta Kappa key in his junior year. His father was often absent in his youth, and there is considerable evidence to suggest that Woollcott was confused about his sexuality. As a young man he'd posed for a photograph in which he wore the clothing of a Victorian matron. He coined two nicknames for himself, "Pretty," and "She-Ancient," and he encouraged his friends to employ them. A prodigious eater, he weighed over 250 pounds, and often wore a scarlet-lined cape. By inclination a homosexual who was afraid to act on his impulses, he was perpetually starved for affection, though his friendship, as Kaufman made clear in his play, could be as much of a trial as a boon. He regularly taunted Kaufman with the epithet "Christ Killer."

Not that Woollcott would ever use such language in front of Irving; the songwriter's gentle yet reserved demeanor simply didn't allow for such rough banter. But Woollcott was nonetheless fascinated by Irving Berlin as an immigrant, Jew, and cantor's son. The critic, who made his living by rushing to judgment, was convinced that these three elements were largely responsible for Berlin's eminence as a songwriter. He thought he detected morose "Jewish" strains in Berlin's ballads, and he was certain that Irving's tendency to be melancholy and aloof was behavior typical of the oppressed Russian Jew. The better he came to know Berlin, the more convinced he was that at the core of this elusive songwriter's being and talent lay his exotic Jewishness.

Thus Woollcott wrote of his sense of wonder concerning the mysterious means by which Berlin "transmuted into music the jumbled sounds of his life—the wash of the river against the blackened piers, the alarums of the street cars, . . . the polyglot hubbub of the curbs and doorsteps of his own East Side, . . . the chants in the synagogues, the whines and squeals of Chinatown, the clink of glass and the crack of revolvers in saloons along the Bowery, [and] above all the plaintive race note, the wail of his sorrowing tribe, the lamentation of a people harried and self-pitying since time out of mind."

By the time Woollcott began his scrutiny of Berlin, the critic was beginning to feel restless with his calling. He had made his name even before the Great War as the *Times'* drama critic, and in 1922 he abruptly left the paper for a rapid succession of posts as a drama critic for the *Sun*, Swope's *World*, and the *Herald*, at an ever-increasing salary, accompanied by an ever-increasing discontent with the critic's trade. He was by nature a dilettante, perpetually intrigued by whatever someone else happened to be doing. In this spirit of generous meddling, he decided to write the first biography of his friend Irving Berlin.

Of course, some of the most significant, rewarding, and difficult episodes of Berlin's career lay well in the future, far beyond the scope of the idiosyncratic book Wollcott was planning. "It is hard to write the biography of a man who is only thirty-six years old as you reach your final chapter," Woollcott would confess. If it seemed early in the day for an evaluation of Irving's career and life, he was, by show business standards, embarking on middle age, and a generation had come to maturity listening to his songs, which faithfully mirrored their attitudes and sentiments.

Furthermore, Berlin had a tireless appeal for the press, so much so that his socializing with journalists amounted to a career in itself. The 1920s was the age in which public relations—the calculated enhancement of a personal image with a view to selling a product—was born. And Berlin played the modern public relations game as skillfully as any other major public figure. He was as meticulous in this pursuit as he was about his songwriting, and he courted and manipulated the press with the finesse of a Tammany Hall politician.

So adept was Berlin at cultivating the trade columnists, reporters, and editors—notably Swope, Woollcott, and *Variety*'s Sime Silverman—that he would have made a formidable elected official, had he been so inclined. In many ways he already *was* a politician, one who owed his position to sheet music sales rather than votes; but the principle was the same: he placed his message before the public, and the public in turn responded. He had his constituency, which needed constant cultivation. The one thing he must never do was to disappoint or defeat their expectations of him—and that was the one thing he never did, until his string of popular successes finally came to an end amid the liberal resurgence of the early 1960s, but by then he was too old and embittered to care.

Berlin stopped short of entering politics, but he helped one of his Tin Pan Alley cronies make a bid for office. James J. "Jimmy" Walker was a slender young fellow who began his career as an Alley plugger and lyricist ("Will You Love Me in December as You Do in May?"). Running for mayor of New York in 1925, he asked Berlin to write a campaign song. He promptly obliged by composing "It's a Walk-in with Walker." Irving's candidate won the race, and he made an ideal mayor for the Jazz Age, a man who mixed city politics and chorus girls with careless abandon.

As a result of Berlin's involvement with civic matters, reporters inevitably came to feel that they made common cause with him. They considered his songs a form of journalism set to music: a repository of popular fads, beliefs, and native wisdom. Berlin's photograph in the paper, generally posed with care, became as well known as his songs; and his likeness—the clouds of dark hair, the commanding eyes, and correct tie—was instantly recognizable. Seen against the background of Berlin's felicitous dealings with newsmen, Woollcott's biography was but another, particularly prestigious, instance of the songwriter's rapport with the press.

A shameless exhibitionist, Woollcott was incapable of doing anything in secret. He invited his subject to collaborate with him—an assignment that Irving, with his reverence for books as tokens of the intellectual world that his youthful poverty had denied him, took seriously indeed. He became Woollcott's chief source of information. Though the tendency to shade and distort could have been overwhelming, Berlin played it straight; he was remarkably candid about his impoverished family, Cherry Street, and his business dealings, even to the point of opening his publishing company's books to Woollcott. Though reticent, Irving Berlin had nothing to hide from his eager, prying friend.

It was amazing how well this improbable couple got along—the hectoring, effete journalist and self-taught minstrel. Yet Berlin found Woollcott to be sympathetic and energizing; the critic could get him to open up as few others could. As their friendship deepened, the songwriter referred to himself not as Irving Berlin but as Izzy Baline, and Woollcott starting calling his subject Izzy. This liberty suggested that Berlin was allowing his friend to see the person he actually was, as opposed to the self-taught songwriter that everyone took him for. In contrast to the methodical Berlin, Woollcott, who often worked in frantic bursts, was nowhere near as careful with the facts he gathered; his "biography" would evolve into an amalgam of sociology, fantasy, and undisguised hero worship.

Of course, having one's biography written by the most celebrated drama critic of the day was a considerable honor. To Irving, the book would set the seal on his career. That it would be yet another by-product of his association with the Round Table served to strengthen his bond with this multifaceted, ever-changing group.

▪ ▪ ▪

In that golden summer of 1922, as Berlin alternately played with the members of the Round Table and prepared for the next season's Music Box revue, there occurred an event scarcely noticed by the world at large, but one laden with profound emotional consequences for Irving. In mid-July his mother, Lena, became ill with pneumonia complicated by chronic nephritis. She was now seventy-two and still living in the Bronx "country" home Izzy had bought for her with the money he'd made from "Alexander's Ragtime Band." Her condition quickly worsened, and beginning July 18, a Dr. H. Schumer visited her daily until her death on the morning of July 21. According to Orthodox Jewish custom, she was buried the same day, at Washington Cemetery in Brooklyn, where her husband Moses had been buried over twenty years before.

Lena's busy son had little time to dwell on her death. But she was, in both actual and symbolic ways, his last link to his childhood, the Old World, Cherry Street, and the immigrant life he'd put behind him. As her health failed and the end of her life became more and more of a certainty, he began composing a new type of song, a lament, expressing his loneliness and melancholy. The year before her death, he'd written "All By Myself," a meditation on solitude and the misery of growing old alone; it was followed by "What'll I Do?" (completed in Neysa's studio) and "All Alone," similarly morbid, yet romantic, complaints. Drawing on an eternal theme, the loss of a loved one, rather than the latest dance craze, they struck a nerve and became some of his most popular and enduring songs from the early 1920s.

"What'll I Do?" was published in early 1924, and it went on to sell more than a million copies of sheet music (and a million records); "All Alone," published in October 1924, set a similar sales pace.

Simply finding the time and tranquility to compose this last song became a problem for Berlin, who, as Woollcott noted, was often moody. The songs still came, but they came slowly, achingly slowly. In search of solitude, he retreated to the Ritz Hotel in Atlantic City, New Jersey, where he lolled on the beach during the day and worked through the night in his suite. But as the song neared completion, his spirits soared. One afternoon, Woollcott, in his dual role of friend and biographer, decided to pay a call on Irving at just that moment. The critic left a vivid sketch of Berlin in the throes of creation:

> At daybreak that day he had just completed the chorus of "All Alone" and the final version of its lyric, scribbled on the back of a menu card, was propped against a siphon which served for the moment as a music-rack. The old busker was uppermost in him and he was possessed to sing it forthwith. If I had not passed by at that moment, the nearest bellhop or chambermaid would been thrown into a flutter by being pressed into service as audience. His accompanist had come down from New York to work with him on the new Music Box numbers and was already drowsing at the piano over a rough, pencilled lead sheet of "All Alone."

This and the other romantic laments Irving was then composing owed much of their popularity to new technology. Suddenly, radio and recordings were spreading his songs more widely than sheet music and live performances ever had. This development was driven home to the songwriter one evening in January 1924, when he listened to John McCormack sing "All Alone" over a small network of radio stations. McCormack reached eight million listeners in one shot—as opposed to the thousand or so patrons who filled the Music Box each evening. His radio performance sparked demand for the recording of "All Alone," which sold 250,000 copies in a month's time. The song went on to sell another million copies in recordings, a million in sheet music, and 160,000 in player-piano rolls.

The potent new combination of radio, recordings, piano rolls, and sheet music benefited Berlin greatly. The varied forms of exposure reinforced one another and whetted the public's demand for music and still more music by Irving Berlin, in whatever form it was available. During its fifty weeks of life, for example, "You'd Be Surprised" sold 783,982 copies of sheet music, 145,505 piano rolls, and 888,790 records. "Say It With Music" displayed similar health; it sold for seventy-five weeks, moving 374,408 copies of sheet music, 102,127 piano rolls, and 1,223,905 records off the shelves. And "All By Myself" proved even more popular, selling during a period of seventy-four weeks 1,053,493 copies of sheet music, 161,650 piano rolls, and 1,225,083 records.

The sudden rise of radio and recordings, which fed on each other with a ferocious hunger, melted Berlin's resistance to ASCAP. Since the organization was determined to collect fees from these new electronic means of distribution—fees that music publishers had tried and failed to get on their own—ASCAP quickly acquired a mission and legitimacy it had previously lacked. Until this time, ASCAP had been hard-pressed to collect even a ten-dollar annual members' fee from songwriters, but now Tin Pan Alley embraced ASCAP. Berlin didn't just join and leave it at that, he cajoled others into joining in his characteristically blunt style. One day he was walking down Broadway when he bumped into Jimmy Monaco, who wrote "You Made Me Love You."

"Jimmy, can you give me ten dollars?" Berlin asked, and when Monaco hesitated, he continued, "Why, Jimmy, what's the matter? Aren't I good for ten dollars?"

Finally Monaco said, "Why, Irving, of course you are."

And Irving said, "Okay, Jimmy. Now you're a member of ASCAP." Berlin himself went on to join ASCAP's board of members.

▪ ▪ ▪

The success of his individual songs was important to Berlin, but he continued to devote most of his ferocious energy to his theater, which had quickly become the centerpiece of his music empire. On October 23, 1922, the second *Music Box Revue* opened. As with the previous year's effort, it ran over three-and-a-half hours, and it consisted of the same gussied-up vaudeville acts that had enlivened its predecessor.

If the songs he composed for the score—including "Pack Up Your Sins and Go to the Devil," "Lady of the Evening," "Bring on the Pepper," and "Dance Your Troubles Away"—sounded slick and fresh, none became a phenomenon or rivaled the previous season's one undoubted hit, "Say It With Music," which was still going strong.

Indeed, the revues were by now becoming better known for their elaborate scenery and costumes than for their music and lyrics. "Pack Up Your Sins and Go to the Devil," for instance, featured an attractive new comedienne named Charlotte Greenwood attired as a red devil and dispatching popular jazz musicians to hell. (So much for Irving's interest in coming to terms with the jazz idiom.) John Steel, a burning Irish tenor who could quickly bring tears to the eyes of the audience, crooned "Lady of the Evening" before a backdrop of rooftops glinting under artificial moonlight. The show's finale featured an optical illusion created by a seemingly endless stream of gold curtains.

Squinting and scowling at this show of finery from the vantage point of his aisle seat, Woollcott decided that the revue's emphasis on Hassard Short's wizardry at the expense of Irving Berlin's music amounted to an artistic miscalculation of the first magnitude. The next morning, in the pages of the *New York Herald*—which had recently hired him away from the *Times* at a widely publicized salary of $15,000 a year—the obese critic complained, "For a time last night it began to look as though none of the somewhat baffled and bewildered players on the stage would be permitted to resort to any such routine and hackneyed entrance as merely walking on the stage." Woollcott, who could be enormously perceptive when he wasn't being a pompous ass, ridiculed the sight: "No, they emerge from tree trunks and bird cages, spring up out of trapdoors and lightly swing down from high trapezes. When this is not possible they walk groggily down interminable staircases of black velvet . . . having to carry with them gowns of silver sequins weighing about a ton each."

The vigorous denunciation suggested that Woollcott had suddenly betrayed Berlin, his friend and literary collaborator, but in all likelihood, there was a different explanation. Inordinately sensitive to appearances, Woollcott was intent on demonstrating that their friendship had not affected his critical judgment. Berlin's reaction to the mauling he received, however, is unrecorded.

Despite Woollcott's cavils, which the other New York dailies gently echoed, the second *Music Box Revue* ran for an impressive span of forty-six weeks. Much of its popularity was traceable to the swanky reputation that the Music Box revues had swiftly acquired. Their audiences were the most exclusive on Broadway. Often consisting of theater people, they liked to compare this year's revue to last year's revue and to imagine what they would do if Berlin would only let them be part of next year's revue. They were cared for in the manner to which they were accustomed. The theater, like others in that gentler era, offered amenities that its prosperous patrons took for granted: uniformed attendants to park their cars and a clerk available at intermission to make their aftertheater supper reservations. There was no more prestigious token that a young society swain could offer his date than tickets to the latest *Music Box Revue*; a visit became *de rigeur* among New York's social elite. Reginald Vanderbilt took his wife-to-be, Gloria Morgan, to see the *Music Box Revue* when they were courting. And in his bitter novel of 1920s America, *The Big Money*, novelist John Dos Passos sends his heroine, Margo Dowling, a former *Follies* chorus girl who later becomes a movie star, to the Music Box in the company of her boyfriend's eager young assistant, Cliff Wegman. "I pretty near had to blackjack a guy to get 'em [tickets] for you," Wegman explains. They have themselves a wonderful time, both during the show and the intermission, spotting celebrities. Dos Passos's evocation of the Music Box's brittle allure indicated the extent to which Berlin's theater and revues had permeated public consciousness as the epitome of show business swank.

▪ ▪ ▪

Irving had occasion to judge how far he'd risen along New York's social and economic ladder four days before Christmas, when Mike Salter died at the age of fifty-four. In years gone by Mike had been a wealthy man, but at the end, he was living in near poverty on the Lower East Side's East 4th Street with his eighty-seven-year-old mother, Rachel; his wife; and five children. Still, he was a figure of some renown, and his passing made the front page of the *New York Herald* the next day. And yet only two men outside the family attended the funeral: an obscure Democratic boss from Coney Island named Kenneth Sutherland and a considerably more prominent songwriter from Manhattan named

Irving Berlin—the only former employee of Nigger Mike's to appear at his pathetic last rites.

"The funeral was to have taken place at a quarter to one," noted the reporter, Water Davenport, of the bleak scene Berlin witnessed. "First Mike's sister had hysterics and it required four or five of the strongest boys from the Atlantic Social Club to carry her out of the room. Then they fetched Mike's wife in and she couldn't stand it. 'For God's sake! Let me speak to him,' she screamed. 'The father of my darlings; the father of my darlings. . . .' "

Mike, in life, had been a big man, and when the ceremony ended, the same able-bodied representatives of the Atlantic Social Club tried to haul his unwieldy coffin out of the apartment and down the stairs, but not until a piano mover took charge did they succeed. As the reporters covering the story began to leave, Berlin whispered to Davenport: "Treat him as kind as you can. He was no angel, maybe, but there are a lot of guys on the street today who would have been in jail if it hadn't been for Nigger Mike."

The earthly remains of Mike Salter were then laid to rest at Washington Cemetery, where Berlin's mother had been interred only five months earlier.

They bore down heavily on Irving, these two deaths, coming so close together, emphasizing a loneliness that no amount of acclaim could assuage. The applause at the Music Box, the thousands of copies of sheet music sold—that was all fine, splendid, in fact, until he came home to his penthouse, his books and art collection, and his toucans. And then he was alone. Single. Childless. A widower for ten years now. Still, if not for Nigger Mike, who had employed him and nagged him into writing his first song, no one, not even Irving, could say what would have become of an uneducated seventeen-year-old busker from Cherry Street named Izzy Baline.

And yet, on the evidence of his activities over the ensuing months, the twin deaths, that of his mother and his surrogate father, Nigger Mike, freed Berlin from ancient obligations even as they plunged him into mourning.

PART THREE

ACCLAIM

1924–1945

■ □ ■ □ ■ □ ■

CHAPTER 10
Mackay's Millions

In June 1923, Irving Berlin treated himself to a trip to Paris before he undertook the demanding task of overseeing the next edition of the *Music Box Review*. Even on vacation, though, he remained preoccupied with his work. Shortly after his arrival, Robert Benchley, one of the stars of the upcoming edition of the revue, and Hassard Short, the director, contacted him and suggested he look up a promising young American singer named Grace Moore. Irving quickly complied; he arranged to call on the young woman at the modest Parisian pension where she was staying, and, as she recalled, "took a good cagey look at my unpalatial surroundings and invited me out to Ciro's for lunch."

Over a glass of wine, the songwriter discovered that Grace was a charming but desperately insecure twenty-four-year-old who had begun her singing career in a Baptist church choir. She had studied music and dreamed of becoming an opera star—much as Irving had dreamed of writing an opera. However, she quickly realized that Irving Berlin's *Music Box Revue* would pay far better than a contemplated operatic engagement. Since she was short of money, she decided to accept his offer to star in the 1923 edition, soon to begin rehearsal in New York.

To formalize the agreement, Berlin wrote out a contract on the table cloth. When the time came to pay the bill, he was surprised to discover that the headwaiter insisted that he pay not only for the meal, but also for the table cloth. "My friends," said Moore, "who had been so elated over my audition at the *Comique*, were bitterly disappointed when I signed the contract with Berlin. But I saw no other way. I had to go back to Broadway to work and save."

Later in his stay, he encountered Crosby Gaige, a journalist turned theatrical producer, whom Berlin knew through the Round Table. When Gaige mentioned that he was acquainted with Erik Satie, the venerable avant garde composer, Berlin asked for an introduction. The producer, glad of an opportunity to curry favor with Irving Berlin, quickly arranged a meeting in Satie's threadbare Left Bank garret. "Satie was old and white-haired and wistful and very, very poor," Gaige wrote of the meeting between the two composers. "Irving was young, black-haired and wistful and very, very rich. Satie spoke no English and Irving spoke no French, but we managed well enough through the mutual friend who had come with us."

Satie and Berlin sat side by side on a piano stool before Satie's mammoth Bechstein, playing. "Of course Irving had to play and sing 'Say It with Music,' and then he asked . . . for a sample of Satie's work."

" 'I will play for you a piece about goldfish,' Satie told us. 'These goldfish live in a round glass aquarium.'

"As his fingers roamed over the keyboard, he produced in tone exactly that picture for us, and we were enchanted."

The price Berlin paid for his Parisian respite became apparent when he returned to New York and the third edition of the revue began preparations. Rehearsals were always a trying experience, but this time they were positively maddening. Robert Benchley, who was anxiously preparing a new, fleshed-out version of his "Treasurer's Report" for the revue, was appalled by the chaos, which seemed to mirror the turmoil of his personal life. For months he had been pursuing a nineteen-year-old female Western Union operator. His sophisticated Round Table friends, who knew of the affair, made no secret of their disdain for the girl, whom they considered too common for a man of his fine and honorable sensibilities. Not that the Round Table disapproved of extramarital relationships in principle, but the girl had to measure up. Caught in a quandary of his own making, Benchley proceeded to compound the problem by persuading Berlin and Harris to put his young girlfriend in the show. Irving was so eager to keep Benchley happy that he gave her a walk-on role in which she was all but overwhelmed by her costume. Even with this arrangement, Benchley despaired. He flatly declared, "Nothing could be more discouraging than a rehearsal shortly preceding the opening of the Music Box."

Berlin—remote, quiet, and contained—appeared helpless to control the course of events. Benchley described his curiously phlegmatic demeanor during rehearsals:

> A little man in a tight-fitting suit, with his hands in his pockets, walks on from the wings. He looks very white in the glare from the foot[light]s. You almost expect to have him thrown out, he seems so casual and like an observer. They don't throw him out, however, because he is Mr. Berlin.
>
> You are suddenly overcome with a feeling of tremendous futility. "Irving Berlin's Fourth Music Box Revue" it already says in the lights out in front of the theatre. And Irving Berlin is little. And the Fourth Music Box Revue is so big. And so far from articulation.

Nor was Benchley the only member of the Round Table to participate in this troubled edition of the revue. George S. Kaufman, as well, contributed a skit, "If Men Played Cards as Women Do," which derived most of its humor from his ingrained misogyny. But the skit was funny enough, and Berlin would have further dealings with Kaufman. The Round Table was thus exerting an increasing influence on Berlin's career, a development all the more surprising, given his penchant for independence.

For all his misgivings, Benchley's monologue turned out to be the comic high point of the evening, but his insecurity about the overall show proved to be well founded. The third edition was shaping up to be the weakest offering at the Music Box Theatre thus far, in terms of the quality of both the comic skits and Berlin's music. He was nowhere near his top form. He would compose but a dozen songs this year, and while they offered highly competent show music, none was particularly distinguished. The sets and costumes, however, promised to be breathtaking as always. One scene, built around Berlin's forgettable tune, "Maid of Mesh," featured a $50,000 mesh curtain fashioned of silver and gold.

The naïve young Grace Moore, however, had no sense of the trouble engulfing the revue and was simply thrilled to be part of the show. "The drawstring that pulled my whole life into shape," she said of the experience. "Here was Broadway at its best, and . . . in being given an opportunity to sing Irving Berlin's simple, lovely songs that suited my voice, I had found the right niche at the right time."

Her niche was a splendid one. Berlin had composed a song for her called "An Orange Grove in California." It was an unpretentious ditty about longing to go where the oranges grow, but the staging was spectacular. Grace and John Steel, the revue's star tenor, strolled through a representation of an orange grove. The grove then disintegrated into orange lights as tiny valves concealed beneath each seat opened and released the scent of orange blossoms into the audience.

Unfortunately for Grace—and to the detriment of the show—the cast did not share Berlin's affection for the opera singer turned Broadway star, and she quickly excited their envy and spite. One cast member, Frank Tinney, who was, incidentally, developing a drinking problem, rigged up offstage chairs to an electric current; when Grace sat down in one, he would turn on the power and watch her jump. More seriously, John Steel, the tenor, felt a keen professional rivalry with her that came to a head on opening night, September 22. At the curtain call, Moore decided to take a bow by herself and found, so she later claimed, that she was "so overcome with emotion" that she couldn't move, not even when Tinney and Steel, fuming offstage, called out, "Why in the hell don't you get up? Are you going to stay out there all night?"

At the conclusion of the premiere, Berlin, sensing that this revue lacked the bravura qualities of its predecessors, was particularly anxious, and he kept a vigil with Grace until dawn, waiting for the press notices. As he feared, most were lackluster. "This revue distinctly lacks exciting features," declared the *World*. "There is a little less lilt than usual in the latest of the composer's scores." However, they did single out Grace Moore as the show's chief redeeming feature. "Grace Moore has tone in her voice to charm the heart out of you," noted one reviewer. And of course Alexander Woollcott was on hand to write of Grace's debut in his overheated prose: "Hats were thrown into the air and cheers resounded from one end of Broadway to the other and a new star was born." On reading this praise, Moore remembered, "I broke down and cried. Irving was sweet and understanding—and audibly patted himself on the back for having guessed right when he persuaded me to give up study in Paris for this Broadway appearance."

But the relief that she and Berlin felt proved to be short-lived. The show's troubles, and Grace's, were just beginning. As the production embarked on its run, she found herself the recipient of a poison pen letter—presumably the handiwork of one of the cast members. "I knew the whole business was a childish explosion of backstage jealousy," Moore wrote, "but it got under my skin none the less and churned up my nervous system."

Several months of this disgraceful treatment took its toll on her performance, with embarrassing results. Grace opened the show with a childishly naughty routine built around Berlin's song, "Tell Me a Bedtime Story," and she often found herself unable to finish her number. "The curtain had to be rung down," she said, "while I tried to pull myself together for my next appearance on the stage."

Finally, Berlin and Harris decided something had to be done to rescue the show. This wasn't the first time an insecure actress bedeviled by rivals had threatened to destroy one of Irving's shows; much the same scenario had consumed Gaby Deslys, who seven years earlier had starred in *Stop! Look! Listen!* Then Berlin was merely the composer, not the producer, and had been forced to stand by while the show disintegrated, but this time, he had the authority to prevail on his actors to attempt to make amends. Displaying compassion for Grace's plight, he instructed Steel to write her a letter of apology, but he spared the egocentric tenor the humiliation of having to deliver it himself; Irving tactfully acted as courier.

When this bit of diplomacy failed to restore Grace to the peak of her form, Harris and Berlin packed her off on a ten-day vacation at a quiet resort in Lakewood, New Jersey. Even this apparently benign gesture turned out to be another practical joke on Moore, for both Harris and Berlin couldn't resist having a bit of fun with her, either. She gratefully accepted the offer, took a train to Lakewood, and had such a good time there that she invited a girlfriend to join her near the end of the stay. "Why, Grace," said her friend on arrival at Lakewood, "I didn't know you were Jewish."

"Why, I didn't either," Moore replied.

And her friend explained: "This is a place where only Jewish people go and only kosher food is served."

Ten days at the Lakewood resort, and Grace Moore from Tennessee hadn't noticed that she was the only non-Jewish guest.

Sam and Irving met Grace on her return to New York, and they expressed their surprise that she'd been able to endure ten days of kosher cuisine. The good-natured singer took this particular jest in stride. In fact, it became something of a rite of passage for her. She proceeded to become associated with the Round Table, and her small apartment served as yet another one of its annexes.

After her return, Berlin decided that the show needed more than a stable cast; it required a stronger score, and he violated the precedent he'd set of avoiding interpolations. However, the song that he did interpolate was his own hit, "What'll I Do?"—the lament he had completed in Neysa McMein's studio under the influence of champagne. Grace sang it with the required combination of delicacy and pathos. Now that he had done all he could to buttress the show, the third *Music Box Revue* gradually settled into a run that would be as long, if not as profitable, as its predecessors.

Yet Irving was not as personally fulfilled as his material success indicated; he passed through his empty, stylish life, defined in equal measure now by show business and the Round Table, wrapped in a cocoon of melancholy and loneliness, as his recent hit songs announced. There was a catch, Berlin discovered, to living in the thrall of the Jazz Age, with its speakeasies, flappers, the Round Table, the Music Box revues, and endless parties: it was exhausting. It made people drink and gamble more than was good for them. It sapped the spirit rather than replenished it.

In January 1924, Irving, worn and harried after the ordeal of restoring this latest revue to working condition, treated himself to a week's vacation in Palm Beach, Florida, with Dorothy Parker and Neysa McMein—though he was involved with neither woman—and Sam Harris. (During this interlude Irving, lonely in the company of two even lonelier women, heard his "All Alone" broadcast over the radio to eight million listeners.) It was characteristic of Berlin's behavior at this indecisive juncture of his life that he would display an admirable, yet annoying, self-restraint amid plenty, as though he were hoarding his emotions for a more worthy (and fresher) romantic partner.

As his self-pity ebbed, he began to appreciate the restorative effects of the vacation. For five full days he lolled on the beach in unconscionable idleness. He read a little, but mainly he daydreamed and marveled at how lazy he had permitted himself to become. He could imagine going on this way forever, relaxing, sunbathing, watching the girls go by, ignoring his trick piano. In time he decided to try his hand at a song about the supreme luxury of idleness. The result, "Lazy," was a workaholic's fantasy of a life of ease. Berlin often insisted that his songs were not autobiographical, and he was correct to the extent that many had no basis in the facts of his life. On the other hand, "Lazy" provided an accurate music-and-word picture of his state of mind even as it described a universal longing.

Irving returned to New York feeling renewed and refreshed. His sense of isolation and loneliness had vanished. He started to go out on the town; he was eager to see new sights and meet new people. Before his Florida tan faded, he met the woman who would be—and there is no other term that properly describes their relationship—the love of his life. However, for a love match that was destined to become one of the most celebrated and controversial society events of the period, it began casually enough, even inauspiciously.

▪ ▪ ▪

One night in early February, Berlin decided to visit his old downtown haunt, Jimmy Kelly's. He had worked there as a singing waiter fifteen years earlier, when he was trying to launch his career as a songwriter. Times had changed, and so had Jimmy Kelly's. It had gone from being a rough-and-ready saloon near Union Square to a fashionable speakeasy at 181 Sullivan Street, in Greenwich Village.

Jimmy Kelly's was popular now with a younger set, a fast crowd in search of a high time during the Prohibition era. Berlin was sufficiently famous that, shortly after he arrived, many of the patrons became aware of his presence. One of them had the nerve to violate his understated yet intimidating privacy and introduce herself to him. Such encounters were his lot now. Nearly everyone who was young and in love at the time danced and petted while well-worn recordings of his love songs played in the background. But this particular admirer's name set her apart; anyone familiar with society would recognize it at once: Ellin Mackay.

Her formidable social standing derived from the fact that her father was the telegraph magnate Clarence Mackay—not only a force in industry but also a mainstay of Long Island society at its most icy and forbidding. Ellin was willowy, blond, and young; she had a good sense of fashion and could afford to dress herself well. With her lanky figure, chiseled features, and widely spaced, burning eyes, she might have been a model or an actress, if she'd been so inclined. As it was, her appearance and her social pedigree gave her entrée into the highest circles of New York society. And she was still young, just about to turn twenty-one. Her education was both exclusive and severely restrictive: governesses at first, later the Spence School in Manhattan, and then St. Timothy's, a boarding school in Maryland's hunt country. The skein began to unravel when she left Barnard after attending for one semester, in the fall of 1922, receiving credit only for a French course. The following year, in her debutante season, her father had formally presented her to society at a ball at the Ritz-Carlton Hotel. She now had a fancy sports car and a trust fund that gave her approximately $50,000 a year to spend as she pleased. Given this support, she was the epitome of *jeunesse dorée*.

All sorts of people were interested in Ellin Mackay: gossip columnists, society doyennes, men in search of a glamorous mate. For a young woman of her background, the true vocation was marriage, the pursuit of the brilliant match—to find it, make it, and keep it. But Ellin Mackay also wanted to write. Her literary aspirations could be acceptable in polite society; during their "enforced retirement from society" (i.e., pregnancy), women like Ellin often wrote novels to make the months pass. Not only is she pretty, society would say of her, but she can *write.* This was fine—artistic ability occasionally went along with money—so long as she didn't take it too far. So long as she didn't try to say anything unsettling, play the tattletale. The strictures and options she faced were, in fact, a trifle bewildering for a girl of twenty-one to contemplate. So much excitement, so much money, and so many tacit codes of society.

In all these respects, she was the ideal Irving Berlin fan and *Music Box Revue* patron. She later confessed that she was smitten with him and soon instigated what was to become a two-year-long pursuit of the most elusive and eligible bachelor in show business.

On the face it, the possibility of their forming a serious relationship seemed remote indeed. Ellin was fifteen years younger than Irving, still a child, really, rebelling against her strict upbringing and education in fancy private schools. She inhabited a world that was, in all important ways, closed to Russian-Jewish immigrants such as Irving Berlin, no matter how successful they became, or how carefully they Anglicized their names. Ellin had grown up on an estate designed by Stanford White that had cost $6 million to construct at the turn of the century. Called Harbor Hill, it was considered the largest private "summer" home in the United States: 648 acres, 50 rooms, a staff of 134 servants, tennis courts, and stables, and a gatekeeper's "cottage" with twenty additional rooms. Irving, in contrast, had grown up in a packed tenement in the heart of the Lower East Side ghetto, on Cherry Street, until he left home at the age of thirteen, at which time he began years of living in decrepit flophouses.

In addition to the vast economic and social disparity of their backgrounds Irving had a record of fruitless entanglements with younger women—generally vivacious but unstable performers such as Elsie Janis, the vaudeville child star, and Dutch Talmadge, the silent-screen actress. Either he'd pined for them, or they'd pined for him, but in any case nothing had come of all the pining except for sob songs. Since the death of his first wife, Dorothy Goetz, in 1912 (when Ellin was only nine), he'd been unable to form a lasting relationship with a woman; by now his apparently permanent loneliness—captured in the poignant, self-pitying lyrics of "All Alone"—had reached the point where it was being broadcast to the entire nation. Thanks to his artistry, the loneliness of this private man had become public knowledge. Without quite meaning to, he'd made himself a target for all manner of beguiling celebrity worshippers and fortune hunters.

On the basis of this history, the likelihood of Ellin's becoming more than just another frustrated suitor was remote indeed. And yet, as Irving would soon discover, there was considerably more grit, substance, and conflict swirling within Ellin Mackay than her youth, money, and frivolous socialite milieu suggested. The fact that she was seen at Jimmy Kelly's—a speakeasy, talking with *a strange man*, in show business, a *Jew*—amounted to a rebellious act of considerable import.

Yet if she had not encountered Berlin here, she was destined to meet him sooner or later at the Round Table or one of its annexes, for she was already on the periphery of that coterie, determined to make her name not as a society figure but as a writer. She had ample precedent to buttress her ambition; her adored aunt, Alice Duer Miller, a Round Table fixture, had managed to combine both pursuits. And Ellin would within several months begin writing for Harold Ross's struggling *New Yorker*, where she would make a name both for herself and the magazine the following year in two notorious articles in which she explained exactly what she, Ellin Mackay, one of *the* Mackays, was doing in a place like Jimmy Kelly's.

"WHY WE GO TO CABARETS," the headline announced, adopting a euphemism for "speakeasies." "A Post-Debutante Explains."

She was breaking society's code now, becoming a tattletale. People from her world viewed the press as a natural antagonist; all journalism was yellow journalism, a gallery of "fools' names and fools' faces." Your name appeared in the paper only three times in your life: when you were born, when you married, and when you died—*not* when you felt like writing an article denouncing your own kind. By allowing *The New Yorker* to take advantage of her name, Ellin had become a traitor to her class. In a restrained diatribe aimed at her Park Avenue and Harbor Hill peers, she wrote:

> Our Elders criticize many things about us, but usually they attribute sins too gaudy to be true. . . . They have swallowed too much of Mr. Scott Fitzgerald and Miss Gertrude Atherton [another novelist]. They believe all the backstairs gossip that is written about us. . . . Cabaret has its place in the elderly mind beside Bohemia and bolshevik, and other vague words that have a sinister significance and no precise definition.

Certainly a "cabaret" was preferable to a conventional society party, she continued, with its "stag line" populated by "extremely unalluring specimens, . . . each poisonous in his individual way." The tone of the piece was malicious, filled with an adolescent self-righteousness, and yet it was fresh and winning. Better by far, she argued, to exercise free choice in an establishment that was open to the public. "We have privacy in a cabaret," Ellin insisted. "What does it matter if an unsavory Irish politician is carrying on a dull and noisy flirtation with the little blonde at the table behind us? We don't have to listen; we are with people we find amusing."

People, she did not have to add, like Irving Berlin.

Their friendship quickly became an open secret among those who knew them. There was no telling where it would end; she risked losing her place in society. Such liaisons between leading figures in society and show business people were not unknown. For years Ellin's father Clarence had been conducting just such an affair with Anna Case, the voluminous opera star, but *in secret*. He knew the rules. Ellin seemed not to. Shortly after she encountered Irving at Jimmy Kelly's, they arranged a second meeting, this time at the apartment of one of Ellin's friends. Word was getting around.

Afraid that Ellin might do something rash—elope with a Jew—Clarence, with his obtuse businessman's mentality, undertook due diligence on this Irving Berlin. He was trying to turn up some dirt, evidence that Berlin was unsatisfactory: other women in his life, unsavory habits, something. Even with the help of private detectives, Clarence discovered nothing to discredit Berlin. Nor did his extensive network of social contacts give him the ammunition he wanted. One day Clarence discussed the problem with a friend, a bank president, who referred him to Crosby Gaige, the producer who had introduced Berlin to Erik Satie. Clarence called Gaige, a complete stranger, and barked, "What is your opinion of Irving Berlin? Do you think he would make a good husband for my daughter?"

To Clarence's disappointment, Gaige replied that he held Irving "in the highest esteem."

But Irving, had Clarence only known, was in no rush to get married. As long as he felt he could see Ellin whenever he liked, she remained a young acquaintance with literary interests; later, when he could not, his feelings about her underwent a transformation. On the evidence of his activities during the next several months, however, he was still far more involved with the demands of his career than with Ellin.

▪ ▪ ▪

Suddenly, a series of pressing external events temporarily supplanted Ellin in Berlin's mind. The first issue concerned a troublesome piece of legislation before Congress. The Dill Bill, as it was called, proposed that radio stations could play copyrighted music without having to pay royalties. A group of veteran songwriters, including Victor Herbert (who would die later in the year), Charles K. Harris, and even Berlin's one-time employer Harry Von Tilzer, banded together and called on Irving, as a representative of the younger generation, to accompany them to Washington, D.C., where they planned to testify before the Senate Patents Committee to demand royalties for radio performances of their music.

To publicize their cause, the songwriters staged an evening of song before three hundred members of the National Press Club. Once again Berlin demonstrated his knack for self-promotion. He'd gone to Washington to publicize a cause and wound up plugging his latest title—the song that had come to him as he'd lolled on the beach in Florida: "Lazy." It didn't fit neatly into any category; "Lazy" wasn't a sob ballad, a love song, or a rag. It was simply a fleeting evocation of a state of mind.

Berlin's presence in Washington attracted the attention of a considerably larger political organization: the Democratic party, then in the throes of trying to select a candidate to run against President Calvin Coolidge in the 1924 presidential election. Intrigued by the political process, especially the panoply of democracy at work, Irving took advantage of Herbert Bayard Swope's invitation to attend the infamous, exciting Democratic National Convention of 1924, which convened on June 25 in New York City's Madison Square Garden.

The ill-starred convention is today best remembered for three things: the punishing heat, which caused chairman Cordell Hull to faint several times; the appearance of a crippled Franklin D. Roosevelt, who nominated Alfred E. Smith as his party's candidate in a famous speech proclaiming Smith a "Happy Warrior"; and the fourteen days and 103 ballots required to select a nominee. During the raucous proceedings, Berlin had occasion to witness the democratic process at its messiest and most confrontational. Swope and his *World* were in the thick of every aspect of the proceedings. He had been instrumental in bringing the convention to New York. Later, when it was underway, his paper pointed out that Smith's principal rival, William McAdoo, had the support of the Ku Klux Klan. And before he delivered the "Happy Warrior" speech, FDR went over the text with Swope, crawling on the floor to retrieve sections the impetuous publisher discarded.

Anna Case, Clarence Mackay's mistress, was also at the convention, draped in a white gown that only made her seem even larger than she was, as she sang the national anthem to the exhausted delegates. Of course Irving had no idea at the time of the indirect role she was to play in his private life.

Swope extended his lobbying on behalf of Al Smith to Berlin, as well, prevailing on the songwriter to come up with some persuasive lyrics to boost Smith's candidacy. Since Smith was already identified with another song, "The Sidewalks of New York," a new tune was the least of his needs, but Swope would not be denied. Irving hadn't written light verse for a newspaper since he'd dashed off a couple of hundred extra verses for his 1909 hit, "My Wife's Gone to the Country," but he was well disposed to Smith because the two had a fair amount in common. Like Berlin, Smith had risen from poverty on the Lower East Side to become something of a popular hero as governor of New York. And not only that, but Al Smith had once done Irving a personal favor when, as a local official, he performed the marriage ceremony of Berlin's partner, Max Winslow.

Irving worked quickly, and the *World* was able to run the resulting song, "We'll All Go Voting for Al," while the convention was still in progress. The song had little measurable impact on the delegates, and at the end of the traumatic convention, Swope and Berlin's candidate, Al Smith, lost the nomination to John W. Davis, who in turn lost the presidential election to Coolidge. For Irving, this shambles of a political convention was just more grist for his songwriting mill, but for his friend Swope, it was a major career setback. Shortly afterward, he decided to leave journalism altogether.

▪ ▪ ▪

While Berlin remained in town and watched the Democratic party come apart at the seams in the heat of a New York summer, his friend and chief propagandist, Alexander Woollcott, was at his country retreat on Neshobe Island, Vermont, toiling on the biography of the songwriter, "whose story," he wrote at the time, "has a strong appeal to my foolish and romantic heart." Woollcott viewed Berlin primarily as a man of the theater. Since the critic lacked formal musical training, he felt less secure trying to evaluate his subject as a composer, so he asked Jerry Kern to contribute "one chapter that says something intelligible about him as a composer, his place in the history of ragtime, his melodic gift, his place as a maker of folk song."

Coming from the influential pen of Alexander Woollcott, this was a summons Kern could scarcely ignore. His reply proved to be the fullest statement yet of the gathering Berlin mythology. Kern began by recalling a visit to London, when he had been asked what were "the chief characteristics of the American nation." Having given the matter some thought, he had his answer ready.

> I replied that the average United States citizen was perfectly epitomized in Irving Berlin's music. . . . Both the typical Yankee and the Berlin tune had humor, originality, pace and popularity; both were wide-awake, and both sometimes a little loud,—but what might unsympathetically be mistaken for brass, was really gold.
>
> Since then, columns have been written about Berlin and his music. Learned expressions like "genre," "con alcune licenza," "melodic architecture," "rhythmic pulsations," etc., etc., have been hurled at the head of modest, shy, little Irving, to his utter bewilderment.

Kern went on to compare Irving Berlin to, of all composers, Richard Wagner.

> Berlin (like Wagner, an inexorable autocritic) molds and blends and ornaments his words and music at one and the same time, each being the outgrowth of the other. He trims and changes and refashions both, many times and oft, but nearly always, strives for simplicity,—never elaboration. He is not bothering much with the seats of the Olympians, but he *is*

> concerned with the lore, the hearts, yes, —and the dancing feet of human folk. . . .
>
> To my mind, there are phrases in Berlin's music as noble and mighty as any clause in the works of the Masters, from Beethoven and Wagner down.
>
> When you remember how the latter used to sit in a darkened room, for hours at a time, waiting for a fragment of melody, sometimes only two or three notes, to come to him, you will agree with my notion that even Wagner would have considered the first three measures in the burthen of "That Mysterious Rag," heaven-sent material. My openly expressed enthusiasm for these five or six notes has amused no one more than Berlin himself. He thinks the theme is pretty good, but any suggestion that it possesses a sheer musical magnificence makes him laugh himself to death. . . .
>
> In short, what I really want to say, my dear Woollcott, is that Irving Berlin has *no* place in American music. HE IS AMERICAN MUSIC; but it will be by his verse and his lovely melodies that he will live and not in his diabolically clever trick accents.

Oblivious to Kern's highbrow praise, Berlin set out, in the fall of 1924, to restore luster to the slightly tarnished reputation of the Music Box revues. Both the composer and his producer, Sam Harris, had their work cut out for them. Once again they could bedazzle the audience with trompe l'oeil scenery and sensational costumes, and once again the score would be exclusively Berlin's, but there was a serious problem. The songs just weren't coming as fast and furiously as they had when Berlin was a young man and ready to conquer Tin Pan Alley with a melody. His few current hits, such as "All Alone" and "Lazy," were formidable, as good as the best he ever wrote, but they did not emerge from the *Music Box Revue* scores and would not serve to lure audiences to them; rather, they were the one-of-a-kind sob ballad rooted in his isolation and melancholia.

Along with the rest of Broadway, Berlin faced the decline of the revue as a popular attraction. Throughout the boisterous 1924–1925 season, the theaters were surfeited with them, but many flopped, notably Ziegfeld's hoary old *Follies*. Buying time to strengthen their entry, Berlin and Harris pushed the opening night back from its traditional late-September date all the way to December 1. Berlin's entry, when it did finally open, rated among the best in this fading genre, but it lacked freshness. The tricks, such as spraying the audience with perfume, were losing novelty. At least Grace Moore was back to charm the audience, and once again Berlin was compelled to interpolate one of his hits for her: "All Alone." She sat at one end of the stage under a tightly focused spotlight, singing it into a telephone, while Oscar Shaw sat at the other, doing the same. It was what the audience expected, a real Grace Moore number, as was Fanny Brice's comic turn, "I Want to Be a Ballet Dancer," which, in her stage-Yiddish accent, came out sounding more like "belly dancer." And finally, there was the number in which the scenery starred: "Alice in Wonderland," a creaky revival of the episode that had appeared in *The Century Girl* of 1916.

Despite the rather tired fare that the fourth edition of the *Music Box Revue* offered, most critics felt that the revue had returned to form, especially after the previous season's lapse. Alexander Woollcott unashamedly declared, "IRVING BERLIN OUTDOES HIMSELF—The Fourth Music Box Revue a Masterpiece of Its Kind." Though in no position to deliver an unbiased assessment of the revue, Woollcott stated that the production was "the best revue which these senses have experienced in ten years of playgoing along Broadway. It was a great night in the land of music halls."

Woollcott was right about one thing, at least: December 1 *was* a great night for show music, though not at the Music Box Theatre. Nearby, at the Liberty, George and Ira Gershwin's *Lady, Be Good!* opened, starring Fred and Adele Astaire. Guy Bolton's libretto was standard light musical comedy romance, but Gershwin's music marked one of the earliest effective uses of jazz in a Broadway musical score, and it contained one song in particular that announced that the songwriting team of George and Ira Gershwin had definitively arrived: the aptly named "Fascinating Rhythm," a demonic concatenation of tricky accents. To sing it was akin to tripping down a spiral staircase without ever falling. The song and the entire show contained an edge, an excitement that had eluded Berlin this time around. Though most of the audience and reviewers were oblivious to the fact, *Lady, Be Good!* pointed the way to the jazzy, brassy future of the Broadway musical, while Berlin's *Fourth Music Box Revue* looked back ever so tastefully to its jumbled, genteel past. The Gershwins' musical entertained audiences for the better part of a year and helped win George Gershwin the cover of *Time* magazine in 1925, but Irving's latest revue expired after 186 performances, the shortest run of the series.

Succumbing at last to the extraordinary and, as it was now apparent, unrealistic demands of turning out a new revue score each year, Berlin and Harris put the Music Box up for rent. Perhaps the final blow came when Grace Moore, who had come to incarnate the spirit of the revues, informed Irving, who had plucked her out of oblivion in Paris only two years earlier and coaxed her through her difficult first season, that she was leaving as soon as her contract expired, determined to resume her operatic career in France. To make matters worse, she gave the distinct impression that she'd acted in the revues solely for the money. Berlin, of course, took money seriously indeed. He couldn't understand what was wrong with the idea of doing something just for the money; with few exceptions, that was what popular music was all about. He tried to persuade Grace to change her mind, telling her she'd lose her dramatic "flare" in opera, but she was not to be dissuaded. With her went the last chance to keep the Music Box revues alive.

But Irving's *theater* was perpetually in demand, even if his latest revue wasn't. In September 1925 a comedy, *Cradle Snatchers*, starring Mary Boland and a youthful Humphrey Bogart, opened successfully at the Music Box and inaugurated a tradition of plays and musicals at the theater without Berlin's involvement. Not for seven years would he mount another show in his own theater. But even without a Berlin show on its boards, the Music Box was generally held in high esteem among producers and performers, a lucky, even charmed, legitimate house.

▪ ▪ ▪

Before the last edition of the *Music Box Revue* concluded, it was seen by two people of special interest to Irving, Ellin Mackay and her grandmother, Marie Louise Hungerford Mackay—a woman who had more in common with Izzy Baline than might be expected.

Marie Louise Hungerford Mackay: the name had been, in the 1890s, illustrious, even notorious. The widow of an alcoholic druggist, she had risen, through her brilliant, tormented second marriage, to become the reigning society hostess of her day. Heads of state regularly attended the salon she held in her Paris apartment. Then the tide of the times had turned against her, and she retired to the upper floors of her son's estate, Harbor Hill, in 1920. She was a small woman but, even in old age, one with great presence. She had penetrating blue eyes and hair that was, as Ellin recalled, "Gray like a steel engraving or a knitted shawl." Since Marie had lived abroad for much of her life, Ellin scarcely knew the woman until she moved into the family estate. "It is hard to begin to know someone when she is seventy-seven," Ellin wrote. "But we managed. We managed very well."

Marie Louise Hungerford Mackay spent many years in retreat from the world. It would have surprised those who recognized the name to discover that she was still alive in 1924 and able to attend a *Music Box Revue.* A frail octogenerian at the time, she brought out her pearls and got into the spirit of the occasion for Ellin's sake. And Ellin loved her grandmother and was fascinated by her willingness to flout convention now as in decades past. Years later Ellin would repay the debt she felt by writing an admiring biography of her beloved grandmother, calling it *Silver Platter*, the story of a spirited, irascible woman who had led a charmed life.

As Ellin was keenly aware, her grandmother had a little secret. She had once lived on the Lower East Side, not far from where the Balines settled. In *Silver Platter* Ellin addressed her grandmother on this point: "Did you remember when you lived nearby on Varick Street and Grand Street in little more comfort than Moses and Leah Baline were to know forty-five years later?" Implying that the Mackays were on a social par with a family of immigrant Russian Jews, the question would have been deeply offensive to Marie Louise Hungerford Mackay.

Indeed, the Mackay name had recently attained social immortality when, on September, 6, 1924, Edward, Prince of Wales, had come to Harbor Hill on his American visit. The lavish party in his honor was the signal event of the Long Island social season. Clarence had decorated the grounds with thousands of colored lanterns and placed hidden floodlights in all the fountains. Paul Whiteman's orchestra, the most prominent exponent of society jazz, was there to entertain the eighty guests. Ellin was one of them, wearing her grandmother's pearls.

During dinner Ellin sat next to the prince and afterward danced with the thirty-year-old heir to the British throne, the great-grandson of Queen Victoria. There was no higher eminence to which a socialite, American or British, could aspire. Any attractive, marriageable young woman who "danced with the Prince of Wales," in the popular phrase of the day, started excited gossip. So there really was no room for common show folk like Irving Berlin in the Mackay's rarefied circle. Despite this history of snobbery and social rancor, Ellin's evening *en famille* at the Music Box turned out to be a great success. Her grandmother "laughed heartily" at the antics of Fanny Brice, who was, of course, thoroughly Jewish. It seemed as though Ellin had managed to secure a measure of family approval for her proposed mate.

Clarence, however, remained adamant: no Tin Pan Alley tunesmith for his daughter. To make Ellin forget this unsuitable match, he bribed her with a European tour. And reverting to the role of the compliant, pampered daughter, she accepted his offer. Together they visited Spain, France, England, Egypt, Algiers, Italy. And when her father had to return to the United States, he left Ellin behind in Europe in the care of a chaperon, Josephine Noel, a faithful family retainer who reported back to Clarence on his daughter's conduct.

If Clarence had hoped that Ellin's extended trip would cause Irving to forget about her, he was wrong. His plan was self-defeating. In her absence the songwriter's feelings about Ellin underwent a sea change. Memory of her troubled him, provoked him, and above all, kept her in the forefront of his thoughts. To express his anxiety over the separation, he wrote, in December, a tune called "Remember"; like his other love songs of the period, it was a self-pitying lament, a paradox that turned back on itself, ending with the admission, suppressed throughout the song, that a loved one has forgotten to remember her admirer.

Berlin was an unhappy suitor, but he was also a professional songwriter, and when he had finished the tune, he wanted to make it into a lucrative hit. "In the song I tried to express a feeling or an emotion that had been embodied in me," he said of "Remember." "It was the newest . . . creation of my brain, and I was a bit sensitive and enthusiastic concerning it."

However, the song met with a poor reaction within his own publishing company. "On Christmas afternoon"—such was Berlin's zeal for work that he did not take even this day off—"I called Max Winslow and Saul Bornstein, my publishing associates, to my studio room in the Music Box Theatre to hear the new song I had composed. I sang it, certain that I had a hit. When I finished," Berlin continued, "Bornstein said that it was not so good. Winslow said it was terrible. I told them I thought the song was good and would be a hit. They tried to persuade me from publishing it and suggested that I throw it into the wastebasket and forget about it."

But he could not bring himself to forget the song, any more than he could forget Ellin. The reaction of his partners to "Remember" precipitated a crisis of confidence in Irving. "During the spring and the summer I remembered 'Remember' and worried about it. I thought I had lost my skill, my talent. I was afraid to write anything for fear Winslow would say it was terrible. I was developing an inferiority complex, which is the greatest hindrance a writer can have. . . . I worried so much that I was becoming a bundle of nerves."

Berlin became obsessed with this one song, "Remember," and the humiliation he had suffered when his partners had panned it. "It seemed that a song was going to be my downfall. That Christmas Day was the worst one I ever spent in my life. Every time I felt worried or troubled I remembered that day and felt worse. I never want another day like that. It was one of mental torture." By now his feelings about the song were fraught with memories of Ellin, and beyond that, the permanent insecurities with which he had lived since his days as an impoverished youth on the Lower East Side.

Finally, though, he found a way to escape from the psychological trap he'd set for himself. "As for 'Remember,' after much worrying and thinking, I decided to publish it against the advice of Winslow and Bornstein and let the public judge." And the public judged the song a hit—just as Berlin had predicted. Once again his judgment was vindicated, his mystical bond with the musical marketplace confirmed and even strengthened after this time of testing.

Once the song had established itself, Berlin performed a complete about-face. To hide his profound insecurity and his delicate yet powerful feelings for Ellin, he denied that he wrote the song out of anything other than commercial calculation. The notion that he'd written it for love, he now claimed, was "ridiculous." He explained: "Just because a man writes sob ballads, he is not writing from his own experiences. It has always been assumed that whenever I've written a ballad I've been through some heartbreaking experience. But the real reason is that the public would rather buy tears than smiles—and right now they happen to want sob ballads."

Here were the two sides of Berlin on display: the sensitive, insecure, suffering musical craftsman and the hard-bitten music publisher. Berlin never attempted to rationalize his contradictory attitudes toward the art and business of songwriting. For now the two were able to coexist. But as he matured, the unyielding publisher and businessman in him would steadily gain the upper hand.

During the months of Irving's creative crisis, Ellin's trip abroad continued. It lasted far longer than either imagined it would: the better part of a year. And while she was away, he had ample time to contemplate the power and influence of the man who stood between him and his beloved: Clarence Hungerford Mackay.

▪ ▪ ▪

The founder of the Mackay dynasty, Ellin's Dublin-born grandfather, John, had, like Moses Baline, come to New York as a penniless immigrant. The year was 1840, and he was nine years old. Two years later his father died, John's schooling ended, and he went to work to help his mother and sisters. He was handicapped by a severe stutter, which gradually lessened as he grew older. Still, throughout his life, he spoke slowly and cautiously, always the man of few words. At sixteen, he became an apprentice in a shipyard, and once he completed his four years' training, he boarded one of the steamers he had helped to build, the *Golden Gate*, on her maiden voyage to San Francisco. There he became fascinated by an obsession among new arrivals in California: mining for gold and silver. He spent the better part of a decade as an itinerant miner in the Sierra foothills. He was happy here, in this hard, elemental existence, and might have remained indefinitely had not news come in 1859 of fabulous silver strikes in the Nevada Territory. When he reached the focus of the mining fever, Virginia City, he and his partner, another Irishman named Jack O'Brien, pitched their last fifty cents into a canyon; they were now penniless.

Virginia City was an exciting but vicious place, well documented by another young fortune hunter and reporter for the local newspaper: Samuel Clemens. John Mackay came to know him quite well. In his early book *Roughing It*, Clemens, writing under his pen name of Mark Twain, noted, "The first twenty-six graves in the Virginia [City] cemetery were occupied by *murdered men*. . . . The reason why there was so much slaughtering done was that in a new mining district the rough element predominates, and a person is not respected until he has 'killed his man.' "

There is no evidence that John Mackay needed to kill anyone to gain respect; he earned it working in the mines with his pick and shovel, at four dollars a day. This was a punishing form of labor, for a mine presented an infernal environment. The temperature ran around 130 degrees of damp, wilting heat. Laborers were forced to wear gloves to swing their picks because the tools were too hot to touch. They suffered severe stomach cramps brought on by the heat. Mackay and the others working in these conditions could devote only fifteen minutes out of every hour to digging; the other forty-five minutes they spent recuperating beside an air vent. After a tour of the Virginia City mines in 1879, General U. S. Grant, no stranger to physical hardship, exclaimed, "That's as close to hell as I ever want to get!"

Mackay eventually moved from digging the mines to preparing the timberwork for them; and then finally, at age thirty, he graduated from manual laborer to contractor, laying tunnels for various owners hoping to strike the mother lode. With a partner named J. M. Walker, he selected and acquired the rights to the so-called Bullion Mine, which, he eventually discovered, was utterly worthless. It consumed Mackay's earnings. Clemens, who was intrigued by the thought of owning a mine himself, offered to exchange jobs with Mackay, who replied, "No, I won't trade, Sam. I've never swindled anybody and I don't intend to start now." That would be, over the decades, his one boast—that he'd never swindled anyone; he'd rather *be* swindled.

Several years and several bad mines later, Mackay found his profitable mine, the Kentuck, which yielded a modest fortune. Mackay could have retired now, cleared out and gone to San Francisco or New York and lived like a gentleman, but he was always happiest in rough surroundings, surrounded by the pungent odor of manual labor. So he stayed on, living in spartan boardinghouses and increasing his fortune.

He joined forces with a new partner, James G. Fair. In 1866 Mrs. Fair introduced Mackay to a young widow, Marie Louise Hungerford Bryant. She was twenty-three, and she had lived as harsh a life as John Mackay. Marie had been born in Brooklyn, and at sixteen she'd married a country doctor, Edmund Bryant, a cousin to the poet William Cullen Bryant. Driven by her husband's restless opportunism, the couple settled in Virginia City. They had two daughters, and then Bryant began to succumb to a poisonous mixture of alcohol and drugs that were easy for a doctor to obtain. One of the daughters died in infancy, the surviving child was lame, and Bryant disintegrated so rapidly that he drifted away from the family and died soon after.

As a nineteen-year-old mother with an invalid child to support, Marie lived in poverty, teaching French to the few in Virginia City who were so inclined and taking in sewing, until she met John Mackay. Since he was already thirty-six years old, the courtship was brief. The only matter to be resolved concerned religion. John was a Roman Catholic, Marie a Methodist; she converted, and they were wed.

Mackay's modest wealth didn't go far in Virginia City; there was little to spend it on. Along with his wife, her daughter, and her mother, he moved into a primitive mountainside cottage where they all lived for the next several years. Marie soon became pregnant, and John Mackay's firstborn was a true son of Virginia City. He was born *in* a mine when his mother unexpectedly went into labor during a visit.

It was after the child, Willie, was born that Marie's love of travel asserted itself. The entire family departed Virginia City for a grand tour of Europe. When they returned to the United States, Mackay went straight to his Virginia City mines, while Marie, the children, and a retinue of servants took over a large house at 805 O'Farrell Street in San Francisco. She now found herself, at thirty-one, the wife of a prosperous mine owner who willingly indulged her taste for luxury and independence. It was here that her second son, Clarence Mackay (Ellin's father), was born, on April 17, 1874.

Marie soon grew bored with San Francisco, and once again she moved, this time to Paris. The contrast between her lavish style of living and that of her husband was astonishing. Consumed with his mining interests, John stayed behind in Virginia City. His mines threw off about a million dollars every month, and four-fifths of that was profit. But "Bonanza" Mackay, as he was now known, lived not in his Virginia City home, which had burned down, or a boardinghouse, but in a borrowed office. His preferred form of recreation was boxing. When he wasn't at his desk, he could generally be found at Bill Davis's South C Street gymnasium, where, stripped to the waist, he would go three rounds with all comers. He boxed in a slow and steady manner, overwhelming his opponent with patience as much as sheer force. He also, in his maturity, took pains to make up for his lack of education, poring over textbooks of English grammar and then, thus fortified, dipping into issues of the scholarly *North American Review.*

While Mackay tried to preserve his body and improve his mind, his wife and children lived in a mansion near the Champs-Élysées and the Arc de Triomphe. Here Marie's chief concern was obtaining entry into the highest circles of French society.

She found it slow going at first, but then one of her off-the-cuff remarks established her reputation. She started a preposterous campaign to decorate the Arc de Triomphe in honor of General Grant, which finally came to nothing. In her frustration, she told a reporter, "Very well, I'll buy their old arch and redecorate it myself!" And when General Grant visited Paris, she gave a ball in his honor that lasted until four o'clock in the morning. Together with her impertinent remark about the Arc de Triomphe, the night made her name. She soon ran the reigning salon of the period, attracting the queen of Spain one day, the president of the French Republic the next. Even her jewelry generated immense publicity; her $300,000 sapphire necklace, designed by Boucheron, was one of the main attractions of the Paris Exhibition of 1878. Fifteen years earlier, she had been a young widow living in a Virginia City boardinghouse; now she was one of the wealthiest, best-known inhabitants of Paris. Finally, Marie attained pseudo-immortality as the thinly disguised heroine of a popular novel of the time, Ludovic Halévy's *L'Abbé Constantin,* the story of a rich young American woman who, after being seen by a local curé as a threat, becomes a benefactor of the Catholic church and all its good works.

Marie's two sons, Willie and Clarence, were raised in this surpassingly wealthy, snobbish, yet essentially empty atmosphere. Wearing the best clothes that could be bought, educated by the best tutors, surrounded by servants, they seemed invulnerable. Not even royalty lived quite so opulently as they did. Though they were American, their frame of reference was entirely European, that of the reactionary and moralistic Second Empire.

The arrogance of limitless wealth eventually led to the undoing of Marie's reputation, at least in France. The unlikely catalyst was her portrait. Jean Louis Ernest Meissonier was the most popular portrait artist in the Paris of the 1880s. He was a small, petulant, haughty man, convinced of his artistic immortality, who worked out of his studio on the Parc Monceau. Wealthy Parisians came to implore him to paint their likeness; he refused many, but he accepted Marie Mackay's commission, for which she agreed to pay a fee of 80,000 francs. When she viewed the result, she was displeased, perhaps with good reason. One critic wrote: "The picture is a gross caricature of the fair sitter, who is a handsome, refined-looking woman, and not the vulgar washerwoman masquerading in a medieval costume that Meissonier has represented her to be." She demanded changes, which the artist refused to make, telling her that he could sell it for much more on the open market than the fee he had charged her. Enraged, Marie paid for her portrait, took it home, and in the presence of a group of friends, set fire to the canvas and let it burn to ashes.

There ensued an uproar in the Parisian press, which attacked Marie Mackay for having the insolence to destroy a work of art. Marie argued that she could do whatever she liked with the portrait since she owned it, but her line of reasoning failed to assuage popular opinion in France. With characteristic impulsiveness, she left Paris permanently and moved her family to London, where she acquired, thanks to the generosity of her distant husband, an equally grand house at 6 Carlton House Terrace. In 1886 she established herself anew as a society hostess by entertaining the Prince of Wales.

After two decades abroad, Marie was as celebrated as her husband. The distance separating husband and wife suited them, allowed them to become more and more their distinctive selves. Once a year, John made a pilgrimage to Europe to visit his wife, having prearranged with his business manager to send a cable summoning him home on urgent business soon after he arrived. The parade of finery that dazzled Marie bored him to the point where he liked to tell his wife's dignified guests of the barnyard animals who'd crowded into his boyhood home back in Dublin. Not even French cooking appealed to him; he taught his wife's chefs to make his preferred meal: corned beef and cabbage. Later, when his wife moved to London, he was even more uncomfortable visiting, for he despised the English with the special hatred of the Irish.

In the spring of 1893, a would-be assassin, enraged by the extravagance of Marie's famous sapphire necklace—its cost, he said, could have fed five hundred families—shot John Mackay in San Francisco. Marie and her two sons rushed to him by boat and by train. The press termed their journey west a "race of death," but by the time Marie reached her husband's bedside, he had begun to recover from the injury. He was soon able to stroll with his family through Chinatown, where Marie patiently heard out acquaintances from the old days—before London and Paris, when she had been an impoverished widow. After this brief visit, Marie once again left John and returned with the boys to London.

The brush with disaster marked a turning point in the family's fortunes. The mines were depleted, and Mackay began to invest in the new field of electronic transmission, especially transoceanic cables. No one knew why Mackay embarked on this new venture in his later years; possibly it was a symbolic attempt to keep in touch with his distant wife and family. In partnership with James Gordon Bennett, proprietor of the *New York Herald*, he founded the Commercial Cable Company, whose steamer, the *Mackay-Bennett*, immediately began laying cable. The new company soon found itself locked into a price war with its chief rival, Western Union, backed by financier Jay Gould. Even Mackay's business partners predicted he would lose everything on the venture. But after a bitter struggle, Gould relented, claiming, "There's no beating John Mackay. If he needs another million or two he goes to his silver mine and digs it up."

One day in October 1895, the aging tycoon received a tragic message on his cable system. It was from Marie, in Paris, informing him that his son Willie had died in a riding accident. He had, Mackay subsequently learned, fallen from his horse during a steeplechase race. Willie's body was brought back to the United States aboard ship and buried in the new Mackay family mausoleum. Clarence—Clarie, to the family—was suddenly called on to fulfill his older brother's role as heir apparent to the Mackay empire. He was only twenty-one at the time, with little interest in anything besides sports, and he abruptly found himself working in an unfamiliar city, New York, in a business about which he was ignorant, for a father he scarcely knew.

As the son of John Mackay, however, he was quickly able to establish himself in New York, and three years later he married Katherine "Kitty" Duer, a flighty and attractive young member of a socially prominent family. (Her sister Alice would become the writer and Round Table habituée.) Although the Duer name commanded respect, the family had for some time been drifting into genteel poverty, and they were glad to have their fortunes refreshed with Mackay's millions.

As a wedding present, his father, now in his late sixties, bestowed on the couple a Louis XIII mansion, designed by Stanford White, located in Roslyn, Long Island. The stones used in the construction came from New York City's dismantled 42nd Street reservoir. The estate, the full square mile of it, had a favored location: the crest of the Wheatley Hills, one of the highest points on Long Island. When the weather was clear, the buildings of New York City, twenty-three miles away, were plainly visible. Because of the spectacular view, the Clarence Mackays christened their palatial home Harbor Hill. It was here that Ellin Mackay grew to maturity, and where she was still living at the time she met Irving Berlin.

The grounds of the Harbor Hill estate were as splendid as the house. There were fountains and a pair of bronze horses—all of French design. Since Clarie fancied himself a sportsman, Harbor Hill boasted extensive athletic facilities: an indoor tennis court housed in a Tudor-style building (one of only two private indoor courts in the country—the other belonged to Jay Gould), an indoor swimming pool and squash court, a trophy room to display the awards Clarence accumulated, and two lawn-tennis courts. As a novelty Clarence installed a mechanical deer that at the touch of a button ran on a track through the woods. It was intended to serve as a moving target, but it also appealed to Kitty Mackay's sense of humor. Once, after spending a long, boring session with her lawyer at Harbor Hill, she asked him to sit on the deer. Since he was intimidated by her, he got on. She pushed a button, and off he went on the deer into the woods, clinging to his briefcase and derby. When the unexpected ride ended, he curtly tipped his hat to her and quietly departed.

While Kitty indulged her taste for pranks, Clarie played polo and bred horses, another gentleman's pursuit. His racing colors were turquoise blue and black, and he was especially proud of them. With his dinner jacket he wore vest buttons and cuff links of turquoise enamel surrounded by small rose diamonds—all designed by Cartier. In addition to horses, he bred dairy cattle, housed in the latest, most up-to-date barn that could be bought, located at the north end of the estate. Each year his livestock won awards at the Nassau County Fair. He lacked for nothing.

Though Clarence acquired other properties, including a town house at 3 East 75th Street in New York City and a leased hunting estate on Gardiners Island, Harbor Hill remained the seat of the Mackay family. Clarie had succeeded, thanks to his father's money, in reproducing the highly artificial world in which he had grown up. As he spent his fortune, it was apparent that Clarie had inherited his mother's scale of values. Unlike her, he had never known any other kind of life, and he was even more rigid and snobbish than she.

In 1900 Clarence and Kitty had their first child, also called Katherine, but known to everyone simply as "K." John Mackay, the patriarch, died of pneumonia in London on July 20, 1902, leaving a fortune estimated in amounts varying from $30 million to $60 million. Clarie attempted to complete projects his father had initiated. The Postal Telegraph and Cable Corporation, as the family business was now called, was in the process of laying a cable reaching from San Francisco to Honolulu. He oversaw the final stages of the project, but as the years passed, it became apparent that he had no idea how to manage the empire he'd inherited, no vision of cable communications, and no feel for business dealings.

His inflexible personal prejudices prevented him from taking advantage of opportunities to expand. Once he was approached by a young man named David Sarnoff, who was working for one of his rivals, the Radio Corporation of America. Young Sarnoff was convinced that the future of electronic communications lay not in transoceanic cables but in home radios. He'd had little success in bringing his own company around to his way of thinking, and now he wanted to start his own firm. All he asked of Mackay was a $10,000 investment: a sizable sum to many, though not for the head of Postal Telegraph. When Mackay gazed on David Sarnoff he saw not an innovative entrepreneur but another Irving Berlin—an upstart Jew—and he sent Sarnoff away. Sarnoff returned to the RCA fold, where his radio plan eventually met with enormous success and propelled him to the leadership of the company. On another occasion Gugliemo Marconi, the principal inventor of wireless transmission and winner of the 1909 Nobel Prize for physics, appeared before Mackay, seeking backing. But Clarence disliked Italians even more than Jews. Years before, his half-sister had married a no-good Italian count, and it became an article of faith with him that all Italians were despicable. So Mackay ignored Marconi as he'd ignored Sarnoff, thus depriving himself of another important business opportunity. He remained frozen in time, forever a man of the nineteenth century. His passions were reserved for private pursuits: sports, religion, and his family. On March 22, 1903, Ellin was born, and four years later, the third and final child completed the family. He was named John, after his grandfather.

Years later, when she was in her forties, Ellin published an autobiographical novel, *Lace Curtain*, about her privileged childhood. In this vivid record of daily life in Harbor Hill's unreal domain, she wrote touchingly of her father and his religious convictions.

> He looked so handsome in his navy-blue jacket and his jaunty panama with the bright band. He squeezed the black bulb and the horn played two notes that might be the beginning of a little tune. It was fun to drive with her father. It was queer to go to confession with him. She knew he went but she never imagined it. He didn't seem like a penitent. It was hard to imagine the hand with the gold signet ring clenched in contrition. To imagine the laughing mouth repeating the solemn words, *Through my fault, through my fault, through my most grievous fault.* Everything about him was gay. Even his business was gay. The map in his office with the little red flags dotted all over the United States.

She was equally taken with Harbor Hill's elaborate network of fountains and gardens.

> The early summer flowers were blooming in the French garden. Pale pink deepened to red in the formal design of the flower

> beds. The creamy gravel paths outlined the bright squares in which the flowers were planted in intricate curves. The French garden was an elaborately patterned carpet between the house and steps that led to the lower terrace. The lower terrace was green and white. The morning shadow of the house deepened the color of the young grass. In the center of the lawn was the white fountain. No water played over the marble. At this hour the fountain was silent. On each side of the terrace the white statues stood at the edge of the wood. . . . Beyond the flowered and grass terraces, the hill dropped against the blue. . . . At the abrupt end of the terrace she could look down at the sky.

Look down at the sky. The illusion derived from Harbor Hill's elevation. Nothing, it seemed, could be higher than the Mackays' position in the scheme of things.

As the ruler of this landscaped kingdom, Clarie looked every inch the patrician. He had clear blue eyes, dark hair, and a large, straw-colored mustache. With the passing of time, he gradually trimmed the mustache back, but when he was younger, it spread in unruly profusion across his lower face. One of Ellin's first memories of her father was the sight of this imposing mustache, obscured by a beer mug he'd raised to his lips. Handsome, wealthy, admired for his athletic prowess if not for his business acumen, surrounded by his family, Clarie seemed blessed beyond measure.

During Ellin's youth, while the Mackays still prospered, the family socialized with the other prominent dynasties who populated their corner of Long Island: the Whitneys, Vanderbilts, and the Theodore Roosevelts. Among all his circle Mackay's greatest admiration was reserved for the former president, whose emphasis on physical fitness and saber rattling strongly appealed to Clarie.

In this homogeneous social environment, the one anomaly of the Mackay family was their religion. However, Clarie's belonging to a religious minority made him even less tolerant of outsiders than some of his Protestant neighbors. Ellin, in particular, came to resent her father's prejudice against Italians and Jews, which, coming from an Irish Catholic, struck her as hypocritical. In her autobiographical novel, a character named Shea, closely patterned after her grandfather,

John Mackay, addresses this incendiary issue. "His voice was loud," she wrote of Shea, "his brogue thick with anger" as he articulates Ellin's reproof to her father.

> Once we were the despised ones. For fifty years and more we were the outsiders. We were the last to come. We were the poor, the ignorant, the unwelcome. Then in the eighties came the big migration of Jews, driven as once we were driven, and we . . . think to build them a ghetto and so ourselves be free. You foolish children. Freedom is born of freedom. . . . I've even heard you speak with scorn of shanty Irish. . . . We live in grand houses here, but it was a shanty I was born in the old country. . . . And I'll thank you to remember the American doctrine that all men are created equal.

Even before Ellin was old enough to question her father's views, the seeds of the family's destruction were being sown. In 1909, when she was only six (and Irving Berlin was publishing his first hit song, "My Wife's Gone to the Country"), Clarie developed throat cancer and underwent surgery on his neck and tongue. The doctor treating him was Joseph Blake, a society physician who lived with his wife and children in Tarrytown, New York. Blake was often at Harbor Hill, attending his patient, and during these visits he started a romantic involvement with Clarence's wife, Kitty. Long after Clarie recovered, the affair between Dr. Blake and Kitty Mackay continued. She was an unlikely candidate for the role of clandestine lover, since she was best known as a society matron who several years earlier had donated $50,000 toward an Episcopalian church in Roslyn. (Unlike her mother-in-law Louise, Kitty did not convert upon her marriage, and her children were uncertain about their religious identity.)

As the affair continued, Clarie and Kitty led increasingly separate lives. At some point he became aware of her philandering and took steps to retaliate. He was understandably hurt and angry, but he adopted a punitive strategy designed to break Kitty rather than restore her to him: he deprived her of their children. In February 1913, while she remained at Harbor Hill, Clarence took "K," who was then thirteen, Ellin, ten, and John, six, to a fifty-room "cottage" in Spring Lake,

New Jersey—the location of a wealthy summer colony—until Katherine broke with her lover. To prevent his wife from retrieving or even communicating with their three children, he surrounded the cottage with private guards, who shadowed every move they made. As the weather grew warmer and the children played tennis, their audience consisted of detectives.

When Kitty refused to yield, Clarence made secret arrangements to take the children abroad, where they would be permanently out of her reach. He booked a suite of twelve rooms, at a cost of $5,000, on the German ocean liner *Imperator*, under the name of "Armore." The family's baggage was sent ahead, without labels, so that no one would discover that the Mackays were about to make a transatlantic voyage. When the time came for Clarence and the children to leave, he gave out a story that they were simply going to Atlantic City for a few days.

On the day of their departure, the children were herded into a large car bound for the New York City pier from which the boat would be leaving. Throughout the journey, detectives clung to the running boards. The driver took a roundabout route, apparently heading for Atlantic City, but at the last minute changed direction and sped toward New York. The *Imperator*'s departure was delayed thirty minutes to accommodate the anonymous party that arrived late at the pier. As Clarence boarded the ship, he was accompanied by two guards who were there to shield him in case his wife tried to serve papers on him or in any way affect his departure.

Clarence's absence was soon noted, his ruse discovered. Reporters from local papers tried calling Kitty at Harbor Hill to get her reaction to Clarence's spiriting away their children to Europe. She was "so taken by surprise," ran one account, "she could not answer for a moment. Then she said, her voice indicating her emotion: 'Why, are you sure about that? I can't believe it. I'm astonished. I don't want to enter into a controversy with you on this matter, but I am certain you are mistaken.' "

Despite its prying, the press had no idea why Clarence had taken such drastic action. It was assumed that Kitty would divorce him simply because he had taken the children without her consent. Her continuing affair with Dr. Joseph Blake was still a secret.

For the children, the unexpected European vacation had its compensations. For Ellin, particularly, it afforded an opportunity to become acquainted with her distant, illustrious widowed grandmother, Marie Louise Hungerford Mackay. Marie still lived in London, an old woman doting on the memory of her firstborn son, Willie. Searching for a replacement for her mother, Ellin tried unsuccessfully to forge a relationship with Marie, but all the young woman would take away with her was a memory of Marie's splendid house and its furnishings. "I remember . . . I ran through the rooms, touching the statues and the pictures, and we pounded up and down the wide stone curves of the stairs," Ellin later wrote. "I remember the house, but I don't really remember you."

In the United States, the Blake family began to crumble under the weight of the affair. Since Dr. Blake frequently and openly visited Kitty at Harbor Hill, their relationship became known throughout the town of Roslyn. In September Catherine Ketchum Blake instigated a million-dollar lawsuit against Kitty Mackay for alienation of Dr. Blake's affection.

To avoid Mrs. Blake's law suit, Kitty fled to Portland, Maine, until it was dropped. However, Catherine Blake soon filed another suit, this time asking her unfaithful husband for a divorce and alimony payments of $1,500 per month.

During this period of intricate legal maneuvering, Kitty Mackay left Harbor Hill and rented a town house on Fifth Avenue in New York. When Clarence finally returned with the children from Europe, *he* rented a town house only a block away, the better to observe her activities.

Provoked by Clarence, Kitty decided she wanted a divorce; her lover was willing to marry her. But Mackay was quick to point out that divorce was not permitted by the Catholic Church, and he was prepared to keep Kitty in marital limbo for the rest of her life. Kitty, of course, was not a Catholic, and she was determined to become the next Mrs. Blake, even though it meant giving up her valued place in society, Harbor Hill, and her three young children.

In February 1914, Kitty quietly traveled to Paris, where Dr. Joseph Blake soon joined her. Now head of the American Red Cross Hospital in Neuilly, a suburb of Paris, he oversaw a staff of twelve doctors. As war loomed, Kitty and her lover took apartments close by one another and awaited completion of their American divorce proceedings. Kitty's, obtained in Connecticut, was the first to come through; Joseph Blake did not receive his until November, by which time Europe was caught up in the Great War. Kitty and Joseph decided to get married immediately, and to avoid interference from Clarence Mackay, Blake took advantage of a wartime dispensation with publishing marriage banns.

On the morning of Friday, November 27, he went to work at the hospital, where he discovered that injured soldiers were arriving in droves. He stayed in the operating room for hours, performing a nonstop series of amputations. Finally, at two-thirty in the afternoon, he left the operating table, scrubbed the blood from his hands, removed his blood-soaked overalls, and drove a Red Cross ambulance to Kitty's apartment on the Avenue Martin. There he met his bride-to-be and several friends and drove them directly to the office of Mayor Boillet, who married Joseph and Kitty in a hurried ceremony. The bride was dressed severely, in a dark blue suit and a marquise hat. After the couple exchanged vows, the Mayor made a speech expressing gratitude to Dr. Blake for the medical assistance he was giving to fallen French warriors.

In wartime there was no opportunity for a honeymoon or any other form of celebration. The newlyweds reentered the Red Cross ambulance, which Kitty herself drove back to the military hospital. Dr. Blake immediately resumed performing amputations on soldiers. The bride, meanwhile, returned to her apartment and took up her wartime work: knitting military jerseys.

The sudden marriage, with its connection both to the Mackay family and its wartime background, made for sensational American headlines that wounded Clarence afresh.

DR. BLAKE, FREE
24 HOURS, WEDS
MRS. MACKAY

Leaves Operating Table in Red
Cross Hospital for Ceremony
in Paris Mayor's Office

DIVORCED BY WIFE FRIDAY

The only advantage for Mackay to come from this public humiliation was the assurance that he was now entitled to custody of the children, his only consolation the knowledge that the family Dr. Blake had left behind was as upset as he. "I cannot understand it all," said Blake's ex-wife, Catherine. "I know Dr. Blake loved his sons as much as I do. But one woman's influence was forcible enough to take him miles away from them, and break up his home."

Now that he had been abandoned by his wife, Clarence gradually underwent a number of changes. He drew his three children ever closer to him, trying, as a divorced parent will, to compensate for the loss of their mother. But the children did not, in Ellin's estimation, appreciate his efforts. "Poor Clarie appeared to them so fierce when he was trying only to protect them," she later wrote. "He had not yet learned that no one, not even a parent, can make another's life safe."

Next, he retreated into a forbidding and ostentatious piousness. He redecorated Harbor Hill as a medieval castle, filled with Gothic and Renaissance works of art by masters such as Botticelli, Bellini, Verrocchio, Donatello, and Raphael; most depicted religious themes. Through prominent art dealers such as Joseph Duveen he obtained French tapestries, flags from the Crusades, and, most notably, a collection of armor rivaled only by William Randolph Hearst's. Walking into the Mackay mansion was comparable to entering a museum. Replicas of knights in authentic armor stood against either wall of the great stone halls, which were draped with tapestries and red velvet hangings.

One other important change came over Clarie. Though he refused to grant his wife a divorce, even after she remarried, he took a lover, and a highly unusual one at that. She was Anna Case, the Metropolitan Opera star. Case was a large woman, outgoing, affectionate, homely, and theatrical: in every way Clarence's opposite. They became acquainted through his involvement in New York's musical world, for, among his other interests, he was a member of the board of the New York Philharmonic and the Met. Just when they began their liaison or how often they were together is not known. A violation of the inhumanly stringent code Mackay had set for himself, his children, and his estranged wife, the affair was conducted entirely in secret.

As for Kitty and Joseph Blake, they spent the war years in Paris, returned to the United States, and began a new family. They would eventually have four offspring, and Kitty gave two of them the names of the children she had lost to Clarence: another Katherine and another John. For the rest of his life, Clarence claimed that all four children were illegitimate.

▪ ▪ ▪

And then, on September 25, 1925, after spending most of the year soul-searching and traveling abroad, Ellin Mackay returned to New York.

■ □ ■ □ ■ □ ■

CHAPTER 11

Ellin

During Ellin's absence, the public's fascination with Irving Berlin's private life steadily mounted. Alexander Woollcott's biography, *The Story of Irving Berlin*, appeared, first in a multipart serialization in *Liberty Magazine* and then as a book adorned with a moody illustration of its subject by Irving's friend, the illustrator Neysa McMein. Published by G. P. Putnam's Sons, the brief volume received a mixed critical reception; Woollcott's florid prose style served his theater reviews well, but his casual approach to research made for a rather slipshod book. Irving naturally responded more subjectively, and he was astounded by Woollcott's spirited re-creation of his life. Although he was already making an art form of elusiveness, he was thoroughly pleased by this type of public exposure and hastened to convey his approval to his friend and first biographer.

Clarence Mackay was said to have acquired a copy, but what he read in its pages could only have confirmed his doubts about the songwriter, for Woollcott's tale emphasized Berlin's immigrant background, impoverished Lower East Side youth, and exotic Jewishness: all traits that the reactionary magnate found repugnant.

In June 1925, *Variety* floated a rumor that Irving and Ellin were "betrothed." In response Clarence rashly vowed that the songwriter would marry Ellin "only over my dead body." The brief controversy was ignored by the more reputable papers, but, thanks in part to Clarence's highly quotable reaction, it did inspire Hearst's gossipy

New York Mirror to run stories purporting to trace the course of her romance with Berlin and describe the friction between the songwriter and Clarence Mackay. One account went so far as to manufacture a confrontation between the songwriter and the telegraph magnate.

"The day you marry my daughter," Clarence supposedly told Irving, "I'll disinherit her."

And Berlin was said to reply, "The day I marry your daughter, I'll settle $2 million on her."

Another fanciful account portrayed Mackay boasting of his ancestry, and Berlin responding, "I can trace mine back to Exodus."

"Is that so?" asked Mackay. "Then there's another Exodus for you now. Get out."

These fabrications were so outlandish that the *Mirror*'s rival, the tabloid *Graphic*, seized the opportunity to editorialize against this example of "irresponsible journalism." Later, the equally reckless *Graphic* would come up with a whopper that exceeded anything the *Mirror* ran about Irving Berlin and Ellin Mackay.

Berlin's romantic trials were now so widely known that they were reenacted in a popular Broadway revue. In George White's *Scandals*, which opened on June 22, 1925, Gordon Dooley portrayed a morose Irving Berlin bewailing the fact that he was "all alone," as enticing chorus girls writhed around his body. The skit was on target, and cruel as it was, there would be still bolder stage lampoons of Irving's and Ellin's on-again, off-again relationship.

As a result of this steady, if unreliable, publicity, reporters gathered on that bright September afternoon when Ellin's ship, the SS *Olympic*, docked in New York. They were primed to cross-examine her about Irving. Ellin, however, sounded chastened by the time she had spent abroad in her father's company. "The truth of the matter," she said at dockside, "is that if I were to marry I would have to surrender the companionship of my father. . . . And I can't bear to think of parting with him."

As she proceeded to deny that there ever had been a serious relationship with Berlin, the reporters became suspicious. How could those reports have gotten started? Ellin attempted to parry the question with Mackay sangfroid. "If you print the story of my engagement, I will simply have to deny it later to my friends. I have not met the young man I would marry to give up my father."

▪ ▪ ▪

Berlin scarcely took notice of Ellin's published remarks because he was grappling with the challenge of writing his first score for a musical comedy. Despite the celebrated mirth of his collaborators, it was not a happy experience for him. "I never knew that musical comedy was so difficult to produce until we began working with the Marx Brothers in 'The Cocoanuts,' " he complained. This show is now remembered as a zany period piece that served as the basis for the Marx Brothers' first movie, but the original production seethed with backstage discord and strain.

Much of the trouble stemmed from the antics of the four brothers themselves: Leonard (Chico), Adolph (Harpo), Julius (Groucho), and Herbert (Zeppo). Together, they'd been knocking around vaudeville for fifteen years, until, in 1924, they scored a major hit on Broadway in *I'll Say She Is!*, a production enlivened by their unique brand of anarchy. Nothing quite like this surreal parody of comic conventions had been seen on Broadway, and the Marx Brothers quickly developed a cult following. One of their chief admirers happened to be Irving Berlin. Much of the brothers' success came from their highly idiosyncratic, free-form way of working. To the Marx Brothers, the gags were everything, and they sacrificed the standard elements of a musical comedy—the script, the score, even the chorus girls—to this end.

After the success of *I'll Say She Is!* the brothers were pursued by a number of Broadway producers who wanted to stage their next show, but the man they wanted was Sam Harris. At Harpo's request, Berlin approached Harris on their behalf. Despite the songwriter's encouragement, Harris hesitated; comedy, he knew, was notoriously unpredictable. Irving asked him to allow the Marx Brothers to come to his office and go through some of their routines. Harris agreed, and the four madcap brothers soon had him in stitches. Still he hesitated. Finally, several days (and, one suspects, several reminders from Irving) later, Harris called the Marx Brothers in Syracuse, where they had gone for an out-of-town engagement of *I'll Say She Is!*, and told them he would become their producer.

Inevitably, Berlin was enlisted to compose the score; George S. Kaufman, his Round Table friend and occasional *Music Box Revue* scenarist, would write the script, a satire on the Florida land boom. As a setting for musical comedies, Florida was now all the rage; as

Kaufman worked on his script, Guy Bolton was writing *Tip-Toes*, a musical set in Palm Beach. In conventional scripts Florida traded on its reputation for playboys and sunshine, but for the Marx Brothers, the location became a haven for swindlers and fortune hunters.

To foster their collaboration, Kaufman and Berlin repaired to Atlantic City, where they took adjoining hotel rooms. The songwriter quickly assembled a dozen tunes—some, like "The Monkey Doodle Doo" of 1913, so old that they were all but forgotten, and some new. Irving's favorite happened to be a love song he'd written several years earlier. Like many of his songs, it had come about as the result of a casual remark, in this case one made by the girlfriend of his musical secretary, Arthur Johnston. In contrast to his boss, Johnston had a formidable reputation as a ladies' man, and his romantic scrapes were the talk of the office. There were so many women in his life he found it difficult to remember their names. At the time, his current girlfriend was called Mona, and she happened to be listening to Johnston and Berlin make idle conversation about how much money a hit song could earn. Impressed by the large sums mentioned, she inquired, "Mr. Berlin, would you write a song about me sometime?" To which Berlin replied, "Why sometime? Why not right now?" He asked her name, and then, leaning back, he began to hum a melody. Once he had that fixed, he devised words to go along with it. Meanwhile, her boyfriend Arthur jotted down the new song on a napkin. "I'll be loving you, Mona," went the lyrics.

There was no sense of lightning striking until 1925, when the hastily conceived, half-finished song came to Irving's attention. By then, however, Johnston had forgotten who Mona was; moreover, Berlin himself had no recollection of the song. After giving the matter some thought, he changed "Mona" to "Always." And the song was reborn.

As he struggled to complete "Always," Irving discovered that Kaufman was not merely indifferent to music but actively hostile to it. This clash of attitudes became a source of misery for Berlin and mirth for Kaufman, who left an acid account of the songwriter's ill-timed attempt to summon enthusiasm for his melody.

> Irving woke me up at five o'clock one morning to sing me a song he had just finished. Now, Irving has a pure but hardly

> strong voice, and, since I am not very strong myself at five o'clock in the morning, I could not catch a word of it. Moving to the edge of the bed, he sat down and sang it again, and again I failed to get it. Just when it looked as though he would have to get in my bed before I could hear it, he managed, on the third try, to put it across. The song was a little number called "Always," and its easy-going rhythms were just up my street. I learned it quickly and as dawn broke we leaned out of the window and sang it to the Atlantic Ocean. . . .
>
> To this day, I do not quite know the difference between Handel's "Largo" and—well—Largo's "Handel." But I have always felt that I knew a little something about lyrics, and I was presumptuous enough then to question Irving's first line, "I'll be loving you always." "Always" was a long time for romance. . . . I suggested, therefore, that the opening line might be a little more in accord with reality—something like "I'll be loving you Thursday." But Irving would have none of it.

Kaufman's lack of enthusiasm caused Irving to lose confidence in the song, and "Always" was deleted from the score of *The Cocoanuts*—though not from its creator's memory.

As preparations for the *The Cocoanuts* progressed, the show's complexity and cost multiplied. "We started to produce a musical comedy which was to cost but $50,000," Berlin noted; the figure brought a smile to Harris's lips. He was, said Berlin, "willing to bet me anything it would cost twice as much. It did that and more." In fact, the budget would eventually reach $250,000.

Money was the least of Irving's worries. As master of the Music Box, he had become accustomed to having the final say over all aspects of a production. Now he was but one more collaborator at the mercy of four eccentric stars. "When we started to rehearse we had our plan well formulated," Irving explained in the *New York Telegram*. "But 'ere long suggestions began to come in from the Marx brothers, from Kaufman, from Harris—in fact, from everybody—and before we knew what had happened the general scheme of things had been turned topsy turvy. My well laid score was opened up and I wrote new songs, new lyrics and eventually we had an entirely different production than had been planned."

Under the strain of coping with this theatrical chaos, Berlin and Kaufman subjected one another to flinty discourtesy. Whenever the music began to play, Kaufman walked out of the theater, and whenever dialogue held the stage, Berlin walked out. The quarreling collaborators suffered further abuse from the Marx Brothers themselves, who took their accustomed liberties with both the songs and the dialogue. The lyrics for Berlin's "A Little Bungalow" were generally mangled or omitted, and the Marx Brothers gradually replaced most of Kaufman's original lines with ad libs. It was during a run-through of this show that Kaufman, himself a master of the ad lib, remarked, "You know, I think I just heard one of my own lines."

Sam Harris, usually adept at theatrical diplomacy, was unable to make peace among the warring factions. His mental clarity had failed him, he became hard of hearing, and he was prone to uttering nonsensical remarks. Despite the efforts of *two* directors, Oscar Eagle and Sammy Lee, to give some semblance of structure to the show, out-of-town tryouts in Boston and Philadelphia lagged; many audience members walked out before the final curtain. In desperation, Kaufman cut deeply into the script and the score, while Berlin complained that the result was more of a comedy than a musical. "I'll tell you what," snapped Kaufman, "You waive the songs and I'll waive the story."

There is reason to believe that by the opening night, December 8, 1925, Irving's mind was more on private matters than the reception accorded *The Cocoanuts*. His romantic relationship with Ellin, for months the subject of considerable gossip and journalistic invention, suddenly entered the public eye when she gave him a "box party" at the theater. The gathering offered a public statement, as if any were needed, concerning the status of their relationship. After the performance, the couple went to the town house of Herbert Bayard Swope, where they celebrated quietly with members of the Round Table. "A fair girl to see and sweetly spoke," noted columnist Franklin P. Adams of Ellin in his private diary. Few doubted that Berlin would marry his rebellious society girlfriend; never before had he been seen so often with the same woman. But the guessing as to the couple's timing—and Clarence's reaction—continued unabated.

Berlin was able to indulge himself in the luxury of party going on the opening night of *The Cocoanuts* because he was, for once, not responsible for every aspect of the production. He needn't have worried because the show, despite the monumental aggravation it had caused nearly everyone involved with it (except the Marx Brothers), was well received by audiences and critics alike. Groucho's quips went over especially well. He flattered a starlet by exclaiming that her eyes shone "like the pants of a blue serge suit," and in the midst of the merriment, he gravely announced, "The next number on the program will be a piccolo solo which we will omit." Harpo relied on deeds rather than words to make an impression, honking his horn and mugging shamelessly. He tried to annoy Groucho with unscripted bits of business, such as chasing a chorus girl across the stage as Groucho tried to complete a scene. But Groucho took Harpo's stunt in stride, telling the audience, "the nine-twenty's right on time."

In fact, the Marx Brothers made so many changes in the script that by June, Sam Harris decided to announce a new and improved "summer edition" of *The Cocoanuts*, featuring four more songs by Irving Berlin. The revised production attracted repeat business and a new round of reviews, which were even more enthusiastic than they had been on opening night. In its various incarnations, the show ran on Broadway for 218 performances before setting out on a lucrative tour lasting two years.

The Cocoanuts would never be counted among the glories of the American musical, now embarking on an extremely fertile period, *without* the help of Irving Berlin, but it was a unique phenomenon. Still, there was no use pretending that Irving's songs were heard to good advantage amid the Marx Brothers' mayhem. It formed part of the joke that they played on the audience—that Irving Berlin had written their music. While the show became a commercial success, Irving's score marked another retreat from the cutting edge of popular song. Lost in romantic reverie, he was far from the synthesis he had achieved in *Yip! Yip! Yaphank*, when his songs and presence had crystalized a moment in history. He had been upstaged by a family of clowns.

▪ ▪ ▪

Once Berlin had put the clamor of the Marx Brothers, George Kaufman, and Sam Harris behind him, he was at last free to concentrate on Ellin. Her published statements to the contrary, they were together almost constantly throughout December, on display at parties, restaurants, and Round Table soirées. All who saw them at this time were aware of the intensity of their devotion to one another. Had he known, Clarence would have disapproved, but Ellin didn't bother to inform him. She lived a double life, now the dutiful daughter, now the rebellious heiress. Her ambivalence suggested that she lacked the inner strength to resist her father's will. She needed Irving to bear the standard of independence for her; he became her liberator.

Irving had no desire to vanquish Clarence; he simply wanted Ellin. It had been over thirteen years since his first wife, Dorothy Goetz, died, after a marriage so brief it had scarcely been a marriage at all. Since then, caution and restraint had marked all his dealings with women; it was not that he lacked passion, but he kept it tightly reined or sublimated it into his music. Now Ellin was to find herself the beneficiary of the powerful emotions Irving had hoarded for fifteen years.

To an immigrant, a self-made man such as Irving Berlin, Ellin Mackay was the ultimate American status symbol: blonde, blue-eyed, wealthy, known in her own right for her journalism. Marriage to Ellin appeared to remedy many of the inadequacies he felt, whether they were real or imagined; becoming her husband would take him as far as he could possibly go into the mainstream of American society. And yet marriage to Ellin implied loss, as well. It would mean that he had taken his largest step thus far toward severing all links to his past—to Russia, Judaism, and the surviving members his family (five older siblings). It was the supreme act of assimilation.

Ellin's path to Irving was also strewn with obstacles. She carried with her the unhappy memories of the lonely years at Harbor Hill after her mother had abandoned the family and the public scandal this action had created. As a reaction, Ellin had a highly developed sense of privacy concerning her personal life. The last thing she wanted to do was create another scandal in the Mackay family by marrying Irving against her father's wishes. Her mother had deeply and permanently wounded her father by running off with another man; now Ellin had to decide if she wanted to repeat this betrayal of Clarence, whom she still loved, in spite of his obvious limitations. It was a difficult decision for Ellin to make because she felt no personal animosity toward her father, only toward his self-important "class" and his stultifying way of life.

Matters came to a head as the couple celebrated New Year's Eve at the Mayfair Hotel in New York City. While dancing with Ellin, Irving announced that he was sailing to Europe in two days, on Saturday, aboard the *Homeric*, with or without her. The plan left no time for them to get married, and Ellin was not in favor of it. A sudden wedding—an elopement—was one thing, but she felt that leaving the country before they wed was too drastic a step. She insisted that he delay their departure until they could be married. The earliest opportunity was the first Monday of the New Year. Irving canceled the *Homeric* reservations.

They spent an anxious weekend apart, Ellin at her father's town house on East 75th Street, Irving at his duplex apartment on West 46th Street. No one else was aware of their plan.

On Monday, January 4, 1926, the first full week of the new year finally began. The weather was foul; tendrils of fog lingered along the Palisades and obscured the upper reaches of city buildings. The temperature was stalled in the forties, and rain, cloaked in mist, drenched workers returning to their offices after the three-day weekend. At City Hall, stylish James J. Walker commenced his first term as mayor of New York City, a position he owed in part to the campaign song written by his friend Irving, "It's a Walk-in with Walker."

Irving himself had been up all night in a state of great anxiety, waiting to make his move. In the morning he finally called Ellin at home, and they made their final plans to marry in a civil ceremony that day. (At the time, couples could be wed in New York without having to take a blood test or endure a waiting period.) After they spoke, Ellin drove herself to Irving's apartment.

While Ellin was en route in her red roadster, Berlin telephoned Winslow to enlist his aid in the matrimonial plans. It was not yet nine o'clock in the morning, and, Winslow later told the press, "I knew there was something up at once, because he usually does not get up until two o'clock in the afternoon. He asked me to come down to the apartment at once and to bring along my wife."

By the time Max and Tillie Winslow arrived at West 46th Street at eleven o'clock, Ellin was with Irving, and they announced their intention to wed immediately. Having been privy to their relationship, Winslow was only mildly surprised. Irving and Max then discussed how they planned to announce the marriage to the press; it was decided that Max would do the talking, Irving the smiling and waving. As the plans took shape, Max telephoned the company's publicity manager, Ben Bloom, and without explaining why, ordered him to hurry to his boss's home.

Once the wedding party—Irving, Ellin, the Winslows, and Ben Bloom—assembled, they went to considerable lengths to appear inconspicuous. They took the subway downtown to the Municipal Building, where the ceremony would be performed. For Ellin, to the manor born, it was the first subway ride of her life.

They arrived at the imposing gray expanse of the Municipal Building and found their way to the office of the deputy city clerk, James McCormick, who was to marry them, only to discover that he was about to leave for lunch. In a classic display of civil service mentality, he refused to delay his meal to perform the brief ceremony.

Suddenly, the confusion that Irving had desperately wanted to avoid engulfed the stranded wedding party. His features—the dark eyes, the thick black hair—were recognized. Well wishers, curiosity seekers, and eventually reporters descended on the scene outside McCormick's office. Impressed by the throng, the stubborn clerk relented, and he agreed to sacrifice a few minutes of his lunch break and perform the ceremony after all. However, he labored under the misapprehension that it was *Winslow* who would be married, with Berlin acting as best man.

As Winslow did his best to set the befuddled McCormick straight, Ellin and Irving hastily completed the necessary documents. Filling out his affadavit for a marriage license, the groom was plainly hurried and nervous; his handwriting slithered across the page like a child's, and the date he supplied for the death of his first wife was off by a year. Eventually Ben Bloom took over for the distracted couple and completed the actual marriage license for them, which they then signed, with Bloom and Winslow acting as witnesses. By now the crowd had grown so large that the wedding party was forced to abandon the Marriage Chapel, where the service was to have taken place, for the private office of the city clerk, who was, naturally, out to lunch.

Even in these functional surroundings, Ellin made a lovely bride, tall and slender in a gray tailored suit and orange cloche hat. Despite their elegance, they were old clothes in which she had hastily dressed before leaving her father's town house that morning, looking as though she were going shopping rather than getting married. Irving was dressed more appropriately for the occasion in a sober dark gray suit, and he was trembling with anxiety.

Knowing how to comport herself in public, Ellin looked older than her twenty-two years, just as Irving looked younger than his thirty-seven; side by side, they seemed to be approximately the same age. But when they responded to McCormick, who performed the ceremony, their voices were strikingly different. Ellin's was high and lilting, with definite upper-class accents, while Irving's was strident and reedy, indelibly marked by the Lower East Side streets of his youth. When he spoke, it sounded as though he were grumbling rather than agreeing to take Ellin for his wife. His tone of voice was deceptive; Irving was completely committed to marrying her.

As soon as McCormick pronounced the couple man and wife (and could, at last, have his lunch) Ellin and Irving dodged the onlookers and reporters they had attracted and scurried downstairs to a bank of public telephones. Ellin's first call was not to her father; she was not prepared to face that difficulty, not yet. Instead, she called her editor at *The New Yorker*, Harold Ross. It seemed that she was concerned that her sudden marriage might cause her to miss the magazine's deadline.

Ross got right on the line. "Hello, Miss Mackay," he said.

She quickly corrected him. "Oh, no, it's Mrs. Berlin. The fact is I shan't be able to get my piece in on time. I'm leaving town in about twenty minutes."

Neither of the Berlins would tell reporters where they were going after the ceremony, but Irving confided to Winslow (who quickly and, as it would turn out, inadvisedly told the press) that he had reserved one of the two presidential suites on the *Leviathan*, cabin 150; the accommodations cost $5,000. And then the couple left the Municipal Building.

They avoided the subway this time, preferring to take a taxi to Irving's apartment, where they resumed spreading the news of their marriage to their friends and relatives—except for Clarence. He did not hear of it until two o'clock in the afternoon, when a friend with connections in the city clerk's office telephoned him at work to advise him that his daughter had married Irving Berlin. Clarence received the news calmly. He dictated a carefully worded statement for his secretary to read when the sensation-hungry reporters called. He then left his office for the day and secluded himself in his town house.

Primed by Max Winslow, the man from *The New York Times* was the first to call Mackay's office. As instructed, his secretary read the statement, which declared that the wedding had occurred without Clarence's "knowledge or approval." To those who had been following accounts of the romance during the past six months, those few words were sufficient to send a signal that a battle was in the making. Ellin's estranged mother, Katherine, living with her second husband, Dr. Joseph Blake, in the Hudson River hamlet of Irvington, New York, was the next family member to be contacted by the press. She wisely refused to comment in public on her daughter's marriage. Privately, she was pleased to see Ellin following in her footsteps and taking this spectacular leap into matrimony.

Throughout that chilly January afternoon, as the rain stopped and started, the newlyweds attempted to cope with the flood of calls to Irving's apartment. By four o'clock, the short winter's day was nearly over, and this narrow corridor of West 46th Street was fast growing dark. Lights appeared in windows along the street, and the trolleys were beginning to fill with people heading home from work. The Berlins decided that the onset of the rush hour was a moment favorable for their getaway. They carefully left the apartment, and, seeing that the street was empty, dashed into a large gray coupe waiting at curbside. Just as the car was about to pull away, they realized that a maid had forgotten to bring their bag. While they waited, reporters suddenly materialized and surrounded the car, holding the impatient couple captive within.

"Have you heard in any way from Mr. Mackay?" called one journalist, asking the question that was uppermost in everyone's minds.

"I can't say anything," Berlin responded in a high, insistent voice. "I can't say where we are going or anything."

Ellin could not resist adding, "You don't expect us to tell you where we are going and then have all of you down there after us, do you?" As a journalist herself, she was clearly more comfortable bandying words with the press than her anxious husband was. By now the wait for the bag was growing tedious, and Ellin loudly complained, "That maid will cause us to miss the train," inadvertantly supplying reporters with a clue concerning the couple's destination. At length the maid appeared with the bag and stuffed it into the car beside the chauffeur. The car pulled away, and the reporters watched it merge into the traffic coursing along Fifth Avenue.

Spurred by Ellin's remark about missing a train, the reporters assumed that the couple would proceed from Pennsylvania Station to one of three destinations: the remote Adirondack Mountains of upstate New York, where Max Winslow was known to have a vacation home; Florida; or Atlantic City. The last choice happened to be correct, and once again the Berlins were dogged by confusion. By the time they reached Penn Station, their train had left. And the *Leviathan*, on which he had booked their $5,000 suite, would not be leaving for a week.

Ever since he'd picked up the phone that morning to propose to Ellin, nothing had gone according to plan, and Irving's anxiety about the manner in which the press would depict his elopement mounted steadily. He was losing control of this, the most significant day of his personal life. He had always insisted on maintaining an iron control over his life; he had fought for it and usually won it: control over his songs, his career, himself. Forced to improvise, Irving declared that they should return to his apartment for dinner. They did so; afterward, they were driven to Atlantic City, arriving at eleven o'clock at night. They spent their wedding night in the same suite at the Ritz where Berlin had written his recent hit songs—it was his good luck suite. To spare the exhausted newlyweds unwelcome publicity, the hotel management permitted them to check in without registering.

In the morning the weather was, if anything, even grayer and rainier than it had been the previous day. Outside the Berlins' tenth-floor oceanfront suite, fog obscured the heaving Atlantic Ocean. At this time of year, the city's famous Boardwalk was nearly deserted.

While the Berlins remained behind closed doors, news of their elopement earned banner headlines on the front pages of most of the New York dailies: precisely the kind of prying, speculative coverage

Irving had been hoping to avoid. Thanks to the voluble Max Winslow, even *The New York Times*, one of the most restrained newspapers, bristled with details that Irving, were he awake to read them, would have found keenly embarrassing.

ELLIN MACKAY WED
TO IRVING BERLIN;
SURPRISES FATHER

Parent Disapproves Society
Girl's Marriage to Jazz
Composer

TELL OF THEIR PLANS, THEN VANISH—
BRIDEGROOM'S RAPID RISE
TO FAME

Irving Berlin a *jazz* composer? The term was now used so loosely that it applied to a broad spectrum of popular music, including, but not limited to, what later came to be defined as jazz. Even though he did not, strictly speaking, compose jazz (and in fact despised it), Berlin's name was now permanently linked to the gaudy age named after it.

A very different newspaper, the *New York American*, played the story much the same way.

IRVING BERLIN WEDS ELLIN MACKAY

Elopers Speed Away
Rich Father Ignored for
Composer by Society Bud

The splashy lead paragraph played up the conflict between Berlin and his new father-in-law:

> Broadway's king of jazz, born Isadore [actually, it was *Israel*] Baline, crossed the labyrinths of social and religious difference and carried off the youngest daughter of Clarence H. Mackay, multimillionaire head of the Post Telegraph Com-

> pany. . . . Even yesterday morning, Berlin told a friend he didn't think she would go through with it. But she did.

The publicity generated a widespread public reaction, which coalesced along two lines of thought. Berlin's cronies on Broadway and Tin Pan Alley, who lionized Irving and rightly considered him one of their own, wished the couple well; in addition, they were generally impressed by his having had the *chutzpah* to carry off one of the country's most prominent "society buds."

The reaction on Park Avenue took a different tone. Ellin's crowd, those listed in the *Social Register*, instantly took a disapproving view of the elopement. Everyone knew Berlin was a dear little man—so talented and successful—but it was just that *those* people were better off marrying one of their own kind. What was Ellin to do, convert to Judaism? An unthinkable recourse. Would she have to speak Yiddish, learn Hebrew, and keep a kosher home, the way *those* people did? And what about children, and their place in society? Ellin had put herself in an impossible situation. Her kind of people insisted that it was simply too difficult to maintain an interfaith marriage. No matter how deeply the two partners were in love, it was bound to break down under the strain of social realities.

It was Ellin, as the traitor to her class, who had to bear the burden of such prejudice. The instant she married Irving, she was no longer welcome in the Mackay circle; she would receive no more invitations to their mammoth summer "cottages" in Newport; their extensive network of their turf, field, tennis, polo, and golf clubs; or their formal social events. The ostracism to which she was immediately subjected was publicly expressed by the society columnist and social arbiter Cholly Knickerbocker (Maury Paul), in the *American*: "Ellin by her marriage has gained a talented husband, a man who made all the world sing. She is to be congratulated. Mr. Berlin has gained nothing—except Ellin." With that cryptic remark, Paul intended to remind his readers that by eloping, Ellin would surely lose her inheritance, which, Paul implied, was the real reason Irving had married her.

While talk of their elopement filtered up and down the city's social strata, Irving and Ellin remained undisturbed in their honeymoon suite, thanks to a false rumor that they were still in Manhattan, hiding in the home of an unspecified "theatrical magnate." However, several reporters who happened to stake out the Ritz in Atlantic City on the off chance that the Berlins might be there spotted the couple striding briskly through the lobby on their way to the windswept Boardwalk. Both were correctly dressed: Irving in a belted polo coat, a dark blue suit, and black derby; Ellin in what one reporter described as a "trim walking suit of dark blue, with a hat to match."

Once again, the unexpected occurred. Another guest at the hotel, W. K. Vanderbilt, Jr., happened by. He was a friend of Ellin's father, and, oblivious to the tension in the family, he stepped forward to offer his best wishes. Following his example, all the other guests in the lobby stepped forward to offer their best wishes, as Ellin smiled, Irving laughed, and the reporters watched.

The well wishers drifted away, but the journalists, beggars at the banquet, stubbornly remained, trying to provoke Irving into saying something about Clarence Mackay. Knowing where an impromptu press conference would lead, Irving demurred; he preferred to let Ellin "do the talking" for them. She, reveling in the attention, began by lightheartedly chiding the press for describing the outfit in which she had been married the day before as consisting of an orange hat and red coat: a combination she would never wear. But the reporters wanted to know what the Society Girl planned to do about her father's certain disapproval of her marriage to the Jazz Composer. Ellin suddenly turned serious. "We are very anxious that Father should give his consent and blessing," she said. "I do hope he is not too angry."

"We are hoping it will be granted," Irving echoed.

And what about a rumor that Ellin received a telegram from her father warning the couple not to seek his blessing? The question elicited an emotional reply from Ellin, while Irving writhed in embarrassment. This was precisely the scene he'd hoped to avoid.

> ELLIN: I haven't heard from Father at all. Of course, I hope he will forgive me, but I can't make any further comment about his attitude. You see, I don't know. We are supremely happy, and that is all that counts.
>
> IRVING: (tugging Ellin's sleeve) Oh, Ellin, this is indelicate. This is indelicate. Let's go, Ellin.

ELLIN: (refusing to move) Don't think our marriage was sudden. We have known each other for years. His songs won me, of course; at the beginning they made me interested in him. Just think. I got married in my very oldest dress. I didn't have time to dress because we were married two hours after we decided to go through with it. Before he called me on the telephone yesterday morning, I had no idea of being married so soon. He just said, "Ellin, I want you to decide one way or the other." So I decided to accept him because I loved him and he loved me. Love means everything. I'm happy because I've done exactly what my heart told me to do.

REPORTER: Will Ellin continue her writing career?

ELLIN: (laughing) Well, I have Irving to support me now.

The interview ended with the couple obliging reporters by posing for photographs. As the flashbulbs popped, Berlin remarked, "This isn't a publicity stunt. This is the real thing."

The Berlins successfully avoided further press scrutiny for the rest of the day. Secluded in their Atlantic City retreat, Ellin remained preoccupied by her father's indifferent response to the marriage. She sent him a special delivery letter inviting him to visit them in Atlantic City, but he failed to respond. The controversy was now a matter of public record, and there were still five more days until they could escape aboard the *Leviathan* to Europe.

The tenacious reporters, meanwhile, had their headlines for the next day, as news of the elopement contined to command the front page of the *Times*:

MRS. BERLIN TO SEEK
BLESSING OF FATHER

FORMER ELLIN MACKAY HOPES FOR
PARDON DESPITE REPORT THAT
HOME IS CLOSED TO HER

On Wednesday, January 6, the Berlins contined to wait for word from Clarence, word that never came. The press continued its vigil, no longer in the lobby of the Ritz, but just outside the door to the

Berlins' suite. At two o'clock in the afternoon, Irving opened the door to inspect the scene. Reporters—fifty of them—were sprawled along the corridor. To the throng, he said sharply, "No statement. We have been awfully misquoted." About what, he would not say. Though plainly exasperated, he still knew the value of favorable publicity (there was a war to be won in the pages of the tabloids as well as the drawing rooms of Park Avenue), and he waved Ellin over to pose for a photograph. Catching sight of the terrifying mob, she recoiled, crying, "oh, heavens." Attempting to salvage another awkward public encounter, Irving put his arm around his young wife and comforted her; he then led her to a private dining room where they underwent the ordeal of being photographed yet again, this time in stony silence.

Immediately afterward, they took a taxi to the Atlantic City railroad station, arriving just ten minutes before the two-thirty train was due to depart for New York—time enough, it turned out, for reporters to swoop down on them once again. The gates to the track opened, and the couple hurried to the last car, walking through the train until they reached their seats. Once she had settled in, Ellin glanced over her shoulder and burst into tears. The reporters had followed them onto the train.

More questions: Had she heard from her father yet? Would there be a religious ceremony?

"I can't say anything now," Irving cautioned.

"Isn't it a bit too early to talk about that?" Ellin asked as she anxiously waited for the train to pull out of the infernal station. "Our plans are so unsettled." The religious question was now uppermost in the reporters' minds because a fantastic rumor had circulated to the effect that the Berlins had written to the Pope to ask for Papal dispensation for the marriage. Another ludicrous tale insisted that Irving would convert to Catholicism as a prelude to the couple remarrying in a ceremony at the Vatican itself.

"Have you heard from Mr. Mackay?" asked a reporter.

"I am sorry to say I have not received any word from him. I am so disappointed that Father didn't come down to see us. I'm supremely happy, but oh, so heartsick," Ellin replied. "I have a very heavy heart." Her unspoken words conveyed still more; as she talked, she "bit her lips as if to keep back tears and fingered her handkerchief nervously."

When their train reached Newark, New Jersey, Irving and Ellin bolted from the seats where the press had held them hostage into the privacy of a chauffeured car, which deposited them at Irving's apartment a little after seven o'clock that evening. There were still more reporters waiting to ambush the couple there, but the Berlins ran from the car to the apartment without pausing to answer a single provocative question. An hour later a crowd still lingered on the dark sidewalk outside Berlin's home, hoping in vain for a glimpse of the famous couple.

At about the same time, Ellin's father returned to his home, where he retired by nine o'clock, refusing to make any more public statements. Privately, he had taken one important step that day; he had instructed his lawyer to draw up a new will excluding Ellin. Her lost share of the Mackay estate came to $10 million. It was the kind of vain, autocratic gesture of which Mackay was so frequently capable. It was also self-defeating, for within several years he would have nothing to leave Ellin or anyone else beyond a legacy of rancor.

There was one other family member who ventured an opinion on the elopement. One of Irving's older sisters, now married and working for a newspaper delivery concern in Montclair, New Jersey, remarked, "I can't understand all the interest in the wedding. I've been expecting Izzy to marry for a year."

▪ ▪ ▪

Such remarks further tantalized the press. Hungry for a statement, reporters repeatedly telephoned Berlin's apartment. When Irving stopped answering the phone, they bombarded him with telegrams that bristled with uncomfortable questions. Running out of patience, Berlin shot back a brusque telegram of his own to all the New York dailies. It concluded:

> WE HAVE NEVER SAID ONE WORD FOR PUBLICATION EXCEPT THAT WE ARE VERY HAPPY STOP THAT STATEMENT WE REPEAT AND BEYOND THAT WE HAVE NOTHING TO SAY.

While in seclusion at the composer's apartment, awaiting the sailing of the *Leviathan*, Irving bestowed a rare and precious gift on

Ellin: the best in his series of romantic ballads, "Always." George S. Kaufman, a confirmed misogynist, had had no use for the song in *The Cocoanuts*, but his disapproval did not deter Berlin from saving it for a more important occasion. The sincerity of spirit in which Irving had written the song endowed it with an uncanny appeal.

Irving did more than dedicate "Always" to Ellin; he assigned her its copyright. The song's royalties, which eventually came to over $300,000, went directly to her. It was his way of giving her a diamond as big as the Ritz, and it helped take the sting out of her being disinherited. It was also a supremely confident gesture for Irving to make, for he never took the expression of such sentiments lightly. When he declared he would be loving Ellin always, he meant exactly that. (Of Arthur Johnston's girlfriend Mona, for whom the song had originally been written, nothing was ever again said.)

On the evening of January 8, Alexander Woollcott gave the couple a quiet farewell party at his apartment. It was located at 412 West 47th Street, which happened to be near the *Leviathan*'s pier on 46th Street. The Berlins stayed at Woollcott's until after midnight, when they went straight aboard the ship. In their presidential suite, they enjoyed the services of two servants, Berlin's butler Ivan and their steward, Robert Sweetlove, who was skilled at ministering to celebrities. The next day, at one o'clock in the afternoon of January 9, five trying days after the wedding, the couple finally sailed for a two-month-long European honeymoon.

Even after they had departed America's shores, controversy beleaguered them. Waiting until Irving and Ellin were safely at sea and unable to respond, Clarence fired off a telegram of his own to the press, reiterating his opposition to the marriage. Thus the Berlins seemed to be fleeing his wrath rather than indulging in the honeymoon to which they were entitled. Ellin, too, contributed to the couple's notoriety. The new issue of *Vogue* magazine, just arriving on newsstands as she was leaving the country, contained her latest broadside against society. This time, she delivered herself of opinions on a wide range of interest to *Vogue* readers, including matters of fashion, debutantes, the opera, and that most pressing concern of the day: the best way to get to Princeton to attend a football game (by train, she advised—and expect plenty of jostling at the university's dining clubs).

Early the next month, more of her writing (under her maiden name) appeared in the following issue of *Vogue*. This time she was writing about a topic her husband knew a thing or two about: a popular dancing fad—not the turkey trot or fox trot this time, but the Charleston—"a strange rhythm in dancing brought from Harlem by Broadway." And by Tin Pan Alley, she might have added, for Berlin could not resist the temptation to capitalize on the craze, as well, with his "Everyone in the World Is Doing the Charleston." Ellin's analysis of the Charleston emphasized how much work it was, as opposed to how much fun and abandon it could generate. "Anyone who has studied the Charleston," she wrote, "who has undergone the strenuous process of 'stretching and limbering' before being permitted to learn a single step, will never again be able to watch with placid, matter-of-fact acceptance the skilful dancing of the chorus in the musical shows. . . . Only those ladies of the chorus who are permanently out of a job could possibly find time for the lurid activities with which they are supposed to occupy their days and nights." Her pronouncements quickly became the subject of lengthy stories in the *Times*. "FORMER ELLIN MACKAY SAYS STEP HAS CAPTURED FIFTH AVENUE, WHICH STRIVES TO LEARN IT," the newspaper headlined. She was now considered a spokeswoman for the younger, more daring members of society—those who spurned stag lines for cabarets, danced the Charleston, and disobeyed their Rhadamanthine elders.

Yet even as Ellin traded on her place in her society, she was being formally stripped of it in a genteel but unmistakable fashion. For years she and the other members of the Mackay and Duer families had been listed in the *Social Register*. To all of them, their place in this catalogue of the people who really mattered was of paramount importance. But then, in January 1926, the *Social Register*'s section entitled "Dilatory Domiciles" contained a note to the effect that Ellin Mackay and Irving Berlin had recently wed. On the face of it, this was a civilized enough statement, but those adept at interpreting the diplomatic language of the *Social Register* divined a darker meaning. Since the *Register* did not refer to "Mr. and Mrs. Irving Berlin," it was apparent to those who cared that Irving would not be taking his place in the *Social Register* beside that of his wife. When pressed for an explanation as to why it was discriminating against Berlin, a spokesman for the *Social Register* said merely that "Irving Berlin has no place in society."

As the *Leviathan* churned through the frigid, gray Atlantic toward Southampton, Irving and Ellin spent most of their time behind the locked doors of the stateroom. The enforced idleness of a midwinter transatlantic crossing quickly became a trial for the hyperactive songwriter. He had a piano at his disposal, but since it was not his prepared model, it was of little use to him. Instead, he wrote radiograms as compulsively as he wrote songs. For a man who had, only days before, been incensed by the meddling of the press, Berlin now displayed a surprising urge to broadcast his feelings and his whereabouts to all and sundry. Significantly, the radiograms were signed not "Ellin and Irving," or "The Berlins," but "The Balines," to suggest that Ellin had married him for who he actually was, not for his reputation—or his money.

The barrage of radiograms directed toward New York had another purpose, as well: to keep alive the publicity Berlin professed to disdain. The only thing worse than being hounded by the press, it seemed, was being ignored. Eventually the *Leviathan*'s captain had enough, and he radioed his own observations of the couple's behavior to New York, together with a bit of gossip: "I've often traveled with honeymooners, but rarely have I been kept busier than by these. They spent a small fortune replying to scores of radiograms. But none of them have come from the bride's father."

After landing at Southampton, Irving and Ellin took a train to London's Waterloo Station. When they arrived, they found the tracks swarming with reporters. Irving was gratified to see that news of his elopement had preceded him to London; once again he could relish the publicity he said he did not want. As they walked along the platform, they were surrounded by a crowd of forty, who sang on cue, "Drink. Drink. Let the toast start / May young hearts never part/ . . . Let every true lover salute his sweetheart."

"Is that for us?" asked Ellin, bewildered. Hearts . . . part . . . sweetheart—her Irving was incapable of such crude rhymes.

One of the serenaders stepped forward. "Mr. Shubert?" he said.

"Shubert?" snapped Berlin, who did not like the producer any better than he had in 1909. A porter explained that the man was actually Irving Berlin, in the company of his wife, Ellin.

"My God," the serenader exclaimed, "we thought he was Mr. Jake Shubert."

It turned out that the crowd consisted of the chorus of Sigmund Romberg's hugely successful operetta *The Student Prince*, there to welcome J. J. Shubert, who had produced the show and who had been on board the *Leviathan*. The singers did not realize that Shubert had left the ship at Cherbourg.

This misunderstanding set the tone for the Berlins' stay in London. They stayed at the Carlton Hotel, where Irving expected to have the pleasure of fending off the press, but English journalists proved to be more respectful of his wishes for privacy than their American counterparts had been. The songwriter yearned to say *no* to reporters, to limit his remarks to a few carefully scrutinized words. But no one asked; he was deprived of the perverse enjoyment of proclaiming his irritation with his popularity. After the excitement of New York, the new year, and the elopement, January in placid London ranked as a disappointment.

Irving tried to distract himself with business. He composed new songs to insert in *The Cocoanuts*, though they could never be heard to great advantage, and met with the English playwright Frederick Lonsdale to discuss a musical collaboration. The distractions of marriage proved too great, and the show hung fire.

After enduring four days of anonymity at the Carlton Hotel, Berlin could no longer contain his impatience. Ellin and he attended London's most popular nightclub, the Kit Cat Club, where Irving's friend Sophie Tucker was performing. In the midst of her act, Tucker waved him onstage and bade him accompany her in his hit sob song, "Remember." As they sang, Ellin, dressed in a short pink skirt, stood on a tabletop, tapping her toes. Reporters gathered at the scene, anticipating conventional remarks about how happy Irving was to visit London on his honeymoon; instead, the songwriter spewed venom at the press. "For nearly two weeks, I've had to protect my wife from insults too bitter for me to speak of," he complained. "We have lived in a nightmare." Referring to their troubled journey to Atlantic City, he said, "When we were going to board a train, one reporter was so insulting that my poor wife burst out crying. So now, if you see any interview reported, it will all be lies." Irving's display of temper indicated that he remained blind to the fact that he had created the storm of publicity, thrived on it, and used it to promote his music business.

Still unable to concentrate on songwriting, he impulsively departed England and traveled to Paris with Ellin. Fearing a crush of journalists, the Berlins remained cloistered for several days at the Hotel Crillon. One afternoon, when Irving happened to look out his window, he discovered a throng of reporters and newsreel cameramen clamoring at the entrance. At last, an opportunity for exposure in the French press. He coaxed Ellin into bearing up under the commotion. "Darling, we'll just have to face it," he told her. "Come on, let's get it over with." They went down to the lobby and, bracing for the onslaught as they came within range of the cameras, suddenly found themselves shunted aside. It turned out that the press had no interest in the honeymooning couple from New York; they were staking out a visiting maharajah.

Once again Berlin tried to compose; he had *two* pianos installed in his hotel suite. Once again he came up dry. At the end of February, he decided to leave Paris as suddenly as he had come, and he returned with Ellin to London, where he declared he would stay for the rest of the year.

After only three days' exposure to chilly London weather, he changed his mind and took Ellin to Madeira, where at last they enjoyed the honeymoon retreat they had previously denied themselves. Irving loved the beaches, the warmth, the Portuguese music, and the relaxation. He wrote several postcards, exulting over the "swell" times he and Ellin were having, as well as the occasional "belly laugh," Irving's artless euphemism for sexual intercourse. Ellin became pregnant. Irving wrote a song to celebrate his happiness, "Always April." It was the best song he ever wrote, or so he said. Few others agreed with his estimation of the tune. Never mind. Irving loved Madeira so dearly that he wanted to buy a villa. Instead, three weeks later, Ellin and he left for Lisbon. And then it was back to London on March 22.

Berlin was sufficiently serious about getting back to work that he sent to New York for his musical secretary, Arthur Johnston. The theory was that his presence, not to mention the expense of bringing him across the Atlantic, would be sufficient to shame Irving into working, but the theory didn't hold. Irving and Arthur sat before the piano in London with little to show for their trouble beyond a few undistinguished numbers to spruce up the score of *The Cocoanuts.*

One of the songs, "Ting-a-ling, the Bells'll Ring," telling of a happy couple about to have their first child, revealed what was uppermost in Irving's mind. Hungry for publicity from his slender output, Berlin dispatched Johnston to New York in June, with orders to publicize the appearance of new songs by Irving Berlin. Although he was sending songs back to the United States, he still had no intention of returning with an obviously pregnant wife to American shores and their prying news reporters. Still, he did not want his first child to be born abroad; he was already giving thought to a novel way of slipping into the country unnoticed.

▪ ▪ ▪

In the United States, the Berlin-Mackay marriage was fast becoming the stuff of legend along Tin Pan Alley, Broadway, and even in Hollywood. Songwriters Al Dubin and Jimmy McHugh rushed out a Tin Pan Alley tribute to the couple, "When a Kid Who Came from the East Side (Found a Sweet Society Rose)." George White, whose *Scandals* had previously parodied Irving's romantic troubles, returned to the theme in June, when a new edition of the revue featured a number called "A Western Union," based on the elopement. In 1928 a play based on the marriage, Crane Wilbur's *The Song Writer*, opened on Broadway, starring Georgie Price as a Jewish songwriter plainly based on Irving and Mayo Methot as the young heiress with whom he falls in love. Although the play had only a brief stage life, MGM made it the basis of an early movie musical, *Children of Pleasure*, released in 1930. This time Larry Gray played the songwriter and Wynne Gibson the heiress. The film contained a full score, but of course Berlin had nothing to do with any aspect of the production, and the songs were written by others.

The popularity of the Berlin name created a series of legal disputes, as well. A car salesman and would-be songwriter by the name of Abraham Brown charged Berlin with plagiarism in connection with the song "All Alone," which Brown charged he'd written two years before Berlin had. Brown insisted he'd shown his uncopyrighted song to one of Berlin's employees, who presumably passed it on to his boss.

While the judge in the case insisted that "no composer of Irving Berlin's stature would stoop to steal a few bars of another man's song" and threw the case out of court, the charge revived rumors that Berlin employed black ghostwriters.

Throughout this summer of legal squabbling, Berlin made desultory stabs at the show he had promised to write with Frederick Lonsdale, but the two fought, and the songwriter gave up on it. With the collapse of this project and the progress of Ellin's pregnancy, he had run out of reasons to stay abroad. After eight months of honeymooning, the longest span of time he had ever spent away from home, he decided to return to New York and the routine of married life. However, Ellin's condition reinforced his desire to be fiercely protective of their privacy; the last thing he wanted was to be greeted by a throng of reporters on a windswept Hudson River pier asking him when the baby was due or, even worse, in what religion the child would be raised.

To avoid the specter of this unpleasantness, Ellin and Irving took a roundabout journey home. They left London for good at the end of August, taking a train to Glasgow, where they boarded the *Montnairn*, a Canadian Pacific steamer, under the assumed names of Mr. and Mrs. J. Johnson. The *Montnairn*, bound for Québec, was no *Leviathan*; there were only six passenger cabins, and Irving had reserved every one of them for his use. Four of them were given over to housing a baby grand piano and other instruments he had accumulated during the months abroad. That, in addition to the thirty-two trunks belonging to the couple, proved sufficient to arouse the curiosity of the crew, who recognized the Berlins and radioed the news to New York. Meanwhile, the ship proceeded calmly through the narrowing funnel of the Gulf of St. Lawrence and down to Québec, where it docked on August 21. The reporters were waiting.

The storm of publicity in which the Berlins had left the country plainly had not dissipated during the months of their absence. Irving's insistence on privacy coupled with his often clumsy efforts at promotion had only served to whet the public's appetite for more news of this charmed, yet afflicted, couple.

"We beg for privacy," said Irving in a written statement. Disguising her swelling stomach in a loose gray dress and a black coat,

Ellin hurried down the gangplank with her husband. Together they dodged the reporters and disappeared into a chauffeured car, which Berlin had arranged to take them to Max Winslow's summer cottage on the shore of the St. Lawrence River. Before the car left, several journalists took note of the license plate number, 3N–29–46, and began to tail the elusive couple. When the car hit traffic, reporters caught up with it and pounded on the windows. Irving, anxious and obdurate, ignored them, as did his pale, drawn wife.

At about eight that night, after a 450-mile drive through the wild Adirondack region, the Berlins arrived at Winslow's cottage in a rainstorm. The foul weather continued the following day, Sunday, until late in the afternoon, when the clouds finally moved off, and the couple could appreciate their scenic surroundings. The cottage, freshly painted green and white, nestled at the end of a long, flower-strewn drive near the shore of the American side of the St. Lawrence River. Ellin, refreshed from a sound night's sleep, emerged wearing a gray dress trimmed with blue and a smart felt hat; no point in disguising her pregnancy now. She was soon joined by Irving, sporting white flannel trousers and a white silk shirt. Reporters were lurking even in this Edenic environment, but Irving waved them away, and they kept their distance. After marching about on the porch and inhaling the fresh, fragrant air, Irving and Max embarked on a late-afternoon fishing expedition for bass and pike in Winslow's motorboat, "Always," named after Berlin's song. Ellin meanwhile went shopping for infant toys. Life, it seemed, had recovered a semblance of normality.

The appearance of tranquility was deceptive. Berlin was in a cold rage over several related matters: the interference of the press, Clarence Mackay's refusal to acknowledge the marriage even though Ellin was now carrying his grandchild, and a report that the old man thought the elopement nothing more than a publicity stunt designed to drum up business for Irving's love songs. "The man is in a highly nervous condition," noted a reporter from the *New York Telegraph* after trying to approach the composer. "He is a very different person from the suave and debonair Berlin who once strolled down Broadway after dark. That genial smile he had when he and his bride sailed on the *Leviathan* . . . has disappeared. He is . . . morose, irritable, and snaps out the word 'no' when approached by those not bosom friends."

This was a Berlin that the press and anyone else who happened to cross his path would be seeing more of: beleaguered and belligerent. Around those he knew well—Winslow and Woollcott, for instance—he was as warm and cozy as always, but he could shift to fury without warning, and those who witnessed his behavior inevitably came away with one overriding question: how could the composer of those lovely, sentimental, romantic ballads such as "Always" and "Remember" suddenly act so crude, glowering and swearing and carrying on as though fate had singled him out for the misfortune of great fame? A large part of the answer was his fierce desire to protect Ellin. He guarded her as jealously as he did his songs, and for the same reason; she was all he had. Anyone, anything, could fail him at any time. His mentality remained permanently that of the survivor, always vigilant, forever wary of anything beyond his control.

Several days later, Irving and Ellin left Winslow's picturesque cottage and boarded a train bound for New York, riding in a closed compartment. Irving's worst fears about his treatment in the press materialized the moment his train arrived at Grand Central Station on August 29. A crowd of several hundred, including photographers and reporters, quickly assembled, though police prevented them from going down to the track level. Unaware of the commotion, the Berlins left their compartment—Ellin in a green hat and dark cloak, Irving in a dark gray suit and a dark green felt hat—and walked to the upper level, where they were spotted and mobbed. Avoiding questions, the nervous couple dashed through the vast expanse of the terminal and into a taxicab on Vanderbilt Avenue. Berlin paused to roll down the window and force a few friendly words to the press, and then he shouted to the driver to take them to his apartment on West 46th Street. "There were a few flashlight explosions as the taxi drew away," remarked a reporter from the *Evening World*, "and Mrs. Berlin shrank back deeper into the cab's interior."

This relatively civilized scene served as a prelude to the chaos that followed. A little after midnight, Berlin, encouraged by the amiable reception he had received at Grand Central Station, went down to the sidewalk in front of his apartment to chat with reporters, as he had in the old days, before his marriage. In his absence, however, the tabloids had been preparing to devote a great deal of space to wild rumors about Berlin's plans to convert to Catholicism; his earlier denials had only given them greater currency, if not credibility. According to the tabloid's warped logic, the impending birth of their child would force Berlin to convert in order to gain Clarence's blessing.

The reporters chose this moment to grill him about the conversion rumors. Irving's instincts told him to flee, but he discovered to his horror that the key to his apartment building did not work. He anxiously began ringing other tenants to let him in, but at that late hour no one answered. Cornered, Irving complained, "Why must I divulge my personal affairs to the public?" He then insisted there would be no conversion, not now, not ever. The tug of war continued for fifteen minutes until he finally managed to rouse one of the tenants, who let him in. Berlin fled.

The next morning, Irving's denials appeared in all the papers. Even his lack of responsiveness made headlines, and when Berlin wouldn't speak, there was always a driver or an elevator operator who'd claimed to have spoken with him and was prepared to offer an opinion of the songwriter's mental state.

Despite Irving's repeated (and truthful) denials of any plan to convert to Catholicism, the *New York Evening Graphic*, in a flagrant abuse of journalistic ethics, went forward with a front-page, banner headline story announcing that Berlin would definitely marry Ellin a second time, in a Roman Catholic ceremony. The article insisted that she was a "faithful communicant of the church," who "took a great deal of pleasure in observing its tenets." To anyone who knew the irrepressible Ellin, this was nonsense; she took far more pleasure in flouting than obeying such conventions. The paper even regarded Berlin's denials as further evidence of the pending conversion: "To admit that it was true would mean more publicity of an unpleasant nature, which might once more incur the displeasure of his stern and hitherto unrelenting father-in-law."

The seemingly authoritative manner in which the *Graphic* delivered its prediction unleashed a furor in several circles: among New York clergy, in Park Avenue salons, and in the newsrooms of the other dailies, which were now inclined to give at least some credence to the *Graphic*'s tale. Berlin was suddenly on the defensive. Nothing he said seemed to make any impression. Even his denials were being twisted and used against him. It was true that since his marriage he had been hypersensitive and ambivalent about the press, often seeking publicity when he declared he wanted to avoid it. At the same time he had done nothing to provoke the shabby treatment, with its undercurrent of anti-Semitism, now accorded him by the *Graphic* and other tabloids.

In despair at gaining a fair hearing in the court of popular opinion, Berlin typed and signed a statement, which was distributed to the New York dailies. Still rabid for news of the songwriter and his pregnant wife, many ran it in facsimile, daring readers to make of it what they would:

> The report that Mrs. Berlin and I are to go through another ceremony, is untrue. I shall deny no more of these false statements.
>
> Irving Berlin

For once, however, Irving was able to have the last word. He returned to a relatively private existence, overseeing his music publishing company and attending to Ellin, who was now nearing the end of her term of pregnancy. On Thursday, November 25, she entered York House, a private hospital on East 74th Street, to have the baby. While Berlin kept an anxious vigil there, he encountered Franklin P. Adams, the columnist, whose wife had given birth at the same hospital several days earlier. "He told me Ellin was to have a child soon," Adams noted in his diary, "so I stopped with him till a nurse came by and told him he had a daughter, and he was greatly overjoyed, and in a few minutes I saw little Mary Ellin, [as the Berlins named their first child] as sweet a little girl as I ever saw."

In an era when a two-week-long stay in the hospital following the birth of a baby was common, Ellin remained at York House, recuperating, for twenty-three days, long enough for rumors to circulate that she had contracted "pernicious anemia" and would have to move to Arizona permanently to recover her health. There was no more truth to this report than there had been to the story of Irving's conversion to Catholicism, but it encouraged public interest in the couple's well-being. To discredit the rumor, Ellin, looking solemn and forlorn after her lengthy stay, displayed her child to photographers. If her father took note of the arrival of his granddaughter, he said nothing to the Berlins about the matter.

Ellin's departure from the hospital several days later proved traumatic. Word that she would finally be taking the baby home spread—probably the work of a hospital employee close to the press—and a crowd of journalists and curiosity seekers braved the cold to catch a glimpse of the celebrated mother and her child. Watching the crowd form as she left the hospital, Ellin cried, "No, no. I won't go out there! I won't!" burst into tears, and fainted. She was taken back to her hospital suite, where she revived. Irving caught up with her there and persuaded her the time had come; she had to leave. She tried again, with her husband shielding her from the throng this time—the popping flashbulbs, the shouted questions. Ellin disappeared into their car, and as they pulled away, Irving was heard to call out, "That's the bane of famous married couples."

After nearly a year of travel and turmoil, Irving returned to his home on West 46th Street with his wife and child. No sooner did they all settle in than he set about writing a song to welcome his new child into the world. Her birth put him in mind of his own childhood, his mother, and his homeland. For one of the few times in his songwriting career, he turned to Russia for musical inspiration and composed his haunting and beautifully modulated "Russian Lullaby."

Written in the key of D minor, the song exuded a heavy Russian feeling, and its augmented chords, together with touches of dissonance, imparted an even darker flavor. This lullaby overflowed both with love and with quiet protest against political repression in the Soviet Union. Yearning, grief, tragedy, protest—the birth of Mary Ellin Berlin had stirred up a rich and surprising complex of emotions in her volatile father.

■ □ ■ □ ■ □ ■

CHAPTER 12

Heartbreak House

Eight days after the Berlins returned home, the songwriter received a late-night phone call from his old friend Belle Baker, the vaudeville singing star. "Irving," she said, "I'm opening in a show tomorrow night, and there isn't a 'Belle Baker song' in the score, and I'm so miserable. What can I do?"

The troubled show to which she referred was *Betsy*, with music and lyrics by the young team of Richard Rodgers and Lorenz Hart, who were fast making a name for themselves on Broadway. Indeed, their rate of production was so rapid that another of their collaborations, *Peggy-Ann*, was scheduled to open the night before *Betsy*. *Peggy-Ann* looked to be a success, but Baker held out little hope for *Betsy*. Both she and her husband Maurice ("Maury") Abrahams were long-standing friends of Irving's; she had helped to make hits of "Cohen Owes Me Ninety-Seven Dollars," "Remember," and "Always." And Berlin had collaborated with her husband years before on an early (and unsuccessful) song. So this was a call of desperation from an old friend.

Irving wanted to help, though he doubted he could be of much use at this late date and hour. "Belle, I'll be very honest with you," he replied. "All I have is a song in my trunk. I've often thought it would be great for you, but I never got around to finishing it."

"Irving, please come over here. Maury is here. We'll feed you, and he'll help—because even something half-finished by you is better than what I've got now, which is nothing!"

Rising to the challenge, Berlin went to Belle's apartment with his incomplete trunk song in hand. It was called "Blue Skies," and he had written only the first eight bars. The two of them sat before the piano in the living room and played the opening bars repeatedly, searching for the bridge, which proved to be exceptionally stubborn. The "middle eight," as the bridge is often called, was reputed to be the toughest part of a song to devise, and "Blue Skies" was no exception. But Berlin stuck with his song through the night, urged on by Belle and Maury, who occasionally dozed off. Finally, about six o'clock in the morning, Irving had his bridge.

Roused from her sleep, Belle, on hearing the now nearly completed song, rushed to the phone and called the show's producer, Florenz Ziegfeld, waking him out of a sound sleep. She shouted that Irving Berlin had just finished a smashing "Belle Baker" song (with considerable encouragement and assistance from her and her husband), and if Flo wouldn't let her sing it at the opening that night, she wouldn't go on. But there was a problem: Rodgers and Hart's contract forbade interpolations. After giving the matter some thought, the pragmatic Ziegfeld replied, "Belle, you can do it, but for God sake, don't tell Rodgers or Hart."

Betsy opened as scheduled that evening, December 28, 1926, and the production was as awful as Baker had feared until, near the end of the show, she sang "Blue Skies" and electrified the audience. They whistled, stamped their feet, and implored Baker to belt out one encore after another until finally, on the twenty-third repetition, she forgot the lyric. Instantly, Berlin, who was sitting in the first row, shot to his feet, shouted out the words, and sang the twenty-fourth encore of the song with her before the enraptured crowd.

Nor was "Blue Skies" a one-night wonder. It had staying power. As with the best of Berlin's efforts, this deceptively simple expression of happiness drew strength from concealed paradox and subtlety. The chorus started out in a minor key, which imparted poignancy and fragility to the mood of happiness, while the lyrics played around with the meaning of "blue"—one of the trickiest words in the popular music lexicon. In the song, "blue" referred at various times to a color, a mood, and even a bird: three types of blue. Yet Berlin accomplished this associative meditation in utterly natural, casual-sounding phrases.

Simple as it was, "Blue Skies" contained enough substance to bear up under those twenty-four encores.

Unfortunately, the success of this one song couldn't save *Betsy*, which lasted for only thirty-nine performances, but it did launch a grim professional rivalry between Berlin and the young songwriting team he had so thoroughly upstaged. Nor did Rodgers or Hart speak to Belle Baker for years afterward.

Irving had often wondered whether Broadway patrons would accept him after his prolonged absence, and he now had his answer. Yet no amount of encores could disguise the fact that he had lost touch with the development of the Broadway musical—the mainstream of popular music. Irving instead returned to Ziegfeld's fold, writing eight songs for the 1927 edition of the *Follies*—still going, but not strong. None of Irving's new songs, many of which were sung by the show's star, Eddie Cantor, came close to making the impression that "Blue Skies" had. The revue closed after only several months, with Cantor and Ziegfeld each blaming the other for its quick demise.

Despite its failure, the score for the 1927 *Follies* marked the beginning of a collaboration between the songwriter and a new musical secretary, Helmy Kresa, that would last—with occasional time off owing to fights and grudges and other strains of working in show business—for the next sixty years, until both of them were too feeble to practice the craft they loved. From this time forward, Helmy was present at the creation of most of Irving's hit songs; he was the man whom Berlin would call in the middle of the night to whistle or hum a few notes of a new song. He was the man who wrote it all down.

Like so many other makers of American music, Helmy Kresa was an immigrant, born in Dresden, Germany. He received his musical education at the Milwaukee Conservatory, putting himself through school with the money he earned as a milkman, but he never lost his German accent, which endowed him with a professorial manner. Although he wrote one hit song himself, "That's My Desire," he regarded it as an accident. He was more comfortable in the role of musical amanuensis, and over the years he served as an arranger both for Berlin and a number of other important songwriters, including Johnny Mercer, Harold Arlen, Cole Porter, Burton Lane, Harry Warren, Irving Caesar, and Harry Ruby—all of whom valued Kresa's skill and tact as an arranger.

Helmy first came to work for Berlin on a temporary basis, to fill in for another arranger in the office who was on vacation. The music company continued to publish songs by other composers, and Kresa's first job was to arrange Harry Woods's "When the Red, Red Robin Comes Bob, Bob, Bobbin' Along." Berlin noticed him right away because Helmy possessed an unusual trait for a trained musician: he believed in simplicity as fervently as his boss did. He didn't try to dress up a tune with fancy harmonies and embellishments; on the contrary, he favored plain harmonies, uncomplicated chords, modest musical statements. He did most of his work in the key of C and would subsequently decide what key the final product should be in, often based on practical considerations such as the vocal limitations of performers. Another endearing quality was his speed; he could polish off a piano part in an hour.

Even with the acquisition of a talented new musical secretary, Berlin languished in his creative slump. He occasionally sought distraction in a succession of glamorous trips—winter in Palm Beach, spring in Europe. He moved to a more private location, 9 Sutton Place, but that too failed to revitalize him. Although he retained an unmatched ability to deliver the isolated hit, other leading composers were advancing the art of the American musical far beyond what Berlin, with his limited musical knowledge, was capable of producing. The 1927–1928 season on Broadway is regarded as the busiest and most creative ever: 270 plays, including Eugene O'Neill's *Strange Interlude*, came to Broadway, and over fifty musicals opened—not one of them by Irving Berlin.

In the course of Berlin's long life, 1927 stands out as the watershed year—the year he came to the end of his crusade to make his place in America. He had his startlingly successful career, his marriage, and his child. And yet this was not a happy or tranquil period for him. In fact, he embarked on a biblical span of seven lean years. In the midst of this fallow period, he gave one of his songs an ominous title, "The Song Is Ended." For a while, this appeared to be a prophecy. Still, a dry spell for Irving Berlin might be reckoned a golden age in the career of another popular composer, for even during this phase, Berlin composed, at widely spaced intervals, some of his best, most complex, and most suggestive songs.

While Berlin foundered, his devoted admirer, Jerome Kern, set a new Broadway standard with his score for *Show Boat.* Like so many other noteworthy Broadway offerings, this production boasted a Round Table pedigree. Late in the summer of 1926, Edna Ferber published a hugely popular novel about the flat-bottomed floating theaters that plied the Mississippi, carrying minstrel shows and melodramas throughout the South. Her story teemed with material rich in promise for stage adaptation: the South, a strong heroine, gambling, and—most notoriously—miscegenation. Kern read the book soon after it appeared, and, thinking it could serve as the basis of a wonderful musical, called Alexander Woollcott and begged the critic to introduce him to Ferber.

Relishing the prospect of functioning as an artistic power broker, Woollcott quickly brought together Ferber and Kern when all three attended the opening of *Criss Cross*, a musical produced by Charles Dillingham. Ferber had her doubts. Musicals, she knew, were frivolous and lighthearted. How would her sprawling novel fit onstage? And what of its social themes, which had no place on Broadway? Though a potboiler, her *Show Boat* was perilously heavy, even tragic material.

Kern persisted. To write the book, he brought in the young Oscar Hammerstein II, who already had several Broadway credits, and the two of them took the project to Florenz Ziegfeld. With his *Follies* in decline, the producer was looking forward to a new phase in his career, presenting musicals in his own theater, inevitably called The Ziegfeld. To build the theater, he enlisted the financial backing of his friend William Randolph Hearst, who was still as stagestruck as he had been a decade earlier, when he had met the young chorus girl Marion Davies. Enthralled with the prospect of presenting a prestigious show in his new theater, Ziegfeld gave the collaborators his blessing.

Kern and Hammerstein worked on the project throughout 1927, while Ziegfeld bombarded them with his trademark telegrams, urging them to hurry. The team required time, for their story encompassed fifty years, three generations, and two races. They were struggling both to streamline the saga for the stage and to integrate songs into the story line. As rehearsals progressed, Ziegfeld drove the cast and himself at a frantic pace, but he himself had little appreciation of the show's merits. As opening night neared, he became convinced it would be a disaster.

When *Show Boat* finally opened at the Ziegfeld Theatre on December 27, 1927, Ziegfeld, unable to bear watching the performance, huddled on the stairway leading to the balcony with his secretary Goldie Clough. Noting a lack of applause for several big numbers in the show, he finally broke down in tears. "They don't like it," he complained. "Goddamn it, I knew they wouldn't."

Ziegfeld was wrong, of course. It was instantly apparent to both critics and audiences that Kern and Hammerstein's extended labors had paid off. Nothing like this musical, with its charm, sweep, sadness, and substance, had ever been seen before on the Broadway stage. *Show Boat* was innovative, but there was nothing tentative about it; every aspect of the production was fully achieved. As theater historian Miles Kreuger has written, "The history of the American Musical Theatre, quite simply, is divided into two eras: everything before *Show Boat*, and everything after *Show Boat*."

The production contained many marvels—Helen Morgan as the alluring and ill-fated Julie, Joseph Urban's lavish but realistic sets, and of course Kern's score. Perhaps its most remarkable characteristic was its deft summation of the American musical from antebellum minstrel show all the way to *Show Boat* itself. The show boat of the title became a metaphor for all this tangled history. Though clearly influenced by the German classical tradition, the score was replete with evocations of African, minstrel, and "coon" musical forms, but Kern refrained from exploiting them. Rather, songs such as "Old Man River" placed them where they belonged, in the sad context of slavery and prejudice. The sense of social outrage underpinning the entire show, though exquisitely muted, imparted an edge to otherwise far-fetched love stories and often arcane theatrical lore that Ferber had unearthed and recreated. Here, at last, was a musical where black chorus members were not required to roll their shiny white eyes while shaking their jet black faces or indulge in other stereotypical "darkie" behavior, and where black and white characters interrelated at a believable level of maturity. The show business conventions of portraying blacks have changed so drastically since 1927 that *Show Boat* now seems, ironically, to belong to the genre that it sought to overturn; but at the time it opened—a time when the Ku Klux Klan ran rampant in the South—the musical was positively revolutionary.

Acclaimed the moment it opened, *Show Boat* remained successful over the years. It was so much ahead of its time that other musicals such as *Oklahoma!*, which it clearly inspired, did not begin to appear until the early 1940s. Eventually even Berlin would get swept up in the trend, but until that time, a full fifteen seasons later, *Show Boat* remained a unique accomplishment. It had such staying power that it enjoyed three separate productions on Broadway, three in London, and three movie versions. (The most successful of the filmed versions was James Whale's lavish 1936 production starring Irene Dunne, Paul Robeson, and Helen Morgan.) Beyond this tangible evidence of its popularity, the musical set precedents both in matters of style—integrating music and story—and theme—social injustice—that defined the Broadway musical for the next thirty years.

As this revolution of social conscience and artistic skill overtook the Broadway stage, Irving Berlin, who generally yielded to no one in his eagerness to exploit new trends, sat and watched. He had a multitude of reasons to refrain from pitting himself against the likes of Kern and Hammerstein. His complete absorption in the strange new world of family life was one; his lack of musical training—a severe handicap when it came to composing an elaborate score—was another. And then there was the dry spell that had plagued him since his marriage to Ellin. The mixture of desperation and inspiration on which he thrived had eluded him for two years now and gave no sign of returning soon.

The last and most subtle reason for Berlin's resistance to writing a "modern" musical was his lack of sympathy with its aims. An innate conservative, he had no interest in criticizing American society (satire was another matter), not after he had spent his life battling to be at its privileged center. A protest song never issued from his trick piano. If people wanted to join in a dance craze, he would be glad to call the tune. If people went to war, he could respond with stirring sentiments. But if people were starving or neglected or abused, he had nothing to offer them beyond the example of his own career.

Broadway was becoming a more elitist environment, increasingly under the sway of people such as Oscar Hammerstein, Jerome Kern, and Cole Porter, who were cultivated, college educated, and acquainted with a wide range of knowledge beyond the theater. The influence of Marx and Freud wafted across Broadway like a heavy incense. This was a world Irving Berlin had never made. As he turned forty, he was suddenly in danger of becoming old-fashioned, or as he put it in his street lingo, "all washed up." His range of knowledge was that of the autodidact, exceedingly deep and narrow, confined to his songs and how to sell them. The world of ideas and theories held no allure for him; he was a tinkerer, a pragmatist, an inspired amateur.

▪ ▪ ▪

Throughout the weary months of creative stagnation, the Berlins coped with domestic trials. On September 4, 1928, Marie Louise Hungerford Mackay, Ellin's adored grandmother, fell ill at the Harbor Hill estate from which Ellin had been banished at the time she eloped with Irving. Marie Louise had lived as a recluse at the estate for a decade, seeing no one but a few close family members. Sensing the end approaching, she telephoned her son Clarie, Ellin's father, who happened to be in London. Word also went out to her three grandchildren, "K," Willie, and Ellin, to rush to Harbor Hill. For Ellin, this would be the first visit to the home where she had spent her girlhood since the trauma of Clarence's disowning her. Before Ellin arrived, or even a priest could be summoned, Mary Louise died.

The loss was great for Ellin, but it was not wholly unexpected. Furthermore, she was sustained by the knowledge that she was again pregnant. However, even that comfort proved to be illusory. Although she gave birth to a son on December 1, he died after only twenty-five brief days of life. His name was Irving Berlin, Jr.

Precisely why the child died is open to question. Medical records indicate that he was suffering from typhoid fever and various complications, but the diagnosis of the attending physician offered scant information as to the cause of death. If anything positive could be said to have come out of this tragedy, it was that Ellin finally heard from her estranged father, who sent a letter of condolence. However, the bereaved parents also heard, amid the conventional expressions of sympathy, anti-Semitic remarks occasioned by the death. Since the child had died on Christmas morning, a few of Ellin's former friends whispered, "It's God's punishment for marrying a Jew."

To recover from the ordeal of losing the child, Irving and Ellin took a vacation in Florida. When he returned to New York early in

1929, he made a tentative effort to revive his songwriting career. Ray Goetz, the brother of Dorothy, Irving's first wife, was now a theatrical producer, and he approached the songwriter with a new project, a musical entitled *Fifty Million Frenchmen.* Berlin agreed to produce the show in his theater, the Music Box, and perhaps even to write the score. Once he realized the story was set in modern-day Paris and filled with decadent aristocrats, social climbers, starving artists, and references to James Joyce's *Ulysses*, he decided he was not the man for the job. Instead, the task fell to a much more appropriate choice, Cole Porter, who was familiar with the show's Parisian milieu. Irving, however, had so little faith in the show's prospects that he changed his mind about producing it at the Music Box, and it moved to the Lyric.

When the show opened late in the year, Irving honored his debt to Goetz by running a paid advertisement to the effect that *Fifty Million Frenchmen* was "the best musical comedy I have seen in years." He claimed it had "more laughs than I have heard in a long time, and one of the best collections of song numbers I have ever listened to. It's worth the price of admission to hear Cole Porter's lyrics." The critics, though, were less enthusiastic, and the show appeared in danger of closing quickly, but Berlin's endorsement was sufficient to build it into a respectable success. His evaluation was curious. It could be interpreted as a slap at Kern's *Show Boat*; furthermore, his published remarks distorted his true feelings about the show, which were negative, but they did offer an impressive demonstration of the weight of his words, and placed Porter permanently in his debt.

As Broadway passed him by, Irving accomplished the arduous miracle of reinventing himself yet again as a songwriter. Too old-fashioned for progressive Broadway, his music was thoroughly up-to-date in conservative Hollywood. In 1927, *The Jazz Singer*, the first movie to fulfill the promise of talkies and musicals, featured Al Jolson singing "Blue Skies." By current standards, his performance was ludicrous; Jolson brought his outsized vaudeville mannerisms to the camera, and when he sang "Blue Skies," his face plastered with ghostly white makeup, he seemed to be leering at a girl just beyond camera range. Despite his archaic style of singing, Jolson was the right performer to introduce the public to the talkies; he personified the movement of vaudeville to Hollywood.

After this early piece of luck with Jolson, Berlin quickly encountered serious problems with the movies. His first effort was "Coquette," a waltz composed for the unsuccessful movie version of the hit play written by George Abbott and Ann Preston Bridges, but the film's failure at the box office hampered his song's chances for success.

To gain a surer foothold in the industry, Irving turned to an old friend from the Lower East Side, Joseph Schenck, who had grown along with the medium; at the time, Schenck was thriving in motion pictures. However, Schenck was no visionary: he had resisted the movies' migration from New York to Los Angeles, and now he was convinced that talking pictures were a fad; the silents were here to stay. Despite his lack of foresight, Schenck had prospered on the strength of his ability to obtain financing and to make the deals that made the movies. He was a member of the young film colony's inner circle, and he had recently built himself a lavish beach house in Santa Monica, beside the homes of other moguls, such as producer Irving Thalberg. In addition, he benefited from excellent connections, for his brother Nicholas was now the power behind the throne at Metro-Goldwyn-Mayer, a position he would hold for the next twenty-five years. Joe, meanwhile, had forged a lasting alliance with United Artists. It was at this studio that he began a relationship with no less a director than D. W. Griffith.

Despite his immense reputation, Griffith's best work was behind him; he was a burnt-out case, plagued by debts, excessive drinking, and unsavory liaisons with young women. Trying to revive the director's waning fortunes, Joe Schenck set him to work on an overwrought romance titled *Lady of the Pavements*, starring Lupe Velez. Griffith made this lavish historical romance as a silent film; later, in the editing process, it was converted into a sound picture, chiefly by adding to the sound track in three different places Berlin's "Where Is the Song of Songs for Me?" Despite Schenck's enthusiastic promotion of the film, it opened to derisory reviews. The movie's failure all but finished Griffith in Hollywood. Berlin preferred to associate himself with successful collaborators, and the spectacle of Griffith, who only a decade earlier had stood at the pinnacle of his profession, falling into disgrace aggravated the songwriter's sense of insecurity. Even with his immense gifts and formidable will, he remained as vulnerable to failure as a novice.

Despite the use of Berlin's music in *Lady of the Pavements*, there is no evidence that he and Griffith ever met, much less "collaborated" on the movie; they had Joe Schenck in common, and that was all. Berlin remained in New York, three thousand miles from the scene of the action. Even when a movie featuring his music was actually filmed in New York, he still kept his distance. The consequences of his absence became embarrassingly apparent when Paramount assembled the Marx Brothers for a screen version of *The Cocoanuts*. This was the first film to contain a complete score by Berlin; in fact, he wrote three new songs for the occasion, most notably "When My Dreams Come True." But it was one thing to write songs, another to film them. As moviemaking, *The Cocoanuts* was crude fare. "Everything is there but nothing comes out," said *Variety*, with considerable accuracy, "excepting the four Marx Brothers." And even they were often out of focus, and Berlin's songs poorly recorded.

Problems of a different sort plagued *The Awakening*, which opened in New York later that year. A romance directed by Victor Fleming, this turgid movie featured one Berlin song, "Marie," that made little impression at the time but gained wide circulation nine years later when Tommy Dorsey recorded a much faster version. While *The Awakening* was a far glossier production than *The Cocoanuts*, it was still a turkey—and no place to launch a hit tune.

The movies were giving Irving Berlin a bad name in Hollywood, reinforcing the notion that he was old hat, a holdover from the *Follies*. And there was some truth to this impression. As a would-be performer who was accustomed to tailoring his songs to individual singers and situations, Berlin acquired a dislike for the slow and scattered process of making a movie. To be at his best, he needed a hands-on approach, where he could instantly gauge the effect of his songs. He was much more in his element when composing a "Blue Skies"—staying up all night, hammering out the song with the performer who would sing it, then hearing the result before an audience hours later, even singing a few lyrics himself. He resented the intrusion of technology between him and audience. By the time one of his songs finally reached the public, it had been subjected to the ministrations of an arranger, an orchestrator, a sound recorder, and a film editor—each of whom diluted his original intentions.

Mammy, the next movie for which he wrote music, circumvented the problem because both the star, Al Jolson, and the story, concerning the fortunes of a touring minstrel show, took Berlin back to his musical roots. Indeed, the story, at least in part, was his own idea. This was Jolson's fourth movie, and Irving supplied one of the infrequent hits he managed to squeeze out during this era: "Let Me Sing and I'm Happy." The declaration of a minstrel singer who relishes the thought of bringing tears to the eyes of his audience, the song was vintage Berlin, and it made an ideal Jolson vehicle. It was funny, coarse, and bold, but it was not the sort of subtle song the movies favored; it was a vaudeville showstopper.

None of the three other songs Irving contributed to *Mammy* were of the same caliber, but one, the forgotten "To My Mammy," became an important curiosity because it asked the question, "How deep is the ocean?/ How high is the sky?" Several years later, as Berlin's confidence began to return, the lines would serve as the genesis of a "new" hit song.

Still looking for a niche in the movies, Berlin became involved with Paramount's *Glorifying the American Girl*, one of the earliest of numerous Hollywood films to exploit and romanticize the Ziegfeld legend. Shot in the Astoria Studios on Long Island, the movie featured cameo appearances by Berlin, financier Otto Kahn, Mayor Jimmy Walker, Charles Dillingham, and even Ziegfeld himself—all of whom were glimpsed as part of a glamorous first-night audience. Snatches of Berlin's music were included in the sound track.

The first movie in which Berlin played an active role was a curiosity named after his hit song "Puttin' on the Ritz." By far the most interesting element in the movie, the song was a marvel of tricky accents and demonic rhythmic patterns. Today it is recalled as a tune evoking the glamor of high society, but that impression derives from a new set of lyrics he gave the song years later. At the time singer Harry Richman made a hit of it—the dying days of vaudeville—"Puttin' on the Ritz" was unmistakably a "coon" song. In faintly condescending terms, the lyrics evoked well-dressed blacks and "high browns."

When the white entertainer Harry Richman sang such lines, he mocked the gaudy rites of Saturday night in Harlem, and indeed, this was how the number was staged in the movie. Twenty-five years later, when "coon" songs were no longer acceptable, Berlin sanitized the lyrics; Lenox Avenue became Park Avenue. In this new guise, the song became a hit all over again when it was sung by Ella Fitzgerald. There was considerable irony in the song's evolution, because Harry Richman, who was white, had sung the "coon" version, while Ella Fitzgerald employed the neutral or "white" lyrics.

The original "Puttin' on the Ritz" polished Richman's image as a charming, if shady socialite. In reality, he fit the familiar pattern of popular entertainers. His parents were Jewish immigrants who had wanted him to play the violin, but he had felt helplessly drawn to show business. Enjoying the fruits of his success as a singer, he ran a popular New York nightclub, Club Richman, and frolicked with the wealthy on Long Island. He was probably better known for his affair with silent-screen star Clara Bow than for his professional accomplishments. With his nasal baritone, double-breasted blazers, and slicked-back hair, Harry Richman was the essence of smarmy charm.

His reputation informed the character he played in the movie, a highly successful but morally flawed singer. "Story is of the usual type," commented *Variety* in a sardonic synopsis. "Starting in poverty, sudden success corrupts the hero, who gets elephantitis of the cranium, goes society, and in the end finds himself just a blind clown. Literally blind here as he loses his sight from bad hootch. Nor does he recover the optics for the clinch, thereby fooling everyone. In many respects the picture is autobiographical, including Richman running a night joint on the side."

To ensure that his songs were heard to the best advantage, Berlin reluctantly left his wife and young daughter and went to the West Coast, where the film was being made. Berlin never really felt at home in Los Angeles, even during the city's pristine infancy, before smog and traffic choked it. An obsessive worker, he had scant interest in the possibilities for distraction that Southern California offered; the concept of recreation was alien to him. The palm tree and poolside life held no interest. He was too keyed up and self-absorbed to relax. To wile away the long nights when he couldn't sleep, he occasionally indulged in marathon high-stakes poker games with Schenck and other motion picture people, but he avoided parties, openings, and nightclubs.

His constant companion was his musical secretary, Arthur Johnston, who quietly hovered in the shadows, should Berlin ever require his services. (Helmy Kresa, meanwhile, remained at his post in Berlin's New York office.) A lifelong urban dweller, Berlin preferred to stay at the Roosevelt Hotel because he liked the feel of asphalt under his feet and could walk from the hotel to various restaurants and appointments. As a sign of his serious intentions about penetrating the film industry, his music publishing company opened a small office at 417 West 5th Street. In a field dominated by men, his first West Coast office manager was an unusual choice, Madeline Hardy, the ex-wife of Oliver Hardy, the obese movie comedian.

While in Hollywood, Berlin immersed himself in the process of making a movie musical, which turned out to be a learning experience for him as well as for many others. Nearly everyone, from Richman to his costar, the slender and youthful Joan Bennett, to the director, Edward H. Sloman, was new to the game. Technology, especially involving music, was still crude. The cast recorded Berlin's songs directly as scenes were filmed, while an orchestra played in the background, concealed behind the scenery or just beyond camera range. Under this inflexible arrangement, there was no dubbing, no chance for Irving or anyone else to perfect the way the songs sounded before matching them to the actors' lips.

This method of filming mercilessly exposed the actors' shortcomings. Richman could sing well enough, but he was a wooden and self-conscious actor. Bennett, meanwhile, gracefully comported herself before the cameras, but when she was called upon to sing, the effort was clearly painful. Berlin, who was on the set every day, patiently tried to make the best of the situation. "He was very sweet to me," Bennett said of Berlin's demeanor. "I sang a duet with Harry Richman, and I'm not a singer. When Richman started to blow his top at me for the way I was singing the duet with him, Mr. Berlin stepped in and put him in his place. He said to Richman, 'What do you mean by picking on her?' "

The film was further hampered by the director's inability to master the rudiments of talking pictures. Sloman had begun his career as an actor and drifted into silent movies when that art form was still in its infancy, gradually emerging as a screenwriter and director of considerable repute. But westerns were his forte, and the special requirements of *Puttin' on the Ritz*, especially the music, defeated him. Sloman's lack of expertise became glaringly apparent during what should have been the most adventurous aspect of the film, an elaborate color sequence devoted to Berlin's "Alice in Wonderland," a song introduced in the last edition of the *Music Box Revue*. Choreographer Maurice Kusell mounted a complex and possibly effective staging of the song, but Sloman's direction slaughtered the spectacle. While Berlin kept a careful eye on the score, he was powerless to alter the movie's primitive visual style.

His inability to control more than a sharply limited area of the complicated business of making a movie frustrated him then, and it would frustrate him throughout his long Hollywood career. "You do it piece by piece," he complained. "You go into a projection room, and you'll see what they call the rushes of the day. It becomes a bit monotonous and boring. And then, when you see the first rough cut, then you out-and-out wish you hadn't done this. A lot of the things that you liked wind up on the cutting room floor."

After frittering away months on *Puttin' on the Ritz* to no avail, Berlin became disgusted with movies and doubtful that he had a place in them after all. Perhaps his critics were right; perhaps he was old hat. It was likely that he would have returned to New York and the music publishing milieu that he knew better than anyone else, if not for an event that irrevocably altered his life and that of the entire nation, as well.

On the evening of October 24, Irving was working late at the United Artists studio on the "Alice in Wonderland" number with Kusell. Word began to circulate around the studio that something serious, possibly catastrophic had occurred on the New York Stock Exchange. Irving suggested to Maurice, "Let's stay up all night and see how the market opens." Staying up all night was a routine matter for Berlin, of course, but Kusell volunteered to accompany him. Throughout the anxious hours of waiting in the studio's commissary, where a funereal mood prevailed, Irving never uttered a word of complaint, even though he was heavily invested in the market. In recent months, inflation had run up the value of his shares to $5 million, on paper, at any rate, and so he followed the fortunes of the market with interest.

When the market opened in New York the next morning, it was

six A.M. in Los Angeles. As the morning progressed, it became obvious that the bottom really had dropped out. Berlin lost his entire investment portfolio in the Crash, but he took the news quite calmly. He had, as yet, no indication that it marked the beginning of vast social changes in the country, and even as the Depression became an inevitable reality, he refused to regard it as a personal or a social tragedy. First and foremost, it was spectacle—the flip side of Lindbergh's solo flight across the Atlantic—and therefore ripe for musical exploitation.

Berlin's initial impression of the stock market crash as the latest craze to sweep the nation gave him an idea for a new movie musical. His story concerned a Wall Street financier ("Larry Day") distracted by a famous and pretty aviatrix ("Vivian Benton") who barges into his office on a bet with a friend. They make a dinner date, but she fails to appear. It turns out she's actually engaged to another man. Undaunted, Larry pursues Vivian aboard an ocean liner and joins her and her girlfriends, who are also pilots, for a transatlantic voyage. During the crossing, Larry learns of the Crash by telephone; with Vivian's encouragement, he returns to New York to try to rebuild his business. And oh yes, they get married.

For all its frivolity, the story contained elements of Berlin's romances with both Dorothy Goetz and Ellin. The scene in which Vivian barges into the financier's office evoked Irving's tempestuous first encounter with Dorothy, and the ocean voyage with a young woman who was a celebrity in her own right traded on his elopement with Ellin. As a story, *Reaching for the Moon*—the title of Berlin's first film scenario—made up in glamour and commercial possibilities what it lacked in logic. It was certainly no worse than any number of hit shows, but Berlin, though a songwriter of genius, lacked the ability of a Wodehouse and a Bolton to create a continuously entertaining plot. Berlin naturally envisioned the movie as a vehicle for his songs, which would provide the principal excuse for making it.

Berlin took his idea to Joe Schenck, who persuaded United Artists to back what seemed a highly promising notion. At the time, studios were in the midst of a musical binge, feeding an apparently insatiable popular appetite for all-talking, all-singing, all-dancing motion pictures. The studio put Douglas Fairbanks into the role of the financier and Bebe Daniels into that of the aviatrix who beguiles him. A much smaller role was carved out for a slim young singer making a name for himself with Paul Whiteman's Rhythm Boys: Bing Crosby.

Crosby's role served no important plot function, but he represented the vanguard of a new type of popular singer who'd gone right from the clubs to the studio, skipping the years of playing to raucous vaudeville houses. He was more of an electronic performer than a live one. Entertainers of the previous generation, such as Jolson, Cantor, and Harry Richman, tended to be larger than life on stage. Audiences could practically smell the greasepaint on them; men like that performed not for the camera but for the folks in the back of the highest balcony at the Palace. But Bing Crosby, born Harry Lillis Crosby, was as cool as those frantic crowd pleasers of the previous generation were hot. So many of them had been Jews from the Lower East Side, and he was from Spokane, Washington. He'd even been to college—Gonzaga University. No immigrant desperation here, no tales of tenement starvation and back alley bluster, only an ingratiating manner—plus impeccable timing and a voice like liquid gold. When Crosby and the next generation of singers (crooners, they would be called—no more belting out the songs) stood before a microphone, their careful underplaying sufficed to put the tune across. Farewell to the wriggling hips and waggling eyebrows of their elders. Of course, Irving, the constant student of performing styles, would have to teach himself to write a new kind of song—subtle and nuanced—for this new type of performer. He would have to write songs that could survive the depredations of microphones and directors and editors—the whole maddening crew responsible for movies being the beastly business they were. And of course, Berlin would acquire the knack; once he did, he would, some years later, write for Crosby again.

Problems developed soon enough with *Reaching for the Moon.* The studio assigned Edmund Goulding to direct the movie and write the dialogue. From the start, Berlin found Goulding impossible to work with, rigid and dogmatic. Sensing that the movie was in trouble, Berlin turned to his old friend Elsie Janis, who had gradually made the transition since the Great War from vaudeville entertainer to film scenarist. Though Janis was able to make a minor contribution to the script, the movie's prospects suffered a further blow when, in the middle of 1930, studios discovered that the public's demand for musicals had suddenly disappeared. (More likely, the studios had rushed so many musicals into release that audiences were surfeited.) Frightened by this development, Goulding jettisoned many of Berlin's songs from the score.

Although just five Berlin songs were recorded for *Reaching for the Moon*, the movie, even in its scaled-down form, proved to be hideously expensive to make. By the time the filming was complete, the costs had come to about a million dollars, a mammoth budget for the times, and one that virtually ruled out the possibility of the movie's returning a profit to the studio. By now Berlin had become so infuriated with Goulding and so frustrated with the entire process of making movies that he walked off the movie and returned to New York, where it was becoming apparent that the Crash heralded major social changes and the Depression was beginning to make itself felt in earnest. This behavior was unique in his career. Even when failure was inevitable, he'd never before abandoned a show before opening night—much less one based on his own idea. That he did so now was a particularly ominous sign for the movie and, by extension, for Berlin's reputation in Hollywood.

The episode left him rattled, and he lost faith in new songs that would later become hits. "Musicals were the rage out there," Berlin later said of his experience with *Reaching for the Moon*, "and then they weren't. Out went the songs. I developed the damnedest feelings of inferiority. I got so I called in anybody to listen to my songs—stockroom boys, secretaries. One blink of an eye and I was stuck. I had two [songs], 'Say It Isn't So' and 'How Deep Is the Ocean?' They're as good ballads as any I've written, but I didn't think they were good enough then." The avalanche of songwriting criticism he received in Hollywood made him feel acutely self-conscious and insecure, and he became more abrasive in his self-defense. "I'll fight and argue over a song," he remarked. "I'll say, 'What the hell do you know about it?' and then I'll go home and write another ending. . . . Oh, I'll overwrite and criticize myself, all right. As a writer gets successful, he sharpens his tools and sometimes they're a little *too* sharp. With experience, you get a little *too* critical and what comes out is a good *songwriter's* song but not a natural song."

In the fall of 1930, United Artists held a press screening of

Reaching for the Moon. Stories about the movie's troubled history and cost overruns were circulating, but Berlin's five songs were still part of the package. However, between the time of the screening and the actual release, on December 29, the studio made a last-ditch effort to change the picture's genre from a musical to a comedy by deleting four more songs. Of Berlin's entire score, only the title number, a melancholy tune in the manner of "Russian Lullaby," remained. If Goulding hoped that by eliminating the music the film would be more acceptable to audiences, he was badly mistaken. The result, shorn of the music, made little sense and contained jarring transitions where tunes had been excised. The film drifted into oblivion, as much a casualty of the Depression as Berlin's vanished stock market investments.

Berlin had come to a bitter pass in his career. With the failure of *Reaching for the Moon*, 1930 proved to be an abysmal year; he had managed to publish only a handful of songs, despite all his efforts. Even though the Depression didn't directly threaten him with imminent financial ruin, it wasn't helping much, either. Worse, he was in danger of losing step with the development of popular music. He lacked a secure foothold either in Hollywood or on Broadway. The isolated hits he turned out were too few and far between to sustain him; sooner or later songs needed shows to back them up. If he wasn't careful, he might wind up like D. W. Griffith, a man who'd outlived his time, a relic.

▪ ▪ ▪

"I saw light after light blotted out by the stock-market crash of 1929," wrote Edna Ferber, an acquaintance of Irving's from the once-vigorous Round Table, as the Depression took hold of New York. "The Empire State Building, the Chrysler spire and a score of star-piercing shafts, glowing with thousands of electric lights in gorgeous designs, had made an Arabian Nights panorama of the New York skyline after dusk. . . . If I ever live to see those lights blazing once more against the sunset sky I shall know that the thing we call the Depression is over."

Such was the grim mood of the city to which Berlin returned from his unhappy encounter with Hollywood. The Depression had a profound impact on Tin Pan Alley, as well, transforming this once-thriving industry beyond recognition. The grim economic environment drove the music business ever further into the studios' smothering embrace. House by house, Tin Pan Alley sold out to Hollywood. MGM acquired Robbins Music. Warner Brothers bought up the venerable M. Witmark & Sons and went to gobble up other publishers—Dreyfus, T. B. Harms, and New World Music. Songwriters increasingly worked under contract to studios rather than music publishers.

This marriage of necessity marked a little-noticed but important development in American popular culture. Since the turn of the century, Tin Pan Alley had regarded itself as the principal custodian of popular myths and fantasies. Now the distinction passed to Hollywood. Pedestrians strolled along West 28th Street, once the scene of a flourishing music industry, without hearing so much as a note. If they wondered whatever became of Tin Pan Alley, they would have discovered it had been bought up by Hollywood.

With one significant exception: Irving Berlin was delighted to sell his songs to the movies, but he refused to sell his publishing company—or his copyrights. His was not merely a minority position, it was unique among the major players. His disappointing experiences working in Hollywood on *Reaching for the Moon* had strengthened his resolve on this point. Irving Berlin, Inc. was not for sale.

His copyrights, he believed, were now more valuable than ever. With his ready cash gone, they were the only thing left to him—along with the Music Box Theatre. He could sell them now at bargain basement prices, or he could hang on to them and wait for better times. Irving decided to wait. And he also decided he'd better write more songs. As the full extent of the Depression became apparent to him, and he recognized that it was more than another craze, he wrote, "I was scared. I had all the money I wanted for the rest of my life. Then, all of a sudden, I didn't. I found I'd have to go back to work and I wasn't sure I could make the grade. I had taken it easy and gone soft and wasn't too certain I could get going again."

▪ ▪ ▪

The Depression's effect on Berlin's music career was subtle, muted, though far-reaching. But its effect on his father-in-law, Clarence

Mackay, proved to be far more drastic. Clarie, who thought he'd forever enjoy his immense inherited wealth, sailed into the collapse completely unprotected. Throughout the late twenties his life-style—the Harbor Hill estate, the European vacations, the cost of supporting his mistress, Anna Case—demanded that he spend at a great rate. In 1928 alone he disgorged over a million dollars to purchase works of art. Since he was getting older and had never enjoyed business, he decided—against the advice of his lawyer—to sell his controlling interest in the Postal Telegraph Company to Sosthenes Behn, president of International Telephone and Telegraph. On March 29, 1928, Postal Telegraph merged into IT&T in a $300 million transaction. Mackay elected to take his multimillion-dollar payment not in cash, or even partly in cash, but entirely in stock.

At first the merger meant little for Clarie beyond moving his office from 253 Broadway to IT&T's building at 67 Broad Street and a change in title from "President" to "Chairman of the Board." The same family portraits hung on the wall, and Clarie was still enamored of medieval flourishes and symbols of power. He wore a special seal ring that portrayed a hand gripping a sword above the legend "*Manu Forti*," and he liked to impress others with the notion that the seal was in memory of his father, who'd "ruled his business with a strong hand."

The Crash, however, swiftly sapped Clarie's hand of its strength. On Black Friday, as his son-in-law quietly waited for news of stock prices in the United Artists commissary, Clarence Mackay watched the value of his stock plummet. In only half an hour, he lost $36 million. His total forfeiture came to several times that amount. As a result, he had the hideous distinction of incurring the largest loss suffered by an individual in the Crash.

The Postal Telegraph Company suffered as well. Within a few short years, it would cease paying dividends altogether. The great empire founded by Clarie's father, John Mackay, once one of the richest in a country filled with riches, had been extinguished, the victim both of a changing economy and Clarie's own shortsightedness.

The loss of the family fortune had a dramatic effect on Mackay's standard of living. Indeed, out in Long Island's Wheatley Hills, an entire way of living, with servants, stables, tennis courts, and private land stretching as far as the eye could see, was quickly passing into oblivion, a giddy memory of the twenties. As for Clarie, he was forced to close up Harbor Hill, store the art treasures he had collected pending an auction, sell his beloved thoroughbred horses, dismiss his staff of 134, shut off the fountains, and move into the estate's gatekeeper's cottage. Harbor Hill, once among the grandest country estates in America, acquired an unofficial new name: Heartbreak House.

As Clarence made the awkward transition from limitless wealth to genteel poverty, his estranged wife, Kitty, reentered his life. Ever since her marriage to Dr. Joseph Blake, Clarence had maintained an elaborate pretense that she was still married to *him* in the eyes of the Catholic church. Resisting his attempts to manipulate her, Kitty, who was not a Catholic, went on to bear four more children.

Now it was her turn to suffer misfortune. As she grew older, she suffered from diabetes and went blind. Then her husband, for whom she had abandoned her first three children and Mackay's millions, abandoned her. Dr. Blake began an affair with a nurse forty years younger than he. In April 1929, he divorced Kitty, now an invalid, to marry the nurse. Kitty's sole consolation was that she kept custody of the four children she'd had with him. Her health continued to deteriorate.

When it became apparent that her mother was near death, Ellin attempted to intercede on her behalf. Ellin arranged for her sister, "K," and Dr. Blake to visit Kitty at her large home at 12 East 87th Street. As it happened, both appeared on the same day, with "K" arriving as Blake was leaving. Coming down the stairs, he patted her on the head and said, "You must be Kathy."

"Yes," said "K."

"Try not to remember your mother this way," Dr. Blake told her. "She was the most beautiful woman in the world."

A year after her divorce from Dr. Blake, on April 21, 1930, Kitty died of complications stemming from cancer and pneumonia. She left a surprising legacy. Shortly before her death she converted to her ex-husband's Roman Catholic faith.

Kitty's gesture of contrition affected Clarence deeply. At eight-thirty on the morning of her funeral, he arrived at St. Vincent Ferrer church at Lexington Avenue and 66th Street, where the service was due to begin at ten A.M. He was accompanied by his two daughters,

"K" and Ellin. He'd seen Ellin on just one other occasion since her elopement, when his mother died.

With the immediate family assembled, Clarence approached Kitty's body, which lay "entombed in bronze beneath a purple pall," according to a newspaper account. It was the Easter season, and on top of her casket Clarence, again displaying his love of symbols, placed a cross woven of lilies. The gesture was his way of forgiving her for having abandoned him. Precisely why Kitty decided to convert to Roman Catholicism in the last months of her life remains a mystery, but no other deed could have been better calculated to cause Clarence finally to absolve her of blame.

Meanwhile, the white-robed Dominican priests who had effected Kitty's deathbed conversion waited at the altar.

As the beginning of the service drew near, more family members arrived: Ellin's brother Willie, and his wife, followed by the four children of Kitty and Dr. Joseph Blake. All teenagers, they politely took their places beside their half-sisters. The next mourner to arrive entered quietly, through a side door, trying not to call attention to himself, but his appearance sent a jolt through the assembled family members. It was Kitty's second husband, Dr. Joseph Blake, his hair and mustache gone gray. A vigorous man, he suddenly looked his age: sixty-eight. Though all eyes were on him, he kept to himself as the funeral mass began.

Afterward, Dr. Blake hurried from the church, back to his twenty-eight-year-old third wife, while Clarence and the rest of the Mackay clan formed a funeral procession to Woodlawn Cemetery, where Katherine Blake was interred in the Duer family plot.

Following the death of her mother, Ellin found her father more approachable. Though she would always think of herself as a woman in rebellion against the hypocrisy of her father's class, she yearned for his approval perhaps more deeply than she was prepared to acknowledge. Eventually she found a way to recover it.

At the beginning of 1931, Clarence's ailing Postal Telegraph Company became the target of a widely publicized lawsuit brought by an opportunist named John S. Hansen, who claimed that Clarence Mackay owed him a $100,000 fee. Hansen noted that he had met Mackay in 1924, when the two were on the same boat crossing the

English Channel, and had offered to secure the Mexican government's permission to allow the Postal Telegraph Company to run its cables through that country. He further maintained that he had kept his end of the bargain, but that Mackay had refused to pay him.

When the matter came to trial in April, Clarence's best defense rested, as it happened, with his daughter, Ellin, who had accompanied him during the channel crossing when he and Hansen allegedly struck the deal. This had been during her year-long 'round-the-world journey to try to forget Irving Berlin. She'd heard the conversation, and as she testified in court, the men had discussed no business whatsoever, much less a complicated transaction involving Mexican cable rights. Thanks to her testimony, Hansen lost his suit, and afterward, Clarence publicly embraced Ellin. Her support set the wheels of reconciliation in motion.

Though Clarence had irrevocably lost control of his business, he made other attempts to put his house in order. Now that Kitty was dead, he no longer had to maintain the pretense that they were still married, and he was at last free to marry his mistress, Anna Case, who had stood by him through the Crash and the loss of his fortune. Since hypocrisy was second nature to Clarence Mackay, the proprieties had to be observed. Before he married Anna, he insisted that she convert from the Dutch Reform faith of her birth to Roman Catholicism. She was confirmed by Cardinal Hayes a month before the wedding. She then married Clarence on July 18, 1931, at St. Mary's Church in Roslyn. As for the three children of Clarence and Kitty, they all loyally attended. But a shade fell over this ceremony as well, for Clarence was slowly dying from a recurrence of the throat cancer of which Dr. Blake had supposedly cured him years before. In place of the robust, exceedingly wealthy man who had supported her in the years before their marriage, Anna was marrying a former millionaire with a proud name who was in failing health.

Since Berlin was in attendance, observers took his presence to mean that Clarence had at last achieved a reconciliation with his son-in-law. And they had, after their fashion. Berlin extended the olive branch of charity to his financially humbled father-in-law by giving the old man a million dollars to make him comfortable in his declining years, there in the gatekeeper's cottage, with Anna Case by his side. His gift was all the more remarkable considering the financial pressure

Berlin himself was under as a result of the Depression and his lack of recent song hits.

Despite the songwriter's generosity, his father-in-law still despised him. No matter what Berlin did, what gestures he made, Clarence would always consider him a Jewish songwriter from the Lower East Side, and no amount of personal generosity could ever change that fact. If anyone benefited from Irving's gallant gesture, it was Ellin, for the acrimony between her husband and her father began to lessen. Irving and Clarie were no longer at war; their relationship was now more of an armed truce. The deposed ruler of Harbor Hill remained as implacable as ever, dwelling in a dream world.

Now more than ever he used the issue of religion to manipulate those around him. Those who remained faithful or converted to Catholicism enjoyed his blessing; those who did not ceased to exist. Since her elopement, Ellin—defiant, too much like her mother—belonged to the latter category: the company of infidels who in the name of selfish pursuits brought disgrace on the House of Mackay. Longing for her father's favor, Ellin, too, began to rethink her commitment to the church. Within a few years she was re-baptized in the Catholic faith and became a regular communicant, at last making peace with this crucial aspect of her heritage. But she was never to repeat her father's folly of forcing her religious convictions on other members of her family.

▪ ▪ ▪

In September 1930, Berlin purchased a lot at 66 East 93 Street, between Madison and Park Avenues. His grandiose scheme was to demolish the existing apartment house and construct, at an estimated cost of $200,000, a new town house for himself and Ellin. It soon became apparent that with the Depression becoming more severe with each passing month and the lights continuing to be extinguished throughout New York, he was stretching himself too thin, and he abandoned the plan.

The austerity measures to which Berlin submitted were slight compared with the ruin that the Depression visited on other prominent show folk with whom he'd worked. Charles Dillingham, the gentleman producer of Irving's first Broadway success, *Watch Your Step*, was forced to mount his first post-Crash musical on a set consisting merely of draperies. As the Depression tightened its grip and audiences shrank, he sank into debt. Esteemed throughout his career for his honesty, he became so desperate for money that he resorted to stealing the box office receipts for Jerome Kern's *The Cat and the Fiddle*, which was running at Dillingham's Globe Theatre. Discovering the theft, Kern was infuriated.

That shabby episode, so out of character for Dillingham, marked the end of the producer's active career. The power and influence he'd wielded was gone, he was broke, and he was soon to die. During the last two years of his life, Charles Dillingham, once the most respected Broadway impresario, lived off the generosity of his former associates, who kept him on a hundred-dollar-a-week stipend.

Florenz Ziegfeld's career followed the same tragic pattern. When the word got around that he'd been ruined by the Crash, Dillingham remarked, "Well, at least that finally makes us even." Staving off creditors at every turn, Ziegfeld mounted the last edition of his *Follies* in July 1931; despite a brave show of sets and stars, it seemed as outdated as the Charleston. By this time Ziegfeld, who'd always played fast and loose with his money and had always gotten away with it, really was destitute. In the winter of 1932, he staged a disastrous musical called *Hot-Cha*, financed by two well-known mobsters, Dutch Schultz and Waxey Gordon. Schultz had tried to get Ziegfeld to call the thing *Laid in Mexico*, but Ziegfeld explained that this little jest might not be entirely acceptable to the general public. They reached a compromise, and it became the *sub*title. Throughout the show's brief run, gangsters were much in evidence, telling the exasperated impresario how to do his job.

In May 1932, Ziegfeld staged his last production, a revival of his greatest Broadway success, *Show Boat*. Many of the participants believed so deeply in the project that they were willing to defer their salaries. For a while, Ziegfeld prospered, but a June heat wave drove audiences from the theater, and the show closed. End of false illusions.

Ziegfeld's avoidance mechanisms were as highly developed as his theatrical instincts, and so he called for more wine and madder music. But he was haunted by a new curse: impotence. He resorted to hormone therapy and then imported willing chorus girls to his home, Burkely Crest, in Hastings, New York, to see whether the treatment had any effect. His health broke under the strain, and he muttered to himself incoherently. His wife, Billie Burke, implored him to join her at her Santa Monica home. On July 5, he boarded the Twentieth-Century Limited, bound for California. He was pale and gaunt, clearly a man nearing the end of his life. Throughout the trip he reminisced disjointedly about his Chicago childhood and his early days in the theater. Long-forgotten memories bubbled to the surface and flashed by as quickly and brightly as the landscape outside the window of his railway car, inflaming his exhausted imagination. Occasionally, he rallied for a brief period and dictated telegrams that were nothing more than gibberish.

He barely survived the cross-country journey, but on arriving in Los Angeles he appeared to recover. It was his last illusion. After only a few days in Santa Monica, he developed pleurisy and entered Cedars of Lebanon Hospital, where he retreated into incoherent ravings. A broken man, he died on July 22 and was buried in a gaudy mausoleum at Forest Lawn Cemetery.

Of the old Broadway warhorses, only the Shuberts remained active, but by 1931 their empire, once valued at $25 million, was in bankruptcy. Still, there was some doubt as to how legitimate their bankruptcy was. Suspicion lingered that the Shuberts had adopted the measure as a ploy to escape paying creditors, for in bankruptcy the Shuberts swiftly consolidated their interests. Lee Shubert subsequently bought back his theaters at a public auction held on the steps of the Wall Street subtreasury building, paying only $400,000. If he raised eyebrows with this tricky maneuver, he confounded his critics with his explanation: "These theaters would be dark today if I hadn't built them." At any rate, the Shubert empire emerged from this possibly imaginary ordeal stronger than ever. The Shuberts hadn't been fans of Berlin's before the Depression, and they weren't about to change their minds now. They remained a force to be reckoned with, and they remained hostile to Berlin.

Neither the Shuberts nor anyone else could fill the vacuum left by the deaths of Ziegfeld and Dillingham—their extravagance and passion for the theater. They represented an era when live productions reached their largest audiences and were at their most influential. Competing now with both radio and the movies, Broadway reduced the size of its output and the scope of its productions. The newspaper columnist Heywood Broun, for instance, mounted a frugal staging of a revue called *Shoot the Works*, to which prominent Broadway figures donated their services simply to gain exposure. Berlin contributed a song called "Begging for Love," only to read the assessment of one unhappy critic: "Berlin received nothing for this number—and it was worth it." So critics were no longer the obliging cheerleaders they'd once been; they now judged shows with a cool and practiced eye, and their readers paid them heed. Expensive productions that would formerly have run for months on the strength of their chorus girls' looks now opened and closed within a week.

Financial hardship transformed the spirit of Broadway as surely as it curtailed its extravagance. Aroused by critics, audiences began to demand more from the shows they saw. In the twenties, frivolity had been its own defense, but now excess seemed irresponsible. The theater should reflect social realities, ran the new dogma, and if possible change them. Show business as a vehicle for social reform: that was a new one on Irving—and on a lot of other Broadway stalwarts, as well. Gone were the days when theater people got together and rented a stage just for the sake of amusing themselves, as the Round Table's members had in 1922. Putting on a show for the thrill of it, the fun of it, the hell of it, was viewed with suspicion—a thing of the past.

A profound disillusionment was abroad in the land. In New York, the reform-minded Judge Samuel Seabury was investigating Irving's friend, Mayor Jimmy Walker. Stories of Walker's infamous "nocturnal cabinet" spread throughout the city, and the spectacle of the mayor's consorting with chorus girls known for their long legs and short résumés only served to encourage them. By his own admission, he preferred to conduct business in the back of a saloon. Judge Seabury's investigation prompted the governor, Franklin D. Roosevelt, to begin another inquiry into Walker's misdealing. In disgrace, Walker resigned his office on August 26, 1932. By then his administration, once a popular marriage of show business and politics, had become a notorious emblem of the way wealth and frivolity combined to corrupt democratic institutions.

One of the first Broadway musicals to mirror this popular disgust with business-as-usual politics opened at Berlin's own theater, the Music Box, on December 26, 1931. The songwriter had nothing to do with this show—one of the few bright spots on the dismal Broadway scene—beyond having the singular fortune to house it and the good sense to learn from it.

No, this achievement belonged to Berlin's admirer George Gershwin. In collaboration with his brother Ira, a lyricist, and George S. Kaufman, Gershwin fashioned a satire on American politics titled *Of Thee I Sing.* All the empty hoopla of a presidential campaign—the rigged convention, the back-room machinations, and the cynical packaging of a First Lady—was exhaustively treated. The result proved to be so successful that it filled the Music Box for 441 performances—far longer than anyone anticipated.

There were repercussions for Berlin. When he decided to mount his own satirical show, which owed much (some said *too* much) to the Gershwin effort, he had to find another theater because *Of Thee I Sing* was still packing them in at the Music Box. Even more impressive, this was the first musical to win a Pulitzer Prize. (Since the prize was given for literature, George Gershwin, the show's driving force, was shortchanged the honor.) The idea that a Broadway show could have anything in common with higher cultural expression and could concern itself with something besides heaving bosoms and silly plots and swell songs came as a new and surprising result of the Depression environment, though not everyone welcomed the trend. "Park Avenue librettos by children of the ghettos," said one rival scribe. Though intended as a disparagement, this was the formula to which Berlin adhered with mounting success for the remainder of the decade.

The success of this musical—all the more remarkable in the Depression climate—placed Berlin in a dilemma. For one of the few times in his varied career, his role as a songwriter conflicted with his role as a theater owner. As the landlord of the Music Box, he enjoyed the stroke of luck that placed one of the season's few hits in his own theater. *Of Thee I Sing*'s commercial success cushioned him from the Depression's worst shocks; without it, he might have lost control of his prized theater. But as a songwriter who jealously guarded his reputation, he was in a different position. Here was this young fellow Gershwin, admittedly talented, possibly even a genius, upstaging him in his own backyard, with the assistance of Sam Harris, who had produced the show. Gershwin was just thirty-four at the time, and he and his brother acquired a reputation as the coming songwriting team on Broadway; Berlin, in contrast, seemed to belong to a bygone era.

While the Gershwins flourished, Berlin continued to suffer from the twin afflictions of low self-confidence and dwindling cash. Even when he wrote a good tune, he lacked faith in it. One recent song, "Say It Isn't So," nearly fell victim to his low self-esteem. After composing it, Irving, certain it was another flop, put it in his drawer. It might have languished there indefinitely, had not Max Winslow, still heading up the professional department of Berlin's office, heard it and liked what he heard. On his own initiative Winslow took the song to Rudy Vallee, now a star on radio.

Irving scorned radio and resisted trying to introduce his songs on the air, but Winslow employed the same dogged approach he'd used to rescue "Alexander's Ragtime Band" from obscurity twenty years before. He went directly to Vallee and said, "Irving's all washed up, or at least he feels like it. He thinks he's written out as a songwriter. But here's a song of his I'd like you to look at and please, sing it for him."

Vallee couldn't decide whether Winslow was telling him the plain truth or making an exceedingly artful pitch, but when he listened to Winslow play "Say It Isn't So," he was seized by it. He readily agreed to sing the song the following Thursday on his weekly radio program. Winslow and Berlin didn't realize it, but the song had struck a nerve with Vallee, who was in the midst of painful divorce proceedings. "The lyrics spoke all I felt," Vallee explained. "There was I singing that song about my girl seeing someone else and going away—it was all true and happening to me." He decided to use Irving's song in a last-ditch attempt to persuade his wife, Fay Webb, to stay with him.

"Thursday evening, as my wife and her father sat in my attorney's office," Vallee said, "my attorney turned on his radio to listen to my radio hour and the poignancy of Irving Berlin's lyric and melody, 'Say It Isn't So.' It hit all three of them with the impact of a bomb! Tears were in Fay's eyes as she listened, and yet she signed the separation agreement."

Though the song failed to accomplish its purpose for Vallee, it succeeded for Berlin: it became an immediate hit—one of the few the songwriter ever launched in the medium of radio. With its success Berlin recovered some of his self-confidence. He returned to his old song "To My Mammy," rescued the intriguing question about how deep the ocean might be, constructed an entire lyric cleverly consisting of nothing *but* questions in the same rhetorical vein, and composed a new melody for them—subdued, slow, with the long, sustained line characteristic of popular music of the thirties. The result, "How Deep Is the Ocean?" became his second hit of 1932 and demonstrated anew the value of the apparently worthless trunk songs he'd made a practice of hoarding throughout his career. When he experienced a vindication of this type, he was quick to note that his "new" hit was just a trunk song or, even more pointedly, salvaged from an admitted flop. "I keep taking lines and other bits out of bad songs," he said of the practice. "And I'll tell you something else—all songwriters do. The only different thing about me is that I advertize the fact that I do it. They don't."

More than timing lay behind the song's success, however. "How Deep Is the Ocean?" offered the clearest demonstration yet of Berlin's growing skill at playing the lyrics off the melody to create a rounded emotional statement. As the text poses one question after another, the music, starting in a minor key, answers by resolving into a major key at the end. The interplay endows the music with psychological weight, supplying the listener with a wealth of complicated, nuanced feeling that extends beyond the literal meaning of the song's lyrics.

Signs of Berlin's recovery lured Joe Schenck to his side. While Irving had been struggling with his loss of confidence, his friend had continued to flourish in Hollywood with United Artists, making money out of costume dramas, gambling it away in Mexico, and then making some more. For Schenck, the Depression presented a marvelous opportunity to pick up bargains. For all his faults, he was loyal to his friends, especially when they had fallen on hard times. He'd felt bad about exposing Berlin to disappointment in the movies, and on a trip to New York he took Irving to lunch.

Over a mutton chop, he brought up the topic that surely hung heavily in Irving's mind. "I hear you're broke," he said. Though not exactly broke, Berlin was certainly hard-pressed; but he was even more upset by his inability to write a string of hits than by his financial straits. Schenck traced Berlin's creative slump to the songwriter's constant worrying about money. "Your talent is just as good as ever," Schenck assured him.

"Sure," Irving said, "but how can I write hit music when I'm upset?"

Schenck then revealed his plan to get Berlin back to work. "I have a building in town that I picked up cheap. It nets me a thousand a week on a lease. You can take over the thousand a week for a year and get down to work."

His scalp tightening, Berlin looked up at his friend. No matter how Schenck described his offer, it amounted to charity, and Berlin would not accept charity, especially from Schenck. To Irving, with his insistence on independence, the offer might have been a challenge, or a threat, possibly a Trojan horse. With a character like Schenck, it was impossible to say. Berlin's eyes were watering now; tears of gratitude, Schenck supposed. But the songwriter took him by surprise. "Joe," he said, "I'll get down to work without the money."

Berlin rose and walked out of the restaurant, leaving Schenck in solitude to ponder the behavior of his obstinate little friend.

Stung by Schenck's offer of charity, Berlin kept his word. He got down to work, sustained work, for the first time in the six years since his marriage. Driven by a mixture of desperation and pride, he was intent on restoring luster to his reputation. He began by thinking of ways to exploit the success of Gershwin's adventurous musical, *Of Thee I Sing*, still going strong in Berlin's own theater. He'd written every other kind of song, from rag to "coon" to sob; he might as well try his hand at social criticism. He was, as always, prepared to *give the people what they wanted.* It now appeared they wanted something that spoke to their sense of deprivation and betrayal. If Berlin wanted an object lesson about the effects of the Depression on the wealthy and powerful in politics, in show business, and in society, he had only to look to the bitter experiences of his friend, former mayor James J. Walker; two of his early mentors, Florenz Ziegfeld and Charles Dillingham; and his father-in-law, Clarence Mackay. Their examples hovered about him like so many morality plays—stark vignettes of once-powerful men abruptly called to account.

Once Berlin decided on a musical that would reflect Depression realities as *Of Thee I Sing* had, he brought in two key members of that show's creative team: George S. Kaufman, who would direct, and Sam Harris, to produce. To ensure the production's glossiness, Berlin resumed his working relationship with Hassard Short, who a decade earlier had turned the Music Box revues into visual spectacles. The neophyte member of the team and, one suspects, its true creative spark plug, was the twenty-eight-year-old playwright Moss Hart, who'd recently made a name for himself by collaborating with Kaufman on the hit comedy *Once in a Lifetime*.

When he began working with Berlin, Hart was in the midst of that first flush of success beside which all subsequent achievements pale. As he related in his penetrating memoir, *Act One*, he, too, had been born in poverty—though in the Bronx, this time, rather than the Lower East Side. Hart was a more sensitive and reflective individual than Berlin, and the younger man's experience of poverty was far darker. For Hart, poverty was the outward manifestation of an inner despair that crushed the soul. But the theater had provided him with a glorious escape from that life before he reached the age of thirty; suddenly he had money and entered the mainstream of American life.

Mixing inspiration from Berlin and criticism from Kaufman, Hart fashioned a story clearly inspired by the political satire in *Of Thee I Sing*, yet it was gentler, more whimsical. Called *Face the Music*, the opening scene takes place in an automat, where busted Vanderbilts and Astors (read *Mackay*) are now forced to dine with the hoi polloi. There a Broadway producer by the name of Hal Reisman (read *Florenz Ziegfeld*) meets the wealthy Mrs. Martin Van Buren Meshbesher, whose husband (read *James J. Walker*) is a corrupt policeman. Cheerfully laundering Meshbesher's hot money, Reisman stages a revue called *Rhinestones of 1932* (read *Follies of 1931*); the production flops and—worse—City Hall becomes the target of an investigation. The tale takes an even more cynical turn when Meshbesher prevails on Reisman to add more Ziegfeld-style flesh to the show, thus reviving its fortunes. (In this last development, life imitated art, for the real Ziegfeld would shortly be at the mercy of his gangster backers and their lasciviousness.)

Hart's story marked a daring departure for Berlin. Never before had he risked antagonizing his audience to this extent. His apparent change of heart did not presage a political awakening; he was simply being a professional, following the shift in the mood of the theatergoing public. Furthermore, the songs he devised were more remarkable for their sweetness than for their bite. When visiting the automat, for instance, the once-wealthy socialites sing "Let's Have Another Cup of Coffee," a tune counseling patience in the face of adversity. The other hit to emerge from his score, "Soft Lights and Sweet Music," marked a return to his rapturous, romantic mood. Through these and other songs in the score, Berlin once again managed to capture the essence of popular feeling by exploring emotions that simmer below the surface rather than by exploiting obvious trends. In his sorrowful ballads of the twenties, he'd caught the mood of melancholy and loneliness lurking behind the decade's frenzied façade; now, in the thirties, he explored a new sense of community and intellectual sophistication trailing in the wake of the Crash.

The task of reinventing himself as a popular songwriter involved protracted labor. Throughout the months he toiled on the score, he was haunted by a fear of failure. *Face the Music* would either be his comeback or offer final confirmation that he was, along with Ziegfeld and Dillingham, washed up. At the outset, he faltered badly. For one thing, the old story about his playing the piano with only one finger, erroneously spawned in London a generation earlier, suddenly cropped up. The next thing he knew they'd drag out the story of the little colored boy who obligingly wrote all his songs for him. Berlin mounted a public relations offensive to salvage his musicianship, playing for anyone who would sit for a moment and listen. Among the journalists he summoned to his office was Percy N. Stone of the *Herald Tribune*, who found Berlin wild with excitement, "jumping from one side of the room to the other," and gesticulating madly as he described his hopes for the new show. And then it was time to disprove the rumor. Berlin sat before the piano and played. Stone duly recorded that Berlin's "long fingers ran up and down the keys in preliminary arpeggios and then struck both major and minor chords. It was a simple demonstration, but it did take in eight fingers and two thumbs." *Quod erat demonstrandum.*

There was another, more serious problem, involving the songs themselves. "For two months I went along as I always have, picking out tunes and fitting in the words," he said.

> I called in some friends and some people in my office who are not "yes men." I showed them what I'd done, and in one voice they shouted "Lousy!" Then my troubles started. I realized I had used tunes and lyrics that had been loafing around in my head; realized I had written them down because they were easy, not because they were good. I grew frightened. "What if I can't write any more good ones?" I thought. I wasn't sure of anything I did. I had to ask everyone's opinion. There was no momentum from the last show to carry me along. I was rusty. I was overanxious.
>
> I grew nervous and I couldn't sleep. I lost ten pounds trying to make songs. We tried to do a revue with a story thread running through it. The whole thing is a satire and my songs had to fit. I couldn't just write anything as I could have done with an ordinary revue. Three times we thought we had it, and three times we had to do it over. . . . And all the time I was frightened to death. If I could have revived any self-assurance it wouldn't have been so tough, but a song writer is only as good as his last show, and I was constantly afraid.

Berlin suffered more shocks once rehearsals began. The chorus girls were so young—many of them hadn't been born when his earliest hits were all the rage on Tin Pan Alley—and he was so old. For the kids who were supposed to bring his music to life, "Alexander's Ragtime Band" or even the relatively recent "All Alone" were no longer part of the living musical language; quaint tunes, they belonged to a different age. He was now a middle-aged man, undergoing the ordeal of a middle-age crisis from which he would emerge either renewed or broken.

To make matters worse, the professional rivalry between Kaufman and Berlin flared up. Kaufman's reputation as a complete man of the theater—director, playwright, and wit—was then at its peak, and yet Berlin had placed his man, Hassard Short, above Kaufman. Theoretically, Short merely designed the sets, but in practice, Berlin charged him with the responsibility of overseeing the entire production. Kaufman displayed his resentment at the first read-through. When the cast enacted scenes from the script, Kaufman gave them his full attention, but just as Berlin started to play the score, the director left the theater. Insulted, Berlin stopped talking to Kaufman, who attempted to apologize for the slight by explaining that he didn't know about music, didn't care about it, and besides, it was Short's job to handle it. None of his excuses endeared him to Berlin, but the men arrived at a chilly entente and rehearsals went forward.

Adding to the anxiety surrounding the production was the cost of mounting it. With *Of Thee I Sing* profitably installed at Berlin's own Music Box, Sam Harris leased the Ziegfeld's former theater, the New Amsterdam. The move proved costly, and the budget swelled to $165,000. This was financial madness; Berlin and Harris could never hope to recoup their costs in the Depression climate. But they wanted more than profit this time: they were seeking to restore their reputations. In their quest, they were assisted by enormous goodwill in the business and in the press. Everyone, it seemed, was pulling for Berlin to return from his five-year absence from Broadway and strut his stuff.

When *Face the Music* opened on February 17, 1932, Berlin's score demonstrated that the veteran songwriter, who had been teetering on the verge of obsolescence, had finally made the leap from the twenties to the thirties. He was in step with the times, composing songs infused with a newfound warmth and elegance. Though some critics faulted the show's similarity to the Gershwins' effort, they welcomed the return of Irving Berlin to the Broadway stage. It was apparent to all that he had at last mastered the popular song idiom of the 1930s.

Despite this favorable reaction, the show enjoyed a comparatively modest run of 165 performances. By July, it was gone, a victim of the Depression-era economics afflicting Broadway. Nonetheless, during its brief life *Face the Music* proved one point beyond dispute: Irving Berlin—ten pounds lighter, considerably poorer, and several years older than when last heard on Broadway—was once again at the top of his trade.

■ □ ■ □ ■ □ ■

CHAPTER 13

Recovery

For Berlin, the success of *Face the Music* triggered an outburst of activity on all fronts: Broadway, motion pictures, and even music publishing. It was an agreeable change. Since his elopement six years before, he had been forced to contend with one intractable problem after another: his father-in-law's opposition to his marriage, the Depression, the difficulty of penetrating Hollywood. All these difficulties had aggravated the profound insecurity lurking at his core. Now, after years of fighting battles within and without, he felt sufficiently confident to seize the initiative and do what *he* wanted, rather than facing yet another dilemma.

He first turned his attention to the task of mounting another Broadway satire—a bigger and better version of *Face the Music*—in his own theater, the Music Box, which the Gershwins had at last vacated. In his opinion, the key to the new show's success would be the young Moss Hart. It was Hart who'd given the earlier show its bite and wit, Hart who understood how to express Depression disillusionment in human terms and in dramatic form. Irving was eager to take his cue from the young dramatist. With the enthusiasm of a veteran song plugger, he pitched Hart—pitched him hard—on the idea of putting together a satirical *revue*, a series of sketches that would not confine themselves to the insular worlds of show business and Tammany Hall but take on international celebrities, world affairs.

Though passé, the revue remained the dramatic form Berlin understood best; but, as Hart wrote, "We both agreed that we had no desire to do a conventional sort of revue with the usual blackout sketches, songs and dances. So we hit upon the idea of writing a topical show right off the front pages of the newspapers." In fact, their topical revue took both its ideas from the papers, and its *form.* This was a novel and striking idea for Broadway—to adapt the newspaper format, with its headlines, gossip, Sunday supplements, and even its comic strips to the stage. And it proved to be inspired, for the newspaper format brought a semblance of unity to what would have otherwise been a series of loosely arranged sketches.

Most importantly, the idea of staging the review as a living newspaper caught Irving's imagination. He had long felt a special affinity for journalists, but had also been on the receiving end of the newspapers' unwelcome prying at the time of his elopement, so he had a score to settle with his colleagues in the press. The new show, titled *As Thousands Cheer*, would serve as his artful vehicle for doing just that.

The partnership nearly foundered when Hart, again short of money, accepted a lucrative screenwriting offer from the producer Irving Thalberg in Hollywood. Fortunately for Berlin, Hart's experience in Hollywood proved as frustrating as his own had been, and a chastened Hart soon returned to New York. To make certain that he would continue to command Hart's undivided attention, Berlin lent him $5,000—an impressive sum in those Depression days—and promised him a comfortable trip to Bermuda, where they would collaborate on the script for the new revue. Humbled by Hollywood and stroked by Berlin, Hart accepted with alacrity.

Although he was generous with Hart, Berlin himself was still short of ready cash as a result of the losses incurred by *Face the Music*, and he had to borrow $10,000 to stage the show. By deferring his own fees as lyricist, composer, and owner of the Music Box, he kept the overall budget to a restrained $96,000. The first edition of the *Music Box Revue*, in contrast, had cost roughly twice as much, but that was in a different era, when money had found its way to Broadway with ease.

Berlin and Hart left for Bermuda in April 1933. "There, in the most idyllic land that one can possibly imagine and one designed by an all-embracing Nature for the convenience and inspiration of writers," Hart said, "we completed the first act and laid out the second in little more than a month." They began by studying newspapers to discover what elements would lend themselves to sketches on stage; certain staples, such as editorials, financial news, and real estate they decided had no place in their revue. But society news certainly did. The well-publicized marital follies of Barbara Hutton, the wealthy heiress, provided grist for the satiric mill. Gandhi lent himself to caricature, as did Aimée Semple MacPherson, John D. Rockefeller, and British royalty. And the comics were a natural, of course. Berlin even had in mind a dandy tune inspired by the weather report: "Heat Wave."

The collaborators discovered their job was made easier by the fact that the behavior of their targets was often so outlandish it was self-satirizing. "There are some persons, you know, who need no distortion to caricature, and the same is true of much of the world's news," Berlin explained. "It is satire in itself and has only to be photographically reproduced to be the most gorgeous kind of irony." And what of the story of a black man lynched by a mob down South? This was surely not the light, satirical fare Irving intended to include, but the songwriter's "Supper Time" demonstrated that a tragedy as well as a farce could inspire a hit song.

Once the revue's twenty-three scenes had been roughed out, Berlin turned his attention to the score. Following his recent practice of hiring members of the Gershwins' team, he brought in their rehearsal pianist, Will Irwin, to act as transcriber. (His usual musical secretary, Helmy Kresa, was assigned the task of arranging Irwin's transcriptions for the orchestra.) A likable and gentle man of twenty-eight, Irwin was in awe of the great Irving Berlin. However, he was in for a shock when he entered the beat-up little cubicle where the songwriter worked and listened to Berlin play the piano. Irwin had been accustomed to George Gershwin's able, pulsing style of pianism, but when Berlin sat down to play, the result defied description—eerie, disjointed meanderings across the keyboard. And then there was the business of the prepared piano with its funny little lever. Once a fixture on Tin Pan Alley, the device was now an anachronism, and younger men like Irwin had never seen one. Berlin had taken to calling his prepared piano "Buick." At one time or another, he owned several "Buicks," and the one in the office was the worse for wear, the ivory discolored almost to the shade of tobacco in places, the wood scarred with countless grooves made by burning cigarettes. And its tone wasn't much better than its disreputable appearance. "The sounds that came of that piano were those of a piano tuner," Irwin recalled. "I'd never heard anything like this."

"What's the matter? Don't you like my playing?" asked Berlin, noticing Irwin's baffled expression.

Irwin thought: How can I say what I think without being fired right now? So he said, carefully, "Mr. Berlin, can you sing the song for me?" And when he sang, Irwin was pleased to hear that "the voice was tiny but absolutely true. Right on the button. I feel that he, perhaps unknowingly, had perfect pitch. So I said, 'Mr. Berlin, why don't we be content with this: you sing it for me, and I'll write it down.' And," Irwin went on to notice, "he was always rhythmically right on the button as to what he wanted, whether it was a dotted quarter note or not a dotted quarter note. So we got along fine from then on."

Still, Berlin's idiosyncracies presented constant challenges. For one thing, he kept strange hours. Berlin would often call Irwin's home at two o'clock in the morning, waking the transcriber out of a sound sleep, to explain that an idea had occurred to him.

"Mr. Berlin, can't it wait until morning?" Irwin would groan.

And Berlin would croak, "No!" But he did have a cup of coffee waiting when Irwin arrived.

Working irregular hours, the two spent four or five days thrashing out a song, and Berlin kept Irwin on a tight leash. While transcribing "Heat Wave," for instance, Irwin tried to incorporate what he called an "inner harmonic thing, a little boom-boom-boom. A little pattern. It worked out beautifully."

Or so he thought. When Berlin heard it, he screamed, "*What are you doing?*" And then, calming down, he added, "Now Will, don't get upset."

The two of them went back and forth over Irwin's little pattern until, at last, Berlin had satisfied himself.

"He finally agreed with me," Irwin recalled, "but not without a fight."

Irwin discovered that Berlin had scant interest in the work of others. A songwriter himself, Irwin longed to demonstrate his wares to the master. Screwing his courage to the sticking place, he asked, "Mr. Berlin, can I play you a tune?" The boss's reply permitted no further discussion:

"Why?"

Irwin later summed up the range of Berlin's musical knowledge this way: "The only person Berlin knew was Berlin."

Berlin's intransigence derived in part from his fear that hearing unpublished songs written by others would expose him to charges of plagiarism, though Will Irwin was the last person to harbor such an intent. Nonetheless, Berlin often appeared to be haunted by past charges that his songs were written by others. Once, when playing for Irwin, the songwriter paused and asked, "Did you ever hear the story of the little nigger boy?" By which Berlin meant his alleged ghostwriter.

"Yes, I have," Irwin conceded.

Referring to the number of hits he'd written over the years, Berlin said, "Do you realize how many little nigger boys I'd have to have?"

But then, when he was in a more relaxed mood, Berlin would unbend slightly and, impressed by the facility with which Irwin wrote down music, confess, "Well, I should study."

By now, however, his young scribe had become a believer in Berlin's eccentric approach to writing hit tunes, and he offered this piece of advice: "Mr. Berlin, I haven't known you too long, but I think you've got an inferiority complex."

Berlin's sense of inadequacy goaded him to attempt a higher level of lyric writing. No more rhyming "n" with "m." No matching "queen" with "supreme" or "Michigan" with "wish again" as in days gone by on the Alley. At the same time, he insisted that the result remain as natural as an off-the-cuff remark. "My songs aim to be conversation set to music," he observed.

The songwriter had put himself in a vise—artistic no less than financial—to compose this score, and while in the throes of creation, he played the part of the cantankerous, contradictory, and self-involved genius. That said, his score for *As Thousands Cheer* was the best work he had ever done for the stage. It consisted of nothing *but* hits: "Easter Parade," "Heat Wave," "Harlem on My Mind," "How's Chances?," "Not for all the Rice in China" (a late addition), and "Supper Time."

Here was a conclusive demonstration that his lean years were at last over.

Of all these songs, "Easter Parade" caused him the most anxiety. It had begun life fifteen years earlier, as the unsuccessful "Smile and Show Your Dimple," written in frank imitation of "Pack Up Your Troubles in Your Old Kit Bag." Although the song had flopped, Berlin had always retained a fondness for the melody, which he saved in his "trunk" and now retrieved for *As Thousands Cheer*. He planned to deploy it in a splashy sketch inspired by the rotogravure section. The idea was to depict the Easter Parade along New York's Fifth Avenue as it appeared in the sepia-toned newspaper photographs of the era. The parade members would first be glimpsed in a tableau vivant behind a scrim; the scrim would lift, and they would spring to life and sing Irving's song. If the song was good enough, the number could be a showstopper.

As Thousands Cheer began rehearsal late in the summer, and Hart, who was not yet the veteran that his collaborator was, fell prey to near panic. It was one thing to imagine and plan the revue in all its gleaming perfection and quite another to engage in the struggle to realize it. In an outward manifestation of his inner ordeal, he grew a skimpy beard that drew its share of comment.

Hart was appalled when he first heard Irving play through one of the new songs, "Heat Wave." How could this artless little ditty hold an audience's attention? Hart asked Irving to run through it again, and still it sounded awful. On reflection, Hart decided the problem might lie with the way Irving sang—or rather, *tried* to sing. "Play 'Always,' " he asked Irving. If that song, a timeless hit and one of Hart's favorites, sounded as bad as "Heat Wave," he would relax. So Irving sang "Always" in that tiny, tinny, raspy voice of his, and Hart couldn't even recognize it. "I thought so," he said, his confidence partly restored.

Of course, Irving wouldn't be responsible for putting "Heat Wave" over. For that he hired one of the most versatile performers of the era, Ethel Waters. Six years earlier she had burst on the scene singing and dancing with abandon in a black Broadway revue called *Africana*. *The New York Times*, in what was then considered a compliment, had compared her to a leading comedienne of the era, proclaiming Waters a "dusky Charlotte Greenwood." Berlin's mingling of black and white actors followed the accepted practice of the day. On Broadway audiences generally welcomed integrated casts; but on the road, and especially in the South, the arrangement could bring down the wrath of the Ku Klux Klan.

Though Ethel Waters was well known, the true star of *As Thousands Cheer* was the celebrated Marilyn Miller. She was a former Ziegfeld protégée, with all that the label implied: a love affair and the great man bestowing gaudy jewelry on her. But Miller, unlike many other Ziegfeld conquests, was never really taken with the impresario-lothario. She had endured rather than adored him in order to claw her way into the *Follies*. Miller had no need of a Svengali, for she was a supremely gifted musical comedy actress in her own right, the beautiful Indiana-born child of vaudeville performers. A professional since the age of six, she could sing, dance, play a scene straight, play it for laughs, and (particularly appropriate for *As Thousands Cheer*) she had a knack for witty impersonations.

Miller was adept at making scenes both onstage and off. Once, she hurled a diamond bracelet Ziegfeld had given her right back in his face. She had further exasperated him by falling for another of his stars, a much younger man named Frank Carter. When Carter died suddenly in an automobile accident, she was backstage, on tour with the *Follies*. On hearing the news, all she said was, "I've never missed a performance, and I'm not going to miss one now." And she didn't.

Her stage successes continued, and she later met Jack Pickford, the husband of Olive Thomas and the man who Ziegfeld, among others, assumed had poisoned her. Miller fell in love with Pickford, and they were married at Pickfair, the renowned Hollywood estate belonging to Jack's sister Mary and her husband, Douglas Fairbanks. The marriage proved to be unhappy and short-lived. Miller remarried, and Jack Pickford later died, of syphilis, it was said, at about the time *As Thousands Cheer* entered rehearsal.

Though temperamental, Miller cooperated with Berlin and Hart, even when they put her on roller skates for what they thought would be the show's spectacular finale: a high-society cocktail party in which the guests skated and sang. In rehearsal she received only bruises for her trouble. Undaunted, the director, Hassard Short, insisted that Miller and the other actors in the scene devote three precious hours each night to roller skating.

Just as the difficult scene was beginning to take shape, the site of rehearsals switched from New York's Amsterdam Theatre to the Forrest Theater in Philadelphia, where the out-of-town tryouts were to take place. On the day of the first full dress rehearsal, Short arrived early, inspected the stage, and commented, "What? No linoleum?"

"Doesn't seem to be any," said Berlin, who accompanied him. "What of it?"

"What of it? It means that they can't skate, that's all. Rough surface—traps—they'd all go over in a heap. They've been rehearsing on a perfectly smooth linoleum surface in New York. We can't do the number."

"But we open on Saturday night," Berlin reminded the director. It was already Thursday. "They can't sing a skating song if they're not on skates. What are we going to do?"

A precise, almost prissy man, Short squared his shoulders and said, "That, my dear sir, is up to you." After a moment, he added, "And I'm not as calm as I seem to be."

Berlin drifted out of the theater, into an alley, where he found Moss Hart, smoking his usual pipe. It was a warm evening, and a sticky haze hung over the entire city. "They can't skate on this stage," Berlin said glumly. "I don't know what to do."

Hart swore quietly. The two men discussed the possibilities, and eventually Hart suggested that Berlin revive a song he had composed months before but had not been able to fit into the show: "Not for All the Rice in China." Berlin retreated to his hotel room to face just the kind of last-minute, all-night challenge on which he thrived. After revising the song, he updated the opening number, in which a chorus explains to the audiences that, for the first time in Broadway history, there will be absolutely no reprise at the end of the show; instead, the last scene will introduce a *new* song: "Not for All the Rice in China."

Berlin worked on his scheme through the night, finishing it at around eight in the morning—just in time for the first public dress rehearsal. The new song made such a favorable impression on the audience that Berlin, Hart, and Short never again thought about roller skates or linoleum.

As Thousands Cheer played so well in Philadelphia that its entire two-week run was sold out. The show quickly acquired favorable word of mouth, and New York critics wrote lengthy features trying to analyze the show's remarkable newspaper format in advance of its opening, incidentally giving it valuable free publicity. Once again Berlin was helped along by general goodwill. As the Depression worsened, Broadway desperately needed a hit, especially at the beginning of the season, and Berlin seemed poised to deliver it. A hit show had a way of energizing not just its fortunate cast and backers but the entire business, and people would start talking about Broadway again the way they used to, in the days before the Crash.

By the time the show was scheduled to open—on September 30, at the Music Box Theatre—Berlin was radiating confidence, but poor Moss Hart was so anxious he could scarcely function. He kept a dinner appointment on opening night at the home of George and Ira Gershwin, though he couldn't bring himself to eat anything. In fact, all three of them had reason to be anxious, for the Gershwin brothers were in the midst of final rehearsals for *their* new show, *Let 'Em Eat Cake*. A follow-up to their hugely successful *Of Thee I Sing*, the satiric musical returned to the fortunes of their mythical president, Wintergreen, and his attempt to win reelection to the White House; it was scheduled to open barely three weeks later.

After the oddly subdued dinner, Hart went to the theater to mingle with the opening-night crowd, the kind of fashionable audience Broadway hadn't seen since the debut of the first *Music Box Revue* a dozen years earlier. "All the people that were always seen at opening nights were there," said Irwin, "bejeweled, bedecked, and so smart." And then the curtain went up on what was possibly the best revue ever presented on the Broadway stage. Said Irwin: "The audience laughed and applauded in all the right places. It was a lovely show. It sailed away."

There was much to marvel at: Marilyn Miller's beauty, Clifton Webb's uncanny imitation of the Prince of Wales, and Hassard Short's inventive staging. He foreswore expensive sets in favor of dramatic lighting effects; he knew how to use cross lighting to impart drama to a scene, and when to use a single spot high overhead to light a single actor. Each of the sketches Hart and Berlin had devised unfolded like a delicious treat, which merely served to raise expectations of more enjoyment to follow.

For a Broadway show, *As Thousands Cheer*'s style was daring, even avant-garde. Berlin's polished songs would have been at home in a Ziegfeld beauty pageant, but the sketches he had written with Hart adopted a bold and abrasive tone. A newspaper headline projected on the proscenium announced each scene, and the sketches took their shots at the reigning celebrities of the day. There were President and Mrs. Hoover leaving the White House, with Herbert bidding farewell to his cabinet with a raspberry. There was the somber spectacle of John D. Rockefeller, Jr., giving Radio City to his father, that emaciated totem of wealth, on the occasion of the latter's ninety-fourth birthday. There was Barbara Hutton (Marilyn Miller), rich beyond the dreams of avarice, asking her beloved Prince Mdivani, "How's Chances?" And Noël Coward, leaving hotel servants utterly befuddled by his eccentric behavior. There was even Joan Crawford attempting to divorce Douglas Fairbanks, Jr.

Politics, finance, society, the arts: a ruthless inner logic lay behind the apparently casual progression of sketches, the logic of the tabloid newspaper. *As Thousands Cheer* made fun of newspapers as surely as it made fun of movie stars and politicians. Indeed, the ultimate target of the revue's satirical barbs was that prowling, oversimplifying, unpredictable fraternity known as the press. The show gave Irving his chance to even the score with journalists, whom he hadn't forgiven for their treatment of him during his elopement. Berlin himself could have been one of the show's targets; eight years earlier, he'd known what it was like to have his personal life—his marriage, his money, his social station—subjected to public scrutiny. The experience had been agony, but it had helped to inspire a hit show.

Although the audience came to see Marilyn Miller, Ethel Waters nearly stole the show because each song Berlin had written for her was a gem. As the headline "HEAT WAVE HITS NEW YORK" appeared, she launched into her torch song, "Heat Wave." When another headline told of violence in the South—"UNKNOWN NEGRO LYNCHED BY FRENZIED MOB"—she displayed her dramatic range in "Supper Time," the magnificently understated lament of the wife of the victim, who must tell her children that they will never see their father again. This was a tragic strain, to be sure, but by no means a protest song. Berlin had so personalized and muted the incendiary racial aspects of the event that what the song lost in bite it gained in universality.

Berlin gave Waters one other song, the sultry "Harlem on My Mind," in which he attempted to anatomize in musical terms what he perceived as the split personality of the American Black. For the number, Waters adopted the persona of a rakehell black expatriate in Paris (similar to Josephine Baker) who yearns for home even at the risk of degradation while she exults in her newly acquired European sophistication. Although "Harlem on My Mind," along with the other numbers Waters sang, contained echoes of the "coon" songs and revues of Berlin's youth, she played them all straight. One need only think of the minstrel staging Berlin had employed to travesty "Mandy" fifteen years before, at the time of the Great War, to recognize the enormous distance he had come in his attitude toward black performers—and the distance that black performers themselves had come.

And of course there was "Easter Parade," Berlin's fifteen-year-old tune with fifteen-week-old lyrics, which closed the first act. When Marilyn Miller and her costar, Clifton Webb, stepped out of the sepia shadows and the parade came to life, the magic of the moment made the show. It was a splendid feeling to sit in the audience of *As Thousands Cheer*, watching the world go by. Despite its satirical edge, the entire show adeptly flattered its audience, making them feel on equal terms with or superior to the public figures who came in for mockery. The laughter it generated induced the audience to feel that they had a measure of control over the world, after all; they knew a thing or two about politicians and celebrities now, how foolish they were, how absurd their lives. In the fall of 1933, this came as reassuring news.

Berlin knew precisely how the show affected audiences because he attended most of the performances, pacing the back of the house, listening to his songs over and over, and trying to gauge the audience's reaction to them. "You gotta watch what they're humming when they come out," he explained to a young assistant. And after the show ended, he drifted through the crowd, a small man, easy to overlook, and listened intently to the comments of the departing patrons, who had no idea their casual remarks were being overheard and scrutinized by the songwriter himself.

As Thousands Cheer became the biggest musical event of the Broadway season. The show had something for everyone. Audiences loved the romantic songs, and critics reveled in Berlin and Hart's satire and clever use of journalistic conventions to frame the entire evening (while remaining oblivious to the revue's satire of *them*). More than most revues, *As Thousands Cheer* depended on the critics for its popular acceptance. At a time when enthusiastic reviews were as scarce as easy credit, the show earned raves, even from *The New York Times'* stern new drama critic, Brooks Atkinson. Like Moss Hart, Atkinson belonged to the new, unsentimental, hard-edged generation finding its voice in the Depression. With society seeming to collapse all around them, they took nothing for granted; they knew life was a serious matter. Atkinson was neither a cheerleader in the manner of Alexander Woollcott nor a crony of Berlin's. He assessed Broadway productions with a cool, even professorial eye, and if producers lost money on account of his stringent standards, that was their problem.

Atkinson looked on this revue, and he found it good—excellent, in fact. "No doubt some one will be able to suggest how 'As Thousands Cheer' could be improved," he wrote, but, "this column can only give its meek approval to every item in the program. . . . As for Mr. Berlin, he has never written better tunes or more sparkling lyrics." The normally restrained critic concluded, "In these circumstances there is nothing a reviewer can do except cheer. Bravo and huzzas!" In the *Herald Tribune*, Percy Hammond found another reason for the revue's success: "Mr. Berlin contributes a lot of satin songs," Hammond said, "But, perhaps fearful that his efforts might be too mellifluous, he collaborates with Moss Hart, a sarcastic chap with an acid, cruel sense of humor. It is an ideal combination. Mr. Berlin . . . holds sex to be sacred, and then Mr. Hart comes along with some brutal and irreverent sketches." The show was, in sum, "Urban, naughty, decent."

One of the few sour notes in the chorus of praise was sounded by *The New Yorker* artist (and occasional Broadway scenarist) Peter Arno. At an opening-night party for the revue at the home of Herbert Swope, stories began to circulate that the sketch in the show involving Gandhi and Aimée Semple MacPherson bore a certain resemblance to a drawing by Arno. Soon after, Arno sued, claiming that Berlin and Hart had plagiarized him. Even if this were the case, which was highly unlikely and probably no more than a bizarre coincidence, Arno would not have been able to copyright the idea. Berlin was occasionally sued—always without success—for plagiarizing songs; this was the first time he'd been sued for plagiarizing an *idea.* In the end, Arno's charge came to nought.

The success of *As Thousands Cheer*'s satire made the failure of the Gershwins' new show, only weeks later, all the more surprising. *Let 'Em Eat Cake* was perhaps the brothers' most accomplished collaboration, but it violated a cardinal rule of Broadway: never stage a sequel. It limped through four weeks before retreating into legend, while Berlin's revue was destined to fill the Music Box Theatre for a full year. The failure of *Let 'Em Eat Cake* signaled that satire's brief, but brilliant vogue on Broadway had come to a full stop.

As Thousands Cheer remained a unique event; it spawned no imitators, even though Berlin and Hart did give serious thought to mounting a sequel of their own, to be called *More Cheers.* They started writing new sketches, publicizing their intentions in the press, and Irving resumed working with Will Irwin, dictating a clutch of new songs. Had anyone besides a few close associates heard the songs, they would have realized that they broke new ground, not only for Berlin but also for popular songwriting. One was a love song called "Cheek to Cheek," the longest and, arguably, the most complex tune Berlin had ever devised; another, entitled "Let Yourself Go," was equally appealing. Instead of winding up in another Broadway revue, the songs temporarily entered Berlin's trunk.

There were several reasons for this sudden about-face. The first was the chilling effect of the commercial failure of the Gershwins' musical. To Berlin, the handwriting was on the wall: a sequel to *As Thousands Cheer* would only tarnish the memory of the original. Still another reason was the prospect of composing once again for Hollywood. Thanks to the success of *As Thousands Cheer*, Berlin's star was in the ascent; people on the coast were prepared to accord him the respect he had been previously denied. Indeed, Hollywood regarded many composers with new appreciation, backed by cash. Faced with persistent hard times on Broadway, Berlin, the Gershwin brothers, and even Jerome Kern, who more than any other composer had defined the American musical, simultaneously abandoned the stage for the dubious blandishments of Hollywood.

And finally, there was the misfortune that befell Marilyn Miller, the obvious choice to star in the sequel. Owing to a blockage of her sinus, she had been born without a sense of smell. After finishing her stint with *As Thousands Cheer*, she entered the hospital for a long-delayed operation to rectify the condition. The procedure was successful. In celebration, her friends showered her with gifts: flowers, perfume, anything scented. Soon after she left the hospital, an infection developed in her sinus cavities, inflamed her brain, and in 1936 she died, amid speculation that syphilis was to blame. (Her husband, Jack Pickford, had died of the disease.) One of the most highly regarded Broadway actresses of the decade, she was just thirty-eight years old at the time of her death.

▪ ▪ ▪

None of these difficulties brought real hardship to Berlin, for the success of *As Thousands Cheer* had rescued him from financial peril. Even with a top ticket price of $4.40, the revue played to standing-room-only audiences throughout its run. As the show's coproducer, he received forty percent of its profits, and he earned further royalties as composer and lyricist. On top of that, he enjoyed still more income from the sale of sheet music of the show's hit songs, published by his own company.

The influx of cash enhanced his life-style but did not drastically alter it. The days when income from hit songs meant a quantum leap in his standard of living were over. He had achieved a plateau of comfort—the spacious Manhattan home, the cook, chauffeur, limousine, antiques, and European vacations—that he would maintain for the rest of his life. Still, he did make overdue refinements and additions. In town, he moved his family from Sutton Place to a new apartment at 130 East End Avenue. Reflecting Ellin's taste rather than his, it was a formal, stately dwelling with impressive views of the East River. There was nothing showbizzy about the place; the antiques and floor-to-ceiling bookshelves quietly suggested the home of a wealthy, cultivated businessman possessed of exacting, if severe taste. The Berlins would live in these surroundings for the next thirteen years.

Irving complemented his comfortable city home with a new place in the country. For just $6,000, he purchased a fifty-two-acre estate in the Catskill Mountains, a two-and-a-half hour drive northwest of New York City. The tiny, exclusive hamlet of Lew Beach, near the town of Livingston, was in a hilly, heavily forested region best known for its trout fishing. Although Irving was no fisherman at the time he acquired this land, in later years he would make desultory attempts at the sport, but the patience it required did not accord with his high-strung disposition. Despite its proximity to Borscht Belt resorts catering primarily to Jewish clientele, the Lew Beach area had a distinctly upper-crust WASP tone. It was an unlikely place to find a celebrity of Berlin's stature, for one did not go there to mingle or to be seen, but to find peace and solitude.

The respite he awarded himself following *As Thousands Cheer* extended to his social activities, as well. Irving had always been fascinated by high society—that had been part of Ellin's desirability, as well as the logical goal of his steady drive toward complete assimilation into the American mainstream. Now, for the first time since marrying Ellin, he felt secure enough to make a concerted effort to penetrate her old-money milieu—a world where Broadway successes counted against an individual if they counted at all.

Though his father-in-law, Clarence, had lost his fortune in the Crash, the Mackay family still enjoyed access to a hunting estate on Gardiners Island, an exclusive preserve nestled between the prongs of eastern Long Island. Clarence's declining health prevented him from using it, but Ellin's brother Willie, who had maintained a cordial relationship with the Berlins throughout their battle with Clarence, often went to Gardiners Island for shooting parties. Willie was the least snobbish and pretentious of the Mackays, including Ellin, and the least concerned with keeping up appearances. He had none of his father's arrogance or rigidity. Next to Berlin, the wizard of Tin Pan Alley, he felt like a "country bumpkin." When he happened to invite his celebrated brother-in-law on a hunting expedition, Willie was surprised by the enthusiasm with which Irving accepted.

On the morning of the hunt, Willie rose at six and went down to the kitchen of the house on Gardiners Island to find Irving awake, dressed, and immersed in a book. As the two men talked, Willie realized his brother-in-law had been up all night; it was easier for Berlin the insomniac to stay up rather than to fall asleep shortly before dawn and drag himself out of bed. And then, when the two of them went out for the hunt itself, Berlin, after peppering Willie with questions and waiting up all night for the event, refused to shoot or even to handle a gun.

The two of them trekked across Gardiners Island, making small talk, occasionally falling silent as they flushed out a covey of quail, and, after Willie had felled one or two of the birds, resuming the conversation. In the process, the two families—the declining Mackays and the ascending Berlins—gradually attained something approaching an equal footing.

Irving reciprocated Willie's hospitality by inviting him to dinner parties populated with the likes of Moss Hart and George S. Kaufman, but Willie decided celebrities weren't to his taste. All theater people really cared about, he concluded, was the impression they made on others. Irving, in contrast, was blessed with more common sense than any other man he'd ever met, and he always got straight to the point.

There was another, private reason for Willie to feel drawn to Berlin, for Clarence Mackay's son fancied himself a musician, too. An amateur, of course, but one devoted to the jazz of the twenties. Willie once sent a recording of his jazz combo to Irving, who made the obligatory polite remarks and then added, "You don't know how lucky you are."

"Why?" Willie asked.

"Because you have something you can do and be occupied."

"Gee, Irving, I never thought of it that way," said Willie, who couldn't tell whether he was being dismissed or complimented.

▪ ▪ ▪

In New York, Irving Berlin's music publishing business continued to prosper. That Irving Berlin, Inc. still existed as an independent entity was worthy of note, for many rival publishers were now adjuncts of motion picture studios; that it managed to thrive in the teeth of the Depression, despite the competition offered by radio, amounted to a minor miracle. Its success had nothing to do with superior business techniques or sophistication; on the contrary, Irving's business succeeded because he *avoided* innovation. He persisted in functioning as a hands-on music publisher, checking music stores on Broadway to make certain they stocked the songs he published. He was often seen running his fingers over the tops of stacks of his sheet music, and if his fingertips came away dusty, he knew his songs weren't selling. He would then return to the office and demand to know the reason why. This humble, personal, yet thorough way of doing business earned him the nickname "The Little Mahatma."

A committed traditionalist, Berlin issued dire warnings concerning the effect of radio on the popular music business. "We have become a world of listeners, rather than singers," he said. "Our songs don't live anymore. They fail to become part of us. Radio has mechanized them all. In the old days Al Jolson sang the same song for years until it meant something—when records were played until they cracked. Today, Paul Whiteman plays a song hit once or twice or a Hollywood hero sings them once in the films and the radio runs them ragged for a couple of weeks—then they're dead." It seemed to him that many of his own hits, were he to attempt to introduce them now, would have no chance of succeeding. " 'Remember' took three months of plugging, before we realized we had a hit," he recalled. "If it hadn't been for the persistence of our campaign it would have died on our hands. But as soon as it caught on, it went up like a fever chart and stayed at the top for a year. If I had written 'Remember' today, it would have been played and forgotten in a month." So damn radio, and, while he was at it, damn the movies. Bring back the good old days of vaudeville and burlesque, he implied; bring back 1911, the year "Alexander's Ragtime Band" established his reputation. Though he forced himself to adapt to changing tastes and technologies, a large part of Irving would always yearn for his formative years, when the whole of Tin Pan Alley occupied a couple of blocks, and he knew everyone and everyone knew him, and this tiny industry had a lock on popular music. Even then, of course, there had been conflicts with sheet music retailers and vaudeville performers, but Berlin tended to forget about those headaches when he reminisced, preferring to edit his memories to make a point.

In the face of the current technological onslaught, Berlin's company reluctantly joined forces with a dozen of the most prominent remaining music publishers in a bold measure. In 1932 they combined their various bookkeeping and distribution operations into a monolithic enterprise known as the Music Dealers Service. Each publisher contributed one thousand dollars, and MDS was in business, selling songs at a uniform price of fifteen cents wholesale, and twenty-five cents retail. MDS bore a perilous resemblance to a monopoly, but publishers were willing to run the risk of legal challenges because they faced the possibility of extinction.

At first, MDS succeeded; later, lawsuits disrupted the cozy arrangement. All the members of MDS decided to fight the legal challenges, *except* for Berlin's company, which in 1934 offered to settle an antitrust suit and dismantle MDS. The last thing he wanted to do was run afoul of the law. His willingness to take an unpopular stand offered fresh proof of his tenacity. He much preferred to study the tastes of "the mob," the customers who would ultimately buy the songs, to cooperating with the competition. The other music publishers began to lose their resolve once Berlin defected from their ranks. One by one they began to side with Berlin's music company against the monopoly they had recently created.

Everything about his music publishing company reflected this honorable, if backward-looking approach to doing business. His newly acquired homes gave concrete expression to his aspirations of dignity and understated wealth, but his company—a little bit of old Tin Pan Alley preserved in the time capsule that Berlin's mind was gradually becoming—remained pure Izzy Baline: street smart, a little rough around the edges, a Mom-and-Pop operation. In 1933 Max Winslow, the man who had "discovered" Irving Berlin, left the business to accept an offer from his brother-in-law, Harry Cohn, head of Columbia Pictures, to run the studio's music department. But Winslow's brother, who was mentally handicapped, kept his job in the shipping department. Under the direction of Harry Dumont, who was assisted by four clerks, this unit could, on a good day, ship as many as 30,000 sheets of music.

Several highly talented individuals also stayed with Berlin. There was the dapper professorial transcriber, Helmy Kresa, who was practically a fixture by now. And there was Dave Dreyer, a rehearsal pianist turned songwriter who made a formidable reputation for himself while he was in Berlin's employ with hit songs like "Me and My Shadow," "Back in Your Own Backyard," and "Cecilia." Though Dreyer toiled in Berlin's shadow, he benefited from the master's peerless knowledge of hit songwriting. When he first demonstrated his song "Cecilia" to his boss, Berlin fastened on the name, which was repeated throughout the song. To his ear, something was not quite right. He suggested that Dreyer emphasize and drag out the second syllable, "Ce*cee-ee*lia," so that it lingered in the listener's mind. Dreyer followed this advice, and that tiny flourish suggested by Berlin was arguably the reason for the song's success.

Berlin occasionally tried to adapt his business to modern times, but innovations occurred in a haphazard manner. In 1931 it was decided—no one could say exactly how—that the company should deal directly with radio, as it had once done with vaudeville. The decision raised the question of who should staff the new department. Eventually, it was decided—again, no one could say how—that a typist and substitute telephone operator named Mynna Granat should be in charge. A pretty, slender woman in her early twenties, Mynna had been working for Berlin's music publishing company since she was nineteen. Her chief ability, outside of her typing and organizational skills, was her relentlessly extroverted personality. She, too, brought her brand of modernization to Berlin's songwriting and publishing business.

Mynna's multiple chores—typing, filing, answering the odd phone call, and trying to organize the radio department—often kept her at the office until as late as nine o'clock at night. By then the place was generally deserted, except when its insomniac boss was at work. At the time, Berlin was in the throes of completing the score for *As Thousands Cheer.* One night during this period Mynna happened to be eating a sandwich at her desk. "I'm at the end of a long hall," she recalled, "and I hear somebody say, 'Is there anybody here who can type?' I jump out the door and I say, 'I can, Mr. Berlin.' He said, 'Good.' How I knew how to put in two pieces of paper and a carbon, I'll never know. He said, 'This is the title of the song.' And he gave it to me. And because I wrote poetry in my fashion, I didn't have to ask and he didn't have to say, 'Next line.' That was a big plus on my part. But I didn't know that he was going to give me ten songs. Which he did. It got to be eleven o'clock. All he said was, 'I will need eighteen copies of each one of these songs by Wednesday.' 'Yes Sir.' And he left.

"Well, luckily, in my trips to the shipping department, I was very nosy, and I had asked Harry Dumont, 'Why is that thing on the floor getting filthy? What is it?' He said, 'It's a machine. You put in paper and you run off copies.' I said, 'Terrific.'

"Later on, I call Nick, the porter, and tell him to pull out the machine and start cleaning. I'm going to have to use it. He said, 'Do you know how?' And I said, 'No, I never did it before.' To make a long story short, I spent about $90 at a stationery store and they taught me how to use it because I spent so much. When I got through copying all the songs eighteen times, I decided to make a table of contents, because I said to myself, 'What if they say they want this song done over or changed?' Then I got labels, and on every label I typed, '*As Thousands Cheer*, Lyrics and Music by Irving Berlin.'

"Then I hear that Mr. Berlin's on the phone asking, 'Who's that girl?' So I get on the phone, and he said, 'This is Mr. Berlin. Will you have everything ready by Wednesday?' I said, 'Yes, sir.' He said, 'Very well, I will call you then.' Wednesday arrives, and he calls and says, 'Be at the Music Box Theatre, backstage, where I will be working. You're coming at three o'clock.' I said, 'Mr. Berlin, I have four packages of songs, I can't carry them.' He said, 'Of course not. Get two or three of the guys from the stock room, get a cab, and come. I'll be backstage waiting for you.'

"Once you get backstage at the Music Box, it's like the movies: Marilyn Miller, Clifton Webb. . . . At any rate, the boys put the packages on this long table, cut them open, and Mr. Berlin says, 'My God, who did this?' 'That girl,' I said. 'It's marvelous!' he said. 'Who taught you this?' I said, 'No one. I thought if I didn't put them in little books, you'd be calling me every day.' "

Mynna's diligence earned her a promotion to Berlin's inner circle—as well as a stern lecture. "Always tell the truth, that's what he taught me," Mynna said. "I was so young, I asked, 'Why?' He said, 'Because then you never have to worry about remembering what you lied about.' " Soon after, Berlin's secretary quit, and Mynna tried out for the job. "Try me for two weeks," she told Berlin. " 'If you don't like me, fire me. What have you got to lose?' Well, he looks at this nut, and he says, 'You are fresh enough to be good. You got the job.' "

Berlin needed a Mynna Granat to help him conduct ordinary business because he was, as she would soon discover, exceedingly forgetful when it came to handling mundane affairs. Yes, he could recall the exact contents of a letter he'd written to Joe Schenck or Flo Ziegfeld years before, not to mention countless lyrics and melodies that had been swirling in his mind for decades, but like many men of genius and drive, he focused on these crucial matters to the exclusion of all else. He was forever leaving his suitcase or briefcase in a train or taxi, his clothes in a hotel, and Mynna was forever devising ways to retrieve the items he had left behind.

"If you gave him an address to go to a party," she recalled, "and he didn't have it with him, he'd get lost." She worried about him when he wasn't under her watchful eye because he never carried money, not even spare change. When he took a cab to the office, he would ask the driver to wait, and then he would find Mynna and instruct her to go down to the street and pay the driver the eighty-five-cent fare, plus tip.

Mynna's chores extended well beyond the office to the entire Berlin family, especially the songwriter's daughters, for whom she functioned as a sometime governess. As Berlin's daughter Mary Ellin grew older, she received her weekly allowance not from her father or mother, but from Mynna. The ritual occurred on Saturdays, when the Berlin chauffeur and bodyguard, a burly Scotsman, would drive the girl to the office; there Mynna would give her $3.50. Occasionally, deductions were made. Before Mary Ellin received her allowance one Saturday, her mother called Mynna and instructed her "to deduct a dollar and a quarter from the allowance."

"What happened?" Mynna asked.

"She lost a library book. And she's got to know that if you lose something that doesn't belong to you, you've got to pay for it."

Some years later, when Mary Ellin turned sixteen, she was permitted to make her first solo purchase, and she chose to buy herself a coat from Bendel's, on 57th Street—under Mynna's supervision, of course. "I told her to pick out the coat, bring it to the office, and if her father approved, she could keep it." Mary Ellin did so one Saturday, when she was off from school.

"In she came with the box," Mynna recalled. "I wasn't going to open it in Mr. Berlin's office. I took off all the wrappings, and because I am what I am, I looked first to see the price, figuring she'd spent two hundred dollars. But I was wrong. It was $29.75. It had a little velvet collar, tailored, lovely. In we go with the coat. Mr. Berlin is expecting her. She tries it on, I make her turn around. He says to her, 'It's a beautiful coat, and I'm very proud of you on your first shopping experience. You did well.' "

As time passed, Berlin became so dependent on Mynna's attentiveness that whenever he bought a new pair of shoes, he gave them to her to break in. She would wear them around the office for several days—only on the carpet, of course—until they were soft enough for Berlin's feet. Indeed, many of Berlin's clothes, which were generally tailor-made for his small, lean frame, became coveted possessions at the office. He passed on his old suits to his employees, and office boys who came by one of Mr. Berlin's old shirts—tailor-made, as well—considered them valuable and useful souvenirs and wore them to work.

Mynna earned Ellin's trust as well as Irving's, and Mrs. Berlin even offered tips on how to handle her husband's flashes of temper. One afternoon Mynna was typing a letter for Berlin, who complained bitterly about some small, possibly imaginary flaw. Ellin happened to be visiting the office at the time. After the contretemps, she took Mynna aside and advised the young secretary, "You should never stoop to someone else's level. You should rise above it."

Ellin's sympathy and lack of affectation endeared her to Mynna. "She was the most wonderful woman I think I've ever met," Mynna recalled. She was especially impressed by Ellin's conscientious devotion to the three Berlin daughters—Mary Ellin, Linda Louise, and Elizabeth—and to her insistence on religious tolerance. "Early in our acquaintance I asked her how she was bringing up the children," Mynna said. "And Mrs. Berlin told me, 'I believe the children should be brought up in their father's faith. My children are going to be brought up as Jews, and when they are fourteen or fifteen I'll teach them about Catholicism, and then they can decide for themselves.' " (Ellin's interest in Judaism amounted to more than mere lip service. Years later, when Eleanor Roosevelt died, she called Mynna, who said, "You sound so terrible, Mrs. Berlin, where are you?" And Ellin replied, "I just left Temple Emanu-el. I said Kaddish.")

Although Ellin became familiar with Judaism, to the point of learning Hebrew and sprinkling her conversation with Yiddish expressions, she stopped short of converting. In fact, in the late 1930s, she returned to the Catholicism she had spurned in her flaming youth. And she sent out a large number of Christmas cards each year, inevitably with Mynna's help. During one of these visits Mynna became aware of Ellin's fondness for expensive antiques, whose prices made Mynna shudder. The table in the library on which they wrote out the cards might have been an important antique, but to Mynna it seemed nothing more than an old scratched-up piece of furniture. And yet she had seen the bill for this same table at the office: several thousand dollars.

After spending an afternoon addressing envelopes on the table, Mynna was invited to stay for dinner with the family.

"The children called their mother 'Mama,' not 'Mother' or 'Mommy,' " Mynna remembered. "Elizabeth, the youngest one, called from her room, 'Mama, can I come out and say hello to Mynna?' And Mama said, 'Not tonight, darling. You have a cold. Just stay in your room.' Linda said, 'I don't have a cold.' And Mrs. Berlin said, 'Well, you may come and join us at dessert.' Now dessert was a chocolate éclair served on a silver platter by a butler. Linda comes in. She's looking at my chocolate éclair. So I have to say, 'Would you like half?' 'Yes,' she says. The butler doesn't say there are five more in the back, so she shared it with me.

"Then I said, 'Mrs. Berlin, as long as I have the opportunity I want to thank for you for that beautiful gift that you sent for Christmas. It's exquisite.' It was a beautiful red purse. Linda said, 'You opened up your present before Christmas?' And I said, 'Yes, because I received it at the office, and I wanted to show it to everyone.' And Linda said, 'But you'll have nothing to open on Christmas morning.'

"Christmas morning, when I got up, I see an envelope under my door. There was a note: 'Just so you'll have something to open up on Christmas morning. Ellin Berlin.' And there was a check for a hundred dollars."

As she became a trusted member of Berlin's extended family, Mynna incidentally received an education in the basics of successful music publishing. Her apprenticeship began the day she started work as Berlin's secretary: "Mr. Berlin said to me, 'I want you to know that a songwriter's most important assets are his copyrights. That's your number one responsibility—always watch mine.' "

Mynna took her boss's emphasis on honesty to heart, and she

gradually familiarized herself with Berlin's copyrights and contracts, among other details of the day-to-day operation of his business. Eventually, her expertise in these matters would lead her to uncover a scandal serious enough to cause Berlin and his associates to break up the firm amid much embarrassment and hollow protestations of innocence. Berlin had been right to worry as he did about the honesty of his associates, because Saul Bornstein, his most trusted business partner, was deceiving him.

Everyone knew Berlin, the creative artist and highly public figure; Bornstein, the bean counter, ran the business on a daily basis. He relished playing the role of the heavy, once firing a salesman for having the temerity to appear at the office with a tan. "My first name is Saul," Bornstein liked to say, "My last name is Bornstein, and my middle name is Oscar. You know what my initials spell."

It was Bornstein that the young songwriters hawking their wares met, not Irving Berlin. Although he was a businessman rather than a tunesmith, Bornstein often tried to pass judgment on songs. When a young songwriter named Burton Lane brought him a tune called "Tony's Wife," Bornstein expressed enthusiasm, but he refused to commit himself because of the title. " 'Tony's wife. The fellows are crazy about Tony's wife.' Jesus, can't you change it to Tony's girl?" Bornstein asked. "It's very risky to call it 'Tony's Wife.' " Lane and Bornstein argued back and forth about the implications of the title, until, at last, Bornstein said, "Well, let's go play it for Irving."

Lane was ushered into the presence of the celebrated composer, where he played his song. Before the last note had faded, Berlin delivered his opinion: "Don't change a note. Don't change a word. It's wonderful." The firm went on to publish the song, which became a hit, and Lane later composed the score for *Finian's Rainbow*.

A worse sin than Bornstein's tin ear was his dishonesty. Over a period of years he made a practice of advancing money to imaginary composers and lyricists in return for nonexistent songs. He would then pocket the money paid out of the company's funds. Bornstein was by no means the only music publishing executive who employed this shady practice, but he had the misfortune of pursuing it in Berlin's office. The written agreements were intended to disguise or legitimize the mythical transactions, but, as Bornstein would later discover to his dismay, the fraudulent contracts had precisely the opposite effect. As the years passed, they left a damning paper trail of his actions.

Bornstein stored the dummy contracts in a big safe in the office, assuming that no one besides himself would possibly take an interest in such arcane matters. He was wrong, as it turned out. There was one other person who possessed a key to the safe, Mynna Granat, and she took an interest in these matters as part of her normal business duties. It was only a matter of time until she stumbled across the all-too-carefully preserved evidence of Bornstein's indiscretions and took it to her boss.

▪ ▪ ▪

That such misdealing could have occurred over a lengthy period of time and at the epicenter of Berlin's music publishing business suggested how overextended the songwriter had become. Somehow, he had to find a way to go on playing the part of successful songwriter, publisher, theater owner, and public figure all at once. The acclaim reached a crescendo in May 1934, as he was turning forty-six. Berlin made the cover of *Time* magazine, joining the ranks of the business tycoons and politicians the magazine normally covered. Here was proof, if any was required, of how fully he had recovered his lost stature. Nine years earlier, Gershwin had made *Time*'s cover, and finally Irving had drawn even with his friend.

The most important aspect of the entire story, the cover portrait, showed Irving bent over the piano, eyes trained on the keyboard; his face was averted from the camera. There was nothing of the showman or entertainer about the pose, which suggested remoteness, inaccessibility, and self-absorption. So this was the studious little man behind all the excitement, it seemed to say. It could have been the formal portrait of a concert pianist—which was precisely the image that its intense, but shy subject wished to project. In the same vein, the caption read, "Jerome Kern was reminded of Wagner." *Wagner?* Kern had indeed made the comparison in the pages of Woollcott's authorized biography, but this was not a widely held or especially valid opinion, especially in light of Wagner's anti-Semitism. At any rate, the observation served its purpose, which was to install Irving Berlin in his niche in the pantheon of American composers.

Portraying Berlin as the Grand Old Man of Tin Pan Alley, the article was among the first to suggest that its subject, "a dark-skinned, crickety little man," having completed a quarter of a century of writing hit songs, had witnessed a momentous era in American history and had faithfully rendered the thoughts and feelings of Americans throughout that period in his lyrics and music. At their best, his songs were time capsules preserving evanescent, long-vanished popular moods and sentiments; in a way that historians, journalists, and even novelists could not, he had managed to capture the voices, accents, and rhythms—the *sounds*—of the American people.

Concurrent with the *Time* cover story, the NBC radio network mounted a multipart retrospective of Berlin's first quarter-century as a songwriter. The five half-hour broadcasts, sponsored by Gulf, took place on Sunday evenings at nine, a choice time period. Among the retrospective's one hundred songs was at least one hit from every year, the lean ones no less than the fat, that Berlin had been in the business:

1910 My Wife's Gone to the Country
1911 Alexander's Ragtime Band
1912 Everybody's Doin' It Now
1913 When I Lost You
1914 When That Midnight Choo Choo Leaves for Alabam'
1915 When I Leave the World Behind
1916 This Is the Life
1917 Down on the Farm
1918 They Were All Out of Step But Jim
1919 A Pretty Girl Is Like a Melody
1920 You'd Be Surprised
1921 Everybody Step
1922 What'll I Do?
1923 All Alone
1924 Remember
1925 Always
1926 Blue Skies
1927 A Russian Lullaby
1928 The Song Is Ended
1929 Puttin' on the Ritz
1930 Let's Have Another Cup of Coffee
1931 Soft Lights and Sweet Music

1932 Say It Isn't So
1933 How Deep Is the Ocean?
1934 Easter Parade

It was a record no other songwriter could equal.

When the series began airing, several weeks before the *Time* story appeared, it instantly removed whatever tarnish still clung to Berlin's national reputation. The songs, said *Time*, "left millions of listeners marveling not only at Berlin's record for hits but also the way he has survived the changing fashions."

To permit his songs—indeed, the pick of his catalogue—to be broadcast on network radio marked a new departure for Berlin, who regularly expressed his displeasure with network broadcasting as a thankless devourer of popular music. The decision proved to be a shrewd one. For most Americans, far from the buzz of Broadway and *As Thousands Cheer*, this radio revue was all they knew of Berlin and what had become of him since the mid-1920s; through it, they renewed their acquaintance with him as if with an aging, but still vigorous relative with whom they had fallen out of touch. "Radio's most valuable asset is the old songs," he explained. "The old songs have a quality of association with the listener." Radio might be a good way to plug a song, but the medium quickly exhausted a songwriter's energies. "After writing these broadcasts," he asked himself, "I wonder how in the world radio can keep on going. Where will it get the material?"

Despite Irving's misgivings, it was apparent to listeners that a remarkable number of Berlin's old songs held up well, even after two decades. They now revealed a timeless quality that outlasted fashion. Considering Berlin's entirely pragmatic approach to his trade, which consisted of faithfully catering to the tastes of the mob, of *giving the people what they wanted*, through whatever the reigning medium of the day happened to be, the songs' durability came as a paradox. Though he wrote for the moment, he lavished extraordinary care on his creations; a large part of his genius consisted of his willingness to take infinite pains in fashioning them. They were built to last.

Suddenly people were talking about Irving Berlin again, and not just on Broadway. His songs had seeped into the national consciousness; after twenty-five years, they seemed to have been there forever.

The retrospective established Berlin as the great musical consolidator, whose melodies had become part of the ineffable glue of society. They were something Americans had in common, like the weather, the Depression, the bittersweet memories of a romance or vanished youth. This unifying aspect of his music helped explain why "Easter Parade" emerged as the biggest hit of *As Thousands Cheer*. As organized expressions of universal escapism, holidays perfectly suited his consensus approach to songwriting. His advancing years lent further strength to his reputation. Through sheer repetition, his better-known songs had acquired incantatory powers that newly minted tunes couldn't hope to match. And their creator was now famous for an entirely new reason: he was famous for having been famous for so long.

In Hollywood, the triple play of the hit Broadway revue, the *Time* cover, and the five-part radio retrospective transformed Irving Berlin from a songwriter to a celebrity. On the strength of his newly enhanced reputation, he planned to return to writing movie scores, this time under circumstances vastly different from his tentative and misguided gropings of the late twenties. When he plotted his reentry into Hollywood, he avoided the obvious choices—Max Winslow at Columbia or his old friend Joe Schenck. Instead, he forged a lasting relationship with quirky little RKO, a studio fighting for its existence.

In December 1934, Berlin left wintry, Depression-weary New York and flew—no train was fast enough for him—to Los Angeles. There he began to lay siege to the motion picture business with all the industry he had formerly brought to bear on Tin Pan Alley. By the time he finished, neither he nor the studio would ever be quite the same.

■ □ ■ □ ■ □ ■

CHAPTER 14

Hollywood Refuge

Since its inception in 1921, RKO—Radio-Keith-Orpheum—had eked out a precarious existence, even by Hollywood standards. It had long been the pawn of rich men wanting to take a flyer on Hollywood. In its first five chaotic years of life, the studio was known as Robertson-Cole Productions, and the lot where it was located, at the corner of Gower and Melrose streets, had formerly belonged to the Hollywood Cemetery. In the mid-twenties, Joseph P. Kennedy, then a powerful Wall Street financier, acquired the studio in part to promote the career of his mistress, Gloria Swanson.

By 1933 RKO was bankrupt, its affairs managed by a bank in New York. Yet these desperate conditions encouraged those who remained at RKO to take risks and attempt solutions that the larger, more staid (and more solvent) studios avoided. So the tone of the studio at the time Berlin arrived was entirely different from that of its established competitors. RKO was small, covering only thirteen acres, and everyone knew everyone else. Its lack of bureaucracy and neighborly atmosphere appealed to Berlin; it was the sort of low-key shambles he was used to back in New York. Even better, the studio was mercifully free of the arrogance and *hauteur* that beset the personnel at its competition. Likened to "a baseball club that had been too long in the cellar," RKO was due for a change in its fortunes.

Among the risk takers on the RKO lot was a young producer named Pandro S. Berman, whose father had been general manager of

RKO's previous incarnation, FBO. The younger Berman became head of the studio when his eccentric predecessor, Merian Cooper, suffered a mild heart attack and took an extended vacation to recuperate. "I'll be on a mountaintop in Hawaii," he told Berman, "but I won't tell you where, so don't try to reach me. You're in charge."

Among the resources that Berman inherited was the great Fred Astaire—or, to Hollywood's way of thinking, the *once* great Fred Astaire. At the time, the value of his stock on the Hollywood fame exchange was severely depressed. Long celebrated on the New York and London stages as the dancing partner of his alluring sister Adele, Astaire had tried—with a distinct lack of success—to make his mark on the movies after Adele retired to marry an English aristocrat. In 1933 he tested for RKO. One executive, on seeing the result, noted, "Can't act. Slightly bald. Also dances." David O. Selznick, the young executive in charge of production at RKO, fretted about Astaire's "enormous ears and bad chin line," though he conceded that "his charm is . . . tremendous." But the pendulum of popular taste had lately begun to swing in Astaire's—and Berlin's—favor, for musicals were once again in fashion in Hollywood, thanks to the surprise success of a hard-edged backstage tale called *42nd Street.* Correctly anticipating a new vogue for singing and dancing, Selznick signed Astaire, bad chin line and all, and brought the nonpareil performer to RKO.

Astaire got off to a tentative start playing secondary roles until Pandro Berman proposed teaming him with a young actress whom the anxious dancer knew slightly; she was named Ginger Rogers. In only two years, she had already appeared in thirteen movies, including the trend-setting *42nd Street.* Rogers wanted to make it as a straight actress; she had no desire to become a glorified chorus girl. But she could dance. And she could sing. And she was lovely to behold, the embodiment of every man's innermost romantic craving.

However, Astaire objected strenuously to the idea of performing with Rogers. "I did not go into pictures with the thought of becoming part of a team," he told Berman, "and if that's what RKO has in mind for me, we'd better end the contract right now." So Astaire wasn't going to share the limelight with anyone else, if he could have his way, and Ginger Rogers was poised to occupy more of the limelight than many an actress might, for everywhere that Ginger went, her mother, Lela, was sure to follow. A classic backstage mother, Lela had groomed her darling daughter for the stage since day one, in Fort Worth, Texas; she read and commented on all scripts submitted to Ginger; she studied Ginger's rushes as obsessively as a trainer watches his prize thoroughbred work out; she vetoed unflattering publicity shots of Ginger; she even took charge of Ginger's costumes.

Though more than mere vanity impelled Astaire to resist performing with Rogers, Berman eventually prevailed. Astaire relented, and a new RKO team was born: Fred Astaire, Ginger Rogers, Lela Rogers, and Astaire's new ally and doppelgänger, the choreographer Hermes Pan, who helped re-create Fred Astaire for the movies. The curious thing about Pan was his extraordinary physical resemblance to Fred Astaire. He'd grown up as Hermes Panagiotopulos in Tennessee, where he'd learned his first dance steps from local blacks. In 1929 he appeared with Ginger Rogers in a short-lived musical called *Top Speed*: he was in the chorus, and she was in her first ingenue role. Even then people were telling him how much he looked like Fred Astaire, with the same open, friendly, finely sculpted features, and of course, the dancing.

With the coming of the Depression and the collapse of the Broadway musical, he gravitated to Hollywood. It was fated that he would eventually find work at RKO, where he was assigned to Astaire himself. Pan knew how to make himself endlessly useful. He worked out routines and solved intricate dance problems with both Astaire and Rogers. But he was always Astaire's man, not Rogers's. When she wasn't available to work with Astaire, Pan filled in for her—an eerie sight, Astaire dancing with a man who looked so much like himself. "You thought you were watching two Fred Astaires," said one observer. When Rogers returned, Pan taught her the routine, and she took her familiar place in Astaire's arms.

To bring harmony to this potentially volatile combination, Berman cannily chose Mark Sandrich as the director. The pipe-smoking, tweedy Sandrich was about as far from the strutting, flamboyant, shouting-through-the-megaphone-and-striding-up-and-down-the-set-in-jodhpurs image affected by various directors as he could get and still manage to command respect from cast and crew.

At the time, studios were still shooting numbers as they had in the days of Berlin's *Puttin' on the Ritz*, with the musicians sawing away just out of camera range and the actors singing along in real time. Impatient with this primitive and confining arrangement, Sandrich devised the playback, a method of recording the songs *before* they were filmed. The advantages of this system were great. Arrangements could be as lush and elaborate as a studio's music director could make them, and all the actors needed to do was lip synch to the playback as the camera rolled. Playback permitted editors to substitute other, more melodious voices at a later time, and encouraged directors to move the camera freely. Suddenly, musical scenes could be filmed anywhere, even out-of-doors.

Assigned by the studio to Astaire, Sandrich took care to develop a movie that would trade on Astaire's persona as a debonair society figure, which the dancer had assumed in his final Broadway show, Cole Porter's *The Gay Divorce*. After acquiring the musical for RKO at a bargain price, Berman gutted the score of all but a few hits; commissioned new songs from a variety of composers; changed the title to *The Gay Divorcée* to placate the Production Code, which in its wisdom insisted that divorce was not a fit subject for Catholic moviegoers; and assigned the leads to Astaire and Rogers. The successful result bought Berman, Sandrich, RKO, and its stars a bit of well-deserved breathing time.

For the next Astaire and Rogers movie, *Top Hat* (the title was Astaire's idea), Berman decided to stick as close to *The Gay Divorcée*'s winning formula as he dared. Same stars, same director, and almost the same plot—indeed, the plot was so similar that nothing seemed to have been altered except the songs and dance routines. The one glittering addition would be Irving Berlin's music. To secure Berlin's services for *Top Hat*, Berman had to make unusual financial concessions. The songwriter demanded a $100,000 fee for his services, a figure he probably could have extracted from a larger studio, but with RKO still in bankruptcy, Berman could offer no more than $75,000. The two struck a deal: Berlin accepted the $75,000 plus ten percent of the movie's gross profits if it earned more than $1,250,000. (Astaire also received ten percent of the movie's profits.) This was an unprecedented arrangement for a studio, to cut a performer in on the profits of a movie, but RKO was that kind of place and Berman that kind of producer. Even better, Berlin retained the copyrights to the songs in the movie's score, a provision no other composer toiling in Hollywood enjoyed. Considering RKO's financial plight and the unlikely prospect that *Top Hat* would ever earn enough money for Berlin to get his percentage, it appeared that all he had won for himself was ten percent of nothing. Most composers would rather get their money up front and let the future take care of itself, but Berlin was by now conditioned to taking the long view of his career; he was fully prepared to make a short-term sacrifice for a long-term gain.

Fired by his profit-sharing deal with RKO and the prospect of working with Fred Astaire, Irving threw himself into the project with an intensity and dedication new to his movie ventures. At the time of his arrival, it seemed he would make short work of the score, for he had brought ten new songs—an entire score—with him from New York.

Two of them—"Cheek to Cheek" and "Let Yourself Go"—were among the most complex he had ever written, yet also among the most seductive, flowing, and romantic. This most conservative of tunesmiths finally burst the bounds of formula hit writing when he came to write "Cheek to Cheek." It was a long song, the longest hit tune Berlin ever wrote: sixty-four bars, twice the conventional length. Its rhyme scheme was simple enough, the usual AABA pattern, but near the end he placed an unusual little episode—almost another song inside of the song—that added eight more bars to the melody's already extravagant length.

By doubling the conventional proportions of a popular song, he invested it with a hypnotic and persuasive quality. It seems to keep turning in on itself and then escaping, and turning on itself once again. It starts off quickly, breathlessly, in fact, with the word *heaven*, almost immediately repeated, and the mood of surging happiness gains further conviction from the song's C major melody. Throughout, the music effectively mirrors the emotions summoned by the lyrics, while maximizing their impact. When the singer confesses his heart is beating so fast he can "hardly speak," for instance, Berlin's melody performs a stretch modulation on the word *speak*, reaching for a chord that sounds strange in the key of C; the music seems to push the singer toward the brink, and then it resolves and brings him back.

There was one other remarkable aspect to "Cheek to Cheek." For all its complexity, Berlin wrote the entire composition, words and music, in a single day. And "Let Yourself Go," also written at lightning speed, was nearly as good as "Cheek to Cheek." However, the rest of the score did not meet their exalted standard. Sandrich insisted that the songs had to be integrated into the movie and advance the story in some way, or failing that, not bring it to a standstill. Adopting a crisis approach, Berlin discarded the other eight songs, holed up in his hotel for the next six weeks, avoiding the studio, composing music by night, in his pajamas and slippers, and writing lyrics by day. As before, the other guests complained about the music emanating from the Berlin suite throughout the night, and the hotel isolated its insomniac guest in the penthouse. There he would stay at his transposing piano for as long as twelve hours at a stretch, without even a meal to disturb his fierce concentration.

Under this regimen he wrote a dozen new tunes to fit the plot of *Top Hat*, including "Top Hat, White Tie and Tails," "No Strings," "Get Thee Behind Me, Satan" (used in a subsequent Astaire-Rogers movie, *Follow the Fleet*), and "The Piccolino." This last song was intended as the big production number for the movie's finale, and as such was something of an anachronism. "I hadn't done a tune like that since the Music Box Revues in the 1920's," Berlin said later. But the elaborate song cost him a great deal of effort to perfect. "I love it, the way you love a child that you've had trouble with. I worked harder on 'Piccolino' than I did on the whole score."

When the time came for Berlin to play the new songs on which he had lavished so much effort before the assembled talent at RKO, the reaction was one of dismay rather than delight. "I was thrilled to meet Irving Berlin," Pan recalled of the bizarre audition, "so I was surprised when I heard him play because he was just a lousy pianist. He played the entire score with his transposing piano, and his bass was clunk-clunk-clunk. And then he would sing the song, and we were all asking ourselves, Is this any good? I remember 'Cheek to Cheek,' especially; the way he sang and played, it sounded so awful."

Once the studio's orchestrators fleshed out the score, however, the result vindicated Berlin. His plaintive, primitive wailing was transformed into a gorgeous, lavish musicality; suddenly it was entirely possible to imagine Fred Astaire singing "Cheek to Cheek" to Ginger

Rogers after all. Of course Berlin owed a debt to Max Steiner, the music director, for his sensitive orchestration, but the orchestrations succeeded as much as they did because the melodies had been there all along, waiting for the right instruments to release them. "It was just magic," said Pan of the orchestrated version. "Melody poured from it. The music automatically flowed."

Berlin could have left the picture to its fate at this point and returned to New York, but he remained at RKO through April, playing the perfectionist, quietly supervising the musical aspects of the production. He carefully listened to the recordings of his songs that Astaire and Rogers made. "He was very critical," said Pan of the songwriter, "very meticulous about getting the right sound and the way he wanted it played. He was free in terms of tempos and letting you paraphrase, just as long as you kept what he felt was in the song." If Berlin did have a strong objection to what he heard, he told the conductor, often running to the piano to demonstrate the musical idea he wanted to convey. "*This* is the sound," he would emphasize. "*This* is the note."

When shooting began, Berlin was constantly on the set, hovering unobtrusively in the background, quietly noticing everything that went on. He often paced, one hand held to his head, the other in his pocket, seeming always to chew gum. Though he said very little, his nervous intensity instantly alerted everyone to his presence. When he did venture a suggestion, he couched it in the most diplomatic terms possible. And he was generally open to Astaire's suggestions concerning the songs. "When Fred wanted to sing 'Cheek to Cheek' almost as though he were talking, Berlin said, 'Oh, that's great, I love it.' He loved the way Fred did that," said Pan.

At Astaire's insistence, a policeman guarded the door to the set, warning away would-be intruders. However, Astaire did have to contend with the Lela factor, for Rogers's mother was constantly in attendance. The two finally locked horns during the filming of the critical "Cheek to Cheek" number. At the final rehearsal, late one afternoon, Ginger arrived on the set in full regalia: a costume highlighted by ostrich feathers. As Astaire and Rogers danced, the flying feathers sent him into a sneezing fit, and after an hour of trying to perform under these conditions, he brought the rehearsal to a halt. In the morning, rather than shooting the scene as scheduled, they rehearsed again, having been promised by the costume designer that Ginger's costume was now under control. Once again Astaire was afflicted with the irresistible urge to sneeze. After hours of struggle, he finally lost his patience and shouted at Rogers, who was startled and burst into tears. All at once Lela, who had been watching, took off after Astaire. There was no way he was going to browbeat Ginger as long as Lela was there to protect her daughter. Astaire continued shouting, now at Lela, who so exasperated him that he left the set. The costume designer again interceded, this time sewing each infernal ostrich feather securely to Ginger's gown. The altered costume no longer caused Astaire to sneeze, and Sandrich was at last able to film the number. None of the tension and rivalry afflicting the performers showed up on the screen, and the sequence showing Astaire courting an ostrich-feather-clad Rogers would be regarded as one of the most romantic interludes ever filmed.

Afterward, Astaire and his ally Hermes Pan, who staged the movie's dance sequences, devised a parody of Berlin's song to taunt Ginger, though her mother was probably their true target:

> Feathers—I hate feathers—
> And I hate them so I can hardly speak,
> And I never find the happiness I seek
> With those chicken feathers dancing cheek to cheek.

Berlin respected Astaire's mania for perfection—in this regard, the two were kindred spirits—and throughout the filming the songwriter was constantly heard to comment, softly, "I love what you're doing, oh, I love it." He later said to Pan, "I'd rather have Fred Astaire introduce one of my songs than any other singer I know—not because he has a great voice, but because his delivery and diction are so good that he can put over a song like nobody else."

For all their apparent dissimilarities, Berlin and Astaire actually had quite a bit in common. They shared humble backgrounds: Fred Astaire, born Austerlitz, was the son of parents of modest means from Omaha, Nebraska. Like Berlin, he had invented a new identity for himself out of the ordinary materials of his life. Like Berlin, he was fascinated by high society and would soon marry into that milieu. And like Berlin, he had come up through vaudeville, taking his lumps and savoring his triumphs along the way. They were both driven perfectionists, working in a popular vernacular they raised to the level of art.

Despite the professional esteem Astaire and Berlin developed for each other, the composer's chronic worrying and pacing and gum chewing made him a figure of fun, at least behind his back. During the filming the need of a new dance song arose at the eleventh hour, Pan recalled. "Berlin said, 'Well, I need to think about it.' I happened to see him the next day alone on the lot, and he said, 'Oh, Pan, I've got that number you and Fred were talking about. Would you like to hear it? I naturally said, 'Oh, I'd love to.' And Berlin said, 'Come on into the office, I'll play it for you.' "

The song was "Isn't This a Lovely Day?"—one of the tunes Berlin had brought from New York.

"And so he played it," Pan said, "and I remembered the first eight bars of the tune. Now, Fred used to play gin rummy with Berlin every week. So I taught Fred the first eight bars of this tune, and Fred had it note for note. The next time they were playing gin, Fred began to sing this new song. Berlin was taken aback. 'Fred,' he asked, 'where did you hear that?' "

Astaire remained nonchalant, Pan remembered. " 'Oh, that?' Fred said. 'It's a tune from the Hit Parade.' " Berlin became increasingly uncomfortable as the sickening feeling that he had inadvertently plagiarized a hit song for his *Top Hat* score descended on him. Finally Astaire could no longer control himself; he burst out laughing and let Irving in on the joke. "You could imagine the shock," Pan remarked.

The completed picture contained only five Berlin songs, but with the lavish treatment Sandrich accorded every single one of them, they put Berlin's stamp on the movie. Of the picture's one hundred minutes, fully thirty were given over to the songs. But Sandrich, the invisible craftsman behind the movie, had done a brilliant job of pacing the numbers; none ran much over six minutes, and only the last one, the monumentally silly "Piccolino," threatened to bring the proceedings to a halt, but by that time the movie was nearly over, and it was time to let out all the stops, anyway.

Despite the heavy calculations that had gone into the making of this movie, on which the fortunes of RKO, Astaire, and Rogers rested, no less than those of Irving Berlin, one last horrible snag arose. Shortly before its late-summer premiere, RKO held a preview screening in Santa Barbara, California, to test audience reaction. Halfway through, patrons began leaving the theater, while Berlin huddled in his seat, feeling miserable. It seemed that his worst nightmare about the movies had finally come to pass. Even now he did not feel as comfortable writing for the screen as for the stage. The process of making a movie forced him to work without a live audience to measure himself against. The flop preview in Santa Barbara appeared to be the inevitable outcome of laboring in isolation.

No sooner had Berlin and the studio begun to mourn *Top Hat* than another preview was held, and this time the audience reacted with delight. When the movie opened at Radio City Music Hall at the end of August, the response of critics and the lines around the block waiting for tickets swiftly confirmed *Top Hat* as one of the year's most successful motion pictures—proof that Hollywood had at last mastered the art of musical comedy. Critics were equally enthralled. *Variety*, the bellwether publication, remarked, "The theatres will hold their own world series with this one. It can't miss and the reasons are three—Fred Astaire, Irving Berlin's songs and sufficient comedy between numbers to hold the film together." The New York *Daily News* went even further: "*Top Hat* is the best thing yet done in a movie musical comedy. The music is Berlin at his best."

The positive reviews had the curious effect of obliterating the memory of his previous movie misfires; *Top Hat* was widely regarded as Irving Berlin's *first* film effort. Though supposedly more permanent than stage productions, movies were falling victim to the same popular amnesia that afflicted the live forms of entertainment they supplanted. From Berlin's perspective, this phenomenon did have its value, for he had never been especially proud of *Puttin' on the Ritz* (the movie) or any other work he'd done for the movies before *Top Hat*. If his early movies were all but forgotten just a few years after they had appeared and he could start all over again with a clean slate, that was fine with him. Berlin now possessed the enviable reputation of having taken Hollywood by storm on the first try.

Movies generally played the Radio City showcase no longer than a week, but *Top Hat* stayed the better part of a month. Made for $620,000, it went on to earn over $3 million—more than enough for Berlin to exercise his profit-taking clause. He wound up earning $300,000 from the movie, three times his original asking price.

Berlin's reward was more than financial. As a young man with a few big hits to his name, he had enhanced his status by writing a Broadway score for the reigning dance team of the day, Irene and Vernon Castle; and now he had accomplished the same feat for Fred Astaire and Ginger Rogers. If his earlier success was remarkable for his extreme youth (he was only twenty-six at the time), the later achievement was equally noteworthy for his maturity; now forty-seven, he continued to meet new musical challenges.

▪ ▪ ▪

Berlin's professional accomplishments could not hold him harmless from human frailty, however. On August 9, only three weeks before *Top Hat* opened, his youngest sister, Sarah Henkin, died tragically in New York. At the time, she was living with her husband, Abraham, who was unemployed, in a grim little apartment at 591 Williams Avenue, in the Brownsville section of Brooklyn. While not especially close to his sister—or to any of his siblings—Irving had eased her situation by giving her an allowance of $100 a month, on which she and her husband had managed to live. But Sarah had been in poor health for several years, asthma being but one of her afflictions, and apparently she suffered from an emotional disorder, as well.

On a warm summer day, she and her husband climbed to the roof of their five-story building in search of sunlight and perhaps a breeze in the stillness of the afternoon. At about one-thirty Sarah asked Abraham to go downstairs to retrieve a chair. As he entered their apartment, he heard screaming coming from the sidewalk below his window. When he looked outside to see what the trouble was, he discovered his wife lying on the pavement. In the brief time that he had left her alone, she had jumped to her death.

On hearing the news of the tragedy, Irving instantly flew to New York. He arrived in time for the funeral, which was scheduled for Sunday. Because of Berlin's fame, the Orthodox Jewish ceremony—held at Brooklyn's Washington Cemetery, the location of the Baline burial plot—attracted its share of photographers and journalists. The songwriter did what he could to throw a veil of secrecy over the proceedings, which only members of the immediate family attended. Not a man given to displaying private emotion, Berlin broke down on this occasion and wept. Photographers waiting for their chance to snap Berlin in mourning were forced to wait until he had entered a car, where he sat between another sister and his older brother, Benjamin, to whom he bore an uncanny physical resemblance.

A spate of headlines about the event appeared in newspapers across the country: "BERLIN'S KIN DIES IN LEAP," "IRVING BERLIN WEEPS AT SISTER'S FUNERAL." For Berlin, who was always acutely aware of his public image, his sister's death was, in addition to being a tragedy, a source of deep embarrassment.

Early Monday morning he flew to Los Angeles, once again exchanging the grim and often hopeless world of his youth for the magic realm of Hollywood, where personal history and circumstances had no meaning. Images of Fred Astaire whirling Ginger Rogers about replaced those of Sarah Henkin being lowered to her final resting place. *Top Hat* was about to open, and he wanted to participate in the last-minute excitement and frenzy.

They represented two extremes of the modern immigrant experience in America, Irving and his ill-fated sister. Whereas he incarnated the fulfillment every immigrant strove to attain, his sister Sarah and the manner of her death told another, darker story. Irving and his distinctive accomplishments would be remembered; Sarah and her all-too-common failure would be forgotten. But the Sarahs of the immigrant world—the *farloyrene menshen*, the lost souls, the ones who lacked the means to articulate and resolve their unfathomable problems—the Sarahs far outnumbered the likes of Irving Berlin.

Sarah's death always remained a private grief; Irving rarely, if ever, referred to it. It was quickly pushed aside, hushed up. His lifelong habit of denying harsh realities, a habit he formed as a boy in order to survive on the streets of the Lower East Side, did not permit him to dwell on misfortune, whether his or anyone else's. Given the circumstances of his childhood, this response was understandable, but it could cause him to appear cold and remote as an adult. Only two months later, when the songwriter was again at RKO, working on a new musical for Ginger Rogers and Fred Astaire, he dashed off a brusque note to Alexander Woollcott, who remained as close a friend as Irving had. Though he apologized for not seeing Alex during the brief trip back East, there was no mention, now or later, of his sister's recent death, which had been the reason for the trip.

Nor was Irving's letter to Woollcott unusual; nearly all the songwriter's correspondence had this same perfunctory air. He was invariably brief and not especially articulate or reflective. Though endlessly resourceful as a lyricist, he made for a singularly lackluster correspondent, who gave nothing of himself on paper and substituted a forced sense of bonhomie for the good intentions he felt. He was essentially a loner; he did not know how to be the confidant, intimate, or kindred spirit of anyone. The endlessly apologetic tone of his correspondence suggests that he wanted to be liked, to cultivate his circle of admirers, but the gift of friendship was one that he finally lacked. His letters—bulletins would be a more accurate description—contained no hint that a man of unusual talent or attainment stood behind them. If he was feeling in a particularly expansive mood, he might venture a remark about the weather (usually fine) or the stock market (looking up, for a change); that was about as far afield as the written observations of the most popular composer in American history ever went. He reserved his brilliance for his songs, his cunning for his business deals.

Increasingly unwilling and unable to express himself outside his music, his behavior often struck those around him as inexplicably, even comically distracted. When Berlin was returning to New York from Los Angeles by rail, a new office boy at the Irving Berlin, Inc., Harold Leventhal, was sent to greet him at Pennsylvania Station and witnessed an example of the songwriter's increasingly quirky behavior. "I was to see that his luggage was collected and that he got into a taxi and came back to the office," Leventhal recalled. "So I met him there and we got into a taxi, and he asks the taxi to stop. He goes out for a paper—and never comes back. I'm sitting there, and I don't have money for a cab. I gave up. I asked the cab driver to come back to the office, and I asked him please to wait. I got the luggage out, ran up to get cash for the cab, and I see he's there. I said, 'Mr. Berlin, I was waiting for you in the taxi.' And he just said, 'Oh, I forgot.' " Nor was this an isolated incident. Berlin would frequently enter and exit cabs in this unpredictable manner, leaving an ever-lengthening trail of forgotten friends and ticking meters behind him.

In unexpected situations Berlin was, if anything, even more evasive. One morning, for instance, a disheveled woman dodged Mynna Granat, Berlin's secretary, and barged into the songwriter's private office, begging for money. She was babbling in Yiddish and appeared to be mentally deranged. Suddenly faced with this unwelcome guest, Berlin reacted not by giving her a few dollars but by fleeing the office in horror.

Mynna summoned Harold Leventhal because she assumed he could speak Yiddish. As Leventhal coaxed the woman from the premises, he told himself that Berlin must understand Yiddish, yet the songwriter had shunned the pathetic woman. "That's always remained with me," said Leventhal, who believed that the helpless old woman who spoke only Yiddish was a manifestation of all that Berlin wished to avoid in his life; his fleeing her demonstrated his habitual denial of who he really was and where he had come from.

One of the few individuals to whom Berlin *could* relate during the late thirties was Fred Astaire, but even Astaire, though properly impressed with Irving's genius as a songwriter, was baffled by his friend's utter self-absorption. In January 1936, when Astaire's young wife, Phyllis, was about to deliver her first child, he asked Irving to help him endure the hours of waiting at the hospital. They wiled away the night as they often did, playing gin rummy. Berlin played card games with the same single-minded intensity that he brought to his songwriting. He would also, on occasion, try out new melodies on Astaire as they played, and just because Astaire was about to become a father, Berlin saw no reason to refrain. "Say," he asked as they held their cards, "What do you think of this for a tune?" He proceeded to whistle and sing it as best he could.

"I like it," Astaire remarked.

"Good," Irving replied. "Gin!"

"He had a good hand and a good idea for a song, and he thought he'd use them both," Astaire later remarked with asperity. Several hours later, Phyllis gave birth to a baby boy, Fred Astaire, Jr.

▪ ▪ ▪

When events demanded, Berlin could force himself to play, briefly, the wacky extrovert. On January 20, 1936, the Hollywood establishment held a testimonial dinner at the Ambassador Hotel to honor the songwriter's twenty-five-year-long career. It was a black-tie affair, and the 155 guests included the most powerful names in the industry: Irving's old friend Joseph Schenck; Darryl Zanuck, who would soon lure the songwriter away from RKO; Al Jolson; Ernst Lubitsch; Pandro S. Berman; Max Winslow; Samuel Goldwyn; and Irving Thalberg. Habitual deal makers, these men would, amid the backslapping and speechifying, be jockeying for the right to use Berlin's songs in various movies.

Fred Astaire was to have served as master of ceremonies, but he was preoccupied with his newborn son. Jerome Kern, who had left Broadway for the movies, took his place supervising the evening's festivities. Two orchestras were present, one led by Johnny Green, a young Harvard-educated composer and arranger, the other by bandleader Ted Lewis. In addition, there were twenty-five composers in attendance, each of whom sang a different hit song Berlin had composed during the previous twenty-five years.

The evening's great surprise was a replica of Nigger Mike's as it had looked—more or less—in its heyday on Pell Street in Chinatown. "When Irving Berlin . . . was led through the swinging doors into the sawdust covered floors of Mike's in Hollywood instead of Chatham Square, New York," noted one reporter, "the little fellow whom they called Izzy in these lean days of his career turned on the tear duct and little beads of emotion crept down his cheeks as he gulped in amazement at the duplication of scenes that were so dear to him."

Three extras made up as bartenders stood at attendance, and a sign said, "Ask Izzy to sing 'Sweet Marie from Sunny Italy' "—his first published song. At the tables sat not the tourists and streetwalkers of the real Nigger Mike's but powerful motion picture executives and assorted songwriters, including Berlin's old rival and collaborator, Al Piantadosi. It was a remarkable sight—all those Hollywood big shots in black tie huddling around little Irving at the piano. Avuncular Jerry Kern gently rested his hand on Irving's shoulder. Joe Schenck, his bulk crammed into a double-breasted dinner jacket, looked for all the world like a gangster on his best behavior.

The only element missing from the entire evening (aside from women; it was strictly a stag dinner) was Nigger Mike Salter himself, dead these fifteen years. His little establishment had finally won the fame he'd always wanted for it in his lifetime. True, it was only a replica some three thousand miles from the original location, but this was another example of Hollywood triumphing over time, space, and logic. Here was a real Hollywood touch, to re-create a slice of life as if it were a scene from a movie: this is your life, Irving Berlin—or a reasonable facsimile thereof.

"Irving was flabbergasted," said the reporter. "He gasped for words which were lost in the tightness of the esophagus, then he came out of it and was 'Little Izzy' again." He forced himself to go along with the charade because it was, in the final analysis, good for business, and he was enough of a businessman to realize that that night's song plugging could become tomorrow's contract. As Piantadosi played, "Little Izzy" sang a selection of his hits, "Alexander's Ragtime Band," "Oh! How I Hate to Get Up in the Morning," "Always," and "Cheek to Cheek." Meanwhile, a battery of newsreel cameras recorded the moment for posterity.

Dinner followed. As master of ceremonies, Kern read aloud excerpts from Alexander Woollcott's biography of Berlin, pausing occasionally to point out people in the book who were present: Al Piantadosi, Max Winslow, and Joe Schenck. The passages that Kern read about Schenck caused the producer embarrassment because they dealt with his former career as a drugstore clerk and opium salesman. An awkward pause ensued. Schenck forced a smile. He tried to explain that selling opium on the Lower East Side was no big deal. The customers, he said, selected their drugs as carefully as women squeezing grapefruit at a market stall. But even as he smiled, his teeth were grinding; he detested having these stupid little stories flung back in his face.

Then the moment Berlin always dreaded arrived; he was called on to speak. As usual, the words failed to come. Finally, he admitted he was having a "hell of a time" and let it go at that. His terror came not from his fear of the crowd, for he loved crowds and needed them as only a lifelong performer could, but because he lacked control over the situation. With control, he was Irving Berlin, the peerless songwriter; without it, he regressed to hapless Izzy Baline. Control separated the beggar, the busker, the refuse of history from the unique phenomenon he had become.

From this time forth talk began to circulate around the industry about the possibility of making a large-scale movie musical based on Irving's "colorful" and "inspiring" story. The canonization of Irving Berlin, Hollywood style, was under way. At this mature phase in the songwriter's career—he was pushing fifty—such rituals contained echoes of earlier rites of passage, and this event, marking Berlin's acceptance by the Hollywood establishment, inevitably recalled his initiation dinner at the Friars' Club and his ascendance to the Broadway establishment twenty-five years before. And yet it was also symptomatic of a certain staleness that had crept into his career. Each milestone had an ineluctable sense of *déjà vu* about it; he was running out of worlds to conquer, both financial and artistic.

In late February 1936, barely six months after *Top Hat* had established Berlin's reputation in Hollywood, *Follow the Fleet*, his second score for a Fred Astaire–Ginger Rogers musical, opened. In line with Berman's conservative instincts, it was closely patterned on the original: same composer, same stars, same director, even the same booking at Radio City Music Hall. And predictably, it met with the same critical and commercial success. This time around, Sandrich made room for seven Berlin tunes, including the haunting meditation disguised as a love song: "Let's Face the Music and Dance."

Although he was spared the reckoning he believed was at hand, his friend George Gershwin was not so lucky. At the time Berlin was writing for RKO, the irrepressible Gershwin was breaking new ground at a furious rate. The previous October his "American folk opera," *Porgy and Bess*, had opened to acclaim on Broadway, where it dissolved the traditional boundaries separating "popular" from "serious" music. As jewel-like as Berlin's recent songs were, none of his recent efforts could compare to his young friend's unprecedented achievement. Nor had Gershwin abandoned the popular arena; he continued, in collaboration with his brother, Ira, to write movie scores and hit songs. The man who'd written *Porgy and Bess* plunged into the remunerative, if vacuous, task of writing the score for *The Goldwyn Follies*, though the job entailed his having to put up with Sam Goldwyn's nagging him like some impossible father figure to write ever more hit songs, the way Irving Berlin did.

As 1936 yielded to 1937, however, Gershwin began to feel ill and moody; no longer was he his usual ebullient self. He suffered from severe headaches, which his doctors were at first inclined to dismiss as manifestations of hysteria. On June 20 Gershwin and his close friend Kay Swift dined with Irving and Ellin (on one of her occasional visits to Hollywood), and during the meal the pounding headache returned. Indeed, the pain was so intense that he required assistance leaving the table. Forty-eight hours later, he entered Cedars of Lebanon Hospital where, on July 11, 1937, he died of a brain tumor at the age of thirty-eight. Berlin, of course, would carry on for decades to come. His narrow field of activity resulted from both his own musical limitations and his enslavement to the musical marketplace. He was, in a broad sense, a victim of his success, doomed to replicate it ad infinitum.

▪ ▪ ▪

Later in 1937 Ellin gave birth to her third child, also a daughter, named Elizabeth Irving. She was to be the last child the couple would have, and their family was now complete. Irving and Ellin's other daughters were swiftly growing up. Mary Ellin was now nearly ten, and Louise almost four. Berlin found himself head of a household comprised of women, a role that had its advantages and its drawbacks. No son would grow up in his shadow, scorning his famous father; but at the same time, there was no one to carry on the Berlin name; it was *sui generis*. In his old age, he would embark on an extended and often frustrated search for surrogate sons who would preserve his musical legacy, if not his name. (Balines, meanwhile, proliferated up and down the Eastern seaboard, but Irving had little to do with them.)

Following the birth of Elizabeth, Irving and Ellin took their first trip abroad since the beginning of the Depression, to England, inevitably. By now the songwriter was a confirmed Anglophile, no matter how many fingers the English insisted he played the piano with. On his return to Hollywood, he immediately resumed his movie work, this time for the remarkable and obtuse Darryl F. Zanuck.

Only the year before, the thirty-four-year-old Zanuck had engineered an enviable coup by luring Berlin to Twentieth Century-Fox. He seemed an unlikely man to have accomplished the feat, for among the Jewish immigrants who had largely been responsible for creating

Hollywood, Darryl Francis Zanuck, born in Wahoo, Nebraska, was an anomaly. Furthermore, he had made his name with gangster pictures starring Edward G. Robinson and James Cagney during his years as production chief at Warner Brothers—not precisely the sort of fare with which Berlin associated himself. What gave Zanuck the edge in his dealings with Berlin was the specter of Joe Schenck hovering in the background. After his departure from Warner Brothers in 1933, Zanuck had worked in tandem with Schenck at United Artists until, in 1935, the two of them bolted and took the reins of a rejuventated Twentieth Century-Fox. Though Berlin now dealt primarly with Zanuck, Schenck's presence at the studio reassured the songwriter that he was among friends.

The relationship between Zanuck and Berlin began simply enough, with the songwriter selling the producer an ancient trunk song called "You're Laughing at Me." Now it was Irving's turn to laugh at Zanuck, because at the time the songwriter had composed this tune, he said, "I thought it was so bad I wouldn't have it published." Yet he later "peddled it to Mr. Zanuck for a great deal of money." The transaction was of course not a demonstration of the song's belatedly discovered worth but an index of Berlin's rising reputation in Hollywood. Zanuck—along with most other studio chiefs—would have been delighted to obtain almost anything by Berlin as a way of establishing a relationship with the songwriter.

The next thing Irving knew, he was writing an entire score for Zanuck, to accompany a big-budget musical called *On the Avenue*, starring Dick Powell, Madeleine Carroll, and Alice Faye. Everything about *On the Avenue* was designed to put the Fred Astaire–Ginger Rogers musicals to shame; it had a larger cast, more lavish sets, more songs by Irving Berlin, a more complicated plot—virtually every element that could be stuffed into one hundred minutes of cinematic entertainment.

The result was, perhaps not altogether unexpectedly, an ambitious misfire, and the culprit was the story, which wavered uncertainly between a satire evoking the smart cynicism of *As Thousands Cheer* and a generic backstage romance between the icy blonde Carroll, who portrays Mimi Caraway, the wealthiest girl in the world, and the affable Powell, playing Gary Blake, an actor who satirizes her father in a stage revue. "People in the public eye must get caricatured," says one character, announcing the movie's theme. "That is the price of fame." There was more than a hint of the Berlin-Mackay romance in the situation, and the promise of pleasurable dramatic conflict looms when Carroll proceeds to buy the offending revue and all the actors in it. Instead of offering a dramatic payoff, the musical slithers every which way. The first scene is set in the girls' dormitory at the University of Southern California, and the second at the Mt. Wilson Observatory, which is staffed by the three manic Ritz Brothers—that was the kind of daffy show it was.

The chaos took its toll. "The brilliant score that Irving Berlin has composed for 'On the Avenue' is the most distinctive feature of the new musical photoplay," said Howard Barnes in the *Herald Tribune*, when the picture opened in February 1937 at Radio City Music Hall, scene of Berlin's two earlier triumphs with Fred Astaire and Ginger Rogers. "The tolerant thing to do would be to discuss the Berlin songs at length. His 'This Year's Kisses,' sung alluringly by Miss Faye, is a notable torch number, and there are four or five more pieces that you will be hearing for a long time in public meeting places and on the radio." Barnes had little to say for the rest of the picture.

By the time *On the Avenue* opened, Irving was already at work on an even more ambitious project Zanuck had conceived following the testimonial dinner highlighting the songwriter's past accomplishments. To Zanuck, Irving Berlin was simply show business incarnate, his life story the history of popular entertainment during the previous twenty-five years, and *Alexander's Ragtime Band* (the movie) was supposed to be an outsized biographical drama of Berlin's life, studded with his hit songs. But that was before Berlin himself became involved in the project. Zanuck naturally enough invited Irving to write the scenario, and the songwriter was glad to comply, as a way of erasing himself from the movie. But even in his omissions and fantasies, Berlin proved to be revealing of himself. He began his pseudo-autobiography not at Nigger Mike's on New York's Lower East Side, but in a honky-tonk saloon in New Orleans, where a small orchestra introduces the title song to the public. And Alexander, rather than being a fictional black bandleader, is now an all-too-real white clarinetist, who imprudently breaks up with his girl and makes his way to Broadway. Just when Berlin seems intent on offering a conventional backstage romance, punctuated with several of his old songs, he takes his Alexander to Camp Upton in time for the Great War, where he meets a certain Irving Berlin. The story behind *Yip! Yip! Yaphank*, of which the songwriter had always remained exceedingly proud, is presented with an abundance of faithful detail.

After this autobiographical interlude, the scenario drifts off into Never Never Land, as Alexander finds himself out of work, a has-been, a holdover from the ragtime era. But then Berlin intrudes upon the story once more, as Alexander approaches the songwriter and his partner, Sam Harris, who give him a job performing in the orchestra at the Music Box Theatre. Eventually, he finds his niche at an "Old Timers' Club," an establishment improbably devoted to reviving ragtime. Through a series of implausible machinations, Alexander enjoys a belated triumph when he is invited to conduct his famous ragtime song before a full orchestra at Carnegie Hall, where he reunites with the girl he scorned years before.

Two motifs dominated Berlin's sprawling story. One was his ever-present urge to return to the past, to the halcyon days of his first triumph, "Alexander's Ragtime Band." The second was his yearning for artistic respectability, signified by the performance of his song in Carnegie Hall. Gershwin had stormed this citadel of high culture, and later Paul Whiteman, but Berlin had been denied the honor. In this movie, at least, he was able to correct the injustice.

Berlin and screenwriter Richard Sherman expanded this already complicated story into a 114-page treatment, which they submitted to Twentieth Century-Fox on March 3. They waited several months for Zanuck's reaction, and when it came, the news was terrible, devastating, in fact. "Mr. Zanuck was quite disappointed with the script," began the notes of a production meeting on May 21, 1937. "This must be a million-dollar picture in every sense of the word." Zanuck continued:

> Audiences will expect to see a WOW! It must [have] the scope of Ziegfeld and Old Chicago—American music as the background of a human drama of real people. Maybe our trouble is that we are trying to tell a phase of American musical evolution

> instead of a story about two boys and a girl. The story of these three is our main plot; the other, the important background. We don't have to be Epic in the old sense of the word; the epic quality should come out in Entertainment. Wherever we go out of our way to mention famous names and all that sort of thing, we are wrong. . . . We musn't lose sight of the fact that audiences know the story; it is not original in the real sense of the world. As it is now, our punches are telegraphed way ahead; there is actually no suspense until the very last part. Having this routine formula, we must write against our scenes rather than *to them.* From a situation story, we must get a character story, the actual situation has to come out of the people. Treat it freshly—make the situations seem unexpected and not by *tricking.*

As the movie evolved away from his original treatment, Berlin excused himself from further screenwriting chores, which were left to the studio's platoon of in-house dramatists. The script underwent further revisions in response to the harsh criticisms leveled by Zanuck; the New Orleans setting yielded to San Francisco, and the movie, which had originally been conceived as a vehicle for Fred MacMurray, was now assigned to Tyrone Power. However, the revised script, according to Zanuck, was, if anything, even worse than its predecessor. "Mr. Zanuck expected the greatest story he ever had," ran the notes to another story conference, this one held on July 7, 1937. "He was very disappointed. The present script is flat, the characters and their motivations are all wrong." And yet: "Somewhere, there is a really great human story in this."

As a moviemaker, Zanuck was far less interested in the musical and historical details with which Berlin had stuffed his story than in the romance, which, he believed, had been slighted. "This can be a great love story," the producer insisted. To Zanuck's disappointment, Berlin's own love story—the tale of his two marriages, with their elements of pathos and grandeur—had no place in the emerging script. Zanuck was further dismayed by the lack of "genuine honesty" in the story—"genuine honesty" being an obsession with the producer. It was hard to describe, but he knew it when he saw it, and as far as he could tell, *Alexander's Ragtime Band* didn't have it.

Despite Zanuck's grievances, the movie began shooting soon afterward. Opening in the summer of 1938, it possessed an indestructible asset that outweighed all its shortcomings: thirty songs by Irving Berlin, including many of his most celebrated hits. On the strength of the songs, the movie blossomed into a solid commercial success, and its popularity added to Berlin's prestige in Hollywood. He had become the mainstream. Said *Variety*: "Consolidated into a single entertainment, the Berlin repertoire taken from various musical shows, films and from the shelves of pop sheet music stores, comprise a symphony as familiar to the average man and woman as the faces of close friends."

So the movie had been a foolproof project all along, no matter what its plot. Yet the treatment given most of the songs in the film left much to be desired. This was the big band era, and swing music was at its apogee. Berlin detested swing as much as he had detested jazz, and for the same reason, that it favored the performer over the composer. Listening to Benny Goodman's version of "Blue Skies," Irving became so incensed at the liberties taken with his song that he complained he'd heard only one or two of his original phrases. He hadn't slaved over the song only to be upstaged by a clarinet. Later, when he met Goodman, he said, at first, "That was the most incredible playing I've ever heard," and then he immediately added, "Never do that again!"

But swing was king, and Alfred Newman's musical direction gave most of the Berlin tunes the lush, suffocating, Hollywood studio swing treatment, thus depriving them of their spontaneity and punch. The musical emasculation scarcely mattered, since the tunes were so well known to the audience that the actors could have whistled them and gotten away with it. Only once did a song by Berlin manage to overcome the movie's embalming, and that occurred when a young actress new to movies, Ethel Merman, who dressed like Fred Astaire, sang about "My Walking Stick." Merman harked back to an earlier generation of performers; she was larger than life, and possessed of a clear, booming voice that went so well with Berlin's tunes.

The songwriter hoped to work with Merman on his next picture for the studio, and he might well have been under the impression that it would feature her, but the movies being the notoriously fickle business that they were, Merman wasn't available. Instead, Berlin found himself working with a little-known actress named Mary Healy, who, after three dreary years as a contract player, desperately hoped that her moment had arrived. "They were trying to get me to sound like Ethel Merman," Healy said of that uncertain period in her career, "because they wanted her for a picture starring Sonja Henie and Tyrone Power without telling me about it."

The movie, eventually called *Second Fiddle*, had already been through a staggering number of incarnations and scripts, as the title changes alone suggested: from *Heart Interest*, *Cupid Goes to Press*, *When Winter Comes* to *Love Is Tops*. Beneath all the fuss and bother was the merest wisp of a romantic comedy based on the recent, widely publicized search for the right actress to play the role of Scarlett O'Hara in the movie version of *Gone With the Wind*. Following the unrepeatable success of the *Alexander's Ragtime Band* retrospective, Berlin doggedly set about discharging this, his final obligation to the studio, to Zanuck, and ultimately, to Joe Schenck.

Though Berlin was his customary dutiful self on the set, the movie, when it opened in July 1939, proved to be as much of a disappointment as *Alexander's Ragtime Band* had been a success. There were manifold reasons for this result, beginning with its flimsy premise, but the score itself would not be numbered among them. "Mr. Berlin might be pardoned for slipping over some dull tunes in a show after all these years of scrivening," commented Howard Barnes in the *Herald Tribune*—Barnes being the one New York critic who generally paid scrupulous attention to Berlin's movie work. "Far from demanding your indulgence, though, he has composed some fetching ballads which do more than anything else in 'Second Fiddle' to keep it beguiling. His 'I Poured My Heart into a Song,' picked out with one finger on a piano at the start and then properly orchestrated, is a honey of a piece." Yet Frank S. Nugent, in the pages of *The New York Times*, condemned the movie for having "an indifferent Berlin score and a plot that blows up all over the place."

The lackluster film terminated the professional relationship between Berlin and Twentieth Century-Fox, but it did little to affect his friendship with Schenck. They continued, as before, to play cards, to take steam baths together, and to reminisce about the old days on the Lower East Side. In financial matters Schenck continued to be as profligate as ever. Mexico, his favored gambling haven, had outlawed that activity in 1935; the move had cost him several hundred thousand dollars. Despite his financial troubles, his star continued to rise—and not just in Hollywood. He made himself highly visible as head of numerous charity drives on behalf of the Red Cross and the National Foundation for Infantile Paralysis. The latter activity put him in the good graces of President Roosevelt, who invited him to visit the White House. By the end of the meeting, he was calling Roosevelt "Chief," and the president was calling him "Joe." In 1938 Schenck distinguished himself by raising nearly $400,000 for the Los Angeles Community Chest. And he visited the president again, this time at the Roosevelt estate in Hyde Park, New York. Joe had demonstrated such talent for good works that the chief wanted him to manage the national campaign for the March of Dimes.

The Internal Revenue Service, however, had a different fix on Joseph Schenck. It noted that his tax returns had been made out not by a reputable accountant but by a story editor at Twentieth Century-Fox, one Joseph H. Moskowitz, and Moskowitz's records of Schenck's financial dealings contained huge gaps. U.S. Treasury Department agents descended on Twentieth Century-Fox, combing the studio's financial records for evidence of Schenck's activities, and they noted a pattern of misdealing that had begun at least as early as 1935. Each year Schenck had underreported his income—which, considering the vast extent of his gambling activities, was almost impossible to ascertain—and each year he had vastly exaggerated his expenses, including, among other items, the cost of maintaining his yacht, the *Carolina*. Ultimately, the Treasury agents determined that Schenck owed his country over $400,000 in back taxes. Schenck might have been able to raise this amount, but there was more. In 1940 a federal grand jury in the Southern District of New York decided to bring charges against Schenck for conspiracy to defraud the government. He happened to be in Chasen's celebrated restaurant when he heard the news that he had been indicted on four counts that carried penalties totaling 167 years in prison, plus heavy fines.

Learning that his closest friend in the motion picture business had run afoul of the law, Berlin became panic-stricken. He had spent many hours gambling with Schenck and had failed to report his winnings. It seemed that it would be only a matter of time until the government caught up with him, as well. Furthermore, Berlin had his own tax case pending with the IRS concerning the money he had made on his score for *Top Hat* in 1935. At stake was $11,092 in back taxes the government claimed Berlin owed. The songwriter had insisted that the money he had made from that picture represented "gain from the sales of capital assets," which could be offset by losses—an argument the Tax Appeals Board was considering.

Feeling doubly vulnerable, Berlin anxiously telephoned one of his several lawyers in New York, expressing his fears that he would be pulled down along with Schenck. Straitlaced Irving cringed at the thought of the adverse publicity a tax scandal could generate. There was some basis for his fears. Years before, Schenck had been marginally involved in the most notorious of Hollywood trials, that of Roscoe M. "Fatty" Arbuckle, whose comedies Schenck had produced. Arbuckle's trial centered on an all-night party during which an actress had died. Schenck had emerged unscathed from that ordeal, but the odds were that he would not be as fortunate on this occasion.

Hastening to dissociate himself from Schenck, Berlin returned to the RKO fold, where he wrote his third and final score for Fred Astaire and Ginger Rogers; the movie was to be called *Carefree*. The songwriter spent January 1938 in Phoenix, Arizona, working on the score, with his wife and transposing piano in tow. By this time he knew the routine of writing for Astaire fairly well, and the work went quickly. The four songs that emerged from his labors—"Change Partners," "I Used to Be Color Blind," "The Night Is Filled with Music," and "The Yam" (the inevitable silly production number)—did not quite match the caliber of his previous RKO efforts, but they were sufficient to maintain his standing.

On his return to Los Angeles from Arizona at the beginning of February, he began the painful business of polishing the songs and supervising the orchestration. In this phase of the project, he was fortunate to collaborate with a rising young orchestrator of exceptional musical resourcefulness, Robert Russell Bennett. It was the beginning of a relationship that would span decades. Like his predecessors, Bennett was forcefully struck by the abyss separating Irving's primitive technical ability and his masterly songwriting. He decided that Berlin *heard* precisely the notes and harmonies he wanted but lacked the skill to find them on the great white expanse of the keyboard with his fingers and *play* them. Working on "Change Partners," Bennett recalled, Irving "came to a spot in this where he played a plain diminished chord." He turned to Bennett "helplessly" and asked, "Is that the right chord?"

"Well," said Bennett, "I don't think it's the chord you hear, somehow or other."

"No, that's not it," Berlin replied. "You play me a chord there."

Bennett played a chord, and another, and another, until he at last struck the one Irving had heard all along but had been unable to find. "That's it!" the songwriter exclaimed. To Bennett, Irving's complete reliance on a musical secretary, rather than undermining the songwriter's reputation, offered proof of his ability; the man was a genius in spite of himself. "I say all great people come into this world without any clothing at all, just naked geniuses of some kind, and out it comes," he philosophized. "They may not be able to express it. . . . They just sit there, and they bring you something, and that's all there is to say about it."

The making of *Carefree* reunited the entire RKO crew responsible for the earlier movies of Fred Astaire and Ginger Rogers, but this effort proved to be the most problematic of the three for which Berlin contributed the score. The book was by far the most daring; for once it skipped the staple backstage romance in favor of a satire of psychoanalysis—not a subject that lent itself easily to musical comedy or for which the resolutely unintrospective Berlin felt any affinity whatsoever. The one dramatic opening he could exploit in musical terms was a "dream sequence" filmed in slow motion. While Astaire danced and sang "Color Blind," the camera decelerated his movements to the point where he seemed to be floating rather than flying, and the result was a piece of magic cinematic fluff.

However, nothing else equaled this sequence for charm and originality, and the movie opened at the end of August to a tepid reception. "It's a disappointing story and the stars alone may save it. Word-of-mouth will be poor," *Variety* tartly commented, with scarcely a mention of Berlin's score. The movie suffered an additional handicap because it competed for box office revenue with the still current *Alexander's Ragtime Band*, which offered considerably more excitement, spectacle, and music by Irving Berlin. Despite these obstacles, *Carefree* did respectable business, pulling in $1,731,000 for the studio, but the budget had grown considerably since the lean days of *Top Hat*, and the film actually lost money.

Finally, the film's peculiar plot suggested that the RKO team was straining for effect the third time around and that the Berlin-Astaire-Rogers combination was flagging, as indeed it was. When Astaire finally kissed Rogers, for the first time in any of their movies together, the gesture had the effect of a kiss-off. After just three short years, the concept had run its course. Although his collaboration with Astaire would continue, this was the last score Berlin wrote for RKO.

The songwriter was now fifty, and he was as impatient as ever with the slow pace of life in a land of eternal sunshine and the protracted, convoluted business of moviemaking. Unlike Gershwin, Kern, and many other composers who had gradually succumbed to the charms of life in Southern California, Irving had never quite adapted. He could never persuade himself to take it easy, to play golf, to sit back and count his money. "I feel slow in Hollywood," he complained. "The tempo there is slow." He'd earned a quick $240,000 in the past twelve months, but it was the next twelve that worried him.

In addition to his growing sense of boredom with Southern California in general and writing for movies in particular, Irving had personal reasons for wanting to return to the East. Ellin and, when school schedules allowed, the children had been spending a fair amount of time with him in Hollywood. Now that pleasant arrangement changed as the health of his father-in-law, Clarence Mackay, deteriorated. Ellin spent an increasing amount of her time in New York.

The slide had begun in earnest in December 1937, when Clarence had undergone emergency surgery at Roosevelt Hospital for appendicitis. He recovered sufficiently to appear occasionally at his old office, at 67 Broad Street, to preside over his shrunken business interests, and on April 16, 1938, he celebrated his sixty-third birthday in relatively good health. Soon after, however, the throat cancer that had plagued him for years took a turn for the worse. He was in and out of the hospital throughout the summer, and when it was apparent that nothing more could be done for him, he returned to the gatekeeper's house at Harbor Hill for the fall. Subsequently, he sought refuge at his New York home at 3 East 75th Street to await the end of his life.

■ □ ■ □ ■ □ ■

CHAPTER 15

Minstrel of Peace

As Clarence Mackay lay near death in New York, and *Alexander's Ragtime Band* illuminated the nation's screens, Berlin sailed for England aboard the *Normandie* in September 1938. A dispute involving the English rights to the songs employed in *Alexander's Ragtime Band* served as the pretext for the songwriter's brief visit, but more than that impelled him to travel across the Atlantic. Hitler's rise had highlighted England's importance to the United States, and Berlin hoped, in the course of doing business, to form his own impressions of the political winds of change sweeping Europe.

After he arrived and checked into Claridge's, the dignified London hotel that he preferred, Berlin turned his attention to business matters. His English publisher, Bert Feldman, was threatening to hold up the foreign release of *Alexander's Ragtime Band*. Feldman claimed that he still owned the English rights to a number of songs included in the film's score, songs that Twentieth Century-Fox refused to pay for. To the songwriter, the dispute served as an object lesson concerning the importance of retaining control over his copyrights, and once Feldman backed down, Berlin set plans in motion to open a London office of his music company and assume responsibility for the publication of his songs directly.

Berlin's business dealings paled into insignificance beside the political strife in Europe. For most Americans, the relentless advance of Adolph Hitler across one national boundary after another was an abstraction, but once Irving arrived in London, with its proximity to the Third Reich, the abstraction suddenly became a terrifying reality. From the vantage point of his suite at Claridge's, Berlin, an inveterate reader of newspapers, carefully followed the unfolding of the Munich crisis at the beginning of October. He read of Prime Minister Neville Chamberlain's return to Heston Airport after a meeting with Hitler, bearing what was later called "that bit of paper," a meaningless Anglo-German accord that the Führer had no intention of honoring. Popular sentiment, to which Berlin was highly attuned, gradually coalesced against Germany and against appeasement. Berlin was no political analyst, but he *was* a dedicated student of popular opinion, and he recognized war fever when he saw it. It was only a matter of time, he supposed, until he would begin writing a type of song he had not turned out since he was a young man: the war song.

Berlin returned to the comparative safety of American shores in October. Just being in New York again, after years of intermittent absence, invigorated him. It was swell to be back in town, back in his own office, back among the crowds he always felt so much at home with, back in every sense where he belonged. In contrast to the sterile luxury and tranquility of Hollywood, New York was a horribly dirty, chaotic, and exasperating place, but Lindy's was down the street, a dozen daily papers were for sale at any newsstand, and countless Chinese restaurants beckoned him: that, plus an endless succession of hit songs, was all Irving needed to feel happy.

Now that he was on his home turf, the terror of war receded slightly. It was just possible that this would be a purely European conflict, that the United States would have no direct involvement in it. Of course many Americans felt as Berlin did; almost no one wanted to go to war. To express this widely shared aspiration, the songwriter, shunning Hollywood and its maddeningly slow and unreal tempo, began giving thought to the tricky task of composing a "peace song" rather than a war song. "I'd like to write a great peace song," he told a visiting journalist, "but it's hard to do, because you have trouble dramatizing peace. Easy to dramatize war. . . . Yet music is so important. It changes thinking, it influences everybody, whether they know it or not."

So Berlin was now a minstrel with a mission; never before had he contemplated writing a song to change or to mold public opinion, rather than articulating it, but he had already lived through one world war, and that was enough. "I worked for a while on a song called 'Thanks, America' but I didn't like it," he recalled. "I tried again with a song called 'Let's Talk About Liberty,' but I didn't get very far with that. I found it was too much like making a speech to music. It then occurred to me to reexamine the old song, 'God Bless America.' "

This was the anthem he had deleted from the score for *Yip! Yip! Yaphank* nearly twenty-one years before, but had kept on file, along with countless other fragments. Had it been left to Berlin to dig out the antique song himself, he might never have found it, but he turned to his secretary, Mynna, and said, "Go to the *Yip! Yip! Yaphank* file and get a copy of 'God Bless America.' " Even Mynna, who was well organized, had a difficult time locating the song, because the transcript had no title, but eventually she was able to produce it for her boss.

He looked at the song, and it was good, though it showed its age. "I had to make one or two changes in the lyrics," Berlin continued, "and they in turn led me to a slight change and, I think, an improvement in the melody. . . . One line in particular; the original line ran: 'Stand beside her and guide her to the right with a light from above.' In 1918 the phrase 'to the right' had no political significance, as it has now. So for obvious reasons I changed the phrase to 'Through the night with a light from above,' and I think that's better." Another change also served to bring the song into alignment with his current thinking: "One of the original lines read, 'Make her victorious on land and foam, God bless America, my home, sweet home.' Well, I didn't want this to be a war song, so I changed that line to 'From the mountains to the prairies to the oceans white with foam, God Bless America, my home, sweet home.' This longer line altered the meter and led to a change in the melody."

Writing the song was half the battle; finding the proper singer and forum in which to introduce it to the public was the other. In this case, Berlin was fortunate that Ted Collins, who managed a popular radio singer named Kate Smith, happened to be looking for a patriotic song for Kate to perform during her Armistice Day broadcast—a song of peace. And the new, improved version of "God Bless America," to Irving's way of thinking, was just such a song.

As for Kate Smith herself, over two hundred pounds of cheerfulness, there were those who loved her and those would just as soon leave her alone. But her enthusiasm had irresistible appeal. At the age of eight she had entertained American troops during the Great War. Later, she was pegged as the next Sophie Tucker, but Kate Smith was always more hick than city smart; her strongest appeal was to rural audiences. The way to reach them was radio, and by the time Irving offered her his song of peace, she was an established presence on CBS, where she had her own show, her own sponsor, (La Palina Cigars), and an avid, if unsophisticated following. Part of the reason she succeeded with them, aside from her rural leanings, was her sexlessness; it was said she offered no threat to the housewives who controlled the radio dial, women who were happy to let their husbands listen to her rather than to some siren of the airwaves. Network radio was a wholesome medium, and Kate Smith was a wholesome singer, and "God Bless America" was a wholesome song.

Exactly how wholesome, Berlin did not fully realize until the night of Friday, November 11, when Kate Smith sang "God Bless America" during her broadcast. Within days of its belated debut, the song began to acquire the status of an unofficial national anthem. The sheet music was suddenly in great demand, and Berlin's publishing company, not having anticipated the song's popularity, raced to catch up with the public's enthusiasm. In any event, a hit was a hit, and Irving had the opportunity to savor this vindication of his songwriting ability. Many another tunesmith harbored a "trunk"—more exactly, a file—bulging with yellowed manuscripts of promising songs that had been discarded from old shows, but no one else had the tenacity and the ability to rescue a tattered effort and make it seem new and timely and convincing.

The feat, all the more remarkable because it was accomplished without the usual tricks of the promotional trade, such as plugging, left even the composer at a loss for a satisfactory explanation. "The reason 'God Bless America' caught on," he tried to explain to *The New York Times* two years after the fact, "is that it happens to have a universal appeal. Any song that had that is bound to be a success; and let me tell you right here that while song plugging may help a good song, it never put over a poor one." The song's apparently inexplicable popularity did serve to confirm one of Berlin's most dearly held beliefs: "The mob is always right. It seems to be able to sense instinctively what is good, and I believe that there are darned few good songs which have not been whistled or sung by the crowd." It was a populist's credo, as well as a merchant's.

Despite his belief in the musical tastes of the mob, the songwriter had underestimated the extraordinary reach and immediacy of network radio, and beyond that, the way it tapped into the depths of the national psyche, for these were turbulent and uncertain months in the United States no less than in England, as the prospect of war, combined with the effects of the prolonged, seemingly endless Depression, induced anxiety throughout society. Less than two weeks earlier, on October 30, the same radio network, CBS, had broadcast an adaptation of H. G. Wells's science fiction story "The War of the Worlds" as a Halloween jest. But the prank lurched out of control as the program's vivid accounts of flying saucers landing in little Grovers Mills, New Jersey, combined with actor-director Orson Welles's all-too-effective presentation, induced mass hysteria and provided a demonstration of the public's unease. For all listeners knew, Hitler had finally unleashed an attack against the United States. Kate Smith's performance of "God Bless America" addressed the same unease, but it had just the opposite effect; it acted as a rallying point. The song's patriotic sentiments, which had seemed so cloying and overwrought two decades earlier, were now exactly right, and Americans clutched at them as if they were a prayer or a security blanket. Without quite meaning to, Welles had exploited the public unease; without quite meaning to, Berlin had calmed it.

▪ ▪ ▪

At eleven P.M. on Saturday, November 12, Clarence Mackay—symbol of the old order—died. He had hovered between life and death for weeks, and his second wife, Anna Case, had remained at his side throughout the ordeal. He was sixty-four years old.

Clarence was no longer the business tycoon and social lion he had been before the Crash, but the Mackay name was still one to conjure with, and his death prompted lengthy newspaper obituaries that rehearsed the Mackay legend and listed some of the dozens of exclusive sporting clubs to which he had belonged: The Racquet and

Tennis, Union, Metropolitan, Union League, Army and Navy, Riding, Knickerbocker, Brook, New York Yacht, Links, City, Turf and Field, Creek, Tuxedo, Meadow Brook, Piping Rock, Westminster Kennel, Sewanhaka, Corinthian Yacht, Nassau Country, Deepdale Golf, St. Andrew's Golf, and National Golf Links—to name a few. That Clarence Mackay had been Irving Berlin's father-in-law was mentioned only in passing, though it was always mentioned; it was one more illustrious (if unwanted) association that would forever attach itself to the Mackay name.

The funeral, which took place at St. Patrick's Cathedral in New York on November 15, was of a scale appropriate to a dignitary or head of state. Hundreds of spectators turned out, restrained by a police detail. Many of them were, of course, hoping to catch sight of his well-known daughter and her even more famous songwriter husband. They were not disappointed. Ellin attended, looking haggard and drawn, her face partially concealed under a flowing veil, her forearms and hands swathed in black velvet, in the company of Irving, who was suddenly looking older himself. To his dying day, Clarence had failed to effect a full reconciliation with Ellin, but no one doubted the depth of his daughter's grief at his passing.

The money Irving had once given Clarence suggested that the songwriter had forgiven his father-in-law, but Berlin never forgot, either. Years later, when opening a bottle from Mackay's wine cellar to share with a friend, Berlin remarked, "My father-in-law would turn over in his grave if he knew that two Jews were drinking his wine."

With Clarence gone, Harbor Hill's days were numbered; for his survivors it was a house filled with memories, many of them bitter. The process of closing down and selling off the contents of the immense mansion had actually begun five years earlier, as if in anticipation of the day when there would be no one willing or financially able to inhabit it. Even before Clarence's death the Metropolitan Museum of Art purchased Clarence's precious medieval artwork. The tapestries and some of the armor that had formerly graced the main gallery of Harbor Hill were now on permanent display in the museum. Later, the British National Gallery acquired various paintings in Clarence's collection, which were sold at bargain rates in a desperate grab for cash to reduce the estate's heavy debts.

The year after Clarence's death, the rest of the furnishings—the china, books, carpets, and artwork in whose midst Ellin had spent her youth—were sold at auction. The armor went on the block in London, fetching $5 million. The art dealer Duveen bought up the statuary; the remaining effects were offered to the American people at Gimbels department store in New York, scene of many Depression-era estate sales.

The Stanford White mansion, which had cost Clarence Mackay's father $6 million to construct, was later beset by vandals, who threatened to reduce it to ruin during World War II. "Police were shorthanded," explained Ellin's brother Willie, who observed Harbor Hill's disintegration from the gatekeeper's cottage, where he then lived. "I couldn't get a watchman for such a large acreage. I thought it wiser to have the place torn down than to try to build it up again." As executor of Clarence Mackay's estate, Willie was the one individual empowered to take this drastic step. He retained a firm known as Mar-Gus to do the job, but he had to wait several months until the wreckers could commence work. At the time, Mar-Gus was busy razing a half-dozen other mansions belonging to the same era as Harbor Hill, in the process bringing Long Island's Gilded Age to its conclusion.

Mar-Gus required six months to complete the demolition of Harbor Hill; there were 50,000 tons of granite slabs to remove, one hundred tons of cast iron. The mansion retained enough of an aura that the task of dismantling it attracted considerable newspaper publicity. "MACKAY'S 'HEARTBREAK HOUSE' FOLLOWS '90'S INTO OBLIVION," announced one headline. Another declared, "MACKAYS = MONEY, MANSION, MISERY" and included a facetious real estate listing:

> HOUSE FOR SALE: 50 rooms, 15 baths, 100 acres. Greenhouse, formal gardens. Equipment and outbuildings suitable for experimental farming. Original cost $2,000,000 but owner satisfied to get back 10% of investment.

Other families have risen and fallen as quickly as the House of Mackay, but few have experienced such great extremes. Clarence had been a religious man, and in his lifetime he had recognized something biblical about the starkness of the family's trajectory. "*I made me great works*," said the Preacher in *Ecclesiastes*. "*I builded me houses; I planted me vineyards: I made me gardens and orchards. . . . I got me servants and maidens, and had servants born in my house; also I had great possessions of great and small cattle. . . . I got me men singers and women singers, and the delights of the sons of men, as musical instruments, and that of all sorts. So I was great. . . . Then I looked on all the works that my hands had wrought and on the labor that I had labored to do: and behold, all was vanity and vexation of spirit, and there was no profit under the sun.*" Such were the sentiments with which Clarence, in his last bitter years, had become familiar.

Where Harbor Hill had stood, a suburban development took root, spreading across the hills that had once afforded Ellin and the rest of the family their glorious view of Manhattan, its distant spires looming in the mist like a city of dreams.

▪ ▪ ▪

Though Berlin was invigorated by his return to New York, the Broadway stage, from which he had been absent for over six years, was severely depressed. The uncertain state of the economy, the flight of talent to the movie industry, even the increased taxes for those in high-income brackets had all combined to dampen the enthusiasm of audiences and producers alike. Neglected by Berlin, Cole Porter, George Gershwin, and Jerome Kern, among other composers, the big, handsome Broadway musical was in danger of becoming a thing of the past.

Despite its recent setbacks, Broadway was still Broadway, as fabled an address in the American imagination as Wall Street or Pennsylvania Avenue—a place where a reputation could be made or retrieved or lost overnight. For Irving Berlin the stage remained the center of the action. It was passion, it was life, it was the unique proving ground that his restless temperament craved. And so, when a well-known lyricist named Buddy DeSylva approached him in the summer of 1939 about collaborating on a Broadway musical—something fun, light, and topical—Irving listened attentively. DeSylva, he knew, had grown up in a theatrical family; his father had worked in vaudeville before retiring from the stage to devote time to his family. Since college, the younger DeSylva had written lyrics for a number of famous collaborators, including Jolson, Gershwin, and Kern.

Irving initially refused to commit himself to DeSylva's proposal, though, because the producer had only vague ideas about the show. While the songwriter marked time, DeSylva turned his attention to other Broadway ventures. In December, his production of *DuBarry Was a Lady* brought Cole Porter, Ethel Merman, Bert Lahr, and a young Betty Grable to Broadway. Their vehicle—a high-society comedy—had been initially created for the movies. Spurned by Hollywood, the project succeeded on the stage.

As a result of this accomplishment, Berlin was inclined to look on the lyricist turned producer with new respect. Even better, DeSylva now had an idea for their show: it would be a satire of the corrupt politics associated with Huey Long, the Louisiana demagogue assassinated in 1935. This idea might have been another Hollywood reject, but it was a workable premise for Broadway, and the songwriter decided to accept DeSylva's invitation to compose the music and lyrics.

Once he had Berlin's commitment, DeSylva assembled the rest of the essential components of the show. Morrie Ryskind, a screenwriter better known for his work with the Marx Brothers, began work on the book, and the show underwent a transformation. It was now less about Huey Long and more about the comic efforts to entrap and embarrass a crusading senator in a "mythical kingdom" called Louisiana. The content of *Louisiana Purchase*, as Ryskind called the show, harked back to Berlin's earlier Broadway satires, especially *Face the Music*. Indeed, the Broadway stage hadn't advanced much beyond it during the songwriter's absence. At the same time, the form looked ahead to the Broadway of the coming decade, for in this production the songs and story were to be fully integrated. For Irving, who would always prefer the revue to all other theatrical genres, this newfangled form posed a distinct challenge. At the age of fifty-one he was prepared to attempt his first musical comedy.

The real pleasure of working on Broadway once again was the opportunity he had to become involved with the aspects of the production from which he had been excluded when he composed for the movies. "Pretty nearly all that's expected of a composer in films is to write five, six or seven songs for a show and then wait for the production to be put together," he explained. "While that is going on they don't need me. Then, when they run off the picture and I hear my songs, I see ways of improving them. But generally I don't get a chance to make changes, because retakes run into too much money. . . . So many processes come between you and the thing you've written. . . . Things are different in the theater. Here, after a show opens, you can still keep polishing, trying little twists you hadn't thought of before. You're close to a stage production. I like that feeling. Why, I walk up and down the rehearsal hall, and I begin to get ideas. Then I go home and sit up most of the night writing."

Berlin did more than polish songs; he functioned as a producer, assembling the most talented people he could find. He entrusted the task of orchestration to Robert Russell Bennett, with whom he had worked at RKO; George Balanchine was enlisted to stage several ballet sequences. Berlin also assumed responsibility for the casting of the show. In this capacity he introduced an unknown actress, Carol Bruce, to a brief, but impressive stardom, a feat that surprised no one more than Carol herself. Still, she looked like a star, tall and thin, with legs that went on forever, and a button of a nose: a dancer's physique. At the time Berlin discovered her, she was singing in a tiny nightclub in Newark, New Jersey. Irving was accompanied that evening by DeSylva, the show's producer, but all Carol could think about was the presence of Berlin. "A basket case of nerves," was how she described herself. "DeSylva didn't mean that much to me—he was a producer. But Irving Berlin!"

After she sang, Berlin invited her over to his table, and they chatted. "I didn't know I had the show that night," she reflected. "I thought it was: 'Don't call us. We'll call you.' " Despite her misgivings, she got the part, whereupon Irving, as she now called her new mentor, became a "surrogate father." And then it was her turn to experience Berlin, the insecure performer. "I came up to his office," she recalled, "still very terrified. Very much in awe of him. With that terrible voice he proceeded to play the score of *Louisiana Purchase* for me, as we tried to establish the key I would sing it in. I spent more than an hour with him at his strange, tinny piano, with his strange, bastardized way of playing and singing. But he was certainly able to convey what he wanted."

Irving continued to hover protectively around his new discovery throughout the rehearsal period. His attentiveness indicated that he had developed something approaching a crush on Carol Bruce. He was, after all, embarking on middle age, and she was a lovely young actress in his thrall. But it was not part of Irving's nature to act out his yearning, however much he felt drawn to her. There were flowers and hugs and cozy chats with Carol—and that was all. It was a romance without sex. The relationship provided an outlet he needed at this time in his life, but there was no question that he remained devoted to Ellin. He would let nothing tarnish his reputation.

He channeled the affection he felt for Carol into the music he wrote for her. He assigned her the two strongest numbers in the show: the title song, "Louisiana Purchase," and a novelty tune called "The Lord Done Fixed Up My Soul." "He was there every minute, every day," she remembered. "As we were getting near to the out-of-town tryouts, he said to me, 'You're going to be a star.' " His prediction proved to be correct. Shortly before the opening night in New York, *Life* magazine came around to do a feature story on Bruce, a star-is-born type of thing. The magazine's reporters and photographers spent a week with her; they took her to a baseball game, they spent time with her at home, they interviewed her mother, and, of course, they photographed her in *Louisiana Purchase*.

Irving continued to lavish attention on Bruce right through opening night, May 28, 1940, at the Imperial Theatre, when the young actress narrowly avoided disaster. She sang her torch song, "The Lord Done Fixed Up My Soul," wearing a costume with an elastic bodice. As she exited the stage she heard the stage manager screaming, about what, she wasn't certain. Her elaborate costume had been caught on a hook, and the next thing she knew, the hook was lifting her into the flies. At that instant, a spotlight turned on her, and the audience was treated to the sight of an acutely uncomfortable Carol Bruce dangling from a hook several feet above the stage.

Irving took the mishap in stride. Encountering Bruce backstage, he asked, "How high would you like to go?" She was too upset to answer.

At the curtain call, Irving and Eddie Cantor, who also attended the opening night, mounted the stage of the Imperial Theatre and asked Bruce to come out by herself. "They flanked me and took my hands," she remembered. "Irving addressed the audience and said, 'I want to tell you all about this young lady. I'm so proud of her. I discovered her, and she exceeded our wildest expectations, and she's gonna be a big star.' I was in an absolute daze."

Berlin and Bruce were not alone in their confidence concerning *Louisiana Purchase*. The musical's reception benefited from the paucity of excitement on Broadway. Reviewers rushed forward to praise the return of Irving Berlin and to canonize its cast, including Victor Moore as the crusading but hapless Southern senator and Vera Zorina as "a bit of trim man-bait." Despite the display of enthusiasm, purists noted that the show, though highly professional and entertaining, lacked a certain conviction. In the pages of *The New York Times*, Brooks Atkinson damned the effort with faint praise: "After an absence of seven years, Mr. Berlin has returned to remind us that he can still write songs without bursting into a fever of perspiration. . . . 'Louisiana Purchase' is a gay, simple, friendly musical comedy with the accomplished ease of a thoroughbred." The problem, according to Atkinson, was that the show lacked the bite of those Broadway satires of the early years of the Depression, especially Gershwin's *Of Thee I Sing*. "Mr. Berlin and Mr. Ryskind have ducked the satiric implications of their topic," the man from the *Times* concluded. "But they have succeeded in putting together a good-humored and enjoyable show."

Irving had demonstrated that his years of involvement with the movie business hadn't dulled his edge; he could still write for the stage, and beyond that, he demonstrated his belated mastery of the art of composing an integrated score for a musical. Yet *Louisiana Purchase*—though it ran for a year on Broadway and was later made into a successful movie starring Bob Hope—lacked the hair-raising resonance of the songwriter's best work. In the end, *Louisiana Purchase* was "merely" a professional effort.

After the opening, Irving suddenly curtailed the attention he had bestowed on his young discovery, Carol Bruce. Now that she was in the first flush of fame, she no longer required it. She could measure her reputation in terms of the magazine covers carrying her picture. "The day the *Life* magazine story came out," she said, "there was a matinée of *Louisiana Purchase*. I got on the trolley—there were still trolley cars at the time—to ride downtown from my apartment at 78th Street to the theater at 45th Street. I didn't take a taxi, I wasn't making that kind of money, only $100 a week, even though I was a big star.

As I was sitting there, we passed a newsstand, and I suddenly saw the cover. I don't know how many newsstands we passed, and *Life* was always prominently displayed. I started screaming, 'That's me!' And the people sitting next to me looked at me like I was mad. That's when Zorina started being cruel to me."

Carol believed that Vera Zorina, who was a much bigger name, regarded all the attention received by the naïve young actress with a jealous eye. "I had to point out to her that every season there's a new discovery," she said. "Last season, *she'd* been on the cover of *Life*. Come on, give me a break, honey." Before the *Life* cover appeared, she recalled, "I went home after the show. My mother would make me take a taxi, then, not a trolley car. And when I got home, I would have an apple and a glass of warm milk, and my mother would tuck me in." After the cover, "I began to have important beaus. I began to be taken to the Stork Club and El Morocco."

Although *Louisiana Purchase* was successful enough to spur Berlin into thinking of another Broadway musical, he lacked collaborators. After the show Buddy DeSylva had immediately become involved with another production, Cole Porter's *Panama Hattie*, leaving Irving to fend for himself. Stranded, the songwriter turned his attention to "God Bless America," a song that had acquired a life of its own. In the year and a half since Kate Smith had introduced it to the American people, it had become something of a national institution. On Memorial Day 1939, it was played at Ebbets Field in Brooklyn, home of the Dodgers; the crowd rose and took off their hats, as they would for the national anthem. That same year, Kate Smith herself breathed new life into "God Bless America" when she sang it at the New York World's Fair. Furthermore, the sheet music had sold over 400,000 copies, and the royalties exceeded $40,000.

Now, in the summer of 1940, the Republicans negotiated with Berlin to feature it at their national convention; the Democrats quickly adopted the same idea for theirs. Though Berlin favored the Republican cause, he could hardly refuse the same privilege to the president's political party. "The Democratic Party is following the Democratic process," he explained, "by complying with more than 10,000 requests from people all over the country." Democrats and Republicans seeking office were not the only ones wishing to ally themselves with Berlin's anthem. A correspondent for the Milwaukee *Deutsche Zeitung*, Elizabeth Schwerin, was moved to translate it into German so that beleaguered German Americans, fearing they would be excluded from the American mainstream, might "manifest their loyalty to the United States." "*Herr, scheutz' Amerika!*" her version began, "*Land meiner Treu.*' "

Recognizing that it would be unseemly for him to continue earning royalties from a song whose primary purpose was patriotic rather than commercial, Berlin established a trust, the God Bless America Fund, to distribute the money earned by the song to charity. This was not a popular idea with his business partner, Saul Bornstein, who opposed the idea of giving any money away, but Berlin's will prevailed. In his selection of the God Bless America Fund's three trustees, the songwriter displayed a masterful knack for public relations. There was Theodore Roosevelt, Jr., whose name was patriotism itself; the boxer Gene Tunney, whose greatest appeal was to the masses; and, as chairman of the trust, his old friend Herbert Swope, whose reputation guaranteed agreeable coverage by the press. There was also a careful religious balance in evidence, for Tunney was Catholic, Swope Jewish, and Roosevelt Protestant. His first inclination was to donate the proceeds from the song to the Red Cross, but Swope recommended the Boy and Girl Scouts; Irving agreed. Over the years, the income from this song would amount to $250,000—all donated to the Boy and Girl Scouts.

This seemingly unassailable patriotic gesture actually enmeshed Berlin in controversy. He discovered that transferring his song from the sphere of show business to politics had its penalties as well as its satisfactions. In place of critics, he acquired political adversaries. "God Bless America" had long been resented by the Left, who found the lyrics jingoistic and presumptuous—Why should God bless America? What about the separation of church and state? Then there was thunder on the Right as well. Two weeks after Berlin announced the creation of the God Bless America Fund, the Reverend Dr. Edgar Franklin Romig, pastor of the West End Collegiate Reformed Church, located right on Broadway in New York City, angrily denounced the anthem in his sermon and generated headlines that threatened a public relations disaster for Irving Berlin. *The New York Times* informed its readers: "SONGS SUCH AS 'GOD BLESS AMERICA' SCORED BY DR. ROMIG AS 'MAWKISH' AND AS 'DOGGEREL.' "

> There is a strange and specious substitute for religion held by many in times of crisis like the present [Dr. Romig warned his congregation]. It is compounded of excessive emotion, wishful thinking, and a facile evading of the rudimentary disciplines . . . and finds its expression in the mawkish iteration of snatches of [a] song like 'God Bless America.'

Dr. Romig's scholarly rhetoric concealed a menacing subtext. A reaction against the song set in, based on the belief that a Tin Pan Alley tunesmith—a mere creature of commerce—was not fit to compose the nation's unofficial anthem. Its critics were also upset that Irving Berlin, an immigrant and a Jew rather than a "real," native-born American, lacked the requisite pedigree to compose such a song.

On Berlin's behalf, Herbert Swope instantly responded to Dr. Romig's attack with an angry letter to *The New York Times*. To Swope, Berlin's ancestry, rather than disqualifying him from writing such a song, was actually his chief recommendation. "As a child in arms he was a fugitive from persecution in Russia," Swope reminded his readers, "finding in America a haven of refuge and hope." Berlin, for his part, repeatedly stated that he had no intention of usurping "The Star-Spangled Banner" as the official national anthem, though many would have been happy to retire that venerable, if unsingable strain in favor of the simpler and more immediate "God Bless America." Both Swope and Dr. Romig, though opposed in all other matters, were correct on one point. "God Bless America" revealed that patriotism was Irving Berlin's true religion. It evoked the same emotional response in him that conventional religious belief summoned in others; it was his rock.

In the politically turbulent summer of 1940, Irving faced political controversy at home, as well. Entering her late thirties, Ellin was finally coming into her own. Now that her three children were older, she had resumed her writing career, publishing short stories at widely spaced intervals and contemplating a novel, eventually titled *Land I Have Chosen*, dedicated to extolling freedom of belief in the United States. Her convictions led her to become an ardent supporter of

President Roosevelt in his campaign for an unprecedented third term in the White House.

Her husband, meanwhile, was of a more conservative turn of mind. He'd endorsed Roosevelt's New Deal because it was the loyal and patriotic thing to do, but at the same time he held the Democrats responsible for raising taxes. On September 5 the Tax Appeals Board in Washington, D.C., decided that Berlin must pay slightly more than $11,000 in back taxes that he still owed on his earnings from *Top Hat*. The songwriter so resented the outcome of the case that he gave vent to his feelings in an unusual lament, "I Paid My Income Tax Today," in which he bewailed his having to render unto Caesar that which was Caesar's. It wasn't the money involved so much as the principle at stake. Irving had no wish to shirk his patriotic duty—several years hence he would donate not thousands but millions of dollars to the war effort in a staggering display of generosity—but the deed would come about as a result of his own decision, not that of a court. In the wake of this galling tax case, Berlin wouldn't have been at all disappointed if Roosevelt's opponent, Wendell Willkie, won the election.

Irving's right-wing tendencies failed to influence Ellin, however. She actively campaigned for Roosevelt, occasionally leaving the security of her apartment for the hazards of open-air political speaking. One afternoon, she left her home in her chauffeured limousine with a stepladder in the trunk. The car pulled up at Lexington and 51st Street. Ellin got out; retrieved the stepladder; mounted it; declared, "Roosevelt is the man we all want and whom America needs"; and climbed down, knowing that she had done her duty.

Before she could pack up the stepladder and drive away, however, a taxi driver took over her rostrum to voice his support, which in turn attracted another cabbie—a Republican, this time—who shouted, "You goddamned Red." By now, Ellin had taken refuge in her limousine, as the traffic built and the contretemps escalated. Eventually the Republican antagonist left the scene, Ellin fetched the stepladder, and headed home to reflect on the hazards entailed by the exercise of her right to free speech.

In addition to her innocuous support of the Democratic party, Ellin joined a more committed organization, the Committee to Defend America by Aiding the Allies. In a radio debate on the question, "Is propaganda endangering the United States?" Ellin, representing the committee, attacked a recent book, *The Wave of the Future*, written by Anne Morrow Lindbergh, wife of the celebrated aviator. Both Lindbergh and Berlin had been icons of the 1920s; that the wife of one hero was now attacking the political beliefs of the wife of another added unusual pungency to the debate. Ellin—along with many others—took strenuous exception to the book's anti-democratic stance. As far as Ellin was concerned, this was an indefensible position, and in the course of the debate, she described Anne Lindbergh as a "sensitive and gentle woman who has been bewildered and frightened by skillful German propaganda. . . . No one can be blamed for being frightened, but it is heart-breaking to find an American woman burying Democracy in quotation marks. She speaks of it tenderly, but she speaks of it as though it were dead. . . . That is not true. Democracy is alive here—it is alive in England. The Nazis have disguised old-fashioned tyranny to look like something new. They have touched the heart of a poet like Mrs. Lindbergh."

In conclusion Ellin insisted that Anne Morrow Lindbergh was virtually a willing dupe of the Nazis. "We must not romanticize the Nazis," she chastened. "They are a group of unscrupulous militants who mean to conquer the world. That is not what I say. That is what they say—'Today we rule Germany, tomorrow the World.' "

Ellin's deeply principled beliefs extended to religion as well as politics. And her insistence on them raised the eyebrows of her husband's closest friend. "I am due back in New York for a strange christening at the hearth in the house of the Irving Berlins," wrote Alexander Woollcott on December 9. "He was brought up as a Jew and she as a Catholic." Now their youngest daughter was being raised as a Protestant. "The youngest of their three daughters—an enchanting child named Elizabeth Berlin—is to be started on her way by a ceremony at which Alice Duer Miller and I will stand as sponsors. I do not know Mrs. Miller's plans but I am wishing that all the days of her life the child may have courage." As a christening present, Woollcott, being a dedicated bibliophile, bestowed a "two-volume edition of the Oxford Dictionary bound in Morocco and stamped with her name in gold."

This ceremony meant there were now three faiths in the Berlin family, one for the mother, another for the father, and a third for the children: proof of Ellin's determination to compensate for the religious intolerance to which she had been subjected as a child.

To Irving, religion—unlike patriotism—was never a matter of great moment, but Ellin's ecumenical spirit took hold of him, as well. Having failed to assemble a worthy successor to *Louisiana Purchase* on Broadway, his thoughts turned once again to the movies. Irving stockpiled ideas as well as songs for shows in his "trunk," and one of his favorites, one that he'd been trying for nearly twenty years to mount, was a loosely structured revue about a successful but lazy entertainer who retires from the New York stage to manage a country inn open only for the holidays. The unusual lodge and the show built around it would naturally be called *Holiday Inn.*

In the face of the threat of war, holidays acquired a new significance; they affirmed the values of hearth, home, and country. A traditionalist, Berlin sensed that people would cling to holidays at a time when the nation's well-being was imperiled. Conceived as escapism, *Holiday Inn* took on a new function; like "God Bless America," it served as a vehicle for endorsing the American way of life at a time when all hell was breaking loose in Europe. *Holiday Inn* was still entertainment; no thought of politics intruded on its timeless appeal. But the threat of war, and what war would mean for the nation, informed every aspect of the movie.

The notion was tailor-made to feature his songs, of course: one for each holiday. He already had "Easter Parade" to his credit, and he made short work of devising melodies to go with other national holidays. There was "Let's Say It with Firecrackers" for the Fourth of July, as well as "Plenty to Be Thankful For," and "Let's Start the New Year Right." However, the song for Christmas—the most emotional and revered holiday in the entire calendar—eluded him. The problem, as he conceived it, was not that he was born a Jew and had remained one, at least nominally. He, too, had nostalgic memories of childhood Christmases on the Lower East Side, and especially of the Christmas tree belonging to his neighbors, the O'Haras. He, too, shared in its charms and warmth. No, the problem was that the Christmas song, as the high point of the show, had to be better than good; it had to be great in the way the "Alexander's Ragtime Band" was great or "God Bless America" was great: simple, universal, and unforgettable.

When the time came to write the song, Irving recalled that being caught in Los Angeles during the holiday season had made him nostalgic for the Christmases of his youth. The palm trees and heat only made him yearn for cold weather and snow. What he wanted, what *everybody* wanted, was a white Christmas; and he designed his chorus to illustrate that universal longing. He made the chorus as simple as he dared. With a subject as potent and evocative as Christmas, a few well-chosen words and images spoke volumes. His show business instincts were in complete command; he never paused to ponder the irony of a cantor's son writing an anthem about a day celebrating the birth of Jesus.

The result of Irving's labors, carried out at night, as usual, filled him with tremendous excitement. It was, he told himself, a "round" song, his term for the rare tune that came to him effortlessly and fully formed. "We working composers all too often, in the interest of expediency, sharpen our pencils, get out that square sheet of paper and become too slick," he later explained. "Those forced efforts are 'square' songs. But sometimes a song is a natural. We may start it to order for a specific scene or show, but our subconscious beings go to work and the song is just there." And "White Christmas" was as natural and "round" a song as he'd ever written.

It was morning when he finished the song. Traffic urgently churned below his window, and in the distance, boats traversed the East River. Instead of going to sleep, he went directly to his office, where his employees gaped at the sight of the boss appearing first thing on a Monday morning. Without pausing to acknowledge them, he found Helmy Kresa, his transcriber, and proclaimed, "I want you to take down a song I wrote over the weekend. Not only is it the best song *I* ever wrote, it's the best song *anybody* ever wrote."

Accustomed to his boss's penchant for boasting, Helmy thought: Oh, you conceited ass.

Irving sat down at the piano to play the song and, in his fashion, sing it. As Helmy wrote down the notes, he revised his opinion. "As he started to sing, I knew right away that the way he juxtaposed the warmth of Southern California with the cold snow would make it a hit," Helmy recalled, "and when he sang the chorus, I knew it really was the greatest song ever written. I was as thrilled as he was." Of course, the real work on the tune was just beginning; the two of them spent weeks, off and on, refining and polishing it, with Irving constantly urging, "Helmy, keep it simple," but neither of them doubted the song would become one of Berlin's most popular efforts.

▪ ▪ ▪

Score and scenario in hand, Berlin struck a deal with Paramount to make the movie of *Holiday Inn*, but before he could report for work at the studio, a pressing matter held him in New York. The tax case of Joe Schenck, after months of preparation, had finally come to trial on March 5.

After proceeding quietly for several weeks, the trial broke into the headlines on the last day of March, when Schenck's lawyers mounted an emotional defense of their client. Schenck had been careless with money all his life, but he and his lawyers had prepared carefully for this legal contest. They were able to field an impressive array of character witnesses who testified to Joe Schenck's integrity. Charlie Chaplin spoke movingly of the embattled early days of United Artists, when he and other film stars brought in Schenck to help settle disputes. The chief justice of the California Supreme Court, Phil S. Gibson, expressed his "good opinion" of Schenck, no matter what controversy now engulfed him. And finally, Irving Berlin took the stand and said that, he, too, had never heard a word spoken against his dear friend Joe Schenck, or his imaginative accountant, Joseph Moskowitz. As the testimonials continued, Schenck sat motionless, feeling his confidence in his eventual acquittal steadily increase. On his lawyer's advice, he did not take the stand in his own defense.

Ignoring the fame and credentials of the defense witnesses, the young prosecutor, Mathias F. Correa, hammered away at discrepancies in Schenck's tax returns—or lack of same. Little details proved more telling than some of the large amounts of money discussed, details such as Moskowitz's deducting over five hundred dollars for Schenck's personal barber, or seventeen dollars for his cigars. Not many people could afford to spend over five hundred dollars a year on a barber, as the members of the jury noted, their resentment against Schenck mounting.

In the end the government made its case. Moskowitz, convicted on one count, was sentenced to a year and a day and fined $10,000.

And Schenck was convicted on two of the four charges brought against him. He, too, was fined $10,000—and sentenced to three years in jail.

"It is not always greatness that takes a person to the top," Schenck said later. "It is a gambling spirit. I used every bit of my ability at dangerous times while abler men slowed down at the dangerous curves." And he always remained grateful for Berlin's show of support: "In the three words that one of my dearest friends, Irving Berlin, used for the title of a song, God Bless America!"

Flag waving aside, the verdict demonstrated that Irving's testifying on Schenck's behalf was not the songwriter's finest hour. Not even Berlin's sterling reputation could salvage Joe Schenck. Irving had testified out of loyalty to his boyhood friend, loyalty that had blinded him to Schenck's blatant dishonesty.

▪ ▪ ▪

At the conclusion of the trial, Berlin returned to Hollywood for the making of *Holiday Inn.* At this stage in his career, he had amassed sufficient clout to assemble the creative team he wanted. He recruited Mark Sandrich, who knew better than any other director how to stage Berlin's songs for the camera; Bing Crosby, to play the charmingly befuddled innkeeper; and Fred Astaire (this time without Ginger Rogers), as Crosby's rival in love.

Driven by his ever-present desire for control, Berlin had won the right to approve every note recorded for the film's score, but that responsibility entailed his prolonged presence on the West Coast. The music director for *Holiday Inn*, the man whose orchestrations were contractually obligated to please Berlin, was Walter Scharf. Like the songwriter's other musical collaborators, Scharf was impressed by the amount of energy and anxiety Irving expended during the final stages of preparation, especially for "White Christmas." "It was as if he were going to have a baby when he was working on that song," Scharf remembered. "I never saw a man so wrapped up in himself. It was all a tremendously traumatic experience for him." The phone would ring, Irving didn't hear it. The sun would rise and set, and Irving didn't notice time passing. Nor did he break for meals, preferring to sustain himself on chewing gum and cigarettes.

Berlin then went over the song with Crosby. "Of course, he's not the one to throw his arms about and get excited," Berlin said later. "When he read the song he just took his pipe out of his mouth and said to me: 'You don't have to worry about this one, Irving.' "

The morning Crosby was scheduled to sing "White Christmas" before the camera, Sandrich and Scharf, aware that their composer had exhausted himself, advised him to get some rest. No need to be on the set until the cameras were ready to roll, they told him. Irving agreed, but he couldn't make himself stay away. "Irving," Scharf said, "don't bother to stick around. We won't be ready for quite some time."

"I won't get in the way," he promised.

The playback started, and Crosby began to produce the silvery tones for which he was famed. As Crosby sang, Scharf happened to notice that one or two of the flats in the background seemed a little out of place. He stole around the back of the set to investigate, and who should he find, crouching low, trying to conceal himself, but Irving Berlin, unable to let go of his creation—his precious song.

"I'm sorry," he said to Scharf, who realized he had no choice but to yield to Berlin's desire to involve himself with every aspect of the film, from writing the songs to sitting in on the story conferences to discussing choreography with Astaire.

Even as Berlin immersed himself in the minutiae of *Holiday Inn*, he brooded on the loss of momentum in his career. *Holiday Inn* would not be released until the following year—another instance of the infernal slowness in the making of motion pictures. "I wrote *Holiday Inn* in 1941 and it wasn't until 1942 or later that people saw it. . . . All that time the songs are hidden away and you have no way of knowing whether the songs will be accepted or rejected. There is even the possibility that someone may duplicate one of your best ideas in the meantime," he complained. "At the end of the year, perhaps longer, they'll tell you how much gross business your picture did and then you will know whether it is a success or not." Meanwhile, another Broadway season was under way, *Louisiana Purchase* had closed, and Berlin had nothing to succeed it. At this juncture, a studio executive happened to mention the name of a hit play in New York. "Whaddya mean?" Berlin snapped.

"What are you getting mad at me for?" the executive said. "It's no competition for you. It isn't even a musical."

"Too bad it isn't one of my shows," he said, as he stormed away.

Irving remained in a foul temper long after he returned to New York. His outbursts became more intense, more at odds with his professionalism and perfectionism. They were a highly unattractive but persistent symptom of the impossible demands he made on himself and the corrosive effects of fame on his personality. The unlikely victim of his next tantrum was the renowned violinist Fritz Kreisler.

Like a number of other virtuosos such as Jascha Heifitz, Kreisler occasionally found time to compose popular songs—"Stars in My Eyes" being the best known—as well as two operettas. Coming across another unpublished song by Kreisler, Berlin decided he had to publish it; no matter how well or badly the song sold, Kreisler's name alone would add measureless prestige to Berlin's music publishing company. A business relationship with the great Kreisler had the class Irving craved.

Impatient as always, Berlin tracked down Kreisler, who was on vacation with his wife, Harriet, in a guest house in the Berkshire Mountains in Massachusetts. A man of polite behavior and fixed habits, Kreisler and his wife came down at the beginning of each day to take breakfast in the dining room with the other guests. One morning, however, Kreisler appeared in the dining room alone and out of sorts. "I've just had a terrible experience," he confessed to another guest sharing the table. After hesitating, Kreisler continued. "I've been on the telephone—a call from New York City from one of your famous song composers. He said that he wanted to buy one of my songs, and I thanked him and said, 'Oh, no, I couldn't do that.' Imagine asking such a thing! Finally, he was offering me fifteen hundred dollars."

It wasn't the generous proposal that had upset Kreisler; it was the famous man's profanity. "The dreadful language he used was so awful," Kreisler lamented. "My mother would not have allowed such a man into our house. No one would have dared to use such words. He began to curse and swear at me. It was really very upsetting." And then quietly, Kreisler added, "The man's name is Irving Berlin. I'm sure you know some of his famous songs."

Kreisler then excused himself, having barely touched his breakfast.

One of the few colleagues to whom Irving remained civil during this stressful period was his best friend and unofficial publicist, Alexander Woollcott, who continued adroitly to ingratiate himself. Over the past decade, Woollcott had moved gradually from journalism to radio, where he hosted two popular programs, "The Town Crier" and "The Early Bookworm." He adored the celebrity that the medium conferred on him, and his signature opening—"This is Woollcott speaking"—became familiar to millions of Americans.

During this troubled interlude in Berlin's career Woollcott did him the favor of organizing a radio tribute to the songwriter, complete with a full choir singing "God Bless America." Even better, he carefully discussed every detail of the tribute in advance with Berlin, so that there would be no surprises; when the time for the broadcast came, all Irving had to do was relax and enjoy the show—which was precisely what he did.

Their friendship renewed, Woollcott invited the Berlins for a long overdue visit to his retreat on Neshobe Island, Lake Bomoseen, Vermont, in July. It was here that the last vestiges of the conviviality that had once marked the Algonquin Round Table could be found. Woollcott's guests played the same distinctive version of croquet that they had shortly after the Great War, only now the balls often disappeared into the woods or the sparkling waters of Lake Bomoseen.

During the long July weekend, the Berlins stayed in Woollcott's comfortable stone "clubhouse," and they cheerfully submitted to the regimen their host prescribed for all his guests: a wake-up swim at sunrise, games in the morning, work in the afternoon, and glorious conversation until late into the night. But all was not well, for, as Irving discovered, his friend was a sick man. Woollcott had recently triumphed in *The Man Who Came to Dinner*, and once the Broadway run ended, he undertook an exhausting national tour. Shortly after arriving in San Francisco, he suffered a heart attack, and the rest of the performances were canceled. Since then, he had spent much of his time at his Vermont retreat, trying to recuperate.

The obese critic's failing health—combined with ominous political developments in Europe—put a damper on the anticipated mood of conviviality. Irving wanted to enjoy himself, but war appeared inevitable and his friend looked deathly ill. The stay would be their last extended period of time together. For all three—Woollcott, Irving, and Ellin—the charmed weekend was the last idyll before war finally did overtake them, the nation, and the world.

■ □ ■ □ ■ □ ■

CHAPTER 16

Minstrel of War

Irving Berlin was fifty-three when President Roosevelt declared war on Japan. By Tin Pan Alley standards, the songwriter hovered on the verge of extreme old age. Had he never written another film score, another Broadway show, another lyric, another *note*, his reputation as the leading popular American songwriter was secure. The list of his enduring creations stretched on and on. "Alexander's Ragtime Band," "God Bless America," "Puttin' on the Ritz," "All Alone," "Remember," "Cheek to Cheek," and "Let's Face the Music and Dance" defined the nation's musical language.

If Berlin had decided to retire about now, people would have understood completely. How nice to leave cold, abrasive New York and sit out the war in Hollywood, holed up at the Beverly Hills Hotel, playing gin rummy and chasing starlets in his spare time. *Holiday Inn*, containing that Christmas song of which he was so fond, would be released the following summer, and he would be able to sit back and watch the money roll in.

Though Hollywood would shortly be teeming with poolside patriots, he could always sing "God Bless America" to the troops now and then. He'd published only half a dozen songs in 1941, but, as their titles indicate, each of them illustrated a war-related theme: "Angels of Mercy," "Any Bonds Today," "Arms for the Love of America," "A Little Church in England," "When That Man Is Dead and Gone," and finally and most plaintively, "When This Crazy World Is Sane Again." No one could say Irving Berlin hadn't done his bit.

Always the zealot when it came to work, Irving had a different notion of what he should be doing with himself at this juncture in his life. The prospect of war sent a shudder of dread through the American people, but it also created a thrill of excitement. Berlin the showman responded to that quickening of the national pulse. "Songs make history and history makes songs," he said. "It needed a French Revolution to make a 'Marsellaise' and the bombardment of Fort McHenry to give voice to 'The Star-Spangled Banner.' " The war simplified everything for him. Now he knew exactly what to do: restage the surprise hit of his youth, *Yip! Yip! Yaphank.*

Berlin was a quarter of a century older now, and he told himself that this time he knew what to expect when mounting an all-soldier show. "When we rehearsed it," he said of the earlier effort, "we were completely unself-conscious because we hadn't a notion of its being at all important." Now, however, he "set out from the start to do something big." In the process, he fulfilled the role, dimly glimpsed a quarter of a century earlier, then forgotten, and then suddenly revived, of a national minstrel. Previously, he had sung of personal dramas—romance and woes and funny little incidents—but now he struggled to give a voice to national and even international issues, to locate himself in history and to make a place for himself in what Henry Luce termed "The American Century."

To set the wheels in motion, Berlin called General George Marshall in Washington to propose his new all-soldier show. Irving was never shy about using a telephone. The instrument, with its ability to narrow any business negotiation to a brief, intense one-on-one, suited him perfectly. He would call anyone, and everyone took his calls, because everyone was delighted to receive a call from the great Irving Berlin; General Marshall was no exception. And when they met soon after, Berlin was gratified to note that on the wall of his office, Marshall had a portrait of General Bell, who had overseen *Yip! Yip! Yaphank.* General Marshall approved Berlin's plan to stage a new morale-boosting revue on Broadway, and the production was under way. Irving promptly decided to call it *This Is the Army.* And in case the Army didn't like it, he had another title in reserve, *This Is the Navy.* Or the *Air Corps.* Whatever. But his heart was with the Army.

Among the earliest members of the energetic young team that Berlin assembled to stage the show was Bob Lissauer. Only twenty-two years old, he had already embarked on a career as a music publisher. Lissauer scarcely knew Berlin; the two had only a nodding acquaintance formed at Lindy's, the show-business restaurant, where they were regular customers. When war was declared, Lissauer was classified 1A, and shortly after that he received a call from Berlin's secretary, Mynna Granat, who said her boss wanted to see him right away at the office, then at 799 Seventh Avenue.

"I hear you're 1A," Berlin said when they met.

"That's right."

"How'd you like to enlist?"

Lissauer explained that he planned to enlist or be drafted.

"Well, I'm putting together a show," Berlin said, "and we're going to handle our own copyrights, set it up as a dummy corporation called 'This Is the Army, Inc.' The Army cannot hold copyrights. We're going to have a company of three hundred soldiers—singers, dancers, actors, musicians, orchestra, stage hands, designers, and everything else. And we need our own music publishing detachment. We've got to get some people in there who specialize in music publishing, and I know what you've managed to do in a short time. All the money is going to Army Emergency Relief."

When Lissauer realized that Berlin wanted him to help manage the music publishing arm of this vast enterprise, he was flattered and relieved. Here was deliverance from the humdrum and possible danger of routine Army life. "You won't be in charge because I've got a lieutenant, Walter Schumann," Berlin explained. "You will be under him, but chances are you'll be a corporal. If you enlist, I will arrange for you to go directly to Camp Upton where the show will be forming, and then we'll come to New York, and we'll do the show for a few weeks." Lissauer enlisted on May 27, 1942, and reported to Camp Upton the next day.

The next person to feel the force of Berlin's personality was Ezra Stone, whom the songwriter chose for the pivotal job of stage director of *This Is the Army*. The twenty-four-year-old Stone was nationally known as the star of the radio program "The Aldrich Family," which had begun life as a Broadway hit in 1938. Most Americans could give a fair imitation of the character who played his mother calling out, "Hen*ry!* Henry Ald*rich!*" While continuing his radio career, Stone made his debut as a director on Broadway in 1939 with a farce called *See My Lawyer*, produced by George Abbott.

When he met Berlin, Stone—a serious, heavyset man—was already in the Army, engaged in morale work. Sensing leadership potential in Stone, the songwriter did his best to inspire him with a sense of mission. "I got the full blast of his charm—very enthusiastic, very warm, very gracious. I was really snowed by him," Stone recalled. Berlin was particularly impressed that Stone had already been assigned to identify potential talent among the inductees and could remove them at will from the combat divisions. "This," said Stone, "Berlin regarded as very important for his use, because the head count was paramount. There had to be three hundred men or more."

Berlin anticipated composing the complete score for the revue at his customary breakneck pace: one month. And he planned to hold rehearsals at Camp Upton, where he had overseen the creation of *Yip! Yip! Yaphank* a generation before. Once rehearsals began, Stone and Berlin were thrown together as weekday residents of Camp Upton. "On Sunday nights I would pick Berlin up at his house on the East Side," Stone said of the arrangement, "and we'd drive out together in my car. We'd spend the week at Upton and leave on Friday afternoon. So I was able to spend my weekends at home, and so was Berlin."

The building in which they worked was called, simply, "T-11." It was an old Civilian Conservation Corps barracks; at one end there was a large common room with a stone fireplace. "That's where Berlin wanted his special piano," Stone said. "It was right next to the latrine, which had a hot water tank that Berlin loved to lean against to warm his back. As he was doing this one night, he said that he could easily be a Bowery bum and let his beard grow. He hadn't shaved that morning, and he was in that kind of mood."

"T-11" quickly became the scene of round-the-clock activity. Private John Koenig, a prominent New York designer, came in each day and worked on the plans for the set. Milton Rosenstock, the musical director, had his room, as well. Brooklyn born "Rosie" had been a child prodigy on the clarinet; he'd studied at the Juilliard School of Music, and he was listed in *Who's Who* by the time he turned twenty-one. He was now a twenty-three-year-old private and grateful to Berlin for giving him the opportunity to continue his musical interests, even in time of war.

After enlisting the talents of Stone, Rosenstock, and Lissauer, Berlin persuaded one other young soldier to become the company's first sergeant. The position required considerable patience and a sense of tact, which, fortunately, Berlin's candidate possessed. His name was Alan Anderson, and he was the son of playwright Maxwell Anderson, who was then at the zenith of his career. The younger Anderson's theatrical pedigree doubtless carried some weight with Berlin, for Maxwell Anderson was synonymous with Broadway's striving for artistic respectability.

From the outset, Berlin, always the showman and never more so than when in uniform, impressed Anderson with the importance of maintaining appearances. "He insisted right from the beginning that we had to be a good military outfit in terms of drilling and looking happy when we were marching around New York," Anderson said of Berlin, "because everywhere we went, we were three hundred Army men, and if we looked like a shambles it would have been a horror for the show. The Army would have dumped it if we hadn't been good salesmen."

Thus far, Berlin's choice of personnel relied heavily on professional entertainers; working on *This Is the Army* would be, for them, an extension of their civilian careers. He displayed real daring, however, in his decision to include black performers in the unit. At the time, the armed forces were segregated, and as a result of Berlin's insistence, the *This Is the Army* unit became the only integrated company in uniform. This extraordinary gesture derived not so much from Berlin's social beliefs as from his show business background and savvy. In his show business milieu, of course, Blacks had long been stars, popular with both black and white audiences. By integrating the revue, Berlin was simply importing familiar conventions into the Army. However, he was not blind to appearances; he knew his gesture would be progressive, at the least, and probably controversial. But he believed in the armed forces as the great leveler in American society. In his youth he had seen the Great War reduce barriers separating Jewish, German, Irish, and Italian ethnic groups in the United States. Yet Blacks had been excluded from this quiet revolution; even in *Yip! Yip! Yaphank*, the black numbers had been performed by whites in blackface in the manner of a minstrel show. His insistence on including Blacks in *This Is the Army* suggested that he believed the Second World War might do for them what the Great War had done for other minorities.

From the start, integrating the company posed problems with the rigid Army bureaucracy. "The black guys had the problem of where they would live, how they would train," Anderson said. "We had an officer who said they should have a platoon of their own. We didn't want to do that, but this guy insisted on it. So we did it that way. They had a couple of good sergeants in their group, and they were a very snappy platoon, actually a small platoon, a squad."

Eventually, black and white members of the *This Is the Army* unit lived as well as worked together. "We had guys who were crackers when they came into the outfit," said Alan Manson, one of the white actors who took to the novel arrangement with enthusiasm. "But after two or three weeks of living together you couldn't say a word against a black man in our company. It really was an enormous experience. Berlin is a fairly conservative guy, but this meant a lot to him."

His advanced ideas on how his men should live notwithstanding, Berlin clung to outdated conventions concerning the material he wanted the black actors to perform. Initially, he expected the first half hour of *This Is the Army* to recreate a minstrel show, which was the way he had kicked off *Yip! Yip! Yaphank*: one hundred and ten men sitting on bleachers, and everyone in blackface. Ezra Stone, the director, was indignant; he knew the minstrel show summoned hideous stereotypes of darkies and "coon" songs—stereotypes that were best forgotten. "Mr. Berlin," he said, "I know the heritage of the minstrel show. Those days are gone. People don't do that anymore."

"No, no, that's nonsense," the songwriter replied.

After considerable discussion, Stone adopted another approach to convince Berlin to skip the minstrel segment: "How can we have one hundred and ten guys in blackface and then get them *out* of blackface for the rest of the show?" Berlin hesitated. Stone's argument gave him a graceful way of backing down. Berlin relented, and the rotund director breathed an enormous sigh of relief. At Berlin's insistence, some remnants of minstrel shows remained, but at least they wouldn't dominate the show.

To give *This Is the Army* the contemporary feel that Stone wanted, the songwriter devised a new song for his black soldiers, something, he declared, "with a real Harlem beat." At first, Stone and the others had no idea what he meant. All they knew was that when they were trying to get some sleep in "T-11," Berlin would plunk away at the piano, night after night. One endless night he played the melody for "Puttin' on the Ritz"—his ode to high-fashion Blacks strutting along Lenox Avenue—over and over again; gradually the song evolved into something new: a different melody with the same rhythm.

When reveille sounded, he announced to the groggy men, "I finally got the number for the colored guys—'That's What the Well-Dressed Man in Harlem Will Wear.' " Turning to a bleary-eyed Ezra Stone, he said, "I want you to call Helmy Kresa." Stone pulled the phone into the hall while Berlin was at the piano and held the receiver as the songwriter played and (in his way) sang to Helmy on the other end. Stone was astonished by the procedure, and he realized with a shock that Irving Berlin could neither read nor write music.

Stone became fascinated by Berlin's high-strung temperament and paradoxical personality. Yet from the first their relationship was highly charged, and the two constantly tested one another. "The rides Berlin and I took back and forth between Camp Upton and New York City took two, two-and-a-half hours," said Stone. "The small talk quickly ran out. I used to turn the radio on. He hated that. I asked him why, and he said, 'Well, I don't like to hear other people's music.' He was half-joking, half-serious."

During one of their trips, George Gershwin's counterpoint song, "Mine," happened to come over the radio, and Stone automatically said, "That's my favorite song." He wanted to bite his tongue as soon as he spoke, but it was too late: "I could feel the blast and the chill."

"Why?" Berlin asked. "Why is it your favorite song, Ezra?"

Stone fumbled for an answer. "Well, I guess because it has two melodies and two sets of lyrics, and it's unique."

"It's an old trick. I've used it many times." And with that he dismissed Stone's—and Gershwin's—challenge to his primacy.

By the end of April, Berlin had completed most of the *This Is the Army*'s rousing score. Although the songwriter had no official rank in the Army and was technically a civilian, he trembled before senior officers as though he were an enlisted man. Berlin's anxiety over confronting military authority soared when General Irving J. Phillipson notified Berlin that he wanted to hear the show. "What if they don't like it?" the songwriter kept asking before the audition. "What if they decide not to go forward?" Observing this behavior, Stone concluded that "it was a pattern of Berlin's mental process to create a crisis and then decide how to solve it."

The audition took place on Governor's Island, in New York Harbor, and immediately afterward, Berlin received word of approval. End of crisis.

Opening night was set for July 4, only two months hence, and the fast-approaching deadline meant that rehearsals were as strenuous as conventional military training, to which they bore an odd resemblance. The company began rehearsing after breakfast, at seven-thirty A.M., and, with breaks for meals, often continued until two in the morning. "Their routine," noted a reporter who visited the company during their feverish preparations, "is that of a regular field company, with not only drill but reveille and even inspections. . . . The cast's sole deviation from normal soldier dress was its shoes, which ranged from shiny tap shoes to ballet slippers. The men's faces ranged in complexion from the deep tan of a field soldier to the smart light green of a recent night-club hoofer."

In June, rehearsals for *This Is the Army* switched from the empty expanses of Camp Upton to the congestion of midtown Manhattan. The actors ran through their lines at the Broadway Theatre, the orchestra practiced at the National, and the dancers worked out at still another theater. Each day, Berlin and Stone would make the rounds of the theaters on bicycle to see how the numbers were progressing. At this point, Berlin was most concerned about the ability of the young musical director, Milton Rosenstock. "Rosie can't cut it," he complained.

And Rosenstock *was* having a difficult time getting a handle on the great man. "I didn't know how to behave myself because I couldn't understand Berlin," Rosenstock recalled. "He played on his special piano in F sharp, and I couldn't understand it. I had never seen a piano like that. He said to me, 'You never did a show. What do you know about show business?' And I said, 'I'm learning, Mr. B., I'm learning.' "

"Mr. B." soon put Rosie through a catechism of the conductor's craft: "Performers need things all the time. Tell me what they need most."

"Tempo," Rosenstock replied.

"Right. Tempo number one. And then what?"

"You have to give them support."

"Right."

"The orchestra is subservient."

At that, Berlin broke into applause. ("I think," said Rosenstock, "it was the first time I ever saw a smile on his face.")

"That's right," Berlin insisted. "You have to understand that. What else?"

"I give up. The arrangements? The balance?"

"Something much more important—loyalty."

"To you?"

"No, not to me," Berlin snapped.

"The way you've been running around here, you need people loyal to you."

"You're wrong, and they're wrong. I don't want people loyal to me," the songwriter explained. "You have to be loyal to the show. And if you are loyal to the show and your considerations are always to the good of the show, and I tell you do something, and you tell me, 'I don't want to do it. I don't think you should do it,' I'll listen. You have an impact on me. In the the business, I'm a certain kind of man. When I go home, I'm another man. One doesn't interfere with the other. The businessman is hard. If somebody can't do something, and I love him, he won't have the job. If somebody I hate, who disgusts me, *can* do the job, he's got it."

There had always been an authoritarian streak in Berlin; it ran side by side with his insecurity, one compensating for the other. The military setting of *This Is the Army* gave him more latitude to exercise his authoritarianism than he had ever before known. He acted as though every word he uttered, every opinion he expressed, had the force of an order, and there was (so he thought) no room for discussion. After all, this was war.

Berlin planned to replace Rosie with the venerable Frank Tours, who had conducted *Yip! Yip! Yaphank*. The songwriter summoned him from retirement in California and spirited him into an orchestra rehearsal under Rosie's direction. Tours watched the young conductor lead the fifty musicians through the overture, and then he signaled to Berlin to meet him in the lobby. There he said, "I'm going back to California, Irving. You don't need me. This man knows much more about it."

The ubiquitous strife afflicting the members of the troupe—and Army life in general—inspired one of Berlin's best songs for the revue. Taking an interest in a feud between Ezra Stone and his captain, Berlin concocted a song called (with heavy irony) "My Captain and I Are Buddies." When this number flopped, he replaced it with a new song destined for wide currency, "The Army's Made a Man of Me." Inevitably, life imitated art, as the song itself became an occasion for still more friction between Berlin and Stone. At issue was the ending; having failed to come up with a concluding couplet, Berlin allowed the song to trail off inconclusively; Stone took it upon himself to complete the lyrics and to sing them during a rehearsal on the stage of the Broadway Theatre.

"The door is open and Berlin walks in," Stone said. "He hears me singing the end of the song with words that he didn't write. I swear to God, it was like a vampire just seemed to fly from that point to the piano. He ripped up the music and said, 'It has always been and always will be, "Words and Music by Irving Berlin." And nobody else!' The next day, he gave me his own version of the ending, which was virtually the same as the one we were using."

The song was completed, but the damage to the relationship between the director and the star had been done. Increasingly, Stone began to act the part of gadfly, an attitude guaranteed to antagonize the songwriter. Even the smallest detail concerning the show could touch off a fresh dispute. During a lunch at Lindy's, for example, Berlin happened to ask Ezra how many house seats he wanted during the revue's limited run.

And Stone replied, "I don't want any, Mr. Berlin."

Stone was being magnanimous; his seats would now contribute money to Army Emergency Relief. But the songwriter considered Stone's attitude symptomatic of a lack of loyalty, both to the show and to Irving Berlin. "You know this is going to be a solid sell-out," he warned, "and you'll want to have some house seats put aside for you and your friends, won't you? You should have twelve."

"No. I don't want the nuisance of having to release house seats every time I'm not going to use them."

Disgusted with Stone's self-righteous attitude, Berlin suddenly brought in another director for advice on staging the show. Joshua Logan was an ebullient young graduate of Princeton who had begun to make his mark as a director and librettist on Broadway. Early in his career, he had been identified as one of the next generation of Broadway kingpins, and then the war had come along and, to his dismay, derailed his career. He was now in military intelligence, and when he learned of a chance to associate himself with the great Irving Berlin, a hero of his, in a successor to *Yip! Yip! Yaphank*, he naturally responded with glee. Reporting for duty with *This Is the Army*, Logan's good-natured enthusiasm won over even Ezra Stone, who welcomed assistance in dealing with Berlin.

Logan found his idol, Irving Berlin, in a mood of high expectation, "at once excitement, glitter, comedy and melody. I fell for him immediately." Despite his irrepressible excitement, Berlin confided that he was deeply troubled about the show, which he feared was little more than a "badly arranged jumble." Logan had just nine days to set it straight. Expecting a shambles, he was astonished by what he saw at rehearsals: "Ten rows of bleachers stretched all across the stage, filled with soldiers, all seemingly great talents. Then song after song, end-man-type jokes, big choruses, acrobatic acts. . . . It was stupefying, and when I turned to Irving, overcome with enthusiasm, he said, 'It's not right, it's not right. You've got to fix it.' "

Logan was at a loss. To his eye, *This Is the Army* amounted to "bulletproof perfection." After several more viewings, though, he essayed minor changes. He asked soldiers singing "I'm Getting Tired So I Can Sleep"—a song that was the essence of torpor—to lean on their elbows rather than sit up straight, but beyond that he found nothing to do.

Opening night, July 4, brought together Broadway excitement and war fever. Today, the stage production of *This Is the Army* is recalled as a blur of synchronized khaki uniforms and hundreds of soldiers singing patriotic slogans and indulging in innocent horseplay. Much of the revue did function on that level, but there was more to it than simple morale boosting. Through his songs, Berlin managed to inject human touches that made life in the armed services comprehensible to civilian audiences.

In the war environment, the normal standards of success or failure did not apply to the production, which was essentially a brilliant fundraising event. With seats ranging in price from $2.20 to $27.50, the opening night alone raised $50,000 for the Army Emergency Relief Fund, as compared with the $83,000 that *Yip! Yip! Yaphank* had earned during its entire run. Plainly, *This Is the Army* was destined to contribute an enormous sum to Army Emergency Relief, and just as plainly, Berlin was destined to cover himself with glory for making it all happen.

However, even success had a way of generating more controversy for Berlin and his revue. The Broadway Theatre, where *This Is the Army* played to packed houses every night, was managed by the Shubert brothers, who were as contemptuous of Berlin in war as they had been in peace. When the brothers realized they must live with Berlin's achievement for the rest of the summer, they hastily attempted to cash in on the show's popularity by demanding a weekly theater rental of $3,000 per week.

Berlin was incensed. At that figure, he calculated, the Shuberts would be making a one hundred percent profit, while he and the rest of the company were donating their services. On July 11, he made a counter offer of $2,000 per week, which would still leave the Shuberts a modest profit. He, in turn, enraged the brothers by threatening to inform the War Department of their excessive demands and then warning them: "Please do not take advantage of this hit."

The vindictive brothers turned the matter over to their lawyer, William Klein, who was appalled by the trouble Irving might cause. "I believe that Berlin's letter is loaded with dynamite," he concluded, dreading the consequences of adverse publicity in the newspapers.

Threatened with a scandal that could impugn the Shuberts' wartime patriotism, Lee hurriedly covered his tracks. At Klein's urging, and with his assistance, he replied to Berlin, claiming, "I have not taken advantage, but rather, the contrary is true, since I was the one who was imposed upon. . . . Although it meant closing a show . . .

and keeping the Broadway Theatre dark for two months before you opened, I cheerfully arranged for the original booking. . . . I never asked . . . for $3000 a week and did not mention any other terms." And in case the War Department was watching this dispute, Lee Shubert went on to insist, "There is little purpose in your going on record, as you put it, with me because the War Department has put the matter in your hands. Since the outbreak of hostilities my own record of assistance to men in the armed forces compares favorably with that of any man's."

The posturing continued as the Shuberts pointed out that they had taken a $1,000 box for the opening night. Of course, Berlin was not to be outdone, not where matters of patriotism and honor and self-sacrifice in time of war were concerned. He reminded the Shuberts that he himself had bought *two* boxes, for $2,000. (Kate Smith, who had championed "God Bless America," went Berlin one better, however, by contributing $10,000 for her two seats.)

Berlin got his way concerning the rental of the Broadway Theatre, but the Shuberts remained spiteful. On August 21, as the show was nearing the end of its second month, still playing to packed houses, still as fresh and magnetic as it had been when it opened, Lee dictated a memorandum for his brother, J. J., reviling their theater's revered tenant: "As far as Irving Berlin is concerned, I would certainly make him pay for everything and not give him any concessions whatsoever. He always was a dirty little rat. He forgets that we gave him his first chance—did everything for him."

Even allowing for a certain amount of theatrical exaggeration, this was a ludicrous statement. The Shuberts' "dirty little rat" happened to be a hero to millions of Americans. But the Shuberts' animosity permitted no acknowledgment of the man's gifts. Ever since the day J. J. had turned his back on a youthful Irving Berlin during an audition in 1909, the Shuberts had been, at best, indifferent to the songwriter's remarkable career.

The success of *This Is the Army* also changed the face of Berlin's music publishing company, dragging it into the war effort. Even though the songwriter was turning over the royalties from the songs to the Army, his pride was at stake, and he plugged the songs as carefully as if he were pocketing every cent. His strategy for increasing the sale of sheet music was to release one song at a time for radio performance. The first, "The Army's Made a Man of Me," was scheduled for an NBC commercial network show. At two-thirty on the afternoon of the show, NBC called Lissauer and informed him that it had been banned by the network's censor.

"Okay," said Lissauer, "tell you what. Mr. Berlin is at the theater, performing in *This Is the Army.* Let me go over and tell him. It's just a few blocks from here."

He shot over to the theater, where he found Berlin backstage, pacing. "Mr. Berlin," he said, "I've got a problem. NBC said they can't do the song because there's a blue line in it." Lissauer repeated the line.

"Sergeant," Berlin said, "do you have a pencil and paper?"

"Yes, sir."

Berlin walked to one side of the house and minutes later returned with a piece of paper on which he had scrawled a new lyric. "Call it in," he ordered.

The relentless radio plugging proved effective, as Berlin knew. Each day, he would call Bob Lissauer to check on the sales of a different title from the score of *This Is the Army.*

"Sir," Lissauer would respond, "we just got the sales figures, and we shipped 19,000 copies of sheet music today."

"Is that all?" Berlin invariably replied.

"Yes, because Monday we sent out 85,000 so the stores don't have to reorder this week."

No matter how many copies were sold, Berlin was never satisfied. Occasionally Lissauer would venture to call up Berlin and announce, "Great news! 'I Left My Heart at the Stage Door Canteen' "—one of the most popular songs in the revue—"just went from number seven to number three on the Hit Parade."

And all Berlin would say was, "What was it you got on 'I'm Getting Tired So I Can Sleep'?" Even when Lissauer boasted that the latter title had made it all the way to number one on the Hit Parade, Berlin failed to offer praise. In fact, he seemed not to care. The eager young Lissauer assumed that there was just no pleasing the old man.

Berlin's insistence on donating the proceeds of the sheet music sales to the Army upset his financial manager, Saul Bornstein, who was appalled by the vast amounts of money the songwriter gave away. In a characterstic ploy, Bornstein tried to influence Lissauer to alter the policy, without Berlin's knowledge. Bornstein summoned the young man and invited him to sit down in front of an enormous desk. "Bob," he said in his best confiding tone, extending his arms to the end of his desk, "I want you to know this desk does not belong to Saul Bornstein. I want you to know that in my heart this belongs to the Army of the United States of America. My heart knows the wonderful things that you fellows are doing, and the sacrifices that you're making."

Lissauer had only one reaction to Bornstein's oration: "Bullshit."

"I want to ask you a question," Bornstein continued. "How many copies of 'I Left My Heart at the Stage Door Canteen' were sold today?"

Recognizing that Bornstein simply wanted to demonstrate how much money they were losing, Lissauer sought refuge in his military status. "There are some things," he said, "that we in the Army are not allowed to discuss." Bornstein ceased to bother Lissauer.

At least one thing about Berlin's company remained unchanged in time of war, however. Mynna Granat continued at her post, although she did have a tie-line to the Pentagon at her disposal, over which she dickered with various officers about the allocation of the precious house seats. She also attended to her boss's needs and whims at the Broadway Theatre. She saw to it that he had clean towels and that the World War I uniform he wore onstage was pressed. "Every night at the performance," she recalled, "I would be with him on the steps of the theater, under a light, going over the mail. Otherwise, I couldn't see him. I couldn't have a seat because they were so expensive, so I sat on the step backstage. And when he came off he would kiss me and say, 'How did I do?' He loved to sing—he loved it."

During the New York run, the Broadway Theatre became a second home for the 359 men in the company. When they were not performing, they would occasionally watch sex-orientation or training films in the theater. It even served as the site of an unusual medical examination. "We lined up in the alley alongside the theater," said Bob Lissauer, "and then we walked in through the stage door, right across the stage for short arm inspection. Everyone gets in front of the doctor. You have to unzip yourself and take out your penis and check for venereal disease." Walter Winchell subsequently found out about the inspection and wrote about it in his column, endowing the group with a certain machismo.

▪ ▪ ▪

As *This Is the Army* neared the end of its Broadway run, *Holiday Inn* prepared to open in New York. At an advance screening for the press, the movie—and Berlin's score—encountered resistance from journalists, who were, understandably, preoccupied with the war. At a reception, Tom Pryor of *Daily Variety* said he didn't think "White Christmas" would make it. Irving asked why. Too schmaltzy, said Pryor. Berlin drew himself up and disagreed, convinced that "White Christmas" would be a big hit.

Despite his assurances to the contrary, Berlin began to grow insecure about his prized song, and subsequent reactions to it confirmed his fears. Prior to the movie's release, he took several members of his office to a screening. Dave Dreyer went along, as did Francis Gilbert, a lawyer in Berlin's employ. Afterward, the gang went to Lindy's restaurant for a postmortem, during which Gilbert declared that the movie would flop. And so, for that matter, would the songs, including "White Christmas." First Pryor, then Gilbert. Irving had by now lost all confidence in "White Christmas." He decided that "Be Careful, It's My Heart"—a charming but lesser effort—would emerge as the movie's one hit song. Rallying to his boss's defense, Dave Dreyer argued that the movie would succeed, but this was a distinctly minority opinion. "I'll bet you a Cavanaugh hat," Gilbert replied. "$25 it'll be a flop."

Once the pluggers in Berlin's office got hold of the sheet music, they, too, were disappointed. Only Bing Crosby, they complained, could pronounce the word "Christmases" with the necessary ease. Dreyer assembled them on a hot summer afternoon and bellowed, "You'll be playing 'White Christmas' all through August." Over the pluggers' groans, Dreyer continued, "I want that song to be number one on the Lucky Strike Hit Parade."

Now that Berlin had managed to get everyone in his office in an uproar over the movie, the actual premiere—at the Paramount Theater in New York, not far from the Broadway Theatre, where he was performing nightly in *This Is the Army*—came as something of an anticlimax, for *Holiday Inn* proved to be a safe and solid success. He reveled in the distinction of having two hit shows in two different mediums before the public. During their simultaneous runs, Berlin displayed widely varied facets of his songwriting ability. In *This Is the Army*, he was a minstrel of war, full of battle cries and rough humor. In *Holiday Inn*, he became a minstrel of peace, singing of romance and nostalgia. The picture served as a bittersweet reminder of what peacetime had been like: a dreamy, far-off place full of snow and sentiment. In the world of this movie, there was no sign of war, no rationing, no sacrifice. Mark Sandrich's direction gave this cinematic greeting card unexpected life and wit, and of course there were Berlin's songs, "Be Careful, It's My Heart," "You're Easy to Dance With," "Let's Start the New Year Right," and "I Can't Tell a Lie." Despite Berlin's early hopes regarding "White Christmas," the haunting song made little impression when the movie opened. The critics admired the way Bing Crosby handled it, but on first hearing, it seemed one of the score's slighter efforts.

During the movie's New York run, Berlin paid close attention to the audience's reaction to his songs, trying with little success to spot the hit. "I've got a song in there which is *so* good," he said to Milt Rosenstock as they walked to the Paramount Theater, where Berlin wanted to catch the midnight show.

"What is it?" Rosie asked.

" 'Be Careful, It's My Heart.' "

Berlin began to sing the tune, and later, in the movie theater, they watched Bing Crosby sing it. And then, Rosie recalled, Crosby sang "this cockamamie little song—'I'm dreaming of a white Christmas. . . .' It was a throwaway."

Although one overwhelming hit song had yet to emerge from *Holiday Inn*, the picture itself was doing well—well enough, at any rate, for Dave Dreyer, who had bet a Cavanaugh hat on the outcome of the movie, to receive his reward. As it happened, Berlin was also wearing a new hat to the office, and Mynna, with her usual attentiveness, took an instant dislike to it. "The brim is too big for your face," she explained. "Dave just got himself a new Cavanaugh hat with a small brim. Please try it on."

Berlin did as told, and then said, in his abstracted way, "Okay, I'll take it," as if, Mynna felt, she were a saleslady in Saks.

He walked out of the office with it, and when Dreyer came looking for his precious new hat, which he had won in a bet, Mynna was forced to explain, "Dave, guess what? Your hat's gone."

In the closing weeks of the year, one of the songs from *Holiday Inn* began to show signs of entering that select circle of undying hits to which "Alexander's Ragtime Band" belonged. "White Christmas," the song so many experts had disparaged, quietly found its way to a special constituency that was immune to all of Berlin's promotional efforts: American soldiers abroad. Around the world, GIs began inundating the Armed Forces Radio Services to play the song. In short order it became, quite spontaneously, the American soldier's anthem of longing and homesickness. Berlin hadn't written the song specifically for soldiers, and this aspect of its appeal caught him by surprise. At any rate, his faith in the song had been vindicated.

Berlin held a press conference to publicize "White Christmas" where it seemed to need a little boost: here at home. As he played for reporters on his battered prepared piano, he noticed his audience's discomfort with the song's introductory verse about warm California Christmases. In view of the song's wartime popularity, the gambit no longer meant much.

As soon as the conference ended, Berlin told Saul Bornstein, "I want you to cut the verse out of the sheet music of 'White Christmas.' From now on, that song goes without a verse. That's an order." Bornstein did as told, but then, Berlin recalled, "The music jobbers who handled sheet music all over the country wrote in and complained like hell—they figured we were cheating them out of a verse."

The songwriter held fast, and his song continued to sell. Even after the war ended, it continued to sell, until it became the most popular song Berlin ever wrote. It simply never fell out of fashion. In its first ten years of existence, it sold three million copies of sheet music and fourteen million records, nine million by Crosby alone. In time it became one of the most valuable copyrights in existence. Irving preferred to gloat over the success in private rather than in the press, but he did permit himself a small display of pride at a luncheon in 1949, when he bumped into *Variety*'s Tom Pryor, who had dared to disparage the song. "Say, Tom," he said. " 'White Christmas' is doing pretty good, eh?"

Although it owed its initial success to the war, the appeal of

"White Christmas" was essentially timeless. It was one of the few songs in the entire Berlin canon belonging to no particular era, place, or musical fashion. It seemed always to have been there, just beneath the surface of the national consciousness, waiting for Berlin to give it final form. It embodied the paradox of the Hollywood dream factory. Here was a Jew, the son of a cantor, writing a classic *goyische* anthem. Many other American Jews, especially in Hollywood, had rushed to assimilate; they had changed their names, their religions, married gentile wives, done whatever they could to slip the bonds of their heritage, and Irving Berlin had gone most of that route himself, though he stopped short of actually converting. But his willingness to embrace Christian themes and imagery in his music was unique. "White Christmas" demonstrated that Berlin had reached the limit of musical assimilation.

▪ ▪ ▪

By summer's end, it was apparent that *This Is the Army* had taken on a life of its own. Originally, Berlin had expected the revue to play four weeks on Broadway. Then, in the first flush of its success, he agreed to extend the run until September 26. At the same time he found himself negotiating the sale of movie rights to Warner Brothers. And finally, the Army was making plans to send the show on a national tour. It appeared that the show would go on—and on. *This Is the Army* had now consumed the better part of his energies for the year, but Irving believed he had a mission to fulfill as long as the war lasted.

The national tour had come about in part because of the enthusiasm of Eleanor Roosevelt. She had loved the show—loved it enough to have seen it *three* times—and she wanted her husband to have the same pleasure. Since the president was unable to travel to New York to watch the revue at the Broadway Theatre, it was only natural that *This Is the Army* come to him. It was an honor that Berlin readily accepted.

The cast, however, soon discovered they would have to blunt some of the revue's rough-and-ready humor for the special matinée performance, scheduled for October 8 at the National Theatre in Washington, D.C. Ezra Stone was approached by a representative of White House security, who was anxious about a sketch concerning KP duty.

In it, Hank Henry, a big, burly comic, appeared onstage wielding a meat cleaver.

"How well do you know Hank Henry?" the security agent asked Stone.

"Oh, very well," Stone told him. "I knew him before the war."

"Has he ever said anything against the president?"

"What's your problem?" Stone demanded.

"Well," the agent said, "you've got him there stage right, and the president's sitting in his box fifteen feet away, and Henry's swinging a meat cleaver."

"No problem. There won't be a meat cleaver," Stone assured him. "Why don't we have him come out chewing on a turkey wing?"

Stone agreed to the suggestion, and he later made one other critical alteration of his own: "I staged all the bows in military fashion. We'd present arms instead of bowing, and then I would give the left face command, and Irving Berlin would come in from the stage left wing. The spotlight would hit him, and we'd present arms to Mr. Berlin." But for the presidential performance, Stone conceded, "I made an error. I knew that we should acknowledge the President of the United States, so my first command was 'Right face.' And Mr. Berlin came in from the other side. He thought I had deliberately insulted him."

In other words, what the audience—and President Roosevelt—saw was the cast saluting Roosevelt while turning their backs on Irving Berlin. The thin-skinned songwriter never forgave Stone for staging what seemed to be a public humiliation in front of the president of the United States of America. No one else in the cast interpreted the incident in the same light; they all figured it was a minor, understandable error in staging. All except for Berlin, that is.

For the moment, there were congratulations all around and a show of unity before President Roosevelt. The day after the command performance, the entire cast and crew were invited to the White House to meet the president. "It was a night none us will ever forget," Alan Manson said. "Roosevelt, crippled as he was, stayed up until 1:30 in the morning, shaking hands with all 359 men in the company. Mrs. Roosevelt and Harry Hopkins were there. No one could go to sleep after that. We just sat up talking about it."

Even as the company was meeting the president, they had to

contend with bigotry both in Washington and, later on, in many of the other cities in which they played. "We always insisted that the black guys stay with us," said Alan Anderson. "And if a place wouldn't take us, all three hundred of us would go where the black guys could go. We wouldn't play in a segregated theater—and that's that. We were invited to a party on occasion, and a couple of times, they didn't include the black guys. We said, 'We're sorry, we're not coming. Forget it.' "

After the ten-day stand in Washington, D.C., the revue went on to Philadelphia, where Berlin and Stone continued their war of nerves. One evening before the show, Stone had dinner at the home of Meyer Davis, the society bandleader. During the visit, he was shown a copy of a manuscript by George Gershwin, complete with corrections; it was for "Bess, You Is My Woman." Stone was impressed, and on his return to the theater, he told Milton Rosenstock all about it. On overhearing the name Gershwin, Berlin emerged from his dressing room and asked, "Well, what's the big deal about that?"

"It was actually in Gershwin's hand," Stone said, unaware that he was treading perilously close to Berlin's chief musical insecurity.

"A musical secretary did that," Berlin insisted and stormed away.

By now Stone could no longer tolerate Berlin's high-handedness. "Some people implied that we should be goddamned glad that we were in this show and not in combat," Stone felt. "I maintained that if what we were doing was needed, then we should have the same treatment as the guy who bakes the bread for the soldiers or is carrying a gun. I couldn't get this concept past anybody, including Berlin. I was making waves, being troublesome. Finally, I took it upon myself to ask for a transfer to combat duty, and the next thing I knew I was being reprimanded by my commanding officer, General Phillipson, for asking for a transfer.

"The same thing happened to a performer in the show named Henry Jones. His wife was dying while we were up in Boston. I wanted his understudy to replace him so he could be with his wife. Berlin said, 'You can't do that to the show.' In spite of Berlin, I was able to get orders cut on Henry and put him on detached service with the music publishing unit of *This Is the Army* in New York. Berlin was very angry with me for having done that."

On December 14, *This Is the Army* opened at the Municipal Auditorium in St. Louis, and the feud between Berlin and Stone finally erupted into the open. After a performance, Berlin called a meeting in his dressing room; Alan Anderson, Milton Rosenstock, and Ezra Stone were in attendance. When they had assembled, Berlin declared that there were, as Stone heard it, "too many Jews in the show and too many of Ezra Stone's friends." Everyone present was astounded. Could Irving Berlin, the son of a cantor, actually be saying this?

Stone retorted, "What about your friends? You've got everybody from the music publishing business." Rosie protested that there were actually more Italians than Jews in the show, if anyone cared to count.

Berlin could not be dissuaded. He explained that he wanted to avoid the appearance that the cast of *This Is the Army* seemed to consist mainly of Jews trying to avoid combat duty by appearing in a morale-boosting show, but in the process he insulted everyone in the room. The cast did contain a number of Jews, but so did civilian show business. Furthermore, Berlin had approved everyone in the cast, so he had only himself to blame if he was unhappy with its ethnic composition.

Stone, meanwhile, was thinking of a spread on Berlin that had just come out in the glossy pages of *Life* magazine, trumpeting the official version of the songwriter's legend. Yet here he was complaining about the number of Jews in the cast. "Publicity—that's all you're interested in," Stone said to Berlin. "You'd sell your grandmother for publicity."

The meeting broke up long after midnight, and Stone, Anderson, and Rosenstock were all profoundly upset by Berlin's diatribe. Of course, the stress of prolonged touring had riled everyone, especially Berlin, with his hair-trigger temper. The men had been together for over six months by this time, and they had been deprived of wives and girlfriends. The Army constantly rode herd on the men to remember that they represented the United States Armed Forces, never more so than when they were offstage. The members of the *This Is the Army* troupe were supposed to be above reproach. Berlin, on the other hand, was accustomed to the constraints of living in the limelight. He had made a point of integrating his company, in part for the sake of appearances, and his concern about the number of Jews in *This Is the*

Army sprang from the same desire to present a balanced company. But he had taken the impulse too far, until it became a vendetta against Stone.

To purge the cast of Jews and so-called "no-talents," he insisted on reconsidering every member of the company. The decree sent shock waves through the troupe; for them, leaving the company could well be a matter of life and death. "I was very, very upset by the feud between Ezra and Mr. Berlin," said Alan Manson, who reveled in his participation in the cast. "I didn't know who was right, but after all, if it weren't for Irving Berlin, we'd all be in the shithouse. I'd been on two infantry shipments to Fort Bragg, and I was pulled off. I was always running into guys I had been at Camp Upton with, and I'd say, 'What about So-and-so?' And they'd say, 'He got killed.' "

It would be several months before Berlin carried out his threat, however. As the national tour worked its way west, Manson, Stone, and the rest of the company remained in a state of suspense about their future.

The manner in which Berlin celebrated Christmas 1942 was appropriate to that of a traveling minstrel. In New York, his wife, Ellin, and his daughters, the oldest of whom was just fifteen, had moved out of their Upper East Side apartment and were living at the Waldorf Astoria Hotel for the duration. Irving did not expect to see his family at all during the holidays, but they took him by surprise with a visit.

Accustomed to traditional holiday celebrations, Ellin arranged for a Christmas tree to be delivered to Berlin's hotel suite in Detroit, where he was performing in *This Is the Army*, and with the girls' assistance she proceeded to decorate the tree while a photographer memorialized the occasion. The photograph of the songwriter, his wife, and family decorating the Christmas tree, when reproduced in the newspapers, served as another plug for "White Christmas." Berlin, the cantor's son, rationalized his participation in the Christmas rite on the basis that it had become an *American* holiday, and as a professional patriot, he made a habit of appropriating all things American to himself. He valued his privacy, and it was highly uncharacteristic of him to put his sheltered family on display. But publicity was publicity was publicity.

Perhaps he would, as Ezra Stone had charged, sell his grandmother for the sake of publicity, but Berlin was after more than press coverage. The people needed heroes; he had offered his services and gotten the job. As long as the war continued, he lived his life on two levels. On one, he was a loving, strict, but remote father and a self-involved, dictatorial entertainer. On another, he was a symbol to millions, both in America and around the world. His life—the rise from poverty, the early hits, the mature successes in the movies—had become transmuted into the stuff of popular legend. His participation in *This Is the Army* magnified all his actions until he became a metaphor for America in the twentieth century. As long as the war lasted, he had a chance to dwell among the archetypes. He was painfully conscious of his enhanced reputation, and he desperately wanted to avoid anything that would tarnish it. All he wanted people to remember about him were the highlights and bold outlines of *This Is the Army.*

In this triumphant mood, the national tour of the revue ended in San Francisco on February 13, 1943. By this time, it had vastly exceeded its financial expectations, having earned $2 million for the Army Emergency Relief Fund.

▪ ▪ ▪

It was a time of fulfillment for Irving, and a time of loss, as well. Several weeks earlier, on January 23, his closest friend, Alexander Woollcott, had arrived at the studios of the Columbia Broadcasting System, at 485 Madison Avenue. It was late on a cold winter's afternoon, and he was scheduled to participate in a round-table discussion for a program called "The People's Platform."

The live broadcast, a discussion of Nazi Germany, began at seven P.M., and within minutes he began to feel that something was seriously wrong. He wrote a note saying, "I'm feeling sick," passed it to the moderator, and slumped before his microphone, suffering from a heart attack. An ambulance was summoned, and Woollcott died several hours later at Roosevelt Hospital. He was fifty-six, just a year older than Berlin.

Woollcott's death left a ragged hole in the Broadway theater. The Round Table over which he had presided in the 1920s had long since vanished, the victim of its members' desire for independence, and his best theater criticism was behind him. Although the erratic work he left behind had slight lasting value, the force of his personality had affected the careers of dozens of creative types, not just Irving Berlin. He was a formidable catalyst. He had intervened in the lives of George S. Kaufman, Edna Ferber, and Dorothy Parker, among others, and almost always for the better. Still, his friendship with Irving had been something special. Together they represented the two extremes of the Broadway spectrum, the effete and the street, and with Woollcott gone, the New York theater lost its most dedicated publicist.

Woollcott had played an important role in Irving's career, and the songwriter found another celebrated wit and ornament of café society to take his place: Cole Porter. His friendship with Porter was as unlikely as his liaison with Woollcott had been. In fact, in years gone by, Berlin had often spoken of Porter mainly with contempt spiked by a touch of envy, and indeed much of the music business looked askance at Porter because he was cut from entirely different cloth than they. He was a WASP, he was from the Midwest (Peru, Indiana), he came from a wealthy family, and he had gone to Yale. All of these characteristics put him on the outs with the self-educated, street-smart immigrants or children of immigrants who populated the entertainment business.

It *was* terribly tempting to dismiss the sleek, well-dressed, well-married Porter as a Yalie dilettante dabbling in Broadway scores, except that Porter's self-evident grace and talent had a way of confuting such an attitude. Within a span of five weeks at the end of 1929, for instance, no fewer than three Cole Porter musicals opened in New York: *Fifty Million Frenchmen* (the production Berlin refused to stage in the Music Box Theatre), *The Battle of Paris*, and *Wake Up and Dream.*

Then came the accident that earned Porter a measure of sympathy no amount of professional success could have won. In 1937 he fell from a horse, crushing his legs. He was crippled for life, enduring constant pain. Berlin, who knew well the uses of adversity, admired the way Cole pulled himself together and continued writing—not only music but also lyrics. That alone made Porter unusual, for nearly all other popular songwriters collaborated. One of the few exceptions to the practice happened to be Berlin himself, and this circumstance helped persuade Irving that he and Cole were kindred spirits.

The resemblance ended there, however. Unlike Berlin, Porter was a trained musician, and even more importantly, Porter wanted to titillate, if not shock, mainstream America. He went out of his way to be clever, progressive, and naughty: all conditions that were alien to Berlin. Porter's music was driven by strong erotic feeling; his most effective songs evoked either preorgasmic excitement and anticipation or postcoital melancholy. He was married to a woman of means, who was older than he, and who probably excused him from conjugal relations. She tolerated his homosexual affairs as he tolerated her lesbian encounters.

There is no evidence to suggest that Berlin was aware of Porter's double life. Berlin was more comfortable with a willfully limited view of Porter, who appealed to him in the same way Woollcott had: as a literate, effete arbiter of café society. And he encouraged Porter not to take himself too seriously. At a party, Ellin introduced Porter to Louis B. Mayer, but when Porter laid eyes on the powerful producer, he blurted out, "He looks like a shark." Later, when Porter wrote a song called "Rosalie" for MGM, Louis Mayer rejected it, and Porter proceeded to write a version he considered to be markedly inferior to the original version. But it was this later version that became a hit. "I wrote that song in hate," Porter complained to Berlin, "and I still hate it."

"Listen, kid," said Berlin, "Take my advice. Never hate a song that has sold half a million copies."

They devised nicknames for one another, as Berlin and Woollcott had; Irving became "The Little Gray Mouse" and Cole "Rat Porter." Through Porter, Irving continued his love affair with upper-class WASP America, and through Berlin, Porter won acceptance in the rough-and-tumble environment of Tin Pan Alley. Porter was as fascinated by Berlin's immigrant background as Berlin was by Porter's WASP credentials. In fact, Porter acknowledged that his WASP pedigree imposed restraints that he yearned to cast aside. He occasionally spoke of writing "Jewish tunes" such as those dictated by his friend Irving. To Porter, "Jewish" music meant sensuous laments in a minor key, a style he consciously tried to emulate.

In defense of his friend Irving Berlin, Porter revealed a warmth of friendship rare in a cutthroat business. During the war, the composer

Harry Warren became Berlin's most vocal critic. When the Allies' bombing raids against Germany became public knowledge, Warren's remark, "They bombed the wrong Berlin," expressed a simmering resentment and gained wide currency. Unlike Berlin, or, for that matter, Cole Porter, whose lives possessed an extra dimension that raised them to the level of allegory, Warren was not a celebrated public figure. He was, however, an enormously successful composer, who is best remembered for his score for the movie *42nd Street.* As Warren's remark indicated, he had a knack for sowing rancor, and his conversation was frequently peppered with slurs against Jews. If he was sincerely anti-Semitic, he was certainly in the wrong business, but his swagger and shamelessness suggest that his remarks constituted more of a provocative pose than a conviction.

In the face of such criticism, Porter hastened to offer Irving a few coy words of encouragement:

> I can't understand all this resentment to my old friend, 'The Little Gray Mouse.' It seems to me that he has every right to go to the limits toward publishing the music of his Army show as every cent earned will help us win the war.
>
> If I had my way he would have been given the Congressional Medal because . . . he is the greatest song-writer of all time—and I don't mean Stephen Foster.
>
> It's really distressing in these days of so much trouble to know that envy still runs rampant even on that supposed lane Tin Pan Alley. I'm sure you will agree about this, dear little mouse.
>
> Love—Rat Porter

▪ ▪ ▪

Porter needn't have worried. By the time he wrote his endorsement, *This Is the Army* had won universal acceptance. After the national tour ended, Irving immediately flew to Los Angeles, where he threw himself into the task of planning the movie version of the revue. Jack L. Warner, the head of Warner Brothers studio, enthusiastically offered $250,000 for the film rights and, as Berlin specified, donated the money to the Army and, in addition, promised to forward all the profits from the motion picture to the same cause.

However, Jack Warner was as reluctant as Saul Bornstein had been to permit untold money to slip from his grasp. As a result, Warner instigated quiet negotiations to lower the studio's expenses. According to the contract, Warner Brothers specified that "the Army will furnish gratis the personnel of the show and the equipment that we can use as well as aid us in securing the services of well-known artists that are in the Army for the production."

In other words, Warner Brothers wanted to pay what they expected to make: nothing.

They *were* getting the services of Irving Berlin for nothing, and the rest of the show's company still earned their wretched Army wages, even though they were acting in a big-time Hollywood movie. Finally, most of the stars whom Warner added to the film to give it box office clout also earned skimpy soldier's pay.

Given all this free labor, the movie's costs were minimal, but Warner Brothers wanted them lower still. Since the movie would be shot in color, the price of film stock was one of the largest expenses that the studio would have to absorb, and Jack Warner tried to persuade Eastman Kodak to donate its film stock to the studio. However, William J. German, writing on behalf of Kodak, reasonably refused the request on the grounds that it might violate the Fair Trade Act.

The wily Jack Warner wrote back, explaining the financial straitjacket Berlin had imposed on the studio: "First, every dollar received for THIS IS THE ARMY, with the exception of actual distribution costs, goes to the Army Emergency Relief Fund. Second, we charged no overhead whatsoever in the production of this picture, and third, only the actual dollars-out-of-pocket that we spent making the film will be recouped by us." And if that argument didn't persuade Kodak, Jack Warner cunningly suggested "a very *secret* gift that no one would ever know about." Especially not the other studios, which might ask for the same favor, ran the implication. Kodak refused to yield to this arm twisting, and Warner Brothers had no choice but to pay for its celluloid.

No sooner had the financial controversy been settled than a fresh series of censorship disputes flared up. Warner Brothers complained that the female impersonators, who were an important element in the show's tone and content, would prevent the movie from being released overseas. "Female impersonators do not exist in Latin America," explained one misinformed studio memorandum to Jack Warner, insisting that they were "highly insulting and revolting to Latin sensibilities and censors. Even could the film be exported, United States soldiers cavorting in dresses would represent ammunition to the enemy's propagandists." As a result of this fear, the studio reduced, though did not entirely eliminate, the roles played by female impersonators, losing a good deal of the show's peculiar charm in the process.

Next, Joseph I. Breen, who enforced Hollywood's Production Code, scrutinized Berlin's lyrics and discovered a troubling and scurrilous innuendo in "Ladies of the Chorus." It would never do, declared Mr. Breen, to have soldiers singing of willing farmers' daughters. He submitted a list of eleven "blue" lines that required rewriting. Such was the grip of Breen's office on the studios that Berlin had no choice but to comply with the demand.

Finally, a conscience-stricken Ezra Stone challenged Berlin on the issue of lyrics. By the time the film went before the camera, Berlin and he were no longer on speaking terms—as every man in the company was acutely aware. The dispute polarized the troupe into factions. Stone sensed his days with *This Is the Army* were numbered; he had fulfilled his role as the stage director and was now dispensable.

Berlin asserted his dominance by insisting on a new ending for the movie, the jubilantly bloodthirsty "Dressed Up to Kill." Stone believed the song was "was terribly wrong from a humanitarian standpoint, but I had no control over it." With another soldier, he worked out a strategy to thwart Berlin by approaching various church organizations to try to enlist their opposition to the battle cry. Stone perceived his crusade in purely moral terms, but it appeared to others in the company that he took a certain satisfaction in having at last found an issue he could use against Berlin, and even subvert him. A man of considerable pride, Stone had a proprietary interest in the show, as did Berlin. But Stone was wrong to think that *This Is the Army* could ever serve as a vehicle for his concerns and passions. Berlin had to exercise final and complete control over the production, as he did with every other aspect of his life.

Though Stone underestimated Berlin's ego, the young director had identified a lyric worth pondering. The songwriter's affinity with the martial spirit had cropped up in earlier songs, where it had seemed as harmless and quaint as a blunderbuss. "Alexander's Ragtime Band," for instance, had celebrated a bugle call that made men "want to go to war." For Irving, music could be as much an incitement to make war as to make love. He understood that war was, in the last analysis, not about singing or joking or fellowship, but about killing, and in "Dressed Up to Kill," he gave vent to the animal energy released in combat.

Fired by Stone, religious groups went after Berlin and Warner Brothers with righteous glee, and by July, the studio was awash with letters and telegrams criticizing the song. Bishop James Baker of Los Angeles spoke for many other clergymen when he cabled Berlin:

> EARNESTLY HOPE YOU WILL CHANGE THE "DRESSED UP TO KILL" SONG & IT IS NOT WORTHY OF YOU OR OF AMERICA AND WILL CREATE ENDLESS CONTROVERSY.

Alarmed by the protests, Jack Warner cabled Berlin, who was in New York for a brief visit.

> THIS MOVEMENT MAY RESULT IN VERY SERIOUS DAMAGE TO THE ENTIRE PRODUCTION AND TO US PERSONALLY BECAUSE WHEN MASS CHURCH ORGANIZATIONS START AFTER YOU YOU HAVENT A LEG TO STAND ON.

Warner proposed that Berlin substitute "Dressed Up to Win" for the original lyrics. Fearing a bad press above all else, Berlin took Jack Warner's suggestion. Although the new lyrics made little sense, the soldiers singing them were still poised with bayonets at the ready, and they created just the same bloodthirsty impression that the song's pious critics had sought to avoid.

As Berlin fought these myriad backstage battles, the 359 members of the show's cast and crew journeyed to Hollywood under military auspices. The unit now bore the formidable title of "Irving Berlin's This Is the Army, Provisional Task Force, Service Supply Force, U.S. Army." Classified as a "troop movement," their presence in the film capital was, officially at any rate, a secret. As such, the company's status ranked among the worst-kept confidences of the war. Their arrival by train on February 14, 1943, was greeted with Hollywood-style hoopla. To oblige cameras recording the event, the men exited the train over and over, creating a cinematic illusion that a thespian battalion had arrived. And when they reached Warner Brothers, they found the streets packed with cheering civilians—all of them studio employees.

The soldier-actors occupied a sprawling, ten-acre camp site close to the studio. Now that they had made it to Hollywood, their lives became a bizarre amalgam of Hollywood razzle-dazzle and military rigor. In the camp, the men lived in heated, electrified tents constructed by the studio's prop department. They ran obstacle courses and performed drills. Under orders from the War Department, they marched in formation to the studio each day through a special entrance and reported for duty to their assigned sound stages. They were not allowed to roam freely, nor were they permitted to approach actresses at the studio. (Off duty, at the Hollywood Canteen, their conduct was another matter.) After completing their scenes, the men marched back to camp.

To relieve overcrowding in their tent city, some of the soldiers found sleeping quarters in private residences. Most moved to humble rooming houses, but at least one found himself assigned to Cole Porter's Bel Air mansion. Once they began to mingle with the stars, they realized they had made it to Hollywood, after all. Alan Manson experienced the joy of hitchhiking with Ingrid Bergman each day to the room he rented in Hollywood for five dollars a week.

The only real Hollywood star that most of the members of the company came to know was a Warner Brothers contract player named Ronald Reagan. Now a lieutenant, he occasionally talked with Berlin during the making of the picture, but the distracted and frantic songwriter could never quite place Ronald Reagan. Was he a soldier, nonprofessional actor, or movie star? "The first several days I was introduced to Irving Berlin," said the future president, "he'd say, 'Glad to meet you!' and I couldn't understand why. But what really surprised me was that afterward he sought me out on the set, and he said, 'Listen, you've got a few things to correct: a little huskiness in the voice and so forth could be improved. But listen! You ought to give this business some thought! When you get out, you could have a future!' And I thanked him for that."

Later, Reagan wondered if Berlin simply hadn't seen any of his movies, which was likely the case, or if "the war had been going on so long I'd simply been forgotten."

Filming proceeded quickly until the day Berlin was scheduled to sing "Oh! How I Hate to Get Up in the Morning" before the cameras, when he suddenly found himself at the center of a humiliating ordeal. The famous scene in *Yip! Yip! Yaphank* in which he was dragged from his tent was re-created with painstaking care for the cameras. Of course, Irving was twenty-five years older. He was still as lean as a whippet, his hair still jet black, but his face was lined and clearly showed the strain of the months of touring with his show. And his voice, on which the success of the entire scene—the high point of the movie—depended, was weaker than ever: high and nasal, and yet at the same time muffled. Noted one brutally honest Warner Brothers memo, "As more than a million persons who saw the show from Manhattan to San Francisco know, Irving Berlin is no singer." He specified that filming start no earlier than three-thirty P.M., when he felt his voice would be stronger. "When it came time to sing his little song," noted an observer, "he blew sky high and forgot his words, like a bewildered child at the blackboard. He fretted about his makeup like a debutante. . . . His spindly legs, wrapped in the puttees of 1917, buckled and trembled. The awkward spell was broken by Michael Curtiz, the director. . . . 'Don't worry, Irving,' he said, '[It] doesn't matter how *you* look. The audiences just want to see Irving Berlin.' "

As he neared the end of the song, his voice faltered so badly that a grip complained, "If the fellow who wrote this song could hear this guy sing it, he'd roll over in his grave."

Berlin's anxiety carried over into every aspect of the production. Warner Brothers provided him with a grand office befitting his celebrity status, but he was too nervous to linger there, preferring to be out among the men in the company, one of whom remarked of Berlin, "He moves with the eccentricity of a bug on water and talks with the rapidity of two sewing circles competing on a quiz program." Even at lunch, Berlin could not sit still; he "nibbled at several tables at once, sometimes ate nothing, always seemed preoccupied, always remembered all the things everybody thought he failed to hear."

The movie's abbreviated filming schedule aggravated Berlin's sense of strain. A perfectionist in matters of timing, he wanted the movie to open on July 4, 1943, exactly one year after its Broadway debut. Because of the controversy surrounding his lyrics, shooting did not commence until March 30 and lasted well into June. The opening was pushed back until August 17, after weeks of frantic, last-minute editing.

The opening of the filmed version of *This Is the Army* prompted a lavish military carnival. The mayor of Los Angeles declared "This Is the Army Day," and, not to be outdone, the governor of California promptly declared "This Is the Army Week." The movie was given simultaneous premieres in three movie theaters. Ten thousand people saw the film at a time. At each location, stars, military bands, and military hardware such as Sherman tanks, jeeps, and 4,000-pound "Block Buster" bombs were on display. The Hollywood Theater became the scene of the greatest demonstration of pomp. Here hundreds of soldiers performed drills, and celebrity seekers could, if they wished, catch a glimpse of one of the film's stars, Lieutenant Ronald Reagan. The movie's New York premiere received the same treatment: stars, guns, and soldiers on parade.

Amid the excitement, there was one missing element: Irving Berlin, who had taken refuge in New York with his family. Succumbing to his familiar opening-night shyness, he chose to stay away from the great event he had labored to create and publicize. This peculiar behavior was pure Berlin, another demonstration of the paradox he had become. Berlin was everywhere; Berlin was nowhere. Bewildered by the songwriter's sudden absence, Jack Warner sent him an exultant telegram conveying some of the flavor of the opening:

> WAS GREATEST SUCCESS OF ANY PREMIERE I HAVE SEEN IN THE YEARS I HAVE BEEN IN SHOW BUSINESS. THE AUDIENCE UNANIMOUSLY ROSE AND APPLAUDED AFTER PICTURE WAS OVER. SORRY YOU WERENT HERE IN PERSON BUT BEING IN THE PICTURE YOURSELF YOU CERTAINLY SCORED. . . . HOPE TO SEE YOU REAL SOON.

The reviews reflected the atmosphere of frenzy surrounding the movie. "Everything about it is b.o. boff," said *Variety*, its distinctive lingo even riper than usual. "After the history of World War II is written, the Warner Bros. filmization will stand out like the Empire

State Bldg. amidst the many other highlights in the motion picture industry's contributions to the home front and war front. It's that kind of an all-embracing job." Virtually a house organ for Berlin publicity, *Variety* had its reasons for arriving at this conclusion. "Firstly, it's socko entertainment. Two, it's a dynamic linking of World War I and II with its respective soldier shows—'Yip Yip Yaphank' and 'This Is the Army,' both by Irving Berlin. Third, it's a fulsome contribution from the entertainment industry for benefit of an altruistic arm of our national defense."

And then there was the movie itself, so bombastic and maladroit that it defied analysis. But there was a war on, and it would have been unpatriotic, perhaps even treasonous, to denigrate the show. As every critic and ordinary moviegoer knew, it was a propaganda film devoted to raising money for charity. No one even pretended to assess its merit objectively. If they had, they might not have been so quick to cheer its sentiments, for among the wartime films Hollywood churned out, *This Is the Army* ranked among the most curious. Since it had begun life as a stage revue, Warner Brothers naturally felt compelled to dress it up with a plot, a love story, and even bits of history lessons before serving it up as a movie. In one of the distracting subplots, Lieutenant Ronald Reagan spends many a dimly lit scene fretting about whether to marry the woman he loves or to devote himself completely to the war effort; only when his intended enlists in the WACs does he reconcile his personal instincts with the nation's needs. As a result of such narrative intrusions, the effectiveness of the original revue—so stirring, simple, and appealing in its own right—was lost.

The film's patronizing treatment of its black cast members proved to be even more deplorable than its understandable propaganda excesses. They might have enjoyed equality offstage, but once they stepped before the cameras, they were required to fulfill stereotypical roles. Yes, Joe Louis offered a cameo appearance to demonstrate his boxing prowess, but two of Berlin's songs shamelessly exploited racist stereotypes. His venerable "Mandy" was once again staged as a transvestite blackface number. Audiences barely had time to recover from the shock of that spectacle before "That's What the Well-Dressed Man in Harlem Will Wear" urged Blacks to enlist because snappy army uniforms would gratify their love of fancy clothes.

At worst an embarrassment, and at best a colossal curiosity by contemporary standards, *This Is the Army* did accomplish the task Berlin, the Army, and Warner Brothers set for it: raising money. For all his anxiety, Irving knew exactly what he was doing. Even while making *This Is the Army*, he recognized that the film was an event, a stunt, a period piece, not a work of art or personal statement. And as a stunt, it exceeded everyone's expectations. Throughout the summer and fall its popularity held, and it earned $9,555,586.44—a sum that Jack Warner proudly, if a trifle reluctantly, donated to Army Emergency Relief.

The movie version of *This Is the Army* attempted to sum up the entire odyssey of the all-soldier show from its World War I origins to America's inevitable victory in World War II. It was planned as the climactic end of the project. In fact, it became just another step in the show's long, complex evolution. A spate of rumors about the future of the outfit soon began to circulate. The men heard that they would be split into two units and sent abroad. One unit, with Ezra, was to go to Algiers; the other, with Berlin, to London. But Berlin said, "There's not going to be any unit that I'm not with."

As the prospect of a foreign tour loomed, Berlin finally carried out his longstanding threat to purge the company of undesirables. "Berlin and I sat down and selected out a hundred and fifty names," Alan Anderson said, "using the whole roster and saying, 'This guy's a fuck-up' and 'This guy I don't think can physically hack it' and 'This one's personality is difficult.' We knew we were going to have to live in close quarters overseas for no one knew how long. It would take considerable cooperation from everybody."

Once the selection process was completed, Alan Manson, Milton Rosenstock, and Alan Anderson all remained with the company and would go abroad with Berlin. Ezra Stone, of course, was left behind.

▪ ▪ ▪

The foreign tour of *This Is the Army*—much like the domestic version—began as a modest undertaking and gradually gathered momentum until it outstripped all the original expectations. The plan, at first, was for the company to play throughout England for three months, after which *This Is the Army* would be disbanded for good. The company reassembled at Camp Upton on September 5, 1943, to rehearse new material for English audiences. Their soldiering, too, remained important, as the men received carbines and took target practice in and around their tap-dance and minstrel routines.

On October 21 the company sailed for Liverpool aboard *The Monarch of Bermuda*, crossing the treacherous, U-Boat-infested waters of the Atlantic as part of a convoy. Their ship was, like other troop carriers, jam-packed, and fresh water was in short supply. To fill their canteens, soldiers were obliged to rise at six A.M. and wait in line; if they were lucky, they would get their water before the faucet was turned off for the day at seven A.M. Feeding the men posed a logistical nightmare; there was time to serve only two meals a day.

When the men weren't waiting in line, they turned their attention to music. There was a spiritual group under the direction of Sergeant Clyde Turner, who baptized the men on the voyage. There were jam sessions, even a string quartet—fifteen separate entertainment units in all. Other ships in the convoy heard the joyful noise and rechristened the ship *Show Boat*. They offered to ferry some of the men over, but the *Monarch*'s captain forbade such a risky maneuver. "There are subs out there looking for us," he cried. "Has everyone gone mad?"

They reached their destination ten days later, but fog prevented them from landing. Berlin flew across the Atlantic ahead of the men and installed himself in a suite at his favorite hotel, Claridge's, where he was shadowed by his bodyguard, coincidentally named Sergeant Arthur Berlin. Arriving behind schedule on November 4, the performers immediately marched aboard a train bound for London, where Berlin met them at the station.

Although the men were tired from the crossing, Berlin subjected them to a pep talk in which he insisted: "Hot or cold, we do it." And there was a lot to do—prepare for the London opening three days hence, broadcast an hour-long program back to the States, and shoot a last-minute scene for the British version of the movie, which Warner Brothers was about to release. The soldiers sent up a groan of protest. "Do you think it's too much?" Berlin anxiously asked. It *was*, but soon the men devised a schedule to meet the demands.

Once again, Irving called on Joshua Logan, who happened to be in London on a military assignment, to polish the staging of the show. And once again Logan found Berlin to be "supercharged" to the point where, Logan later wrote, "He had convinced himself that he had brought me there—conjured up my appearance in London personally because he wanted a new and bawdy scene in the show and I was the only director with the evil mind to do it."

Irving's notion of a bawdy scene consisted of a comic sketch in which a soldier who yearns to sleep with his wife must first get past his mother-in-law. The risqué aspect came from the fact that the English version of *This Is the Army*, as with the American, employed female impersonators.

There remained only one problem: getting Logan officially transferred to the show. Accustomed to having his way with every aspect of the production, Berlin was surprised and angered to learn that Logan's commanding officer—a certain Colonel Chappell—refused to reassign the director. Incredulous, Berlin immediately called General "Hap" Arnold at the Pentagon to complain, and Arnold yielded to Berlin. But Logan's CO still held firm: no transfer. By then Berlin was beyond indignation, in a storm against both General Arnold and General Eisenhower for letting him down. Sure there was a war on, but Berlin had his priorities.

Finally, he called Logan's CO himself. "Colonel Chappell," he said, "This is Irving Berlin." A pause. Berlin became impatient. "Hello, hello," he snapped.

And then Chappell replied, "Did you say you were Irving Berlin? *The* Irving Berlin?"

"That's right. Now I want Logan."

To which the star-struck Chappell responded, "Anything you say, Mr. Berlin. Jesus Christ, *Irving Berlin!*"

As Logan worked on the "bawdy" sketch, Irving found time to write a new song for the English edition of *This Is the Army*, "My British Buddy," a humorous attempt to foster Anglo-American relations in a war marked as much by discord and rivalry among the Allies as by cooperation. Even before his arrival in London, Berlin had tried to write a song emphasizing transatlantic cooperation, but the earlier effort, "England and America," ("Standing side by side, / Bound together by ancient ties / That the oceans can't divide!") fell a little flat. It was too pompous, too much in the mold of "God Bless America" to suit the occasion; the gentle sarcasm of "My British Buddy" better expressed the prevailing mood.

Berlin arranged for a British music publishing company to handle the song on a charitable basis, exactly as his own music company was doing in New York. But he soon ran up against another obstacle: with wartime restrictions there was not enough paper available to print the song. More phone calls from Irving ensued, together with explanations that the song was part of the war effort, and the paper appeared.

He also knew from his experience in the First World War that soldiers were liable to twist songs into clever but unprintable parodies. For this reason, the sheet music contained the following warning: "The performance of any parodied version of this composition is strictly prohibited." Nonetheless, a rueful travesty soon appeared:

> My Russian Buddy . . . He says he winning the war and that's
> okay with me.
> My Irish Buddy . . . He's as neutral as can be.
> My Yankee Buddy . . . He gets ten bob a day, and I get two
> and three.

Since *Yip! Yip! Yaphank* hadn't traveled across the Atlantic in 1918, wary English audiences required some background as to the nature and purpose of its successor, *This Is the Army.* An emotional program note offered the Army's explanation of the revue's mission. "If you find 'This Is The Army' entertaining," read the note, in part, "it will have served an important purpose. Entertainment is an essential to high morale, a fact which is understood, surely, throughout the British Empire, where astonishing esprit stood alone, for a time, against the barbaric effort to conquer the civilized world." An additional note informed audience members that in case of an air raid, they could, if they wished, leave the theater, but they were warned that "the performance will continue and members are advised in their own interests to remain in the building."

Opening night for *This Is the Army* at the London Palladium proved to be every bit as rapturous as the opening night in New York. Berlin sang "Oh! How I Hate to Get Up in the Morning," just as he had in the domestic tour, and his new song, "My British Buddy," went over well with the audience—as the Associated Press reported on November 13:

> A New American song is sweeping over London and its psychological punch is equal to another big chunk of lend-lease or a fresh troopship of soldiers.
>
> It is Irving Berlin's "My British Buddy," heard for the first time when his all-soldier musical hit, "This Is the Army," was given its premiere here Wednesday night.
>
> Mr. Berlin sang it himself, clad in his authentic trappings of a sergeant in the last war—a broad-brimmed campaign hat, baggy breeches, wrapped leggings and a high-colored tunic.
>
> Mr. Berlin thought it up one night when he was walking the London streets in a blackout at a time when the Germans were attacking Britain from the air. It seemed to him, he said, that he had found the right spirit of British-American comradeship, the sort of spirit that did not need prompting or rhetoric. . . .
>
> Mr. Berlin has presented the rights to the song hit to the British Service Charities Committee, Lady Louis Mountbatten, co-chairman of the committee, announced.

Lunching with Edwina Mountbatten and her husband, Lord Louis, several days after the opening, Berlin was moved to reflect on the time he had unexpectedly encountered Louis's father, Prince Louis Battenberg, thirty-seven years earlier. At the time, he was still Izzy Baline, an unknown singing waiter in Nigger Mike's, and Prince Louis Battenberg was visiting royalty. The encounter had been young Izzy's first brush with fame. Once news of the more recent meeting got out, a joke began to circulate: Berlin had supposedly told Lord Louis, "I see I'm not the only one here who's changed his name."

For prominent Americans, wartime London was remarkable for the easy access they enjoyed to the highest echelons of British society. Berlin's dining with the Mountbattens was but one instance of this extraordinary openness; another was the arrival of an envelope from the "Prime Minister and First Lord of the Treasury." Within, the songwriter found an invitation to have lunch with Winston Churchill at 10 Downing Street. Without realizing it, Irving had stumbled into a notable instance of mistaken identity.

Throughout the course of the war, Churchill had been entertained by dispatches written by the celebrated Oxford don *Isaiah* Berlin, who was assigned to the British Embassy in Washington. On hearing that the writer he so admired was visiting London, Churchill hastened to invite Isaiah Berlin to lunch. Through a bureaucratic mix-up, however, the invitation went out to the songwriter rather than the political commentator.

On the appointed day, Berlin presented himself at the prime minister's residence, where he was escorted to a comfortable room and given a cigar and a glass of brandy. In time, Churchill appeared, still under the impression that his guest was Isaiah Berlin. The prime minister wasted little time on pleasantries. "How is war production in the United States?" he demanded.

Berlin was taken aback by the question. He was a composer and performer, not a war correspondent. "Oh, we're doing fine," he hesitantly answered.

"What do you think Roosevelt's chances of reelection are?"

Uncomfortable at being called on to play political pundit, he gave the obvious answer. "I think he'll win again."

"Good," Churchill replied. "Good."

"But if he won't run again," Irving offered, "I don't think I'll vote at all."

For the first time, he had Churchill's interest, not that he welcomed it. "You mean you think you'll have a vote?" Churchill asked, a note of wonder—or was it British irony?—creeping into his voice.

"I sincerely hope so," Irving said.

"That would be wonderful," Churchill replied, appearing to sum up. "If only Anglo-American cooperation reached such a point that we could vote in each other's elections. Professor, you have my admiration. You must stay for lunch."

Throughout lunch at 10 Downing Street, Irving was haunted by the feeling that he was well out of his depth. Why had Churchill addressed him as "professor?" He stopped trying to reply to Churchill's probing questions and fell silent. Eventually Churchill turned his back on his taciturn guest. The awkward lunch finally came to a conclusion, and as Churchill left the room, he whispered loudly to an aide, "Berlin's just like most bureaucrats. Wonderful on paper but disappointing when you meet them face to face."

Unaware of Irving's true identity and purpose in London, Churchill belonged to a tiny minority. *This Is the Army*'s brief run at the Palladium accomplished its mission: it raised money, promoted goodwill between the Americans and the British, and showered Berlin with publicity. The English had loved him and his music since his first visit thirty years before, and the revue's success demonstrated that they still did. His picture was everywhere, his war songs on the lips of embattled Englishmen.

During its London run, the company of *This Is the Army* was fortunate enough to escape danger from serious air raids during their stand at the Palladium. In case they were tempted to assume that their special status as performers excused them from the hazards of war, an object lesson cleared up that misconception. Just one week after they left London, buzz bombs began to fall over the city, destroying, among other buildings, the Red Cross barracks in which the cast and crew of *This Is the Army* had stayed. Sixty GIs, none of them company members, died in that blast, but the tragedy served to remind the performers of their vulnerability.

After London, the revue toured the provinces—Manchester, Birmingham, Glasgow, Belfast—and returned to London to perform for General Eisenhower on February 6, 1944. At the time, everyone believed that *This Is the Army* had finally reached the end. "But Ike was so moved by the show that he came backstage afterward," Manson said. "He had this Kansas voice; if you closed your eyes you'd think it was Clark Gable. He said, 'I know you think you're just doing a show and that you feel maybe you're not really soldiers, but don't ever think for one minute that you're not doing a job. This thing is so important. We're going to see that you guys go down and play for the boys around the world.' "

On February 8 Eisenhower wrote to General Marshall proposing that *This Is the Army* should play to soldiers on all fronts. A week later, the company took a train to Liverpool, where they boarded the SS *Ormonde* and sailed to Algiers, arriving on the first of March. After two weeks of performing in North Africa, the troupe sailed for Naples. "We moved into the destroyed palace of Victor Emmanuel on the Naples waterfront, which had received twenty-two direct hits," remembered Alan Manson. "While we were there, we had a twenty-third hit. The Nazis were bombing the harbor. No one was ever injured in our company, but the point was we were in the thick of it." War was not the only hazard the men faced in Italy; on March 23 Mt. Vesuvius erupted, adding to the chaotic situation they faced.

The company finally found temporary shelter in the small San Carlo Opera House in Naples, where they played for the first half of April. "The men were brought down in relays to see the show. They didn't know what they were getting," said Manson. "They thought they were going to see an accordion player and a broad shaking her ass. But we gave them an enormous show, with 150 men"—and, of course, Irving Berlin, whose poignant rendition of "Oh! How I Hate to Get Up in the Morning" was a highlight of each performance. By this time, the song had become more than an anthem of disgust with reveille; it was a protest against the monstrous war that had overtaken all their lives.

By early June, Allied troops had taken Rome, and Berlin's company came riding into the city on trucks six days behind the victorious forces. Later that month, *This Is the Army* took up residence at the Royal Opera House, performing twice daily. In addition, the tireless songwriter found time to make thirty-five solo appearances in military hospitals, where he performed Italian melodies he had learned as a boy on the Lower East Side.

Despite the merriment he tried to summon, entertaining the wounded was a grim business, and Berlin arrived at a new understanding of the soldiers, who were young enough to be his children. "The boys in this war are different from those in the last war," he told *The New York Times*.

> In 1918 the boys in the trenches sang together. But the fellow in a foxhole is not apt to sing by himself. Believe me, he has other things to think about. Dropping bombs are not good accompaniments, even for war songs.
>
> Remember how the doughboys went across during the last war? They marched down the Avenue singing Over There or It's a Long Way to Tipperary. They were anxious to get over there and make the world safe for democracy, and they sang about it. Today the boys are grimmer. . . .
>
> In Italy, we would occasionally play for civilians, the

proceeds going to some local charity. I shall never forget a performance in Rome where I don't believe one-tenth of the audience could understand a word of the show. If anyone does not think that music is the universal language I wish he could have attended that performance at the Royal Opera House.

I spoke through an interpreter at the end of the show. I told how as a kid who had been born in Russia my folks went to America and settled in an Italian neighborhood. We youngsters knew no distinction of race or creed and I used to sing Jewish songs for them and they sang Italian songs for me. By the time I was through talking the audience and I were singing songs we both knew in chorus. Music knows no boundary lines and is one of the greatest forces in bringing the people of different nations together. And that is one of things the world will need after this war is over.

During his stay in Rome, Berlin, whose wife had returned to the Catholic church, persuaded an American chaplain to arrange an audience with Pope Pius XII. "I had heard many stories in Rome of the help the Pope had given the Jews, and I took this opportunity of thanking the Pope," he later explained. After the war, a spirited debate would arise as to whether this Pope had done anything substantial to help the Jews, but for Berlin, with his reverence for symbolism, a gesture or a slogan was often as good as a deed.

At the conclusion of the Italian tour, Irving left the company of *This Is the Army*, on July 26, 1944, to return to New York. There he stripped off his khaki quasi-uniform and started dressing as stylishly as he had before the war. And he sat once again at his desk in his Seventh Avenue office, beneath the portrait of Stephen Foster, whose example had been with him throughout his songwriting career. But his mind remained on the revue. "While we were overseas," said Manson, "Mr. Berlin got the names of all our parents and the wives of those who were married, and he either wrote or called every family in the company to say, 'Your boy is fine, and he sends love.' "

The company's tour, without Berlin, passed through one devastated theater of war after another, always attracting large and appreciative audiences. "We're playing in a very small opera house in a charmingly grubby two-horse town," wrote John Koenig, the set designer, at a time when their location was a military secret. "I've seen

ABOVE: **Berlin's friendship with the violinist Jascha Heifetz began when the two were members of the Algonquin Round Table.** (*The Story of Irving Berlin*, Alexander Woollcott, Putnam, 1925.)

RIGHT: **The Songwriter and the Jazz Singer: Berlin with Al Jolson.** (Courtesy of ASCAP)

George Gershwin wanted to be musical secretary to his idol, Irving Berlin, who considered the younger man much too talented for the job. (Courtesy of ASCAP)

ABOVE: **Vaudeville star Harry Richman performs the title song in the 1929 motion picture *Puttin' On the Ritz*.** (Museum of Modern Art/Film Stills Archive)

Richman (left) with *Puttin' On the Ritz* costar, Joan Bennett, and Berlin. (Museum of Modern Art/Film Stills Archive)

The finale of *Top Hat*—"The Piccolino." (Museum of Modern Art/Film Stills Archive)

FACING PAGE: **Berlin with Fred Astaire and Ginger Rogers during the making of *Top Hat* (1935). The songwriter admired Astaire above all other performers.** (Museum of Modern Art/Film Stills Archive)

Irving Berlin in early 1937, at the time he completed his score for Twentieth Century-Fox's *On the Avenue*. (USC Library, Special Collections, Hearst Newspaper Collection/Twentieth Century-Fox)

ABOVE: Irving Berlin, at age fifty, performs at a testimonial dinner held in his honor in Hollywood. The event took place within a replica of The Pelham Café, where he had worked as a singing waiter in his youth. Jerome Kern rests his hand on Berlin's shoulder as burly Joseph Schenck (standing between Berlin and piano) looks on. (Courtesy of ASCAP)

Mynna Granat—Irving Berlin's secretary and Saul Bornstein's nemesis—in 1943. (Mynna Granat Dreyer)

Berlin accompanies his grieving wife, Ellin, to the funeral of her father, Clarence H. Mackay, at St. Patrick's Cathedral in New York. Clarence opposed his daughter's marriage to the Tin Pan Alley songwriter, and the enmity between Berlin and his father-in-law ended only with Mackay's death on November 12, 1938. (Wide World Photos)

Irving Berlin (in costume) with Ezra Stone, the young director of *This Is the Army*; the two men had a highly charged relationship. (Theatre Collection, Museum of the City of New York)

FACING PAGE: Exhausted from months of touring with *This Is the Army*, Berlin went before the cameras in Hollywood to sing "Oh! How I Hate to Get Up in the Morning." His voice was so weak, however, that a technician was heard to say, "If the fellow who wrote this song could hear this guy sing it, he'd roll over in his grave." (Theatre Collection, Museum of the City of New York)

Berlin chats with one of the "girls" in the chorus of the original Broadway version of *This Is the Army*. The sight of soldiers cavorting in drag delighted theater audiences but caused concern at Warner Brothers, the studio producing the motion picture adaptation of the revue. (Theatre Collection, Museum of the City of New York)

A white Christmas. Touring the country with *This Is the Army*, Berlin paused to celebrate Christmas, 1942 in a Detroit hotel room with his family: (left to right) Ellin, Mary Ellin, Linda, and Elizabeth. (USC Library, Special Collections, Hearst Newspaper Collection)

The all-soldier cast of *This Is the Army* sings "Mandy" on Broadway—1942. Irving Berlin's wartime revue raised nearly $10,000,000 for the Army. (Theatre Collection, Museum of the City of New York)

BELOW: **Irving and Ellin shortly after the outbreak of World War II.** (USC Library, Special Collections, Hearst Newspaper Collection)

He likes Ike: accompanied by his wife Ellin, Berlin receives a citation from President Dwight Eisenhower. The songwriter composed three songs boosting Ike's candidacy. (Courtesy of ASCAP)

Ethel Merman as Annie Oakley in the original Broadway production of *Annie Get Your Gun*, 1946. (Theatre Collection, Museum of the City of New York)

For over sixty years, Berlin, who could neither read music nor write it, dictated his songs to his musical secretary, Helmy Kresa. (Helmy Kresa)

ABOVE: **Four years after triumphing in *Annie Get Your Gun*, Ethel Merman returned to Broadway to star in Berlin's political satire *Call Me Madam*** (Theatre Collection, Museum of the City of New York)

After Judy Garland dropped out, Betty Hutton assumed the starring role in the troubled Hollywood version of *Annie Get Your Gun* and rescued the movie from disaster. (Museum of Modern Art/Film Stills Archive)

At Berlin's insistence, Marilyn Monroe sang "Heat Wave" in the 1954 motion picture, *There's No Business Like Show Business*. (Museum of Modern Art/Film Stills Archive)

FACING PAGE: **The Kennedys walk out of the Washington premiere of *Mr. President*, the musical Irving Berlin wrote in the vain hope of capitalizing on their glamour and popularity.** (John Fitzgerald Kennedy Library, Boston, Massachusetts)

Irving Berlin with his oldest daughter, Mary Ellin, at the Stork Club in New York, 1949. Shortly afterward, she flew to Nevada to seek a divorce from her first husband, Dennis Burden. (USC Library, Special Collections, Hearst Newspaper Collection)

Ever the showman, Irving Berlin sings the score of his last, unsuccessful Broadway production, *Mr. President*, 1962. (Theatre Collection, Museum of the City of New York)

'This Is the Army' so many times, I now prefer to watch the audience reaction instead. . . . We open with three national anthems, 'La Marsellaise,' 'God Save the King,' and 'The Star-Spangled Banner.' Then our twenty-six-piece orchestra beats out the overture and we're off. . . . The GI's are not timid with applause; they whistle, yell and roar approval. Daumier would have loved the way they hang over the boxes, those behind craning forward; and all their physical reactions to a good gag. But there's something almost too concentrated and frantic about their enjoyment, something too hysterical in their laughter."

They reached Cairo, Egypt, on August 3, where they performed through the end of the month in the Cairo Opera House. They passed most of September and October in Iran, performing in such exotic locales as Ahwaz, Andimeshk, Khurramabad, Hamadan, Kazvin, Teheran, Arak, and Khorramasahr. At the conclusion of this leg of the tour, Berlin once again returned to his traveling show.

By year's end, the men were exhausted from their travels. It would soon be 1945, three years after they had reported for duty on *This Is the Army*, and there was still no end in sight to their rigorous touring schedule. When Berlin rejoined the company in New Guinea on December 30, he carried orders that they were to proceed into the Pacific and certain danger.

"I was worried," said Rosie of this next leg of the tour. "We all were. We were going to travel island to island, in the battle zone. We'd have our meetings, and a certain officer would say, 'Do this, do that,' and I would see Berlin sitting back, not saying anything. I asked myself, What the hell is the matter with him?"

Rosie went to see the songwriter that night, and he said, "Mr. B., you're sitting back and this guy's running everything. We can't even get a word in. Why the quiet?"

"We need certain things—we need a ship, we need equipment, and this man can get it for us," Berlin explained.

"Do we need him that much?"

And he said, "Yup."

Eventually, the officer obtained everything they needed, and once he did, Berlin called a meeting, and said, "Lieutenant, we are so grateful for what you've done. We have our own organization, and we will now run it our way. Thank you very much."

The officer sat there, as Rosie recalled, "with his mouth open."

"I thought I was going to do it."

"Oh, no," Berlin told him. "You were gonna put us together."

"Well, who's going to run it?"

The point was well taken, for Berlin had no official status in the Army and could not start giving orders. "Then the most fantastic thing happened," Rosenstock said. "We had a major with us. He knew nothing, but he knew the Army. We sat down with this major, and Berlin told him, 'This is the way this outfit runs now. There will be no decision as far as the show's concerned without the full okay of five people. This committee will run the show.' And that's the way the whole thing ran, and it ran very well."

Few theatrical troupes have suffered as many hardships as did the company of *This Is the Army*, traveling the Pacific in time of war, but the beleaguered soldier-actors prevailed through a combination of ingenuity and enthusiasm. Part of the credit belonged to the men themselves, by now welded into a band with a fanatical devotion to their cause, a fanaticism required to survive, and part belonged to Berlin himself, whose indomitable will had made the worldwide tour possible. The overcrowding aboard decrepit ships, inferior food, isolation, constant danger, and lack of women had all subjected the members of the company to an unusual degree of stress. Without Berlin's example of persistence in the face of seemingly insurmountable obstacles, the company would have quickly disintegrated. With it, however, they could be resourceful and tenacious, even when their surroundings mocked their efforts, battered their health, and reduced the show from a Broadway smash to theater of the absurd.

During their year-end stand in New Guinea, for instance, the men received vaccinations hours before they were to give a show, and by the time the curtain went up, they were already suffering symptoms. Rosie, the conductor, felt his knees buckle, and he could barely lift his arms. Musicians tried blowing on their instruments, but were too weak to produce any sound. "The smart clicks of the tap dances disappeared into a soft shoe routine. The chorus went horribly flat, and the comedians broke into an unprecedented amount of doubletalk," Rosie recalled. The show stumbled to a conclusion, and the next day's performance was canceled while the men recovered from their vaccinations.

When the show finally did take place, the audience was enormous:

fifteen thousand tired, homesick GIs. Here they were, halfway 'round the world from home, stuck in a feverish nightmare of dampness and danger. And suddenly they had the opportunity to see the man whose songs they'd grown up hearing and singing: Irving Berlin. And not just Berlin, but an entire Broadway show, complete with orchestra, all of it in the jungle. The only disappointment they felt was the lack of real women in the cast.

At the end of the show, Berlin naturally gave an encore. The GIs could not be denied, after all. They had a request. "God Bless America," Berlin thought. But no, they told their commanding officer they wanted to hear Berlin sing his great hit, "Over There." Berlin, nonplussed, said he'd be pleased to sing the song "written by my friend, the late George M. Cohan." And he went on to sing "Over There" in a voice so wan, so uncertain that it sounded as though his mouth were full of marbles. But the soldiers loved it, anyway.

For Irving, the experience of performing far from home offered unexpected rewards. One night, he was invited to an enlisted men's club, where the men serenaded him with his own "White Christmas." The song was not only on the lips of American soldiers; the songwriter also heard it sung by the residents of New Guinea in a language he did not even understand. Still, the tune was unforgettable: "White Christmas," there in the tropics.

It was a wonderful experience, performing in the jungle this way, but it was also slightly mad. No other songwriter of Berlin's stature would have attempted to lead his own military troupe around the world. No other popular entertainer was willing to put his life on the line so regularly for the sake of the war effort. The exploits of *This Is the Army* revealed still more facets of this multitalented man. His willingness to plunge in and deal with the smallest detail of organizing the production, the Army's obstinate bureaucracy, as well as the maddening Pacific climate—all this revealed his affinity with generals and politicians. His stamina and resourcefulness suggested once again how formidable a political leader Berlin would have made, if he had chosen that route, if he hadn't started singing as a small boy with his father in *shul* and stumbled across his musical genius.

Departing the New Guinea jungle for the vast expanses of the Pacific, the company discovered they had merely exchanged one set of hardships for another. In January 1945, they acquired what Anderson termed "a rotten old Dutch freighter that no Japanese commander would waste his time on. It was very small, 260 feet long. And we chugged all over the Pacific in it until June."

The boat, *El Libertador*, was designed to carry twenty-five passengers; now it had to transport one hundred and fifty weary players. To squeeze aboard, the company jettisoned scenery, generators, costumes, props, and even irreplaceable musical instruments. The equipment that the troupe did take along quickly showed the effects of the region's persistent humidity. Stringed instruments required repairs every third day. Wind instruments, unless coated with vaseline, rusted just as quickly; and the few remaining costumes rotted away. The weather bedeviled the men, as well. It seemed to rain nearly every evening, just as they were landing at a new destination and beginning to unload their equipment or trying to find a dry place to sleep.

Berlin flourished in these strenuous conditions. He relished the camaraderie among the men. Their youth and unquenchable enthusiasm proved infectious, and he himself exhibited remarkable physical stamina. For exercise, he would don a bathing suit and jump off the ship into the glimmering waters of the Pacific. Besides swimming, his chief form of physical activity, he often explained, was worrying and pacing. The only giveaway to his age was the pair of horn-rimmed glasses he wore when banging out a brief communiqué on a battered typewriter with one finger. (Throughout his life, his typing remained as primitive—and effective—as his piano playing.) As the war neared its end, the indefatigable composer added new songs reflecting the progress of *This Is the Army* around the globe: "The Fifth Army's Where My Heart Is," "Heaven Watch the Philippines," "I Get Along with the Aussies." In all, he wrote thirty-four songs that appeared at one time or another in the score. The last was titled, appropriately enough, "Oh, To Be Home Again."

Still, the conditions under which he and the men labored were strenuous. Most days they put on a show, then packed up, returned to the ship, sailed to the next harbor, unpacked, tried to sleep, and the next day staged another show—or two. They repeated the cycle through Milne Bay, Oro Bay, the Admiralty Islands, Lae, Finschafen, Hollandia, Samar—wherever members of the Army, Navy, Marines, or Air Corps were to be found; all the world was their stage.

When they were not battling nature, they often had to cope with the prejudices of the men they were trying to entertain. "In the Pacific, they tried to separate the black guys from the rest of the outfit," Anderson recalled. "We had to produce a paper that said, General Marshall gives us orders to travel together. And they listened to us because they didn't want us to go back to General Marshall. So we were not segregated in living quarters, or in eating, or working."

United on the issue of race, the company bickered over the subject of rank. Matters came to a head in the spring of 1945, when the cast was drifting from one remote outpost in the Pacific to the next. Berlin had tried and failed to obtain all the promotions his men wanted. To distance himself from the matter, over which he had little influence in the first place, he let Alan Anderson deliver the bad news. Though many of the men had remained privates throughout the war, they still were soldiers, and they had no choice but to continue.

Berlin, in contrast, possessed no rank, but this apparent shortcoming proved to be an asset of considerable value, for his lack of official status permitted him to come and go as he pleased. (He could also sleep as late as he liked.) The unusual arrangement became especially useful when, shortly after the dispute over promotions, a cable from Paramount Pictures summoned Berlin to Hollywood to supervise the score of *Blue Skies*, which was about to go before the cameras.

An amalgam of old Berlin tunes, the quaint and gentle movie starred Bing Crosby and Joan Caulfield. Without official military status, Berlin was in the enviable position of departing the dank, cramped quarters of their rustbucket for the unreal luxury of Hollywood. In New York, Mynna Granat arranged for her boss to hitch rides on military flights that brought him to Hollywood within several days.

Berlin slipped back into the show business milieu as though four years of war had never intervened. At the end of July, he held a press conference to publicize both *This Is the Army*, lest it be forgotten at home, and the forthcoming movie. He even found time to demonstrate a new song for reporters, "The Horse and the Flea"—intended for *Blue Skies* but never used—"with his inimitable piano plunking and tin-whistle voice." Remarked one observer, "It is a nifty tune, although perhaps Bing Crosby . . . will do it more justice."

While Berlin plunked and sang in Hollywood, the cast and crew of *This Is the Army* reached Guam on August 2, 1945. Four days later, the Enola Gay took off from that island to drop the first atomic bomb. The men had no knowledge of the event that would bring the war in the Pacific to a traumatic conclusion.

The final leg of the troupe's round-the-world journey sparked a remarkable burst of energy. In a span of ten days at Leyte, in the Philippines, the company gave thirty-six performances before a total of 77,000 GIs. While they were in Okinawa, a typhoon struck on September 16, 1945, but they escaped without injury. The following week, they departed for Iwo Jima, where they spent two days, before pressing on to Eniwetok, Runit, and Kwajalein. They finally reached Hawaii on October 10.

Berlin planned to rejoin the company for the closing days of the tour, but getting there with the war having only just ended proved to be a difficult task. Once again, he used his outstanding military connections. "When Mr. Berlin had to go to Hawaii," said Mynna, "I picked up my phone to the Pentagon, and I could not get a plane in any part of the service. Everything was packed full. Mr. Berlin said, 'I have to be there.' He had to make arrangements for where the men were going to live, where they were going to eat, and so on. I called Eddie Rickenbacker and said, 'Mr. Berlin has got to get to Honolulu. No one can help him.' He said, 'Tell Mr. Berlin to be at the airport. He's got a plane.' "

At the final performance of *This Is the Army* in Haleakala, on the island of Maui, on October 22, Irving Berlin sang "Oh! How I Hate to Get Up in the Morning" one last time and concluded his appearance with a speech in which he said he hoped he would never again have to write another war song.

In all, approximately 2,500,000 soldiers and civilians had seen *This Is the Army* somewhere in the world between its Broadway debut on July 4, 1942, and its Hawaiian finale in 1945. Two weeks later, the soldiers flew to San Francisco in four detachments, and a final formation took place at three-fifteen P.M., Saturday, October 27, 1945, at Hamilton Field. *This Is the Army* had come to the end of its astonishing run.

Several of the soldiers who had played important roles in the show from the beginning were not there to relish the melancholy pleasure of the final formation in San Francisco, at the end of a victorious war.

Ezra Stone, victim of a bitter power struggle with Berlin, was long gone. Milt Rosenstock, the conductor, had fallen ill near the end of the tour and had left early. But Alan Manson, who had joined the cast shortly after completing his basic training over four years earlier, was still with the company at the end.

The exhausted soldiers dispersing throughout the country could count themselves among the fortunate. Although the show had visited most of the theaters of operation in the war, none of its members had been killed. For many, the disbanding of the troupe marked the end of the great adventure of their lives. More than most shows, *This Is the Army* belonged to its time and to the men who performed in it. As such, it became obsolete the moment the war ended. The movie version was merely a souvenir of the show itself; the songs, good as they were, were irrevocably linked to the war. The essence of the show resided with the men themselves, and each took a piece of it away with him. They were now confronted with a more modest task than entertaining war-weary servicemen posted around the world: they would try to resume their lives where they had left them off four years before.

Irving Berlin enjoyed a grander homecoming. Shortly after his return, he traveled to Washington and appeared at the office of his wartime patron, General George Marshall. President Harry Truman had conferred the Medal of Merit, the nation's second highest honor, on the songwriter, and now Marshall himself fastened the award to the lapel of the exceedingly proud songwriter. In addition, Berlin received a citation reading, "He has set a high standard of devotion to his country and has won for himself the thanks and appreciation of the U.S. Army for highly meritorious service."

The brief ceremony—stiff, dry, and military though it was—marked the sweetest moment in Berlin's entire career. In receiving the Medal of Merit, he finally, at the advanced age of fifty-seven, completed his drive for assimilation. Attaining that goal was worth the financial sacrifice he had made during the war, for it was a matter of honor—*koved*, in Yiddish. Honor was the one distinction Berlin took more seriously than wealth, and the one he had harbored the most doubts about attaining in his adopted country. Thanks to the war, his goals and the nation's had become one. Honor was his at last.

PART FOUR

RETREAT

1946–1989

■ □ ■ □ ■ □ ■

CHAPTER 17

One-Upmanship

As the Second World War ended, the Broadway stage began to hum once again with vigor and originality. A courtesan in her youth, later a flapper, Broadway now embarked on a respectable, if slightly overbearing, middle age. Songwriters and librettists who had exiled themselves to Hollywood during the thirties began to converge on New York. Whether they cared to admit it or not, all were drawn by the artistic and financial success enjoyed by composer Richard Rodgers and lyricist Oscar Hammerstein II, whose *Oklahoma!* (1943) and *Carousel* (1945) finally set the American musical on the course first suggested by Jerome Kern's *Show Boat* in 1927.

On the strength of these achievements, Rodgers and Hammerstein became the reigning force in musical theater. As audiences of the time knew, the name Hammerstein bore approximately the same relationship to Broadway that the name Roosevelt did to American politics. Oscar Hammerstein's grandfather had been an important opera impresario, and his father had managed the Victoria Theatre. Even his uncle had been a successful Broadway producer. If ever a man was born to the Broadway stage, Oscar Hammerstein II was he. His partner, Richard Rodgers, had been composing Broadway scores for two decades, first in collaboration with the brilliant, if volatile, Lorenz Hart, and, following Hart's death, Hammerstein.

Broadway and its audiences had changed during the years of Depression and war. The naughty, lavish revues, once its staple, had dwindled to a tiny handful; conditioned by movies, theatergoers wanted stories of substance. As Rodgers and Hammerstein repeatedly (and profitably) demonstrated, audiences responded to a treacly blend of self-conscious Americana and heartening liberal sermons with as much enthusiasm as an earlier generation had brought to the spectacle of flashing thighs and heaving bosoms. Even as Rodgers and Hammerstein raised the Broadway musical to the level of operetta and imbued it with a social conscience, they grew wealthy.

As the talent migrating east noted, the economics no less than the aesthetics of Broadway had undergone a crucial transformation. It was now cheap to mount a full-scale musical, cheap compared to making a movie, that is. A decent movie musical could easily cost over a million dollars to make, while the trend-setting *Oklahoma!* had been mounted for just $75,000 and would run for over two thousand performances. And the hit shows would inevitably be sold to the movies, thus earning more money, more royalties, more of everything.

Later, the development of the long-playing record, accommodating an entire score on a single platter, meant that songwriters and lyricists suddenly had an important new market for their wares: the "original cast album." Rodgers and Hammerstein again played the role of innovators, when Decca released the score of *Oklahoma!* in a long-playing version, thus establishing the practice for Broadway shows. The happy confluence of all these forces—artistic, economic, and technological—meant that the Broadway musical was in the midst of a new flowering.

Among the first veterans of the Broadway stage to attempt a comeback was Jerome Kern, whom Rodgers and Hammerstein were happy to acknowledge as their inspiration, so happy that they wanted him to write the score of their next show, which they planned to produce. Their story—highly embroidered—told of Phoebe Annie Oakley Moses, the unlettered sharpshooter who emerged from Darke County, Ohio, to entertain the United States at the turn of the century, and her rival Frank Butler, who became her husband and manager.

Even for a Broadway musical, *Annie Get Your Gun*, as the show was called, had a bizarre history. It began to take shape during the war, when Dorothy Fields, a lyricist and the daughter of the venerable comedian Lew Fields, listened to her husband describe a drunken soldier he'd recently seen. This soldier, a marksman, was displaying all the silly prizes he'd won at the booths at Coney Island. "As if out of the sky, from Heaven, comes this idea," she remembered. "Annie Oakley—the *sharpshooter!* With Ethel Merman to play her!" And it *was* a good idea, especially for its time, charged with the sexual implications of a woman who used her phallic gun with mastery, as well as satirical observations about show business. During the war, people could relate to the notion of a woman with a gun; women, if not in the battlefield, had become a potent part of the wartime work force.

With her older brother Herbert, a librettist, Dorothy first approached the producer Mike Todd with the idea, and when he scoffed, she buttonholed Oscar Hammerstein at an ASCAP meeting. Hammerstein instantly agreed, as did his partner Rodgers, but Ethel Merman posed a greater obstacle. Merman (Merm, to those who knew her, Ethel Agnes Zimmerman on her birth certificate) had a reputation as a rabble-rouser that rivaled her reputation as a singer with a clarion voice and perfect elocution. Mention Merm to a theater crowd, and people would roll their eyes and shake their heads. Soon they'd rehearse their Ethel Merman stories: her miserable affair with stockbroker Alter Goetz (one terse mention in Walter Winchell's column, "Al Goetz prefers his wife to Ethel Merman," and the affair was over); her foul mouth, so foul that even men tired of matching her dirty joke for dirty joke; and her arrogance: if the hairstyle of a certain chorus boy bothered her, she didn't ask him to change it, she had him fired. In real life, none of these qualities was much fun, but onstage, seen through the prism of the character of Annie Oakley, they could be the stuff of high comedy.

But there was another obstacle. Merman had just had a baby by Caesarian section, and she was now languishing in a New York hospital, slowly recuperating, in no condition to discuss business. Undaunted, Dorothy Fields talked her way to the star's bedside, leaned over, and whispered, "Merm, would you think of yourself as Annie Oakley?" Too tired to argue, Merm said she would do it.

Dorothy and her brother Herbert immediately began work on the book. Rodgers and Hammerstein, their euphonious, polysyllabic name a virtual guarantee of Broadway success, lobbied to lure Jerome Kern back from Hollywood to write the score. They were already planning to produce a revival of Kern's *Show Boat*, which worked in their favor, but it was Rodgers's telegram that did the trick:

> IT WOULD BE ONE OF THE GREATEST HONORS OF MY LIFE IF YOU WOULD CONSENT TO WRITE THE MUSIC FOR THIS SHOW.

Though Kern accepted the offer to compose the score for *Annie Get Your Gun*, he harbored serious doubts about the wisdom of returning to New York. He suffered from high blood pressure, and his doctor had put him on notice to take things easy. His last Broadway show, *Very Warm for May*, had proved an embarrassing flop six years earlier; all that work, and it had closed after fifty-nine performances. At this point in his life, he wondered if he needed the *tsuris* of another Broadway show.

On November 3, 1945, Kern arrived in New York after an arduous train ride from Los Angeles and installed himself at the St. Regis Hotel. The following day, he dined at the Hotel Astor with the librettist Guy Bolton, chatting amiably about the new musical on which he was about to embark. Afterward, he walked uptown. Reaching Park Avenue and 57th Street, he suddenly collapsed on the sidewalk.

Unconscious, he was transported by ambulance to City Hospital, the same hospital where Stephen Foster had died. It was but a few blocks from the house on East 56th Street in which Kern had been born. Still insensate from the effects of a stroke, he lay in a charity ward with fifty other inmates, most of them indigent. No one suspected who he was; he carried no identification except for an ASCAP card inscribed with a number. Eventually, the hospital tracked down the number, identified the patient as the celebrated Jerome Kern, master composer of the American musical. A screen was placed around his bed, and a nurse kept watch over him.

Meanwhile, Rodgers and Hammerstein began to wonder what had become of their Jerry, who had failed to show up at various rehearsals and meetings. Their discovery of his condition triggered a pilgrimage of friends and celebrities to City Hospital. When Kern's daughter arrived from California, she arranged for her father—who was still unconscious—to be moved uptown to posher quarters at Doctors Hospital, where he lingered for several days before dying on November 11.

"That was the worst week of my life. The worst week of everybody's life," Dorothy Fields later remarked. Still, something had to be done; the show must go on. The tears dried soon enough. "After the funeral," she continued, "we were all sitting at a restaurant, and we started discussing who could possibly replace somebody as gifted as Kern." There was Kern, not yet cold in his grave, and Dick Rodgers, consummate professional that he was, already had his replacement in mind, almost as if Dick had been thinking of the man all along, even *before* Kern had died. But Dick's choice posed a problem. "It means Dorothy can't do the lyrics," he said, never one to spare an ego or to cushion bad news.

At this point, Dorothy couldn't have cared less about writing lyrics; she just wanted to see the show staged. "I have enough to do with the book," she said. "Who is it?" And Rodgers replied with a single word capable of solving all their problems:

"Irving."

And why not? With Kern and Gershwin dead, and Rodgers and Hammerstein unwilling to write the score and lyrics, only Irving Berlin and Cole Porter came readily to mind as composers of stature. *Annie Get Your Gun* was definitely *not* a Porter show. Too corny, too *American.* And so, a process of elimination left Berlin as the best available replacement. However, it was a choice fraught with hazard, for Berlin had no place on the new, postwar Broadway. Rodgers and Hammerstein represented the Broadway establishment; compared to them, Berlin was a loose cannon. The theatrical form with which he was most closely associated, the revue, was in decline. Unchallenged as the craftsman of the outsized, one-of-a-kind hit such as "God Bless America," he had yet to prove himself in musical comedy; *Louisiana Purchase* had been a commercial success six years before, but it failed to make a lasting impression. And *This Is the Army* cast Berlin as an overseas crusader rather than a Broadway composer. Still, he was a phenomenon.

Berlin's first reaction to the offer was one of fear—fear that he would lack the star billing to which he had become accustomed. "I don't know whether I'd want to do a show that isn't 'Irving Berlin's Whatever,' " he complained.

"Irving, sorry, but this is our idea, our play," came the reply. "It can't be 'Irving Berlin's *Annie Oakley.*' "

"Let me think about it over the weekend," the songwriter said. "If I decide to relinquish the billing I've always had, then we'll talk about it."

For the moment, Berlin refused even to read the Fields siblings' first act; he wanted to make his decision without any influence whatsoever. The character of Annie Oakley and the idea animating the show meant absolutely nothing to him. "He thought Annie Oakley was something you punched holes in, a free ticket," said Dave Dreyer, the songwriter who worked for Berlin.

Over the weekend Berlin reflected on his situation. It had been splendid traveling the globe for the last few years, playing the role of the archetypal minstrel, then coming home to collect a medal for services rendered. Now it was time for him to return to the real world, the "real world" in his case being Broadway. During the last five years, he'd lived a strangely inverted existence, in which show business was blood, sweat, and tears, and the war had been, for him, an all-expenses-paid, round-the-world tour. But it didn't pay the rent; he'd donated all the money his wartime revue had earned, nearly $10 million, to the United States Army. And now Rodgers and Hammerstein offered the chance for him to make some real money he could keep. He could hardly find better auspices under which to return to the stage, or better and more willing librettists than Herbert and Dorothy Fields with whom to collaborate. Once he swallowed his disappointment that the marquee wouldn't read "Irving Berlin's *Annie Oakley*," the opportunity had strong appeal.

On Monday, Berlin called back, still noncommittal, but asking to see what Herbert and Dorothy Fields had written. The following Friday, he sat down with Rodgers, two eminent composers going head to head to thrash things out. Now Berlin was hesitating because of the show's form; he still felt uncomfortable with a narrative musical, a "situation show," as he called it; that was Rodgers's forte. Rodgers insisted that "situations," far from inhibiting songwriting, were a tremendous aid. Irving "wouldn't have to find ideas in the sky. They'd be on paper, they'd be in the book, which would be a lot of help."

Irving had his doubts, not the least of which was the task of measuring up to Richard Rodgers's standard, for he would be pitting himself against the acknowledged master of the narrative musical. Nothing would be worse than coming in a poor second to Rodgers, with the critics declaring that if only Rodgers had composed the score, how much better it would have been. Seeing Berlin continue to balk, Rodgers recalled, "I begged him to go home with the book and fool around over the weekend and see how things worked, whether he got any ideas, whether it felt comfortable for him."

Berlin took the incomplete script and retreated to an Atlantic City hotel with his arranger, Helmy Kresa. There he faced a final obstacle concerning the type of music he was supposed to compose: "hillbilly stuff," he called it. Of course, he knew nothing about hillbilly music, but he reached the conclusion that it had no place in *Annie Get Your Gun*; ultimately, it was a musical about show business, not hillbillies, and show tunes did have a place. And that was a type of music he happened to know one or two things about. Suddenly, the master song, that endless, evolving compilation of melodies he carried in his head, which he alone could hear and which had eluded him for years at a time, seemed to be his for the listening. Within a week, he roughed out half a dozen songs. "Doin' What Comes Naturally" introduced the earthy, crude Annie Oakley. In "You Can't Get a Man with a Gun," she lamented her inability to find love while wielding a weapon. "They Say It's Wonderful" was the obligatory ballad that Annie and Frank sing when they do at last find each other.

Finally, "There's No Business Like Show Business," sung by Butler's troupe, served little plot function, but it was nonetheless a subtle and sophisticated tour de force. Its principal melody—a rather ordinary one—consists of only three tones: a businesslike tune about show business. Then Irving begins to work his tricks. In the bridge, the melody suddenly becomes a scale, or nearly a scale, in contrast to the tightly knit opening. In the fourth and final statement of the melody, illustrating anxiety about a flop show, the dominant chord Berlin sounds underscores the uncertainty; the ear cannot tell where this chord may lead. A trained musician would call this effect a "circle of fifths"; Berlin would say it simply sounded right to him. Even more impressive than the architecture of the melody is his use of syncopation to unify these disparate parts. The introduction of syncopation gives the entire tune a relentless, anxious, pulsing feeling perfectly suited to its meaning. It was a stroke of genius to syncopate the song; take it away, and the melody was too limp to contain much interest and conviction, but with it, "There's No Business Like Show Business" became an anthem fit to take its place beside "God Bless America."

Berlin played through this, the first crop of songs, before an audience consisting of Rodgers, Hammerstein, Dorothy Fields, and the show's new director, Joshua Logan, whom Rodgers had recently brought in. Berlin counted the addition of Logan as another plus. They had worked well together on *This Is the Army*, and Logan was one of the few directors Irving trusted. And Logan was just as delighted at the turn of events. At the time *Annie Get Your Gun* had come up, he had been thinking of himself as a "doddering thirty-seven-year-old has-been." Indeed, he had some justification to fear for his health, because an eye injury threatened his sight, and he was undergoing treatment. So he was delighted to find himself once again in his element, exercising his talents on Broadway, thanks to Dick Rodgers.

Logan and the rest of them knew enough to make allowances for Irving's quaint manner of performing, and they were enthralled by what they heard. And Berlin *knew* they were enthralled, because he studied their faces closely to observe their reactions. "He would grab me by the collar and sing a lyric into my face the moment I stepped into the room," Logan wrote. "Only by fixing his eyes on the listener could he sense if the song worked. If one blinked too often or one's eyes glazed for a second, Irving was apt to put the song away." Every minute flinch of cheek muscle and shift of the eyes spoke to the songwriter—Did this little joke in the lyrics work? Was that transition in the melody sufficiently startling?—and helped him gauge the level of interest in this, his first and most crucial audience. Berlin liked what he saw. Wait until Merman gets hold of those dynamite lyrics, their smiles said; wait until an orchestrator fleshes out that magnificent harmony.

During this period, a supercharged Berlin moved restlessly from his Upper East Side home to his office and to his Catskills retreat, tinkering constantly with the songs and trying them out on the members of the show's creative team. He devoted particular attention to "There's No Business Like Show Business." When he dictated the lyrics to his secretary, Mynna Granat, however, she muttered, "You call that a song, Mr. Berlin? This isn't a song. This is nothing." Berlin cautioned her not to comment and to keep typing, and insisted that the song would become one of his biggest hits, but her words eroded his confidence. When they were done, she proceeded to file it away.

The next time Irving sang the song for Logan and Rodgers—leaning into their faces—he thought he detected a certain lack of interest.

"What's the matter? Don't you like the song?" he asked.

"No, no," Logan and the others protested. "That song's already a smash."

"Yes, but the way you looked, so skittish."

And the audition concluded with that plaintive observation.

In the next run-through, Irving omitted the song altogether. At the end, Dick Rodgers approached him and said quietly, "Irving, you left out a number that I like. Why?"

Berlin replied: "Well, the last time I played the score, when I came to that song, I looked at your face, and you weren't enjoying yourself, and I thought you didn't like it, so I decided to cut it."

"Well, I'm crazy about it," Rodgers complained. "Put it back."

"We can't scream louder every time we hear it," Logan added.

Berlin's reply gave everyone pause: "I don't think I could find it right now. It's in a pile." *In a pile?* Mynna, he explained with a shrug, would need time to track it down.

At the urging of Logan and Rodgers, she immediately began searching for the song but couldn't find it anywhere. Soon they were all ransacking Berlin's office for a copy of "There's No Business Like Show Business," which Mynna eventually found lurking under a phone book, as good a place as any to file away that nothing of a song she herself had never particularly cared for.

Once the song was restored to the score, Logan felt the need of another tune in the second act, a duet for Merman and Ray Middleton, who would play her love interest, Frank Butler. Hesitating to raise the issue directly with Berlin, Logan cautiously whispered his request to Oscar Hammerstein during a meeting at Hammerstein's home on East 63rd Street. Berlin was sitting on the opposite side of the room at the time, but he managed to overhear the remark. "Another song?" he whispered, and suddenly announced, "Listen, everybody, Josh wants another song."

The question now was *where* to place the duet, since Oakley and

Butler were not on speaking terms in the second act. Rodgers proposed some sort of quarreling song, or a song of challenge. "Challenge!" Berlin shouted. "Of course! *Meeting over!*" Berlin knew precisely what he had to do: "I've got to go home and write a challenge song."

Logan taxied to his apartment at 56th Street and Park Avenue, a journey lasting only minutes, and when he walked in the door, his phone was ringing. "Hello, Josh," said Berlin in his high, creaky voice, "How's this?" The songwriter proceeded to croak the entire chorus for "Anything You Can Do," a comic gem of a challenge song for Annie Oakley and Frank Butler to sing together while maintaining their feud. The task of devising it had consumed all of fifteen minutes.

"Where the hell did you write that?" Logan asked.

"In the taxicab. I had to, didn't I? We go into rehearsal Monday."

Conceived on a moment's notice, the song summed up the entire meaning of Irving's working for his rival, Richard Rodgers: "Anything you can do, I can do better." The idea of competing against Rodgers, outdoing Rodgers, obsessed Berlin before, during and even after *Annie Get Your Gun.* Months later, on the evening that *Oklahoma!* was to give its two-thousandth performance, Rodgers invited Irving and Josh Logan to watch the show. As the three of them walked along West 44th Street to the theater, Irving began talking shop, asking Dick how the *Oklahoma!* album was selling in England.

"It's doing extremely well," Rodgers told Irving. "We didn't really expect to sell there at all because, you know, they don't have the same interest in the subject that Americans do, but we sell, oh, five hundred albums a month, which is really a lot over there."

"That's marvelous, really marvelous," cackled Berlin, who considered five hundred of anything a trivial amount, even for England. "I suppose it's doing well here?"

"Well, I hate to brag," said Rodgers with false humility, "but I think it's the most successful album ever."

But Irving had his comeback ready: "Do you realize that 'White Christmas' is still on the Hit Parade?"

"God, that's marvelous," said Dick, a distinct chill in his voice belying his enthusiasm.

Berlin couldn't stop there. " 'White Christmas' " he said, "has sold more sheet music than any other piece of sheet music ever printed, even in the days of Victor Herbert: five million copies."

"Five million copies," Rodgers forced himself to say. "That's *mar*velous."

At which point Irving tugged Josh on the sleeve and said, "Do you see how far back I had to go in this conversation to bring up 'White Christmas'?"

Despite this competitive undertone, Berlin, Rodgers, and Hammerstein reveled in the prospect of bringing in another hit, but the revelry ended with the show's first orchestra rehearsal. In the business of orchestration, Irving had deferred to Rodgers, who entrusted the task of expanding and elaborating the score to Philip Lang. Because of Lang's solid reputation, no one gave much thought to how he was proceeding. Rehearsals in New York ended; in a mood of high expectation the cast, crew, and costumes all traveled to New Haven to begin out-of-town tryouts. Now it was the turn of a new figure to loom large in the process of assembling the musical, the conductor. In this case, the assignment fell to Jay Blackton, once again, Rodgers's choice. Blackton was a small, intense man—and a perfectionist. Stricken with polio before he was a year old, he had, with his mother's encouragement, studied piano and done quite well at it. As he liked to say, his musical ability meant he would be able to earn his living sitting down. After attending Juilliard and knocking around opera and then radio for several years, he had found his niche when he conducted the orchestra for *Oklahoma!* After that experience he was, as he recalled, "sucked into Broadway."

On the night before the orchestra rehearsal, Blackton, in his room at the Taft Hotel in New Haven, called Lang and asked to see the orchestration of Berlin's score. Lang sent the music over, and Blackton began to study it. "The more I looked, the worse I felt," Blackton recalled. The problem was not Irving's tunes, but Lang's unsympathetic orchestration; in Lang's version, the songs lost their charm. "By now it was three o'clock in the morning," Blackton said. "I called Phil Lang; he was asleep. The next day, I started my rehearsal. Phil came down and watched as Dorothy kept poking me in the ribs and saying, 'Jay, what's going on here?' She was beginning to get flustered, and I kept muttering, 'Don't worry, I'll take care of it.' "

Blackton dreaded hearing Irving's reaction and did whatever he could to keep the songwriter away from the orchestra, but of course Berlin quickly became aware of the problem. His songs, his precious songs, with which he had dazzled his collaborators, sounded awful. Rodgers and Berlin went to lunch at a nearby restaurant, Kaysey's, to consider the problem. "For God's sake," Irving said, "what are we going to do? This will never work." By the end of the meal they decided to call the best orchestrator they could name, Robert Russell Bennett, who had worked successfully with Berlin at RKO. The following morning, Bennett arrived, and he immediately took over responsibility from Lang. Bennett's new orchestration rescued Berlin's score from disaster.

After a successful tryout in New Haven, the show moved to Boston for a three-week stand, where Berlin, always the perfectionist, took pains to polish songs that others already considered finished. "Out of the blue I got a little shaky about 'Doin' What Comes Naturally,' he said." "I often get that way about a song that is going fine, but I thought—maybe I could improve this one. I worked like a dog. Oscar Hammerstein said, 'It's wonderful as it stands. Why don't you leave it alone?' And there's nothing so tough as to give a performer a new lyric so that she had to remember part of the old and part of the new. Anyway, I picked a matinée and gave it to Ethel. Then I went back to her dressing room, and there was that lyric, as she was making up, in front of her, and by God, she did it absolutely letter-perfect. The thing was, it didn't go. The audience reaction didn't compare. And we went back to the original. Once you change something, the audience tells you, even if they applaud, they tell you."

At the end of April 1946, *Annie Get Your Gun* returned to New York, where it was to undergo two final days of run-throughs before opening at the Imperial Theatre. Havoc struck again, when crew members were hanging the scenery; suddenly bricks began to tumble, and a steel girder buckled. Dick Rodgers was onstage when he heard a loud crack, and the next thing he knew a stagehand was pushing him out of harm's way. The auditorium was quickly evacuated. To the disbelief of Rodgers, Logan, Merman, and Berlin, the entire theater appeared to be on the verge of collapse.

Rodgers later spoke to the engineers inspecting the damage. "They told us we couldn't possibly open the show for weeks," he recalled. "Well, this was really disaster. Oscar and I went see Lee Shubert, whose theater the Imperial was, and he moved things around. He took a show out of Philadelphia, sent it to New Haven, and got us the Shubert Theatre in Philadelphia."

During the two-week respite in Philadelphia while the Imperial Theatre underwent repairs, rumors started to circulate that the real reason the show's opening had been delayed was not because the Imperial Theatre required mending—that story was simply a clever dodge designed to disguise the fact that the musical itself was in serious trouble. Though groundless, the rumors succeeded in giving *Annie Get Your Gun* an advance reputation as a troubled show.

After surviving the sudden death of its original composer, the traumatic replacement of its orchestrator, and the near collapse of its theater, *Annie Get Your Gun* finally opened in New York on May 16, at the refurbished Imperial. Inevitably the evening occasioned anxiety. Logan, Merman, and everyone else associated with the show had become accustomed to out-of-town audiences that laughed uproariously at Annie Oakley's stunts and Berlin's lyrics, especially the line, "You can't shoot a male in the tail like a quail." But the Broadway crowd held back; polite chortles replaced outright belly laughs. The script introduced the characters in bold strokes:

> ANNIE: Look it over, Mister. Look it over keerful. Lift up his wings. See? No buckshot in that bird. Jes' one little hole in his head.
>
> WILSON: Mighty pretty shooting!
>
> ANNIE: Might pretty eatin', too. Fer evvy one I get ye, ye gotta give me two nickels and a dime.
>
> WILSON: Can't hurt to try them. I'll take two dozen.
>
> ANNIE: How many is that?
>
> WILSON: Twenty-four.
>
> ANNIE: (to her brothers and sisters) Who do we know kin count up to twenty-four?

The production lacked the psychological depth and complexity of *Show Boat*, not to mention the delicacy and nuance characteristic of Jerome Kern, and the freshness of *Oklahoma!* Furthermore, its songs failed to interrelate, as they did in the best Broadway scores. As one jest after another met with a lukewarm response, Irving paced, Rodgers sat in silence, and Logan tormented himself with thoughts such as, "Why is that lady laughing? She must be a backer. Berlin's finished. Merman's lost her voice." What had happened to their surefire hit?

He was slow to recognize that the pallid reaction resulted not from an unexpected weakness in the show but from the audience's frustrated expectations; first-nighters expected another Rodgers and Hammerstein music drama replete with operatic aspirations and social commentary. What they got, to their initial dismay, was a knockabout Irving Berlin musical filled with bits, routines, *shtick*.

Only Merman seemed not to mind the audience's muted reaction. At intermission, Logan sought her out backstage. "How are you able to play to them?" he asked.

Said Merman: "Easy. You may think I'm playing the part, but inside I'm saying, 'Screw you! You jerks! If you were as good as I am, you'd be up here!' "

By the second act, however, the audience came to the belated realization that the evening was closer in spirit to vaudeville than to Wagner, and they began to demonstrate their enjoyment in an appropriate manner: laughing, shouting, applauding. If *Annie Get Your Gun*'s lack of innovation and social commentary came as a disappointment to connoisseurs of the Broadway musical, its humor and enthusiasm had an irresistible appeal for audiences, if not for critics. Those who expected the show to mark the next phase in the evolution of the American musical, after *Oklahoma!* and *Carousel*, were destined to be disappointed; Berlin's music and lyrics strove only to entertain, and in that they succeeded brilliantly. "A good professional musical," commented *The New York Times*, with a "pleasant score by Irving Berlin. . . . The colors are pretty, the dancing is amiable and unaffected, and Broadway by this time is well used to a book which doesn't get anywhere in particular." Other critics, whose expectations were not quite so high, reacted more favorably. "BULL'S EYE" said the headline for Howard Barnes's appraisal in the *Herald Tribune*: "The new Rodgers-Hammerstein production has every hallmark of distinction. . . . The Irving Berlin songs form a fascinating web of wit and melody."

The main complaint lodged against Berlin's score for *Annie Get Your Gun* by students of the American musical was that it was merely an assorted collection of hits, unlike the more operatic scores by Rodgers and Hammerstein. In a word, it was old-fashioned. Yes, it was old-fashioned, Berlin acknowledged, "nothing but good old-fashioned hits." An operatic score in the manner of Rodgers and Hammerstein remained, for him, an unattainable goal; he knew his arena, and within its confines, he was the unchallenged master. "Aren't we lucky that the critics only *write about* the music and don't try to *write* it themselves?" he complained.

Though bitter over his failure to become the critics' darling in the manner of Rodgers and Hammerstein, an exponent of the progressive postwar American musical, Berlin consoled himself with the knowledge that his score was an enormous commercial success. The show spawned nine hits in all: "Anything You Can Do," "Doin' What Comes Naturally," "The Girl That I Marry," "I Got the Sun in the Morning," "I Got Lost in His Arms," "I'm an Indian, Too," "There's No Business Like Show Business" (the song he had intended to cut from the score), "They Say It's Wonderful," and "You Can't Get a Man with a Gun." The number of hits set a record for Berlin; neither he, nor, for that matter, anyone else, had ever written a Broadway score with more hit songs than *Annie Get Your Gun* contained.

As always for the songwriter, the real pleasure to be had from the show's success came not from scanning the reviews—the good, the bad, and the indifferent—but from counting the money his labors had earned him. *Annie Get Your Gun* had a healthy run on Broadway, lasting 1,147 performances; his thirty percent share of the proceeds brought him $2,500 a week; his music publishing company would eventually make approximately $500,000 from selling sheet music of the score; and his royalties from the original cast album, a Decca recording, exceeded $100,000. He earned further royalties from a profitable national tour, starring Mary Martin, and from the production's four-year-long run at the London Coliseum in a production starring Dolores Gray.

Of greater importance to Irving than these statistics was the sale of the motion picture rights. Approaching these crucial negotiations, his competitive instincts were in full cry. "He's always been motivated by the thought that anything he did had to be better than anything he had ever done, and, if possible, better than anyone else had ever done before," noted Dave Dreyer of his boss at this juncture. "It would have to cost more; . . . he would have to get more than he had ever got, or that anyone else had ever got. He was the most fantastic maneuverer for money you ever saw in your life. He outmaneuvered all those sharpies in Hollywood as if they were Boy Scouts."

The first "sharpie" Irving encountered was producer Arthur Freed, who was in charge of a semi-independent unit at MGM devoted to producing musical comedies. Freed combined the flair of stage impresarios with the financial pragmatism of a contemporary motion picture executive. His background, too, brought together an unusual amalgam of traditions. He was a southern Jew, born Arthur Grossman in Charleston, South Carolina, and he had been educated at Phillips Exeter Academy in New Hampshire. After Exeter, he took off in another unlikely direction, working as a song plugger in Chicago. In this capacity he came to know the Marx Brothers, who were then riding the vaudeville circuit. Inevitably, Freed gravitated to New York, where he began writing songs for restaurants. No sooner had he begun to establish himself than he left for the West Coast, where he managed a theater, wrote scores, and eventually burrowed his way into motion pictures. Because of his dual experience in songwriting and producing, he was well suited to the task of bringing *Annie Get Your Gun* to the screen.

Negotiations between the two parties dragged on for the better part of a year; not until June 13, 1947, did Berlin, along with Herbert and Dorothy Fields, sign an agreement with MGM delivering the motion picture rights to the studio. Freed was both exhausted and impressed by the way Berlin handled himself. "It took longer to write one of Irving's contracts than it did the script," the producer said, "but after it was done, he forgot about the contract and gave you anything you wanted." The amount of the sale—$650,000, payable in five annual installments—was a record for a musical.

▪ ▪ ▪

This sudden wealth wrought extensive changes in the songwriter's life, beginning with his acquisition of an opulent new home. For a number of years Ellin and he had admired an oversized town house on Beekman Place, a quiet cul-de-sac near the United Nations. The home belonged to the banker James V. Forrestal. About to become Secretary of Defense under President Truman, he had put the property up for sale. In early June, the financial success of *Annie Get Your Gun* assured, Berlin felt confident enough to buy it. He and his wife would live there for the rest of their lives.

The five imposing stories of red brick that came into Berlin's possession in 1946 were covered by a mansard copper-green roof, and its favored site included a compact garden. The house was located on a slip, so that three sides were exposed, two facing quiet streets, the other overlooking the gray expanse of the East River. His new home was the most obvious testament to his wealth and success that he ever permitted himself; in every socioeconomic way it was about as far as he could get from the Lower East Side, and it abounded in the one luxury that had been in short supply in his youth: space.

The process of moving into the new home proved to be a tedious and protracted business—not the kind of endeavor for which he had much patience. At the beginning of September 1946 he left Ellin in charge of the matter and flew to London, where he spent a month catching up on the activities of the English branch of his music publishing company and laying plans for that country's production of *Annie Get Your Gun*. On October 1 his plane landed at New York's LaGuardia airport, where his wife met him. The new house, he discovered, was still not ready.

As Irving waited to move, his next film opened. But *Blue Skies*, yet another musical recycling his catalogue, in Technicolor this time, was not to be the cinematic answer to Broadway's *Annie Get Your Gun*. Begun during the war, the movie had since suffered a variety of misfortunes beyond the songwriter's control. Most seriously, its talented and reliable director, Mark Sandrich, who had imparted gloss and wit to the Fred Astaire–Ginger Rogers movies at RKO, as well as *Holiday Inn*, died at the beginning of production, and his replacement, Stuart Heisler, was not of the same caliber. Then there were casting problems: at first Fred Astaire was going to be in it, then he wasn't. And then, ten days before the movie went before the cameras, he was—saying it would be his last motion picture appearance.

When Berlin previewed the result, he was disappointed. Attempting to put on a brave show of confidence for the press concerning the prospects of *Blue Skies*, he admitted, "If I start to pick the picture to pieces I can find all kinds of flaws." As expected, the film received tepid, occasionally scornful reviews when it opened on October 16.

Berlin's standards held up well, but the guiding hand of Mark Sandrich was sorely missed.

Although *Annie Get Your Gun* continued to pack the Imperial Theatre on Broadway, the failure of this movie to make a similar impression in Hollywood triggered a prolonged spell of anxiety in the songwriter. Approaching sixty, he was increasingly gripped by the fear that his muse would desert him, or, as he was given to telling his friends, that he would reach out for it and find that it wasn't there. He had expected a movie such as *Blue Skies*, which traded on his old songs, to counteract the uncertainty of trying to turn out new hits every season, but if the old songs failed to find an audience, what then?

Eleven days after *Blue Skies* opened, an unlooked-for honor offered Irving temporary relief from his self-doubt. The Roosevelt Memorial Association held a dinner on October 27 to bestow its distinguished service medal on five eminent recipients. Four of them were war heroes—General Dwight D. Eisenhower, Admiral William F. Halsey, General Douglas MacArthur, and Admiral Chester W. Nimitz. The fifth man held no military rank; he was an entertainer who had seen nearly as much action during the Second World War as some of these generals: Irving Berlin, a songwriter among soldiers.

After the guests had assembled at the Theodore Roosevelt Home at 28 East 20th Street and eaten a predictably bland meal of cream of mushroom soup and breast of chicken, it was time for the speeches. Still fretting over the poor reception accorded *Blue Skies*, Berlin was even more nervous than usual when facing an audience poised to hear his spoken utterances. Before the meal, he had said, only half in jest, "I will play and sing every song I ever wrote if you don't make me make a speech." And now, when the time came for him to address the crowd, he was nearly dumbstruck: "After hearing the citation, I really can't even be funny. I could not be funny, anyway. . . . I can't be as emotional as I would like. . . . I am too full of great humility and pride, and I really don't know how to express myself."

At the end of the evening, Berlin took refuge behind his favorite instrument, where he felt slightly more comfortable.

> MR. BERLIN: I see a copy of one of my songs on the piano [ran a transcript of his remarks]. I wish I could read it. (Laughter)

MR. HAYS: [the Association's presiding member] Sit down, and we will see.

MR. BERLIN: . . . My singing won't be very much better than the little, feeble talk I tried to make, but I am really not nervous about my singing, because I know you don't expect very much. (Laughter)

The abashed songwriter proceeded to perform "Blue Skies" and "White Christmas" as only he could, in his faint foghorn of a voice. His vocal cords seemed to gain strength, however, when he contemplated his third and final selection, the inevitable "God Bless America."

MR. BERLIN: When I wrote it in 1918, I might frankly say that I had no idea of patriotism for that particular song at the time. . . . I wrote it to be the finale of a show which we were doing at Camp Upton, . . . and after finishing the song I thought it was a little bit too patriotic, and I thought it was a little too obvious for the soldiers to sing, [but] it has a wonderful meaning to me now. (Mr. Berlin then sang "God Bless America," the audience joining him on the second chorus.)

For a few blissful moments, he exulted in his affinity for and worship of all the old soldiers in his audience.

▪ ▪ ▪

The evening's glow faded quickly. Weeks after he entertained the generals, a long-dormant scandal in his own music publishing company erupted. The affair began casually enough on a Saturday afternoon when Mynna Granat was having lunch—sent up by Lindy's, as usual—at her desk in Berlin's office at 799 Seventh Avenue. This was the "new" office the songwriter had opened four years earlier, during the run of *This Is the Army.* Occupying an entire floor, it was distinctly posher than the Broadway quarters he also maintained; instead of the gray walls and scarred furniture of the older place, 799 Seventh was decorated with bright colors, paintings, and comfortable furnishings.

As she finished her lunch, Mynna decided to catch up on her filing. She opened the company safe and began to peruse the contracts contained within, contracts stored over a period of time by Saul Bornstein, who continued to direct the company's business activities. Idly studying the documents, she discovered that the company had paid out numerous advances to nonexistent songwriters for nonexistent songs. This was certainly not the way Irving Berlin conducted his business, Mynna knew. The unavoidable implication was that Bornstein had pocketed the money himself, or taken kickbacks from others involved in the scheme.

Mynna decided to raise the issue with Dave Dreyer, whom she had recently married—the outcome of an office romance they had been carrying on during the previous few years.

After considering Mynna's discovery, Dreyer spoke with Berlin about the dummy contracts; the songwriter was skeptical but not entirely surprised. Soon after, he told Dreyer, "I talked to my lawyer about it, and I need evidence."

"Well," Dreyer replied, "Mynna has the key to the safe."

The following Sunday, when Bornstein was not likely to be in the office, Dreyer and Mynna combed the safe for the suspicious contracts, gathered them, and presented the evidence to Berlin.

They heard nothing further about the matter for several weeks. And then, Mynna recalled, one afternoon, as Berlin was dictating letters to her, "In walks Bornstein. He starts screaming at me: '*Where did you get these papers from?*' "

Berlin rose from his desk and ordered Bornstein, "Don't you dare insult her." Bornstein stepped back, astonished to see his partner siding with this . . . secretary . . . against him. "After all," Berlin continued, "I've been suspicious for many, many years. I needed proof, and now I've got it. Goddammit, you and I are through."

Whereupon Berlin stormed into his office and slammed the door after him.

The two antagonists met shortly after the confrontation, and Berlin offered Bornstein a way to leave the company and save face. It was, under the circumstances, a generous deal. Berlin would retain the copyrights to—and thus the right to publish—his own songs, and Bornstein could take the copyrights to all *other* songs published by Berlin's company. Those non-Berlin songs amounted to a large share of the business—not half, but enough for Bornstein to become the proprietor of a lucrative music publishing company without having to do anything except agree to Berlin's conditions.

Bornstein knew he had no choice but to take the deal Berlin offered. The business broke up. Bornstein took over the plush office at 799 Seventh Avenue, where he established the Bourne Music Company, running it successfully until his death in 1957. Berlin retained his other office, at 1650 Broadway, for himself. There he was joined by the loyal Dreyers and most of his "professional" staff. Alfred Chandler, who had worked for Berlin since 1940, became the new business manager and assumed many of Bornstein's former responsibilities.

Mynna and Dave were not to stay with Berlin much longer, however. Shortly after the breakup of the office, Mynna had the misfortune to run afoul of Ellin Berlin over a minor matter. Mrs. Berlin asked Mynna to obtain theater tickets to a Broadway show—not one of Irving's. Mynna called around and eventually obtained two tickets, and as she gave them to Mr. Berlin, she boasted that she had "done the impossible" for his wife.

"One doesn't speak about Mrs. Berlin in that tone of voice," explained Helmy Kresa, who had a keener sense than Mynna of his boss's limits. "Whenever Mrs. Berlin gave me her hand I clicked my heels in the old German way."

Berlin was infuriated by Mynna's patronizing attitude toward Ellin and resolved to fire her, and Ellin acquiesced because, one suspects, she resented Mynna's familiarity with Berlin. Over the years, Mynna had insinuated herself into just about every area of the Berlins' life, and the family, responding to her generous nature, had taken care of her. But now that Mynna was married to Dave Dreyer, it was time for her to move out on her own. Soon after the incident Dave Dreyer quit Berlin's company to start his own publishing firm, and Berlin, appreciative of all that Dreyer had done for him over the years, gave him $25,000 to help him start the business. Mynna left, as well, to join her husband.

With the purge of Bornstein and the departure of the Dreyers, Berlin's company was a different place: smaller and, despite the songwriter's popularity, further from the mainstream than ever. Without Mynna, Winslow, and Bornstein, many of the songwriter's links to the music business—the ranks of pluggers, publicity men, and salesmen—were severed. Of course, the sheet music business was not what it had been even ten years earlier; the era of the million-copy song was gone forever; these days, the big money was in recordings and motion picture deals. Sheet music was fast becoming an anachronism, a souvenir of the great days of Tin Pan Alley. So Berlin no longer had need of maintaining a full-scale business; it was enough that his company keep his songs in circulation (especially "White Christmas," which sold more sheet music than *any other song*, as Berlin had reminded Richard Rodgers); watch over his copyrights, renewing them as necessary; and collect royalties.

As much a businessman as a composer, he was, by 1946, an exemplar of the American dream in a new and materialistic way that loudly supplanted the idealism of the songwriter in wartime. Irving Berlin, it seemed to the press, had it all: three presentable, well-behaved daughters; a wife of beauty and accomplishment; and, of course, professional success on a scale unprecedented for an American composer. Such was the image he sought to project, and like many myths, it contained many elements of truth. As a paradigm of the American dream, his continuing fame suggested that the dream continued unabated into the postwar era, a potent and durable force, but also, to its critics, a shallow and mercenary one. But it was equally true that no amount of worldly success could alter Berlin's fundamental character; beneath the preening and the custom tailoring and the Bermuda tan, he remained as insecure and naïve as Izzy Baline had been in his days as a singing waiter.

This irreducible mixture came to the fore when the songwriter encountered Eugene O'Neill. At the time, they were the two great men of the American theater, but as individuals they were utterly different. Flush with the success of *Annie Get Your Gun*, Berlin gave off the sweet scent of popular entertainment, while O'Neill emanated the musty odor of serious literature. Berlin himself was aware of the gulf and intimidated by O'Neill's stature—not merely by the playwright's fame, for Irving dealt with celebrities every day, but by O'Neill's aura of somber grandeur. Ten years earlier, O'Neill had won the Nobel Prize for Literature, and Berlin was acutely aware that he possessed no comparable accolade. But they had, as the songwriter would discover, at least some common ground: the playwright's long-standing admiration for Berlin's songs, particularly his "sob songs" from the twenties. They shared, as well, a mutual friend in the playwright Russel Crouse—"Buck" to those who knew him.

After several years of promising to introduce Berlin to O'Neill, Crouse finally kept his word on Saturday, November 23. The playwright arrived early at the Crouses' with his wife Carlotta; the four of them ate a dinner of beef stew. Later, about nine in the evening, the Berlins arrived, followed by Crouse's theatrical partner, Howard Lindsay, and Lindsay's wife, the actress Dorothy Stickney.

Berlin had worked himself into a state of anxiety over the prospect of meeting O'Neill. "I was worried about what I was going to say to him," he recalled. "I'd read a few of his plays but didn't really know his work, not the way my wife does. I figured on saying . . . how much I respected him." Leaving their car, he instructed his driver to wait; they would be staying only fifteen minutes or so. "As soon as we got there," Irving continued, "I found he was interested in my old songs, he knew them, he knew them all, even some I'd forgotten." O'Neill asked Irving if he happened to recall "I Love a Piano." And of course Irving did. They sat down together on the bench in front of the Crouses' piano and immediately began to sing that they knew a fine way to treat a Steinway, their voices gathering conviction as they went. "He had to sing in one key because that's how I play," Berlin remembered, but O'Neill scarcely noticed the limitation. They proceeded to sing and play other Berlin songs with mounting glee—such was the spell cast by the songwriter's melodies.

The playing and the singing and the reminiscing lasted for hours, with Berlin and O'Neill continually asking each other, "Do you remember such-and-such?" Having exhausted their repertoire of Berlin's songs, they went on to sing tunes by other composers—anything whose lyrics O'Neill could recall—and the playwright possessed a formidable memory for lyrics. At some point during the evening, their hostess, Anna Crouse, called Bennett Cerf, the publisher, and his wife, Phyllis, and invited them to drop over and join in the festivities; the Cerfs arrived within minutes to lend their voices. And as they all sang, Berlin, drawing on a lifetime of experience in the music business, described what performer had made this or that song famous, who had published it, when it had been published, how many copies it had sold, and so on into the night for his delighted companions. He was, as everyone there recognized, Tin Pan Alley incarnate.

At midnight, the Berlins' driver, suffering from the cold weather, rang the doorbell, seeking to discover what had happened to his employers; the singing continued, however, and the Berlins stayed until three o'clock in the morning. On the strength of Berlin's impromptu performance, the evening became a triumph—though not one line of dialogue from *Anna Christie, The Emperor Jones*, or any other play by O'Neill had been uttered. Even after the guests departed, the playwright remained in a state of high excitement. Soon after, his wife wrote to Anna Crouse, "Gene couldn't get to sleep until four he was so full of pleasure & song & delicious stew!"

To his surprise, Berlin came away with a warm memory of O'Neill, who turned out to bear scant resemblance to the glowering, intimidating genius of repute. Above all, the songwriter valued the respect he believed O'Neill held for him; perhaps, Berlin thought, the two of them had more in common than he had dared to believe. Perhaps he, too, belonged to the select fraternity of genius.

In any event, he felt secure enough to invite the O'Neills, together with the Crouses and Lindsays, to attend a performance of *Annie Get Your Gun* in mid-December. Now it was the playwright's turn to suffer pangs of doubt, for he dreaded going to the theater, dreaded watching second-rate drama, and above all, dreaded being recognized, pointed at, exhibited. In this instance, however, he found himself enjoying Ethel Merman's antics so much that he forgot himself and stayed until the end of the show—a rare occurrence for O'Neill—and afterward went backstage to congratulate the star on her bravura performance. The only unpleasant moment during the evening occurred when O'Neill, dazzled by the sight of the chorus girls who had come to gape at him, stared at one particularly attractive young well-wisher as his ferociously protective wife stood by, paralyzed with jealousy.

▪ ▪ ▪

Reviewing the events of 1946, Berlin was entitled to feel a swelling sense of satisfaction. His successful return to Broadway, combined with the purchase of his imposing new home, indicated how swiftly he had found his place in postwar America. But for the songwriter, the accomplishment of *Annie Get Your Gun* marked an end rather than a beginning, the culmination of a drive to return to the New York stage that had begun as early as 1940, with *Louisiana Purchase*. He was now, as he had not been since the early years of the Depression, emotionally and physically exhausted. The year 1947 would see a dramatic drop-off in the number of songs he published; fewer than a dozen would appear, and none of them as dizzyingly successful as his score for *Annie Get Your Gun* had been. And in 1948, he would publish only five new tunes, none of them particularly distinguished.

He embarked upon a two-year-long period of consolidation and stock taking. Perhaps he had gone to the well once too often, and it was time to allow his inner resources to replenish themselves. Contemplating his rise to the pinnacle of society occasioned much earnest reflection on how far he'd risen, and he felt a need to reexamine his origins, as a way of enumerating the milestones he had passed along the route and explaining to himself how he had come to be the phenomenon he was.

These thoughts were with him on a chilly evening in February 1947, when he was dining at *Le Pavillon*, an exclusive French restaurant in New York City. His elaborate meal consisted, in part, of wild duck and crepes stuffed with crab meat, and his companion was Ward Morehouse, a playwright and drama columnist for the *New York Sun*. A beefy, amiable man, Morehouse was a throwback to the era when theater critics socialized regularly with the celebrities about whom they wrote.

"When I was a kid," Irving said over coffee to Morehouse, "I never knew there was food like this in the world." And he went on to reminisce about his boyhood on Cherry Street—the overcrowding, the fifteen-cent-a-night flophouses, Nigger Mike's: the entire shabby panoply of his youth. On impulse, he invited Morehouse to accompany him on a short tour of Chinatown, to see what, if any, scenes of the songwriter's formative years still existed.

Irving paid the check (he considered it unethical to allow a journalist to buy him a meal; employees and friends were another matter), tipped the unctuous waiter and captain, and, followed by Morehouse, hurried into his limousine. The car glided down Fifth Avenue to Madison Square, swerved onto Broadway, past Union Square, once home to the office of Waterson, Berlin & Snyder, as well as the rest of Tin Pan Alley, and turned east on Chambers Street, as Berlin began to have second thoughts. "I don't know what we're going to find down there," he muttered. "We'll just have to see."

By now they were on the Lower East Side; but it was no longer the rowdy neighborhood of Izzy Baline's childhood. Immigrants like the Balines had grown up, moved away, died off. "The streets were silent and strangely empty," according to Morehouse. "Squares and rectangles of light showed wanly in tenement windows." Finally Berlin spotted a familiar sight. "That's Cherry Street," he told the driver. "Stop there. We'll get out."

The car came to a halt, and its two passengers entered the night, Morehouse tentatively, Berlin with the swagger of one striding across his own turf. Memories assaulted him; he began gesticulating widely. There was Levy's saloon, and that used to be a German delicatessen, but we didn't go there, we went to the kosher place around the corner. . . . And the junk shop! The place where he'd sold off pieces of the samovar his mother had brought from Russia for five cents . . . where was it? Somewhere around here; he couldn't be sure, not in the dark. It was a long time ago, nearly half a century.

At last they came to his boyhood address, 330 Cherry Street, changed beyond recognition by a new façade. Even Cherry Street had come up in the world. Hat in hand, he stood at the curbside and looked up, silently remembering. At length, he said, "This was my house," as a note of wonderment crept into his voice.

They reentered the car and approached the Bowery, in whose tawdry saloons Izzy Baline had sung for pennies pitched at his feet; they drove past the site of the notorious Cobdock Hotel, where, he recalled, prostitutes earned their living with visiting sailors. At length they came to 12 Pell Street, where the Pelham Café, otherwise known as Nigger Mike's, had stood—the *real* Nigger Mike's, not Hollywood's re-creation of the bar. The building was still there, but the café was gone. A barely visible "FOR RENT" sign hung in the dusty window. Unable to tear himself from the forlorn piece of real estate, he planted himself in the doorway, trying to get a glimpse of the interior, as if shades from his past hovered within, or the dying notes of a ragtime tune once hammered out by Lukie Johnson still echoed in the air.

Chinatown had changed along with the rest of the Lower East Side. Instead of the headquarters of the notorious Hip Sing Tong, the Chinese gang, neon lights beckoned families of tourists in search of a meal or souvenirs. Irving ignored them in favor of a bleak Chinese mission on Doyers Street, insisting to the somewhat hesitant and self-conscious journalist that they enter.

Within, they found fifty or so elderly men, asleep or listening to the comforting drone of prayers intoned by a minister. Berlin and Morehouse, conspicuous in their natty threads, their clean-shaven cheeks, took a seat in the rear. Of course, Berlin was quickly noticed, recognized by the minister, who began to croon "White Christmas" to his semiconscious regulars—and to the man who had composed the song. Uptown, at about the same time, a far wealthier crowd was cheering Ethel Merman in *Annie Get Your Gun.*

When the minister finished singing, there was no applause, none whatsoever. Irving rose to his feet and made a small bow as the members of the mission turned to stare at him in haunting silence. Then one old man in the front row smiled at the visitors. A tear coursed down the cheek of the wizened man behind him. And another old man, on crutches, stirred slightly. Suddenly, a loud voice shattered the mood:

"Sure, that's him. That's Berlin himself. Didn't I tell you folks you'd get a lot for your money? Didn't I tell you I'd give you a lot of surprises and excitement? Didn't I? Didn't I?"

During the song, several sightseers and their tactless guide had entered the mission. The voice belonged to the tour guide, who harangued his group as Mike Salter himself had done in the days when he conducted tours of Chinatown's high spots.

Berlin and his companion immediately fled the mission, but the tour guide caught up with them, as the members of his group, who also recognized Berlin but were content to leave him in peace, waited uncomfortably. The guide implored the songwriter to address the group, but Berlin turned around and snapped, "Go away. I've done my act for tonight." And then, to Morehouse, he said under his breath, "We'll pick up the car and go over to Jimmy Kelly's in the Village."

As they entered, a small orchestra struck up "Alexander's Ragtime Band": it was the kind of tribute he expected and appreciated. After all these years, he still liked the melody, the song that had invented Irving Berlin in the public mind. Savoring a brandy at the restaurant where he had met Ellin over twenty years earlier, Berlin continued the stream of reminiscence. "I really had an easy time as a kid, honest," he insisted to Morehouse, as the sweet alcohol took effect. "My struggles didn't actually begin until after I'd written 'Alexander's Ragtime Band.' It's been a struggle ever since to keep [the] success going." And he began to brood on the less-than-glorious *Blue Skies.* "I've never been in a tougher spot than I'm in right now," he said, a rare touch of self-pity creeping into his voice. If only life consisted of writing one hit show after another, without the flops in between.

Irving's former employer, Jimmy Kelly, joined them at the table. "When I went to work for Jimmy," Berlin said to Morehouse with a wink, "he was a damn good boss." He turned to Kelly, adding, "Weren't you, Jimmy?"

"Hell. Those were the good old days, all right," said the ageless prizefighter. "When it's quiet down here I get to thinking a lot about you, Izzy, and about Nigger Mike. He was a peculiar guy. You could have the shirt off his back if he liked you."

Glancing at his watch, Morehouse realized time had passed quickly; it was one o'clock in the morning, not at all late for Irving. They went back to the car once again and wound up the evening at the Stork Club, having come full circle, from wealth to poverty and back to wealth in the span of a few hours. "You know," Berlin said at the end of the evening, "if something happened and I found I had to go back to work, to start working at Kelly's all over again, I think I could do it."

CHAPTER 18

Tycoon

Joe Schenck went to jail quoting his friend Irving Berlin—"God Bless America!" He emerged only four months later, determined to resume his career in motion pictures. As a result of his conviction for income-tax evasion, however, he was forced to resign the chairmanship of Twentieth Century-Fox; he later returned as an executive producer with the same company. Although he no longer wielded the same power that he had before the tax case brought him down, the industry still paid heed to the name Joe Schenck, if only because his brother Nick ran the holding company that owned another studio—MGM.

In February 1947, Irving Berlin flew to California for a reunion with his old patron and ally. The setting was Joe Schenck's home in Palm Springs, whose dry, healthful climate and proximity to Los Angeles attracted retired silent-film stars and studio executives, as well as the odd gangster; Schenck, soon to turn seventy, blended right in with the raffish scene.

At the time, Irving was experimenting with a solution to his insomnia: Nembutal, a prescription sleeping pill. Before another night of tossing and turning, he dosed himself as usual and fell asleep. At about three o'clock in the morning, a frightful cacophony shattered the desert silence. Brandishing a revolver, Schenck charged the swimming pool, where a St. Bernard was thrashing about in the water, afraid of drowning. There were several guests staying at Schenck's home that night, including Moss Hart, and all of them had rushed to the pool—all except Irving, who, thanks to his sleeping pills, remained unconscious. Over a late breakfast the following morning, he complained, "The same old story. Took three Nembutals and didn't catch a wink." In the future, Nembutal would pose greater problems for Berlin to master.

More than simple nostalgia had prompted the desert rendezvous; Irving had movies in mind, and he proposed to Joe that they make another anthology of his hits, something lavish, say in the manner of *Alexander's Ragtime Band* of ten years before, only in Technicolor. Call it *Easter Parade.* A great song in 1933, and still a great song today. How could it miss? That was fine with Joe—anything was fine with Joe when it came to his old friend Irving, who had testified for him at the tax trial.

In addition, the songwriter insisted on taking a *percentage* of the movie's profits. Extraordinary as the demand seemed, he had a significant precedent to back him up. In the early 1930s, he had been able to obtain a percentage deal at RKO, thanks to the studio's desperate financial situation, and he prized the dignified arrangement, for it signified that a movie containing his songs was literally *his* picture. The pride of ownership brought out the best in him. Irving figured he knew as much about marketing a movie as composing a score; he was, after all, a music publisher as well as a songwriter. He'd made a career out of knowing what Americans wanted to hear. For him, Hollywood was simply the audiovisual successor to Tin Pan Alley. Still, in postwar Hollywood the demand amounted to heresy; studios refused to permit performers, composers, and the like the privilege of profit sharing. Yet even *that* unprecedented condition was fine with Joe; nothing was too good for Irving, author of "God Bless America." "Irving never lost money for anybody," Schenck was fond of saying. The two men shook hands on the deal.

Berlin flew back to New York to await receipt of the contract, and Schenck conferred with other studio executives at Twentieth Century-Fox—executives who didn't know Irving the way Schenck knew Irving and who said, not at all surprisingly, that there was no way they were going to give the songwriter a share of the profits. But they would pay him more up front, a lot more. Schenck wired this slight alteration in their handshake deal to Irving, who sent a terse reply: "Dear Joe—You and I shook hands on a deal for 'Easter Parade,' so let's forget about it."

At MGM, Louis B. Mayer promptly bid $500,000 for *Easter Parade*, more than Twentieth Century-Fox had offered. What made the offer intriguing was that Joe's brother Nick was the power behind Mayer at MGM; thus, the two brothers were in effect bidding against one another for the songwriter's services. At first, Berlin scorned both offers. In high dudgeon, he wired back to MGM, "Dear Louis—why should I ask one thing from Twentieth and do another for you?" Now both Mayer and Nick Schenck were feared men in Hollywood; no one refused them, especially when they waved money around, but Irving did. As a result of his telegrams flying back and forth across the country, Berlin was fast acquiring a reputation in Hollywood as a difficult man to deal with—actually, "sonofabitch" was the term commonly used in connection with his name, and there was a trace of admiration attached to the epithet.

Then, to the surprise of all concerned, Mayer caved in: Berlin could have his percentage as well as the half-million bucks. Joe Schenck (and Twentieth Century-Fox) lost out, and MGM obtained the right to make *Easter Parade*. Arthur Freed, who was already in charge of the film version of *Annie Get Your Gun* at MGM, would produce both movies. Eager to make the songwriter feel at home, MGM gave him a special office called "The Berlin Room," where he quickly installed himself at one of his prepared pianos. Irving was pleased, and his income soared: as a result of his motion picture deals, he earned $640,000 in 1947, and that was after taxes.

Now that Mayer had secured the songwriter's services, the producer rushed the musical into production so that it would be ready for Easter of the following year. By April, Berlin and the screenwriting team of Albert Hackett and Frances Goodrich were on the studio's payroll and at work on the picture. While the score consisted primarily of new interpretations of old songs, Berlin did consent to write eight additional tunes for the movie, although at least several of the "new" songs—including "A Couple of Swells," the best of the lot—were, in fact, trunk songs.

Requiring the services of a transcriber, the songwriter discovered to his dismay that Helmy Kresa was too ill to travel. Freed arranged for Johnny Green to replace Kresa—if Irving, who was known to be fussy about these things, would agree. The New York-born, Harvard-educated Green had written hit songs ("Coquette," "Out of Nowhere," "Body and Soul," "I Cover the Waterfront"), led his own band, and made a distinguished career for himself as a conductor and music director in Hollywood. And he had long been acquainted with Berlin. A small, feisty man, Green yielded to no one in the field of music ("I'm not a prodigy, just impertinent")—except Berlin, whom he revered. Yet there was a problem: Green had left MGM at the end of 1946 in a dispute. Freed intervened and negotiated Green's return in April, at several times his former salary, to become music director for *Easter Parade.*

"Irving," Green said at the outset, "I'm very good at this kind of thing, and I would be delighted to do it, without implying for one moment that I can make you as happy as Helmy can."

"My God, the great Johnny Green being my musical secretary," Berlin magnanimously replied.

"Who knows what the great Johnny Green can learn from being your musical secretary?"

Irving slapped his knee, put his arm around Green, and agreed to work with him.

The two of them spent many hours in the Berlin Room at MGM, Green taking down the master's tunes. Eventually Green got up the nerve to voice a few musically informed opinions and met with the same reaction as his many predecessors had. "Irving," he began, "I have a small suggestion to make—if you don't mind."

"Of course not, Johnny."

Green proceeded to explain his idea in musical terms: "You played a third in the bass. I really think it has a thick sound, and coming out of what you're coming out of and going into what you're going into, you would do much better with a fifth. You avoid the muddiness."

Irving considered. All this talk of thirds and fifths—the patter of trained musicians—mattered little to him; *sounds* were what counted.

"Let me hear it my way, the way I did it." Green played it Irving's way. "Now play it your way," Irving said. And Green played it his way. "Let me hear my way again." Green complied, as they went back and forth between the two versions three, four, five times. And when they were done, Irving delivered his final pronouncement:

"Leave it the way I wrote it."

Thus Green learned there would be no collaboration involved in the composition of a song, despite Berlin's musical illiteracy. "Whether it's a word of lyric, a line of melody, a line of countermelody, a harmonic progression," Green realized, "it was written by Irving Berlin."

In addition to laboring on the movie's score, Berlin took it upon himself to consult frequently with the screenwriters, Frances Goodrich and Albert Hackett. It was this married team's first musical script, and they set their tale in the show business world of 1912. Irving was one of the few people still active in the business who had been around in 1912, and he made numerous suggestions to emphasize the movie's fidelity to its period. "Sometimes he would come with an idea and a song to illustrate," Goodrich recalled, and the three of them would try to work it into the story. Irving thought highly of the young team, and he was eager for their script to avoid the saccharine tone that had plagued *Blue Skies*, but in his zeal for authenticity, he ran afoul of the director, Charles Walters, who privately complained to Freed that the script was, if anything, too authentic and harsh. It was important for all concerned to recognize that they were not setting out to make the next *42nd Street; Easter Parade* was to be light, escapist fare, whose darkest emotion was nostalgia.

Agreeing with Walters's point of view, Freed hastily brought in a young screenwriter named Sidney Sheldon, later better known as a popular novelist. Although he was only in his mid-twenties, Sheldon had written several Broadway shows, three of which had run simultaneously, and he was now devoting his energies to churning out movie scripts at the same breathless rate. When Goodrich and Hackett, considering their work complete, went on a European vacation, he set about revising their script so that it conformed to the relentlessly cheerful tone of the typical MGM musical.

Berlin courted Sheldon as diligently as he had Goodrich and Hackett. The youthful screenwriter, accustomed to being excluded from important meetings, was astonished by the songwriter's enthusiasm, which seemed more appropriate to a twenty-year-old tyro than to the grand old man of American popular music. Indeed, Irving's enthusiasm extended beyond *Easter Parade*. Even before that script was finished, he tried to interest Sheldon in writing the screenplays for other musicals. Late one morning, he came into the screenwriter's office and announced, "I have an idea for a show," and he spent forty-five minutes describing the story. Finally, Sheldon was forced to cut him off. "Irving," he said carefully, "I'm sorry I have to interrupt you, but I have a luncheon date."

"Where are you having lunch?" he asked.

"In Beverly Hills."

"I'll ride with you," Irving instantly replied, even though they were scheduled to meet again one hour later.

He rode in Sheldon's car so the two could talk, as Berlin's chauffeur followed them, ready to pick up the songwriter when Sheldon reached his destination. The ride permitted Berlin an extra ten minutes to explicate his idea.

In this formative period, *Easter Parade* was planned as a vehicle for Gene Kelly and Judy Garland. Irving had hoped that his favorite male performer, Fred Astaire, would play the lead, but the dancer had recently embarked on a period of half-hearted retirement. After a month of preparation, however, Kelly broke his ankle while rehearsing, he said. (Actually, he had sustained the injury playing touch football in his backyard.)

News of the accident quickly reached others working on the movie. Berlin was the first to call Freed. "What are we going to do, Arthur?" he asked.

Accustomed to Irving's frequent seizures of anxiety, Freed replied, "Don't worry. I'll handle it."

Soon after, when Sheldon heard that Kelly had broken his ankle, he was incredulous. "That's a joke when you're shooting a picture," he observed. "They only do that in Warner Brothers musicals, where a dancer breaks his leg, or the singer loses her voice. I asked Arthur, 'What are you going to do, postpone?' "

"No," Freed told him, "I sent the script to Fred Astaire, and if Fred likes it, we'll start shooting."

Sheldon, who was then twenty-six, was appalled at the idea of Astaire, who was approaching fifty, assuming the role. "Arthur," he warned, "You can't put Judy Garland opposite a grandfather. The audience will be rooting for them *not* to get together."

To which Freed curtly replied, "Write the script."

After a polite delay, Astaire, grandfather or not, decided to cut his retirement short, much to Berlin's delight. Three days later, he began rehearsing the musical numbers with Garland.

Stars generally recorded their songs before filming, and during this phase, Berlin and Freed hovered constantly in the background, always alert. On occasion they became overexcited and made nuisances of themselves. During the prerecording of "A Couple of Swells," Johnny Green recalled, "We were ready to go, the red light was on, I said 'Roll 'em'—and bang the door opens and Freed and Berlin walk in. I gestured to them, 'Shhhh,' and said, 'Slate it again, please. . . .' Judy and Fred are ready. We start. Suddenly I hear Arthur jingling his coins in his pocket, . . . then I hear Arthur remarking to Berlin in one breath: 'Aren't they great!' " Freed slapped his knee; Berlin slapped *his* knee. When the recording was played back, it preserved Astaire and Garland's singing along with Freed's remarks and the knee slapping of Freed and Berlin. The stars erupted into laughter and set about recording the song again—in quieter circumstances.

The actual shooting began on November 25, 1947, and ended on February 9, 1948, with the filming of an elaborate shot of St. Patrick's Cathedral on Fifth Avenue. The scene, depicting the Easter Parade, required the presence of seven hundred extras and one hundred 1912-vintage vehicles. Although the result was astonishingly realistic, the scene was actually shot not in New York City but on a studio lot containing a replica of two blocks of Fifth Avenue. The rest of the vista—primarily background—was added later by the studio's special effects department. This sort of spectacle, along with Irving's fee, the stars' salaries, and the cost of color film, all combined to push the budget of *Easter Parade* above $2,500,000.

As the movie neared completion, Irving flew home to New York; it was good to feel the asphalt beneath his feet once again and to be rid of that infernal Los Angeles sunshine. He turned his attention to Broadway, not as a songwriter this time, but as an investor in Tom Heggen's wartime drama *Mister Roberts*, produced by Leland Hayward. Irving had never before invested in someone else's production, but he was willing to entrust his cash to this risky enterprise because of his faith in its director, Joshua Logan. He followed the play's development closely, traveling to Baltimore to watch an out-of-town tryout, which reassured him that his money was safe. When it opened, the play would prove to be hugely successful—yet another coup for Berlin.

In California, meanwhile, Arthur Freed was racing to meet the holiday deadline for *Easter Parade*. On February 28, fewer than three weeks after completion of the principal photography, the movie was to be shown at the Westwood Village Theatre in Los Angeles. Berlin returned to the West Coast to be present, though he disliked the ordeal of previewing as much as he had when he first began writing motion picture scores, and for the same reason: by the time the movie was shown to an audience, it was too late for him to change the music.

To the relief of Berlin, Freed, and MGM, the preview audience greeted *Easter Parade* with enthusiasm. Though it missed its Easter release date, the movie became the musical hit of the summer of 1948. It was, in *Variety*'s estimation, "Socko screen entertainment," and returned $6,800,000 to the studio.

The commercial acceptance of *Easter Parade* justified the extraordinary deal Berlin had cut with MGM. The last time he had enjoyed a film success of similar magnitude was with *Holiday Inn*, a full six years before, and while no hit of the caliber of "White Christmas" emerged from the new score, the movie demonstrated that the Berlin name—and the Berlin catalogue—retained their fascination for Americans in the postwar era.

▪ ▪ ▪

On May 11, Irving Berlin turned sixty. Reluctant to display himself in public, especially to mark his advancing years, he retreated to his Catskill estate, where he was inundated with letters and telegrams, and where a number of friends turned up to throw him a birthday party. As their gift to the songwriter, Richard Rodgers and Oscar Hammerstein II established a scholarship in his name at the Juilliard School of Music in New York City, where serious students of composition would obtain the musical education Berlin had been unable and unwilling to acquire for himself.

Entering his seventh decade, Irving Berlin was as fit and well-groomed as ever; he still spent hours with his barber each week and continued to wear carefully chosen custom-tailored suits, usually of dark blue. There were a few signs of age, however. He wore glasses now, and lines bisected his face. He still found it impossible to relax, to assume anything less than total control over his business, his finances, himself. Insomnia continued to plague him; while others slept, he was up nights worrying. By day, he was often cranky, seemingly without reason. When an acquaintance met him one morning on the street, he said, "Irving, you look as if you slept well last night."

"Yes," he said, "but I dreamed that I didn't."

He had played many roles in his time: orphan of history, minstrel, widower, lover, benefactor. Now he was settling into his newest part—tycoon—with the zeal he had brought to the earlier phases. He had always been concerned about money, but as he reached this milestone in his life, the subject came to dominate his thinking—even his feeling. As he grew ever wealthier, he suffered from a sense of inner impoverishment; often there seemed to be nothing *but* money in his life. He had been generous in the past, when he'd had less money at his disposal. Now that he had more, his generosity evaporated, replaced by the fear that others would consider him a soft touch and try to take advantage of him. He watched over his newly acquired wealth with greater care than he had exercised in the past. Instead of writing songs, he called his business manager, Alfred Chandler, at home every evening to catch up on the day's business. Not one call, but as many as six or even ten each night, until Berlin had satisfied himself that every deal had been scrutinized, every penny accounted for.

At the same time, he suspected that whenever people discussed Irving Berlin, all they could think of was how much money he must have. Small incidents fed this concern. Returning from a short Caribbean vacation, he happened to run into a press agent, Gary Stevens, whom he knew at a distance. Impressed by the songwriter's deep tan, Stevens essayed a joke: "Oh, by the way, how was everything down at Fort Knox?" Berlin cringed; it was just the sort of remark he dreaded hearing. Soon after, he bumped into Phil Silvers, the comedian, who was exiting the Irving Trust Company building. Silvers quipped, "Irving, I just put some money in your bank." Once again, not the kind of remark Berlin liked to hear. "For Christ's sake," Irving complained, "that guy was never funny."

Berlin as Fort Knox, Berlin as a bank: this was not the sort of reputation the image-conscious songwriter wanted to possess, yet his behavior often encouraged it. When he entered his bank in New York, an eager officer told him how delighted they were he was maintaining such a large account with them. Once Berlin realized he had a substantial chunk of money sitting in a bank earning little or no interest, he immediately withdrew the entire sum and reinvested it elsewhere. Thereafter, bank officers were instructed *never* to talk to Mr. Berlin about his money. His anxiety about money had more serious repercussions for those in his employ. When one of the song pluggers on his staff suddenly suffered a heart attack and asked for his Christmas bonus in advance to pay his medical bills, Berlin refused, even though his employees had no health insurance or pensions. "We're not running a charity here," he insisted. The reply stunned the afflicted song plugger. (Irving was more responsive about his gambling debts. When he got behind in a high-stakes card game, he would call Alfred Chandler and instruct him to hurry over with cash immediately so that the game could continue.)

His fear of being taken advantage of extended even to his own wife. When Ellin passed her driving test, she went to Chandler to request money from her husband to purchase a small car, such as a Ford, "so that I can get around the city without the chauffeured limousine." When Chandler relayed the request, Berlin snapped, "Tell her to buy it herself. She has her own goddamned money."

He was simultaneously boasting and complaining. Ellin did have her own money, and she had earned it from her writing.

▪ ▪ ▪

> The wind blew cold. The great bulk of Pride's Tower could not shelter the steps on which Veronica stood. The dried leaves on the surface of the thick, deep ivy rustled against the walls of the terrace. The shining green was gone from the leaves of the vine. She closed her eyes, not to see the winter that surrounded her. . . .

On this note of fallen glory began Ellin Berlin's new novel, *Lace Curtain*. Published by Doubleday in 1948, it was her second book, and its appearance demonstrated that the songwriter's wife was now meeting with striking professional success of her own.

Four years earlier, at the age of forty, she had published her first novel, *Land I Have Chosen.* Fraught with glancing references to her own life and background, the story concerned two women, one a spoiled daughter of Long Island society, the other a sympathetic German actress with the misfortune to be married to a man who is secretly a Nazi. Eventually, the spoiled society woman steals away the actress's disreputable husband. In the guise of this worldly romantic yarn, her novel offered a liberal ideological tract.

With its romantic interest and timely theme, this earlier novel received generally respectful reviews and sold well, in part because of her husband's knack for promotion. At the end of a ceremonial and rather predictable interview with *The New York Times* about his career, he abruptly changed the subject to his wife's book, *Land I Have Chosen.* He suddenly picked up the phone and called a local bookstore. "When music publishers put out a song," he explained to the clerk at the store, "we always call up to find out how it's going. Don't tell Mrs. Berlin I called, but I would like to find out how her book is selling." The interviewer saw Berlin's face break into a grin. "Selling better than Somerset Maugham!" he declared. "Gee! Can you imagine, she never told me. Gosh, if one of my songs sold better than Kern's I'd be walking on air." Now all the exclaiming and gee-goshing was an act, of course—outselling Kern was a routine occurrence for Berlin and no reason for celebration—but it was a good act, and the *Times* did him the favor of running it. Once again, the songwriter had displayed his masterful way with a plug.

Assisted by Irving's astute salesmanship, Ellin's first novel eventually sold an impressive 450,000 copies in various editions. The motion picture rights went for $150,000; the figure was touted as a record sum for a novel, and even if it was not, it was still a formidable amount.

Encouraged by the success of this book, she began work on *Lace Curtain,* and when word of her story began to circulate, it stirred interest, as well. Ellin Berlin, it appeared, was planning to write about a mixed-faith marriage; there could be little doubt as to her source of inspiration. However, Ellin chose to tell a rather more conventional story about a marriage between a Protestant and a Catholic. "That was not our problem," Berlin said when the novel appeared. "But," he added, "I think the book is largely autobiographical." By which he meant that his wife's story, for those who cared to look beneath its polite surface, teemed with references to the obstacles Ellin had to overcome in her marriage to Irving, and more than that, her passionate feelings about the subject of religious tolerance.

Ellin's marriage was not the only one to occupy her thoughts—and the Berlin household—at that moment. In the summer of 1948, just as *Lace Curtain* was appearing in bookstores, his eldest daughter, Mary Ellin, announced her engagement to Dennis S. Burden, a former Navy pilot who was now a student at Columbia University. She was just twenty-one, and her haste to marry contained more than a hint that she was eager to escape the occasionally oppressive aura of her famous father. She was neither as spoiled nor as neglected as some children of celebrities were, but her marriage to the socially prominent Burden, of New York and Newport, Rhode Island, would keep her away from the glare of fame, cloistered in a milieu of social eminence that would have comforted her late grandfather, Clarence Mackay.

Coming on the heels of the publication of *Lace Curtain*, the July 3 wedding of Mary Ellin Berlin and Dennis Burden provided Ellin an important forum in which to demonstrate her convictions about religious coexistence. The day began with a wedding breakfast in honor of the couple, during which Rabbi Morris Lazaron offered his blessing. Later that day, at the Berlin home at 17 Beekman Place, a different sort of clergyman, the Reverend George B. Ford, performed the actual ceremony, as Ellin and Irving and assorted Mackay and Burden relatives looked on.

The father of the bride, for his part, did not view his daughter's marriage as an unmixed blessing. It was, to his way of thinking, still another expense. And yet he felt that everyone, especially the Burden clan, had expected Irving Berlin, the Midas of modern music, to pay for a lavish wedding. "Who the hell do they think we are?" he complained about the cost of the affair, "the Vanderbilts?"

Owing to the prominence of the bride's parents, the wedding touched off a brief flurry of chatter in the gossip columns—a distant echo of the furor Irving and Ellin had created when they eloped twenty-two years earlier. "BURDEN-BERLIN MATCH BRINGS TOGETHER THREE GREAT FAITHS," declared a headline in the *New York Post*; the mixed-religion issue, so inflammatory two decades earlier, was still worthy of note, but the press now viewed it as cause for satisfaction, rather than alarm. At the *Daily News*, the marriage moved an editorial writer to marvel that only in America could immigrants and socialites intermarry so freely; *Time* responded by labeling the star-struck rhapsody "the season's most snobbish editorial."

▪ ▪ ▪

In December, Irving left New York to resume what was for him a more gratifying role: entertaining American troops. He had made a fortune in recent months, and now it was time to discharge his patriotic duty. His itinerary took him to the most politically sensitive area in Europe: Berlin. Earlier in the year, the Soviet Union had blockaded the city, prompting the United States to begin flying vital supplies across Germany to its isolated inhabitants. The airlift continued through Christmas, and one of the supply planes landing at Berlin's Tempelhof airport contained, instead of coal, a load of American celebrities, including Bob Hope, television hostess Jinx Falkenburg (of "The Tex and Jinx Show"), and, burdened by an overcoat that seemed to double his size, Irving Berlin, here in the city whose name he had taken as his own over forty years before.

When the plane landed and the door opened, Irving Berlin and Bob Hope grasped an astonished Falkenburg by the arms and tossed her down the coal chute. The prank was all in good fun, but Irving was fond of treating the prim Falkenburg to rough gestures like that. Later, when she tried to persuade him to appear on her television show and began to lay down conditions he disliked, he shocked her into silence by warning, "Don't fuck with me, Jinx."

Afterward, the songwriter flew to London and caught up with his English office. There he received a message from an unexpected quarter: Robert Sherwood, the American playwright, who was then living in England. The eminent playwright, it seemed, had given birth to an idea for a Broadway musical that he wished to discuss with the eminent songwriter.

Normally, Irving dismissed others' suggestions for shows out of hand, but he made an exception in the case of Sherwood, whom he had known for nearly thirty years. Both men traced their theatrical lineage to the long-vanished Round Table. Sherwood had even acted in a small role in *No Sirree*, the Round Table revue for which Berlin had conducted the orchestra. Since then, Sherwood had graduated from an assistant editor at *Life* magazine to a respected playwright, frequently mentioned in the same breath as Eugene O'Neill. Combining seriousness with mainstream appeal, Sherwood was a hero to many, an author that journalists, in particular, revered. He was a great big man, six foot seven—more than a foot taller than Berlin—and while generally solemn, he could unexpectedly give way to fits of whimsy and mirth.

The songwriter traveled to Sherwood's home in Surrey, thirty miles from London. There the playwright divulged his idea for a musical; it would revolve around the Statue of Liberty. Arriving in New York harbor during the war aboard a troop ship, Sherwood explained, he had witnessed the electrifying effect of the monument on soldiers. Research on the statue's history convinced the playwright that there was an engaging story to be told, for after it had been shipped to New York, a gift of the French People, the Statue of Liberty lay in pieces on the dock for lack of money to assemble it. It was then that newspaper publisher Joseph Pulitzer began a circulation-boosting campaign to raise funds to erect the statue.

Such was the historical background, but Sherwood wanted to elaborate on it. In his version, Pulitzer's rival, James Gordon Bennett, publisher of the *New York Herald*, sends a reporter to Paris to find the French girl who had posed for the statue; she happens to be a demimondaine straight out of a lithograph by Toulouse-Lautrec. The *Herald* reporter proceeds to spirit her away to New York, where she is feted as the living symbol of liberty.

As even this brief synopsis suggests, Sherwood's premise was complicated and literary; it was nearly impossible to summarize, required masses of exposition, and would prove infuriatingly difficult to dramatize within the conventions of the Broadway musical. On his return to the United States, Berlin did some research of his own on the Statue of Liberty, and he discovered that the actual model for the statue was not the pleasantly tawdry music-hall gypsy of Sherwood's imagination but the mother of the sculptor, Frédéric Auguste Bartholdi. The discovery threw the proposed story off track, and Sherwood struggled to make something interesting out of the rivalry between Bennett and Pulitzer.

Nonetheless, Berlin was happy to associate himself with Sherwood's aura of high purpose because the songwriter hoped the production would at last fulfill his desire to be taken seriously. His seriousness was shared by all those he assembled or who gravitated toward the project in the early months of 1949. In addition to its serious subject matter, there was its serious writer, Sherwood, its serious director, Moss Hart (who would come to share writing credit with Sherwood), and its serious choreographer, Jerome Robbins. Given this assemblage of talent, there appeared to be little doubt *Miss Liberty* would be a serious contribution to the American musical theater.

Berlin and Sherwood believed so deeply in their project that they decided to produce the show themselves. This time, there would be no Ziegfeld, no Rodgers and Hammerstein to watch over Berlin; he would be free to do as he pleased, answerable only to himself. However, Irving would also assume a financial risk amounting to several hundred thousand dollars; in addition, he would be lacking the standard of judgment that enlightened producers, such as Rodgers and Hammerstein, could have offered.

On the other hand, the moment seemed exactly right for a show such as *Miss Liberty*, for this was the high summer of postwar American imperialism. As World War II receded from the political horizon, the nation was as stable as it had been at any time during Berlin's career, and New York was now the unchallenged center of American cultural life. A rare unanimity reigned in public discourse, and if darker issues—McCarthyism, the Cold War—smoldered just beneath the surface of public life, the prevailing tone was sunny, even complacent. What better time and place for a celebration of the spirit of liberty that the United States had won for itself during the hard years of war?

Once preparations for *Miss Liberty* got underway, however, problems immediately developed. Berlin and Sherwood found it next to impossible to collaborate on their Broadway show. Expecting to open the production on the Fourth of July, the songwriter composed most of his score *before* receiving Sherwood's book. This procedure was destined to complicate the tricky business of integrating songs into the story—as always, Berlin's *bête noire*. And the script, when it did come, lacked dramatic flair.

Worse, Sherwood, invoking the sanctity of a playwright's text, refused to change a word. That was not the way to develop a successful musical libretto, at least not on Broadway. Dorothy and Herbert Fields, in contrast, had constantly attended rehearsals and performances of *Annie Get Your Gun* and had tirelessly written and rewritten their libretto until every joke, every nuance of characterization was sharply etched.

Much of the strain of working on the intractable material was borne by the performers themselves. Here Berlin was ill-served by his decision to serve as his own producer, for in his desire to keep expenses low, he avoided high-priced Broadway stars such as Ethel Merman or Mary Martin in favor of younger, less experienced, and less costly performers. A case in point was Allyn McLerie, a talented young dancer who had recently come to prominence in the popular Broadway musical *Where's Charley?* (1948).

Now, cast in the role of model Monique DuPont and thus charged with the responsibility of providing *Miss Liberty*'s sex appeal, McLerie sensed something seriously wrong the moment rehearsals commenced. "The book," she said, "was very lugubrious." Seeking to introduce a bit of levity into the proceedings, she asked Moss Hart if she could smile occasionally.

"Yes, dear. Do that," he told her.

"But *where?*"

"I don't know," he said. "You'll find a way."

This was no way for a star to be born. "Everything was sad," she recalled of those dismal early rehearsals. "Everything was bad." Even the surroundings reinforced the sense of sad futility clinging to the show, for rehearsals took place in a chilly, seedy practice hall on a dreary side street off Eighth Avenue.

When Sherwood did deign to attend rehearsals, it was painfully apparent to the cast members that he had been drinking heavily. At one point he broke into song, not one of Berlin's hits, but "When the Red, Red Robin Comes Bob, Bob, Bobbin' Along," all the while balancing uncertainly on his knees, kissing McLerie's toes. Despite his truancy, Sherwood retained the affection of cast members; instead of rewrites, he offered welcome comic relief.

Berlin, for his part, hovered nervously on the fringes of this muddle, constantly munching on sour balls, which he would occasionally distribute to favored cast members. Others, such as Eddie

Albert, who played Horace Miller, a bumbling photographer, felt subtly excluded. When Albert asked Berlin for a dime to make a phone call, Berlin refused even that small courtesy. Helmy Kresa, now recovered from his health problems, was again at the songwriter's side, poised to take down a melody, should any occur to Berlin, but good musical ideas were in short supply. Irving's score, in comparison to the robust crowd-pleasers he had written for *Annie Get Your Gun* three years earlier, was brittle and tentative. The songs tried to be satirical and ribald, but they were also awkward and obvious, especially by his standards. They were not absolutely awful, but everyone expected more from Irving Berlin—especially the composer himself.

He was under fantastic pressure to meet the old standard he had set for himself, as well as the new standard set by his principal rivals, Rodgers and Hammerstein. On April 7, as rehearsals for *Miss Liberty* dragged on, their musical drama *South Pacific* opened at the Majestic Theatre. Starring Mary Martin and Ezio Pinza, the show, under the direction of Joshua Logan, racked up the largest advance sale in Broadway history—a thought particularly galling to the fiercely competitive Berlin. Its carefully interwoven tales of American service men (and women) serving in the Pacific theater during the Second World War was everything *Miss Liberty* was not; *South Pacific* was exotic, romantic, thought provoking, and hugely entertaining. And it was *serious*; it would later win the Pulitzer Prize, only the second musical to capture the award (Gershwin's *Of Thee I Sing* had been the first). Unlike Rodgers and Hammerstein, Berlin had actually *been* in the Pacific during the war, touring with *This Is the Army*; he had a few observations on that experience worth sharing, but the opportunity had gone instead to Logan, Rodgers, and Hammerstein: the men with whom he had worked on *Annie Get Your Gun*. And while they triumphed, Irving was burdened with the lifeless story of the Statue of Liberty.

Desperate to prove himself, Berlin became unusually defensive about his songs. Whereas he had been so sensitive to the opinion of his collaborators that he had nearly dropped "There's No Business Like Show Business" from *Annie Get Your Gun*, he now insisted that all of his songs for *Miss Liberty* were guaranteed hits, no matter what anyone else thought. He was especially enthralled with his "Give Me Your Tired, Your Poor," a musical setting of the verses written by

Emma Lazarus for the Statue of Liberty. To his way of thinking, this self-important song was destined to become a patriotic anthem to rank with "God Bless America."

Berlin suffered a blow to his pride when he tried out "Give Me Your Tired, Your Poor" on Gordon Jenkins, a respected songwriter and arranger. As Jenkins entered the Berlin office with Helmy one afternoon, Berlin himself suddenly appeared. "Listen, you guys," he ordered. "Just stand there and listen to this." Berlin suddenly fell to his knees, his arms upraised, in a posture worthy of the vaudeville stage, and began to sing his version of the Emma Lazarus poem: "Give me your tired, your poor, your huddled masses yearning to breathe free. . . ." He was so moved by his own performance that tears filled his eyes. He was determined to prove that at the age of sixty-one he still had it in him to write hit songs and hit shows.

When he finished singing, he said, still on his knees, "By God, I'll tell you guys one thing: no one's ever thought of using those lines in a song, and I can tell you it's going to stop 'em cold. It'll really shake 'em up. The whole house will just sit there in silence. God, what an idea!"

Jenkins, however, had another reaction. "I hate to tell you this, Mr. Berlin, but all those words *have* been used before in a song."

The songwriter jumped to his feet and shouted at Jenkins, "You're a goddamned liar! No one's ever done it before!"

"Mr. Berlin," Jenkins continued, "I used those words in a song three years ago." As Berlin continued to scream, Jenkins explained that he had set the same Emma Lazarus verses to music in his *Manhattan Tower*, a popular song-and-narrative recording issued by Decca in 1946. As Jenkins tried to speak, Berlin continued to hurl abuse at him: Jenkins was a goddamned liar, a lying prick. Finally, he told Jenkins: "Get the fuck out," and went back to his office, slamming the door after him.

Surprised but composed, Jenkins quietly said good-bye to Helmy, who could manage nothing more than an embarrassed grunt in reply. It was not the first time he had seen his boss fly into a rage, nor would it be the last. Despite the revelation that Gordon Jenkins had set the same Emma Lazarus poem to music only three years earlier, Berlin kept the song in the *Miss Liberty* score.

▪ ▪ ▪

The songwriter's irrational outburst indicated that he was laboring under an extraordinary degree of stress. The problems afflicting *Miss Liberty* comprised only a part of his professional worries. In Hollywood his prize musical comedy *Annie Get Your Gun*, which had seemed to be a sure thing, was ensnared in a nightmarish series of misfortunes that had brought production to a halt.

The pressure on everyone concerned with the $3 million movie to measure up to the success of the original Broadway version was immense and, as it turned out, overwhelming. Arthur Freed was producing once again, and his choice of director for the movie was ill-advised. Busby Berkeley was celebrated for his lavish, eye-filling Depression-era musicals, but his love of artifice was of little use on this occasion. *Annie Get Your Gun* required a gritty, American feel that escaped him.

Judy Garland was starring, at a salary of $6,000 a week, but she was not the same Garland who had been so radiant in *Easter Parade*. At twenty-six, she was becoming increasingly addicted to tranquilizers and sleeping pills, uppers and downers: Nembutal, Seconal, and Benzedrine, among others. Nor was she alone in her consumption of them; the pills had hit Hollywood hard, and stars, who felt under tremendous pressure to be up, to emote on cue, to give more than they thought they had, obtained them however they could. Garland's case was especially dramatic. As her dependency on drugs increased, she lost weight, and her behavior became increasingly erratic. Shortly before beginning work on *Annie Get Your Gun*, she submitted to a series of shock treatments, which stabilized her moods, but only temporarily.

Rehearsals commenced on March 7. Garland recorded the entire score—eleven songs in all. Less than a month later, on April 4, production began. On only the second day, Howard Keel, playing the role of Frank Butler, fell from a horse and broke an ankle. That was a serious mishap, to be sure, but the schedule could be rearranged to accommodate his recovery. Garland's drug addiction posed a far more alarming problem. She made no effort to conceal her dependency. Watching the dailies, she would get up from her seat, casually walk over to the water cooler, and wash down a handful of Benzedrine. When the time came to shoot "I'm an Indian, Too," she was so woozy that she was unable to stand without assistance. Watching the pathetic display, Freed rose from his chair and lashed the incoherent actress with the most appalling language, as embarrassed crew members tried to avert their eyes.

Given all these difficulties, it was no surprise that the dailies were disappointing. The effect of Garland's drug addiction could not be concealed. She looked pale and unwell on film, and she was; her hair was coming out in clumps. She was simply lost as Annie Oakley, with none of the bigger-than-life quality the role required.

At the beginning of May, a distraught Freed fired Berkeley. "He was shooting the whole thing like a stage play," Freed explained. "Everyone would come out of the wings, say their lines and back away upstage for their exits." Following Berkeley's departure, Garland lost all confidence in her performance. She arrived late, left early, burst into tears at the least provocation, then spent hours apologizing for her unprofessional behavior. Through it all, the filming of "I'm an Indian, Too" dragged on, six grueling days in all. When the ordeal ended on May 10, MGM fired her, as well.

After reading the notice of dismissal, she fell to the floor of her dressing room and wailed, "No! No! No!" How could they do this to her? Judy Garland had never lost money for anybody, least of all MGM. When she reached her home, she collected herself sufficiently to send a brief communiqué to the studio. "I shall never come back," she warned, "now or ever." She meant those words; shortly after writing them, she took an overdose of sleeping pills.

Production of *Annie Get Your Gun* immediately shut down; no reasons were given. Within days, the studio paid $150,000 to "borrow" the madcap comedienne Betty Hutton from Paramount and cast her in the prized role of Annie Oakley. However, there was still no director attached to the project, and filming would not resume for months. Later in May, Garland entered Peter Bent Brigham Hospital in Boston to recuperate from the ordeal, to cut back on the pills and the booze, to try to get her life in order.

Through it all, Berlin, preoccupied with *Miss Liberty*, could do nothing but make anxious telephone calls to Arthur Freed on the West Coast and keep abreast of the succession of calamities overtaking *Annie Get Your Gun*: Keel's broken ankle, Garland's odd behavior, Berkeley's firing, Garland's firing, Garland's probable suicide attempt. And there was a new problem, as well: Frank Morgan, the actor portraying Buffalo Bill, suddenly died. Never in all his years in the business had Irving seen difficulties equal to those afflicting *Annie Get Your Gun*; it seemed entirely possible that the movie would never be made. There really *was* no business like show business.

▪ ▪ ▪

Meanwhile, on the East Coast, more prosaic—though equally serious—problems continued to trouble *Miss Liberty*. The director, Moss Hart, was on the point of quitting over Sherwood's refusal to change the script. The two of them would meet; Hart would say, "Bob, I don't like this scene"; Sherwood would reply, "Well, I do"; and the meeting would come to an end. There was little Irving could do about that problem, either.

"They were all geniuses," McLerie said of the show's ill-matched creators, "and they were so happy about being geniuses that they didn't get down to brass tacks." Distracted by the problems afflicting *Annie Get Your Gun*, Irving constantly changed his mind about *Miss Liberty*'s prospects. "He always took the opinion of the last person he talked to," McLerie recalled, "whether it was Helmy or the usher."

At the time, McLerie was married to Adolph Green, the lyricist and librettist, and he occasionally dropped in on rehearsals in Philadelphia. Catching up with Berlin at the rear of the theater, Green complimented the songwriter on the score, and Irving felt a surge of self-confidence. "I want every song in this show to be a hit song," he said, summoning the memory of the success he had enjoyed with his previous Broadway score.

"If it's as good as *Annie Get Your Gun* you have no problem," Green said.

"No, no," Irving shot back. "In *Annie Get Your Gun* I had to defer to the book. These songs will be hits all by themselves."

Few agreed with Irving's confident assessment. "Being a book and lyric writer," McLerie said, "Adolph was probably going mad, because the show simply wasn't happening. I was kind of crazed. I remember sitting on a roof in one of my scenes, singing a duet called, 'You Can Have Him,' and holding onto my face and thinking that if I *didn't* hold on, it would fly into pieces. I was so embarrassed to be out there." To her way of thinking, the script gave her no part to play. More experienced actresses were able to fill in a role, but, McLerie said, "I wasn't up to making her out of nothing. I wasn't that good. I didn't know what to do."

The one number that McLerie *did* feel comfortable performing never made it into the show, though it was arguably the most tantalizing song in the score: "Mr. Monotony." Dwelling on a romantic triangle, the song was sexy, moody, and reminiscent of the Beat ethos then breaking into public awareness; evoking jazz, black tights, and romantic torment, it was unlike anything Irving had previously written. He'd intended it for his score for *Easter Parade*, and Judy Garland had recorded and filmed it, but there was no place for a disturbing torch song in that relentlessly cheerful movie, and it had been deleted at the last minute. Now it was McLerie's chance to introduce the song. In his frantic search for trustworthy opinions about the show, Berlin humbled himself and invited Rodgers and Hammerstein, his former producers, to view one of the tryout performances, and afterward they told him, "You must have the courage to cut out the one showstopper because it is bad for the character of the girl singing it." He followed this advice, thus depriving his show of the most distinguished song in the score.

As the Broadway opening loomed, and the Philadelphia tryout audiences came to consist of an ever-larger percentage of New Yorkers seeking an early impression of the show, Sherwood rallied, cut back on his drinking, and began rewriting the script with Moss Hart. This state of affairs meant that actors were performing scenes they knew could be dropped at any time and were forced constantly to memorize new scenes—which also might be cut. Watching the show disintegrate before his eyes, Sherwood complained to a visiting journalist, "I hate opening-night audiences. They're too damned chic. These people cannot wait to rush back to New York and say, 'Well, I saw the new Berlin show. Needs plenty of work.' "

Only Berlin persisted in his optimism. Five days before the show opened in New York, he rashly predicted to *The New York Times* that at least four songs from the *Miss Liberty* score would become hits: "Let's Take an Old-Fashioned Walk," "Little Fish in a Big Pond,"

"Homework," and "Just One Way to Say I Love You." "Give Me Your Tired, Your Poor," his setting of the Emma Lazarus poem, would belong to a different category altogether, beyond that of a mere hit. He was already laying plans for a "Give Me Your Tired" foundation, patterned after his "God Bless America" foundation, to distribute the song's royalties to charity.

With all the last-minute rewriting, *Miss Liberty* missed its Fourth of July deadline, but it still bore the honor—and the weight—of inaugurating the 1949–1950 Broadway season. On Friday, July 15, *Miss Liberty* faced its demanding first-night audience at the Imperial Theatre, on the stage where *Annie Get Your Gun* had triumphed just three years before.

The role of chief judge and executioner of *Miss Liberty* fell to Brooks Atkinson of *The New York Times*. The bird watcher and former war correspondent had steadily consolidated his position as the arbiter of success and failure on Broadway. He hadn't reviewed *Annie Get Your Gun*, so it was difficult to say with much certainty whether he was predisposed to like or dislike Berlin's work, but it was assumed that his progressive tastes would not permit him to place the songwriter in the same category as, for instance, Rodgers and Hammerstein. But even if *Miss Liberty* was not hailed as the next *South Pacific*, a degree of success seemed assured. For decades, New Yorkers had been accustomed to reading accounts of Irving Berlin's latest triumphs, and now, in the glorious summer of 1949, his name was synonymous with achievement, and anything less than an instant, unequivocal smash would have seemed out of character. Everyone knew the man wrote hits as relentlessly as the New York Yankees won pennants.

Acutely aware of this reputation, Berlin was caught unprepared for Atkinson's broad condemnation in the *Times* the next morning. "To come right out and say so in public," he wrote, " 'Miss Liberty' is a disappointing musical comedy. It is built on an old-fashioned model and it is put together without sparkle or originality." Atkinson reserved his harshest criticism for Sherwood's book, and in contrast he let Berlin off lightly: "No doubt everyone in America will be familiar sooner or later with Mr. Berlin's romantic melody, 'Let's Take an Old-Fashioned Walk. . . .' Mr. Berlin has also written some good numbers for dancing. But still the impression persists that this is not one of Mr. Berlin's most memorable scores and that he has written other songs in the past in very similar idioms." In sum, he found *Miss Liberty* to be nothing more than a "routine show." And the following week, in a further consideration of the show, he gave the dagger one last twist. "In view of their special gifts as writers," he said of Sherwood and Berlin, "they have missed the opportunity of their Broadway careers."

Nor was Atkinson's judgment unique; other daily critics echoed his reservations.

On the strength of its advance sale, the show played on Broadway until April 1950, but it failed to generate excitement. Costing $215,000 to produce, it earned back most—though not all—of its investment through ticket sales. Despite Berlin's best efforts, it was never sold to the movies, which might have made up the difference, and the expected income from publishing the score failed to materialize, as well.

Contrary to Berlin's predictions, and in a dramatic reversal of the precedent set by *Annie Get Your Gun*, none of the songs in *Miss Liberty* became a smash hit, to be sung and cherished in homes across the country—not one. The "Give Me Your Tired" foundation proved unnecessary, a well-intended but vainglorious gesture. Berlin had written his share of flops over the years, of course, and he had contributed dozens of forgettable songs to Broadway shows, but this marked the first time in his Broadway career, a career stretching back to *Watch Your Step* of 1914, that his entire *score* had flopped. The simple magic of his music—its ability to evoke, intoxicate, thrill, startle, or soothe, to touch lightly on universals of human experience and longing—was nowhere in evidence.

The show's failure seemed all the more conspicuous because Broadway was coming off its most exciting season since 1927. In addition to *South Pacific*, Cole Porter's *Kiss Me, Kate* had opened at the end of 1948, Jule Styne's *High Button Shoes* less than a year before that. Drama on Broadway was also at its zenith; *Death of a Salesman, The Madwoman of Chaillot*, *Anne of a Thousand Days*, and *Edward, My Son* were all on the boards. Collectively, these productions demonstrated that an increasingly sophisticated Broadway establishment had left behind Irving Berlin and his creaky little *Miss Liberty*. For once he had reached out and found that it wasn't there, after all.

As if the failure of this production were not trial enough for Berlin to bear, a disagreeable domestic problem arose. As the ill-fated *Miss Liberty* opened, his eldest daughter's marriage began to unravel. For all of Ellin's good wishes and expressions of religious tolerance, the union had proved singularly unhappy. Just one year after she had wed, Mary Ellin, accompanied by her mother, flew to Nevada. They spent six weeks in that state to fulfill its residency requirement, after which she filed for divorce from Dennis Burden on the grounds of "extreme mental cruelty." A decree was granted on August 11. Afterward, Mary Ellin returned to the family. She later married Marvin Barrett, a writer and teacher, and this time the marriage succeeded.

In the space of only a few weeks, Berlin had suffered two setbacks to his pride, one overwhelmingly public, the other entirely private, but nonetheless significant. It was with the greatest relief that he learned that *Annie Get Your Gun*, the tormented production that had been shut down throughout the summer, resumed filming in Hollywood on October 10. This was the first positive news Berlin had received in months, and it buoyed his spirits. Of course, the prospects for the cinematic version of *Annie Get Your Gun* remained in doubt. It had already consumed over half its $3 million budget, and it was still far from completion. Both the new star, Betty Hutton, and the new director, George Sidney, were acutely aware of the problems preceding their involvement with the picture, and neither felt entirely comfortable with the other. Despite the potential for friction, shooting proceeded nonstop throughout the fall, and by December 16 the task was at last completed. Six months late and nearly a million dollars over budget, *Annie Get Your Gun* finally wrapped. MGM set a release date for the following May.

Berlin had no direct involvement with the movie because he was preoccupied with writing the score for yet another Broadway show, one that he hoped would repair some of the damage *Miss Liberty* had done to his reputation. This time, his goals were relatively modest. He wouldn't try to outdo *Annie Get Your Gun* or Rodgers and Hammerstein. Instead of devising self-conscious anthems and tiresome sermons, he returned to the fundamentals of his trade: a simple story, a star for whom to write, and no ambition greater than that of entertaining his audience.

■ □ ■ □ ■ □ ■

CHAPTER 19

Irving Likes Ike

As a young man, Howard Lindsay, educated at Boston Latin School and Harvard on scholarship, seriously considered entering the ministry. Instead, the stage became his pulpit. Over the years, he acted, directed, and wrote plays on Broadway, but there remained something clerical, even pedantic, about his manner. He was solemn and courtly, with an actorish voice like aged brandy; anyone meeting him would quickly realize that Howard Lindsay belonged to the aristocracy of the theatrical profession in the days when the expression meant something.

For all his virtues and his diligence, he might have remained a journeyman in his trade were it not for his collaboration with Russel Crouse, a former press agent and journalist turned playwright and librettist. Lindsay and Crouse, as they were always known, began working together in 1934, on Cole Porter's *Anything Goes*. Lindsay was already forty-five years old, a seasoned director, Crouse four years younger. Starring Ethel Merman as Reno Sweeney, the show became the musical smash of the season, and the Lindsay and Crouse partnership was launched. Five years later, their carefully crafted adaptation of *Life With Father*, starring Lindsay and his wife, Dorothy Stickney, became the longest-running play in the history of Broadway, lasting 3,224 performances. Despite their hard-won craftsmanship and professionalism, the team lacked a distinctive dramatic voice; they were in the business of devising Broadway vehicles—literate, intriguing scenarios—rather than expressing their own ideas and emotions.

In the summer of 1949, as Irving Berlin's *Miss Liberty* foundered on Broadway, the sixty-year-old Lindsay was vacationing with his wife at a resort in Glenwood Springs, Colorado. As he stared at the splendid mountain scenery, his attention happened to be snagged by a familiar figure lounging at the pool: Ethel Merman, the creator of Reno Sweeney and Annie Oakley on Broadway, wearing a yellow bandanna. And *not* working. Being a complete man of the theater, Lindsay immediately began thinking of a show for her.

Earlier in the day, he had read a *Time* magazine account of a woman whose name was on everyone's lips at the time; she was Perle Mesta, the so-called Hostess with the Mostes' of Washington, D.C., during the Truman era. *Time* reported that Truman had recently named the dowdy but spirited Mesta as the ambassador to the grand duchy of Luxembourg. The thought made Lindsay laugh with pleasure—not Truman's appointment, but the idea of no-nonsense, all-American Ethel Merman playing a Perle Mesta-type ambassador in a staid European country. Lindsay called his collaborator, "Buck" Crouse, who was taking *his* vacation at his country home in Anasquam, Massachusetts, and outlined the idea, to which Buck responded with equal enthusiasm. And on that pleasant summer afternoon in Glenwood Springs, a show was born.

After talking with Buck, Lindsay shouted to Merman, "Hey, Ethel, how would you like to play Perle Mesta?"

And Merman replied, "Who's Perle Mesta?" Lindsay explained, and Merman agreed to play the role.

Several weeks later, when Lindsay and Crouse brought the idea to Berlin—Ethel Merman playing Perle Mesta, it's surefire, it can't fail, she's perfect for the part—the songwriter reacted favorably. He was eager to recover from the disaster of *Miss Liberty*, to reassert his preeminence. Irving recognized his career on Broadway might conclude with this show; he knew he was out of touch with the younger half of his audience, not only its music but its concerns, but being the proud and competitive man that he was, he wanted to end his Broadway career with one last hit. An autumnal air hung over the show. Berlin, Merman, and Lindsay and Crouse were all veterans, and any new project became for them, inevitably, an excursion into memory.

Although he agreed to write the score, Irving had a familiar question for Lindsay and Crouse: "Who's Perle Mesta?" Ellin, a former socialite, did know, and Irving checked with her, and later Lindsay and Crouse sent over clippings about the society hostess. Initially, Berlin was wary of basing an entire show on a living person ("We weren't quite sure whether we'd get hung or shot or something," he said); his previous Broadway efforts had been based on historical figures such as Annie Oakley, or purely fictional creations. Not since *As Thousands Cheer* had he ventured to portray actual people. Perle, however, was game; during a dinner with Ellin, Irving, Margaret Truman, and Lindsay and Crouse, all she wanted to know was who would portray her onstage.

Perle Mesta's willingness to cooperate, though pleasant, was not crucial to the show; if she had objected, the character could always have been changed out of recognition. A novel financing arrangement actually clinched the deal. Producer Leland Hayward, with whom Berlin had previously enjoyed good luck investing in *Mister Roberts*, persuaded Mannie Sachs, an executive at RCA records, to underwrite the production's entire cost: $250,000. The arrangement offered a dramatic demonstration of the influence the recording industry now exerted over Broadway musicals. To obtain the backing, Berlin and the rest of the principals would take a twenty percent reduction in their royalties until RCA earned back its investment. What made the arrangement all the more remarkable was that Merman was then under contract to Decca, which refused to let her record for its arch competitor. On RCA's recording, Dinah Shore sang the role of the ambassador, and Decca retaliated with a recording of its own, featuring Ethel Merman. Thus, *two* albums emerged from the show—and neither one was a hit.

Once the deal had been struck, Berlin wrote the score during the fall of 1949, while nervously making the rounds, as usual, of his Beekman Place home, his Catskills estate, and his Broadway office. It was then the turn of Helmy Kresa to transcribe the songs and to add, under Berlin's supervision, harmonies, ornaments, and other small touches. The process continued as Helmy turned over the transcriptions to an orchestrator for further elaboration; in this instance, Don Walker was responsible for adapting the score to a full Broadway orchestra.

Leaving his songs to become what they would, Berlin flew to Paris with his wife and children at the end of the year for a brief vacation. On January 2, 1950, the family arrived in London, where they stayed, as always, at Claridge's. By now Irving felt so confident of his new show that he was boasting to the English press about it. Still no title yet, Berlin said as he anxiously twisted a piece of paper in his fingers, though it was based on the American "ambassadress" Perle Mesta. But, he added, "we don't say it is Mrs. Mesta."

▪ ▪ ▪

Shortly after the Berlin family returned from their European holiday, the movie version of *Annie Get Your Gun*—long delayed, plagued by endless problems—held its first preview, in Long Beach, California. The enthusiastic audience reaction to the screening brought MGM to the belated realization that the troubled movie had the earmarks of a hit, after all. The new Annie, Betty Hutton, received an extremely favorable reaction on the response cards, as did Berlin's lyrics and music.

Industry anticipation built throughout the winter and spring. The material was one thing, it appeared, and the making of the movie another; in the end, the material—Berlin's songs and Herbert and Dorothy Fields's story—had prevailed. When the movie finally opened, on May 23, the general reception equaled the advance publicity. All the headlines said the same thing in slightly different ways: " 'ANNIE GET YOUR GUN' IS BETTER THAN EVER," " 'ANNIE GET YOUR GUN' SUPERB MUSICAL COMEDY ENTERTAINMENT," " 'ANNIE' IN A CLASS BY ITSELF AS FILM FUN," " 'ANNIE' PLINKS THE BULL'S-EYE," and, to sum up, "EASTERN REVIEWERS HAIL FILM VERSION OF 'ANNIE.' " The first run of the film proved to be so successful that it was rereleased in 1956, and eventually earned over $8 million in a marketplace hard hit by the arrival of television. For a movie that almost never got made, whose director and star had been replaced in the midst of filming, *Annie Get Your Gun* had come to a gratifying finale.

Reassured by this screen success, Berlin turned his attention to his new Broadway show, which had finally acquired a title: *Call Me Madam*. Rehearsals, which began on August 14 at the Golden Theater in New York, were a trifle dull; the director, George Abbott—*Mr.* Abbott to everyone—approached a new production as if he had been called in to quash a rebellion in a remote corner of the British Empire.

Only Howard Lindsay was foolish enough to challenge Abbott's authority. The playwright discovered that the director had had the temerity to change a few lines of dialogue. On hearing the actors recite the altered text, Lindsay remarked, "Well, I hope we still have the same title." His talent for confrontation honed by years of ordering about demanding, insecure actors, Abbott dismissed the company and conferred privately with both Lindsay and Crouse in the lobby. He explained in tones that brooked no interference that if he decided changes had to be made, they would be made. Period. Seeing they had no choice in the matter, the writers agreed to the inevitable.

Rehearsals proceeded under Abbott's grim and purposeful regimen until late September, when the production entered tryouts in New Haven. That was when lightning finally struck, and the lightning rod, as it turned out, was a dead spot in the middle of the second act. It is axiomatic in the theater that second acts require work, rewriting, revision, and sometimes tantrums and shouting matches complete with flying spittle and threats to fire, to quit, and never to work in another show again so-help-me-God—and *Call Me Madam* was no exception in this regard. Its second act was soporific. Much of the difficulty came from Berlin's problem number, "Mr. Monotony," which had already been excised from two previous productions. Ethel Merman was having no better luck with this moody excursion into the neurotic side of romance than Judy Garland and Allyn Ann McLerie had before her, and at the end of a performance, she said, "I've gone along, I've cooperated, I've sung the song and it doesn't fit. It's out." Realizing that it was impossible to force Merman to perform a song she hated, Berlin cut it, along with another misfire entitled "Free," one of the self-congratulatory hymns to democracy of which he had grown so inordinately fond. "We gotta have something to lift the second act," Merman called out in her clarion voice, as Berlin hastened from the auditorium, pausing only to say, over his shoulder, "You're right."

Merman sought solace at an Episcopal church, where she took Communion, while Berlin sequestered himself in his suite at the Taft Hotel. He devised a new song, "Something to Dance About"—a good tune, but not enough to rescue the second act from the doldrums. The prospect of bringing in another flop like *Miss Liberty* weighed heavily on him. The show's bright spot at the time was not its famous song-starved star but foppish young Russell Nype, who played the role of Merman's press attaché. With his crew cut and glasses—Broadway's notion of an Ivy League look—he was the show's discovery, a neophyte among all the old hands. However, Nype was doing so well with his first act number, "It's a Lovely Day Today," that he feared Merman would get him fired. He was just a kid getting $150 a week and hoping for a break, after all, while Merman was the queen of Broadway. Nype failed to realize that anyone who sang a Berlin song as successfully as he did was not about to be fired from a Berlin show. Irving was quite taken with this young man, and he would stop Nype on the street just to hear the actor relate how well "It's a Lovely Day Today" had gone the night before. (The songwriter was aware that Nype was popular with the chorus girls, as well, one of whom startled the young actor by admitting, "Mr. Berlin said that if we got you, we'd have a virgin"—an intriguing thought, but, Nype said, emphatically not true.) Unable to rid herself of the scene-stealing Nype, Merman did the next best thing; she asked Berlin to write a duet for her to sing with "the kid," much as he had written a duet, "Anything You Can Do," for her to sing with her costar in *Annie Get Your Gun*. The songwriter agreed to give it a try.

At the time, Irving's brilliant but neglected counterpoint number, "Play a Simple Melody"—written back in 1914 for his first Broadway score, *Watch Your Step*—was enjoying sudden popularity thanks to a recent recording, called "Simple Melody," made by Bing Crosby and his son Gary. Well, said Mr. Abbott to the songwriter, why not try a new counterpoint tune for the duet, one part for Merman and the other for the kid to sing? Berlin hadn't produced a counterpoint song in twenty-six years, not since his last *Music Box Review*, but the belated success of "Simple Melody" offered a powerful incentive to make an attempt.

Once again Irving retreated to his hotel suite while the cast, director, and writers waited. As it happened, Buck Crouse's room was directly above Berlin's, and throughout the night of September 11 the writer could hear the sounds of the piano wafting up through the floor. Two mornings after Berlin had slipped from view, Abbott wrote, Crouse "hurried into the theatre with a big grin and said gleefully, 'I think he's got something. I keep hearing the same tune over and over.' " Indeed Berlin did have something; it was called "You're Just in Love." It was a counterpoint number, as Abbott had suggested, and it would be the last great song of Berlin's career.

The first person to hear the completed song, however, was not Merman, nor Abbott, nor Leland Hayward—not even Lindsay and Crouse. Young Russell Nype was lounging in his room at the Taft Hotel when the phone rang; he picked it up. Mr. Berlin was calling: "Would you come down to the suite? I've just written a number for you."

Nype hastened to the songwriter's suite, where Berlin, having worked through the night and possibly the previous night as well, answered the door wearing pajamas and a bathrobe. His hair, Nype noticed, was as black and shiny as shoe polish. The young actor cautiously entered, his eyes settling on Helmy Kresa, who was waiting at the piano. "I'll sing this for you first," Berlin said. Nype sat down and listened to the songwriter croak the words to Merman's part of the duet, as Kresa played. Berlin then gave Nype the other part, and the two of them sang together. Everything clicked, and when they were finished, Berlin warned, "Don't tell Ethel you heard this number before her." With that, the pajama party ended.

Later that day, Abbott, Hayward, Merman, and Nype convened in Berlin's suite, where the songwriter, now dressed, sang the duet for them, Nype doing as he'd been told and pretending he was hearing it all for the first time. When they were done, Merman delivered a succinct verdict on the duet: "We'll never get offstage."

Call Me Madam had come to New Haven as a ramshackle production; it left reinvigorated, with a real chance of becoming a hit show. The course of its development illustrated one of the key myths of Broadway, a myth that persisted despite numerous exceptions. The myth was that shows gained strength during their out-of-town tryouts. Let the audience walk out of the four-and-a-half-hour version in Philadelphia and yawn at the three-and-a-half-hour version in New Haven. The show rolls on, losing bloat along the way, until it reaches New York, where the first-nighters cheer the two-hour-and-forty-five-minute Broadway version—the only version that matters, in the last analysis.

In reality, some shows peaked too early, strutting their best stuff in the sticks. Others peaked too late, stubbornly refusing to jell until weeks *after* opening night. But *Call Me Madam*, under the guidance of its aging masters, appeared to be right on course. The first performance in Boston vindicated Merman's prediction concerning Berlin's new counterpoint duet: the audience demanded seven encores of "You're Just in Love." Modern audiences were not normally given to such spontaneous displays; it was thought that they had gone out with vaudeville, but Merman and young Nype, now receiving his first intoxicating taste of celebrity, were happy to oblige. Their song knit together the score, and, by extension, the entire show.

Though Berlin's score was now virtually complete, the production continued its sporadic evolution. During a late rehearsal, Abbott requested a reprise of "It's a Lovely Day Today." "Why don't you knock out some sort of choral arrangement," he said to the conductor, Jay Blackton. On the surface, this sounded like a simple request, but it concealed a formidable challenge. Blackton busied himself in his dressing room with this assignment for the next hour. He then met with the chorus in a darkened hotel restaurant to rehearse the number. "I taught it to them by rote from this manuscript I'd just written," he said. "Abbott didn't know it. Nobody knew it. So I had to teach the kids while Berlin would come in and out, and he liked it." When it seemed to be done, he said, "Let's call Jerry," meaning Jerome Robbins, the choreographer.

"That was a big test," said Blackton. "Jerry was multitalented, and he was tough—a repressed sort of fellow, a loner, remote. He took forever to decide on a step, but what he'd come up with was amazing. So we did it for Jerry. He listened to it once and said, 'What the hell am I going to do with that?' Imagine how I felt! There's my chorus standing there bright and eager, selling it because they love it. But he was a genius. After trials and errors, Jerry staged it, and left it note for note as I had written it."

Subsequently, Lindsay and Crouse attempted to refine their libretto, but Merman refused to cooperate. "Boys, as of right now," she said, "I am Miss Birds Eye of 1950. I am frozen. Not a new comma." There would be no new dances, choral arrangements, gags, or duets to disrupt the final tryout performances of the show. The days were short now; rehearsals, which had seemed so abundant back in August, trickled down to a handful. *Call Me Madam* was scheduled to open in New York on October 12.

Shortly before the curtain rose at the Imperial Theatre, Buck Crouse approached the star backstage. "Are you nervous, Ethel?" he asked. Ethel Merman, resplendent in her Mainbocher gown, gave an Ethel Merman response: "No, the audience has paid their money. They're the ones that should be nervous." Irving, chronic worrier that he was, could not bring himself to share her bravado; his show was facing the same battery of critics who had condemned *Miss Liberty* the year before.

This time, however, Berlin and his collaborators offered a production that did not strangle on its own obscure aspirations. *Call Me Madam* was, by turns, robust, cynical, and romantic. Beneath its glittering exterior, the show related a bittersweet tale of sex as a tool of diplomacy and the corrosive influence of money on politics, as Merman's character, Sally Adams, buys herself an ambassadorial post with her father's wealth. But the audience had not come for the sake of the plot; they were there to see the star, to behold the spectacle of Ethel Merman positioning herself center stage and delivering her lines and songs directly to the audience, without bothering to look at the other actors. There were, as well, endearing touches of humor, such as her surprise at discovering that little Lichtenburg, the country to which she is posted, is, in reality, not the same color it was on the map; there were the topical references, such as the cozy phone calls she makes to a president whom she affectionately calls "Harry" and the small talk about "Margaret"; and, finally, there was Berlin's score, which managed to fuse the vitality of that moribund genre, vaudeville, with the narrative demands of the contemporary musical.

Even Brooks Atkinson of *The New York Times* was won over by the result: "When Miss Merman and he [Russell Nype] sing 'You're Just in Love,' which is Mr. Berlin's top achievement for the evening, 'Call Me Madam' throws a little stardust around the theatre and sets the audience to roaring." As *Call Me Madam* began its eighteen-month run, all the good things for which songwriters pray happened to Berlin. Darryl F. Zanuck purchased the motion picture rights for Twentieth Century-Fox. Berlin's share, $75,000, was but a fraction of what he had received for his *Annie Get Your Gun* score, but at the same time he received a flat fee of $600,000 from Zanuck for still another cinematic anthology to be titled *There's No Business Like Show Business.* Ethel Merman, whose film career had been as lackluster as her Broadway career was brilliant, persuaded Zanuck to allow her to star in both movies. (Russell Nype, to his bitter regret, was not so fortunate in his dealings with the studio; in the filmed version of *Call Me Madam*, the part he created would be played by Donald O'Connor.)

A national tour of *Call Me Madam*, which commenced in 1952, offered an additional bonus for the songwriter. Once the show earned back its investment for RCA records, Berlin's income doubled. In addition to his fee as composer and lyricist, he received a further ten percent of the show's net profits; under this arrangement, he was earning between $1,500 and $2,500 a week from the road company, plus an average of $1,700 weekly from the Broadway production. And of course, there was income from the sheet music his company published, the recording royalties, and the motion picture agreement to take into account.

At this stage of his life, Irving, always careful with his money, was more concerned with estate planning than with spending. Since he had a stock portfolio whose value approached $2 million, the show's income, while welcome, was not crucial to his business affairs. Of his extra ten percent, he gave three percent to each of his daughters, placing the money in trust for the younger two, Linda and Elizabeth, while Mary Ellin, the oldest, received her share directly. The remaining one percent he gave to the conductor, Jay Blackton.

▪ ▪ ▪

As Dwight Eisenhower edged toward declaring himself a candidate in the 1952 presidential election, one song in particular from *Call Me Madam*, "They Like Ike," enjoyed a popularity extending well beyond the walls of the Imperial Theatre on Broadway. It demonstrated once again Berlin's urge to ingratiate himself with politicians. Eisenhower had especially strong appeal. He had been a war hero, and Berlin, his hatred of reveille notwithstanding, respected all things military. As a Republican, Eisenhower was less likely to raise taxes than a Democrat, and taxes was another issue about which Berlin held firm opinions.

Irving's enthusiasm for Eisenhower was so great that Ellin, who had been a Democrat (and a left-wing Democrat, at that) since she was old enough to vote, switched her allegiance to the Republican party—and thereby repudiated McCarthyite suspicion that her earlier sympathies might have been influenced by Communist ideology. She announced her support of his candidacy by signing a letter printed in *The New York Times*; the text called for the "election of General Eisenhower" because "Peace and security are the most important issues facing the American people."

A coalition of Eisenhower backers announced plans to feature "They Like Ike" at an enormous fundraising rally at Madison Square Garden in New York City on February 8, 1952. So excited was the songwriter by the prospect that he overcame his shyness and agreed to entertain the crowd—if there were a crowd. Since Eisenhower remained abroad, in France, where he promised to listen to the event via shortwave radio, observers predicted that the gathering, called a "Serenade to Ike," would play to a half-empty Garden. To make matters worse, it could not get underway until after a prizefight ended.

The observers were wrong. By the time the bout ended, and television personality Tex McCreary opened the meeting at eleven-thirty P.M., a crowd of fifteen thousand had assembled to cheer the Eisenhower candidacy. The rally offered an example of American political ballyhoo at its ripest; there were bathing beauties and long-winded speeches, cries of "I like Ike," each one a plug for Berlin's song as well as for the candidate, and of course there were banners and slogans, the most popular being "Holler with a dollar"—designed to elicit contributions.

After the American Legion drum and bugle corps led the crowd through "The Battle Hymn of the Republic," the stage was given over to the show business figures who had turned out to support Eisenhower. Ethel Merman belted out Berlin's "There's No Business Like Show Business" to the assembly; Mary Martin sang "I'm in Love with a Wonderful Guy," accompanied by the song's composer, Richard Rodgers; and Clark Gable offered a few words in support of Ike.

The late-hour festivities culminated with the appearance of Irving Berlin, who sang a rewritten version of his Eisenhower song, now entitled "*I* Like Ike." As the song approached its conclusion, the diminutive songwriter with a genius for coining phrases suddenly yielded his microphone to a man who appeared to be Harry Truman. Harry Truman at a Republican rally? He wasn't, of course; it was an actor from the cast of *Call Me Madam* named Irving Fisher, who happened to bear a striking resemblance to the outgoing president. Fisher then sang "I like Ike" as the audience of fifteen thousand roared in approval.

The moment offered fresh evidence of Berlin's promotional genius, his knack for knowing exactly how and when to cross the line between show business and politics. The plug simultaneously boosted his Broadway show, his hit song, and his favorite candidate. Think of any one component, and the other two immediately came to mind. In fact, the plug was a little *too* perfect. Once Dwight Eisenhower declared his candidacy for president of the United States, the television networks announced they were banning "They Like Ike" from the airwaves because it contained a partisan political message. Sales of the song, from which Berlin had been reaping a healthy profit, plummeted.

The abrupt action roused Berlin's wrath, and he retaliated by refusing to cooperate with the beast. When Ed Sullivan, the host of a popular variety show on CBS, attempted to stage a televised tribute to Irving Berlin, the songwriter sent in his lawyers to block the event. Even after they received assurances that the tribute had been called off, Berlin complained, "I don't trust that sonofabitch."

Although the networks continued to shun "They Like Ike," Berlin's song persisted throughout the campaign season. With its strident melody playing in the background, Eisenhower went on to win the Republican nomination and the presidency. Two years later, with Eisenhower in midterm, Irving reaffirmed his feelings in "I Still Like Ike." A hit song written to elect a president; a president whose nickname constantly evoked the song: Irving had managed to devise the ultimate plug.

Nor did the President forget to honor his debt to Berlin. On July, 17, 1954, the Berlins appeared for an outdoor ceremony at the White House, where Eisenhower announced his intention to bestow a medal on the songwriter, "in recognition of his services in composing many popular songs, including 'God Bless America.' " Berlin gave a speech —a few words forced out with effort—as Ellin stood silently beside him. "All the royalties of 'God Bless America,' " *The New York Times* reminded its readers in an editorial published the next day, "went to a trust fund for the Girl and Boy Scouts of America. Every penny of the proceeds of 'This Is the Army,' produced in 1942, went to the Army Emergency Relief. For these and other reasons, there couldn't be a more popular law than the one that now gives Mr. Berlin his medal. May he wear it for many years to come." Irving could not actually wear it, however, until it had been struck, and that required an Act of Congress as well as an appropriation of $1,500. Congress went along; it was the Eisenhower era, after all, and unanimity was the order of the day. The songwriter finally received his medal—twice the size of a silver dollar, with Berlin's profile adorning one side—in another White House ceremony the following February.

Berlin's music, in turn, helped to shape and promote Eisenhower's public image as president. Aligning himself as he did with Eisenhower, Berlin's mood, his public utterances, and his songs mirrored the era's subtle changes, from initial triumph to satisfaction, and from satisfaction to complacency, and, finally, as the decade neared its end, from complacency to obstinacy. Phrasemaker, minstrel, political force of vast if unmeasurable influence, Irving Berlin continued to be a potent presence in American life in the second half of the twentieth century.

▪ ▪ ▪

Immediately following the Madison Square Garden rally, Berlin was again forced to turn his attention from the heady sphere of politics to domestic grief. His sister Ruth, formerly Rebecca, who lived in Newark, New Jersey, had for some time been suffering from cancer; the end could come at any time. Earlier, as her condition worsened, her son, Irving Berlin Kahn, had made an appointment to see his famous uncle.

"What can I do for you?" Berlin asked the young man when they met.

"Well," he said, "your sister is dying of cancer. Her medical bills are getting very expensive. I was wondering if you could help her to pay them."

"She's my sister," the songwriter said, "but she's your mother. When you use up all your money taking care of her and you run out, then I'll help out." But not, he implied, until then. Since there was nothing else to say, Irving Kahn started to leave. "By the way," called the songwriter after him. "Don't call yourself Irving *Berlin* Kahn. Use the initial. Please don't use my name." With that warning ringing in his ears, Berlin's nephew left the office.

Berlin was not always as miserly as this exchange indicated, but he detested being asked for money directly. He preferred to give when *he* wanted to, and on his own terms. However, he was extremely sensitive about his name, which he continued to regard as if it were a trademark that must not be violated. There was little, of course, that Irving Berlin Kahn could do about that problem. (Kahn later became a highly successful cable television entrepreneur.)

On February 12, four days after the Madison Square Garden Rally, Berlin's sister (and Kahn's mother) succumbed to the cancer. She was sixty-eight years old. Of the six children of Lena and Moses Baline, only three survived: Benjamin, Augusta (or Gussie), and the baby of the family—sixty-four-year-old Irving Berlin. The following year, on May 12, 1953, his brother Benjamin, who owned a fur shop in New London, Connecticut, died.

The songwriter warded off intimations of his own mortality by concentrating obsessively on business. No detail, it seemed, was too trivial to escape his notice; even an unauthorized children's version of "Oh! How I Hate to Get Up in the Morning" prompted him to create an uproar. Arthur Shimkin, the president of Bell Records (predecessor of Arista), planned to release the song on his company's juvenile label, Golden Records, and he realized the lyrics required a slight alteration to make them suitable for younger listeners. A children's song could not contain a threat to "*murder* the bugler." On the spur of the moment, Shimkin altered the lyrics to: "Someday I'll *be* the bugler / Some day I'll be waking them up instead."

The record executive then met with Berlin to seek approval for the change, "for the sake of children and their teachers."

The instant he heard what Shimkin had done, Berlin flapped his arms and glared. "Young man," he declared, "that song is an American hymn," and he proceeded to lecture Shimkin on its historical importance, as the embarrassed record producer edged toward the door and finally escaped.

Two weeks later, Shimkin discovered to his dismay that his altered version had been pressed and shipped to various points of sale around the country; there was no stopping it now. As the threat of a major lawsuit loomed, he telephoned Helmy Kresa in New York for help. Helmy didn't know what to do either, and he refused to tell Berlin about the problem. "Didn't you hear what happened to the Greek messenger bearing bad news?" he asked.

The record producer then wrote a simple letter of explanation, expressing the hope that Berlin would understand the situation. He immediately received a ten-page-long telegram from Berlin's lawyer, ordering Golden Records to cease and desist and quoting masses of copyright law to support this demand. Shimkin wrote back once more, and this time he hardened his position. If you sue, he warned Berlin, how will it look in the newspapers—"Irving Berlin Sues Children's Record Company for Deleting the Words 'Murder' and 'Dead' from Record"?

Fearing adverse publicity, Berlin relented, and the recording was sold as planned.

Shimkin thought he had heard the last of the irascible songwriter, but four years later they again crossed swords. In 1956 Tommy and Jimmy Dorsey released a successful recording of Berlin's venerable "Marie" (1928) on Bell Records. As a courtesy, Shimkin sent a copy to the songwriter's office.

On Yom Kippur—the holiest day in the Jewish calendar, a day when much of the entertainment industry is shut down—Shimkin was at home with his family. The telephone rang; Shimkin answered. A familiar voice: "This is Irving Berlin calling from Chicago to tell you that I have the copy of the Dorsey recording, and I think it's wonderful. I'm calling my office to order five hundred copies to send to all the disk jockeys with my personal note that I think this is the best version of 'Marie' ever made so that they should play it."

"Thank you," Shimkin said automatically. He waited for Berlin to continue, but he heard only breathing at the other end of the line.

When Berlin resumed speaking, his voice was an octave lower. "And Arthur," he said, "don't think I forgot. You're the little bastard that blackmailed me on 'Oh! How I Hate to Get Up in the Morning.' " And he hung up.

Shimkin heard one last time from the songwriter when Tommy

Dorsey, who had breathed new life into "Marie," recorded another Berlin song for Bell. Once again, Shimkin sent a copy to Berlin's office as a courtesy, and once again, Berlin called. But this time, he was enraged. "You tell that Irish bastard"—meaning Dorsey—"not to fuck around with my song," Berlin said, and he demanded that Dorsey rerecord the song with its original ending.

A somewhat abashed Shimkin telephoned Dorsey at his home in Stamford, Connecticut. "I played it for the old man," Shimkin said, and repeated the rest of Berlin's remarks.

Dorsey, who also had a fierce temper, replied, "You tell that Jew bastard that I fucked around with 'Marie,' and without that there wouldn't have been any song!" Dorsey then recorded the song exactly as Berlin had written it. Both versions flopped.

Berlin played a more active role when he learned that Eddie Fisher was scheduled to record one of his songs. Fisher was then near the height of his popularity, but Berlin became anxious after hearing stories that the singer had a poor memory for lyrics. To make certain Fisher sang the song correctly, the songwriter dispatched a secretary to a recording session with the printed lyrics. While Fisher sang, the secretary sat in front of him, holding up the words as Fisher did take after take—fifteen in all—until he got Irving Berlin's words right.

Since Fisher was willing to comply with Berlin's demands, the songwriter briefly took him under his wing. He gave Fisher the opportunity to sing the last song in the Berlin catalogue to become a hit, "Count Your Blessings Instead of Sheep," at a banquet in October 1954, commemorating the arrival of the first Jews in America. Berlin instructed Fisher to announce that the song was dedicated to "our greatest blessing, our President."

Berlin was unable to exert comparable influence over Elvis Presley, though. When he heard Elvis's rendition of "White Christmas," he was appalled. He immediately ordered his staff to telephone radio stations around the country to ask them not to play this barbaric rock-and-roll version, which he considered a sacrilege. Berlin's hostility toward Presley seemed to be but another in a growing list of grudges, but it foretold the songwriter's alienation from the mainstream of popular music, and, by extension, popular performers, popular trends, popular thought—the environment on which his music depended. At the time, Presley, though a phenomenon, seemed to exist at the freakish edge of popular music, and show business veterans like Berlin were inclined to dismiss the singer as an aberration. They failed to recognize that the passionate, primitive, gyrating Presley was a harbinger of all that was to dominate the next wave of popular music; his brand of rock and roll enjoyed the same reputation for immorality and scandal that ragtime had in its day. Berlin and the other members of the Tin Pan Alley establishment, all of them growing old and lulled by their past successes, were also slow to catch on to the deeper meaning of the Presley phenomenon: from now on, it was the singer, not the song, that mattered.

▪ ▪ ▪

Yet for a time Berlin could take comfort in the knowledge that Hollywood continued to endorse his traditional values. In 1953 he boasted of having *three* movies in various stages of development: the film version of *Call Me Madam; There's No Business Like Show Business*, the anthology starring Ethel Merman; and *White Christmas*, still another compilation of his antique songs. With a jerry-built plot pegged to the most popular song in Berlin's catalogue—"White Christmas" sold 300,000 copies of sheet music a year regardless of fashion or fad—the movie, starring Bing Crosby, Danny Kaye, and Rosemary Clooney, was scheduled to open in time for Christmas 1954. It promised to make a substantial contribution to Berlin's wealth; Paramount had paid him $300,000 for the right to use his songs, and promised him a thirty percent interest in the movie's net profit.

Irving refused to be content with this bounty—or to acknowledge the possibility that he had saturated the marketplace with his songs, his patriotism, himself. With his catalogue nearly played out, he now pinned his hopes on selling the motion picture rights to *Miss Liberty*, whose score had languished in obscurity since the show closed on Broadway. In the absence of a trusted associate, Berlin tried to sell the show himself. *White Christmas* and *There's No Business Like Show Business* were about to open, and he was in a fugue of anxiety and excitement. He'd cut lucrative deals for himself in the past, and there seemed to be no reason why he couldn't do it again.

He first approached Arthur Freed at MGM with the idea, stressing that the show's lack of hit status meant the studio could acquire it at a bargain price. When Freed balked, Berlin laid siege to Columbia Pictures. On September 10, 1953, he discussed the project with Columbia producer Jerry Wald. The songwriter began by boasting that *Miss Liberty* contained his best work "since *Annie Get Your Gun.*"

At that, Wald felt called on to bring the conversation down to earth. "Irving," he said, "I'll tell you what I've discovered. If you have the property, you seem always able to attract the people. I've noticed this. We have *From Here to Eternity*, and we've certainly got the stars for the picture."

Berlin refused to be drawn into a digression concerning another movie; he was there to sell *Miss Liberty*. "The thing that was wrong with the show [was that] it had a leaden story," he said. "It doesn't have to. It's all the story of the Statue of Liberty, and it's a great story. And it has two very big song hits."

"I have the album, Irving, which I've played many times."

"It was crap. It was nothing. Done with amateurs, you know. You can't tell by that. You've got to know what's in it."

Said Wald, "One of the fundamental things wrong with the show, I think, is that you had Eddie Albert, who is not primarily in musical comedy."

"The whole set up was wrong," Berlin agreed, and he made his pitch. "Here it is in a nutshell. . . . The price is $200,000 and not less. That's the property." Berlin launched into a detailed discussion of the changes he wished to make to the story; he even proposed how it should be filmed. "If you've got a commitment with Cinerama, this is a thing to do with Cinerama."

"CinemaScope," Wald corrected.

"I mean CinemaScope. . . . In the test, if you haven't seen it, they've got a shot of the New York harbor with the Statue of Liberty."

"I've seen it. It's magnificent." Now it was Wald's turn to make a proposal. "Irving, I want to ask you something. If we did this deal, would you write us some new—"

"No! No! No!" Berlin shouted, thus closing the door on his best chance, perhaps his only chance, for selling the project to Columbia.

Wald tried again. "Suppose we wanted some extra old songs of yours and some new songs. How do we go about that?"

"If you wanted one old song in there I'd be delighted to give it to you." He reminded Wald that he—Berlin—had included rights to "That International Rag" (1913) for nothing as part of the *Call Me Madam* deal at Twentieth Century-Fox. "My bit of *Call Me Madam* was $75,000," Berlin added. "Which you can put in your eye."

Berlin then coached the producer on what to say to Harry Cohn, the boss of Columbia Pictures. "Tell him nobody is breaking down my door to get it, outside of Metro," Berlin advised. "They want it a little cheaper, but they can't get it."

Berlin refused to say why. The truth was that he had been trying to persuade Arthur Freed at MGM to buy the rights to *Miss Liberty* for the past two years without success, and Columbia was his second or third or fourth choice. Still, he insisted, "I'm not trying to sell it." And he offered a fanciful rationale for his position: "Moss Hart and Sherwood—I said to them both frankly when Metro came along—I said, 'Boys, think it over. Anything you okay, I'll okay.' And they said, 'No. They're buying just because of your score and don't sell it to them unless you are satisfied with the price.' And if you get this and do it right, it's a very cheap property because they pay me $500,000 to do a show. . . . You've got to tell Harry he's got to make up his mind. This cannot be a cheap picture."

Wald still refused to commit himself, and Berlin resorted to plugging "Give Me Your Tired, Your Poor," the setting he had composed for Emma Lazarus's verses. "In my opinion, that hymn is as good as 'God Bless America,' or anything I've ever done," he insisted.

"I think it's a very impressive piece of work, Irving," Wald said tactfully.

"Yes, and in Cinerama it's just terrific."

After all his boasting about *Miss Liberty*, the songwriter suddenly allowed a disconcerting truth to slip into the conversation.

> BERLIN: It wasn't a complete failure, you know.
>
> WALD: Oh, I know. I think it ran a year, didn't it?
>
> BERLIN: It ran a year, and the only way it was a failure was that it cost so goddamn much money. We still owe about ten percent of the backers—not mine! Because I took a third of it and put up every goddamn nickel.

Nothing could have been more calculated to disrupt the favorable outcome of all that had gone before than Berlin's reminding Wald of the show's sorry history, but it was too late, the harm had been done.

Irving waited months for Columbia to make a commitment. Wald himself was of two minds about the project, and eventually he concluded that it was a "good thing gone wrong." Finally, it was apparent that despite Berlin's high-pressure salesmanship, no movie would ever be made from *Miss Liberty*. But it would not be for lack of trying on the part of the indefatigable songwriter. Berlin's dealings with motion picture executives like Wald brought out the worst in the songwriter. He became as coarse and garrulous and two-dimensional as he believed the executives were. "They all say its commercialism," he said in his own defense, "but you just try and buy a picture by Picasso and see what they charge for it. That's pretty commercial, too." Not that he was comparing himself to Picasso, but, he insisted, "We're living in a country that is a commercial country." And he was its premier commercial composer.

In his longing to be commercial, to be tough, he often sacrificed the enthusiasms and intuitions that had always been his real strength. In his zeal to impress studios with the box-office appeal of his songs, Berlin lost sight of the fact that well-heeled motion picture executives were not his true constituency; ordinary Americans were, and as he became increasingly isolated from their experiences and emotions in the 1950s, he gradually surrendered his ability to write songs that spoke to them. Increasingly, he frittered away his energies in interminable bickering over money.

Even his other movie projects, when they reached audiences, showed signs of age. Paramount's *White Christmas* lacked freshness, and the story, involving a reunion of veterans (Crosby and Kaye) at a country inn run by their beloved retired general, shamelessly cribbed from *Holiday Inn*'s plot. The restrained professionalism of the cast and director, Michael Curtiz, imparted an air of old pros going through their highly polished routines once again. Just two months after Paramount released *White Christmas*, Twentieth Century-Fox flung *There's No Business Like Show Business* at the public, and this elaborate paean to showfolk proved to be as frenetic as its rival was stodgy.

The making of *There's No Business Like Show Business* had posed numerous difficulties. Zanuck originally assigned Lamar Trotti, a screenwriter responsible for numerous musicals at the studio, to the project. Trotti had mastered the studio's formula. Silly plot gimmicks, the good girl–bad girl duality, a relentlessly moralizing tone—such was Trotti's stock-in-trade. And then, as had happened to so many others involved with Berlin's postwar projects, Trotti died before he could complete the job. Zanuck offered the assignment to a young writing team, Phoebe and Henry Ephron, but Phoebe, especially, had a distinct lack of sympathy for the material. "I won't go to see it," Phoebe told her husband, "why should I write it?" Henry promised her that she wouldn't have to see the result, and the Ephrons reluctantly accepted the task. "I think it was the hardest job we ever did," Henry wrote.

Shortly before the film began production, a new star joined the cast as a direct result of Irving's intervention: Marilyn Monroe. He had seen her photograph during a dinner at Joe Schenck's home, and her plushy, come-hither look fascinated him. She seemed to be the next Rita Hayworth, only more available, closer to a tramp than a satin-clad starlet. He had an inspiration: Marilyn would be perfect, absolutely perfect singing his tongue-in-cheek torch song, "Heat Wave," in *There's No Business Like Show Business.* He implored Schenck to call her—not tomorrow, but at that moment—even though it was two o'clock in the morning. (Schenck was long accustomed to Berlin's impatience; he once bet the songwriter fifty dollars that he couldn't sit in a chair for five consecutive minutes; within two minutes Berlin was pacing.)

"That crazy Schenck called me at two in the morning," Marilyn later complained to the Ephrons. "And then he put Berlin on the phone." And Berlin urged her to sing "Heat Wave." Despite his plea, Marilyn refused to accept the insubstantial part until Zanuck dangled the prospect of starring in Billy Wilder's new film, *The Seven Year Itch,* before her. For the sake of working with Wilder, she agreed to appear in *There's No Business Like Show Business.* She was to play Ethel Merman's daughter, but neither Merman nor Monroe would stand for the arrangement, so the Ephrons hurriedly rewrote the entire script. Monroe now portrayed the kind of character the studio felt she did best: a sex object.

The addition of Monroe instantly complicated the task of making the picture. She made no secret of her unhappiness about her recent marriage to Joe DiMaggio, the way he would come home with a large group of friends and sit around with them, playing gin rummy and watching television and ignoring her, Marilyn Monroe. It was the one thing she could not tolerate, being ignored. The unhappy actress would arrive hours late for work, or not at all, depending on her mood, to the intense irritation of Ethel Merman. And even if Marilyn had been on time, she would have touched off a bitter rivalry with Merman simply by being young and beautiful. Merman hated to be seen with her and compared to her; she was everything Merman feared in a Hollywood actress: a gorgeous young blonde who couldn't sing and who would steal the picture.

When the movie opened at the end of 1954, its scale, further exaggerated by the wide-screen effect known as CinemaScope, proved so vast that no one, not even Marilyn Monroe singing "Heat Wave" in a gaudy tropical costume, could steal it. Berlin's songs whizzed past at such a rate that more discriminating audiences became bewildered and a trifle annoyed. Ethel Merman was lost amid the chaos of subplots about the life of a vaudeville family and the profusion of characters. "If anyone raises feeble protest that this has been shown before," commented *New York Times* film critic Bosley Crowther, "we hasten to add that it has never—but never!—been shown on such a scale." Intended as a celebration of the music of Irving Berlin, *There's No Business Like Show Business* instead became its cinematic epitaph. Never again would he write a movie score.

The songwriter's fall from grace in Hollywood was so swift, so dramatic, as to defy logic. But there were reasons behind it. His catalogue was depleted, for one thing; he had finally run out of enough songs to support another large-scale film retrospective. In addition, the executives who had been his most influential links to the motion picture business had been pushed aside to make room for younger men. And finally, the studios themselves, caught between television and recent antitrust rulings, no longer monopolized the entertainment industry. For all these reasons, then, his base of support in Hollywood eroded beyond recovery.

▪ ▪ ▪

His movie career at a standstill, Berlin slumped into a depression, refusing even to talk. At the beginning of 1955, Ellin and he took a ten-day vacation in Haiti, but the change of scenery failed to alleviate his melancholy. Only the unexpected presence of Noël Coward at the resort where the Berlins were staying promised to cheer the beleaguered songwriter. Coward was traveling with the dress designer Ginette Spanier, who, on being introduced to the famous Irving Berlin, was surprised to find "a little old man who was feeling very, very sad."

Although he was too depressed to exchange *mots* with Coward, he later brightened when he happened to hear the notes of "White Christmas" being picked out on a piano. Recognizing the playful Noël Coward at the keyboard, the songwriter strolled over. When Coward finished another song, Irving inquired, "Who wrote that tune?"

"You did," Coward said. Berlin was so depressed he had forgotten the song was his.

By now a knot of guests had formed around the piano, many of them imploring Coward to sing one of his own songs. Coward was no Irving Berlin, but he did write and perform cabaret-style songs from time to time. Still, he shook his head. "No," he said. "This is Irving Berlin's night."

As the songwriter retreated to his table, Coward launched into an impromptu Irving Berlin recital, and when he finished, the resort rang with cheers. Irving stayed at his table while Ellin approached Coward. "Noël, darling," she said, "You will never know what you have done for Irving today." A Caribbean resort . . . a famous, depressed American songwriter . . . a famous English dramatist . . . a grateful wife: the incident might have come from a play by Coward himself.

▪ ▪ ▪

On his return to New York, Irving briefly recovered his spirits. Tan and fit, he made a brave show, smiling for the press and talking about the new musical comedy he would write for the Broadway stage in time for the 1956 season. Inspired by Alva Johnston's book *The Legendary Mizners*, it would dramatize the story of the brothers, Addison, the flamboyant architect, and Wilson, the witty playwright. Irving was one of the few people still around who had actually known Wilson Mizner, and for that reason the idea appealed to him, but working on the show with his collaborators, George S. Kaufman and S. N. Behrman, proved to be an unhappy experience. According to Kaufman, they felt they were in danger of becoming "writers who mask sterility with incessant productivity": a condition that aptly described the most recent years of Berlin's professional life.

Irving had little time to dwell on this disappointment, for he soon faced a new challenge: a nasty lawsuit charging that he had plagiarized "You're Just in Love," the hit counterpoint song from *Call Me Madam.* Normally these plagiarism suits came to nothing, but his accuser on this occasion, Alfred L. Smith, was an especially persistent adversary. A gold stamper by trade, Smith insisted that a song he'd written in 1947 called "I Fell in Love" was pirated by Berlin. Both songs, he claimed, contained a distinctive "Hebraic chant."

When the matter came to trial before the New York State Supreme Court, Smith's argument proved to be riddled with inconsistencies. Berlin's lawyers produced an expert who testified that the envelope containing Smith's manuscript had been opened and resealed at least once. There was a strong implication that Smith had altered his song *after* Berlin's "You're Just in Love" became a hit. Nor did the logic behind Smith's charge bear scrutiny. With its intricate counterpoint structure, "You're Just in Love" was among the most complex and distinctive songs in Berlin's entire catalogue. Smith admitted he lacked musical training, and it seemed unlikely that he would have been capable of devising this tune on his own. Furthermore, any number of people, including Helmy Kresa and Russel Crouse, had seen or heard Berlin compose it on or shortly after September 11, during the frantic New Haven tryouts of *Call Me Madam.* And finally, the song was specific to that show; it had been tailored to suit a unique dramatic situation. Given these circumstances, "You're Just in Love" offered a singularly poor basis for a plagiarism suit, and Smith's accusation gradually acquired the aura of an elaborate hoax.

Hoax or not, Berlin went to extraordinary lengths to dispel any suspicion about the song—and to attract publicity. In fact, once he realized that he had nothing to fear from the trial, that Smith's cockamamie allegations could not possibly threaten his eminence, he turned the proceedings to his own advantage. Taking the stand, he patiently described the course of his career, listed his hits starting with "Alexander's Ragtime Band," and told how he had come to write "You're Just in Love" at the request of George Abbott. Finally, he offered to demonstrate his *modus operandi.* "With one finger he struck different pieces of a near-by wooden shelf as though he were picking keys laboriously," a reporter observed.

The next day, March 31, he sat before a piano and launched into a boisterous version of the disputed song. The sound of Berlin's high-pitched voice accompanied by the piano ricocheted through the courtroom. It was his best performance since his appearance at the Madison Square Garden rally. His nervous, effervescent brand of charm had worked down at Nigger Mike's in 1907, it had worked in *This Is the Army* during the forties, and it still worked in 1955, here in this sedate courtroom usually populated by serious legal types droning on interminably. Berlin knew how to work a crowd, any crowd, how to get them on his side and make skeptics into fans.

The next morning, the display generated headlines:

MUSICAL MYTH BLASTED

BERLIN SHOWS IN COURT THAT HE
IS NO ONE-FINGER PIANIST

Berlin had deftly managed to explode *two* fictions at the same time—the first, that he'd plagiarized the song, and the second, the rumor dating back to his visit to England over forty years earlier that he could only play the piano with one finger.

It surprised no one, therefore, when Justice Martin M. Frank, on April 27, ruled in favor of the defendant, primarily because—well, because he was Irving Berlin. "The proof in this case does not justify, nor does common sense permit, the inference that Mr. Berlin would jeopardize the singular place he has earned from the achievements of a lifetime," Frank wrote.

Though he had finally managed to put to rest the rumor that he did not write his own songs, Berlin was plagued by other, more insidious gossip, against which he had no clear defense. For several years now, the entertainment world on both coasts had given if not credence then at least serious consideration to the rumor that Irving Berlin was, astonishingly, addicted to drugs. Reports came from all directions. During rehearsals for *Call Me Madam*, for instance, Ethel Merman claimed he was "on the hard stuff," and she did not mean whiskey. But Merman was a notorious gossip and noted for her cutting remarks.

Another, more troubling source was Milton "Mezz" Mezzrow, a jazz musician whose musical avocation served as a cover for his drug dealing. Prone to boast about the famous musicians he supplied, he claimed he once sold a kilo of marijuana to Berlin, which would have cost about five hundred dollars at the time. Eventually Mezz was tried and convicted and went to jail for selling marijuana, and he subsequently died in Paris. But the rumor about Berlin that he had helped to spread lived on.

In its most luxuriant form, the rumor suggested that Berlin had started using drugs when he was a singing waiter in Chinatown, in the days when opium was sold legally. The rumor also involved Joe Schenck, who had worked at the drugstore that sold opium, and who supposedly supplied Berlin. The story that Berlin was some kind of an addict offered a convenient explanation for his behavioral quirks—his shyness, nervousness, and sudden flashes of temper. Furthermore, so many other musicians did use drugs; why would Berlin be any different?

But to those who knew him best, the rumors were false. Berlin was the way he was not because of drugs but because of his temperament. Associates like his faithful transcriber Helmy Kresa and his one-time secretary Mynna Dreyer, people who were with him at all hours of the day and night over a period of years, were aware of the stories; the tale was so prevalent that it was impossible to avoid. But at the same time, they knew there was no truth to it. "To my knowledge he never used drugs," Kresa insists, ascribing the rumor to professional jealousy.

To the extent that Berlin had a problem, it involved not marijuana or other street drugs, but the common prescription drug Nembutal, which he began using after the Second World War in his lifelong quest for a sound night's sleep. Berlin made no secret of his use of Nembutal; he referred to it in interviews when he joked about his insomnia. However, as his tolerance for Nembutal increased, and he began taking ever-larger doses of the drug, his dependency on it became a cause for concern rather than laughter.

Rather than buy the Nembutal himself from the Upper East Side drugstore that he patronized, he usually dispatched one of his employees on the mission. On at least one occasion, Irving became so anxious waiting for the prescription to be delivered that he paced up and down the street in a rainstorm until the errand boy finally appeared with it. He was aware of the impression such behavior might make and feared his frequent recourse to Nembutal might lead to public embarrassment or even blackmail. When government narcotics agents, making a routine inspection of Berlin's pharmacy, discovered his many prescriptions, the druggist explained that his famous customer was a sick man and didn't want anyone knowing about it. The agents accepted the story.

When Irving heard about the incident, however, he worried. His anxieties increased when the two owners of the drugstore asked his business manager, Al Chandler, if Berlin would consider making them a $7,500 business loan. As he did on numerous occasions, Chandler relayed the request for money to his boss. "What the hell are they trying to do, shake us down?" he said with considerable irritation.

As the rumors about Berlin's eccentricities and irascibility spread, the songwriter retreated from the public eye, and the rumors expanded to fill the information vacuum. The world was still hungry for news of Irving Berlin, his music, his wife, his children, hungry for more reminiscences of growing up impoverished on the Lower East Side, and possibly another "White Christmas" languishing in his trunk, awaiting only his desire to call it forth.

In the absence of new songs, his hits received considerable air play throughout the mid and late fifties, and were widely recorded, and as a result, he continued to receive generous royalty payments. Indeed, royalties proved to be the one area where his preeminence still went unchallenged. ASCAP collected and distributed royalties according to a complex formula, and Berlin's share was higher than any other songwriter's. In 1950 he collected $72,000, in 1952, $87,000. Only Cole Porter came close to equaling those figures. ASCAP subsequently introduced a new system of allocating royalties, and Berlin's income from this source went higher still:

	Irving Berlin	*Cole Porter*
1954	$101,000	65,000
1955	100,000	65,750
1956	102,000	71,500

This was the fruit of a lifetime's endeavor, his entire catalogue working for him.

Berlin profited from writing both words and music, whereas most other songwriters (Porter being an important exception) formed teams and shared their take. For instance, Rodgers and Hammerstein, Berlin's main rivals during this era, collected about $70,000 annually, but they naturally divided the amount between them.

Now that he was no longer able to write scores for Broadway or Hollywood, Berlin relied almost exclusively on his ASCAP income. In October 1954, he remarked, "Without ASCAP's performance revenue I couldn't survive. . . . I would have to close shop and see my thirty-year-old organization go down the drain." He had few new songs of merit to offer, and as he counted his money in the form of quarterly earnings statements from ASCAP, he devoted ever less time to composing. He ceased making live performances or showing up at the White House. Most destructively, he continued his pointless feud with television.

Unaware of the intensity of Berlin's feelings regarding the medium, the BBC decided to commemorate the songwriter's seventieth birthday on May 11, 1958, with a ninety-minute dramatized biography with music. (It was a measure of Berlin's depressed reputation in Hollywood that no comparable *American* ceremony was planned to mark the occasion; the English, it seemed, had a better sense of the songwriter's role in musical history.) The BBC's program was not the conventional sedate tribute with a few singers sitting around a set crooning old favorites. It was a hugely ambitious undertaking; the producer, Ernest Maxin, announced his intention to stage a "TV musical on the Hollywood scale." It was touted as being among the most elaborate and costly productions the BBC had ever mounted. The show would feature not only Berlin's songs but also dramatic portrayals of characters from his life, everyone from Lena Baline to Mike Salter, Dorothy Goetz, Ted Snyder, George Gershwin, up to and including Ellin and Clarence

Mackay, as well as Irving Berlin himself, played by a young American actor named Gaylord Cavallero, who, with his sleek black hair and intense dark eyes, bore a passing resemblance to the songwriter.

The BBC put the program into production and gave it considerable publicity. At the eleventh hour, however, the subject of this tribute began having second thoughts about the BBC's intentions. He realized that the British network had mounted an entire production, the equivalent of a movie, without consulting him. Lacking control over the situation, he descended into sullen fury. Performing his songs was one thing, and Berlin approved of that aspect of the show, but the dramatization of his life was another, and on that issue, he was unalterably opposed to any attempt to impersonate him or his wife or his mother or anyone else in his life.

Several days before the broadcast, Berlin's office contacted the BBC, which at first politely resisted any attempt to meddle, but on May 8, one of Berlin's lawyers sent a lengthy telegram insisting that the BBC restrict its tribute to the songs only. At the last minute, the network yielded to the demand and restructured its Hollywood-style show. Out went the story and characters (said Gaylord Cavallero, who was to have portrayed Berlin, "I must be the unluckiest actor in the world"), in went an extra half hour of music. And it was in that hastily revised version that the tribute was broadcast across England. The cantankerous songwriter subsequently tried to justify thwarting the well-intended BBC tribute: "It would be an invasion of my privacy. The BBC never asked my permission to do this. I would find it very embarrassing. I don't want my life story told while I'm alive. When I'm dead, they can tell it all they want."

Berlin's quarrel with the BBC was a symptom of far more serious problems with which he was struggling in private. After decades of ceaseless composing, performing, and agitating on behalf of his music, he was on the brink of physical and emotional breakdown. Since the outbreak of the Second World War and the inception of *This Is the Army*, he had gone from score to score, from Broadway to Hollywood and back again without respite, and the only complaints he suffered, seemingly, were insomnia and a hair-trigger temper. The unending stress eventually took its toll, and he found himself a patient in a private hospital on the Upper East Side of New York, with three nurses caring for him around the clock.

He was suffering from depression, exhaustion, and malnutrition: the legacy of years of overwork and overuse of sleeping pills. His collapse placed a considerable strain on Ellin, who confided in one of the nurses that perhaps the most difficult part of being married to Irving Berlin was contending with his outbursts of temper. That peril had always existed in her marriage—the possibility that she had exchanged one tyrant, her father, for another, Irving. But meekness was not Ellin's style, and she had generally been able to hold her own against her husband. Their three daughters were not as well equipped to handle Irving's temper as she was, however, and Ellin conceded that it had been difficult for her to shield the children from Irving's tantrums. Though his violence was purely verbal, it was nonetheless terrifying for that.

Later, when Irving began to recover, he, too, became friendly with the same nurse, and his regrets concerned not his family but his work. He expressed remorse over having bought tunes over the years from little-known songwriters for small change, published the songs, and never having given these relatively anonymous craftsmen the recognition and recompense they deserved. As a music publisher, Berlin was not at all unique in this regard. On Tin Pan Alley, musical thievery had been the order of the day, but to Berlin, with his unyielding respect for the integrity of a songwriter's work (his own, especially), the practice violated the stringent code of business ethics he followed. He had always insisted on obtaining full credit for himself; he knew he should have been as careful to *give* credit when credit was due.

More than the hollow panoply of a birthday tribute, Berlin's stay in the hospital marked a turning point in his life. When he recovered and went home, he was a man entering his seventies, and he was forced to acknowledge the reality of aging and to reign in his expectations for the future. It was apparent now that this best work, his most memorable accomplishments, were well behind him. The realization was, for him, enormously depressing. But his life wasn't over, of course, though he would have to take things easier now, a day at a time, and more importantly, he would need to recover a sense of purpose to illuminate the years to come.

■ □ ■ □ ■ □ ■

CHAPTER 20

The Cheering Stops

There was no symbol more evocative of Irving Berlin's songwriting career than his transposing piano—the upright, tinny-sounding, cigarette-scarred "Buick" on which he picked out his tunes. After five decades of constant use, its ivory keys, once smooth and white, were discolored, its finish scratched and peeling. Perhaps the device had outlived its usefulness, and at age seventy, so, perhaps, had he. As he embarked on his uneasy retirement in the late 1950s, he placed the instrument in storage, a muse languishing in the darkness. It was a gesture of resignation, even despair.

Well-meaning friends such as Irving Hoffman, a press agent, and Sam Shaw, a photographer, rallied to his side, urging him to take up a hobby. Irving, they said, try golf—but at seventy he figured he was too old to play. Irving, try fishing—there was excellent fishing around his country home, and he tried his luck in nearby streams, but he lacked the patience of the true fisherman, and he soon gave it up. Irving, they finally said, try *painting*—and he did try, and he was intrigued by it, though so critical of his efforts that he failed to appreciate the simple pleasure of manipulating color on a canvas. "I couldn't just enjoy it as a Sunday painter," he said. "I'm very tough on myself, sometimes too tough." Although painting would continue to exert a fascination for him, despite his penchant for self-criticism, he recognized that there was only one activity that engaged all his faculties:

"I've always thought of myself as a songwriter. What else would I want to be?" he mused as he contemplated life in his seventies—and beyond. "I'm a songwriter, like dozens and dozens of others, and as long as I'm able, whether the songs are good or bad, I'll continue to write them, because songwriting is not alone a business or a hobby with me. It's everything."

Those were brave words and sad words, as well, because he could no longer write the songs that were everything to him—not just the hit songs, but any songs at all. No hits, no flops, nothing. Between 1957 and 1962—five barren, angst-ridden years—the nation's preeminent songwriter published but a single title, an anthem called "Israel," a "God Bless America" for the Jewish state, and it failed to catch on.

The man who only several years before had been among the most famous show business figures in the world, a celebrity who had fought to keep his name everywhere—on movie marquees, on the radio, and on records—dropped from sight. "I got really sick," Berlin said of his lost years. "I suffered severe bouts of depression. I worried about everything when, really, I had nothing to worry about." He passed his days in a shadow existence. "As the months went by," wrote *Life*'s theater critic, Tom Prideaux, of his troubled friend, "you spent more and more time alone in your own rooms on the top floor of your Manhattan town house on Beekman Place. You suffered from a nervous skin disease that locked you in a fiery straitjacket of pain"—by which Prideaux meant shingles, a debilitating condition caused by a virus that produces excruciating blisters.

During the epoch of his withdrawal from the world, Berlin dwelled in solitude in his Manhattan aerie. He had his own kitchen, and he took his meals by himself. On the infrequent occasions that he went out for a walk, it was always at night, when he would not be recognized. He tried composing songs now and then, and he broke through his isolation to talk with friends on the phone, even singing a few verses to gauge what they thought, but nothing he did seemed to strike a spark. His was a cruel and fickle business—appealing to the hearts and imagination of the public. In the past, when he had succeeded, and they all loved him, he had felt invulnerable, as if he could go on forever; but now that he was faltering, and they ignored him, his self-confidence dissolved into a foul mixture of anger and despair. He had always lacked an innate sense of worth, and that gnawing sense of inadequacy had been the thorn in his side driving him to feats of greatness, but in his weakened physical condition he lacked the fury to resume the struggle.

Ellin, meanwhile, lived a separate existence on the lower floors of the cavernous house, spending her time on charity work for the Girl Scouts and writing another book, a memoir of her once-celebrated, now-forgotten grandmother, Marie Hungerford Mackay.

Her husband also doted on the past: the songs he had written, the performers he had known, and the shows on which they had worked—so famous in their time and now forgotten. To forestall his own oblivion, he began to establish a network of men who became his confidantes and later his spokesmen. They tended to be scholarly and serious, these men. The roster included, at one time or another, Stanley Green and Edward Jablonski, both respected chroniclers of popular entertainment; and a group of veteran songwriters, Harry Ruby (his friend from Camp Upton days), Abe Olman, and Harold Arlen. With no male heir to carry on for him, to set about dutifully preserving his legacy for future generations, he turned to these men as to surrogate sons. He would telephone them at home, at any hour of the day or night, once a week on average, sometimes several times a day when something bothered him; and they would discuss various items appearing in the trade publications, *Variety* and *Billboard*, or swap gossip about the doings at the latest ASCAP board meeting. Occasionally, when Irving Berlin refused to talk to the world at large, which generally appeared to him in the guise of eager, ingratiating reporters seeking his opinions, one of the surrogates would volunteer to speak on his behalf, relating Berlin's little jokes and barbs and reminiscences—the observations of a deposed and embittered monarch startled by the way the world was carrying on without him.

The youngest member of this select group was an apprentice producer at Columbia Records named Miles Kreuger, who possessed a keen sense of show business history complemented by a phenomenal memory. When he came across two private recordings that Berlin had made in 1913—one of which contained the legendary song he had sung on the occasion of his initiation into the Friars, "What Am I Gonna Do?"—he immediately recognized their importance. He hurriedly ordered pressings made and sent them to Berlin without realizing the impact his gift would have. When the songwriter received them, it was as though his youth—the best part of it, at any rate—had returned.

Visiting Helmy Kresa at Berlin's office soon after, Kreuger received a phone call from the Old Man himself, who was at home. Aware of the songwriter's reclusiveness, Kreuger recoiled in astonishment when Helmy told him who was on the line. "I knew Richard Rodgers, I knew Harold Arlen, and I knew Cole Porter, but they were mere mortals," he said. "This was a man from another century." Which was how Irving Berlin, once the perennial man of his times, now appeared to young people in the early sixties. As Helmy handed him the receiver, Kreuger felt he had stepped into an Alfred Hitchcock movie in which someone was pushing an object menacingly close to the camera. He's going to be deaf, Kreuger told himself, he's going to be senile, he's going to be old, and what will I say to him?

He cautiously said hello, and then he heard a "high-pitched, animated voice that sounded as though it belonged to a hysterical teenager":

"Hi!" the voice said. "It's Irving Berlin! I want to thank you for those records you gave me. I made those records privately, but you know how it is, you move from one place to another, and you lose things, you put things in a closet, and things get broken. I lay awake at night thinking about those records all those years, and if I could only hear them again." Kreuger was startled. Had Berlin actually *lain awake at night thinking about recordings he had made in 1913?* Berlin made other curious observations. "Listen," he said, "I got a daughter who's a Cole Porter fan, and Cole writes pretty good stuff. But I want her to know that when it's really necessary her old man can write some pretty sophisticated tunes himself." And he proceeded to ask Kreuger to make a copy of the songs he wrote for "Freddy," because "those were pretty sophisticated tunes, if I do say so myself."

It took the young record producer a moment to realize that Freddy's last name was Astaire. "Of course, Mr. Berlin, I'd be happy to," he said.

"What could I give you?" Berlin asked. "I mean anything."

"You don't have to give me anything," Kreuger replied. It was the correct response.

"Listen, Helmy's got something for you. It isn't much, but it's a token of my appreciation."

At the conclusion of the call, Helmy gave Kreuger an envelope containing a photograph of the songwriter, who had previously autographed it. "To Miles Kreuger," the message read, "with deep appreciation of giving me the recordings I made in 1913 of the Friars' Speech." It was dated 1961.

"Of course," Kreuger later reflected, "I've gone through life hearing the stories about the little boy in Harlem who writes Berlin's songs. He must have been off that day because Berlin obviously chose the wrong preposition; it's not 'appreciation of' as Berlin wrote, but 'for.' I was touched by that; he didn't have anybody correct his grammar, he just wrote his personal sentiments. I look at that picture every single day of my life."

Thereafter, they talked frequently on the phone, and Kreuger sensed that Berlin was suffering from a sense of inferiority in relation to other songwriters, a conviction that "he wasn't as educated as Richard Rodgers, as melodically gifted as Jerome Kern, or as witty as Cole Porter." Berlin, he decided, feared comparisons because he felt unworthy of his stature, and as a result of his inner self-doubt, he had a perpetual craving for self-affirmation.

The relationship between master and disciple foundered for just this reason, when the scholarly Kreuger inquired about the fate of the score that had been deleted from Berlin's botched movie, *Reaching for the Moon.* Even though forty years had intervened, the memory of this debacle still rankled the songwriter, and Berlin suddenly turned antagonistic. "Miles, I'm really astonished by this," he said. "This line of questioning is strange. You want to change history to suit your own meaning and interpretation of it." When Kreuger pleaded that nothing was further from his mind, Berlin replied, "Aw, you're just like all the rest of them. Frankly, I'm disappointed. I didn't think you'd do that."

Kreuger hadn't intended to provoke Berlin, of course. He'd simply made the mistake of reminding the songwriter of *Reaching for the Moon.* Berlin never spoke to him again.

▪ ▪ ▪

It so happened that Kreuger's boss at Columbia Records was the distinguished record producer Goddard Lieberson, who exerted an oblique but powerful influence on the Broadway musical. A few years before, after previewing Alan Jay Lerner and Frederick Loewe's score for *My Fair Lady*, Lieberson had persuaded *his* employers, CBS, to invest $360,000 in the show. A huge gamble, Lieberson's strategy had paid off handsomely, for the show became a mammoth hit. *My Fair Lady* was still playing on Broadway and would eventually gross over $20 million: now there was a sum to inflame Irving's imagination. Furthermore, Columbia's original cast album of *My Fair Lady*, produced by Lieberson at a cost of $22,000, earned another fortune for CBS. Say what people would about the rise of television and the death of the musical, the success of *My Fair Lady* demonstrated how rich the rewards of bringing in a Broadway hit still were. Beyond the money, Lieberson's handling of the original cast album was a sonic marvel; he did not simply record the songs, he *reproduced* their theatrical aura.

As the songwriter's painful case of shingles relented, he wished to give birth to one last show that would imitate this success. He'd been written off many times before—when the ragtime craze ended, during his creative slump following his marriage to Ellin, after the failure of *Miss Liberty*—and each time he'd fought his way all the way back. But the world had changed drastically in the past few years: now John Glenn circled the globe every three hours, and a handsome young Irish-Catholic president and his even more glamorous wife were installed in the White House. Berlin repeatedly asked himself how a songwriter might capture the new spirit they represented. He occasionally telephoned Howard Lindsay and Russel Crouse, his collaborators on *Call Me Madam*, to discuss ideas with them—something for Ethel Merman, something timely and topical. But Merman wouldn't do it; Irving Berlin or no Irving Berlin, she'd had enough of Broadway for the time being.

In May 1961, Lindsay and Crouse mentioned an idea that set Berlin's mind spinning. For some time the writing team had been turning over an idea for a show about a president retiring from office. Lindsay and Crouse were probably thinking of Eisenhower when they began; eventually they realized that Ike no longer had much box-office appeal (if he ever had), but his glamorous successor Jack Kennedy certainly did, and Jackie even more so, and their lovable children scampering all over the White House completed the perfect domestic situation. Not even Lamar Trotti, the Twentieth Century-Fox screenwriter who had made a career out of inventing adorable show business families, could have devised a more stage-worthy clan.

The idea of writing a show about a president proved endlessly flattering to Irving's fragile ego. Ever since *Louisiana Purchase* (1940), his earliest narrative Broadway musical, he had drawn inspiration from political stories, but he had never before written about the most important political figure of all. To do so now suggested he had himself reached the summit of his own profession, that he was, as a headline would shortly label him, " 'Mr. President' of Tin Pan Alley." Furthermore, he'd always conducted his career in a manner that paralleled a politician's calling. He wrote songs speaking to public issues and concerns of the moment, and he tallied the sales of his music as if the figures were votes. Of course he wasn't at all close to President Kennedy, and he remained a confirmed Republican, but the lack of any real sympathy with his subject scarcely seemed to matter at the time.

After a decade's absence from Broadway, Berlin felt sufficiently invigorated and confident to choose this premise as his vehicle for a comeback worthy of the Grand Old Man of Tin Pan Alley. He came down at last from his top-floor apartment. He began showing up at his office once again. He looked good, in touch, as sharp as ever. And, in the most positive action he had taken in years, he took his transposing piano out of storage. In short, he came out of retirement.

He departed for his Catskills estate, once again a man with a vocation, and amid the splendid summer scenery mulled over the score for the new musical. "It would have been easy to have gone into the trunk for the songs, but I wanted to see if I could still reach up and find it there," Berlin said, as he tried to grasp the air above his head. So he sat down and wrote a few ballads. Played them for Lindsay and Crouse, who liked them. Pulled in Joshua Logan, director of *Annie Get Your Gun*, and Leland Hayward, producer of *Call Me Madam.* It was a good feeling to be working with the old team again, everyone a pro. "Once you get started on a show," Berlin said, "you just keep going."

As the word circulated that Berlin & Co. were at work on a new Broadway show, now called *Mr. President*, Goddard Lieberson endowed the enterprise with his imprimatur when he agreed to underwrite and produce the original cast album for Columbia Records *and* to lend the producers $200,000. To outsiders, Lieberson's involvement signaled another smash hit in the making. Perhaps the new musical, to be called *Mr. President*, would be the next *My Fair Lady*; on Broadway, anything was possible. Privately, however, the record producer resented the arrangement. He described the process of obtaining the rights to Broadway shows as "verging on hysteria." He explained that "for a producer to ask a record company for money is immoral, for a record company to give it is ignorance." In the case of *Mr. President*, then, Columbia Records displayed both ignorance and immorality—but it got the rights to the show. As for the cost of mounting the stage production, estimated at $400,000, Hayward, Lindsay and Crouse, Logan, and Berlin all put up the money themselves and owned equal shares of the property.

The Broadway Establishment (or what was left of it) had joined forces to mount a musical about the new Political Establishment, and the thoroughly Establishment credentials of *Mr. President* appeared to guarantee its success. At another time, that might have been just the way it happened, but this was 1962: strange winds of controversy were blowing across the land. Nothing—least of all the brilliant image projected by Kennedys—was quite what it seemed, and the Establishment was fast falling out of favor. Berlin emerged from his Beekman Place retreat assuming that the national consensus on which he had always depended for the success of his songs still held, but that consensus had evaporated during his absence, and his musical's Establishment bias would prove its undoing.

No one foresaw that eventuality when the show began taking shape in April 1962. At the time, *Mr. President* appeared to be a sure thing. Even before the stars were announced, over a million dollars worth of tickets were sold, and Hayward was predicting the advance sale would set a Broadway record. In his public utterances, Irving was a bit more cautious. "I wouldn't pay a million dollars for something I'd never seen," he said. He noted his prolonged absence from Broadway, worried aloud about whether he had gotten rusty in the interim, and his becoming modesty made people want him to succeed all the more.

Always a fast worker, he finished his score by May: twenty-two songs, most of them in a comic vein. Thereafter, he devoted the better part of his energies to publicizing the show and his return to the public eye; each interview he gave boosted the show's advance sale as well as his own self-confidence. There he was, in shirt sleeves, talking in his rapid-fire manner, demonstrating new songs on his transposing piano. He was nothing like the gargoyle of Beekman Place rumors had made him out to be. The journalists came away impressed.

Variety decided to make the story of Berlin's return to Broadway its own; the editors there sank their teeth into the event as if they hadn't had a bone to chew on since talking pictures came in. On July 18, a banner headline in inch-high letters announced:

BERLIN'S B'WAY BOUNCE-BACK
HE RESIGNS FROM HIS RETIREMENT

The announcement positioned *Mr. President* as the outstanding event of the upcoming Broadway season. The songwriter himself was quoted, in italics, as saying, "*I'm going right to work on another show immediately*," whether or not *Mr. President* succeeded. All that talk about retirement, Irving said, had been a huge "mistake."

His ebullience turned to combativeness when *Mad*, the impudent humor magazine whose brand of satire appealed mainly to young readers, parodied the lyrics to some of his favorite songs. In 1961 the magazine published a special issue, "Sing Along with *Mad*," containing a "collection of parody lyrics to 57 old standards which reflect the idiotic world we live in today." Inevitably, Berlin was heavily represented. There was, for instance, a nimble burlesque of *Easter Parade* entitled "Beauty Parade":

Don't wear that bikini,
The one that's teeny-weeny,
Your looks are not important
In the Beauty Parade.

There was also a new set of lyrics for "Cheek to Cheek," now retitled "Sheik to Sheik," that began as follows:

Heaven, we're in heaven and our earth with rich black oil
just seems to leak
And we always find the happiness we seek
When we're talking dough together sheik to sheik.

And "Always," the most sacred song in the entire Berlin canon, the minimalist tone poem whose copyright he had given to Ellin as a wedding present, became the basis for a spoof of psychiatry:

He'll be seeing me
Always!
2:15 to 3:00
Always!
I've become aware
He's a millionaire;
He'll get daily care
Always! Always!

These and fifty-four other song parodies—all equally ludicrous—prompted Berlin to band together with a dozen other music publishers to sue the magazine for copyright infringement. It was one thing to be ignored, he had learned to deal with that indignity, but it was another to be mocked. To his way of thinking, there was no end to the ways that the disrespectful editors of *Mad* magazine had offended him: they had printed his lyrics—or lyrics closely resembling them—without payment and without his permission, which he would never have granted; they had corrupted the value of his original songs; they had, as his lawyer would shortly claim in court, committed "The worst kind of piracy. Piracy on the High C's."

The suit sent out legal shock waves extending well beyond the songwriter's private concerns. Ultimately, the right to publish satire, an important tenet of the First Amendment, was at stake. If the music publishers won, the entire genre of satire and parody of known models under copyright protection could be severely curtailed. However, if

Mad won, the legal status quo would remain in force, and Berlin would suffer a blow to his vanity. It was up to the courts to decide, and they took their time. The publishers' suit against *Mad* was filed in April, but Irving found that the judicial wheels ground exceedingly slowly, almost imperceptibly, in fact. It would be two years until a resolution was reached.

As the suit dragged on, *Mr. President* went into rehearsal. As usual, Berlin did more than compose the score; he cast the show, as well, and that was where the trouble started. To play the pivotal role of the outgoing Irish-American president, he selected Robert Ryan. It was a peculiar choice, for Ryan was best known as a movie actor with a charming, brooding presence. Whether Ryan could sing well enough or generate the energy a Broadway show required was open to question.

Berlin exercised far better judgment when it came to the part of Ryan's fashionable wife, the Jackie Kennedy stand-in. For years, the songwriter had wanted to work with Nanette Fabray, an intelligent, poised, and stylish actress with twenty years' experience on Broadway to her credit. In the past, whenever Berlin had been casting a new show, Fabray was unavailable, but now timing worked in his favor. She had recently had a baby, and she was caring for the infant in Los Angeles, surrounded by diapers and bottles, and it seemed that her career was over. "Do you think I'll ever work again?" she would ask her husband, screenwriter Randy MacDougall. "People have forgotten me. I've been pregnant."

As she was feeding her baby one day, the phone rang. It was Irving Berlin, and he hadn't forgotten her; in fact he was offering her the female lead in *Mr. President.* Without reading the script or hearing a song, she gratefully accepted. She packed up the family, drove with them across the country, and installed herself at the Carlyle Hotel in Manhattan on a year's lease. Given its enormous advance sale, *Mr. President* was expected to play on Broadway twice that long.

The script for the show was waiting for her when she arrived. While she met with Lindsay and Crouse, her husband sat down and read it through, and when she came back from the meeting, he was stricken with gloom. "Nan," be said, "do you really *have* to do this show?"

"What do you mean?"

"It's the worst script I have ever read," he told her. "It's nothing."

A sense of despair seized Fabray. "Is it salvageable?" she asked.

"I don't think so. It doesn't make sense. The characters are nothing. Have you heard the score?"

"Well," Fabray said, "I'm going to hear it this afternoon."

Later that day, she kept her appointment to hear the score at Berlin's studio. "I went there in a semi-coma," she said, "and I sat down on a sofa, and in came this adorable, wonderful man."

"I'm gonna play you the score," Irving announced. "The first thing I want to sing to you is the love song. *Your* love song." And he added, "I love this song."

He shifted the lever on his "Buick," and he sang the love song in "this high, thin little voice of his." And when he was through, the actress burst into tears. "He thought I was crying because I was so moved by the moment and how pretty the song was," she realized, "but actually it was the contrast between his enthusiasm and the terrible news I had heard about the script. I was so overwrought. He jumped up and came over and kissed me right on my hearing aid. I thought he had broken my head."

She hastily explained that she had to wear the device because she was hard of hearing, and Irving became terrified that he had damaged her ear. After she reassured him that he had not, they *both* cried over his love song. "Yes," she said, "he thought it was that beautiful."

He played through the rest of the songs—"a darling score," she thought. Her admiration for the man returned. "Irving knows how to make a note give the musical inflection that will make a lyric be either funny or sad or warm or loving," she said, "and that's what great composing is all about. If you're telling a joke, there's always a comma before the punch line. He is able to put that comma in the music to make the punch line perfect for the singer."

Then he asked Nanette what she thought of the script. Deciding "not to be terribly honest" about the matter, Fabray claimed she hadn't read it, yet.

Irving sensed her uncertainty and admitted, "Well, it does need work."

Reassured by Berlin's assessment ("I thought, at least he recognizes that"), Fabray began rehearsals. Fortunately, Josh Logan, the director, was in a good form. That was not always the case with him, for he was a manic-depressive and prone to fits of extreme melancholy, but at the time, he was in an "up" cycle—warm and cheerful with the cast, and attentive both to Fabray and her young son, whom he carried on his hip all through rehearsals. (One of her son's earliest memories was of a big man toting him around, constantly asking, "What do you think?")

Lindsay and Crouse refused to listen to criticism of their handiwork or to alter so much as a syllable. They were in for a shock when the production held its first out-of-town tryout, in Boston, at the end of August. In the first scene, Robert Ryan, as President Stephen Decatur Henderson, puts a piece of paper in a typewriter and begins to write his memoirs, as various members of his family walk in and introduce themselves. Every line, it seemed, began with a name: "Hi, Stephen," "Hi, Nell" (Mrs. Henderson), and so on for two or three minutes—Hi, Bob . . . Hi, John . . . Well, Stephen . . . Yes, Nell . . . Bye, Stephen. . . . And when it was finally over, the scene received, as Fabray recalled, "one of the biggest, longest, and most destructive laughs I've ever heard in my life."

The rest of the show never recovered from that disastrous opening, and as for Berlin's songs, they failed to help the muddled story. The comic numbers weren't all that funny, the sentimental songs embarrassingly outmoded. As a whole, the score was weaker than his previous Broadway flop, *Miss Liberty*; it was, in fact, the weakest, the stalest, the most tuneless score he had ever written. Even his attempts to be up-to-date, such as his "Washington Twist" number, proved lame.

The critics jumped all over the show, especially the *Record American*'s Elliot Norton. Esteemed as the Brooks Atkinson of Boston, Norton was often the first reputable critic to pass judgment on Broadway-bound productions, and as a result he usually wielded his power with caution. On this occasion, however, he summed up his reaction to *Mr. President* in one stark word: "Dreadful." It was not a description he used lightly. "Dreadful is the only word," he explained, "Anything milder would be misleading, not to say dishonest." And he singled out for special condemnation the songwriter whose comeback this was to be: "Never in his whole career has Irving Berlin written so many corny songs."

Humbled by the critical drubbing, Lindsay and Crouse revised their script, but Berlin refused to remove any of his songs. In fact, he added a number called "Empty Pockets Filled with Love." It was a counterpoint song, vaguely reminiscent of "You're Just in Love," the tune that had rescued *Call Me Madam*, but the trick—a good one in its time—had lost its magic. The show's prime movers mounted a publicity campaign in its defense. Berlin ran interference in the press, claiming that he'd been expecting the show to receive "mixed" notices all along, and he insisted *Mr. President* was basically a sound production. "It will play two years on Broadway—you watch." He was correct on that point; its prodigious advance sale guaranteed the show a lengthy run no matter what the critics said.

Despite the feisty attitude he adopted for public consumption, Berlin was gravely concerned about the show's prospects. Suddenly he seemed frail, fully his seventy-four years. "We have a terrible problem," he quietly admitted to cast members, "but we'll fix it, we'll fix it." The task seemed a hopeless one. No longer did he boast of writing more shows after *Mr. President*; he now said, with a certain sadness and dignity, "This will probably be my last show."

He solicited opinions as to how the show might be fixed from anyone he could lure to Boston. Cadres of show doctors set about rewriting the script of *Mr. President* and slipping it under Logan's door. Displaying considerably more *chutzpah*, Fabray's husband slipped *his* version under Lindsay's and Crouse's doors. Even when advice was offered, none was taken.

The problems besetting the show, while serious, were not (by Broadway standards) unusual or even insoluble. If Florenz Ziegfeld had been alive to see the pass that *Mr. President* had come to, he would have replaced Lindsay and Crouse, replaced Robert Ryan, interpolated hit songs into Berlin's score, and, when all else failed, overwhelmed the audience with spectacle and gossamer-clad female thighs. If Rodgers and Hammerstein had been running the show, they would have leavened the book with sadness and a well-intentioned "message" that sent the audience out into the night with a tear in the eye and a catch in the throat. And if the Irving Berlin of the 1930s, the era of *As Thousands Cheer*, had been present, he would have been quick to temper the idolatry of the Kennedys with stinging satire. But that Irving was no longer around, though his formidable reputation continued to haunt the cautious and sentimental old man who had written the show's score. As *Mr. President* concluded its problematic Boston run, no one involved with the show was willing to shout *No!* and take the necessary steps to rescue it from mediocrity.

On September 25, *Mr. President* opened at the National Theatre in Washington, D.C. Because *Mr. President* was transparently based on the Kennedys and promised to enhance their image, the family had decided to embrace the show. Jack Kennedy, especially, had long been in thrall of show business, and if Irving Berlin had written a thinly disguised musical about the Kennedy clan, then the president was going to make it his own.

Irving Berlin had participated in quite a few glamorous opening nights in his time, but nothing in his experience matched the Washington premiere of *Mr. President*. The Kennedys bought out the entire National Theatre for a benefit performance on behalf of two charities favored by the family. The evening became a festival of money, glamour, and publicity—everything that the Kennedys and America of the early 1960s represented. "This was going to be the biggest party of all time," Fabray realized. Politicians mingled with socialites, socialites with press lords, press lords with foreign dignitaries. Lyndon and Lady Bird Johnson were there, CBS chief William Paley was there, *Time* founder Henry Luce was there with his wife, Clare Boothe Luce. So were various dignitaries representing the French government. And the Kennedys were there in force: Rose and Bobby and several Kennedy sisters were scattered around the theater. And of course the president was *supposed* to be there; the fabled rocking chair awaited his graceful physique in a box at stage right. (Johnson's box was at stage left.)

Washington is a town haunted by ghosts, and one of those ghosts was the memory of the assassination of President Lincoln as he watched a play at Ford's Theatre. As a result, security was especially tight that night. Before the performance began, the Secret Service men sealed off the National Theatre as well as the block on which it was located. Inside the theater, they examined every object within reach, including

Fabray's Tampax. "They had taken it apart and couldn't get it back together again," she noted. "It was just lying there, this little thing."

The diversion offered the cast members one of the few laughs they would have, for it was to be a night of dreadful gaffes. After all the preparations on his behalf, President Kennedy failed to appear, although his equally glamorous wife Jackie was present. Leland Hayward ordered the conductor, Jay Blackton, to delay the show. He was supposed to strike up "Hail to the Chief" the instant he saw Hayward wave a handkerchief, but the signal never came. In frustration, Hayward began swearing, and he finally gave up and told Blackton, "He hasn't shown up yet. We have to get to the overture."

As Blackton lifted his baton and the orchestra began to play, the audience, mistaking the overture for "The Star-Spangled Banner," rose to its feet. "I saw this out of the corner of my eye," Blackton said, "and I didn't know what to do. I had to keep going. I couldn't turn around and say, 'No, this isn't the "Star-Spangled Banner." Please sit down.' That was Leland's job." After eighteen bars or so, the audience realized that they were not at a baseball game, that the orchestra wasn't playing the national anthem, and they sheepishly sat down.

Now it was the script's turn to subvert the show. In an early scene, Robert Ryan, as the president, asks his wife, "Well, what did you think of the conversation with Charles de Gaulle? He's got a mind like a steel trap." And she responds, "Yes, and it snapped shut years ago."

It was an old joke and not an especially effective one. Before the performance, when Fabray learned that the French ambassador would be in the audience, she had pleaded with Lindsay and Crouse to delete the line. "We will offend everybody in the theater," she warned, but the writers were inflexible and ordered her to follow their script as they had written it. "I delivered the line as carefully as I could," Fabray said, "I tried to make it sound like I was kidding, but no matter what I did, a shock went through the audience and then a few people booed and hissed. And the show was only four minutes old."

As the first act stumbled on, the actors endured the unsettling sensation of vying for the audience's attention with the sight of the president's empty box. The Secret Service agents were milling and the audience was buzzing, gossiping about the nature of the emergency that had detained the president. Even the cast members lost track of the performance. "Along with everyone else, I wasn't watching the conductor," Fabray said, "I was watching the President's box to see what was happening there. People were running in and out." Actually, it was not a government crisis that kept Kennedy from *Mr. President* but the heavyweight title bout between Floyd Patterson and Sonny Liston. Kennedy had stayed behind to watch the match on closed-circuit television in the White House.

At the end of the first act, the president's box was still conspicuously empty. The intermission came and went, the lights dimmed, and the second act started without him. And then, fifteen minutes into the act, Blackton noticed the oboe player waggling his eyebrows. The conductor glanced over his shoulder and realized that Kennedy had finally arrived. Rather than settling the audience, his presence created further commotion, as Dean Rusk and various aides ostentatiously tiptoed in and out of the box to confer with him. Eventually Kennedy and his wife slipped out of the theater; their surreptitious disappearance announced that the president had not the slightest interest in *Mr. President*.

The evening wore on, and Robert Ryan's limitations as a performer became painfully apparent. "His dramatic scenes were wonderfully timed," Fabray commented, "but when it came to comedy, he didn't know how to carry a laugh. He would stand there frozen until the last person had finished laughing before he gave his next line." Even worse, the biggest laugh he received was unintentional. At the end of the performance, he sang a patriotic anthem called "This Is a Great Country." It could have been a new "God Bless America," the audience humming the tune as they left the theater, but Ryan flubbed the lines introducing the song. The audience snickered at his confusion, and the drama of the moment was destroyed.

After the curtain rang down, Berlin and the cast underwent another ordeal, that of attending a reception given by Ambassador and Lady Ormsby-Gore at the British Embassy. President Kennedy, who had vanished mysteriously during the performance, now materialized again, sitting at a table with Jackie and the French ambassador. When Nanette Fabray was introduced to the little group, the unfortunate joke about de Gaulle that she had been forced to make during the show returned to haunt her. The president rose and said, "Hello, how are you?" Jackie rose and said, "Hello, how are you?" She then introduced

Fabray to the French ambassador. Instead of rising or making a polite remark, he refused even to look at the actress who had dared to insult Charles de Gaulle. Confounded by this display of Gallic temperament, the actress tried to apologize for the remark she had been forced to say onstage, but she found herself tongue-tied.

While the ambassador snubbed Fabray, Irving Berlin, the driving force behind the entire show, sat in a corner, looking shrunken and feeling miserable. "He knew what a disaster this was," Fabray said, "and he tried to carry on, tried to be kind, gentle, and supportive. When you know what you're doing is a disaster, you have to put up a front."

The humiliation continued the following morning, when each of the three Washington newspapers accorded *Mr. President* a negative review. The rich and powerful audience in attendance at the National Theatre the night before earned considerable space in the gossip columns, but no amount of fancy trappings could hide the fact that the show they had gathered to see was a flop.

There ensued a flurry of frantic but pointless last-minute changes before *Mr. President* finally opened in New York on October 20. After the trauma the cast had endured on the road in Boston and in Washington, the mercifully uneventful Broadway debut came as an anticlimax. Everyone connected with the production realized they were immune to further criticism because of the immense advance sale, now reckoned at more than $2,650,000. With this cushion, there was little incentive for Berlin or anyone else to tamper with *Mr. President*. "It was the ticket of the year," Fabray remarked, "but the word was out that the show was in terrible trouble, and even though we didn't get very good reviews in New York, we came off better than we would have because people were prepared for the world's biggest turkey."

Although the New York reviews were not as bad as the cast feared—or had come to expect—they were nonetheless distressing. The headline of Walter Kerr's searching notice in the *New York Herald Tribune* set the tone:

BERLIN'S "MR. PRESIDENT"—MUCH TALENT, LITTLE CHEER

As before, the songwriter came in for the lion's share of criticism, for by now the show was considered his—not Ryan's or Fabray's or

Hayward's or Lindsay and Crouse's—but Irving Berlin's, and so he was called to account. "Mr. Berlin's hand seems to rise and fall thoughtlessly, as though he weren't looking at the keys," Kerr wrote, and he faulted Berlin for ignoring the rudiments of the songwriter's trade: "More seriously, the words—which always were simple, but simply evocative—are prosaic, mere wooden soldiers keeping up with the beat. . . . 'It gets lonely in the White House when you're being attacked. And the loyal opposition gets into the act' isn't good Berlin, it is just weak editorial writing. Strangely, the number of harsh, consonant line-ending[s] which are turned into rhymes increases wildly, and against all the old-fashioned rules for song writing." And *Time* magazine adopted a spiteful tone, comparing the enterprise to the maiden voyage of the *Titanic*, with Berlin, Logan, and others as the passengers: ("As it ploughed through the murky theatrical waters of Boston and Washington, iceberg-cool critics put sizeable holes in its hull . . ."). The following week *Time* declared *Mr. President* "the worst musical on Broadway." Suddenly, Berlin bashing was in favor.

Reviews this bad would have closed most other Broadway productions, but Berlin could always rely on the remarkable advance sale. Misfortune plagued the production even after its opening night, however. Within days of the Broadway premiere, the Cuban missile crisis brought the world to the brink of disaster. Kennedy's grim confrontation with Soviet premier Nikita Khrushchev altered popular perceptions of the presidency; so it was not entirely parties and flirting and fashion and cultural events, after all. Berlin's benign view of life within the walls of the White House was more than old-fashioned; it was willfully naïve.

Six months after its opening, ticket demand for *Mr. President* suddenly waned. Irving began plugging Columbia's original cast recording of his score, insisting that the album was even better than the actual show. The ploy failed to work; neither the album nor the show prospered. After all the publicity and the historic advance sale, *Mr. President* ran not for five years, as its backers once speculated, or even for two years, as its detractors feared, but for just eight months. "The day our advance sales ran out," Fabray said, "was the day we closed."

Five months later, an assassin's bullet fired in Dallas put an end to the Kennedy era and any lingering memories of amusements designed to capitalize on it. *Mr. President* and, by extension, Irving Berlin, became but two more casualties of the rapid-fire changes taking place throughout the sixties. At the touch of a trigger, today's pop icons were transformed into tomorrow's martyrs. History was playing cruel pranks on the songwriter. The popular consensus from which he had always drawn inspiration for his songs and on which he had relied for his popularity yielded to a highly polarized climate, and he, along with his patriotic anthems and his jolly, hearty war songs, found himself entrenched on the wrong side of the barricades. "You can't sell patriotism," he lamented, "unless the people feel patriotic. For that matter, you can't sell people anything they don't want."

Although he was the most conspicuous casualty of the revolution overtaking the music business, he was not alone. The old guard was in decline; Oscar Hammerstein II had died in 1960, and Cole Porter, Berlin's principal comrade at this time, would die in 1964. Many of the survivors who continued to toil on Broadway found themselves repeating Berlin's debacle on a smaller scale. Trapped by his reputation as a stodgy and meretricious tunesmith, the songwriter ceased to reinvent himself. For a man of his age, there was no use in even trying to catch on or catch up with the sixties' adulation of youth and all its excesses. "You don't have to stop yourself [from writing songs]," Berlin said on a radio interview on November 7, as the full extent of the show's failure was becoming apparent. "The people who have to listen to your songs tell you to stop."

The music business passed him by along with politics. The record companies, artists, composers, and musicians gradually migrated to the West Coast, where Tin Pan Alley reconstituted itself on Sunset Boulevard, three thousand miles and worlds away from Beekman Place. With few exceptions, a Broadway show was no longer the place to launch a hit song. Many young rock-and-roll musicians refused to touch material they hadn't written themselves; they had no interest in recording other people's song lyrics, ideas, emotions, least of all those of a seventy-five-year-old man who wore a suit and tie each day of his life and pored over his quarterly ASCAP statements with the meticulousness of an accountant. Popular music was once again on the cutting edge of social change, but it was *protest* music. Berlin had been an intensely political songwriter since his stay at Camp Upton during the First World War, but he had always sought and supported the status quo in his music; he had never written a song protesting anything except, perhaps, income taxes. But now he could no longer locate the status quo; it had ceased to exist.

▪ ▪ ▪

Although the public response to *Mr. President* did Berlin's reputation more harm than good, the songwriter refused to admit that he was no longer a force in popular music. Unlike so many other songwriters, even highly successful ones, he owned the publication rights to virtually all his titles, and because of this fortunate situation, he was in a unique position to initiate a movie retrospective. Skeptics noted that he hadn't written a film score in nearly a decade, but to Berlin that observation implied there was a whole new motion-picture audience out there who had never been exposed to an Irving Berlin song on film. Surely it would be possible to shed his staid image and adorn the enormous Berlin catalogue—a catalogue that encapsulated an entire culture in song—with the flamboyant raiment of the sixties.

To launch an undertaking of this magnitude, the songwriter required potent allies, and of all his studio contacts, Arthur Freed, who had been responsible for making so many memorable musicals at MGM, including Irving's *Easter Parade*, remained the most influential. Soon to be elected president of the Academy of Motion Picture Arts and Sciences, Freed was well liked, well known, well connected: the ideal man to restore Irving Berlin to prominence in Hollywood.

In 1963, after Berlin had recovered from the ordeal of *Mr. President*, the two men began discussing their proposed film retrospective. It would be called *Say It With Music*, after the song Irving had written in 1921, which had become associated with the Music Box revues of that era. And it would be a big-budget picture; Freed was thinking $6 million, and the figure would probably go higher.

The two men agreed on the scale of the movie, but they differed sharply about its story. Apparently unaware of Berlin's recent donnybrook with the BBC, Freed wished to make a musical biography of Berlin. Studios had churned out a number of successful biographical movies about popular composers—Cole Porter, the team of Harry Ruby and Bert Kalmar, and Jerome Kern—employing their songs throughout the story. The durable legend of Berlin's career—the rise from busker to Tin Pan Alley and Broadway, the death of his first wife, the famous courtship of Ellin Mackay—offered splendid material for another exercise in cinematic hagiography.

Irving grew crotchety at the thought: "What the hell would I do with a handsome leading man impersonating me? I'm not handsome." Freed had no choice but to abandon his original plan and consent to develop an original story bearing no resemblance whatsoever to Berlin's life, even though the resulting movie would contain nothing *but* Berlin's songs. The compromise placed an extraordinary burden on the script to be an ingenious and compelling creation in its own right.

Sensing that Freed's interest might be flagging in the face of these obstacles, Irving proceeded to tantalize his friend. He appeared in Freed's office at MGM one day, a portfolio under one arm. "What's that?" the producer asked. A new score, the songwriter said. "I've got to hear it," Freed responded. But that would be too easy. Instead, Berlin said that he didn't want anyone hearing his new score just now, even though he was walking around the corridors of MGM with the music. Rising to the bait, Freed pleaded with Irving to play the songs—there was a piano right there in the office. Berlin pointed out that it was not a *transposing* piano, and thus was of little use to him.

By now Freed was frantic. Please Irving, play something, anything—just one song. So Berlin sat at the piano and played *one* song in his old-fashioned song plugger's way, leaning so close to his listener's face that Freed could see the cracks between Irving's teeth, the hairs in his nostrils. And he loved Irving's song, absolutely loved it. Irving Berlin *was* show business. And even though the piano didn't suit him, Irving was persuaded to play a few more songs, and a few more, and by the time he was finished, Freed had decided to buy the motion picture rights to the new score, together with various older songs, for a million dollars. It had been, for Berlin, a rather successful audition.

Freed used his pivotal position in the industry's power structure to interest the Hollywood establishment in the project. At the Milestone Award dinner, given by the Screen Producers Guild on March 3 at the Beverly Hilton Hotel, he arranged for Berlin to receive the Guild's Laurel Award, thus ensuring that Berlin would actually attend the event. Freed persuaded Frank Sinatra—a probable star of the contemplated movie—to sing a medley of Berlin songs at the dinner. He cajoled Los Angeles Mayor Sam Yorty into making March 3 "Irving Berlin Day" and local radio stations to play nothing but Irving Berlin songs during that day. And finally, he made certain to number among the dinner's toastmasters several of the most dominant producers in Hollywood: Sam Goldwyn, Adolph Zukor, and Jack Warner.

The dinner went smoothly, the seduction of Hollywood worked as planned, and immediately thereafter, Berlin and Freed began negotiating the financial arrangements underpinning *Say It With Music*. Irving instructed his Los Angeles attorney, George Cohen, to demand one million dollars for the rights to the songs, as Freed had promised. Instead, MGM offered Berlin twenty-five percent of the movie's net profit. The two sides eventually settled on the following arrangement: Berlin would get the million dollars—to be paid in ten annual installments. That the songwriter was willing to accept this condition at his advanced age indicated that he was confident that he would still be around a decade hence to collect the last payment.

Say It With Music now gave every sign of being a favored, top-priority studio project, to be rushed into production. On April 30, MGM declared its intention to film *Say It With Music* for release in 1964. At the Academy Awards that year, Freed, who understood the protocol and purpose of plugging as well as Berlin, arranged for Ethel Merman to participate in an elaborate tribute to the songwriter featuring songs beginning, inevitably, with "Alexander's Ragtime Band" and ending, just as inevitably, with "There's No Business Like Show Business," the hit she had introduced in *Annie Get Your Gun*.

Within weeks of that presentation, Freed announced that he had signed Vincente Minnelli to direct *Say It With Music*, which was to star Frank Sinatra and Judy Garland. In addition, other performers associated with Berlin, including Merman, Bing Crosby, Fred Astaire, as well as various celebrities of the moment, such as Pat Boone, Bobby Darin, Johnny Mathis, and Connie Francis, were to appear in smaller roles. All this talent cost a great deal of money, of course, and the picture's budget vaulted to $15 million—more than twice its original cost.

Gleefully observing the accumulation of talent and money, Berlin dashed off ten songs for inclusion in the score, which would now consist of at least twenty-five of his tunes, and for a man of seventy-five, the new tunes weren't half bad. In fact, they weren't bad for a man of thirty-five. "I Used to Play by Ear" showed the master in a mordant, playful mood, and "The Ten Best Undressed Women in the World" evoked the sensual spirit of Ziegfeld. *Say It With Music*, it seemed, was shaping up to be the cinematic equivalent of the old *Follies*, and this was a vernacular that Irving could understand, all stars and spectacle and his songs—and the story be damned.

Still, the actors couldn't sing for two hours straight; there had to be some narrative framework. Freed assigned Arthur Laurents the unenviable task of trying to devise a script for the extravaganza. A playwright, Laurents had written the books for two other musicals, *Gypsy* and *West Side Story*. Such impressive credentials won him a salary of $250,000, and it was now his task to devise a story worthy of the songs, the stars, and most importantly, MGM's $15 million investment.

The soaring prospects for *Say It With Music* appeared to be a harbinger of a late-life renaissance for the songwriter. Returning to New York, he took patriarchal pride in the fact that his middle daughter, Linda, who had married several years before, was to give birth. He passed a giddy summer in the Catskills, where he monitored the progress of *Say It With Music*. Stars entered and exited the cast of the musical at a dizzying rate. Garland was replaced by Julie Andrews; Sophia Loren joined the production, as Freed explained that the Italian actress would be making her "musical debut." Frank Sinatra yielded the male lead to Robert Goulet. Jerome Robbins was to have choreographed a few numbers, but at the last minute he dropped out. Garland and Sinatra would be missed, but the movie continued to gather momentum.

On September 11, Berlin flew to London to take part in another happy occasion: the marriage of his youngest daughter, Elizabeth, to Edmund Fisher, son of a well-known British ornithologist, James Fisher. The union offered evidence that his daughter had inherited his lifelong Anglophilia. Since Berlin had remained a durable figure in England throughout the years, the wedding received ample play in the British, if not the American, press. During his stay abroad, he was in fine spirits, plugging *Say It With Music* (his high, raspy voice, wrote a journalist, sounded "like an egg, softly cracked"), and then giving his daughter away in a formal ceremony at the most socially "correct" church in London, St. George's in Hanover Square.

Soon after his return to New York, his spirits still high, problems began to trouble *Say It With Music.* They gathered slowly at first, a few insubstantial clouds on a summer's day, but they would eventually darken and spread across the entire horizon. At the beginning of November, Laurents delivered a treatment, and several weeks after that, the preliminary script for *Say It With Music.* For sheer theatricality, it was worthy of Ziegfeld at the impresario's ripest. Laurents had decided to tell the story of an international wastrel who conducts love affairs with beautiful women in four countries—Sophia Loren in Italy, Julie Andrews in England, Brigitte Bardot in France, and Ann-Margret in the United States. This, of course, would never do. The international settings violated the essentially American character of Berlin's songs, and the leading man's romantic exploits, though a superficial reflection of the spirit of the sixties, desecrated the songwriter's straitlaced image; a playboy had no place in an Irving Berlin movie.

Lacking a suitable script, the picture could not begin shooting. Its stars dispersed, and the juggernaut that had been *Say It With Music* came to an eerie standstill; both Freed and MGM ceased to speculate about stars or a new release date. Unable to rectify the problem, Irving retreated to his Catskills estate, where he paced the forest floor as anxiously as he had paced the carpet in his Broadway office.

On the heels of this disappointment, Berlin finally learned of a decision in his long-standing plagiarism suit against *Mad* magazine, and the news was not good. On March 23, 1964, Judge Irving R. Kaufman of the United States Court of Appeals ruled in favor of the humor magazine; there had been no copyright infringement. "Parody and satire are deserving of substantial freedom both as entertainment and as a form of social and literary criticism," he declared. Berlin had based his claim of infringement, in part, on the fact that the *Mad* parodies employed the same *meter* as his lyrics had, but this argument, if anything, worked against him. "We doubt that even so eminent a composer as Irving Berlin should be permitted to claim a property interest in iambic pentameter," wrote the judge.

The decision, and the judge's singling out of Berlin for a lecture from the bench, made the songwriter seem quite the curmudgeon for getting mad at *Mad.* More than ever he was out of tune with the times. There was painful irony in the legal decision, as well, for Berlin himself had wrung a fair amount of coin from satire, beginning with his earliest professional efforts, creating blue parodies of popular songs during his days as a singing waiter, and, years later, in his highly successful Depression-era Broadway revue, *As Thousands Cheer.* Now it was *Mad*'s turn to benefit from the same protection Berlin and countless other songwriters and performers had enjoyed over the years.

▪ ▪ ▪

Throughout the summer of 1964, Arthur Freed agitated on behalf of Irving Berlin and *Say It With Music.* The producer asked another screenwriter, Leonard Gershe, to concoct a new story, and in Gershe's hands, the script became even more grandiose and fragmented, virtually a parody of the Hollywood spectacular. Thirsting for novelty in the title sequence, Gershe and Freed proposed splitting the screen into seven distinct sections, each capable of displaying a separate image. They envisioned seven different Berlin songs playing simultaneously on this screen, one of which would be sung by the cast of a popular television comedy, *The Beverly Hillbillies.* A memorandum explained, "On the sound track these numbers will be orchestrated so as to build to a great musical climax all merging into 'Say It With Music,' which will come up strong behind the main title."

After this appalling opening, Freed and Gershe planned to introduce Fred Astaire, who would function as a "kind of Greek chorus" commenting on the action. He would first appear in front of the Plaza Hotel in New York, philosophizing to the effect that the more things change, the more they stay the same. The story would then shift to a romance between one William Bladen, modeled on the broadcasting tycoon William Paley, and Diana, a writer for *Time* magazine, based on the journalist Shana Alexander, who plans to write a cover story on the reclusive Bladen.

Freed eventually came to his senses and scrapped the elaborate artifice he had concocted with Gershe. He next brought in the team of Betty Comden and Adolph Green to pull off the seemingly impossible stunt of devising a story for *Say It With Music.* Word of their involvement encouraged Berlin, and he repeatedly called them to express his gratitude. "This is it," he would tell them, at last the movie was getting off the ground. But Comden and Greene also struggled to find a way to unify the picture. They resorted to telling three stories, one set in 1911, another in 1925, and still another in 1965, as a way of displaying Berlin's songs to best advantage. It was a clever idea, though it contained many of the same faults as its predecessors.

As the writers fussed and Irving fretted, time passed swiftly; suddenly it was 1966. Management changes marked by vicious infighting roiled MGM, but Freed managed to retain his influence. Neither he nor Berlin would consider abandoning the quixotic crusade that *Say It With Music* had come to represent for them. However, the lack of a satisfactory script continued to bedevil the movie. Two drafts and $150,000 later, Comden and Green left the project, replaced by George Wells.

At the beginning of the year, even Berlin's attention began to wander from the project. He was able to indulge himself in the pleasant distraction offered by a revival of *Annie Get Your Gun.* Richard Rodgers, who, along with his late partner Oscar Hammerstein II, had produced the original version of the musical on Broadway twenty years earlier, had recently become president of the Music Theater of Lincoln Center, New York's lavish, if somewhat forbidding, new cultural center. His plan to revive *Annie Get Your Gun* depended on obtaining permission from two individuals who had been crucial to its success: Ethel Merman and Irving Berlin.

The prospective revival afforded Berlin an opportunity to see his best Broadway score performed in a temple of high culture. Only a few Tin Pan Alley composers had breeched the barrier separating the concert hall from the saloon, Gershwin being the most prominent example, but Berlin never had, though he coveted the respectability such acceptance bestowed. Here, at last, was his chance, and he grabbed it.

Once he had made his decision, he immediately called Merman himself, though she tried to act coy in the face of his enthusiasm. "Wait a minute, Irving," she told him. "You don't just call up a person and ask if they want to do 'Annie Get Your Gun' just like that. I'll have to think about it." She quickly agreed, of course; a reunion of Berlin and Merman under the auspices of Richard Rodgers and Lincoln Center had a compelling logic to it. Of course she was too old for the part, but her voice was remarkably intact. Even though she no longer resembled the young, naïve Annie Oakley of Darke County, Ohio, she could still fill the theater with hillbilly twang.

The Lincoln Center version of *Annie Get Your Gun* would not be identical to the 1946 production; both score and script were slightly revised for the occasion. Dorothy Fields streamlined her original script; Berlin cut two numbers ("I'll Share It All with You" and "Who Do You Love, I Hope") and added a new verse for "There's No Business Like Show Business." Irving also took the trouble to compose a new number for the show, "An Old Fashioned Wedding," another counterpoint song in the tradition of "Play A Simple Melody" and "You're Just in Love." His repeatedly turning to the contrapuntal form when he needed a surefire showstopper suggested that he considered this type of song, of all the varied forms he had ever tried, to be his musical signature.

The revival began rehearsals in April, with everyone involved excited, star struck, and self-conscious. There was much exclaiming over the fact that all concerned were aging well, didn't look a day older, were just as good as ever, and rock and roll be damned. Merman and Berlin, on greeting each other, demonstrated how well they could play their favorite roles, Salty Ethel and Spunky Irving:

"Irving!" she announced, "you look great! What are you doing for sex?"

And Berlin shot back, "Well, Ethel, if you can get it up, I can get it in."

That was good, the press agents liked that sort of repartee; it confirmed that Merman and Berlin still had what it took to put on a show. And when the songwriter predicted that the revival would be even better than the Broadway original, no one dared contradict him. He had earned the right to preen.

Despite the dignified auspices under which it was produced, the new version of *Annie Get Your Gun* followed the well-worn path of a traditional Broadway musical. It opened out of town, in this instance, well out of town, in Toronto, Canada, on May 9, and moved to Lincoln

Center on the last day of the month, where it would play during the summer before moving on to a brief road tour of the Midwest.

Shortly before the New York opening, Berlin turned seventy-eight, and the birthday, rather than being an occasion for bitterness, as these unwelcome anniversaries had become for him, found him in a philosophical mood. He had spent a good deal of time gazing at the broad East River from his lofty Beekman Place home, and had come to the conclusion that the river was one of the few constants in his life since his arrival in New York at the age of five. "I've always lived near this river," he repeated numerous times. "It's a more swanky neighborhood than in the old days, but the same tugboats pass by the windows." The river exerted such fascination for him, in fact, that he even gave thought to writing a new musical about it. He tried some songs, a few "bits and pieces," he called them, but then he gave up, realizing that at his age the project was too large to attempt.

Three weeks later, the new *Annie Get Your Gun* had its New York opening. Just before the curtain went up, Ethel Merman, waiting in her dressing room, received a package from Tiffany's. She unwrapped it and found within a miniature gold blossom along with a note written by Irving. "A sweet-smelling rose," he wrote, "starts a run in the nose / So a metal petal / for Etel." The present, together with its bittersweet verse, showed that Irving, despite all the reverses he had suffered in the last dozen years, was at the top of his form.

During the performance, attention focused on the composer's new song, "An Old Fashioned Wedding." When Bruce Yarnell, who played the role of Frank Butler, began to sing it, the tune did sound terribly outdated, with its evocations of a quaint little chapel and orange blossoms. The audience's worst fears seemed to be confirmed, until Ethel Merman began to chant *her* part of the duet—drowning out Yarnell with demands for champagne, caviar, and a big church—and the song fulfilled its destiny, which no one but Berlin himself had predicted, as a showstopper. Of course they weren't applauding an entire new score or even a movie; it was just one song, but it was enough to prove that Irving Berlin, at age seventy-eight, still possessed a little of the theatrical and musical magic that had made him an exceptional popular composer.

The heady experience of hearing applause after years of silence and contempt took him back, further back, even, than the original *Annie Get Your Gun.* "I haven't felt such warmth and affection," he said, "since *This Is the Army.*" The production received universal approbation from the critics, and at the end of its tour returned to Broadway for an additional run of several months' duration.

The revival and everything connected with it had its expected tonic effect on Berlin, and the songwriter once again turned his attention to that troubled spectacular, *Say It With Music.* Late in 1967, Arthur Freed formed an alliance with Blake Edwards, a producer and director who was married to Julie Andrews. Under the terms of the agreement, the two men were to produce the movie, Edwards would direct, and Julie Andrews would, of course, have the female lead. Since her wholesome presence had recently helped to make the film version of *The Sound of Music* an enormous success at the box office, she was able to command a considerable salary: one million dollars for ten weeks' work, an additional seventy-five thousand for each additional week's work, and ten percent of the film's gross profits over $10 million. Filming was to commence in September 1969. The agreement came closer to making *Say It With Music* a reality than it had been at any time during the six years Freed and Berlin had been pushing the project.

Days after signing the agreement, the songwriter reluctantly agreed to participate in another stunt designed to keep his name before the public and thereby increase the picture's chances of actually getting made. Ed Sullivan, the television variety show host whose notice Berlin had once angrily spurned, planned to devote his broadcast of May 5, 1968, to an eightieth birthday tribute to the songwriter.

Eighty! That simple fact filled Berlin not with joy but with dread and anxiety, for though he had aged, his pugnacious spirit remained intact. He felt himself to be a young man unaccountably trapped in an old man's frail body. True, he took satisfaction in the fruits of old age: his grandchildren, his long and stable marriage, and the honors he had accumulated during his career, but he was not happy playing the role of an old-timer, an *alte kocker.* Nor was he comfortable with the idea of marking his eightieth birthday on national television.

The occasion, which promised to be another elaborate confirmation of past glories, was in a direct line of descent from his 1911 induction in the Friars. At eighty, he experienced the same overwhelming mixture of gratitude and anxiety that he had felt at twenty-three, and he was beginning to suspect that he was being honored not for who he was and what he had done but for how long he had lived. He would have to exhibit himself, and he was sufficiently vain to resent the fact that he looked old. Worse, he would have to say something. It had always been true of Berlin that although he could sing (after a fashion) and compose, he could not speak. Without his transposing piano and his musical secretary by his side, he was still a dumbstruck kid from Cherry Street.

The program began with Lyndon Johnson offering birthday greetings—and what other Tin Pan Alley tunesmith, what other *composer*, for that matter, could get the president to wish him happy birthday on television? Meanwhile, Irving agonized backstage, awaiting his appearance at the end of the show. When the time came, the stage filled with row upon row of Boy Scouts and Girl Scouts, and then the songwriter himself appeared, this little man, so easy to overlook, who had made it all happen. He led the children as best he could with that scratchy, back-alley voice of his in "God Bless America." And then Sullivan wheeled out a birthday cake bearing eighty brilliant candles. Yes, it was corny, and in 1968 his patriotic anthem was more than old-fashioned, it seemed downright reactionary, but the scene of the old man and the boys and girls and the birthday cake elicited both tears and smiles from the audience. In the end, that was all Irving Berlin had ever wanted to do.

The success of the Sullivan tribute, especially "God Bless America," encouraged the songwriter to entertain the possibility that he and everything he stood for, the old values, the old ways, were about to return to favor. "Patriotism goes out of style every once in a while in this country," he said, "and it becomes fashionable to be unpatriotic, because in America nobody stops you from being unpatriotic. But it comes bouncing back. The hard core of this country still stands up and shivers when you play 'The Star-Spangled Banner.' "

His claim was premature. With disenchantment spreading throughout the country, "God Bless America" had become the anthem of imperialism, and there was little Irving could do to counteract that impression. Listening to the growing number of anti-Vietnam war songs on the radio, he complained to his friends that the current political climate left him caught, as he put it, with his music and lyrics down. Neither hawk nor dove, Irving was simply a supporter of the United States' position, whatever it happened to be. He recognized controversy when he saw it, and he shied away from writing a song that referred to the undeclared conflict. He feared that any musical statement he made would return to haunt him, the way his songs from *This Is the Army*—"The Army's Made a Man of Me" and "This Is the Army, Mr. Jones," among other martial titles—now pegged him as a reactionary. The only *anti*war song in his catalogue was his bizarre isolationist polemic of 1914, "Stay Down Here Where You Belong," and the only performer willing to record it was the equally bizarre Tiny Tim, who warbled it in his peculiar falsetto.

Berlin did make one small but significant concession to the antiwar movement: he revised the lyrics to "Alexander's Ragtime Band," changing the original line, which spoke of a bugle that sounded "so natural that you want to go to war" to "so natural that you want to hear some more." But that was the *only* concession the songwriter was willing to make to the tenor of the times.

Irving paid the penalty for his obstinacy in Hollywood, where people were forever revising the past to suit the whims of the present. In recent years, MGM, where *Say It With Music* was about to begin shooting, had become a notoriously unstable place. Early in 1969, Edgar Bronfman, heir to the Seagrams Distilleries fortune, took charge of the studio, but MGM's finances were out of control, and by the end of the year, he was forced to cede control to Las Vegas investor Kerk Kerkorian. Struggling to pull the studio back from the brink of chaos, Kerkorian appointed a controversial new president: James T. Aubrey, Jr. Later on, the songwriter would blame the system for doing him in, or changing times, but actually, it all came down to the character of this one man, and what Irving Berlin represented to him.

As the CBS programming chief during the first half of the decade, Aubrey—slender, elegant, cool, thoroughly a man of the sixties—had made his name by lowering the standards of programming while elevating the network's popularity. This Princeton-educated autocrat openly despised anything prestigious, traditional, or expensive, much preferring the simplest and cheapest solutions to programming problems. His regime was identified with one show in particular, "The Beverly Hillbillies," a piece of fluff that elicited gasps of outrage from critics even as it shot to the top of the ratings. The Aubrey name was magic at CBS in those years; he made money for everyone, and he did precisely as he pleased. In the process he earned a beguiling nickname: the Smiling Cobra. But then something went wrong. Rumors about income-tax problems and a lurid personal life circulated along Broadcast Row. In February 1965, the chairman of CBS, William Paley, and his respected second-in-command, Frank Stanton, summarily fired him.

The Aubrey name was still magic in Hollywood, however; the rumors and sudden firing made him seem, if anything, even more glamorous. It was at this point in his career that Kerkorian installed the Smiling Cobra as the next head of MGM. Inheriting a company in desperate financial straits, Aubrey set about dismantling the once-great studio. He arranged to auction the studio's entire collection of costumes and props, everything from trolleys to the shoes worn by Dorothy in *The Wizard of Oz*; he sold off part of the studio's back lots; peddled MGM Records to a foreign company, Polygram; ordered the destruction of the studio's vast music library (keeping but a single score per film); disposed of its script library; and finally, he came to *Say It With Music*, starring Julie Andrews. Here was a picture that had been in development for seven years, and that worked against it. It would cost at least $15 million to make, and that went against it even more strongly. And it featured old songs by the biggest has-been Aubrey could name, Irving Berlin, and *that* was the final blow. Without ever meeting with Berlin or Arthur Freed, Aubrey canceled the motion picture.

Berlin responded to the setback—so arbitrary, so final—with impotent rage. His lawyer fired off an angry letter to MGM insisting that the studio continue to pay the songwriter every penny it owed him under their original agreement. And the studio complied, not that the money gave Berlin much gratification at this point in his life. "It's fine to be able . . . to get a million dollars," he said. "You don't get to keep a hell of a lot of it. It's much more important to me if they had made the picture. And they could have. It was to be Arthur's and my swan song in motion pictures. But those 'civilians,' as I call them, . . . they were stupid!"

The final, irrevocable collapse of *Say It With Music* marked the formal end of Berlin's career in Hollywood, much as the quasi failure of *Mr. President* seven years before had terminated his Broadway career. He retreated once again to his Catskills home, where he sought solace in solitude and did his best to put on a smiling, avuncular face for his small group of friends and associates. Over the course of his sixty-two-year-long career, he had attained an unequaled position as a songwriter; Irving Berlin would always be Irving Berlin, and "God Bless America" would last as long as America—but it was generally assumed that he now belonged to American musical *history*; no one wanted to hear new material from Irving Berlin. He had been banished from the mainstream of popular entertainment that he had once dominated, and he was not equipped to endure his exile gracefully. He was no happier in retirement now than he had been ten years earlier, but unlike the previous period of retreat, which he had largely brought on himself, there was no chance that he could reemerge. For the rest of his life, he would be famous, he would be celebrated, he would even be venerated, but he would also be unemployed.

Berlin's second and final withdrawal from the world marked the beginning of the most bizarre phase of an already remarkable life. Even if the marketplace had rejected him, legions of fans, music historians, and producers repeatedly attempted to reach the songwriter. Some wished to pay him tribute, some sought only to satisfy their curiosity, and still others wished to assess his entire career. Battling them all, Berlin willed himself into a mysterious anonymity.

CHAPTER 21

Coda

At four-thirty in the afternoon on Monday, October 25, 1971, the telephone rang in the New York apartment of James T. Maher. At the time, he was three years into a mammoth project: collaborating on a comprehensive survey of American popular song with his friend Alec Wilder, a well-regarded composer and lyricist. Answering the phone, Maher heard a thin, high-pitched voice, and he realized with a shock that his caller was perhaps the last person from whom he ever expected to hear.

"This is Irving Berlin," the songwriter shouted. "We got that crap you sent. Who the hell do you think you stupid bastards are?"

Jim Maher, as it happened, was a historian and writer of some distinction. And Wilder, for his part, enjoyed a considerable reputation among the vestiges of New York's literary and café society. At sixty-four, he had lived for years at the Algonquin Hotel, was widely read, and was familiar with nearly every type of music, from symphony to jazz to song. He had conducted extensive interviews for his survey of popular music with many major songwriters and other figures in the business, with one important exception: Irving Berlin.

For three years Berlin had resisted his persistent attempts to arrange a meeting, until, several weeks before, he suddenly telephoned Wilder, expressing great enthusiasm for the forthcoming book. The two of them chatted amiably for an hour about the project. "I'll tell you the truth," Berlin confided, "I only wrote six or eight songs. I just kept writing them over and over again. But I had them all fooled! Nobody noticed." It was one of his stock lines, the kind of shoptalk with which he often regaled listeners, and Wilder was entranced. Soon after their conversation, Berlin loaned him a leather-bound volume containing the sheet music for hundreds of Berlin tunes, and he promised to arrange a meeting soon.

Shortly after this apparent breakthrough, one of Berlin's lawyers asked to see Wilder's eighty-page section about the songwriter. Although he had serious reservations about allowing Berlin an advance look at the text, Maher complied. After that, he heard nothing from Berlin until the phone call.

Such were the two "stupid bastards" and the "crap" they had sent Irving Berlin.

At first, Maher tried to placate Berlin, and through the shouting he said how delighted he was that the songwriter had decided to favor him with a call.

"I don't give a damn about all that," Berlin screamed. "My secretary read me your letter and all that shit you and Wilder are writing. Let me tell you right off the whole goddamn thing is stupid and pretentious. All that stupid, stupid analysis—that's a lot of crap. Wilder is trying too hard to be a 'tune detective.' " As Maher realized, the epithet referred to musicologist Sigmund Spaeth, who had once hosted a popular radio show billing him as "The Tune Detective."

Berlin assumed that Wilder, a latter-day tune detective, was attempting to prove that the songwriter had plagiarized songs throughout his career. A patient, scholarly man, Maher tried unsuccessfully to explain to Berlin that Wilder had no such subversive designs. In fact, the chapter on Berlin consisted of a painstaking and often worshipful evaluation. "In the course of his prodigious output he has written a great many memorable songs. . . . I am frankly astounded by the sophistication of Berlin's theater songs" ran a typical Wilder observation. It was true that he occasionally expressed reservations about a particular song, such as "Always" ("It is, frankly, not a favorite of mine"), but he was never less than respectful. Nothing in his examination of the songs detracted from Berlin's professional stature.

But Wilder and Maher had failed to realize how deeply Berlin resented and dreaded their book, which gave every indication of becoming the standard work in the field when it was published. He took such violent exception to it because, with its scholarly tone, its Oxford University Press aegis, and its penchant for comparing songwriters with one another, it hit on nearly every worry that Berlin had about his musical abilities.

"I had a guy," Berlin continued, "a very good musician, who has worked for me for over forty years, who really *knows* music—who knows what the hell he's talking about—and I had him read it, too." The man was, Maher guessed, Berlin's veteran transcriber, Helmy Kresa. "And he agrees with me. It's a lotta goddamn crap."

In particular, Wilder's faint disparagement of Berlin's precious "Always" aroused the songwriter's wrath: "Who the hell cares what *he* thinks! That's just his opinion. Who the hell is Wilder, anyway? My God, what's the matter with you guys? The whole goddamn thing is full of mistakes. I never saw such a piece of shit. I'll tell you one thing, it's a rotten job of research. And if it was you that did it, it's a goddamn disgrace. *You're* a disgrace! I've run into some stupid bastards, but you two take the cake."

By now Maher was badly shaken. He had been quietly going about his work, and then, without warning, a maniac—or so it seemed—had called and begun ranting. "There was no music in that voice," Maher later reflected, "only the sour malevolence of a mean spirit."

"And goddammit," Berlin then said, "you didn't even *ask* me."

Maher tried to explain that for three years he had tried to contact Berlin by mail and by phone, but there was no stopping his enraged caller, who said he didn't believe that any other figures discussed in the book had cooperated with Wilder. When Maher insisted they all had, the songwriter expressed astonishment that Harold Arlen, a friend to both Berlin and Wilder, had granted Oxford the right to quote his music.

"If he let you do that," Berlin said, "he's a goddamn dumb schmuck, and so is Dick Rodgers. Both of them! You know, you guys are lying to me. I goddamn well don't believe for one minute that they let you use their music. That's bullshit!" As he resumed his attack on Wilder, a plaintive tone crept into his protests:

"I could tell him some things he ought to know, for Christ's sake.

And that song of mine he thought sounded like Harold Arlen—that's all wrong. I'll show him and get him straightened out. Jesus, he's got that stuff all wrong. I wrote *my* songs first: *get that straight!* And listen to me—I'll tell you one other thing, goddammit—I sure as hell don't need Wilder to tell me whether a song is good or not. . . . I've got clippings here, goddamn books full of them, about my songs. People like Virgil Thomson wrote about my songs, and *he* thought that ["Always"] was a good song, and by God, it is. A damn good song, even if your friend doesn't think so."

Maher had to begin the same sentence five times until Berlin was quiet long enough for the editor to complete it. Wilder, Maher said, was "merely saying that some of your songs were better than others, but the main thing was that they kept getting better and better as the years passed."

"I don't know who the hell Wilder is," Berlin responded. "I'll tell you this, though: he's what we call a fucking longhair."

At that moment, Maher's doorbell rang. He asked Berlin to wait, and the songwriter began yelling even louder than before and to breathe heavily. "He even," Maher noted, "began to laugh in a weird way while he was panting."

"Who the hell do you think I am?" Berlin was saying as Maher desperately tried to get from the phone to the door. "I read all that stuff that says I'm Jesus Christ. Well, I think that's a lot of goddamned crap, too. Crap!"

The doorbell sounded again; Maher's visitors—two writers working on another book—were waiting. "Would you *please* hang on, Mr. Berlin," Maher asked.

"I'm through," Berlin said. "What I don't understand is how the hell you guys could write a book like this, and how a publisher [like Oxford] with the reputation they've got would want to publish it. Tell Wilder to call me."

Berlin slammed down the receiver, and Maher ran to greet his guests. As he opened the door, they noticed immediately that he was pale and shaking, as though he had seen a ghost. "What in the world is the matter?" they asked, and Maher proceeded to explain the nature of the "ghost" who had given him such a shock.

It had been a harsh, even brutal encounter. Perhaps the most remarkable aspect of the entire harangue was how unnecessary it had been, for, as Berlin, his lawyers, his secretary, and whoever else had seen the galleys were well aware, the book he condemned overflowed with praise for him. But he found it nonetheless intolerable that a "fucking longhair" named Wilder would dare to pass judgment on him, even *favorable* judgment.

News of the dispute spread quickly through the musicians' and critics' grapevine: Berlin was on a tear again, he really took poor Jim Maher's head off that time. However, instead of protecting his name, the tantrum harmed Berlin's reputation. His propensity for making abusive phone calls—and there would be other instances—had a chilling effect on any discussion of his music. For many journalists and acquaintances of Berlin, publicly discussing the songwriter meant running the risk of incurring his permanent enmity. With the exception of Alec Wilder, writers in the field either ignored him or took refuge in show business platitudes and recycled a few well-known facts, lest they receive one of the irate phone calls. Once again, Irving Berlin had become the gargoyle of Beekman Place.

Fortunately, Berlin's threats against *American Popular Song*—for all the distress they caused Maher and Wilder—came to nothing. The following year, Oxford University Press published the book, and it was overflowing with admiration for the man who despised it. By the time of Wilder's death, in 1980, this massive, encyclopedic study had come to be considered the definitive work on the subject of popular American songwriting.

▪ ▪ ▪

It was evident that as he entered his eighties, the songwriter was not going gently into that good night. Berlin raged against others who he considered to have encroached on his domain, as he had raged against Alec Wilder. Soon after his confrontation with Jim Maher, he created another memorable fracas that sent shock waves through New York's music community.

On this occasion, his target was an innocuous new organization called the Songwriters' Hall of Fame. In 1969, Berlin and Richard Rodgers had been the first two individuals elected to this society, and Berlin had welcomed the idea: how nice to be honored. But three years later, in a bid for some sorely needed press attention, the Songwriters Hall of Fame decided to induct twenty-seven composers. When Berlin learned of this plan, he became incensed. He called his friend Abe Olman, a music publisher who, along with Johnny Mercer, had been one of the organization's prime movers, and shouted, "You've just destroyed the Songwriters' Hall of Fame. By opening it up to everybody, you have destroyed its exclusivity." He continued to fulminate, and at the end of the conversation, he declared, "I will no longer support this group."

He lashed out at others associated with the Songwriters' Hall of Fame—wounding and astonishing everyone with whom he spoke. And after he had finished, he refused to have anything further to do with the organization. And the stories about Berlin's vituperative behavior continued to spread.

These outbursts had an indelible ugliness about them, but for all the misery he brought to others, none was more tormented than Berlin himself, who was trapped in a maelstrom of insecurity—perennially afraid that friends, family, and business associates were all liable to take advantage of his wealth and fame. At the same time, he felt more removed from the action with each passing year, more likely to be forgotten, closer to the oblivion that had claimed the reputations of so many other popular songwriters. And his obsession with preserving his musical legacy made him a victim of his own success, a prisoner of himself.

▪ ▪ ▪

One respite Berlin permitted himself from the endless task of allaying the demands of his ego was painting. This happened to be the hobby of choice for many songwriters. Berlin's friend Harold Arlen was a dedicated Sunday painter, and during the course of his short life, George Gershwin had displayed, in addition to his musical genius, a formidable visual ability. So there were ample precedents for Berlin's turning to this pastime. After flirting with painting during his period of retreat in the late fifties, Irving embraced it in the seventies, donning a smock and mixing pigment with the same fierce concentration he had brought to the task of songwriting. The results, however, were somewhat different, as Berlin himself had the good grace to acknowledge. "As a painter," he quipped, "I'm a pretty good songwriter."

Indeed, his canvases were remarkably crude, even for an untrained, "primitive" painter. First he would cover a wooden palette with a heavy layer of oil, generally in a primary color, and then he would glue the painted palette to a canvas. He would then decorate the shape, to make it suggest, with a few lines, a penguin or a stork. Occasionally he would frame a snapshot of a friend in the eye of the palette, and then give away the result to the invariably startled, grateful, and speechless subject.

Many of the recipients of Berlin's canvases were professional acquaintances or celebrities with whom he had worked, people such as Fred Astaire and Hermes Pan. Astaire's oil showed an umbrella and a beak, and contained a caption, "Isn't this a lovely day to be caught in the rain?"—a line from the song Berlin had written for Astaire to sing to Ginger Rogers in *Top Hat* nearly forty years before.

Not all his canvases conformed to this childish example. At least one of his oils was so dark and haunting that it reminded a friend of the Holocaust. Berlin decided to keep it rather than give it away. Nor did he believe in giving away his other artwork for all time. When the recipient of an Irving Berlin original died, it was not at all unusual for a representative of the artist to appear at the deceased's home and reclaim the work, as if it were a copyright that Berlin licensed and controlled rather than an outright gift.

Inevitably, the songwriter gave thought to organizing a show of his oils, but his telephone friends wisely discouraged him. It was obvious that his efforts were crude, and it was equally obvious that painting offered Berlin a refuge from the extraordinary demands he had made on himself as a songwriter. Better to keep it an entirely private pursuit, a true hobby.

Seeking some sort of audience, Berlin would permit his grandchildren to watch him paint, and in fact, that was how they came to see him, as an old man working with brushes and tubes of oil paint. When one of this granddaughters was asked to write a composition for school, she drew on the experience in an essay entitled, "An Afternoon with My Grandfather." On reading it, her teacher asked, "Who is your grandfather?"

"Irving Berlin is my grandfather," the child answered.

"Irving Berlin?" the teacher said with some astonishment. "What does he do?"

And the girl replied, "He paints!"

▪ ▪ ▪

There was one other escape he permitted himself: ceaseless phone calls to the same group of surrogate sons he had been cultivating since the late fifties. As the years passed, he spoke most frequently with Harold Arlen; in addition to being professional songwriters and amateur painters, the two men were both sons of cantors.

Their conversations frequently centered on complications in Arlen's personal life. When Arlen's wife, Anya, died, various friends encouraged him to begin dating women and to consider remarrying, but by that time he had contracted Parkinson's disease, and his nose and eyes ran. Inevitably, his illness interfered with his social life. Dorothy Fields (the librettist for *Annie Get Your Gun*), also widowed, set her sights on Arlen as a husband. She was a formidable woman, with her whiskey voice and flashing eyes, and Arlen was reluctant, perhaps even afraid, to marry her, and he asked Irving for advice.

Arlen explained that he felt much different about his late wife than he had, for instance, about his parents. He hadn't *chosen* his parents, he said, and he always knew they would die someday. But he *had* chosen to marry Anya, and their relationship was irreplaceable.

Berlin, married over fifty years himself, approved of his attitude. "Tell Dorothy to go fuck herself," he advised.

▪ ▪ ▪

Berlin's insistence on standing alone, whether in music or in one's personal life, had its admirable side, as well. The motion picture studios and music company conglomerates, who owned the preponderance of copyrights on popular songs, generally licensed them to television commercials selling everything from deodorant to cars. To his credit, the aging Berlin refused to allow his songs to be thus degraded, even though the decision meant financial sacrifice. "I don't want to hear my song in a fucking hair spray commercial," he said.

In a world of bottom-line imperatives, Berlin's publishing company, now occupying a modest suite of offices at 1650 Broadway, had become one of the most remarkable anomalies in the music business. It was true that he could no longer claim the highest royalty payments in the land; by the mid-sixties, various rock-and-roll performers who composed their own material, particularly the Beatles, had surpassed him and all the other songwriters of his era. But his songs still received airplay, and they were still being recorded. "White Christmas" alone had sold forty million recordings and over five-and-and-a-half million copies of sheet music, and it continued to sell at a fast pace.

His music publishing company was obviously worth many millions of dollars, though no one ventured to guess exactly how many, and he constantly received offers to sell his treasured, priceless catalogue. He could name his price, write his own check, demand anything he wanted. At his age, others reasoned, what did he need the headaches for?

Berlin always refused to sell, at any price. Except for the few copyrights he had donated ("God Bless America" to the Girl and Boy Scouts, "Always" to Ellin), the songs were his alone, and he clung to them as tenaciously as he did to life itself. His resistance to changes in the marketplace and the realities of his advanced age amounted to an extraordinary assertion of his willpower. The will had always been there, of course; it had enabled him to survive his early years on the Lower East Side, the death of his first wife, and the vicissitudes of his career, but it had usually been cloaked in glamour and charm. Now it was naked, and it was not a pretty sight, but it *was* impressive. In a fast-moving world, where nearly everyone and everything seemed interchangeable, Irving Berlin endured—unalterable, inviolate, seemingly eternal.

▪ ▪ ▪

Though he now spent more time rusticating in the Catskills than pacing the carpet in his office, he kept in constant touch by phone with Helmy and the others he employed, and it was a point of pride with him that he continued to make all his deals himself. Rather, he would *refuse* to make them. He frequently denied others permission to use to his individual songs—the rights to which belonged to him and him alone—in movies or on television or even in Broadway shows, even though he would be paid for their use through ASCAP. Nor were these fly-by-night offers that he turned down. One originated with perhaps the only other figure who could rival his stature on Broadway, the director George Abbott, who had done such an able job staging *Call Me Madam*.

George called his friend Irving and said, "I'd like to do a musical using a lot of your songs that have never been in a show." There were, Abbott knew, hundreds from which to choose. It would be a great event, a show that could have performed the resurrection of Berlin that *Say It With Music* had failed to bring about. And Abbott was the only person in the American theater community with the prestige to make it happen.

Berlin wouldn't consider the idea. Wouldn't even discuss it. "I'm not available for work," he told Abbott. And what if Abbott took care of everything, and Berlin didn't have to work? "I don't want any of my things done if I can't work on them," the songwriter said, precluding even that possibility. Copyright law, if not popular sentiment, was on Berlin's side. Abbott could, if he wished, stage a mixture of songs by Irving Berlin and other composers, and as long as Irving received his royalties, there was little he could do. But once Abbott decided to stage a show with a score *exclusively* by Berlin, the director was required to obtain the songwriter's permission.

Occasionally, however, greed did get the better of Berlin. In the late sixties, Simon and Schuster approached the songwriter with an attractive and flattering proposal: the publishing company wished to bring out a two-volume edition of Irving Berlin's lyrics with an introduction by Leonard Bernstein. The compilation would be priced at fifty dollars. At first Berlin looked favorably on the idea, but when he heard that Simon and Schuster was approaching other songwriters, as well, he wanted to assure himself that his advance was larger than theirs. He demanded $100,000 from the company—a figure vastly exceeding the amount the book could earn. He refused to budge from this figure, and as a result, neither this nor any other compendium of his lyrics has ever been published.

Berlin's lifelong habit of making his own deals was well known throughout the entertainment business, and it was now regarded as either an old man's harmless idiosyncrasy or a grave mistake. Irving Lazar, the diminutive powerhouse of an agent for all manner of celebrities, was of the latter opinion. Over lunch at Romanoff's in Hollywood, he questioned Berlin about his curious way of conducting business. "Why do you go around selling your own stuff?" he asked. "Why don't you have me as your agent? It's more dignified. You don't have to sing it to anybody. That's so cheap, so second-rate."

"Listen," he said to Swifty Lazar, "If you were me, would you hire Swifty Lazar to be your agent?" Swifty said he would not. "So what are you bothering me for?"

▪ ▪ ▪

Alone, Berlin continued to scrutinize his copyrights and the receipts from the Music Box Theatre, which he had built with Sam Harris half a century ago. After all these years, the Music Box was thriving, still considered a lucky Broadway house. Harris had died years before, and his widow subsequently sold his share to the Shubert organization, which now owned the theater in partnership with Berlin. The alliance brought to an end the long-standing rancor between the songwriter and the powerful Shubert brothers. His last visit to the theater took place in 1970, when Ellin and he attended a performance of the hit play *Sleuth*.

Despite his near invisibility, he insisted—over the phone—that he was not "hiding out from anybody." And he continued to cherish a fond daydream of returning to center stage. A successful revival of the 1925 flapper musical *No, No, Nanette* on Broadway in January 1971 encouraged the songwriter to believe that perhaps his style of music was at last coming back into favor. Although he was in his mid-eighties, he pulled old songs out of his trunk and began fashioning a score, but as he got deeper into the task, he lost confidence. "At my age, it's hard to go to auditions and rehearsals and the rest," he explained. "Besides, you get frightened. You can stand success, but you're afraid of failure."

With these words, he plunged ever deeper into privacy. His presence was often in demand, even if his music was not, but he invariably refused to oblige, even when the cause was close to his heart. In June 1972, one hundred surviving members of the cast of *This Is the Army* assembled in the Belasco Room of Sardi's Restaurant in New York's theater district to celebrate the thirtieth anniversary of the show that had given Berlin his greatest satisfaction. Alan Manson attended, as did Ezra Stone, Joshua Logan, and Alan Anderson, but not Irving Berlin. While the cast reminisced and drank, he kept to himself at his Catskills estate.

Whether in the country or in his New York town house, his routine was the same. He passed his days as if in a trance, walking, watching television, and painting, and rarely speaking to anyone, even his wife. On rare occasions, he played the piano, but he had ceased composing, though he expressed the hope that he could write just one more song before he died.

▪ ▪ ▪

On January 25, 1978, Berlin's older sister Gussie (Chasse) died in New York. The youngest of the eight Balines who had come to America in 1893, Irving was now the sole surviving member of the immigrant family.

▪ ▪ ▪

Advancing into his nineties, he attracted a new kind of fame; he went from being a celebrity, with all the potential for controversy and exploitation that the role implied, to an object of veneration. In place of the broad-based, mass-media acclaim he had once courted and enjoyed, he spontaneously attracted a tiny but intense following of apostles dedicated to keeping the flame of Irving Berlin ablaze. Their dedication to him took the form not of headline-grabbing tributes and black-tie banquets populated by press agents, but of intimate rites imbued with a religious sincerity and fervor. At his age, this was probably the only form of tribute that the songwriter could comfortably withstand.

The leader of these apostles, John Wallowitch, assumed the role quite by accident. A Juilliard-trained composer and cabaret singer, Wallowitch had lived in Berlin's neighborhood for twenty years and had long been a devotee of the songwriter. "It makes you believe in God, to think that He could create someone like Irving Berlin," Wallowitch said. Walking his dog, he would occasionally pass Berlin on the street when the songwriter was out for a walk. Eventually they developed a nodding acquaintance, and the songwriter came to fancy Wallowitch's dog. "I wish I had a dog like that," he told Wallowitch, "but my wife won't let me." Later, Wallowitch became more daring and asked Berlin about one of his earliest songs, "Sadie Salome, Go Home." "How do you know about these songs?" Berlin asked, and then he joked, "You must be an old-timer."

One Christmas Eve, Wallowitch was walking his dog past the Berlin town house; he was singing "White Christmas" to himself, and he suddenly burst into tears. Thereafter, singing the song in front of the house became a Christmas Eve ritual for Wallowitch—"a way of contacting the muses," he said. He later asked a few friends to join him in the observance, and they would collect in front of Berlin's home and serenade the reclusive songwriter. Eventually, their number grew to seventeen.

Christmas Eve, 1983, was particularly cold—four degrees, with a nasty wind whipping off the East River. A friend suggested that they should try ringing Berlin's doorbell. "I found myself overcome with fear," Wallowitch said. "After what seemed an eternity I pushed the doorbell, and the house, which is usually dark, suddenly lit up like a Christmas tree. On the third floor, a shade was being pulled. We sang 'Always,' repeated 'White Christmas,' and then the front door opened."

"Mr. Berlin wants to thank you," said a maid.

"We're here to thank *him*," Wallowitch replied.

The maid invited the freezing serenaders into the kitchen, where they were astonished to see Berlin himself, wearing pajamas, bathrobe, and slippers, his dark eyes large and bright. "I want to thank you," he told the group. "That's the nicest Christmas present I've ever had."

The songwriter hugged all the men; it was, they noted, a good, strong hug, and then he kissed all the women.

Afterward, the ecstatic little band returned to Wallowitch's apartment, where they sang songs by Irving Berlin for two and a half hours without once repeating themselves. It had been, for them, a mystical experience; it was also the last time the songwriter ever appeared before an audience.

▪ ▪ ▪

On rare occasions, Berlin was seen taking a constitutional in the neighborhood, accompanied by a bodyguard, and he presented a cranky and forbidding aspect to the world, chasing away children who strayed across his path and refusing to acknowledge the greetings of local residents. Indeed, at least one neighbor found him so disagreeable that whenever she saw him, she crossed the street to avoid an unpleasant encounter. Most neighbors, however, had no idea that America's great songwriter was alive, much less living in their midst.

In fact, the famous, forgotten recluse gave every sign of being in good physical condition for a man of his age. And he was *not* senile; he had, as his phone friends invariably put it, "all his marbles." Berlin summarized his condition much the same way. "My health is perfect," he would say, "from the neck up." Actually, that wasn't quite accurate. His eyesight was failing now, and his business documents were read to him. He could walk by himself, though he required help getting out of a chair. He detested all these reminders of aging.

He emerged from his petulant mood when he spoke with one of the members of his extensive network of telephone friends, though their number was steadily dwindling. He had outlived many of his friends and colleagues and rivals: Arthur Freed, Ethel Merman, Al Jolson, Eddie Cantor, Cole Porter, Lorenz Hart, Oscar Hammerstein II, Florenz Ziegfeld, Richard Rodgers, Marilyn Miller, Joshua Logan, Joe Schenck, Max Winslow, Grace Moore, Jerome Kern, George Gershwin, Victor Herbert, and Ted Snyder, among many others. Berlin was now one of the last surviving representatives of a vanished epoch of American popular culture.

He was especially bereft when Harold Arlen died, in November 1986. Unable to muster the strength to attend a memorial service held in Arlen's honor, he instead sent a message to be read on his behalf. "We would talk on the phone for hours," Berlin recalled, "never about songs. Conversation would start when one of us would ask, 'How did you sleep last night?' This would continue until we were both worn out and too tired to sleep."

The death of Fred Astaire on June 22, 1987, came as an even greater blow, for Irving had long considered him to be the most capable, exacting, and professional performer with whom he had ever worked. Both exercised great discipline and self-restraint, and both were fond of reminiscing. "Why didn't you ever kiss your leading ladies in the movies?" Irving had once asked him, and Fred replied, "Who do you think I am, Clark Gable?" On hearing of his beloved friend's demise, Irving immediately called Stanley Green, who found him incoherent with grief. In Astaire's death, the songwriter glimpsed his own.

▪ ▪ ▪

Berlin gained some relief from the terror of extinction in managing his publishing company, whose affairs he persisted in supervising by phone. One remarkable, though hardly welcome, aspect of his longevity was that the copyrights on his early songs were beginning to expire. Under United States copyright law, his music and lyrics were protected for seventy-five years, after which they entered the public domain. In 1984 dozens of his titles began to escape his control, and in 1986 the song that had launched his career, "Alexander's Ragtime Band," became public property.

In response to these unavoidable losses, he zealously guarded the songs still protected by copyright, generally refusing to license them to anyone. One noteworthy instance of his tenacity occurred in the mid-eighties, when the director Steven Spielberg tried to negotiate for the rights to use "Always" in a motion picture. Berlin refused, and Spielberg, assuming that the songwriter wanted more money, repeatedly increased his offer—to no avail. Finally Berlin ended discussions with the explanation that he was reserving the song for one of his own projects. So it was no to Spielberg, and with few minor exceptions, no, no, *no* to anyone else making a similar request.

Since he no longer set foot in his office, he worried that his employees were shirking their responsibilities in his absence. When he called at lunchtime and discovered that Helmy Kresa, who had been in his employ for sixty years and was himself in his eighties, had gone home for the day, he became greatly annoyed. The next day, Helmy recalled, Berlin "raised hell and told me that I should stay until three o'clock and not take an early train." And Helmy, as always, heeded the words of his boss.

▪ ▪ ▪

He granted regular access to only a few. Ellin naturally came first, and he jealously guarded her attention. He became agitated if she spent what he considered to be too much time with anyone else, even a maid. The two of them would have dinner every evening at five, and she would dress for the occasion, although, as she explained to a maid, "I really only have to fix the left side of my hair because Irving sits to the left of me at dinner, and it is the only side he will see."

A cardiologist visited every week, and the two would make small talk as the doctor proceeded with his examination. Another regular visitor to the Berlin household was his barber, who arrived every month to cut his famous customer's hair, which, though sprinkled with gray, was still remarkably thick. Occasionally the barber would complain that Berlin had let his hair grow too long, but the songwriter would merely shrug and say, "So? Where am I going?" And if the barber happened to forget himself and begin humming a popular song as he trimmed his customer's hair, Berlin would tell him to shut up.

There were few other visitors at Beekman Place. No friends dropped by to chat, no family members visited, no grandchildren arrived to distract him from his reveries of the past. Berlin's eruptions of anger had succeeded in driving them all away.

His growing misanthropy all but eliminated his name from the press. In July 1986, when he, along with a small number of other prominent immigrants, was selected to receive a medal from President Reagan as part of a Liberty Weekend celebration, Berlin was the only honoree not to attend the open-air ceremony in New York Harbor. Instead, he watched coverage of the event at home on television.

At the conclusion, as if to compensate for his absence, he telephoned the producer, David Wolper, whose extravagant presentation had drawn some criticism. "I watched all four days of it," he told Wolper, "and I wouldn't have changed a thing. Don't believe what you read in the press that it was too glitzy. When I wrote 'God Bless America,' they said it was too corny, but it's still around. You did it exactly the way I would have done it." The showman in Berlin lived on, even though he was now too frail, too shy, to show himself.

▪ ▪ ▪

As a result of his prolonged absence from the public eye, it became ever more widely assumed that Irving Berlin was no longer alive, although no one could pin down the exact date of his death, of course. Berlin's refusal to communicate with the press and his insistence on privacy contributed to the widespread ignorance about him.

As his ninety-ninth birthday approached, ASCAP decided to take out a full-page advertisement in *The New York Times* to commemorate the occasion, but before doing so, the organization decided to check with Berlin. On hearing of the plan, he was enraged. "Do you realize how much a full-page ad in the *Times* costs?" he said. "I pay you to administer my money, not to squander it. The answer is no."

Although he could exercise control over this one outlet, he was powerless to stem the flow of articles appearing in newspapers around the country, most of them expressing a sense of wonder, even confusion, about what had become of the songwriter after all these years. "BERLIN, AT 99, A RECLUSIVE IMMORTAL," read the headline for *The New York Times* article on the event. It came as something of a shock to realize that he was still around. Many younger people didn't know who he was, or they couldn't place him; they thought "White Christmas" was a folk song, "God Bless America" the work of an anonymous artisan, and they had never heard of "Always" or "Remember." Older people, for whom these songs were lifelong companions, were also surprised to learn that the songwriter was alive. Irving Berlin was ninety-nine, imagine that.

Once again, John Wallowitch was on the scene to mark the occasion, having become Berlin's self-appointed ambassador to the press. At 5:42 A.M. on May 11, Wallowitch and his group positioned themselves in front of the town house and sang "Happy Birthday" to Berlin. There was no reaction, except for the sight of two third-floor window shades going up. Still, for Wallowitch, that was enough.

Later in the day, Berlin quietly celebrated his ninety-ninth birthday with his wife and daughter Elizabeth. That night, New York City's mayor, Edward Koch, held a considerably more lavish party in Berlin's honor at Gracie Mansion, the mayor's official residence; although the guest of honor lived close by, he chose not to attend.

▪ ▪ ▪

The muted excitement surrounding Berlin's ninety-ninth birthday was merely a prologue to the ballyhoo that threatened to burst forth if he lived to the age of one hundred. In New York and Los Angeles, numerous promoters began to plan ways to capitalize on the occasion, but the songwriter, determined to minimize the publicity, gave his reluctant blessing to only one event. Morton Gould, then the president of ASCAP's board, called Berlin to ask his permission to hold a benefit tribute in Carnegie Hall.

"What's your hurry?" Berlin asked. "Why do you have to talk about it now?"

As Gould waited for an answer, Berlin considered. He had been similarly honored for the last fifty years. All the tributes had been different, each a reflection of its era, and yet the songs they chose to highlight were generally the same, and by now the tributes seemed to blend into one endless medley of Irving Berlin standards. The songwriter had no more need of being honored, but the public's urge to honor him had grown to the point where it had to be satisfied in some way. If he withheld permission from ASCAP, it was likely that any number of unauthorized tributes would rush to fill the vacuum, a possibility he could not endure, and so he finally agreed to ASCAP's plan as the most bearable alternative.

He warned ASCAP not to expect him to appear onstage or anywhere else in public, for he was far too sensitive about his feeble appearance. He wanted people to remember him in his prime, as a compact, intense, vigorous man with thick black hair and burning eyes, not as an old man in a wheelchair, a death's head suddenly appearing at a celebration, startling the revelers. "I don't want people to stare at me and say, 'See how old he looks,' " he told his phone friends.

As the ASCAP celebration took shape, and the roster of celebrities who agreed to appear lengthened, the songwriter took pleasure in taunting the organization. "You know," he warned, "I might screw up all your plans. I might die before my hundredth birthday."

In preparation for the day, Wednesday, May 11, 1988, on which Irving Berlin began his second century, solemn retrospectives and frenzied appreciations spewed forth in the press. The *New York Daily News*, displaying the keenest appreciation for the songwriter's appeal, assigned its "Inquiring Photographer" to ask the usual varied assemblage of New Yorkers to respond to the question, "What does Irving Berlin mean to you?" Replied one subject: "He means everything to me. His songs will live forever. I'll soon be 91. I recall his songs for a show about the army base at Yaphank, L.I., where I was discharged in 1919." In addition, the paper asked its readers to vote for their five favorite songs chosen from a list of one hundred composed by the master. "On the 2,165 ballots we received," the *Daily News* revealed, " 'God Bless America' and 'White Christmas' were each marked on 1,328—or 61.3%. You probably think we're making this up. We aren't."

At the same time, the only sour note to be heard was sounded in the same *Daily News*, where the brash columnist Jimmy Breslin took it upon himself to explain, "WHY I DON'T LIKE IRVING." Playing the role of heckler at the banquet, Breslin announced, "You can't get me to say I like the guy no matter how old and revered he is." Indeed, he expressed the hope that when Berlin read the column he would "froth." Breslin's main gripe against Berlin, it turned out, was that the songwriter had once refused the columnist permission to quote three words from "A Pretty Girl Is Like a Melody" in a novel Breslin was completing. "Because of him, like some kind of censor, I had to change the book," Breslin complained, "Nice guy. . . . Now I know the man is 100 and I know he's revered, but I'm betting he was like this when he was 60."

If Breslin spoke for many who had suffered unpleasant encounters with the songwriter over the years, the staid Carnegie Hall tribute presented the authorized version of the Berlin legacy to an audience that had paid up to one thousand dollars a seat for the privilege of attending.

The stage featured an outsized keyboard fitted with silver and gold keys. Against this glittering backdrop, Shirley MacLaine sang the evening's first song, "Let Me Sing and I'm Happy," and then Walter Cronkite, the former CBS anchorman, strolled to a lectern and, in his familiar, mellifluous voice, set the evening's tone. "Irving Berlin helped write the story of this country by capturing the best of who we are and the dreams that shape our lives," he recited. "Irving Berlin has written over 1,500 songs, and it is there we find our history, our holidays, our homes and our hearts." Cronkite was succeeded by a varied group of entertainers who performed highlights from Berlin's catalogue, although many who appeared had no special association with his songs or even with his music.

Since the event was to be broadcast several weeks later by CBS, the requirements of television taping meant that the gala came to a halt between songs, as the audience fidgeted and cameras and technicians jockeyed for new positions. Despite these annoyances, there were brief interludes when the evening came alive, when Berlin's songs sounded as impudent and compelling as they had in a vaudeville theater. Nell Carter brought old-fashioned fervor to "Alexander's Ragtime Band," and Rosemary Clooney intoned "White Christmas" with perfect pitch and diction.

In addition to the bravura moments, there were numerous curiosities offered up in the name of Irving Berlin. Leonard Bernstein sat before a piano and sang, in a low nasal voice, what he said was the first song he could recall hearing as a child, "A Russian Lullaby." Garrison Keillor, the essayist and humorist, spoke, rather than sang, the lyrics for "All Alone," which he aptly termed a "poem of eighty-one words without one unnecessary word." And to meet the scrutiny of television cameras, Frank Sinatra sang his number—"Always"—twice.

Three hours after it began, the evening ended in an appropriately grandiose and patriotic manner as the entertainers surrendered the stage to the United States Army Chorus, which sang "This Is the Army." Then the aisles filled with Girl and Boy Scouts, and opera singer Marilyn Horne led the assembled throng through "God Bless America." Thus ended the public celebration of Berlin's one hundredth birthday—none of it seen by the man in whose honor it had been staged. ASCAP proposed to transmit the proceedings to Berlin's Beekman Place home via closed-circuit television, but Berlin had no interest in watching, and he declined the offer. His refusal to participate in the ceremony in any form, even to comment on it through intermediaries, imparted an awkward quality to the entire evening. The tribute, it seemed, was haunted by a reticent and embittered wraith.

The night before, at midnight, the unofficial observance had taken place. At Beekman Place, John Wallowitch and his contingent assembled in front of Berlin's home, once again serenading the songwriter, hoping to catch even a glimpse of his face. They sang "Happy Birthday." They sang "Always." They called out to him. On the third floor, a shade lifted, and the light behind it was extinguished. Someone was looking down at them; in all likehood it was Berlin himself, enveloped in darkness.

A voice called out: "Sorry," it said. "He looked outside and decided it was too cold."

▪ ▪ ▪

Less than three months after Irving's one hundredth birthday ceremonies, Ellin Berlin died. She had been in poor health for several years, the victim of numerous strokes. After suffering a series of seizures at home, she was rushed to nearby Doctors Hospital, where she was pronounced dead of natural causes shortly after midnight on July 29, 1988, at the age of eighty-five. She had, of course, been everything to her husband, and he had loved her, just as the song he presented for her shortly after their marriage six decades earlier declared, "always." The strength he drew from their marriage, and the victory he had won over her father's prejudices revealed the best part of his nature. A scourge to his business associates and friends, especially in his later years, Irving had been ever the doting husband.

Ellin's will, drawn in 1982, named her husband as her sole legatee and her executor. Since Berlin was now virtually blind and could write his name only with assistance, he decided to renounce the role of executor. However, he still possessed sufficient presence of mind to inquire about who would replace him. On being informed of the name of the bank, he said, "Fine, that's my bank."

She left an extensive estate to her husband—nearly $10 million, including their Beekman Place residence, which had been listed in her name. The mansion was conservatively valued at $5,500,000. The remainder of her holdings included $250,000 in stocks and bonds, $75,000 in cash, and over $2 million in so-called "tangible personal property" such as jewelry.

Although Ellin hadn't published a book for thirty years, she was recalled in numerous obituaries as both a writer and the wife of a famous songwriter. In her lifetime, she had never been one to boast of her literary attainments. "What I am," she once said, "is a professional wife, mother and grandmother, for God's sake. That's my job. The other is my avocation." As for the scandalous circumstances of her elopement, she had little to say in her later years beyond one simple and defiant observation: "Certainly I married out of my social order. I married *up*."

Even as she married up, however, she had returned to her father's Roman Catholic faith. Her funeral service, at St. Patrick's Cathedral on Fifth Avenue, where her father's funeral service had taken place fifty years before, recalled the opulence of Clarence Mackay's era. The day of the service, August 2, brought with it oppressively hot and humid weather. Within the famous cathedral's vast, ornate interior, a mixture of casually dressed tourists and the faithful were milling about when the huge double doors of the main entrance swung open with a groan and a shaft of sunlight suddenly penetrated the shadows. Moments later, eight pallbearers carried a plain wooden coffin containing the mortal remains of Ellin Mackay Berlin over the cathedral's perilous stone steps and into the vestibule. They gently placed the coffin on a small trolley and wheeled it up the nave toward the sanctuary at the eastern end of the cathedral, accompanied by a small group of mourners comprised primarily of members of the immediate family.

There were a few celebrities in evidence, however: former New York mayor John Lindsay, Kitty Carlisle Hart, and Helen Gurley Brown. There was also an honor guard representing the Girl Scouts of America. A complement of newspaper and television reporters hovered about the cathedral's entrances and even in the south transept, hoping for a glimpse of Ellin's reclusive husband.

Amid the buzzing of the perplexed onlookers, the funeral mass began. Reverend Anthony DallaVilla, cathedral rector, eulogized Ellin Berlin with reference to the song her husband had written about her: "She will be remembered and loved, 'Always, always.' " Near the end of the rite, Cardinal John O'Connor unexpectedly appeared to give his blessing, later explaining that although he hadn't known either of the Berlins, he, too, wished to pay tribute. "No man could have given the joy to the world that Irving Berlin gave had he not had the love and support of a wonderful woman," he said as incense wafted through the cathedral. "I came today to thank her for this great contribution to the world."

Thus was Ellin mourned in a setting as splendid, public, and formal as that in which she had lived her life.

Avoiding the publicity his presence was certain to attract, Berlin did not attend the ceremony, preferring to remain, as he had for most of the previous twenty-five years, in seclusion at his Beekman Place home, overlooking the vast, gray river in sight of which he had spent so much of his life.

▪ ▪ ▪

His chronic reluctance to place himself on display deepened the mystique surrounding him to an impenetrable opacity. Americans craved news of his activities, but he refused to offer any gesture or remark for public consumption—not a single word. Even his network of friends ceased to hear from him and were at a loss to speak on his behalf. A captive of his deteriorating body, he remained secluded within the walls of his house. Without Ellin to bolster him, he deteriorated at an ever-accelerating pace. By the summer of 1989, he was under the care of nurses around the clock. On the afternoon of Friday, September 22, four months after his one hundred first birthday, Irving Berlin died quietly at home on Beekman Place.

His son-in-law, Alton Peters, made the announcement to the press. Asked whether Berlin had died from illness, Peters responded, "No, he was one hundred one years old. He just fell asleep."

▪ ▪ ▪

News of Berlin's death dominated the national news throughout the weekend and inspired an outpouring of newspaper and television obituaries, retrospectives, and tributes in honor of the immigrant who had, through talent and force of will, become the nation's songwriter. On Broadway, where his rousing scores had attracted patrons to theaters since 1914, Berlin was accorded the traditional memorial: just before curtain time, marquee lights, normally a dazzling white that turned night into day, flickered and dimmed to a melancholy yellow for a brief interval. Across town, on Beekman Place, John Wallowitch led his friends in a requiem serenade outside the Berlin home. Politicians, too, paid their respects. Former president Ronald Reagan, whom the songwriter had advised during World War II to give some thought to acting professionally, offered his condolences. Attending a luncheon in Boston, President George Bush led a crowd in singing "God Bless America" and then released a statement describing Irving Berlin as a "legendary man whose words and music will help define the history of our nation."

In contrast to these public utterances, Berlin's funeral was an entirely private, even obscure, affair. Family members attended a small service held at the Frank E. Campbell Chapel, a traditional Manhattan site of last rites for celebrities. The songwriter's burial, held on September 26 at Woodlawn Cemetery in the Bronx, was even more private, with only his three daughters and a handful of loyal employees in attendance. As a reform rabbi, Daniel Wolk of Congregation Emanu-el in suburban Westchester, officiated, the body of Irving Berlin, America's greatest songwriter, was interred beside that of his wife.

Since Berlin had been fiercely private and vigilant about his finances during the final decades of his life, the contents of his will and his plans for the vast number of copyrights he held had long occasioned speculation. The terms of his will, a highly detailed, thirty-page document drawn in May 1968, continued the pattern of his extreme caution and frugality concerning the administration of his business affairs. Naming the Morgan Guaranty Trust Company of New York as his executor, Berlin left instructions for modest cash bequests to several longtime employees. Helmy Kresa, for instance, who had been Berlin's principal transcriber for over sixty years, received only $10,000. Various surviving relatives of Berlin's—nieces and nephews and grandchildren and the like—were put down for slightly larger amounts.

Berlin's three daughters became the beneficiaries of the bulk of his estate, to share equally among them; their inheritance included property—notably the Beekman Place house and the Catskills estate—in addition to the priceless copyrights of their father's songs. On the subject of his extensive catalogue, Berlin urged from the grave that his songs be administered and, if necessary, sold as a unit rather than being fragmented. Reflecting his painstaking attention to business matters, he took further precautions, as well. Although he permitted the publication and licensing of unpublished songs that might be lurking in his trunk at the time of his death, he laid down strict conditions: no more than two songs could be licensed for performance at a time, there could be no changes made to individual songs, and no interpolations in unpublished scores. Finally, on the longstanding issue of dramatizing his life story—an idea he had resisted as long as he was alive, but which inevitably became the subject of renewed interest at the time of his death—he asked that his daughters give their approval to any such project.

Through the instruments of the law, Berlin was able, in death as in life, to maintain his iron grip on the songs that had meant everything to him. Although millions would continue to sing his lyrics and to hum his unforgettable melodies, and the press would continue to recount the legends surrounding him, there would be no further word from Irving Berlin, only an unbroken silence extending into eternity.

Chronology

■

SONGS BY IRVING BERLIN

The following chronology lists Irving Berlin's songs by approximate date of creation. Since it is often difficult to ascertain precisely when he composed or completed many of his works, I have grouped them by five-year periods. Although I have endeavored to make this list as complete and accurate as possible, heretofore unknown songs by Berlin may eventually surface.

Many of these songs were published and reissued haphazardly; as a result, there are occasional variations in the spelling and punctuation of their titles—especially in the use of question marks, exclamation points, and parentheses. Where possible, I have followed the spelling and punctuation as they appeared on the covers of the original sheet music.

In some cases, Berlin's songs were copyrighted years after he composed them. Therefore, this compilation does not relate to copyright dates. It is purely for historical purposes, to give a sense of Berlin's evolution as a songwriter over a period of decades.

The names of Berlin's collaborators are noted in italics.

1907–1911

After the Honeymoon
(Ted Snyder)
Alexander and His Clarinet
(Ted Snyder)
Alexander's Ragtime Band
Angelo
Angels
(Ted Snyder)
Before I Go and Marry I Will Have a Talk with You

The Best of Friends Must Part
Bring Back My Lena to Me
(Ted Snyder)
Bring Back My Lovin' Man
Bring Me a Ring in the Spring
Business Is Business, Rosey Cohen
Call Me Up Some Rainy Afternoon
Christmas Time Seems Years and Years Away
(Ted Snyder)
Colored Romeo
(Ted Snyder)
Cuddle Up
Dat's-A My Gal
Dat Draggy Rag
Dear Mayme, I Love You
(Ted Snyder)
Do Your Duty, Doctor
(Ted Snyder)
Dog-Gone That Chilly Man
Don't Put Out the Light
(Edgar Leslie)
Don't Take Your Beau to the Seashore
(E. Ray Goetz)
Dorando
Down to the Folies Bergere
(Vincent Bryan and Ted Snyder)
Dreams, Just Dreams
(Ted Snyder)
Ephraham Played Upon the Piano
(Vincent Bryan)
Everybody's Doin' It Now
Goodbye, Girlie, And Remember Me
(George W. Meyer)
The Grizzly Bear
(George Bottsford)
He Promised Me
Herman, Let's Dance That Beautiful Waltz
(Ted Snyder)
How Do You Do It, Mabel, On Twenty Dollars a Week?
I Beg Your Pardon, Dear Old Broadway
If I Didn't Go Home at All
(Edgar Leslie)
If I Thought You Wouldn't Tell
(Ted Snyder)
If the Managers Only Thought the Same As Mother
(Ted Snyder)
I Just Came Back to Say Goodbye
I Love You More Each Day
(Ted Snyder)
I'm a Happy Married Man
(Ted Snyder)
I'm Going on a Long Vacation
(Ted Snyder)
Innocent Bessie Brown
Is There Anything Else that I Can Do For You?
(Ted Snyder)
I Wish You Was My Gal, Molly
(Ted Snyder)
Just Like the Rose
(Al Piantadosi)
Kiss Me, My Honey, Kiss Me
(Ted Snyder)
Marie from Sunny Italy
(M. Nicholson)
Meet Me Tonight
Molly, Oh! Molly
My Melody Dream
My Wife's Gone to the Country, Hurrah! Hurrah!
(George Whiting and Ted Snyder)
Next To Your Mother Who Do You Love?
(Ted Snyder)
No One Could Do It Like My Father
(Ted Snyder)
Oh, How That German Could Love
(Ted Snyder)
Oh, That Beautiful Rag
(Ted Snyder)
Oh! Where Is My Wife Tonight?
(George Whiting and Ted Snyder)
One O'Clock in the Morning I Get Lonesome
(Ted Snyder)
Piano Man *(Ted Snyder)*

Queenie
(Maurice Abrahams)
The Ragtime Violin
Real Girl
Run Home and Tell Your Mother
Sadie Salome, Go Home
(Edgar Leslie)
She Was a Dear Little Girl
(Ted Snyder)
Sombrero Land
(E. Ray Goetz and Ted Snyder)
Some Little Something About You
(Ted Snyder)
Someone Just Like You, Dear
(Ted Snyder)
Someone's Waiting for Me
(Edgar Leslie)
Spanish Love
(Vincent Bryan and Ted Snyder)
Stop! Stop! Stop! Come Over and Love Me Some More
Stop That Rag (Keep on Playing)
(Ted Snyder)
Sweet Italian Love
(Ted Snyder)
Sweet Marie, Make a Rag-a-Time-a-Dance with Me
(Ted Snyder)
Telling Lies
(Henrietta Blank and Fred E. Belcher)
Thank You, Kind Sir, Said She
(Ted Snyder)
That Dying Rag
(Bernie Adler)
That Kazzatsky Dance
That Mesmerizing Mendelssohn Tune
That Monkey Tune
That Mysterious Rag
(Ted Snyder)
That Opera Rag
(Ted Snyder)
There's a Girl in Havana
(E. Ray Goetz and Ted Snyder)
Try It On Your Piano
Virginia Lou
(Earl Taylor)
We'll Wait, Wait, Wait, Wait
(Edgar Leslie)
What Am I Gonna Do?
When I Hear You Play That Piano, Bill
(Ted Snyder)
When I'm Alone I'm Lonesome
When You Kiss an Italian Girl
When You're in Town (In My Home Town)
Whistling Rag
Wild Cherries Rag
(Ted Snyder)
Wishing
(Ted Snyder)
Woodman, Woodman, Spare That Tree
(Vincent Bryan)
Yankee Love
(E. Ray Goetz)
Yiddisha Eyes
(Ted Snyder)
Yiddisha Nightingale
Yiddle on Your Fiddle Play Some Ragtime
You've Built a Fire Down in My Heart
You've Got Me Hypnotized

1912–1916

Abie Sings an Irish Song
Alexander's Bag-Pipe Band
(E. Ray Goetz and A. B. Sloane)
Along Came Ruth
Always Treat Her Like a Baby
And Father Wanted Me to Learn a Trade
Anna Liza's Wedding Day
Antonio, You'd Better Come Home
The Apple Tree and the Bumble Bee
Araby
At the Devil's Ball
At the Picture Show
(E. Ray Goetz)

Becky's Got a Job in a Musical Show
The Belle of the Barber's Ball
Blow Your Horn
Brand New
(Ted Snyder)
Call Again
Chatter, Chatter
The Chicken Walk
Cohen Owes Me Ninety-Seven Dollars
Come Back to Me, My Melody
(Ted Snyder)
Come to the Land of the Argentine
Daddy, Come Home
Do It Again
Don't Leave Your Wife Alone
Down in Chattanooga
Down in My Heart
Elevator Man, Going Up! Going Up! Going Up!
England Every Time for Me
Everything in America Is Ragtime
Father's Beard
Following the Girl Behind the Smile
(E. Ray Goetz)
Follow Me Around
Follow the Crowd
The Friars Parade
The Funny Little Melody
Furnishing a Home for Two
The Garden of Yesterday
Ginger
(E. Ray Goetz)
The Girl on the Magazine Cover
God Gave You to Me
Goody, Goody, Goody, Goody, Good
Happy Little Country Girl
The Haunted House
He Played It on his Fid, Fid, Fiddle-De-Dee
(E. Ray Goetz)
He's a Devil in His Own Home Town
(Grant Clarke)
He's a Rag Picker
He's Getting Too Darn Big for a One-Horse Town
He's So Good to Me
Hiram's Band
(E. Ray Goetz)
Homeward Bound
Hurry Back to My Bamboo Shack
If All the Girls I Knew Were Like You
If I Had You
If That's Your Idea of a Wonderful Time (Take Me Home)
If You Don't Want Me (Why Do You Hang Around)
If You Don't Want My Peaches (You'd Better Stop Shaking My Tree)
I Hate You
I Love a Piano
I Love to Dance
I Love to Have the Boys Around Me
I Love to Quarrel with You
I Love to Stay at Home
I Never Would Do in Society
(E. Ray Goetz)
I'm a Dancing Teacher Now
I'm Afraid, Pretty Maid, I'm Afraid
I'm Down in Honolulu Looking Them Over
I'm Going Back to Dixie
(Ted Snyder)
I'm Going Back to the Farm
I'm Not Prepared
In Florida Among the Palms
In My Harem
It Isn't What He Said, But the Way He Said It
I've Got a Sweet Tooth Bothering Me
I've Got to Go Back to Texas
I've Got to Have Some Lovin' Now
I Want to Be in Dixie
I Want to Go Back to Michigan (Down on the Farm)
I Was Aviating Around
(Vincent Bryan)
Jake! Jake! The Yiddisher Ball Player
(Blanche Merrill)

Keep Away From the Fellow Who Owns an Automobile
Keep on Walking
The Ki-I-Youdling Dog
(Jean Schwartz)
Kiss Your Sailor Boy Goodbye
The Law Must Be Obeyed
Lead Me to Love
(Ted Snyder)
Lead Me to that Beautiful Band
(E. Ray Goetz)
Let's Go Around the Town
A Little Bit of Everything
The Little Girl Who Couldn't Care
(E. Ray Goetz)
Lock Me in Your Harem and Throw Away the Key
Lonely Moon
(E. Ray Goetz)
Look at Them Doing It
Metropolitan Nights
The Million Dollar Ball
(E. Ray Goetz)
The Minstrel Parade
The Monkey Doodle Doo
Morning Exercise
Move Over
My Bird of Paradise
My Heather Belle
(E. Ray Goetz)
My Sweet Italian Man
Office Hours
The Old Maid's Ball
Opera Burlesque on the Sextette (from *Lucia Di Lammermoor*)
A Pair of Ordinary Coons
Pick, Pick, Pick on the Mandolin, Antonio
Play a Simple Melody
Polka
Pullman Porters Parade
(Maurice Abrahams)
Ragtime Finale
The Ragtime Jockey Man
Ragtime Mocking Bird
Ragtime Opera Melody
Ragtime Soldier Man
Rum Tum Tiddle
Sailor Song
San Francisco Bound
Settle Down in a One-Horse Town
Show Us How to Do the Fox Trot
Si's Been Drinking Cider
Skating Song
Snookey Ookums
Somebody's Coming to My House
Spring and Fall
Stay Down Here Where You Belong
Stop! Look! Listen!
The Sun Dollars
The Syncopated Walk
Take a Little Tip from Father
(Ted Snyder)
Take Me Back
Take Off A Little Bit
Teach Me How to Love
That Hula Hula
That International Rag
That Society Bear
That's How I Love You
That's My Idea of Paradise
There's a Girl in Arizona
(Grant Clarke and Edgar Leslie)
They Always Follow Me Around
They're on Their Way to Mexico
They've Got Me Doin' It Now
This Is the Life
Tra-La, La, La!
A True Born Soldier Man
Until I Fell in Love With You
The Voice of Belgium
Wait Until Your Daddy Comes Home
Watch Your Step
We Have Much to Be Thankful For
Welcome Home
What Is Love?
When I Discovered You
(E. Ray Goetz)
When I Get Back to the U.S.A.
When I Leave the World Behind
When I Lost You
When I'm Out with You
When I'm Thinking of You, I'm Thinking of a Wonderful Love

When It Rains, Sweetheart, When It Rains
When It's Night Time in Dixie Land
When Johnson's Quartet Harmonize
When the Black Sheep Returns to the Fold
When the Midnight Choo Choo Leaves for Alabam'
When You're Down in Louisville (Call on Me)
While the Band Played an American Rag
Why Don't They Give Us a Chance?
The Yiddisha Professor
You Better Come Home
You Picked a Bad Day to Say Goodbye
You've Got Your Mother's Big Blue Eyes

1917–1921

After You Get It, You Don't Want It
All By Myself
At the Court Around the Corner
A Bad Chinaman from Shanghai
Beautiful Faces Need Beautiful Clothes
Behind the Fan
Bells
Bevo
The Blue Devils of France
But! She's Just a Little Bit Crazy
Chinese Firecrackers
Cinderella Lost Her Slipper
The Circus Is Coming to Town
Come Along Sextette
Come Along to Toy Town
C-U-B-A (I'll See You In)
Dance and Grow Thin
(George W. Meyer)
The Devil Has Brought Up All the Coal
Ding Dong
Down Where the Jack O'Lanterns Grow
(George M. Cohan)
Dream on, Little Soldier Boy
(Jean Havez)
Drowsy Head
(Vaughn De Leath)
Ever Since I Put on a Uniform
Everybody Step
Everything Is Rosy Now for Rosie
(Grant Clarke)
The Eyes of Youth See the Truth
(George M. Cohan)
For Your Country and My Country
From Here to Shanghai
The Girls of My Dreams
Goodbye, France
The Hand That Rocked My Cradle Rules My Heart
Harem Life
Home Again Blues
(Harry Akst)
How Can I Forget
I Can Always Find a Little Sunshine in the Y.M.C.A.
I'd Rather See a Minstrel Show
If I Had My Way, I'd Live among the Gypsies
I Have Just One Heart for Just One Boy
I Left My Door Open and My Daddy Walked Out
I Like It
I Lost My Heart in Dixieland
I'll Take You Back to Italy
I'm a Dumbbell
I'm a Vamp from East Broadway
(Harry Ruby)
I'm Gonna Do It If I Like It
I'm Gonna Pin a Medal on the Girl I Left Behind
I'm the Guy Who Guards the Harem
I Never Knew
(Elsie Janis)
In a Cozy Kitchenette Apartment
It Takes an Irishman to Make Love
(Elsie Janis)
It's the Little Bit of Irish
I've Got My Captain Working for Me Now

I Wonder
I Wouldn't Give That for the Man Who Couldn't Dance
Just Another Kill
Kitchen Police
King of Broadway
The Leg of Nations
The Legend of the Pearls
Let's All Be Americans Now
(Edgar Leslie and George W. Meyer)
Letter Boxes
Lindy
Look Out for That Bolsheviki Man
Mandy
A Man Is Only a Man
Mary Brown
Mr. Jazz Himself
My Ben Ali Haggin Girl
My Little Book of Poetry
My Sweetie
My Tamborine Girl
The New Moon
Nobody Knows (And Nobody Seems to Care)
Oh! How I Hate to Get Up in the Morning
Over the Sea, Boys
The Passion Flower
Pickaninny Mose
A Play without a Bedroom
Polly, Pretty Polly
(George M. Cohan)
Poor Little Rich Girl's Dog
Pretty Birdie
A Pretty Girl Is Like a Melody
Ragtime Razor Brigade
Relatives
The Road that Leads to Love
Say It With Music
The Schoolhouse Blues
Send a Lot of Jazz Bands Over There
Show Me the Way
Smile and Show Your Dimple
Someone Else May Be There
The Sterling Silver Moon
A Streak of Blues
Sweeter Than Sugar (Is My Sweetie)
Syncopated Cocktail
Tell Me, Little Gypsy
The Syncopated Vamp
That Goody Melody
That's My Idea of Paradise
There are Two Eyes in Dixie
There's a Corner Up in Heaven
There's Something Nice about the South
The Wedding of Words and Music
They Call It Dancing
Until I Fell in Love with You
Was There Ever a Pal Like You?
Wasn't It Yesterday?
We're on Our Way to France
When My Baby Smiles
When the Curtain Falls
Whose Little Heart Are You Breaking Now?
You Cannot Make Your Shimmy Shake on Tea
(Rennold Wolf)
You'd Be Surprised
You're So Beautiful

1922–1926

Alice in Wonderland
All Alone
Always
Always April
At Peace with the World
Bandanna Ball
Because I Love You
The Bellhops
Blue Skies
Bring on the Pepper
The Call of the South
Can't You Tell?
Chanson Printaniere
Climbing the Scale
Crinoline Days
Dance Your Troubles Away
De Tant Amour—De Tant D'Ivresse
Diamond Horse-Shoe
Don't Send Me Back to Petrograd

Don't Wait too Long
Everyone in the World Is Doing the Charleston
Five O'Clock Tea
Florida By the Sea
Funny Feet
Gentlemen Prefer Blondes
The Happy New Year Blues
He Doesn't Know What It's All About
Homesick
How Many Times?
I'm Looking for a Daddy Long Legs
I'm on My Way Home
In the Shade of a Sheltering Tree
It's a Walk-in with Walker
I Want to Be a Ballet Dancer
Just a Little Longer
Lady of the Evening
Lazy
Learn to Do the Strut
Listening
A Little Bungalow
Little Butterfly
The Little Red Lacquer Cage
Lucky Boy
Maid of Mesh
Minstrel Days
Montmartre
My Baby's Come Back to Me
One Girl
An Orange Grove in California
Pack Up Your Sins and Go to the Devil
Porcelain Maid
Rainy Day Sue
Remember
Rock-A-Bye Baby
Sixteen, Sweet Sixteen
Some Sunny Day
Take a Little Wife
Take 'im Away, He's Breaking My Heart
Tango Melody
Tell All the Folks in Kentucky (I'm Coming Home)
Tell Her in the Springtime
Tell Me a Bedtime Story
Tell Me with a Melody
That's a Good Girl
They're Blaming the Charleston
Ting-a-Ling, the Bells'll Ring
Tokio Blues
Too Many Sweethearts
Unlucky in Love
Venetian Isles
The Waltz of Long Ago
We Should Care
We'll All Go Voting for Al
We'll Never Know
What'll I Do?
What's There about Me?
When We're Running a Little Hotel of Our Own
When You Walked Out Someone Else Walked Right In
Where is My Little Old New York?
Who
Why Do You Want to Know Why?
Will She Come from the East?
With a Family Reputation
You Forgot to Remember

1927–1931

Any Love Today?
Begging for Love
Better Times with Al
Broker's Ensemble
Chase All Your Cares and Go to Sleep, Baby
Coquette
Do You Believe Your Eyes, or Do You Believe Your Baby?
How About Me?
How Can I Change My Luck?
How Much I Love You
I Can't Do Without You
I Don't Want to Be Married
I Love My Neighbor
I'm the Head Man
In the Morning
In Those Good Old Bowery Days
Is That Nice

It All Belongs to Me
It's Up to the Band
I Want You for Myself
It's Yours
Jimmy
Jungle Jingle
Just A Little While
Knights of the Road
Learn to Sing a Love Song
Let Me Sing and I'm Happy
The Little Things in Life
Looking at You (Across the Breakfast Table)
Marie
Me
Memory That's Soon Forgotten
My Castle
My Little Feller
My New York
My Rhinestone Girl
Nora
Ooh, Maybe It's You
The Police of New York
Puttin' On the Ritz
Rainbow of Girls
Reaching for the Moon
Ribbons and Bows
Roses of Yesterday
Russian Lullabye
Shaking the Blues Away
Soft Lights and Sweet Music
The Song Is Ended
Sunshine
Swanee Shuffle
Sweet Baby
Tickling the Ivories
To Be Forgotten
Toast to Prohibition
To My Mammy
Together We Two
Torch Song
Two Cheers Instead of Three
Waiting at the End of the Road
What a Lucky Break for Me
What Does It Matter?
What Makes Me Love You?
When My Dreams Come True
When the Folks High-Up Do the Mean Low Down
Where Is the Song of Songs for Me?
Why I Love My Baby
Why Should He Fly at So Much a Week?
With You
Yascha Michaeloffsky's Melody
You Got to Have It in Hollywood
You Must Be Born with It

1932–1936

Butterfingers
But Where Are You?
Cheek to Cheek
City Hall
Debts
Drinking Song
Easter Parade
Eighteenth Amendment Repealed (*melody by Stephen Foster*)
The Funnies
Follow the Fleet
Get Thee Behind Me, Satan
Harlem on My Mind
Heat Wave
How Deep Is the Ocean
How's Chances?
I Can't Remember
I'd Rather Lead a Band
I'll Miss You in the Evening
I'm Playing with Fire
I'm Putting All My Eggs in One Basket
I Never Had a Chance
I Say It's Spinach
Isn't This a Lovely Day
Let Yourself Go
Let's Face the Music and Dance
Let's Have Another Cup of Coffee
Lonely Heart
Lunching at the Automat
Majestic Sails at Midnight
Man Bites Dog
Manhattan Madness
Maybe I Love You Too Much

Maybe It's Because I Love You
Metropolitan Opening
Moonlight Maneuvers
Moon Over Napoli
No Strings (I'm Fancy Free)
Not for All the Rice in China
Nudist Colony
On a Roof in Manhattan
Our Wedding Day
The Piccolino
Revolt in Cuba
Say It Isn't So
Skate with Me
So Help Me
Society Wedding
Stop Press
Supper Time
To Be Or Not To Be
Top Hat, White Tie and Tails
We'll All Be in Heaven When the Dollar Goes to Hell
We Saw the Sea

1937–1941

Angels of Mercy
Any Bonds Today?
Arms for the Love of America
Back to Back
Change Partners
Dance with Me (Tonight at the Mardi Gras)
Fools Fall in Love
Girl on the Police Gazette
God Bless America
He Ain't Got Rhythm
I'd Love to Be Shot from a Cannon with You
If You Believe
I Poured My Heart into a Song
I'm Sorry for Myself
It'll Come to You
It's a Lovely Day Tomorrow
I Used to Be Color Blind
I've Got My Love to Keep Me Warm
Latins Know How
A Little Old Church in England
The Lord Done Fixed up My Soul
Louisiana Purchase
Marching Along with Time
My Walking Stick
The Night Is Filled with Music
Now It Can Be Told
An Old Fashioned Tune Is Always New
On the Steps of Grant's Tomb
Outside of That I Love You
Sex Marches On
Slumming on Park Avenue
The Song of the Metronome
Swing Sister
This Year's Kisses
What Chance Have I with Love?
When That Man Is Dead and Gone
When This Crazy World Is Sane Again
When Winter Comes
Wild about You
The Yam
You Can't Brush Me Off
You're Laughing at Me
You're Lonely and I'm Lonely

1942–1946

A Couple of Song and Dance Men
Abraham
Adoption Dance
All of My Life
American Eagles
Anything You Can Do
The Army's Made a Man of Me
Be Careful, It's My Heart
Colonel Buffalo Bill
Doin' What Comes Naturally
Everybody Knew But Me
The Fifth Army's Where My Heart Is
Getting Nowhere (Running Around in Circles)
The Girl That I Marry
Happy Holiday
Heaven Watch the Philippines
Holiday Inn
How About a Cheer for the Navy

I Can't Tell a Lie
I Get Along with the Aussies
I Got Lost in His Arms
I Got the Sun in the Morning
I Left My Heart at the Stage Door Canteen
I'll Capture Your Heart Singing
I'll Dance Rings around You
I'll Share It All with You
I'm a Bad, Bad Man
I'm an Indian, Too
I'm Getting Tired So I Can Sleep
I Paid My Income Tax Today
I Threw a Kiss in the Ocean
Jap-German Sextette
Just a Blue Serge Suit
The Kick in the Pants
Ladies of the Chorus
Let's Go West Again
Let's Say It with Firecrackers
Let's Start the New Year Right
Me and My Melinda
Moonshine Lullaby
My British Buddy
My Defenses Are Down
My Sergeant and I Are Buddies
Oh! To Be Home Again
Plenty to Be Thankful For
The President's Birthday Ball
The Race Horse and the Flea
A Serenade to an Old Fashioned Girl
Song of Freedom
Take It in Your Stride
That Russian Winter
That's What the Well-Dressed Man in Harlem Will Wear
There Are No Wings on a Foxhole
There's No Business Like Show Business
They Say It's Wonderful
This Is the Army, Mr. Jones
This Time
Ve Don't Like It
What Are We Gonna Do with All the Jeeps?
What Does He Look Like?
White Christmas
Who Do You Love, I Hope
With My Head in the Clouds
You Can't Get a Man with a Gun
You Keep Coming Back Like a Song
You're Easy to Dance With

1947–1951

The Best Thing for You
Better Luck Next Time
Business for a Good Girl Is Bad
Can You Use Any Money Today?
A Couple of Swells
Drum Crazy
Extra! Extra!
Falling Out of Love Can Be Fun
A Fella with an Umbrella
Follow the Leader Jig
Free
The Freedom Train
Give Me Your Tired, Your Poor *(Emma Lazarus)*
Happy Easter
Help Me to Help My Neighbor
Homework
The Honorable Profession of the Fourth Estate
The Hostess with the Mostes' on the Ball
I'd Like My Picture Took
I'm Beginning to Miss You
In Acapulco
It Only Happens When I Dance with You
It's a Lovely Day Today
Just One Way to Say I Love You
Kate
Let's Take an Old Fashioned Walk
Lichtenburg
Little Fish in a Big Pond
Love and the Weather
A Man Chases a Girl
Marrying for Love
Me An' My Bundle
Miss Liberty
The Most Expensive Statue in the World

Mr. Monotony
Mrs. Sally Adams
The Ocarina
Once Upon a Time Today
Only for Americans
Our Day of Independence
Paris Wakes Up and Smiles
The Policemen's Ball
The Pulitzer Prize
Sing a Song of Sing Sing
Something to Dance About
Steppin' Out with My Baby
The Train
They Like Ike
Washington Square Dance
What Can You Do with a General?
What Do I Have to Do to Get My Picture in the Paper?
You Can Have Him
You're Just in Love

1952–1956

Aesop, that Able Fable Man
Anybody Can Write
The Best Things Happen While You're Dancing
Choreography
Count Your Blessings Instead of Sheep
For the Very First Time
Gee, I Wish I Was Back in the Army
I Like Ike
I'm Not Afraid
I Never Want to See You Again
Ike for Four More Years
I Still Like Ike
It Takes More than Love to Keep a Lady Warm
Klondike Kate
Love Leads to Marriage
Love, You Didn't Do Right by Me
The Old Man
The Most
Opening the Mizner Story
Out of the This World, Into My Arms
Please Let Me Come Back to You
A Sailor's Not a Sailor
Sisters
Sittin' in the Sun
Smiling Geisha
Snow
When a One-Star General's Daughter Meets a Four-Star General's Son
When It's Peach Blossom Time in Lichtenburg
You're a Sentimental Guy
You're a Sucker for a Dame

1957–1961

I Keep Running Away from You
I'll Know Better the Next Time
Irving Berlin Barrett
Israel
Sam, Sam, the Man What Am
Sayonara
Silver Platter
Song for Elizabeth Esther Barrett
When Love Was All
You Can't Lose the Blues with Colors

1962–1966

Don't Be Afraid of Romance
Empty Pockets Filled with Love
The First Lady
Glad to be Home
A Guy on Monday
I'm Gonna Get Him
In Our Hide-Away
Is He the Only Man in the World?
It Gets Lonely in the White House
It's Always the Same
I Used to Play by Ear
I've Got to Be Around
Laugh It Up
Let's Go Back to the Waltz
Long As I Can Take You Home
A Man to Cook For

Meat and Potatoes
Mr. President
An Old Fashioned Wedding
Once Every Four Years
A One-Man Woman
Outside of Loving You, I Like You
Pigtails and Freckles
Poor Joe
The P.X.
The Secret Service
Song for Belly Dancer
The Ten Best Undressed Women in the World
They Love Me
This Is a Great Country
Wait Until You're Married
The Washington Twist
Whisper It
Who Needs the Birds and the Bees?
You Need a Hobby

SCORES PRINCIPALLY BY IRVING BERLIN

Dates for each show's opening follow the title.

STAGE

Watch Your Step
December 8, 1914
Stop! Look! Listen!
December 25, 1915
The Century Girl (with Victor Herbert)
November 6, 1916
Yip! Yip! Yaphank
August 19, 1918
Ziegfeld Follies
June 16, 1919
Music Box Revue
September 22, 1921
Music Box Revue
October 23, 1922
Music Box Revue
September 22, 1923
Music Box Revue
December 1, 1924
The Cocoanuts
December 8, 1925
Face the Music
February 17, 1932
As Thousands Cheer
September 30, 1933
Louisiana Purchase
May 28, 1940
This Is the Army
July 4, 1942
Annie Get Your Gun
May 16, 1946
Miss Liberty
July 15, 1949
Call Me Madam
October 12, 1950
Mr. President
October 20, 1962

FILMS

Puttin' on the Ritz 1929
The Cocoanuts 1929
Top Hat 1935
Follow the Fleet 1936
On the Avenue 1937
Carefree 1938
Alexander's Ragtime Band 1938
Second Fiddle 1939

Holiday Inn 1942
This Is the Army 1943
Blue Skies 1946
Easter Parade 1948
Annie Get Your Gun 1950
Call Me Madam 1953
White Christmas 1954
There's No Business Like Show Business 1954

Select Bibliography

■

ABBOTT, GEORGE. *Mister Abbott.* New York: Random House, 1963.

ADAMS, FRANKLIN P. *The Diary of Our Own Samuel Pepys.* New York: Simon & Schuster, 1935 (2 volumes).

ADAMS, SAMUEL HOPKINS. *Alexander Woollcott.* New York: Reynal & Hitchcock, 1945.

ATKINSON, BROOKS. *Broadway.* New York: Macmillan, 1970.

BALLIET, WHITNEY. *Alec Wilder and His Friends.* Boston: Houghton Mifflin, 1974.

BERLIN, EDWARD A. *Reflections and Research on Ragtime.* Brooklyn, N.Y.: Institute for Studies in American Music, 1987.

BERLIN, ELLIN. *Lace Curtain.* Garden City, N.Y.: Doubleday, 1948.

———. *Land I Have Chosen.* Garden City, N.Y.: Doubleday, 1944.

———. *Silver Platter.* Garden City, N.Y.: Doubleday, 1957.

BLESH, RUDI. *They All Played Ragtime.* New York: Alfred A. Knopf, 1950.

BORDMAN, GERALD. *American Musical Theatre: A Chronicle*, expanded ed. New York: Oxford University Press, 1986.

———. *Jerome Kern.* New York: Oxford University Press, 1980.

BROWNLOW, KEVIN. *The Parade's Gone By . . . .* New York: Ballantine Books, 1969.

CAREY, GARY. *Anita Loos.* New York: Alfred A. Knopf, 1988.

CASTLE, IRENE. *My Husband.* New York: Charles Scribner's Sons, 1919.

CASTLE, VERNON and IRENE. *Modern Dancing by Mr. and Mrs. Vernon Castle.* New York: Harper, 1914.

CHASE, GILBERT. *America's Music from the Pilgrims to the Present.* New York: McGraw-Hill, 1966.

CHASE, ILKA. *Past Imperfect.* Garden City, N.Y.: Doubleday, 1942.

COHAN, GEORGE. *Twenty Years on Broadway.* New York: Harper & Brothers, 1924.

COLLIER, PETER, and DAVID HOROWITZ. *The Kennedys.* New York: Summit Books, 1984.

DOS PASSOS, JOHN. *The Big Money.* New York: NAL Books, 1969. (Originally published 1936.)

EDWARDS, ANNE. *Early Reagan.* New York: Morrow, 1987.

EPHRON, HENRY. *We Thought We Could Do Anything.* New York: W. W. Norton, 1977.

ERENBERG, LEWIS A. *Steppin' Out.* Westport, Conn.: Greenwood Press, 1981.

FERBER, EDNA. *A Peculiar Treasure.* New York: Doubleday, 1939.

FINE, JO RENEE. *The Synagogues of New York's Lower East Side.* New York: New York University Press, 1978.

FORDIN, HUGH. *The World of Entertainment.* Garden City, N.Y.: Doubleday, 1975.

FRANK, GEROLD. *Judy.* New York: Harper & Row, 1975.

FREEDLAND, MICHAEL. *Irving Berlin.* New York: Stein & Day, 1974.

———. *A Salute to Irving Berlin.* London: W. H. Allen, 1986.

———. *Jerome Kern.* New York: Stein & Day, 1981.

GAIGE, CROSBY. *Footlights and Highlights.* New York: E. P. Dutton, 1948.

GARDINER, JAMES. *Gaby Deslys.* London: Sidgwick & Jackson, 1986.

GOLD, MICHAEL. *Jews Without Money.* New York: Horace Liveright, 1930.

GOLDBERG, ISAAC. *Tin Pan Alley.* New York: John Day, 1930.

GOLDSMITH, BARBARA. *Little Gloria . . . Happy at Last.* New York: Alfred A. Knopf, 1980.

GREEN, STANLEY. *The World of Musical Comedy*, rev. ed. Cranbury, N.J.: A. S. Barnes, 1968.

GUILES, FRED LAWRENCE. *Marion Davies.* New York: McGraw-Hill, 1972.

HAMM, CHARLES. *Yesterdays.* New York: Norton, 1979.

HART, MOSS. *Act One.* New York: Random House, 1959.

HASSE, JOHN EDWARD, ed. *Ragtime.* New York: Schirmir Books, 1985.

HEMSTREET, CHARLES. *Nooks and Corners of the Old New York.* New York: Charles Scribner's Sons, 1899.

HIGHAM, CHARLES. *Ziegfeld.* Chicago: Henry Regnery, 1972.

HINDUS, MILTON. *The Old East Side.* Philadelphia: Jewish Publication Society of America, 1969.

HOYT, EDWIN P. *Alexander Woollcott.* New York: Abelard-Schuman, 1968.

HOWE, IRVING. *World of Our Fathers.* New York: Harcourt Brace & Jovanovich, 1976.

JABLONSKI, EDWARD. *Gershwin.* Garden City, N.Y.: Doubleday, 1987.

JANIS, ELSIE. *So Far, So Good.* New York: E. P. Dutton, 1932.

JASEN, DAVID. *Tin Pan Alley.* New York: Donald I. Fine, 1988.

KAHN, E. J., JR. *The World of Swope.* New York: Simon & Schuster, 1965.

KANTER, KENNETH AARON. *The Jews on Tin Pan Alley.* New York: Ktav Publishing House, 1982.

KAUFMAN, BEATRICE, and JOSEPH HENNESSEY, eds. *The Letters of Alexander Woollcott.* New York: Viking, 1944.

KREUGER, MILES. *Show Boat.* New York: Oxford University Press, 1977.

LANDMAN, LEO. *The Cantor.* New York: Yeshiva University Press, 1972.

LEWIS, OSCAR. *The Silver Kings.* New York: Alfred A. Knopf, 1947.

LOGAN, JOSHUA. *Josh.* New York: Delacorte Press, 1976.

LOOS, ANITA. *The Talmadge Girls.* New York: Viking, 1978.

MARKS, EDWARD B. *They All Sang.* New York: Viking, 1935.

MAST, GERALD. *Can't Help Singing.* Woodstock, N.Y.: The Overlook Press, 1987.

MCCABE, JOHN. *George M. Cohan.* Garden City, N.Y.: Doubleday, 1973.

MEADE, MARION. *Dorothy Parker.* New York: Villard Books, 1987.

MEREDITH, SCOTT. *George S. Kaufman and His Friends.* Garden City, N.Y.: Doubleday, 1974.

MERMAN, ETHEL, with GEORGE EELLS. *Merman: An Autobiography.* New York: Simon and Schuster, 1978.

MEYER, HAZEL. *The Gold in Tin Pan Alley.* Philadelphia: J. B. Lippincott, 1958.

MOORE, GRACE. *You're Only Human Once.* Garden City, N.Y.: Doubleday, 1944.

MOTTO, VINCE. *The Irving Berlin Catalogue.* Quicksburg, Va.: The Sheet Music Exchange, 1988.

REAGAN, RONALD, and RICHARD G. HUBLER. *Where's the Rest of Me?* New York: Karz Publishers, 1981. (Originally published 1965.)

RISCHIN, MOSES. *The Promised City.* Cambridge, Mass.: Harvard University Press, 1962.

RIIS, JACOB. *How the Other Half Lives.* Cambridge, Mass.: Harvard University Press, 1970. (Originally published 1890.)

———. *The Children of the Poor.* New York: Johnson Reprint Corporation, 1970. (Originally published 1892.)

ROSKOLENKO, HARRY. *When I Was Last on Cherry Street.* New York: Stein & Day, 1965.

SANJEK, RUSSELL. *American Popular Music and Its Business,* vol. 3. New York: Oxford University Press, 1988.

SCHICKEL, RICHARD. *D. W. Griffith.* New York: Simon & Schuster, 1984.

SCHWARTZ, CHARLES. *Cole Porter.* New York: Dial Press, 1977.

SELDES, GILBERT. *The Seven Lively Arts.* New York: Harper & Brothers, 1924.

SHEAFFER, LOUIS. *O'Neill: Son and Artist.* Boston: Little, Brown, 1968.

The Songs of Irving Berlin. New York: Irving Berlin Music Corp., n.d.

SPAETH, SIGMUND. *The Facts of Life in Popular Song.* New York: Whittlesey House, 1934.

———. *A History of Popular Music in America.* New York: Random House, 1948.

SMITH, HARRY B. *First Nights and First Editions.* Boston: Little, Brown, 1931.

SWANBERG, W. A. *Citizen Hearst.* New York: Collier Books, 1961.

TALESE, GAY. *The Kingdom and the Power.* Garden City: Doubleday, 1978.

TEICHMANN, HOWARD. *George S. Kaufman.* New York: Atheneum: 1972.

———. *Smart Aleck.* New York: Morrow, 1976.

THOMAS, BOB. *Astaire.* New York: St. Martin's Press, 1984.

———. *I Got Rhythm! The Ethel Merman Story.* New York: Putnam, 1985.

TWAIN, MARK. *Roughing It.* New York: New American Library, 1962.

VALLÉE, RUDY. *Let the Chips Fall . . . .* Harrisburg, Pa.: Stackpole Books, 1975.

WHITCOMB, IAN. *After the Ball.* New York: Simon & Schuster, 1973.

———. *Irving Berlin and Ragtime America.* London: Century Hutchinson, 1987.

WILDER, ALEC. *American Popular Song.* Edited and with an Introduction by James T. Maher. New York: Oxford University Press, 1972.

WILK, MAX. *They're Playing Our Song.* New York: Atheneum, 1973.

WODEHOUSE, P. G., and GUY BOLTON. *Bring on the Girls!* New York: Simon & Schuster, 1953.

WOOLLCOTT, ALEXANDER. *The Story of Irving Berlin.* New York: G. P. Putnam's Sons, 1925.

Notes on Sources

Abbreviations for archives and frequently cited sources:

PUBLICATIONS:

EB Edward A. Berlin, *Reflections and Research on Ragtime*
GB Gerald Bordman, *American Musical Theatre*
MF Michael Freedland, *Irving Berlin*
RS Russell Sanjek, *American Popular Music and Its Business*
IW Ian Whitcomb, *Irving Berlin and Ragtime America*
AW Alexander Woollcott, *The Story of Irving Berlin*

ARCHIVES:

BL Mackay Collection, Bryant Library, Roslyn, Long Island.
Columbia Columbia University Oral History Collection, New York.
Houghton Alexander Woollcott papers, Houghton Library, Harvard University, Cambridge, Mass.
LCL Performing Arts Research Center, The New York Public Library at Lincoln Center, New York.
NYPL Microforms Division, New York Public Library.
Shubert Shubert Archives, New York.
Time Inc. Time Inc. archives, New York.
USC Archives of Performing Arts, University of Southern California, Los Angeles.

CHAPTER 1: **Lost Souls**

3 SS *Rhynland: New York Times*, September 14, 1893; Customs List of Steerage Passengers aboard the *Rhynland*, *ZI-131, Rolls #618, #1433, *NYPL.* (Hereafter referred to as "Customs list.")

3 cheapest passage: Howe, *World of Our Fathers*, p. 39.

4 Ellis Island: *ibid.*, p. 43 (note); *MF*, pp. 6–7.

4 family of Moses Beilin: Customs list.

4 photograph of Moses: reproduced in Ellin Berlin, *Silver Platter.*

5 September 14: *ibid.*

5 "We spoke only Yiddish": Kanter, *The Jews on Tin Pan Alley*, p. 134.

5 adopt American ways: Riis, *How the Other Half Lives*, p. 97.

6 "lost souls": Howe, *World of Our Fathers*, p. 77.

6 Monroe Street: *AW*, p. 10.

6 "a gray stone world": quoted in Howe, *World of Our Fathers*, p. 72.

7 "great prisonlike structures": quoted in Rischin, *The Promised City*, pp. 82–83.

7 "The story of inhuman packing": Riis, *The Children of the Poor*, p. 36.

7 330 Cherry Street: *New York Sun*, February 24, 1947; *AW*, *passim.*

7 Cherry Street was so disreputable: Riis, *How the Other Half Lives*, p. 32.

8 Number 1 Cherry: Hemstreet, *Nooks and Corners of Old New York*, p. 51; Roskolenko, *Last Time I Was on Cherry Street*, p. 242.

8 "pigsty reaching up": *ibid.*, p. 243.

8 "You never miss": quoted in *IW*, p. 21.

9 Under his reign: Howe, *World of Our Fathers*, p. 7.

9 Moses had been born: 1900 U.S. Census, *ZI-263, Roll #1084, taken June 5, 1900, *NYPL.* (Hereafter referred to as "1900 Census.")

9 Mohilev: Berlin gives Mohilev as his place of birth on each of three documents he signed under oath to obtain his immigration and naturalization papers. 1) Declaration of Intention, September 23, 1915, Supreme Court, New York County, #118640. 2) Petition for Naturalization, October 15, 1917, #71726. 3) Oath of Allegiance, February 6, 1918, #118640. All the above from Old Records Division, Manhattan County Clerk's Office. He also gives Mohilev as his birthplace on his marriage license, January 4, 1926, Office Record #246.

10 As a *chazzan:* Landman, *The Cantor*, pp. 83–93.

10 Moses' grandfather: *AW*, p. 13.

10 He was lying on a blanket: *ibid.*, p. 9.

10 part-time *shomer: MF*, p. 10.

11 Three of the daughters: 1900 Census.

11 Izzy worked: *AW*, pp. 3–5.

11 "I used to go there": *New York Sun*, February 24, 1947.

11 deposit the coins: *AW*, p. 18.

12 "He just dreams": *MF*, p. 12.

12 "I suppose it was singing": *ibid.*, p. 13.

12 "I did not have": *Saturday Evening Post*, January 14, 1944.

13 In September 1900: Death certificate of Moses Baline, Manhattan, Cert. #22124.

13 "of chronic bronchitis": *ibid.*

CHAPTER 2: **Prince and Pauper**

14 "he contributed less": *AW*, p. 21.

15 lodging houses: Riis, *How the Other Half Lives*, pp. 59, 134; *AW*, p. 23.

15 Fifteen cents: *AW*, p. 30; *New York Sun*, February 24, 1947.

15 "You got a cubby-hole": *ibid.*

15 When he signed: *AW*, p. 24.

16 Occasionally a neighbor: *ibid.*, pp. 21–22.

16 range of saloons: *ibid.*, p. 29; *New York Sun*, February 24, 1947.

17 "A terrible joint": *New York Sun*, February 24, 1947.

17 57 Bowery: *ibid.*

17 "The bums and riffraff": *ibid.*

18 1902 season: *GB*, p. 183.

18 "boomer": *AW*, p. 25; Whitcomb, *After the Ball*, p. 48.

18 Harry Von Tilzer: *IW*, p. 62; *AW*, p. 25; Hamm, *Yesterdays*, p. 308.

19 "Alexander (Don't You Love Your Baby No More?)": *IW*, p. 62.

19 The offices: *EB*, pp. 44–46; Hamm, *Yesterdays*, p. 285.

19 Tony Pastor's famous music hall: *AW*, p. 25; Marks, *They All Sang*, p. 12; *MF*, p. 20.

19 Izzy's job: *AW*, pp. 25–26.

20 Chuck Connors: *IW*, p. 25; *AW*, pp. 28–29.

20 "There are houses": Riis, *How the Other Half Lives*, p. 65.

20 Olliffe's Drugstore: *AW*, pp. 178–179; *New York Sun*, February 25, 1947.

20 Blind Sol: *MF*, p. 18; *AW*, pp. 29–30.

21 The Pelham Café: *IW*, pp. 26–27; *AW*, pp. 40–48; *EB*, p. 42.

22 Chinatown Gertie: *AW*, pp. 54–55.

22 Sulky: *AW*, p. 49.

22 Lukie Johnson: *EB*, p. 42.

22 blue parodies: *Variety*, December 25, 1914.

23 Olliffe's: *AW*, p. 180.

23 seven dollars: *New York Sun*, February 24, 1947.

23 Schenck was studying: *New York Evening Journal*, April 4, 1914.

23 "Now a singing waiter": quoted in *IW*, p. 28.

23 "sort of took": *ibid.*

24 "captured New York": *New York World*, November 20, 1905; *AW*, p. 51.

24 "rough tweed suit": *New York World*, November 19, 1905.

24 "Prince, you can do": *New York World*, November 20, 1905.

25 "two waiters": *ibid.*

25 Herbert Bayard Swope: Kahn, *The World of Swope*, pp. 110–112; *AW*, pp. 51–52.

26 One evening Casey picked a fight: *AW*, pp. 55–57.

26 "Once you start": *MF*, p. 27.

26 attracting still more publicity: Singing waiters were a standard feature in Chinatown and other areas of New York that catered to the tourist trade. Another singing waiter, Isidore Itzkowitz, who was four years younger than Israel Baline, won an amateur contest at a Bowery theater and launched himself in vaudeville under the name Eddie Cantor.

27 "Marie from Sunny Italy": *AW*, pp. 66–68; *New Yorker*, February 12, 1944; *New York Daily News*, September 7, 1947; *New York Sun*, February 24, 1947; *MF*, pp. 28–30.

27 Izzy's share: *IW*, p. 31.

28 "It went": *New York World Telegram*, February 29, 1936.

28 Izzy and Winslow: *AW*, p. 129; *Variety*, December 25, 1914.

29 diamond pinky ring: *MF*, p. 30.

29 Bullhead Lawrence removed: *ibid; IW*, p. 31; *New York Sun*, February 24, 1947.

CHAPTER 3: **Tin Pan Alley**

30 Jimmy Kelly: *New York Sun*, February 24, 1947; *AW*, p. 64; *Variety*, December 25, 1914.

30 "The headquarters": *New York Sun*, February 24, 1947.

31 "Queenie, My Own": *IW*, p. 32; *MF*, p. 31.

31 The Boys and Betty: GB, p. 246.

32 "Winslow's Singles": *RS*, p. 36.

32 Edgar Leslie: Author's interviews with Ian Whitcomb.

33 Seminary Music Company: *IW*, p. 33.

33 Henry Waterson: *ibid; New York Times*, August 11, 1933; Author's interview with Al Brackman.

33 The younger man, Snyder: Jasen, *Tin Pan Alley*, p. 33.

34 Dorando: *AW*, p. 72; Wilk, *They're Playing Our Song*, p. 268; *IW*, p. 35.

34 Amy Butler: Jasen, *Tin Pan Alley*, p. 33.

34 "Just you trot": *AW*, p. 72.

35 "We did it to see": *IW*, p. 37.

35 Instead, Berlin proposed: *AW*, p. 73.

36 Stephen Foster: Whitcomb, *After the Ball*, p. 306.

36 "It's hard": *IW*, p. 52.

36 "world famous 'Sweet Adeline' ": Whitcomb, *After the Ball*, p. 47.

36 Temperance: *New York Times*, February 21, 1988.

37 "After the Ball": Whitcomb, *After the Ball*, pp. 3–4.

37 F. W. Woolworth chain: *RS*, p. 34. Occasional price wars drove down the cost even further. In 1907, a department store in New York cut the price of sheet music to a penny but sold 20,000 copies in just two hours.

38 I have heard it: *Green Book Magazine*, February 1915.

39 "When writing popular songs": quoted in Hamm, *Yesterdays*, p. 290.

39 Then Stephen Foster popularized: Wilder, *American Popular Song*, pp. 3–6; Mast, *Can't Help Singin'*, pp. 26–30; *GB*, p. 13.

41 hanging his portrait: Whitcomb, *After the Ball*, p. 306.

41 "You've got to have": Reminiscences of Cary Morgan, *Columbia*.

41 "The best songs": Marks, *They All Sang*, p. 3.

42 Three or four pianos: Quoted in Hamm, *Yesterdays*, p. 289.

42 Monroe Rosenfeld: Jasen, *Tin Pan Alley*, p. 16; *IW*, pp. 60–61; Whitcomb, *After the Ball*, p. 44.

43 "One night, in a barber shop": quoted in *IW*, pp. 66–67; *AW*, p. 81.

44 WEATHER NOTES: quoted in *IW*, p. 65.

44 In an impressive display: *ibid.*, p. 67.

45 "Song writing all depends": *New York World*, July 10, 1910.

45 "My Blue Heaven": *IW*, p. 68.

45 "Night after night": *Vancouver World*, May 1912.

45 It sold even more copies: *New York World*, July 10, 1910.

46 "Of course sentimental ballads": *New York World*, July 10, 1910.

48 "When you're a singer": BBC interview with Irving Berlin, September 25, 1963. (Hereafter referred to as "BBC interview.")

CHAPTER 4: **Reinventing Ragtime**

49 Shubert brothers: *GB*, p. 208; *MF*, 38; *Shubert*.

50 "quite tedious": Talese, *The Kingdom and the Power*, p. 439.

50 Seeking a spot: *AW*, p. 83.

51 Fanny Brice: *GB*, p. 257.

51 The Girl and the Wizard: GB, pp. 250–251.

52 On January 6, 1910: *GB*, pp. 254–255.

52 Thus the 600,000 copies: *Vancouver World*, May 1912.

52 The Man Who: *New York World*, July 10, 1910.

53 Berlin and Snyder sang: *GB*, pp. 257–258; *AW*, p. 84.

54 In October 1910 he accompanied his boss: *IW*, pp. 72–73.

56 Montgomery and Stone: Whitcomb interviews.

56 "nigger keys": Author's interviews with Helmy Kresa.

57 "The key of C": Interview with Irving Berlin, WBAL radio, November 7, 1962. (Hereafter referred to as "WBAL interview.") The author wishes to thank Stanley Green for providing a transcript.

57 "transposing piano": *AW*, p. 35; Jack Hirshberg's interview with Irving Berlin, 1954. (Hereafter referred to as "Hirshberg interview.") The author wishes to thank Mr. Hirshberg for making this material available.

57 "I get an idea": *Green Book Magazine*, February 1915.

58 "I know rhythm": *ibid.*

58 "I am working": *ibid.*

58 "There is the fellow": WBAL interview.

59 Ben Harney: *EB*, p. 31; *GB*, p. 297.

60 "Syncopation is the soul": *Theatre Magazine*, January 1916.

60 "Short choruses": *Green Book Magazine*, February 1915.

61 Folies Bergère: AW, p. 89.

61 "You think it's good?": *MF*, pp. 42–43.

61 Florenz Ziegfeld: *GB*, pp. 146–147; Higham, *Ziegfeld, passim;* Smith, *First Nights and First Editions*, pp. 241–242.

62 "Mr. Ziegfeld was not especially enthusiastic": Smith, *First Nights and First Editions*, p. 241.

64 He was also superstitious: *GB*, p. 231.

64 "He treated Berlin": Author's interview with Goldie Clough.

65 "He's laying": *ibid.*

65 "A skinny little guy": *ibid.*

65 "It was built": WBAL interview.

65 Writing both words and music: *Green Book Magazine*, February 1915.

66 He persuaded Snyder: *Variety*, December 25, 1914.

67 Emma Carus: *IW*, p. 79.

67 "in only a mild": *Green Book Magazine*, February 1915.

68 "The reason our American composers": *Theatre Magazine*, February 1915.

68 "the musical sensation": quoted in *IW*, p. 79.

68 And I got an answer: quoted in *Stereo Review*, February 1988.

69 "Songwriters don't steal": *Green Book Magazine*, April 1916.

70 Lukie Johnson: *EB*, p. 42.

70 "You know": *IW*, p. 75.

70 dictionary definition: *The Random House Dictionary of the English Language*. (New York: Random House, 1969) p. 1187.

CHAPTER 5: **Love and Death**

72 Broadway chronicler Rennold Wolf: *AW*, p. 94.

72 "Jew boy": *ibid.*, p. 95.

73 "Mr. Berlin's 'Friar-speech' ": *Variety*, December 25, 1914.

73 latest dance steps: *IW*, p. 170.

74 Outside the theater: *AW*, p. 92.

74 "To see this slim little kid": *Variety*, September 16, 1911.

75 Gee, Izzy": *AW*, p. 93.

75 834 Beck Street: Death Certificate of Lena Berlin, July 21, 1922, Bronx, N.Y. #4716. Department of Health of the City of New York, Bureau of Records.

75 "I want you to come": *MF*, pp. 49–50.

76 216 West 112th Street: Application of Irving Baline [sic] . . . to assume the name of Irving Berlin, Old Records Division, Manhattan County Clerk's Office, November 21, 1911. #5084. (Hereafter referred to as "Name application.")

76 he petitioned the New York State Supreme Court: Name application.

76 "The musical compositions": *ibid.*

77 Waterson, Berlin & Snyder: Business Name Index, Old Records Division, New York County Clerk's Office.

77 "You know, Irvy": *IW*, p. 81.

77 he earned a share: *ibid.*, p. 80.

77 "If I loaf": *Vancouver World*, May 1912.

77 "long enough for me": *ibid.*

78 "I don't write church lyrics": *IW*, p. 140.

78 " 'ragged' more money": quoted in *Vancouver World*, May 1912.

78 exploit ragtime's popularity: "Alexander's Bag-Pipe Band" appeared in *Hokey-Pokey*, a revue mounted by the popular clowns, Weber and Fields. *GB*, p. 274.

78 "If I live long enough": quoted in Blesh, *They All Played Ragtime*, p. 72.

78 "I'm going to prove": *Theatre Magazine*, February 1915.

78 "A grand opera": *Theatre Magazine*, January 1916.

79 *The Sun Dodgers: GB*, p. 283.

79 "presentment condemning": *EB*, p. 66.

80 " 'Everybody's Doin' It' is an example": *Green Book Magazine*, February 1915.

80 "reckless and uncontrolled dances": *IW*, pp. 147, 168–169.

81 "She had hardly begun": *MF*, pp. 47–48.

82 Dorothy's father: Death Certificate of Dorothy Berlin. #21248, New York Department of Records and Information Services—Municipal Archives (hereafter referred to as "Death Certificate"); *New York Telegraph*, July 18, 1912; *Buffalo Morning Express*, July 20, 1912.

82 they were married: *Buffalo Morning Express*, July 20, 1912.

82 72nd Street and Riverside Drive: *New York Telegraph*, July 18, 1912.

83 "The doctors and the decorators": *AW*, p. 103.

83 Everybody is doing it": *New York Telegraph*, April 30, 1912.

83 Dr. L. Korff: Death Certificate.

83 At five o'clock: *Buffalo Morning Express*, July 20, 1912.

83 pawn ticket for jewelry: *MF*, p. 55.

86 London revue: *New York Telegraph*, September 12, 1912.

86 United Songwriters of America: Wilk, *They're Playing Our Song*, pp. 263–264.

86 Popular song *Green Book Magazine*, April 1916.

87 "under a nervous strain": *Green Book Magazine*, February 1915.

87 "in desperate need": *ibid.*

87 I liked its freakishness: *ibid.*

89 There is no doubt: *Times* (London), February 8, 1913.

89 500,000 copies in England: *IW*, p. 142.

89 press conference: *IW*, p. 166.

90 "I hum the songs": *Daily Express* (London), June 20, 1913.

90 £20,000 A YEAR: *ibid.*

91 "It is almost impossible": *ibid.*

91 "to announce": *Times* (London), July 8, 1913.

91 "I was foolish": *New York Herald Tribune*, February 23, 1932.

92 "The Swanky Yankee": *ibid.*

92 I discovered that all of my songs: *Green Book Magazine*, February 1915.

92 "I sweat blood": *Theatre Magazine*, February 1915.

93 "once they have seen": *Times* (London), July 8, 1913.

CHAPTER 6: **Broadway Bound**

98 James Reese Europe: *EB*, p. 63; *New York Times*, July 9, 1989; *RS*, pp. 25–26.

98 "There never was": *EB*, p. 61.

98 the Castles built an empire: *IW*, 170–172; *RS*, pp. 25–26; Erenberg, *Steppin' Out*, pp. 158–167.

100 "If Vernon ever looked": Erenberg, *Steppin' Out*, p. 166.

100 The Merry Widow: *GB*, pp. 236, 297.

100 Charles Dillingham: *GB*, p. 196.

101 Round the Clock: Smith, *First Nights and First Editions*, pp. 279–280.

101 "Book (if any)": *GB*, p. 303.

101 "It was the first time": *New York Herald Tribune*, May 16, 1948.

102 summer of 1914: *Variety*, December 25, 1914.

102 He is a genius: Smith, *First Nights and First Editions*, pp. 280–281.

103 Observing his show: Author's interview with Stanley Green.

103 "I went to church": Smith, *First Nights and First Editions*, p. 282.

104 "My songs were all ragtime": *New York Herald Tribune*, May 16, 1948.

104 "piano and ten": Marks, *They All Sang*, p. 174.

104 "In this way American": WBAL interview.

105 As the curtain rose: Script for *Watch Your Step* by Harry B. Smith in Theater Collection of the Museum of the City of New York; *GB*, p. 303.

107 This trick: Berlin's subtle musical message was, to judge from the reviews *Watch Your Step* received, largely lost on the audience, who accepted it as merely one more stunt, and coming after the spectular opera parody, it suffered by comparison. In fact, "Play a Simple Melody" was neglected for nearly fifty years, until Bing Crosby recorded a popular version with his son in 1950, and the song's place of honor in Berlin's catalogue was finally recognized. By then, *Watch Your Step* was all but forgotten, and the Castles were scarcely more than a brilliant memory.

107 "The musical part": *Saturday Review*, October 1, 1966.

108 "would probably not have believed": *Variety*, December 25, 1914.

108 "Seldom has a successful first night": *ibid.*

109 Thirty years later: Irving Berlin to George Frazier, December 16, 1942. *Time Inc.*

109 'WATCH YOUR STEP': *New York Times*, December 9, 1914.

110 "stands out like the Times building": quoted in *IW*, pp. 172–173. In contrast to *Variety*, *Billboard* emphasized Berlin's "Aladdin-like transition—from piano player in a Bowery dance hall to the authorship of Watch Your Step. . . . How forcefully are we reminded that this is a country of wondrous opportunities." The music trade publication predicted that Berlin would go on to even better things, "but the biggest night of his life would seem to be last Tuesday when his 'piece' swung into competition 'On Broadway.' " And yet *Billboard* struggled to place a label on exactly what Berlin had wrought: "musical melange," perhaps, or "vaudeville." As entertaining as his music was, "it is noticed that bits, snatches and excerpts have been made to form a melange of everything else he had done all rolled into the revisional and provisional score."

The Evening Sun expressed similar reservations in more serious tones, declaring that *Watch Your Step* "is ephemeral as art, but is permanent as a landmark." The *New York Clipper*, an influential theatrical weekly, made the most decisive reckoning; Berlin, it maintained, had succeeded "brilliantly," and "to name the tunes that achieved popularity would be to print the entire table of the musical numbers."

110 The only trick: *GB*, pp. 302–303.

110 175 performances: Following the practice of musical shows of the day, *Watch Your Step* was augmented by interpolations after it opened. Perhaps the most significant is "Lead Me to Love," which went into the show a month and a half later. Since the song was written with Ted Snyder, with whom Berlin had stopped collaborating by this time, it was, in all likelihood, a trunk song. Another late arrival was "I've Got to Go Back to Texas," a song Berlin did not bother to copyright until 1916. (James T. Maher to author.)

111 George Bernard Shaw: *MF*, p. 65.

111 "Reel" 1: Young Irving: *Music and Theatre Gossip*, February 1915.

CHAPTER 7: **The Great American Composer?**

114 Berlin accorded: Whitcomb interview.

114 Now Berlin discovered: Brackman interview.

115 he owned three shares: Old Records Division, New York County Clerks Office, File #05303–14C.

115 "I never had": *Theatre Magazine*, February 1915.

116 He purchased: *American Magazine*, December 1920.

116 "many thousands": *ibid.*

116 He invested: *ibid.*

116 "Many nights": Janis, *So Far, So Good!* p. 166.

116 "There was one song": *ibid.*

117 As much as she: *ibid.*, pp. 167–168.

117 On the evenings: *ibid.*

118 "The five most important": *Sunday News*, September 7, 1947.

118 "Oh, Mr. Berlin": *AW*, p. 151.

119 Berlin was so fond: *IW*, p. 177.

120 The song first occurred: *AW*, p. 100.

120 "There's a great idea": *MF*, p. 65.

120 When she introduced: *New York Times*, May 4, 1915.

120 The problem was: *Green Book Magazine*, April 1916. Berlin does not specifically name Jolson as a recipient of a fee in the passage describing (and lamenting) the practice, but elsewhere in the same article he lists the names of performers for whom "there's nothing much a publisher won[']t do," and the implication of a payoff is clear. The list includes: Eva Tanguay, Nora Bayes, Irene Franklin, Blanche Ring, Jolson, Kitty Gordon, Fritzy Scheff, Elizabeth Brice (who had appeared in *Watch*

Your Step), and Emma Carus, who had helped popularize "Alexander's Ragtime Band." Considering his familiarity with at least three of these performers, it can be assumed that Berlin spoke from personal knowledge.

121 The document had been: *AW*, p. 101; *IW*, pp. 177–178; *MF*, p. 65.

121 "Our popular song writers": *American Magazine*, December 1920.

121 "It's not a matter": *Theater Magazine*, January 1916.

122 The publisher sells: *Green Book Magazine*, April 1916.

123 This cutthroat competition: *ibid.*

123 "the amateur has no": *ibid.*

123 Fred and Adele Austerlitz: Thomas, *Astaire*, pp. 39–44.

124 The teenager's father: Jablonski, *Gershwin*, pp. 9–18.

125 "Not bad": *ibid.*, p. 16; *MF*, pp. 67–68.

126 "If the rights": *RS*, p. 39.

126 The year before: *MF*, p. 62.

127 "Every time I see": *New York Times*, May 11, 1958.

128 The following year: *IW*, p. 197.

128 "Popular songs reflect": Marks, *They All Sang*, p. 188.

129 He commenced: Old Records Division, New York County Clerk's Office, Volume 290, p. 176, February 6, 1918. #118640.

129 The beginning of 1916: Castle, *My Husband*, p. 66.

129 *Billboard* disclosed plans: *IW*, p. 179.

130 One of the actual: Gardiner, *Gaby Deslys*, p. 121.

131 "I can't go out": Guiles, *Marion Davies*, pp. 45–46.

131 Later, when she: Gardiner, *Gaby Deslys*, p. 121.

131 for the next forty-five: *IW*, p. 179.

131 "Contains a wealth": *New York Clipper*, January 1, 1916.

132 "There is no": *IW*, p. 180.

132 Initially, the show: Gardiner, *Gaby Deslys*, pp. 122–123. There is good reason to believe that *Stop! Look! Listen!* marked the beginning of the end of her career, if not her life. Gaby Deslys died only four years later, in 1920, of pneumonia, though there were persistent rumors that syphilis contributed to the decline of her health.

133 The famous theater: Mast, *Can't Help Singing*, p. 57.

134 Along Broadway: *New York Clipper*, November 8, 1916.

134 "Folks shook their heads": *New York Times*, November 7, 1916.

134 On being introduced: Clough interview.

135 "Victor was constantly": *ibid.*

135 "Victor, I'm a bit": *MF*, p. 69.

136 "I tried to learn": *New York Times*, October 14, 1962.

136 As the theater: Max Hoffman conducted subsequent performances.

137 Audiences beheld stars: *The Century Girl* program, Theater Collection, Museum of the City of New York; Higham, *Ziegfeld*, p. 118.

137 "garden of a": *ibid.*

137 "even down in": *New York Times*, November 7, 1916.

137 "The curse is off": *ibid.*

138 The centerpiece of the second: *ibid.*

138 "must be lopped": *ibid.*

139 " 'THE CENTURY GIRL' ": *New York Times*, November 7, 1916.

140 "part of his genius": Author's interview with Irving Caesar.

141 "Come around to the studio": *Liberty Magazine*, July 5, 1941.

142 "The Virtuous Vamp": Carey, *Anita Loos*, *passim*; Brownlow, *The Parade's Gone By . . .*, p. 549.

142 "I sometimes used": Loos, *The Talmadge Girls*, pp. 40–41.

143 Yet Dutch hesitated: *ibid.*, p. 41.

144 His first effort: *American Heritage*, August 1967.

145 "There is a gramophone": Castle, *My Husband*, pp. 65–66.

145 "THE GREAT AMERICAN COMPOSER": *Vanity Fair*, April 1917.

145 He signed on again: *GB*, p. 314.

146 The predictably slapdash: *GB*, p. 329; *New York Clipper*, January 9, 1918.

146 Vernon Castle became: Castle, *My Husband*, p. 3.

147 Living in obscurity: *EB*, p. 81.

147 Two years later: *New York Times*, July 9, 1989.

147 As early as January: *EB*, p. 28; *RS*, p. 29.

147 "Assassinators of Syncopation": *IW*, p. 200.

149 "I hereby declare": Old Records Division, New York County Clerk's Office, Volume 290, p. 176, February 6, 1918, Petition #717126, Certificate of Naturalization #835183.

149 "painful shock": *AW*, 113.

CHAPTER 8:
Sergeant Berlin

150 "I found out quickly": *American Heritage*, August 1967.

150 Once drafted: *AW*, p. 125.

152 "I really wasn't fitted": *AW*, pp. 114–115.

152 "Berlin gets into the Army": Wilk, *They're Playing Our Song*, p. 274.

152 "wanted to be a good soldier": *American Heritage*, August 1967.

152 "Well," said the officer: *AW*, pp. 118–119.

153 "There is a song": *Stereo Review*, February 1988.

154 "We want a new community": *MF*, pp. 72–73.

154 "the Navy did a show": *American Heritage*, August 1967.

154 "Here's the thing": Wilk, *They're Playing Our Song*, p. 275.

154 In May the Navy: *GB*, p. 333.

155 Once the extent: *MF*, p. 73–74.

155 "He'd come up to me": Wilk, *They're Playing Our Song*, p. 275.

156 "There were so many": *ibid.*

156 "Just a little sticky": *American Heritage*, August 1967.

156 She surprised everyone: Dutch soon divorced the tobacco importer and resumed acting, but her screen career ended with the silents in 1929. She married three more times and became an alcoholic. Meeting Berlin's former love object years later, Anita Loos found her a "lonely lost soul, too lacking in resources to function as a living woman."

157 They bivouacked at the 71st Regiment: *IW*, p. 198; *American Heritage*, August 1967.

158 "became a carefree mob": *Theatre Magazine*, October 1918.

158 "Of course there was": *ibid.*

159 "Every soldier in the audience": *ibid.*

160 "fairly stopped the proceedings": *ibid.*

160 The soldiers suddenly streamed: *American Heritage*, August 1967.

160 "I have heard": *Variety*, August 23, 1918.

161 "It may well be": *New York Times*, July 12, 1942.

161 "Yes," she answered: *MF*, p. 77.

161 'YIP! YIP! YAPHANK' MAKES ROUSING HIT: *New York Times*, August

20, 1918; *Brooklyn Eagle*, August 20, 1918.

162 On closing night: *IW*, p. 200.

163 "I'll give five hundred dollars": *MF*, p. 80.

163 Yet he did fear: *IW*, pp. 209–210; Whitcomb interview.

164 Since his last meeting with Berlin: Jablonski, *Gershwin*, pp. 35–36.

165 This time he turned: *New Yorker*, March 19, 1938.

165 As a first step: Old Records Division, New York County Clerk's Office, File #05303–14C, #04884–19C.

166 Each of the men: *RS*, p. 36.

166 "You no sooner step out": *AW*, pp. 160–161.

166 "Slim-waisted": *ibid.*

166 the only time he could tolerate: *New Yorker*, December 18, 1926. Johnston later became a successful Hollywood composer, known best for his association with Bing Crosby.

166 "Men who, when Berlin": *AW*, pp. 168–170.

167 "nine rules for writing": *American Magazine*, December 1920.

168 If he found a song wanting: Author's interviews with Mynna Granat.

170 "the best individual song": Irving Berlin to George Frazier, December 16, 1942. *Time Inc.*

170 "Nothing could be more commonplace": *American Magazine*, December 1920.

171 At the year's end: Hamm, *Yesterdays*, p. 336.

171 Other songs by Berlin: *New York Clipper*, June 18, 1919. Such was the show as it appeared on opening night, but no Ziegfeld *Follies* stayed still. Week by week, interpolations modified the performance, as the restless Ziegfeld battled to keep his show *au courant.*

171 "This edition of the 'Follies' ": *ibid.*

171 In 1917: *GB*, pp. 340–342.

172 "He doesn't love me": Higham, *Ziegfeld*, pp. 114, 138–141.

CHAPTER 9:
From the Music Box to the Round Table

175 His gambling instincts: Meredith, *George S. Kaufman and His Friends*, p. 270.

175 Cohan was married: *New York Journal*, July 2, 1932; *New York Post*, July 4, 1941; *New York Times*, July 4, 1941; *AW*, pp. 174–175.

176 "If you ever want to build": *AW*, p. 173. Woollcott casually assumes that "three or four years" passed between the time Berlin suggested the theater's title and Harris purchased the property on which it would be built, a chronology placing their first meeting in 1916. But Woollcott is extremely casual about dates, and it strains credulity that several years and a war intervened.

176 "That would be": *MF*, p. 89.

176 "Irving, you remember": *AW*, pp. 173–174. Fifty years after the fact, Berlin came up with a slightly different version of this incident. "I went up to Sam's office and he said, 'I bought 100 feet of the Astor property on 45th Street. You're my partner.' " (*New York Times*, September 23, 1971). Since Woollcott was on good terms with both Berlin and Harris and was writing soon after these events occurred, he may be considered a more reliable source in this instance. The papers of Sam Harris, which might have proved a useful resource, were destroyed after the producer's death. According to one archivist's recollection, they were unceremoniously dumped on the sidewalk.

177 Designed by C. Howard Crane: *Architectural Review*, February 1, 1922.

178 "It stinks from class": *New York Times*, September 23, 1971.

178 "Joe, I'm in trouble": *MF*, p. 90.

179 While Berlin fretted: *AW*, p. 181.

179 A breakdown of the revue's budget: *AW*, pp. 186–187.

180 The young man: *MF*, p. 91.

181 "What's that?" *AW*, pp. 182–183.

182 On September 22: *AW*, pp. 184–185; *New York Times*, September 23, 1971.

183 "How could it miss?": *New York Clipper*, September 28, 1921.

184 "The climax to this episode": *ibid.*

185 "We had a terrible time": WBAL interview.

185 The cost of keeping: The following is a tally of basic weekly expenses involved in running the Music Box. (*AW*, p. 187)

Theater staff salaries	$2,279.10
Company salaries	10,225.60
Trade bills	1,311.81
Rent	2,000.00
Orchestra salaries	1,541.86
Royalties	1,378.12
Wardrobe	291.56
Miscellaneous	128.97

185 DAINTY PLAYHOUSETTE: *New York Herald*, September 24, 1921.

186 "The Music Box was opened" *New York Times*, September 23, 1921.

186 "[Berlin] has written": *ibid.*

186 The revue ran: *AW*, p. 187.

187 Whenever the opening: *ibid.*, p. 207.

187 He moved downtown: 1925 New York State Census, New York County Clerk's Office.

188 There was a broad corridor: Wodehouse and Bolton, *Bring on the Girls!* p. 179.

189 "which immediately proceeded to strike": *ibid.* pp. 168–181.

190 It was true that he earned: *AW*, p. 147.

190 The show eventually opened: *GB*, p. 385.

190 "JAZZ GRAND OPERA": *New York Sun*, February 17, 1922.

192 "Their standards were high": Ferber, *A Peculiar Treasure*, pp. 292–293.

192 Shortly after joining: *GB*, p. 368.

193 "Well, for five hundred": Meade, *Dorothy Parker*, p. 95.

193 Since then, Swope: Kahn, *The World of Swope, passim.*

194 The best-known chronicler: Teichmann, *George S. Kaufman*, pp. 290–291.

195 "Beautiful, grave": Hoyt, *Alexander Woollcott*, p. 160.

195 "A bleak, high-ceilinged room": *ibid.*

195 "While we all sat": Wilk, *They're Playing Our Song*, p. 279.

196 The Round Table rallied: *AW*, pp. 82–83.

197 He coined two nicknames: For instance, see the letter Woollcott wrote to Round Table member Edna Ferber in *The Letters of Alexander Woollcott*, p. 76.

197 "transmuted into music": *ibid.*, pp. 6–7.

198 "It is hard to write": *AW*, p. 222.

200 In mid-July: Death Certificate of Lena Berlin, July 21, 1922, Bronx, N.Y. #4716. Department of Health of the City of New York, Bureau of Records. Her husband Moses was originally buried elsewhere in Washington Cemetery, and on June 17, 1924, he was moved to the Baline family plot. The Death Certificate gives her last name as "Berlin" rather than "Baline," suggesting that she, too, had changed her name.

201 At daybreak that day: *AW*, p. 154.

201 This development was driven home: *ibid.*, p. 149.

202 During its fifty weeks: *ibid.*, p. 147.

202 "Jimmy, can you give": Author's interview with Gerald Marx.

203 "Pack Up Your Sins": *GB*, pp. 374–375.

203 "For a time last night": *New York Herald*, October 24, 1922.

204 Reginald Vanderbilt: Goldsmith, *Little Gloria . . . Happy at Last*, p. 93.

204 "I pretty near": Dos Passos, *The Big Money*, p. 347.

205 "The funeral was": *AW*, pp. 58–61.

CHAPTER 10: **Mackay's Millions**

209 "took a good cagey look": Moore, *You're Only Human Once*, p. 81.

209 "My friends": *ibid.*

210 "Satie was old": Gaige, *Footlights and Highlights*, p. 186. Gaige places this encounter in 1922, but internal evidence suggests that it actually took place two years later.

210 For months he had been pursuing: Meade, *Dorothy Parker*, p. 120.

211 "Nothing could be more": *AW*, pp. 204–206.

211 A little man: *ibid.*

211 "Maid of Mesh": *GB*, p. 381.

212 "The drawstring that pulled": Moore, *You're Only Human Once*, p. 82.

212 Grace and John Steel: *GB*, p. 381.

212 "so overcome with emotion": *ibid.*, p. 84.

212 "This revue distinctly lacks": *New York World*, September 24, 1923.

212 "Hats were thrown": quoted in Moore, *You're Only Human Once*, p. 82.

213 "I broke down": Moore, *You're Only Human Once*, p. 82.

213 "I knew the": *ibid.*, p. 84.

213 "The curtain had": *ibid.*, p. 85.

213 "Why, Grace": *ibid.*

214 Worn and harried: Meade, *Dorothy Parker*, p. 122.

215 Times had changed: *Time Inc.*

217 She later confessed: *New York Post*, April 10, 1975.

218 "WHY WE GO TO CABARETS": *New Yorker*, November 28 and December 12, 1925.

218 Our Elders criticize: *ibid.*

219 "What is your opinion": Gaige, *Footlights and Highlights*, pp. 185–186.

220 To publicize their cause: *MF*, pp. 98–99.

221 Swope and his *World:* Kahn, *The World of Swope*, pp. 284–287.

222 "whose story," he wrote: Kaufman, ed., *The Letters of Alexander Woollcott*, p. 77.

222 I replied that the average: *AW*, pp. 214–216.

224 Grace Moore was back: Moore, *You're Only Human Once*, p. 97; *GB*, p. 397.

224 "IRVING BERLIN OUTDOES HIMSELF": *New York World*, December 2, 1924.

224 Nearby, at the Liberty: *GB*, pp. 395–397; Jablonski, *Gershwin*, pp. 182–187.

225 He tried to persuade: Moore, *You're Only Human Once*, p. 100. She eventually did make a success of her operatic career but died in a plane crash in 1947.

225 Not for seven years: Other productions that opened at the Music Box during this interlude included: *Chicago*, December 30, 1926; *Paris Bound*, December 27, 1927; *The Little Show*, April 30, 1929; *Topaze*, February 12, 1930; *Once in a Lifetime*, September 24, 1930; and, most notably, *Of Thee I Sing*, George Gershwin's Pulitzer Prize-winning musical.

226 "It is hard to begin": Ellin Berlin, *Silver Platter*, p. 12.

226 a frail octogenarian: *ibid.*, p. 14.

226 "Did you remember": *ibid.*

226 The lavish party: *ibid.*, pp. 441–443.

227 "In the song I tried": *New York Telegraph*, December 27, 1925.

228 "During the Spring": *ibid.*

228 "As for 'Remember' ": *ibid.*

228 "Just because a man": *MF*, p. 105.

229 The founder of the Mackay dynasty: Lewis, *Silver Kings*, pp. 65–70.

230 "The first twenty-six": Twain, *Roughing It*, p. 255.

230 "That's as close": Lewis, *Silver Kings*, p. 23.

230 "No, I won't trade": *ibid.*, p. 69.

231 In 1866 Mrs. Fair: *ibid.*, pp. 47–57, 73–80.

232 "Very well, I'll buy": *ibid.*, p. 88.

233 "The picture is": *ibid.*, p. 94–95.

234 "race of death": *ibid.*, p. 99.

234 "There's no beating": *ibid.*, p. 107.

235 Much information about the Mackay estate has been drawn from unpublished descriptive material in the Mackay family collection of the Long Island Historical Society.

235 As a novelty: Author's interview with Evelyn Haynes.

236 His inflexible personal prejudices: Mackay Collection, *BL.*

237 On another occasion: *ibid.*

237 He looked so handsome: Ellin Berlin, *Lace Curtain*, p. 32.

237 The early summer flowers: *ibid.*, p. 104.

239 "His voice was loud": *ibid.*, p. 199.

239 In 1909, when she was only six: Mackay Collection, *BL.*

240 "so taken by surprise": Unidentified newspaper clipping, dated 1913, Mackay Collection, *BL.*

241 "I remember . . . I ran": Ellin Berlin, *Silver Platter*, p. 12.

242 On the morning of Friday: *New York American*, November 29, 1914.

242 DR. BLAKE, FREE: *ibid.*

243 "I cannot understand": Unidentified newspaper clipping, dated 1914, Mackay Collection, *BL.*

243 "Poor Clarie appeared": Ellin Berlin, *Silver Platter*, p. 437.

243 Retreating into a forbidding . . . piousness: Mackay Collection, *BL.*

243 They would eventually have: Haynes interview. Katherine rarely saw the Mackay children again, and when she did, they were cool to her, as one incident illustrates. Years after she married Dr. Joseph Blake, Katherine happened to recognize her oldest child, "K," at the Colony Restaurant in New York. Katherine impulsively rushed over to her daughter and kissed her. "K" then called the maître d' and said to him, "I don't know this woman. Would you please tell her to leave me alone."

CHAPTER 11: **Ellin**

245 he was thoroughly pleased: Woollcott Collection, *Houghton.*

245 "only over my dead body": *Variety*, January 6, 1926.

246 "The day you marry": *MF*, p. 108.

246 "irresponsible journalism": *Variety*, January 6, 1926.

246 In George White's *Scandals: GB*, p. 402.

246 "The truth of the matter": *MF*, p. 105.

247 "I never knew": *New York Telegram*, March 11, 1926.

247 Nothing quite like: *GB*, p. 386.

247 After the success: Meredith, *George S. Kaufman and His Friends*, p. 270.

247 As a setting: *GB*, p. 408.

248 To foster their collaboration: Meredith, *George S. Kaufman and His Friends*, p. 276.

248 In contrast to his boss: Granat interviews.

248 "Mr. Berlin, would you write": Jasen, *Tin Pan Alley*, pp. 72–73.

248 Irving woke me: quoted in Teichmann, *George S. Kaufman*, pp. 300–301.

249 "We started to produce": *New York Telegram*, March 11, 1926.

249 "When we started to rehearse": *ibid.*

250 Whenever the music: Teichmann, *George S. Kaufman*, pp. 91–93.

250 "I'll tell you what": Meredith, *George S. Kaufman and His Friends*, p. 277.

250 His romantic relationship: *Variety*, January 6, 1926.

250 "A fair girl": Adams, *The Diary of Our Own Samuel Pepys*, p. 573.

251 "like the pants": *GB*, p. 408.

251 "summer edition": Meredith, *George S. Kaufman and His Friends*, p. 280.

251 Her published statements: *New York Times*, January 5, 1926.

253 Matters came to a head: *New York Times*, January 5–6, 1926; *MF*, pp. 109–119.

253 On Monday, January 4: *New York Times*, January 5, 1926.

253 "I knew there was": *ibid.*

255 "Hello, Miss Mackay": *ibid.*

256 "knowledge or approval": *ibid.*

256 Ellin's estranged mother: *ibid.*

256 "Have you heard": *ibid.*

258 "ELLIN MACKAY WED": *ibid.*

258 "IRVING BERLIN WEDS ELLIN MACKAY": *New York American*, January 5, 1926.

258 Broadway's king of jazz: *ibid.*

259 "Ellin by her marriage": *New York American*, February 10, 1926.

260 "trim walking suit": *New York Times*, January 6, 1926.

260 "We are very anxious": *ibid.*

260 I haven't heard: *ibid.*

261 "MRS. BERLIN TO SEEK": *ibid.*

262 "No statement": *New York Times*, January 7, 1926.

262 "I can't say anything now": *ibid.*

263 Her lost share: *Time Inc.*

263 "I can't understand": *MF*, p. 115.

263 "WE HAVE NEVER SAID": *New York Times*, January 8, 1926.

263 While in seclusion: *MF*, p. 119.

264 On the evening of January 8: Telegram from Irving Berlin to Alexander Woollcott, January 12, 1926. Woollcott Collection, *Houghton.*

264 In their presidential suite: *New York Times*, January 10, 1926.

264 The new issue of *Vogue: New York Times*, January 9, 1926.

265 "a strange rhythm": *Vogue*, February 15, 1926; *New York Times*, February 7, 1926.

265 "FORMER ELLIN MAC-

KAY": *New York Times*, February 7, 1926.

265 "Dilatory Domiciles": *New York Times*, February 4, 1926; *New York Social Register*, 1926.

266 "The Balines": Woollcott Collection *Houghton.*

266 "I've often traveled": *MF*, p. 121.

266 "Drink. Drink. Let the toast start": *ibid.*, pp. 124–125.

267 Irving tried to distract: Berlin wrote of his activities in Europe to Alexander Woollcott (*Houghton*). See also *MF*, p. 127.

267 "For nearly two weeks": *ibid.*

268 "Darling, we'll": *Saturday Evening Post*, January 9, 1943.

268 "belly laugh": Woollcott Collection *Houghton.*

268 Berlin was sufficiently serious: *New York American*, June 1926.

269 "A Western Union": *GB*, p. 413.

269 A car salesman: *New York World*, June 26, 1926; *New York Evening Post*, June 25, 1926.

270 They left London: *New York Post*, August 21, 1926.

270 "We beg for privacy": *MF*, pp. 135–136.

271 At about eight that night: *New York Evening Post*, August 21, 1926; *New York Tribune*, *New York American*, and the *News*, August 23, 1926.

271 "The man is in a highly nervous": *New York Telegraph*, August 24, 1926.

272 "There were a few flashlight": *New York Evening World*, August 30, 1929.

273 "Why must I divulge": *New York Sun*, August 30, 1926.

273 "faithful communicant": *New York Evening Graphic*, August 31, 1926.

274 The report that Mrs. Berlin: *New York Mirror*, September 1, 1926.

274 "He told me Ellin": Adams, *The Diary of Our Own Samuel Pepys*, p. 679.

274 In an era when: Unidentified newspaper clippings, *LCL.*

275 "No. No. I won't": *New York Telegraph*, December 16, 1926.

CHAPTER 12: **Heartbreak House**

276 "Irving," she said: Wilk, *They're Playing Our Song*, pp. 281–282.

277 *Betsy* opened as scheduled: *GB*, p. 420.

278 None of Irving's new songs: *GB*, p. 427.

278 Like so many other makers: Author's interviews with Helmy Kresa; Jasen, *Tin Pan Alley*, p. 76–77.

280 To build the theater: Swanberg, *Citizen Hearst*, p. 465.

281 "They don't like it": Higham, *Ziegfeld*, p. 184.

281 "The history of the American": Notes for EMI recording of the musical, 1988. CDS 7 49108 1/2/4.

282 It was so much ahead: For extended discussions of *Show Boat*, see Bordman, *Jerome Kern*, pp. 275–292 and Kreuger, *Show Boat, passim.*

283 On September 4, 1928: Ellin Berlin, *Silver Platter*, pp. 444–445; Mackay Collection, *BL.*

283 Irving Berlin, Jr.: Death Certificate of Irving Berlin, Jr., Manhattan Municipal Archives, #31637.

283 "It's God's punishment": *MF*, p. 146; Kanter, *The Jews on Tin Pan Alley*, p. 142.

284 "the best musical comedy": *MF*, p. 146; Schwartz, *Cole Porter*, p. 109.

285 His first effort: *Films in Review*, May 1958.

285 "Where Is the Song": *ibid.*

285 Despite Schenck's enthusiastic: Schickel, *D. W. Griffith,* pp. 503–505, 544–545.

286 "Everything is there": *Variety,* May 24, 1929.

287 This was Jolson's fourth movie: *Films in Review,* May 1958.

287 Shot in the Astoria Studios: *ibid.;* Higham, *Ziegfeld,* pp. 199–200.

288 In reality, he fit: Erenberg, *Steppin' Out,* p. 245.

288 "Story is of the usual": *Variety,* February 14, 1930.

288 An obsessive worker: Author's interviews with Maurice Kusell and Mynna Granat.

289 "He was very sweet": Author's interview with Joan Bennett.

289 Sloman had begun: Brownlow, *The Parade's Gone By . . . ,* pp. 181–185.

290 "You do it": BBC interview.

290 "Let's stay up": Kusell interview.

290 $5 million: Kanter, *The Jews on Tin Pan Alley,* p. 142.

291 took the news: Kusell interview.

291 His story concerned: *Variety,* January 7, 1931.

293 Frightened by this development: Author's interviews with Miles Kreuger; Kusell interview.

293 "Musicals were the rage": *New York Times,* May 11, 1958.

294 Of Berlin's entire score: Kreuger interview.

294 "I saw light after light": Ferber, *A Peculiar Treasure,* p. 323.

295 House by house: *RS,* pp. 109–110.

295 "I was scared": *MF,* p. 149.

296 Throughout the late: Mackay Collection, *BL.*

296 "Manu Forti": ibid.

297 "You must be Kathy": Haynes interview.

297 A year after her divorce: Mackay Collection, *BL.*

298 "entombed in bronze": Unidentified newspaper clipping, April 23, 1930, Mackay Collection, *BL.*

298 At the beginning of 1931: *New York Times,* April 23, 1931; *MF,* p. 152.

299 Before he married Anna: Mackay Collection, *BL.*

300 Despite the songwriter's generosity: Granat interviews.

300 In September, 1930: *New York Times,* September 16, 1930.

301 As the Depression tightened: Bordman, *Jerome Kern,* p. 323; *GB,* pp. 429, 459, 469, 475, 488.

301 "Well, at least": Higham, *Ziegfeld,* p. 202.

301 In the winter of 1932: *GB,* p. 476.

301 Throughout the show's: Higham, *Ziegfeld,* pp. 211–212.

302 His health broke: Bordman, *Jerome Kern,* pp. 325–326; *GB,* pp. 476–477; Higham, *Ziegfeld,* pp. 215–223.

302 "These theaters would be dark": Atkinson, *Broadway,* p. 414; *GB,* p. 461.

303 "Berlin received nothing": *GB,* pp. 469–470; *MF,* p. 152.

304 Of Thee I Sing: GB, pp. 473–474.

304 "Park Avenue librettos": *ibid.,* p. 476.

305 "Irving's all washed up": *MF,* pp. 153–154.

305 "Thursday evening": Vallée, *Let the Chips Fall . . . ,* p. 58.

306 He returned to his old song: *MF,* p. 154.

306 "I keep taking lines": *ibid.*

306 "I hear you're broke": *Liberty Magazine,* July 19, 1941.

308 As he related: For more on Hart, see the Moss Hart papers at the

State Historical Society of Wisconsin in Madison.

308 Called *Face the Music: GB*, pp. 475–476.

309 "jumping from one side": *New York Herald Tribune*, February 23, 1932.

310 "For two months": *ibid.*

310 For the kids: *ibid.*

310 Kaufman displayed his resentment: Meredith, *George S. Kaufman and His Friends*, p. 75.

311 When *Face the Music* opened: *GB*, pp. 475–476.

CHAPTER 13: **Recovery**

313 "We both agreed": *New York Times*, October 8, 1932.

313 The partnership nearly foundered: *ibid.*

313 he had to borrow $10,000: *Saturday Evening Post*, January 9, 1943.

313 By deferring his own fees: *Time Inc.*

313 "There, in the most": *New York Times*, October 8, 1932.

314 "There are some persons": *New York Herald Tribune*, October 1, 1933.

314 A likable and gentle young man: Author's interviews with Will Irwin.

315 "The sounds that came": *ibid.*

316 "My songs aim": Isaac Goldberg, "Words and Music from Irving Berlin," Unidentified newspaper clipping, 1934, *LCL.*

317 It had begun life: *MF*, pp. 155–156.

317 fell prey to near-panic: *New York Herald Tribune*, October 1, 1933.

317 "Play 'Always' ": *Time*, April 28, 1952.

317 "dusky Charlotte Greenwood": quoted in *GB*, p. 426.

318 She was a former Ziegfeld: Higham, *Ziegfeld, passim; GB*, p. 306; Kreuger interview.

318 Miller was adept: Higham, *Ziegfeld*, pp. 125–126.

318 "I've never missed": *ibid.*, p. 136.

318 Jack Pickford: *ibid.*, pp. 148, 187, 226.

319 "What? No linoleum?": *New York Herald Tribune*, November 5, 1933.

320 He kept a dinner appointment: *New York Times*, October 8, 1933.

320 "All the people": Irwin interviews.

321 There were President and Mrs. Hoover: *GB*, p. 484.

322 "You gotta watch": Author's interview with Harold Leventhal.

323 "No doubt some one": *New York Times*, October 2, 1933.

323 "Mr. Berlin contributes": *New York Herald Tribune*, October 2, 1933.

323 At an opening-night party: Correspondence between Irving Berlin and Clare Booth Luce, dated October 4, 9, and 12, 1933, in the Library of Congress, Manuscript Division, Washington, D.C. The author wishes to thank Sylvia Morris for bringing the matter to light.

324 Berlin and Hart did give: "Irving Berlin Plans Successor to 'As Thousands Cheer,' " Unidentified newspaper clipping, *LCL.*

324 resumed working with Will Irwin: Irwin interviews.

324 Owing to a blockage: Kreuger interview.

325 As the show's coproducer: *Saturday Evening Post*, January 9, 1943.

325 For just $6,000: *ibid.*

326 Ellin's brother Willie: Author's confidential interview.

327 Irving reciprocated: *ibid.*

327 :"You don't know": *ibid.*

328 "The Little Mahatma": Author's interview with Saul Chaplin.

328 "We have become": *MF*, pp. 167–168.

328 In 1932 they combined: *RS*, pp. 190–192.

329 One by one they began: The matter soon took another surprising turn. It had been widely assumed that the judge in the case *Mayer* v. *MDS et al.*, would accept the generous settlement offer, but he didn't buy the argument that MDS was, after all, a monopoly. Still, the brush with the law had exposed the publishers' scheme to scrutiny, and MDS's role was greatly reduced, much to Berlin's satisfaction.

329 In 1933, Max Winslow: *RS*, p. 36.

329 And there was Dave Dreyer: Granat interviews. Mynna Granat later married Dave Dreyer.

330 Mynna's multiple chores: *ibid.*

330 "I'm at the end": *ibid.*

332 "If you gave him": *ibid.*

333 "You should never stoop": *ibid.*

334 "The children called": *ibid.*

335 "My first name": Author's interview with Arthur Shimkin.

335 "Tony's Wife": Author's interview with Burton Lane.

335 Over a period of years: Granat and confidential interviews.

336 "Jerome Kern was reminded": *Time*, May 28, 1934.

338 "left millions of listeners": *ibid.*

338 "Radio's most valuable asset": *MF*, pp. 157–158.

339 In December 1934: *New York World Telegram*, April 19, 1935.

CHAPTER 14:
Hollywood Refuge

340 In the mid-twenties, Joseph P. Kennedy: Collier and Horowitz, *The Kennedys*, pp. 51–55.

340 "a baseball club": Thomas, *Astaire*, p. 105.

341 "I'll be on a mountaintop": *ibid.*, p. 112.

341 "Can't act. Slightly bald": *ibid.*, pp. 98–99.

341 In only two years: *ibid.*, p. 106.

341 "I did not go into pictures": *ibid.*, p. 113.

342 A classic backstage mother: *ibid.*, p. 129.

342 The curious thing about Pan: Author's interview with Hermes Pan; *GB*, pp. 456–457.

342 "You thought you were": Thomas, *Astaire*, pp. 107, 139.

343 Sandrich devised the playback: *ibid.*, pp. 116–117.

343 For the next Astaire and Rogers movie: *ibid.*, pp. 111–120.

343 The songwriter demanded: S. Green interview.

344 Fired by his profit-sharing deal: Author's interview with Pandro S. Berman.

345 Sandrich insisted: Thomas, *Astaire*, p. 127.

345 Adopting a crisis approach: *New York World*, April 19, 1935.

345 "I hadn't done a tune": *New York Times*, November 19, 1974.

345 "I was thrilled": Pan interview.

346 It was just magic": *ibid.*

346 "He was very critical": *ibid.*

346 At Astaire's insistence: Thomas, *Astaire*, pp. 129–130.

347 "I love what you're doing": Pan interview.

348 "Berlin said, 'Well,": *ibid.*

348 Of the picture's one hundred minutes: *Variety*, August 29, 1935.

349 Shortly before its late-summer premiere: *MF*, p. 160.

349 "The theatres will hold": *Variety*, August 29, 1935.

349 "*Top Hat* is the best": Quoted in Thomas, *Astaire*, p. 131.

349 first film effort: *Variety*, August 29, 1935.

350 Made for $620,000: S. Green interview; Thomas, *Astaire*, p. 131.

350 On August 9, only three weeks: *New York Evening Journal*, August 9, 1935.

351 "BERLIN'S KIN": *New York Daily News*, August 12, 1935; *New York Evening Journal*, August 12, 1935.

351 Irving rarely, if ever: Granat interview.

351 Only two months later: Irving Berlin to Alexander Woollcott, October 8, 1935. Woollcott Collection, *Houghton*.

352 "I was to see": Leventhal interview.

353 One morning, for instance, a disheveled woman: *ibid.*

353 "Say," he asked: *MF*, p. 161; Thomas, *Astaire*, p. 137.

353 On January 20, 1936: *New York Times*, January 19, 1936; *Hollywood Reporter*, January 21, 1936.

354 "When Irving Berlin . . . was led": *Variety*, January 29, 1936.

355 "Irving was flabbergasted": *ibid.*

356 And predictably, it met with: *Variety*, February 26, 1936.

357 He suffered from severe headaches: Jablonski, *George Gershwin*, pp. 314–325; *MF*, p. 175.

357 Late in 1937: *Liberty Magazine*, July 19, 1941.

358 "You're Laughing at Me": *MF*, p. 168.

359 "The brilliant score": *New York Herald Tribune*, February 5, 1937.

359 He began his pseudo-autobiography: Twentieth Century-Fox Collection, *USC*.

360 "Mr. Zanuck was quite disappointed": *ibid.*

361 "Mr. Zanuck expected": *ibid.*

361 "This can be": *ibid.*

362 "Consolidated into a single entertainment": *Variety*, June 1, 1938.

362 "That was the most incredible": Author's confidential interview.

363 "They were trying to get": Author's interview with Mary Healy.

363 The movie, eventually called *Second Fiddle:* Twentieth Century-Fox Collection, *USC*.

363 "Mr. Berlin might be pardoned": *New York Herald Tribune*, July 1, 1939.

363 "an indifferent Berlin score": *New York Times*, July 1, 1939.

363 In financial matters Schenck continued: *Liberty Magazine*, July 19, 1941.

365 "gain from the sales": *New York Times*, September 6, 1940.

365 Feeling doubly vulnerable: Author's confidential interview.

365 The songwriter spent January 1938: *MF*, p. 166.

366 "came to a spot": Wilk, *They're Playing Our Song*, p. 265.

366 "It's a disappointing story": *Variety*, August 31, 1938.

367 pulling in $1,731,000: Thomas, *Astaire*, pp. 168–169.

367 "I feel slow in Hollywood": *New York Journal American*, September 4, 1938.

367 The slide had begun in earnest in December 1937: *New York Times*, November 13, 1938.

CHAPTER 15: **Minstrel of Peace**

368 His English publisher: *New York Times*, September 14, 1938.

369 "I'd like to write": *New York Journal American*, September 4, 1938.

370 "I worked for a while": *New York Times*, October 27, 1940.

370 "Go to the *Yip! Yip! Yaphank* file": Granat interviews.

370 "I had to make": *New York Times*, October 27, 1940.

371 "The reason 'God Bless America' caught on": *New York Times*, July 28, 1940.

372 At eleven P.M.: *New York Times*, November 13, 1938.

372 newspaper obituaries: *ibid.*

373 "My father-in-law would turn over": Author's confidential interview.

373 Even before Clarence's death: Unidentified newspaper clipping, Mackay Collection, *BL*.

374 "Police were shorthanded": *ibid.*

374 HOUSE FOR SALE: *ibid.*

375 Buddy DeSylva: *GB*, p. 412.

376 *DuBarry Was a Lady*: ibid., p. 518.

376 "Pretty nearly all that's expected": *New York Times*, May 26, 1940.

377 "A basket case of nerves": Author's interview with Carol Bruce.

378 But it was not part: Shimkin interview.

378 "He was there every minute": Bruce interview.

378 As she exited: *ibid.*

378 "They flanked me": *ibid.*

378 "a bit of trim man-bait": *New York Times*, January 1, 1942.

379 "After an absence of seven years": *New York Times*, May 29, 1940.

379 "The day the *Life* magazine story": Bruce interview.

380 On Memorial Day 1939: *MF*, p. 178.

380 Now, in the summer of 1940: *ibid.*

380 "The Democratic Party": *ibid.*, p. 182.

381 "*Herr, scheutz' Amerika!*": *New York Times*, September 22, 1940.

381 the God Bless America Fund: Granat interviews.

381 In his selection: Kahn, *Swope*, pp. 112–113. Later trustees, who replaced the original three, demonstrated a similar flair for popularity: Joe DiMaggio, Mrs. Ralph Bunche, and Theodore R. Jackson (one of Berlin's lawyers).

382 "SONGS SUCH AS 'GOD BLESS AMERICA' ": *New York Times*, July 29, 1940.

382 "As a child in arms": *New York Times*, July 31, 1940.

383 On September 5: *New York Times*, September 6, 1940.

383 "Roosevelt is the man": *MF*, p. 185.

384 "sensitive and gentle woman": *ibid.*, pp. 186–187.

384 "I am due back": *The Letters of Alexander Woollcott*, p. 266.

385 He, too, had nostalgic memories: *Saturday Evening Post*, January 14, 1944.

386 "We working composers": *ibid.*

386 "I want you": Kresa interviews.

387 the trial broke into the headlines: *New York Times*, April 1, 1941.

387 Moskowitz, convicted on one count: *Liberty Magazine*, July 19, 1941.

388 "It is not always greatness": *Liberty Magazine*, June 28, 1941.

388 "It was as if he were going": *MF*, pp. 190–191.

389 "I wrote *Holiday Inn* in 1941": *ibid.*, p. 236.

389 "Whaddya mean?": *ibid.*

390 "I've just had a terrible experience": Author's confidential interview.

391 The obese critic's failing health: Woollcott Collection, *Houghton*.

CHAPTER 16: **Minstrel of War**

393 "Songs make history": *New York Times*, May 17, 1942.

393 And when they met: *American Heritage*, August 1967.

394 "I hear you're 1A": Author's interview with Robert Lissauer.

395 "I got the full blast": Author's interview with Ezra Stone.

395 Brooklyn born "Rosie": Author's interview with Milton Rosenstock.

396 "He insisted right from the beginning": Author's interview with Alan Anderson.

397 "We had guys who were crackers": Author's interview with Alan Manson.

397 "Mr. Berlin," he said: Stone interview.

398 "I finally got the number": *ibid.*

399 "Their routine," noted a reporter": *New Yorker*, June 20, 1942.

399 "I didn't know how to behave myself": Rosenstock interview.

401 "I'm going back": *ibid.*

401 Taking an interest in a feud: Stone interview.

401 "The door is open": *ibid.*

402 "at once excitement, glitter": Logan, *Josh*, pp. 157–158.

403 With seats ranging in price: *New York Times*, July 4, 1942.

403 When the brothers realized: William Klein to Lee Shubert, July 14, 1942, *Shubert.* This memo restates the important points of the dispute.

403 "Please do not take": *ibid.*

403 "I believe that Berlin's letter": *ibid.*

403 "I have not taken advantage": Lee Shubert to Irving Berlin, July 14, 1942. *Shubert.*

404 $10,000 for her two seats: *New York Times*, July 4, 1942.

404 "As far as Irving Berlin": Lee Shubert, Memorandum, August 21, 1942. *Shubert.*

405 it had been banned: Lissauer interview.

406 "Bob," he said in his best confiding tone: *ibid.*

406 "Every night at the performance": Granat interviews.

406 "We lined up in the alley": Lissauer interview.

407 At a reception, Tom Pryor: Author's interview with Thomas Pryor.

407 "I'll bet you a Cavanaugh hat": Granat interview.

408 "I've got a song": Rosenstock interview.

408 "The brim is too big": Granat interview.

409 "I want you to cut": Wilk, *They're Playing Our Song*, pp. 276–277.

409 "Say, Tom": Pryor interview.

410 movie rights to Warner Brothers: Warner Bros. Archives, *USC*.

410 October 8 at the National Theater: Alan Anderson: "*This Is the Army* Itinerary, 1942–1945." (Hereafter referred to as "Itinerary.") The author is grateful to Mr. Anderson for furnishing this detailed record of the production's performances.

411 "How well do you know Hank Henry?": Stone interview.

411 "It was a night": Manson interview.

412 "We always insisted": Anderson interview.

412 After the ten-day stand: Itinerary.

412 "Well, what's the big deal": Stone interview.

413 On December 14: Itinerary.

413 "too many Jews": Stone interview.

413 Everyone present was astounded: Anderson interview.

413 "Publicity—that's all": Stone interview.

414 "I was very, very upset": Manson interview.

414 Accustomed to traditional holiday celebrations: *Saturday Evening Post*, January 14, 1944.

415 February 13, 1943: Itinerary.

415 Several weeks earlier, on January 23: *New York Times*, January 24, 1943.

416 Berlin had often spoken of Porter: Irwin interviews.

417 "I wrote that song": *MF*, pp. 164–165.

417 "Jewish tunes": Schwartz, *Cole Porter*, p. 118.

418 "They bombed the wrong Berlin": Whitcomb interview. Warren was also known for another unpleasant jibe concerning Berlin: "The guy's secret was he carried around a portable Wailing Wall."

418 I can't understand all this resentment: *MF*, pp. 206–207.

418 Jack L. Warner, the head of Warner Brothers: Jack Warner to John Taylor, July 1, 1942. Warner Bros. Archives, *USC;* Irving Berlin to Alexander Woollcott, September 18, 1942, Woollcott Collection, *Houghton*. See also Edwards, *Early Reagan*, pp. 271–272.

419 "the Army will furnish gratis": Jack Warner to John Taylor, July 1, 1942. Warner Bros. Archives, *USC*.

419 Since the movie: William J. German to J. L. Warner, July 12, 1943. Warner Bros. Archives, *USC*.

419 "First, every dollar received": J. L. Warner to William J. German, July 19, 1943, *ibid.*

419 "Female impersonators": Carl Schaefer to J. L. Warner, December 17, 1942, *ibid.*

420 Next, Joseph I. Breen: Breen to J. L. Warner, February 25, 1943, *ibid.*

420 Finally, a conscience-stricken Ezra Stone: Stone interview.

421 EARNESTLY HOPE YOU WILL CHANGE: Bishop James C. Baker of Los Angeles to Irving Berlin. See also R. Burton Sheppard to Warner Bros., August 2, 1943; Jack Warner to Irving Berlin and Hal Wallis, July 2, 1943. Warner Bros. Archives, *USC*.

For further discussion of the controversy surrounding the lyrics in *This Is the Army*, including charges of racism, see Clayton R. Koppes and Gregory D. Black, "Blacks, Loyalty, and Motion-Picture Propaganda in World War II," *Journal of American History*, September 1986.

422 The soldier-actors occupied: Undated descriptive material, Warner Bros. Archives, *USC;* Edwards, *Early Reagan*, p. 272.

422 Cole Porter's Bel Air mansion: Edwards, *Early Reagan*, p. 272.

422 Alan Manson experienced the joy: Manson interview.

422 "The first several days": This interview with President Reagan was kindly conducted at my request by his official biographer, Edmund Morris, on June 28, 1988, Washington, D.C.

423 "the war had been going on so long": Reagan, *Where's the Rest of Me?* p. 122.

423 "As more than a million persons": Undated descriptive material, Warner Bros. Archives, *USC*.

423 'Don't worry, Irving': *ibid.*

423 "If the fellow": Reagan, *Where's the Rest of Me?* pp. 121–122.

423 "He moves with the eccentricity": Undated descriptive material, Warner Bros. Archives, *USC*.

424 The mayor of Los Angeles declared: Edwards, *Early Reagan*, pp. 274–275.

424 WAS GREATEST SUCCESS: Jack

Warner to Irving Berlin, August 17, 1943. Warner Bros. Archives, *USC.*

424 "Everything about it": *Variety*, August 4, 1943.

426 it earned $9,555,586: Estimates vary slightly. Letter to Sam Schneider, September 24, 1954, Warner Bros. Archives, *USC; Saturday Review*, January 26, 1946.

426 "Berlin and I sat down": Anderson interview.

426 The company reassembled: Itinerary.

427 On October 21 the company sailed: Itinerary; *Saturday Review*, January 26, 1946.

427 Sergeant Arthur Berlin: *MF*, p. 214.

427 Arriving behind schedule: Letter from Alan Anderson to author, June 8, 1988.

427 "Do you think it's too much?" *Saturday Evening Post*, January 26, 1946.

428 "He had convinced himself": Logan, *Josh*, p. 165.

428 "Colonel Chappell," he said: *ibid.*, p. 166.

428 "England and America": This song was neither performed nor copyrighted. The lyrics appeared in the *New York Times*, November 21, 1943.

429 My Russian Buddy: *MF*, p. 229.

430 A New American song: *New York Times*, November 14, 1943.

430 "I see I'm not the only": *MF*, p. 216.

430 Throughout the course of the war: *Sunday Times* (London), September 8, 1946; *Time Inc.; MF*, pp. 220–221.

431 Just one week after: *Saturday Review*, January 26, 1946.

432 After London: Itinerary.

432 "But Ike was so moved": Manson interview.

432 On February 8: Itinerary.

432 We moved into the destroyed palace": Manson interview.

433 on March 23: Itinerary.

433 "The men were brought down": Manson interview.

433 By early June: Itinerary.

433 "The boys in this war": *New York Times*, August 20, 1944.

434 "I had heard many stories": *MF*, p. 226.

434 At the conclusion: Itinerary.

434 "While we were overseas": Manson interview.

434 "We're playing in a very small": *New York Times*, February 25, 1944.

435 They reached Cairo: Itinerary.

435 "I was worried": Rosenstock interview.

436 "The smart clicks": *Saturday Review*, January 26, 1946.

437 "written by my friend": *American Heritage*, August 1967.

437 One night, he was invited: *Saturday Evening Post*, December 19, 1954.

438 "a rotten old Dutch freighter": Anderson interview.

438 They repeated the cycle: Itinerary.

439 "In the Pacific": Anderson interview.

439 In New York: Granat interviews.

439 "with his inimitable piano": Associated Press dispatch, July 21, 1945.

439 August 2, 1945: Itinerary.

440 "When Mr. Berlin had to go": Granat interviews.

440 In all, approximately 2,500,000: *Saturday Review*, January 26, 1946.

440 Two weeks later: Itinerary.

441 "He has set a high standard": *MF*, p. 229.

CHAPTER 17: **One-upmanship**

445 Rodgers and Hammerstein became: *GB*, p. 346.

446 A decent movie musical: *ibid.*, p. 536.

446 Decca released: *ibid.*, p. 568.

447 "As if out of the sky": Wilk, *They're Playing Our Song*, p. 289.

447 Ethel Agnes Zimmerman: Thomas, *I Got Rhythm!* p. 16.

447 hairstyle of a certain chorus boy: Author's interview with Russell Nype; Thomas, *I Got Rhythm!* p. 39.

447 "Merm, would you think": Wilk, *They're Playing Our Song*, p. 289.

448 "IT WOULD BE ONE": Freedland, *Jerome Kern*, p. 169.

448 Very Warm for May: GB, p. 517.

448 On November 3, 1945: Freedland, *Jerome Kern*, pp. 170–172.

449 "That was the worst week": Wilk, *They're Playing Our Song*, pp. 289–290.

450 "He thought Annie Oakley": *New York Times*, May 11, 1958.

450 On Monday, Berlin called: Wilk, *They're Playing Our Song*, pp. 289–290; Reminiscences of Dorothy Fields, *Columbia*.

451 "I begged him": Reminiscences of Richard Rodgers, *Columbia*.

451 "hillbilly stuff": Thomas, *I Got Rhythm!* p. 94.

452 "doddering thirty-seven": Logan, *Josh*, pp. 178–179.

452 "He would grab me": *ibid.*

452 "You call that a song": Granat interviews.

453 "What's the matter?": Rodgers reminiscences, *Columbia;* Joshua Logan tells much the same story in his *Josh*, p. 183.

453 Soon they were all ransacking: Granat interviews.

453 "Another song?" he whispered: Logan, *Josh*, pp. 183–184. Logan relates the same story in Wilk, *They're Playing Our Song*, pp. 291–292.

454 "It's doing extremely well": Reminiscences of Joshua Logan, *Columbia*.

455 "sucked into Broadway": Author's interviews with Jay Blackton.

456 Bennett's new orchestration: In the playbill for the show, Lang, Bennett, and Ted Royal share credit for the orchestrations, but Bennett's work prevailed. (Blackton interviews; Rodgers reminiscences, *Columbia.*)

456 "Out of the blue": "Interview with Irving Berlin," *USC*.

456 Havoc struck again: Thomas, *I Got Rhythm!* p. 97; Logan, *Josh*, p. 185.

456 "They told us": Rodgers reminiscences, *Columbia*.

457 rumors started to circulate: Logan, *Josh*, p. 185.

457 ANNIE: Look it over: Quoted in *GB*, p. 552.

457 "Why is that lady": Logan, *Josh*, p. 186.

458 "How are you able": *ibid.*

458 A good professional musical": *New York Times*, May 17, 1946. Lewis Nichols wrote the notice.

458 "BULL'S EYE": *New York Herald Tribune*, May 17, 1946.

459 "Aren't we lucky": Logan, *Josh*, p. 187.

459 Annie Get Your Gun had a healthy run: Warner Bros. Collection, *USC*.

459 "He's always been motivated": *New York Times*, May 11, 1958.

460 His background: Kanter, *The Jews of Tin Pan Alley*, p. 59.

460 "It took longer": *New York Times*, May 11, 1958.

460 The amount of the sale: "Brief

of Contract," June 13, 1947, Freed Collection, *USC; New York Herald Tribune*, May 16, 1948.

460 For a number of years: Hirshberg interview.

460 In early June: *New York Times*, June 12, 1946.

461 "If I start to pick": *New York Sun*, October 15, 1946.

462 "I will play and sing": Program and Transcript of the Roosevelt dinner, Archives of the Roosevelt Memorial Association, Long Island, N.Y.

463 long-dormant scandal: Granat interviews.

464 "I talked to my lawyer": *ibid.*

465 Alfred Chandler: Author's confidential interview.

465 "One doesn't speak": Kresa interviews.

465 Dave Dreyer quit: Granat interviews.

467 The playwright arrived early: Sheaffer, *O'Neill: Son and Artist*, pp. 587–588; Letter from Louis Sheaffer to author.

467 "I was worried": *ibid.*

469 "When I was a kid": *New York Sun*, February 24, 1947.

471 Within, they found fifty: *ibid.*

CHAPTER 18: **Tycoon**

474 "The same old story": *Time*, April 28, 1952.

474 "Irving never lost money": *ibid.*

475 At MGM, Louis B. Mayer: *New York Times*, May 11, 1958; Thomas, *Astaire*, p. 207.

475 "The Berlin Room": Fordin, *The World of Entertainment*, p. 224.

475 he earned $640,000: *MF*, p. 242.

475 By April, Berlin: Freed Collection, *USC*.

475 trunk songs: Seven of the "new" songs made it into the final version of the movie: "Better Luck Next Time," "A Couple of Swells," "Drum Crazy," "A Fella with an Umbrella," "It Only Happens When I Dance with You," "Steppin' Out with My Baby," and "Happy Easter."

476 "I'm not a prodigy": Author's interview with Johnny Green.

476 "Irving," Green said: *ibid.*

477 "Sometimes he would come": Fordin, *The World of Entertainment*, pp. 223–226.

478 "I have an idea": Author's interview with Sidney Sheldon.

478 "What are we going to do": Fordin, *The World of Entertainment*, p. 226.

478 "That's a joke": Sheldon interview.

479 "We were ready": Fordin, *The World of Entertainment*, pp. 228–229.

479 He turned his attention: Irving Berlin to Leland Hayward, February 16, 1948, *LCL*.

480 "Socko screen entertainment": *Variety*, May 26, 1948; Fordin, *The World of Entertainment*, p. 234.

480 birthday party: *New York Herald Tribune*, May 16, 1948.

481 "Irving, you look": *MF*, p. 247.

481 he called his business manager: Author's confidential interview.

481 Returning from a short: Author's interview with Gary Stevens.

481 Silvers quipped: Author's confidential interview.

482 When he entered his bank: *ibid.*

482 "We're not running": *ibid.*

482 "so that I can get around": *ibid.*

482 "When music publishers": *New York Times*, May 20, 1944.

482 450,000 copies: *New York Herald Tribune*, May 26, 1948.

482 The motion picture: *New York Times*, July 30, 1988.

482 "That was not our problem": *MF*, p. 249.

483 "Who the hell": Author's confidential interview.

484 "BURDEN-BERLIN MATCH": *Time*, June 7, 1948.

485 When the plane landed: *The Sketch*, January 5, 1949.

485 "Don't fuck": Author's confidential interview.

485 Robert Sherwood, the American playwright: *New York Times*, July 29, 1983.

485 his idea for a musical: Memo from Robert E. Sherwood, May 13, 1954, Freed Collection, *USC*.

486 Berlin did some research: Transcript of telephone conversation between Irving Berlin and Gerald Wald, September 10, 1953, Wald Collection, *USC* (hereafter referred to as "Wald transcript"); Jerry Wald to William Goetz, June 9, 1954, Wald Collection, *USC*.

488 Allyn McLerie: Now known professionally as Allyn Ann McLerie.

488 "The book," she said: Author's interview with Allyn Ann McLerie.

488 he broke into song: *ibid.*

489 When Albert asked Berlin: Author's interview with Eddie Albert.

489 On April 7: *GB*, pp. 567–568.

490 "Listen, you guys": Gordon Jenkins to James T. Maher, August 11, 1978. Written reminiscence furnished by Maher.

491 Judy Garland was starring: Frank, *Judy*, pp. 247–248.

491 Rehearsals commenced: Fordin, *The World of Entertainment*, pp. 274–276.

492 "He was shooting": *ibid.*, p. 276.

492 When the ordeal ended: *ibid.*, pp. 276–277; Frank, *Judy*, pp. 249–253.

492 Production of *Annie Get Your Gun:* Fordin, *The World of Entertainment*, p. 278.

493 "Bob, I don't like": McLerie interview.

493 "I want every song": *ibid.*

493 "Being a book": *ibid.*

494 He'd intended it: Fordin, *The World of Entertainment*, p. 233.

494 "You must have": *ibid.*

494 "I hate opening-night": *New Yorker*, June 25, 1949.

494 Five days before: *New York Times*, July 10, 1949.

495 "To come right out": *New York Times*, July 16, 1949.

496 "In view of their": *New York Times*, July 24, 1949.

496 most exciting season: *GB*, p. 562.

496 For once he had: A revival of *Miss Liberty* at the Goodspeed Opera House in East Haddam, Connecticut, in July 1983, offered further confirmation, if any was needed, of the show's flaws. Concluded *Times* reviewer Mel Gussow on that occasion: "One can almost see the Statue of Liberty wince." (*New York Times*, July 29, 1983)

497 They spent six weeks: *New York Herald Tribune*, September 14, 1949.

497 Six months late: Fordin, *The World of Entertainment*, p. 281; *Annie Get Your Gun* production files, Arthur Freed Collection, *USC*.

CHAPTER 19: **Irving Likes Ike**

498 Lindsay and Crouse: Kreuger interview; Author's interview with Dorothy Stickney (Mrs. Howard Lindsay); *GB*, p. 490. For more on Lindsay and

Crouse, see their papers at the State Historical Society of Wisconsin, Madison. Both men died in 1968.

499 In the summer of 1949: Thomas, *I Got Rhythm!* pp. 104–105.

500 "We weren't quite sure": "Interview with Irving Berlin," *USC*.

500 Producer Leland Hayward: *RS*, p. 239.

501 "We don't say": *Evening Standard* (London), January 3, 1950.

501 The enthusiastic audience reaction: Freed Collection, *USC*.

501 "EASTERN REVIEWERS": *Los Angeles Times*, May 25, 1950.

501 The first run of the film: Fordin, *The World of Entertainment*, p. 283.

502 "Well, I hope": Thomas, *I Got Rhythm!* pp. 106–107.

502 "I've gone along": *ibid.*, p. 110.

503 "Mr. Berlin said": Nype interview.

503 she asked Berlin to write: Thomas, *I Got Rhythm!* p. 110.

503 "Play A Simple Melody": For a discussion of Berlin's counterpoint songs, see "Mr. American Music" by Henry Hewes in *The Saturday Review*, October 1, 1966.

503 "hurried into the theatre": Abbott, *Mister Abbott*, p. 228.

504 "You're Just in Love": Thomas, *I Got Rhythm!*, p. 110–111.

504 "Would you come down": Nype interview.

504 "We'll never get": Thomas, *I Got Rhythm!*, p. 111.

505 the audience demanded: *GB*, p. 574.

505 "Why don't you knock": Blackton interviews.

505 "Boys, as of right now": Thomas, *I Got Rhythm!* p. 111.

506 "Are you nervous": Stickney interview.

506 "When Miss Merman": *New York Times*, October 13, 1950.

506 Darryl F. Zanuck purchased: Wald transcript, *USC; Variety*, December 15, 1954.

507 Ethel Merman, whose film career: Thomas, *I Got Rhythm!*, p. 130.

507 In addition to his fee: *Call Me Madam* production file, *LCL*.

507 stock portfolio: Author's confidential interview.

507 Of his extra ten percent: *ibid.*

508 She announced her support: *MF*, p. 261.

508 A coalition of Eisenhower backers: *New York Times*, February 9, 1952.

509 the television networks announced: *GB*, p. 574–575.

509 "I don't trust": Author's confidential interview.

509 "in recognition of his services": *New York Times*, July 18, 1954.

510 Act of Congress: *New York Times*, February 19, 1955.

510 "What can I do": Author's confidential interview.

511 On February 12: *New York Times*, February 16, 1952.

511 May 12, 1953: *New York Times*, May 13, 1953.

511 unauthorized children's version: Shimkin interview.

511 "Young man," he declared: *ibid.*

512 "This is Irving Berlin calling": *ibid.*

513 Fisher was then: Author's confidential interview.

513 "our greatest blessing": *MF*, p. 267.

513 When he heard Elvis's rendition: Author's interview with Walter Wager.

514 With a jerry-built plot: *Time*, April 28, 1952.

514 Paramount had paid: *Variety*, December 15, 1954.

514 He first approached Arthur Freed: Irving Berlin to Arthur Freed, August 7, 1951, Freed Collection, *USC*.

515 On September 10, 1953: Wald transcript, *USC*.

516 "fundamental things wrong . . .": Jerry Wald to William Goetz, June 9, 1954, Wald Collection, *USC*.

517 "They all say": Hirshberg interview.

518 "I won't go": Ephron, *We Thought We Could Do Anything*, pp. 123–124.

518 he once bet: *Time*, April 28, 1952.

518 "And then he put Berlin": Ephron, *We Thought We Could Do Anything*, p. 125.

519 She made no secret: *ibid.*, pp. 125–126.

519 The unhappy actress: Thomas, *I Got Rhythm!* p. 131.

519 "If anyone raises": *New York Times*, December 17, 1954.

520 vacation in Haiti: *New York Herald Tribune*, January 15, 1955.

520 "a little old man": *MF*, pp. 269–270.

521 "writers who mask": Meredith, *George S. Kaufman and His Friends*, pp. 636–637.

521 nasty lawsuit: *New York Times*, March 31, 1955.

522 MUSICAL MYTH: *New York Times*, April 1, 1955.

522 "The proof in this case": *Alfred L. Smith* v. *Irving Berlin*, April 27, 1955, Supreme Court, Special Term, New York County, Part V., 207 Misc. 862.

523 "on the hard stuff": Nype interview.

523 Milton "Mezz" Mezzrow: Author's interview with Ernest Anderson.

523 "To my knowledge": Kresa interviews.

524 Irving became so anxious: Author's confidential interview.

524 In 1950, he collected: *RS*, p. 304.

524 Berlin's income: *ibid.*, p. 412.

525 "Without ASCAP's performance": *ibid.*, p. 397.

525 "TV musical": *BBC Radio Times*, May 9, 1958.

526 Berlin's office contacted: *ibid.*

526 "It would be": *MF*, p. 275.

526 he found himself a patient: Author's confidential interview.

CHAPTER 20: **The Cheering Stops**

528 he placed the instrument: *New York Times*, October 14, 1962.

528 "I couldn't just enjoy": The title of Berlin's 1957 song, "You Can't Lose the Blues with Colors," probably alludes to his attempt to cure his depression with painting.

529 "I've always thought": *New York Times*, May 11, 1958.

529 "I got really sick": *Daily Express* (London), September 13, 1963.

529 "As the months": *Life*, May 3, 1963.

530 He would telephone: Brackman interview.

531 "I knew Richard Rodgers": Kreuger interview.

531 "he wasn't as educated": *ibid.*

533 Goddard Lieberson: *RS*, p. 352.

533 In May 1961: *New York Times*, October 14, 1962.

534 " 'Mr. President' ": *ibid.*

534 "It would have been easy": *New York Herald Tribune*, June 4, 1962.

534 "Once you get started": *New York Times*, October 14, 1962.

535 "verging on hysteria": *RS*, p. 354.

535 In the case of *Mr. President: Variety*, July 18, 1962.

535 "I wouldn't pay": *New York Herald Tribune*, April 23, 1962.

536 BERLIN'S B'WAY: *Variety*, July 18, 1962.

536 *"I'm going right": ibid.*

537 "The worst kind": *MF*, p. 290.

538 "Do you think": Author's interview with Nanette Fabray.

540 "Hi, Stephen": *ibid.*

541 "Dreadful is the only word": Quoted in the London *Daily Mail*, August 29, 1962.

541 "Empty Pockets Filled with Love": *Variety*, September 19, 1962.

541 "It will play": *ibid.*

541 "We have a terrible problem": *MF*, p. 286.

542 "This was going to be": Fabray interview.

542 Politicians mingled: *Variety*, October 3, 1962.

543 "They had taken it apart": Fabray interview.

543 "He hasn't shown": Blackton interview.

543 "Well, what did you think": Fabray interview.

544 Floyd Patterson and Sonny Liston: *Variety*, October 3, 1962.

544 The conductor glanced: Blackton interview.

544 Eventually Kennedy: Fabray interview.

544 "His dramatic scenes": *ibid.*

544 "Hello, how are you?": *ibid.*

545 $2,650,000: *MF*, p. 284.

545 "It was the ticket": Fabray interview.

545 BERLIN'S "MR. PRESIDENT": *New York Herald Tribune*, October 22, 1962.

546 "As it ploughed": Quoted in *MF*, p. 284.

546 Irving began plugging: *RS*, p. 353.

546 "The day our advance": Fabray interview.

547 "You can't sell patriotism": *MF*, p. 285.

547 "You don't have to stop": WBAL interview.

548 Soon to be elected president: Fordin, *That's Entertainment!*, p. 518.

549 "What the hell": *MF*, p. 297.

549 "What's that?": *New York Times*, May 8, 1988.

549 Freed used: Fordin, *That's Entertainment!*, p. 518.

550 The two sides: *ibid.*, p. 519. Berlin would collect the full amount, though MGM tried to reserve "non-exclusive" rights after the ten-year period lapsed. In 1975, Berlin finally removed this condition, and the songs were his alone (*Variety*, June 4, 1975).

550 On April 30: *Box Office*, May 6, 1963.

550 All this talent: *New Musical Express* (London), June 21, 1963.

551 Freed assigned Arthur Laurents: *New York Times*, June 17, 1963.

551 Stars entered: *New York Times*, November 11, 1963.

551 "like an egg": *Daily Express* (London), September 13, 1963.

552 At the beginning of November: Freed Collection, *USC*.

552 Freed and MGM ceased: *Hollywood Reporter*, August 26, 1964.

552 "Parody and satire": *New York Times*, March 24, 1964.

553 "On the sound track": Freed Collection, *USC*.

553 The story: *ibid.*

553 "This is it": Fordin, *That's Entertainment!* p. 521.

554 Two drafts and $150,000: Freed Collection, *USC*.

554 "Wait a minute, Irving": *New York Herald Tribune,* April 15, 1966.

556 "I've always lived": *MF,* p. 293.

556 "A sweet-smelling rose": Merman, *Merman,* p. 241.

557 "I haven't felt": *Life,* June 10, 1966.

557 The production received: *New York Times,* June 1, 1966; *World Journal Tribune,* September 22, 1966.

557 Late in 1967: Memorandum Agreement, May 8, 1968, Freed Collection, *USC;* Fordin, *That's Entertainment!* p. 522.

558 Meanwhile, Irving agonized: *New York Times,* May 6, 1968.

558 "Patriotism goes out": *New York Daily Column,* April 26, 1968.

558 Listening to the growing number: Harry Ruby Collection, *USC.*

560 The Aubrey name: *Life,* September 10, 1965; Fordin, *The World of Entertainment,* p. 523.

560 His lawyer fired off: George Cohen to Saul Rittenberg, April 24, 1969; Saul Rittenberg to George Cohen, May 27, 1969. Freed Collection, *USC.*

560 "It's fine to be able": Fordin, *The World of Entertainment,* p. 524.

CHAPTER 21: **Coda**

562 At four-thirty in the afternoon: Author's interview with James T. Maher.

562 "This is Irving Berlin": *ibid.* The following conversation is drawn from notes furnished by James T. Maher, hereafter referred to as "Maher notes."

563 "The Tune Detective": In his day, Spaeth had been the bane of many a songwriter because of his uncanny ability to discover themes in popular songs that were derived, whether accidentally or not, from traditional music. For instance, he once assembled a list of over a hundred popular songs (such as "How Dry I Am") that opened with the same four notes. However, Spaeth had great admiration for Berlin, who, he wrote, "has been criticized by his competitors, maligned by his inferiors and snubbed by those who consider themselves musically superior. All of them would gladly pay a fortune for his unerring grasp of popular taste and his unique ability to satisfy it."

563 "In the course": Wilder, *American Popular Song,* pp. 91–93, 103.

564 "I had a guy": Maher notes.

564 "You've just destroyed": Maher, Brackman interviews. The author wishes to thank Lesley Alderman for further research on the controversy.

568 "As a painter": *New York Times,* May 8, 1988; author's confidential interviews.

568 "Isn't this a lovely day": Pan interview.

568 "Who is your grandfather?": Wilk, *They're Playing Our Song,* p. 295.

569 Arlen's personal life: Author's confidential interviews.

569 "Tell Dorothy": *ibid.*

569 "I don't want to hear": *ibid.*

570 "White Christmas": *RS,* p. 473.

571 "I'd like to do a musical": Author's interview with George Abbott.

571 He demanded $100,000: Author's confidential interview.

572 "Why do you go around": *New York Times,* May 8, 1988.

572 Harris had died: *New York Times,* March 7, 1950.

572 His last visit: *New Yorker,* April 17, 1978.

572 "hiding out": *ibid.*

572 "At my age": *ibid.*

572 In June 1972: *New York Times,* June 16, 1972. The cast of *This Is the Army* continued to hold reunions at five-year intervals, though Berlin never attended any of the subsequent gatherings, either.

573 he expressed the hope: Author's interview with Magda Volgas.

573 On January 25, 1978: *New York Times*, January 28, 1978.

573 "It makes you believe": Author's interview with John Wallowitch.

575 "My health is perfect": Kresa and confidential interviews.

575 "Why didn't you ever kiss": Author's confidential interview.

576 Steven Spielberg: *New York Times*, May 12, 1988.

576 "raised hell": Kresa interviews. Helmy Kresa finally retired shortly before Berlin turned one hundred.

577 "I really only have": Author's confidential interview.

577 "So? Where am I going?": Author's confidential interview.

577 "I watched all four days": Author's interview with David Wolper.

578 "Do you realize": S. Green interview.

578 At 5:42 A.M. on May 11: Wallowitch interview.

579 "What's your hurry?": Lane interview.

579 "I don't want": Author's interview with Oscar Brand.

579 "What does Irving Berlin": *New York Daily News*, May 11, 1988.

580 "WHY I DON'T LIKE IRVING": *New York Daily News*, May 19, 1988.

580 Carnegie Hall tribute: *New York Times*, *New York Daily News*, May 12, 1988.

582 A voice called: *New York Daily News*, May 12, 1988.

582 "Fine, that's my bank": Will of Ellin Berlin, January 19, 1982, Surrogate's Court, County of New York.

582 She left an extensive estate: Inventory of Assets, Estate of Ellin Berlin, Surrogate's Court, County of New York, #3743–1988.

582 "What I am": *New York Post*, April 10, 1975.

583 "She will be remembered": *Newsday*, *New York Post*, August 3, 1988; *New York Times*, July 30, 1988.

584 care of nurses: Author's confidential interview.

584 Irving Berlin died quietly: *New York Times*, September 23, 1989.

584 "No, he was 101": *Variety*, September 27, 1989.

585 The songwriter's burial: *New York Times*, September 27, 1989.

585 The terms of his will: Will of Irving Berlin, October 17, 1989, Surrogate's Court, County of New York.

Index